J. M. Steadman

Summer, 1966

D0220997

Style, Rhetoric, and Rhythm

ESSAYS BY MORRIS W. CROLL

Style, Rhetoric, and Rhythm

ESSAYS BY MORRIS W. CROLL

EDITED BY J. MAX PATRICK
AND ROBERT O. EVANS,
WITH JOHN M. WALLACE
AND R. J. SCHOECK

PRINCETON, NEW JERSEY
PRINCETON UNIVERSITY PRESS
1966

Copyright © 1966 by Princeton University Press

ALL RIGHTS RESERVED

L.C. Card: 65-14310

Publication of this book has been aided by
the Annan Fund of Princeton University

Printed in the United States of America
by Princeton University Press, Princeton, New Jersey

Preface

This edition of the best works of Morris William Croll has had a long gestation. Over a dozen years ago, with the warm encouragement of the most eminent Renaissance and seventeenth-century specialists and the backing of Professor Donald Stauffer, then chairman of the Princeton English Department, I announced my intention of collecting and seeking a publisher for the articles written by Professor Croll. The ideal and obvious publisher was the Press of Princeton University, where he had spent almost his entire academic life. However, for various reasons, the idea was impractical for the Press at that time, and was rejected. I nevertheless refrained from submitting the project elsewhere. Postwar times were uncertain, but I was confident that publishing circumstances would improve, that the need for making Croll's work available would continue, and that the Press at Princeton would recognize that the merits of these scattered articles, several of them very difficult to obtain, fully justified publication in spite of the problems involved.

A decade passed, during which I collected the works and began the necessary editorial work on them—that is, to bring them up to date by adding references to scholarship on the diversity of Croll's subjects that had appeared since his essays were published. With one of those extraordinary coincidences which occur not only in scientific discovery but also in literary scholarship, just as I was redrafting the project for a second presentation to Princeton University Press, I discovered that one of my own former pupils had submitted a similar suggestion to the Press and that Professor John M. Wallace of Johns Hopkins University was also planning an edition; and about a month later two other scholars wrote to me asking if I were still planning to collect and publish Croll's writings—if not, they would do so themselves.

By this time I had come to realize that the task of editing was not a simple one of gathering and reprinting, with an updating bibliography. A check revealed that, although the scholarship and accuracy of the main texts were of a high order, Professor Croll had been very cavalier—to put it mildly—about his footnotes, especially in the earlier articles. In at least one instance he seems to have left the footnotes to be written by his undergraduate pupils. In short, the whole apparatus of notes and quotations had to be checked and corrected where necessary—an enormous labor, inasmuch as Croll rivalled Bacon in taking all knowledge as his province. Recognizing my own incompetence to perform all this work and aware that the expertise of specialists was needed to bring the footnotes and bibliographical matter up to date, I was happy to enlist the cooperation of Professors Robert O. Evans, John M. Wallace, and R. J. Schoeck in the editing. It proved to be a happy cooperation. Each of these scholars took the prime responsibility for checking and editing one or more of the essays; then I coordinated, integrated, and added— sometimes greatly—to what they had done. It was also sometimes necessary to transfer bracketed material added in the footnotes by one editor to more appropriate positions in essays edited by the others. Such transfers and my own additions have been made silently, so that credit is not always given where it is due. The ultimate responsibility for any faults that remain is mine, but credit for the merits of the editing must be shared.

Some changes in the main texts of Croll's essays have also been made silently—rectification of typographical errors, additions of some authors' first names, and similar minor clarifications; but any major alterations in his main texts, such as correction of dating errors, have been duly noted. Croll made no fetish of consistency: his spellings and reference forms vary, even on the same page; he did not hesitate to quote from different editions of an author within an essay; sometimes, particularly in "The Rhythm of English Verse," he was obviously willing to quote, though inaccurately, from memory (for example, in Calverley's *Ode to Tobacco*); and to achieve a fluid style and expressive cadence, he was willing to omit marks of punctuation where we would now impose them. Such features are typical of the man and seem to be intentional. Accordingly we have hesitated to impose on them the rigid uniformity of modern scholarship except when changes were unavoidable.

More liberty has been taken with the footnotes—justified by the fact that Croll obviously slighted them. They have frequently been reworded and standardized for clarity; references have been filled out; when an edition he used could not be found, citations were sometimes changed to more available texts. Such changes are made silently. The notes, as a result, may not be in his own words, but they are true to his intention. Added material has been put in brackets. In most cases it has been possible to check and, if necessary, to correct the original references. But in some instances we have had to leave the notes in their original form.

Croll's other published works do not merit reprinting here. His earliest production, "Tom Jones," in *Papers Read before the Novel Club of Cleveland* (Cleveland, 1899, pp. 36-47) is merely a pleasant appreciation. His University of Pennsylvania dissertation, *The Works of Fulke Greville* (Philadelphia, 1903, 59 pages), contains some valuable insights, but the best of them were repeated, developed, or modified in later articles. *English Lyrics from Dryden to Burns* (New York, 1912) is a textbook anthology with a rather conventional introduction. A brief entry, "John Florio," in *Modern Language Notes*, xxxiv (1919), 376, drew scholars' attention to a previously unrecorded work by Florio—the first book of William Vaughan's translation of Boccalini, *The New-Found Politicke*. In 1930-1931 Croll published in *Modern Philology* reviews of Williamson, *The Donne Tradition*, White, *English Devotional Literature*, and Nethercot, *Abraham Cowley*. At the 1917 meeting of the Modern Language Association, Croll delivered a paper on "The Cadences of the Collects," material which, in revised form, appears in the present volume. As chairman of the MLA Committee on Metrical Notation, appointed in 1922, he helped prepare the report which was published in *PMLA*, xxxix (1923), lxxxvii-xciv: it recommended both the traditional macron-breve symbols for meter and the method of musical symbols which Croll employed in his own articles on metrics.

T 73.36
U.C.L.A.
...dents' Store
R 1 2 5 0
Exchanges or Refunds
...his Label Is Removed

Professor Croll's papers and lecture notes are preserved in Princeton University Library. They contain little, if anything, which he polished to publishable form. It is to be hoped that the present collection will inspire some qualified scholar to select and edit the best portions of these unperfected works.

J. Max Patrick
NEW YORK UNIVERSITY

Biographical Note

MORRIS WILLIAM CROLL was born at Gettysburg, Pennsylvania, April 16, 1872, the son of Luther Henry and Jane Crawford Smyth Croll. His father was Professor of Mathematics at Pennsylvania (Gettysburg) College, which Morris attended in due course, receiving the A.B. degree in 1889 and the A.M. in 1892. In 1931 his old college was to award him an honorary Litt.D. He continued his studies at Harvard, from which he received an A.B. in 1894 and an A.M. in 1895. From 1895 to 1899 he taught in the University School, Cleveland, Ohio. Completing graduate study at the University of Pennsylvania, he wrote his dissertation on the works of Fulke Greville under the direction of Professor Felix Schelling, receiving his Ph.D. in 1901. From 1901 to 1905 he was an Associate Editor of the *Lippincott-Worcester Dictionary*. Returning to teaching, he was brought to Princeton in 1905 by President Woodrow Wilson as one of the fifty "preceptor guys" in the new plan of undergraduate instruction. He was promoted from Instructor in English Literature to Assistant Professor in 1906, to Associate Professor in 1918, to Professor in 1921. He retired in February 1932. Early in World War I he served on Herbert Hoover's Commission for the Relief of Belgium, for which in September 1919 he was awarded the Cross of King Albert. Professor Croll never married. For the last years of his life he resided with his sister, Miss Elsie L. Croll, at 40 Bayard Lane, Princeton. Never robust in health, after his retirement he became less and less active, with long periods of confinement to his rooms. He died at Saranac Lake, New York, where he was spending the summer, on August 17, 1947.

In the fall of 1916 Mr. Croll met his preceptorial in English Romanticism in a cubbyhole at the top of the old School of Science. His tall, somewhat stooping figure suggested Sargent's portrait of R. L. S. at Bournemouth. A general impression of physical frailty grew on acquaintance, but this was not the effect of any slackness in his manner. One was first struck by his soft and precise enunciation, with an occasional sibilant emphasis just rising above a whisper. This furnished a striking contrast to the vigorous and sometimes explosive delivery of J. Duncan Spaeth, the lecturer in the course. There was nothing of the pundit in his comments, but the quiet note of authority that marked matters of special interest to him commanded respect. Because he was gentle in criticism of the callow responses of his students, his rare displays of irritation were more effective in consequence. Perhaps most notable in his presentation of literature was the pervasive evidence of a sensitive appreciation.

In the autumn after the United States entered the war, many senior classes contained only a handful of students. Professor Croll's course in Poetics and a group permitted to enroll for Advanced Composition, five in all, met in his rooms, 6 North Reunion. His graduate courses in the immediate postwar years, English Prose Style 1500-1680 and the English Lyric, not much larger, foregathered in his study at 7½ Greenholm. He was probably at his best with these small, intimate groups. In both undergraduate and graduate courses might be noted his impatience with lecture notes or reading from a prepared manuscript. On more than one occasion, beginning with a manuscript, he tossed it aside and continued the discussion without again consulting it. The only one of his courses in which the formal presentation of the subject permitted the writer to take highly organized class notes was Poetics. But even here what he remembers is rather Croll's reading of Bridges's "Whither, O splendid ship" and Yeats's "The Lake Isle of Innisfree," with an exposition of their metrical subtleties, than the historical and critical outline of lyric production. His method, of necessity, became more formalized when he met larger classes in the late twenties.

The writer particularly recalls the older man's sympathetic assistance when he was in great perplexity about his obligation to military service. Mr. Croll felt sadly that he was himself barred from active participation in the war effort. In the early summer of 1918 he worked on a Pennsylvania farm for six weeks, until the unwonted exertion wore him down, compelling him to complete rest for the remainder of the season. In September of that year he wrote from Bread Loaf Inn, Vermont: "It was a great pleasure to hear from you and know of your being at work on the great business. *Nothing* else is worth a young man's doing now, and I resent the *single* year (less!) which prevents me from being drafted in it. I'd rather be a private in the trenches than anything else in the world. And if I could only stand it—or have a shadow of a chance of standing it—I'd not balk at the morality of lying about my age."

Professor Croll must have enjoyed a period of comparative vigor in 1923, for in the latter half of the year he took sabbatical leave, traveling in England, and on his return after Christmas he appeared in good health and spirits.

He read widely, but his personal taste was conservative. One recalls a summer when he reported his reading as including *Lalla Rookh* and Trollope, and an afternoon when he was found deeply immersed in Scott's *Anne of Geierstein*. He was a founder of the Freneau Club, a student literary society which invited writers to the campus to read from their work and to discuss it informally. After a visit from Sinclair Lewis, Mr. Croll wrote: "His lecture was in good colyum style—to the delight of the U.G.'s. But *Main Street* is hard reading for all that. After all and all, the classics are still the classics—hey?" Nevertheless, his response to undergraduate creative efforts was unforced and generous. *A Book of Princeton Verse II*, 1919, in whose publication he was the moving spirit, carried on the tradition of Princeton poetry that had been marked by two previous collections. For this volume Professor Croll was assisted in gathering contributions by James Creese, '18, and with them were associated Henry Van Dyke and Maxwell Struthers Burt, the former writing the Preface. Of the thirty-four authors included, several were well known beyond the campus, but young aspirants were chiefly and liberally represented.

After the summer of 1927 the writer was seldom in Princeton, and on infrequent later visits Professor Croll was not often in the village. There was worsening news of his completely failing health. At Reunion 1943 the members of our Advanced Composition class in attendance telephoned Miss Elsie and begged to call on Saturday afternoon. She gave her permission, but stipulated that the visit be brief. Morris Croll was his gracious self, cordially welcoming his former students, but he was obviously very frail. The last note in the writer's possession was written a fortnight later from Saranac Lake, thanking us for a book we had brought him.

Professor Croll's most important book was the edition, with Harry Clemons, of Lyly's *Euphues*, which appeared in 1916. The work tentatively entitled *From Montaigne to Dryden*, a study of prose style in the seventeenth century, achieved only partial publication in journal and *Festschrift* articles. His interest in the musical basis of verse suggested an intellectual kinship with Sidney Lanier, and, like Lanier, Croll played the flute, though with something less than the mastery of the author of *The Science of English Verse*. *The Rhythm of English Verse* existed only in mimeographed form and has not hitherto been printed, perhaps because of the difficulty and expense of reproducing the metrical notation devised for it. Professor Croll's contributions, both to metrics and, especially, to "Attic" prose, have been extensively cited, but it has not been easy to lay one's hands on them. Their gathering in this volume is not only a fitting memorial to a fine scholar, but a sorely needed aid to contemporary scholarship.

Atlanta, Georgia   THOMAS H. ENGLISH
                                                      EMORY UNIVERSITY

Contents

CONTENTS

Abbreviations

Abbreviations of titles of periodicals, etc. are standard ones as used in *PMLA*. In the notes, Croll's articles are referred to as follows:

APL: "Attic Prose: Lipsius, Montaigne, Bacon"

APS: " 'Attic Prose' in the Seventeenth Century"

BS: "The Baroque Style in Prose"

Cadence: "The Cadence of English Oratorical Prose"

Lipse: "Juste Lipse et le Mouvement Anticicéronien à la Fin du XVIe et au Début du XVIIe Siècle"

Muret: "Muret and the History of 'Attic' Prose"

Music & Metrics: "Music and Metrics: A Reconsideration"

Rhythm: "The Rhythm of English Verse"

Sources: "The Sources of the Euphuistic Rhetoric" (Introduction to *Euphues*)

PART I

The Anti-Ciceronian Movement:
"Attic" and Baroque Prose Style

So that readers may follow the development of Croll's ideas, these five essays are printed here in the order in which he prepared them for publication. However, it should be borne in mind that Muret initiated the Anti-Ciceronian movement, that Lipsius was his follower, and that Croll later acknowledged that Essay One needed revision in part. Accordingly, those interested in grasping his developed ideas and in following the movement chronologically are advised to begin with Essays Two and Three, and to read Essay One in the light of the recapitulation in the opening part of Essay Four.

Foreword to Essay One

Croll's essay remains standard; recent studies of Renaissance neo-Stoicism have confirmed its estimate of Lipsius' importance and emphasized the contribution of philosophy to the making of seventeenth-century Senecan style.[1] The most significant modification of its thesis is George Williamson's argument that Lipsius' own style was more Tacitean than Senecan.[2] José Ruysschaert has uncovered details of Lipsius' reading while in Rome and of his rivalry with Muret;[3] E. Catherine Dunn has discerned in the *Epistolica Institutio* Lipsius' intention to free the *ars dictamini* from the stranglehold of the classical oration, and to renew the ancient connection between letter-writing and the conversational manner of the dialogue;[4] Wesley Trimpi has gone further, and has been able to offer another reason for the remarkable popularity of Senecan style by showing how Lipsius and others vastly widened the scope of the familiar epistle until it became competent to discuss subjects, both human and divine, which formerly had been reserved for other genres.[5]

With the exception of *The Senecan Amble*, later essays have served less to correct Croll's opinions than to underline the essential rightness of his approach. By establishing for students of seventeenth-century prose a program and a method he achieved for them what he credited Lipsius with doing for the Anti-Ciceronians. More than most

---

[1] Jason A. Saunders, *Justus Lipsius: The Philosophy of Renaissance Stoicism* (New York, 1955) gives a sixty-page life of Lipsius and a bibliography that lists most of the scholarship on him since the publication of Croll's study in *Revue du Seizième Siècle*, II (July 1914), 200-242. See also "Lipsius" in the index of D. C. Cabeen, *A Critical Bibliography of French Literature*, Vol. II: *The Sixteenth Century*, ed. Alexander H. Schutz (Syracuse, 1956). For editions of Lipsius' works, see F. van der Haeghen, *Biblioteca Belgica*, Vols. XV-XVII (Ghent, 1880-1890).

[2] *The Senecan Amble: A Study in Prose Form from Bacon to Collier* (Chicago, 1951), pp. 121-149. See the Foreword to *BS* below.

[3] "Le Séjour de Juste Lipse à Rome (1568-1570)," *Bulletin de l'Institut Historique de Rome*, XXIV (1947-1948), 139-192; "Une Édition du Tacite de Juste Lipse, avec Annotations de Muret, Conservée à la Mazarine," *Revue Belge de Philologie et d'Histoire*, XXIII (1944), 251-254.

[4] "Lipsius and the Art of Letter-Writing," *Studies in the Renaissance*, III (1956), 145-156.

[5] "Jonson and the Neo-Latin Authorities for the Plain Style," *PMLA*, LXXVII (1962), 21-26. In his book, *Ben Jonson's Poems: A Study of the Plain Style* (Stanford, 1962), Trimpi has relied heavily on Croll's essays. This book is hereafter referred to as "Trimpi."

3

scholars in 1914, he realized that the Renaissance had a theory for everything, and that the history of prose style could be more accurately plotted by reference to the professed aims of the writers themselves than by an eclectic criticism of tendencies, influences, native sources, and internal evidence. The point is enforced by comparing Croll's present essay with G. P. Krapp's still valuable work of the following year. Krapp distinguished numerous trends and qualities in "literary prose," but he made only one reference to Seneca—a statement that the English stylists "knew Seneca and studied him almost as zealously as they did Cicero"[6]—and did not realize that the doctrine of imitation was capable of such dramatic variations. Croll perceived that a literary revolution began with the imitation of new models, although in the essay on Muret he retracted much of his emphasis on this fact.

Croll's familiarity with the work of classicists, who customarily discussed Roman stylistic theory in terms of its Grecian origins, was certainly in part responsible for the innovations he wrought in the study of Renaissance prose. But if in one respect he began a revolution himself, in another he belonged to an older generation than ours—Burkhardtian in its sense of the newness of the Renaissance, although, like us, indisposed to regard all its later manifestations as decadent. Scholars now separate the modern and medieval components of the Renaissance with extreme circumspection; for Croll, however, the Anti-Ciceronian movement was modern. Having related Euphuism emphatically to medieval sermons—as he was later to link all vernacular expression at about 1550 to medievalism—he saw in the program initiated by Muret and Lipsius, and established in the vernacular by Montaigne and Bacon, the birth of the modern mind. In the Anti-Ciceronians, he writes, "we seem to hear the first words of the theory of individual style." And it is the growth of this theory in the subsequent history of Senecan prose which he outlined in the closing pages of this essay. The impulse toward personal freedom in thought and language seems to have remained the sole psychological explanation that Croll offered for the new style, and his belief in it

[6] *The Rise of English Literary Prose* (New York, 1915), p. 275.

4

grew with years. It led him later to misunderstand the plain style in the Restoration, which he judged to be a mere revision of Senecanism, effected by the influences of Descartes, Baconian science, and *mondanité*. However, to take "the heat and fever out of the imaginative naturalism of Montaigne, Bacon, and Browne," is to create a rival style, not to introduce "certain changes within the *cadres*" of Senecan prose,[7] and one concludes that Croll's theory is applicable chiefly to those early humanists from whom it was first derived. Here, other scholars (notably Arnold Stein in his early essays on Donne, and Floyd Gray on Montaigne)[8] have not hesitated to follow him. His belief that the Anti-Ciceronians attempted to catch the movement of thought in all the ardor of its first conception in the mind remains truer of the geniuses than of the common run of their disciples. Croll's error is in favor of quality, and it is no more than the usual irony of scholarship that the wings of his theory have been trimmed by the very instruments which he forged.

To read the present essay after the later and hitherto more accessible studies is to wonder if Croll ever spent an apprenticeship in his subject, for his understanding of Anti-Ciceronianism seems to have sprung Minerva-like into being. Not only are his judgments of the major authors fully formed, but many of the crucial texts which he was to quote again are mustered here. Muret is given his rightful priority, the minor classical writers associated with the movement are enumerated, "Attic" is loosely defined—together with the rhetorical dangers inherent in Senecan style—and the two other members of Croll's triumvirate, Montaigne and Bacon, complete a substantial survey.

His later studies added the classical background, discussed the origin and success of the movement in greater detail, and distinguished carefully the principal differences between Senecan styles; the freedom of his generalizations increased with the command of his sources, yet his fundamental apprehension of the nature of Anti-

[7] Review of R. F. Jones, "Science and Prose Style," *PQ*, x (1931), 185.
[8] Arnold Stein, "Donne and the Couplet," *PMLA* (1942), 676-696; "Donne's Obscurity and the Elizabethan Tradition," *ELH*, xiii (1946), 98-118. Floyd Gray, *Le Style de Montaigne* (Paris, 1958).

Ciceronianism remained the same. This is illustrated by his omission to develop more fully the implications of his character of Lipsius, in which he had drawn attention to the weaknesses of the master's temperament, his tendency to doubt rather than to assert, his scruples and self-distrust. Croll compares him, as he was to do again, with the philosophic solitaries like Montaigne, Burton, and Browne, who were "groping" for originality of thought. Not until Don Cameron Allen's "Style and Certitude" was the significance of these remarks explored.[9] Allen boldly linked the Senecan style with the doubters and all those afflicted with "the disease of reason" and claimed that its defeat of the transcendental Ciceronian style, which had flourished for a brief period at the dawn of humanism, marked the end of an intellectual system men could believe in. The later "African" style of Browne and Taylor was evolved by Anti-Ciceronians who had solved their doubts by a return to faith—a suggestion which in part explains how these authors could have been mistaken for Ciceronians for so long. Croll twice suggested, indeed, in later essays, that the connections between melancholy and Senecan style would bear investigation, and one might have expected that his hypothesis about the birth of the modern mind would have made such an investigation congenial. Croll, however, discovered in the scepticism of the moral scientists their implicit confidence in man's strength and happiness as the fetters of the old world were wrenched apart, and it was to the explanation of this side of their achievement that he devoted his own great energies.

JOHN M. WALLACE
THE JOHNS HOPKINS UNIVERSITY

[9] *ELH*, xv (1948), 167-175.

Juste Lipse et le Mouvement Anticicéronien à la Fin du XVIe et au Début du XVIIe Siècle*

EDITED BY JOHN M. WALLACE

✧ I ✧

L'Homme

JOEST LIPS (1547-1606) ou, comme on l'appelle généralement, Juste Lipse, fut considéré à son époque comme l'un des triumvirs littéraires dont le travail et le talent contribuèrent, à la fin du XVIe siècle, à faire passer la suprématie de l'érudition de l'Italie aux pays du Nord. C'est ainsi qu'en parle à sa mort le panégyriste officiel qui rapporte évidemment là un lieu commun de la critique, et son biographe moderne, dans l'excellent livre où il fait revivre cette ancienne opinion, le place au même rang que Scaliger et Casaubon.[1] Il faut remarquer cependant que, de nos jours, sa réputation est tombée bien au-dessous de la leur et, quand ils ne l'ont pas négligée dans la critique des forces littéraires de son temps, les savants modernes ont eu quelque malin plaisir à rappeler que le triumvirat romain comprenait un élément de faiblesse.[2]

* Published in *Revue du Seizième Siècle*, II (July 1914), 200-242. In *Muret*, n.5, Croll acknowledges need "for revision at several points." There is a partial summary in *APL*, II.

[1] Charles Nisard, *Le Triumvirat Littéraire au XVIe Siècle*: *Juste Lipse, Joseph Scaliger, et Isaac Casaubon* (Paris, 1852), pp. 1-148. [Nisard, p. 3, cites the article on Lipsius in Antoine Teissier, *Les Éloges des Hommes Savants Tirés de l'Histoire de M. de Thou* (Leiden, 1715), IV, 526.] L'ouvrage de Émile Amiel, *Un Publiciste du XVIe Siècle*: *Juste-Lipse* (Paris, 1884) a moins de valeur.

[My responsibility for the notes to this essay is limited to the verification and correction of Croll's own footnotes. Almost all the supplementary material has been contributed by J. Max Patrick. I am also grateful to Cornell University for a grant that enabled me to check some of the rarer books in Washington. J.M.W.]

[2] Voir l'article de Mark Pattison sur Lipse dans *The Encyclopaedia Britannica*, 9e éd. (Edinburgh, 1875). [However, J. Dana's trans. of Lipsius' *De Bibliotecis Syntagma* was published in 1907 in Chicago as *A Brief Outline of the History of Libraries* and Albert Steuer wrote a slight, uncritical dissertation, *Die Philosophie des Justus Lipsius* (Münster, 1911). Partly owing to Croll, attention to Lipsius has increased

De telles variations d'opinion sont intéressantes. Il est toujours possible que le jugement de la posterité soit moins exact que celui des contemporains; je dirai plus, il semble probable que le siècle qui a le mieux connu les hommes les a le plus justement appréciés, et notre curiosité s'efforce de découvrir dans les tendances, dans les simples circonstances, ou peut-être dans le seul goût qu'ont les hommes pour les contrastes frappants, les causes possibles d'une injustice posthume. Il n'est certes pas difficile de trouver de pareilles raisons au discrédit dont a souffert Lipse. Tout d'abord, ses opinions et sa conduite dans les affaires d'Église et d'État n'y furent pas étrangères. Catholique d'éducation, il fut enlevé à cet enseignement par ses parents qui craignaient de le voir devenir la victime des théories et des desseins des Jésuites et, pendant onze ou douze ans, il fut professeur à l'Université calviniste de Leyde. Il dut, d'une façon quelconque, y affirmer des principes protestants; cependant, c'est là même qu'il écrivait son fameux ouvrage, *Politicorum, sive Civilis Doctrinæ Libri Sex* (1589), dans lequel il approuvait la persécution des hérétiques par le feu et l'épée, sous prétexte que l'ordre et la paix sont les objets essentiels de la société humaine. Ses paroles, "Ure et seca," firent scandale dans toute l'Europe protestante; il semble pourtant que ce soit de son plein gré qu'il abandonna sa chaire en 1591 et se remit entre les mains de la colonie jésuite de Louvain. À partir de ce moment jusqu'à sa mort, en 1606, il servit fidèlement avec sa plume la cause de la Contre-réforme.

L'avantage de ces changements au cours de sa vie fut de lui

since 1914; for example, in addition to the works mentioned in the Introduction to this essay, Léontine Zanta, *La Renaissance du Stoïcisme au XVIe Siècle* (Paris, 1914); Basil Anderton, "A Stoic of Louvain," *Sketches from a Library Window* (Cambridge, 1922), pp. 10-30; Guido Capitolo, *La Filosofia Stoica nel Secolo XVI in Francia* (Naples, 1931); V. Nordman, *Justus Lipsius als Geschichtsforscher und Geschichtslehrer* (Helsinki, 1932); and the editions by Croll's one-time pupil, Rudolf Kirk listed in n.4 below. Other related studies are: F. L. Schoell, *Études sur l'Humanisme Continental en Angleterre* (Paris, 1926); C. B. Hilberry, *Ben Jonson's Ethics in Relation to Stoic and Humanistic Thought* (Chicago, 1933); Philip A. Smith, "Bishop Hall, 'Our English Seneca'," *PMLA*, LXIII (1948), 1191-1204; H. W. Sams, "Anti-Stoicism in Seventeenth- and Early Eighteenth-Century England," *SP*, XLI (1944), 65-78; Audrey Chew, "Joseph Hall and Neo-Stoicism," *PMLA*, LXV (1950), 1130-1145; Ralph G. Palmer, *Seneca's* De Remediis Fortuitorum *and the Elizabethans* (Chicago, 1953); Jonas A. Barish, *Ben Jonson and the Language of Prose Comedy* (Cambridge, Mass., 1960); George Williamson, *Seventeenth Century Contexts* (Chicago, 1961), especially the essay on "The Rhetorical Pattern of Neo-Classical Wit"; Julien-Eymard d'Angers, "Le Stoïcisme dans l'Œuvre de J.-L. Guez de Balzac," *Revue des Sciences Humaines*, N.S. LXXXIII July-Sept. 1956), 269-300. See also works listed in *APS*, n.36.]

permettre d'entretenir des relations littéraires avec les membres des deux partis et avec tous les pays européens, du Danemark à l'Espagne, en même temps qu'il étendait son influence plus loin qu'aucun autre homme de son époque. Mais, d'un autre côté, les protestants, qui admiraient et imitaient son style, ne pouvaient guère, après qu'il les eut quittés pour les Jésuites, lui accorder leurs louanges cordiales, tandis que, par cette espèce de fatalité qui poursuit souvent l'homme qui varie, ses amis jésuites furent parfois tentés de déprécier son travail de littérateur et de savant, parce qu'il était inspiré par des tendances et une méthode qu'ils blâmaient. C'est ce que montrent les écrits d'un certain nombre de Jésuites, maîtres de rhétorique, ceux du Père Bouhours, entre autres, et du Père Vavasseur; d'autre part, l'évêque Joseph Hall est un excellent exemple de ces hommes qui furent ses disciples littéraires bien que conduits, par leur attachement à leur cause, à couvrir de ridicule et de mépris ses ouvrages religieux.[3]

En second lieu, son caractère, son tempérament, son attitude morale et intellectuelle sont demeurés sans attrait pour un certain nombre de rares lecteurs modernes qui se sont intéressés à ses œuvres. Il n'y eut rien d'héroïque chez Lipse. Il n'a jamais soutenu une opinion pour laquelle il eût cru devoir mourir, ou même lutter très sérieusement. Sa nature était de celles qui doutent plus aisément qu'elles n'affirment et qui examinent de façon aussi sceptique leurs propres opinions et celles des autres; catholiques et protestants n'étaient sans doute pas tellement différents à ses yeux en ce qui concerne la vérité de leurs dogmes respectifs, et sa soumission à l'autorité des jésuites, vers le milieu de sa vie, paraît avoir été quelque chose comme une façon d'échapper à l'impossible tâche de faire un choix intellectuel. Dans ses opinions littéraires, il montre la

---

[3] Joseph Hall, dans ses *Epistles*, I.5-6 (*Works*, Oxford, 1837, VI, 134-143) raille les traités de Lipse, *Diva Virgo Hallensis Beneficia Ejus et Miracula* (1604) et *Diva Sichemiensis sive Aspricollis* (1605). Il cite un passage où Lipse affirme qu'un jour de l'année 1603 vingt mille personnes ont visité l'une des deux petites chapelles où la Vierge opérait des guérisons miraculeuses. Voici le commentaire de Hall: "Oh, what pity it is, that so high a wit should, in the last act, be subject to dotage! All the masculine brood of that brain we cherished, and, if need were, admired: but these his silly virgins, the feeble issue of distempered age, who can abide?" (p. 137). Scaliger qui, à l'Université de Leyde, succéda à Lipse se trouva fort embarrassé par certains louanges qu'il avait faites de l'érudition de Lipse (voir une lettre adressée à Casaubon et citée par Jacob Bernays, *Joseph Justus Scaliger*, Berlin, 1855, pp. 171-172). Scaliger, cependant, était aussi un adversaire littéraire: il essaya de s'associer aux opinions "romantiques," au sujet de la seconde période de la latinité (voir Nisard, pp. 128-130).

même incertitude, la même hésitation; fondateur d'une école de prose, il devint le premier partisan de l'opposition et indiqua la route à suivre à maint critique hostile de la génération suivante.

Blâmer de tels hommes est chose facile; leurs craintes, leurs scrupules et leurs gémissements semblent petits à côté des nobles enthousiasmes des premiers humanistes et il y a certainement quelque chose de faible et de bien peu viril dans les efforts de Lipse pour échapper à la responsabilité des temps malheureux où il vivait, quelque chose d'hypocondriaque, comme Nisard le fait remarquer dans les lamentables tableaux qu'il fait des massacres, de la dévastation et de l'anarchie dont il fut témoin en Allemagne et dans les Pays-Bas.[4] Pourtant, il serait injuste de juger Lipse sans se rappeler qu'en effet la vie pouvait paraître aussi noire qu'il le dit pendant les dernières années du XVIe siècle, que la politique européenne, religieuse et séculière, avait changé depuis la Renaissance et que les difficultés intellectuelles des esprits sérieux augmentaient tous les jours. L'enthousiasme naïf de Pic de la Mirandole, de Colet ou de Mélanchton est absolument invraisemblable chez un homme de la génération de Lipse: le comparer à eux, c'est ne voir que le plus mauvais côté de sa nature. La comparaison, du reste, est inutile et fausse et sa vie morale prend, d'un autre côté, un intérêt et un sens tout spécial si nous le voyons sous son vrai jour, parmi les hommes les plus modernes de son temps, le précurseur des générations qui viendront. Lipse est un des premiers spécimens d'un type nouveau, auquel appartiennent Montaigne, Balzac, Burton, Sir Thomas Browne et même Pascal: hommes désillusionnés et mélancoliques, las du bruit de la vie, spectateurs contemplatifs, moralistes stoïciens, égoïstes qui se plaisent à étaler leur "moi" faible et sans héroïsme.

La troisième cause du déclin de la réputation de Lipse comme

---

[4] Surtout dans son traité *De Constantia, Libri Duo, qui Alloquium Praecipue Continent in Publicis Malis* (1584). Cet intéressant opuscule fut traduit en anglais par Sir John Stradling en 1595 [and also by R. G. in 1654 and Nathaniel Wanley in 1670]; il montre l'influence de Montaigne qui s'en servit et, sans doute, réfuta les opinions qui s'y trouvent dans ses *Essais*, particulièrement iii, ix-x. Voir l'ouvrage de Pierre Villey, *Les Sources et l'Évolution des Essais de Montaigne*, 2e éd. (Paris, 1933), i, 178. Suivant M. Villey (ii, 65-66) l'œuvre joua un rôle important dans la renaissance de la philosophie stoïcienne à la fin du XVIe siècle. Naturellement, cette renaissance aida au changement qui se fit dans la prose et que nous étudions ici. [See the editions by Rudolf Kirk of *Tvvo Bookes of Constancie, by Justus Lipsius*, trans. Sir John Stradling (New Brunswick, N.J., 1939), and of two related works, *Heaven upon Earth* and *Characters of Vertues and Vices*, by Joseph Hall (1948), and *The Moral Philosophie of the Stoicks, Written in French by Guillaume Du Vair, Englished by Thomas James* (1951).]

savant se trouve dans la nature, vraie ou supposée, de ses études classiques. Mark Pattison a formulé l'accusation, avec sa brusquerie habituelle, lorsqu'il a dit que l'intérêt que Lipse prenait aux classiques était uniquement celui d'un rhéteur.[5] Naturellement, ayant sous les yeux ses ouvrages politiques, ses lettres, ses biographies et ses traités philosophiques, Pattison devait forcer là sa pensée; ce qu'il a voulu dire, c'est que Lipse a peu ajouté à ce que nous savions de la vie extérieure de Rome, de ses institutions judiciaires et militaires, de sa topographie, en un mot à cet ensemble de faits chers à l'archéologue, et il implique par ses paroles qu'en comparaison de Scaliger et de Casaubon, par exemple, Lipse s'intéressait peu aux réalités de la vie romaine.

Voilà sans doute un jugement extraordinaire. Le caractère général des recherches savantes du XVIIe siècle, comparées aux efforts des premiers humanistes, c'est d'avoir rapproché les Grecs et les Romains de la vie contemporaine, grâce en partie à une connaissance plus intime de leur existence journalière et grâce aussi à un sentiment nouveau de la continuité de la culture intellectuelle depuis les anciens jusqu'aux temps modernes, en passant par la littérature des Pères de l'Église et par l'Église du moyen âge. Au lieu de les contempler avec respect et vénération, figures grandies et indistinctes dans une mystérieuse splendeur, séparées de nous par une brèche dans l'histoire, on commença à les voir avec leurs proportions réelles et à mesurer leurs actions à l'échelle de la vie moderne. L'effort des savants fut de moderniser les anciens, tandis que leurs prédécesseurs s'étaient attachés à se romaniser ou à s'helléniser eux-mêmes. Appliquées aux grands contemporains de Lipse, ces remarques ne pourraient soulever aucune controverse; Pattison en reconnaît la justesse à propos d'Isaac Casaubon; s'il n'a pas su voir qu'elles convenaient parfaitement à Lipse, c'est en raison de cette forte tendance pragmatique qui a caractérisé l'érudition anglaise jusqu'à une époque très récente. Il ne pouvait pas s'intéresser beaucoup à Lipse, parce que Lipse s'intéressait moins à la vie extérieure de l'antiquité qu'à sa vie intérieure et morale. Car Lipse était avant

[5] *Encyclopaedia Britannica*, art. "Lipsius." [Apparently Croll was unaware as yet of John Edward Sandys, *A History of Classical Scholarship*, 3 vols. (Cambridge, 1900-1908), where Lipsius' merits as a classicist are recognized. His ed. of Tacitus placed him in the front rank of Latin scholars, in Sandys' judgment. According to Saunders (p. 59), "there is scarcely a problem relating to Roman antiquities on which his criticism and judgment have not thrown lasting light. . . . To Lipsius belongs the glory of having given to literary and historical studies a fruitful and enduring stimulus."]

tout un moraliste et un philosophe. À l'époque malheureuse que fut la sienne, il trouva sa consolation, non point dans l'enseignement religieux de ses maîtres les Jésuites, mais dans la doctrine stoïcienne de la résignation calme et du détachement intérieur. Le traducteur anglais de son traité sur la *Constance* s'en rendit si bien compte qu'il crut nécessaire, dans sa préface, de demander pardon au lecteur de l'absence de toute note chrétienne dans les maximes et il se peut que ce besoin de justifier son auteur reflète le sentiment d'alarme excité dans les cercles orthodoxes par un autre ouvrage de Lipse, son *Thraseas*, qui ne fut pas publié et dans lequel il soutenait, entre autres doctrines stoïciennes, le droit au suicide.[6] Bien qu'il semble que ce livre n'ait jamais été imprimé, le scandale poursuivit l'auteur toute sa vie. Son traité sur le stoïcisme, *Manuductionis ad Stoicam Philosophiam*, et son édition des œuvres de Sénèque confirmèrent la réputation que ses premiers ouvrages lui avaient value, et le Jésuite—qui fut son apologiste—dut examiner, entre autres questions douteuses, *An Lipsius Stoicae Sectae*.[7] La réponse évasive du Père Scribanius équivaut presque à celle que Lipse lui-même fait dans une des lettres que nous venons de citer: il avait choisi le refuge, de tous temps vénéré, des infortunés qui, depuis Abélard jusqu'à Montaigne, s'étaient trouvés, dans le domaine intellectuel, "naître sous une loi, attachés à une autre." C'est-à-dire qu'en tant que chrétien, il faisait sa soumission à l'Église, mais qu'en tant que philosophe, il suivait les anciens.

La vérité, c'est que Lipse étudia l'antiquité dans l'intention d'y trouver une consolation et une règle de vie. Tacite et Sénèque lui fournirent des modèles de style, mais il fut attiré vers eux, dans le principe, parce que l'un d'eux était "pater prudentiae" et l'autre "fons sapientiae."[8] Il diffère de Scaliger et de Casaubon, non pas parce que son sens des réalités de la vie antique était moins vif que le leur, mais parce que son sens des besoins moraux et intellectuels de son époque l'était beaucoup plus. Nous voyons en lui l'un des chefs intellectuels de cette génération qui subit la première

---

[6] Voir ses *Epistolarum Selectarum Centuria II, Miscellanea*, II.22,28 (épître à Plantin, son imprimeur), dans *Opera Omnia* (Antwerp, 1637), II, 79, 82. [Unless otherwise noted, this ed. is used for quotations from Lipsius. He recurred to the subject of suicide in *Manuductionis ad Stoicam Philosophiam Libri Tres* (1604), III.22-23; see the discussion by Saunders, pp. 111-116.]

[7] C. Scribanius, *Justi Lipsi Defensio Posthuma* (Antwerp, 1608). [Croll quotes the title of Ch. XI; in Lipsius, *Opera*, II, 315. The ed. of *L. Annaei Senecae Philosophi Opera* appeared in 1605.]

[8] *Ep. ad Italos et Hispanos*, 89, dans *Opera*, II, 315.

la réaction contre les espérances et les enthousiasmes de la Renaissance. La philosophie stoïcienne, avec sa théorie de la supériorité de l'esprit sur les circonstances, qui, de divers côtés, éveilla tant d'échos entre 1575 et 1675, qui inspira les plus beaux passages de Chapman, de Greville et de Donne, par exemple, qui retentit de façon différente dans la sombre école espagnole de Quevedo et de Balthazar Gracián et dans les maximes de Montaigne, fut exposée par Lipse dans ses traités et dans ses lettres avant qu'aucun de ses contemporains ou successeurs aient formulé leurs opinions.

✧ II ✧

Sa Rhétorique

Ce qui nous intéresse surtout ici, c'est le rôle que Lipse joua en guidant la prose dans la direction qu'elle prit au XVIIe siècle. Il était né bon écrivain, et ses lettres, ses traités auraient pris place dans la littérature auprès des *Essais* de Montaigne, bien qu'à un rang inférieur, s'ils avaient été écrits dans une langue vivante; mais c'était aussi un maître de rhétorique, dont l'idéal et les méthodes étaient bien définis. Un certain nombre d'autres écrivains de son temps, en particulier Bacon et Montaigne, eurent les mêmes opinions et le même goût littéraire que lui, et, à vrai dire, il ne fait que représenter une tendance générale de la prose en Europe; seulement, il semble bien qu'il soit le seul homme de sa génération qui ait formulé la rhétorique de ce nouveau mouvement, qui l'ait enseignée et défendue ouvertement. Voilà comment s'explique le retentissement considérable qu'eut son style à son époque et pendant les cinquante années qui suivirent sa mort; et c'est pour cette raison aussi qu'il mérite, dans la critique moderne, une place plus importante que celle qui lui est généralement faite.

Lorsque commença la vie publique de Lipse, le cicéronianisme était encore florissant. Avant le milieu du XVIe siècle, il avait été attaqué par deux des plus grands chefs intellectuels de la Renaissance: en 1538 par Érasme, dans son fameux dialogue *Ciceronianus*, et un peu plus tard par Ramus, l'ennemi d'Aristote, dans un traité nommé *Oratio de Studiis Philosophiae et Eloquentiae Conjungendis* (1546). Cette critique, pleine de bon sens, dirigée contre le mouvement cicéronien par les apôtres de la liberté et de la lumière paraît concluante à l'esprit moderne et la force de leur ironie irrésistible. La victoire de la raison ne fut cependant qu'apparente et sans résultat, et dans le troisième quart du siècle, Ascham, Cheke et Car en Angleterre, Mélanchton, Sturm et Camerarius en Allemagne et les disciples de Bembo à Rome marchaient encore dans les sentiers battus de l'humanisme orthodoxe.

Cette résistance remarquable d'un dogme étroit,[9] et surtout son grand succès auprès des humanistes des églises de la Réforme s'explique par un défaut dans le programme de ses adversaires, ou, pour mieux dire, par leur défaut complet de programme. Ils attaquaient le régime de l'absolutisme sans offrir une constitution qui le remplaçât. La seule méthode qu'ils surent proposer pour substituer à l'imitation exclusive de Cicéron fut le choix, pour chaque écrivain, d'un modèle parmi les maîtres de l'antiquité, ou bien un éclectisme vague, qui réunirait les qualités de différents auteurs. Mais le XVIe siècle savait qu'il n'était pas capable d'une liberté sans frein. Il savait, ou tout au moins pressentait vaguement, qu'il était exposé au danger de retomber dans l'abîme de barbarie auquel sa culture avait récemment, et péniblement, échappé. La ligne de démarcation entre le bon et le mauvais latin, entre le style véritablement classique et les formes corrompues du latin du moyen âge n'était pas encore nettement établie dans l'esprit des hommes, et le charme de la rhétorique des sophistes grecs, de la recherche

[9] Il faut se rappeler que, dans la controverse de la Renaissance, on entendait par cicéronianisme non seulement l'admiration et l'imitation de Cicéron mais l'imitation exclusive de cet auteur, et, par anticicéronianisme, toute opposition à cette théorie. Tous les anticicéroniens, Lipse, Montaigne et Bacon, proclamaient, et très sincèrement, que Cicéron était le plus grand maître de la rhétorique latine, quoique tous aient préféré d'autres modèles.

Sur le cicéronianisme, voir John Edward Sandys, "The History of Ciceronianism" dans *Harvard Lectures on the Revival of Learning* (Cambridge, 1905), pp. 145-173; Izora Scott, *Controversies over the Imitation of Cicero as a Model for Style and Some Phases of their Influence on the Schools of the Renaissance* (New York, 1910), pp. 106-111; Eduard Norden, *Die Antike Kuntsprosa vom VI. Jahrhundert von Chr. bis in die Zeit der Renaissance* (Leipzig, 1898 and Darmstadt, 1958), II, 773-782. Aucun de ces livres ne s'étend sur le dernier mouvement anticicéronien que nous étudions ici et qui fut couronné de succès. On trouvera quelques remarques intéressantes sur le cicéronianisme dans W. H. Woodward, *Vittorino da Feltre and Other Humanist Educators* (Cambridge, 1897), pp. 10-13. [For further background, see Croll's later essays below and their Forewords; G. L. Hendrickson, "The Origin and Meaning of the Ancient Characters of Style," *American Journal of Philology*, XXVI (1905), 248-290; Trimpi, pp. 28-59 and *passim*; J. W. Duff's chapter on "Augustan Prose and Livy" in *A Literary History of Rome from the Origins to the Close of the Golden Age* (London, 1953); Wilbur Samuel Howell, *Logic and Rhetoric in England, 1500-1700* (Princeton, 1956); Sister Miriam Joseph, *Shakespeare's Use of the Arts of Language* (New York, 1947); Williamson, *Senecan Amble*, Ch. I and *passim*. See also *Sources*, n.12 and n.22.]

d'Apulée, du latin provincial des Pères de l'Église attirait encore par trop des esprits restés médiévaux au fond.

Les dangers qui assaillaient tous ceux qui s'écartaient du chemin étroit de la langue purement classique sont rendus évidents par la prose des différents pays au XVIe siècle. Les écrivains qui visent à l'élégance de la forme tombent généralement dans l'imitation des procédés trop faciles de la rhétorique des Pères de l'Église, tandis que ceux qui préfèrent se montrer simples et directs sont ordinairement grossiers et vulgaires, ou simplement insipides et impossible à lire. Ce fut donc un excellent instinct qui poussa les humanistes à faire du dogme cicéronien comme une haie autour de leur jardin et à le cultiver conformément aux règles qu'il prescrivait.

Pendant le dernier quart du siècle même, alors que de nouvelles attaques contre le cicéronianisme commençaient de plusieurs côtés, la plupart des chefs échouèrent parce qu'ils ne purent pas, ou n'osèrent pas opposer au cicéronianisme de programme d'imitation bien défini. Muret,[10] l'ami de Lipse, tombé en disgrâce dans son pays à cause de l'aide qu'il apporta à la Ligue, conduisait à Rome, sous la protection de la curie, une campagne contre la superstition de la rhétorique, laquelle, à ce moment, restait surtout liée à la Réforme. Dans ses *Variae Lectiones* de 1580, il étale, d'un air de défi, une longue liste d'auteurs latins pour qu'on les imite, sans distinction de mérite; il est vrai que sa liste montre une préférence précisément pour les auteurs de l'âge d'argent que Lipse commençait à défendre, et, dans une lettre écrite à peu près à la même époque, nous le voyons se plaindre amèrement des obstacles que les Jésuites dressent sur sa route quand il veut enseigner Tacite à ses élèves. Mais, parmi les nombreux modèles qu'il propose, Tacite et Sénèque côtoient des écrivains d'un tout autre caractère; comment l'élève doit-il faire son choix? Comment son goût sera-t-il formé et guidé, pour lui permettre d'établir la distinction qui convient?

La réponse d'un moderne à cette question serait naturellement que nul guide, nul modèle de ce genre n'est nécessaire au succès de l'élève dans la rhétorique, car son style doit être personnel, et

---

[10] Voir Charles Dejob, *Marc Antoine Muret: un Professeur Français en Italie dans la Seconde Moitié due Seizième Siècle* (Paris, 1881). [Cf. *APS*, n.38 and *Muret*, I, par. 2 and n.4. In *Revue Critique d'Histoire et de Littérature*, XVI, N.S. XIII (June 19, 1882), 483-488, Pierre de Nolhac's review of Dejob's book points out its errors and omissions]; et voir Nisard pour les relations de Muret avec Lipse.

un instinct infaillible lui indiquera le prototype dont il a besoin, s'il ne lui tient lieu de tout modèle. L'un des résultats de la révolte contre le cicéronianisme, que nous étudions ici, fut en effet de préparer la voie à la théorie moderne de l'individualisme; mais ce n'était pas, à l'époque, une théorie sage ni sûre. Les générations qui virent la fin du XVIe et le commencement du XVIIe siècle ne pouvaient ni se passer d'une doctrine d'imitation, ni se fier à leur propre instinct de la forme: leur sens de la forme n'était pas encore un instinct; ils percevaient la forme de certains modèles classiques et s'appuyaient sur une autorité reconnue, pas encore sur des lois naturelles. Le danger de rejeter toute espèce de dogme apparaît clairement lorsque, continuant à lire la liste de Muret, nous y trouvons le nom d'Apulée.

Ce qui distingue Lipse, c'est qu'il indique au mouvement la route à suivre pour se libérer du cicéronianisme. Il découvrit une méthode qui semblait concilier les deux forces opposées de son temps: le besoin d'autorités et de conventions d'une part, le désir de la nouveauté de l'autre. Il ne se rendit cependant pas maître de sa méthode dès le début; le style particulier qui le caractérisa plus tard n'était pas encore formé lorsqu'il se présenta au public, en 1569, avec un ouvrage de critique de textes intitulé *Variae Lectiones*. L'ouvrage était précédé d'une longue dédicace, sous forme de lettre adressée à son protecteur le cardinal Granvelle et écrite en périodes cicéroniennes claires et limpides. Nisard—excellent cicéronien lui-même—loue fort cette préface et prétend que Lipse n'écrivit jamais aussi bien; pour nous, l'intérêt de cette lettre est simplement de nous montrer Saül chez les prophètes, Lipse commençant sa carrière comme disciple de Mélanchton, de Sturm, et de Bembo. Il n'avait toutefois que vingt-et-un ans quand l'ouvrage parut; après un intervalle de huit ans, il publia un volume du même genre, *Quaestiones Epistolicae* [1577], où le changement survenu dans son goût est déjà visible.[10a] Plaute est désormais son auteur de prédilection. Il est clair que dans les vieux mots, dans le réalisme piquant de l'auteur comique, il a trouvé le moyen d'échapper à l'ennui créé par un purisme suranné; il avoue, en effet, que ce vieux style a plus de saveur pour lui que celui de Cicéron et ajoute, en parlant de

---

[10a] [Croll's error, that *Variae Lectiones* was published in 1567, when Lipsius was twenty, has been corrected in the text and his "intervalle de sept ans" has been changed to "huit ans." Originally there were four books in *Variae Lectiones*, but Lipsius shortened the work to *Variarum Lectionum Libri Tres* (Antwerp, 1577).]

son propre style, que le plan de son ouvrage ne lui permet pas d'employer la diction souple, agréable et nombreuse consacrée par l'usage, mais lui impose, au contraire, un mode d'expression plus précis et plus mordant. Ceci est dit avec un semblant d'humilité, et il cherche à se réfugier sous le couvert orthodoxe des lettres de Cicéron; mais il est évident qu'il est déjà arrivé à un tournant décisif.[11]

Ces paroles du reste ne sont pas tout à fait sincères; la conversion à laquelle elles font allusion n'a sans doute point été amenée par l'étude de Plaute et des lettres de Cicéron, mais en partie par ses entretiens avec Muret à Rome en 1567 et en partie par les recherches, déjà très avancées, qu'il faisait pour sa fameuse édition de Tacite. Cette œuvre parut, sous sa première forme, en 1575, alors que Lipse avait vingt-huit ans. À cette époque, il avait découvert ce qui sera le but des travaux de toute sa vie, et, désormais, tous ses efforts d'éditeur et de critique s'appliqueront à reconstituer les textes, à défendre le style et à expliquer la philosophie des auteurs romains du premier siècle de l'Empire. Dix ans plus tard, son nouveau style est déjà fameux, il doit lutter contre ses adversaires et ses imitateurs et a déjà commencé le grand ouvrage qui fait pendant à son Tacite, l'édition des œuvres de Sénèque, qui acheva, en 1605, le monument qu'il avait consacré à la mémoire de l'âge d'argent.

Le dessein de Lipse est très nettement indiqué dans un éloge

---

[11] [*Quaestiones Epistolicae*, better known as *Epistolicae Quaestiones*, is described by Saunders (p. 17) as "a collection of letters to various scholars and friends, concerning philological and literary nuances and practices, and full of scholarly conjectures respecting ancient authors and manuscript discoveries." In it, Saunders continues, citing v.26: Lipsius' "preference for the later Latin writers and their style became obvious. He tells us that the teaching which he proposes in this text 'does not permit a style, extended and suave, such as you find in Cicero. What it wants is brevity, piquancy, and a sufficiency of ancient references'" (III.16).] Une lettre écrite à un ami [Janus Lernutus, in June 1577] montre qu'en réalité il était beaucoup plus avancé dans sa théorie du style qu'il ne veut bien l'admettre publiquement. Voici ce qu'il dit (*Ep. Misc.* I.13, dans *Opera*, II, 16) de son nouvel ouvrage: *De quibus quid judicaturi sitis, timeo. Alia enim quaedam a prioribus meis haec scriptio, cui nitor ille abest, et luxuria, et Tulliani cincinni: pressa ubique, nec scio an quaesita nimis brevitas. Quae me tamen nunc capit. Timanthem pictorem celebrant, quod in ejus operibus plus semper aliquid intellegeretur, quam pingeretur: velim in mea scriptione.* C'est une description de Sénèque et de ses imitateurs. [Croll cites this passage in English in *APL*, II, par. 7. Cf. Williamson, *Senecan Amble*, p. 123; F. I. Merchant, "Seneca the Philosopher and his Theory of Style," *AJP*, XXVI (1905), 44-59; E. V. Arnold, *Roman Stoicism* (Cambridge, 1911); C. N. Smiley, "Seneca and the Stoic Theory of Literary Style," *Wisconsin Studies in Language and Literature*, III (1919), 50-61; J. F. D'Alton, *Roman Literary Theory and Criticism* (London, 1931).]

extraordinaire publié l'année qui suivit sa mort par Gaugericus Rivius, un juge de Malines, qui se dit le disciple du maître. La valeur de cet ouvrage ne consiste pas seulement dans son sujet, mais aussi dans le fait que son style est plein de toutes les erreurs de goût signalées par Lipse chez ses imitateurs. Dans le passage le plus important, Rivius s'exprime ainsi:

"Voilà la scène sur laquelle Lipse joua le rôle principal, non point paresseusement et en vain, mais bien réellement; et (quoique cette erreur ou cette maladie se soit grandement répandue de nos jours) jamais on ne le vit s'appliquer à re- chercher avec un zèle inquiet, où pouvait bien avoir été la cuisine d'Apicius, l'Apollon de Lucullus, ou le lupanar de Messaline; combien on pouvait mettre de guirlandes à la statue de Marsyas, si le menton de Poppée était beau et bien fait, de quel pays, Thessalie ou Numidie, venait le cheval de Curtius, si le vin de Palerme était plus délicat que celui de Chios, ou mille autres bagatelles, mille autres niaiseries de ce genre. Mais, déclarant qu'il vivait pour l'État,[12] et que l'État n'était pas à lui seul, il décida dès l'abord de sauver la vie de ses semblables par son travail, de redonner par ses soins la santé aux malades, de rendre leurs possessions premières à ceux qu'on avait injustement dépouillés et de les libérer de leurs fers. C'est pourquoi il visita toutes les prisons et remarqua Sénèque,[13] le poète tragique, Velleius Paterculus, le fameux Pline, ce panégyriste jadis célèbre de l'empereur Trajan, et beaucoup d'autres encore qui portaient les chaînes et le cos- tume des prisonniers et se tenaient là, dans la boue et la saleté, marqués au fer rouge, rasés, à demi morts. Dans la même foule, il aperçut encore Valère Maxime, si peu semblable à lui-même, si peu semblable à son nom.[14] . . . Et deux prison- niers surtout se distinguaient, qu'on avait injustement punis. . . . Lucius Annaeus Seneca et Gaius Cornelius Tacitus, hommes qui avaient occupé le rang de consuls, sortis on ne sait de quel barathre, de quel antre de Polyphème, ou plutôt de quelle caverne, peuplée de tigres et de panthères. . . . A Lipse, qui eut pitié d'eux et demanda pourquoi des hommes qui

[12] Il entend probablement *Respublica litterarum*.
[13] Il plaisante sur la condition tragique de la réputation de Sénèque.
[14] Lipse publia des annotations sur Valère Maxime en 1585 et des remarques sur Velleius Paterculus en 1591.

avaient, comme citoyens, travaillé pour le bien public étaient prisonniers, pourquoi on mettait dans les fers et pourquoi *on enchaînait ceux qui s'étaient attaché toute l'humanité* par leurs services et auraient dû être entre les mains et sur le cœur des princes; pourquoi *on souillait ceux qui avaient fait briller au delà des limites du monde*, au delà de la nature, la lumière éclatante de la prudence et de la sagesse; à Lipse, ils n'expliquèrent qu'une chose: c'est qu'au point de vue de ceux qui sont à la fois ignorants et influents, rien ne distingue un grand d'un médiocre talent, car ces puissants de la terre ne peuvent souffrir qu'on s'élève à leur niveau, et chez les coupables, l'innocence elle-même devient une espèce de crime et est considérée comme telle. Eux-mêmes cependant [Tacite et Sénèque] étaient laborieux, graves, sobres dans leurs discours, ennemis de la pompe et de la perfidie des cours et amis de la vérité. En conséquence, ils n'étaient ni dupes, ni trompeurs.[15]

"Le style de ces grands hommes lui plut, bien que, sous ce rapport, on les ait dit particulièrement désagréables. Et voilà que, par un coup de sa baguette magique, il les affranchit et leur rendit tous leurs droits de citoyens, de citoyens, ai-je dit? Il fit encore davantage: quand tous les membres qui leur restaient furent guéris, ils reçurent la pourpre et tous les ornements attachés au rang, comme en vertu du "postliminium"; puis, dans cet état, ils s'en retournèrent au Sénat. Sénèque et Tacite, ayant ainsi été secourus, afin de rendre le bien pour le bien, comme il sied à des hommes libres et bons, secoururent leur protecteur Lipse pendant toute sa vie, l'aidant de leur présence et de leurs conseils."[16]

Ce passage ajoute quelque chose à ce que nous savions de la carrière de Lipse et nous éclaire d'une façon intéressante sur les

[15] J'ai indiqué en italique dans ce paragraphe deux pointes ou *acumina*, caractéristiques de l'école anticicéronienne. La concision et la subtilité de Lipse devint, chez son imitateur, de l'obscurité et de l'extravagance; l'anticicéronianisme tourne au *concettismo*.

[16] Gaugericus Rivius, *Justi Lipsi Principatus Litterarius*, dans Lipse, *Opera*, I, lxxxii-lxxxiii. Dans la traduction, l'extravagance du style est atténuée pour qu'on puisse comprendre. L'ouvrage parut avec un volume d'œuvres diverses de Lipse et d'éloges sur lui, publié l'année (1607) qui suivit sa mort par son editeur Joannis Moretus. Il contient un très beau portrait orné de figures symboliques. [For an account of this work, *Justi Lipsi Sapientiae et Litterarum Antistitis Fama Posthuma* (Anvers, 1607), see F. van der Haeghen, *Bibliographie Lipsienne* (Ghent, 1886-1888), III, 315-317.]

œuvres secondaires qui occupèrent les intervalles entre ses grands travaux. Dans la liste donnée par Rivius, un lecteur familier avec la littérature anglaise et continentale du XVIIe siècle reconnaîtra les noms d'auteurs fort populaires à cette époque, et très souvent cités, qui étaient méprisés ou inconnus au XVIe siècle et sont plus ou moins retombés dans l'oubli depuis. Il comprend mieux alors pourquoi Jonson et Balthasar Gracián citent fréquemment Velleius Paterculus, pourquoi Montaigne et Burton connaissent si bien Valère Maxime et pourquoi on a tant étudié et imité en Espagne, en France et en Angleterre le panégyrique de Trajan par Pline le jeune.[17] Et l'on peut dire aussi que Lipse, comme lui et ses contemporains le publient, aida par son influence à créer cette admiration pour Salluste, qui fut l'un des traits du goût au commencement du XVIIe siècle. Bref, Lipse choisit le rôle de défenseur de la latinité de l'âge d'argent, d'interprète auprès de son époque des phases du mouvement anticicéronien qui commença pendant la vie même de Cicéron et triompha pendant le siècle qui suivit sa mort. C'est vers ce mouvement qu'il dirige l'attention de ses contemporains, leur donnant par là un moyen sûr d'échapper à leur propre cicéronianisme. Comment devons-nous alors comprendre le terme "âge d'argent de la latinité" ainsi employé et quels sont les caractères du style de ses auteurs qui le différencie du style de Cicéron et lui permit de servir de type à une école de prose moderne?

En ce qui concerne les détails de construction et d'ornement, nous répondrons en analysant soigneusement le style de Lipse et ses préceptes; mais, en ce qui concerne l'inspiration du premier mouvement anticicéronien et ses tendances, c'est dans les lettres qu'il écrivit à ses amis et où il exposait ses théories qu'il faut chercher ses opinions. Par exemple, il écrivit en 1586: "Je désire publier quelque chose qui fasse savoir tout ce que je pense au sujet

[17] Comparer "A Panegyrick to King Charles" de Sir Henry Wotton dans *Reliquiae Wottonianae* (London, 1672), pp. 135-158, qui dit y imiter Pline, et l'analyse et l'éloge du "Panegyrique de Trajan" par Dom Jean Goulu (l'adversaire de Guez de Balzac) dans la seconde partie de ses *Lettres de Phyllarque à Ariste* (Paris, 1628); aussi les *Commentaribus* de Lipse, *Opera*, IV, 283 et suiv. Le goût que l'on montra pour cet ouvrage et l'admiration de Tacite résultent en grande partie de ce qu'on étudiait l'art d'être courtisan avec grande application dans tous les pays européens à la fin du XVIe siècle. Le mouvement anticicéronien, la réaction catholique et la monarchie nouvelle sont reliés les uns aux autres d'une façon intéressante. Dans sa préface au lecteur, Lipse s'excuse du peu d'importance attribuée à la langue dans son livre et suppose que quelqu'un vient lui rappeler que Pline était un maître de politique et *conveniebat Aulae, cui scribis*. [See *APS*, n.58.]

de l'imitation. Car il est trop tard pour que moi je change: cet arbre, qu'il ait poussé droit ou de travers, s'est endurci dans sa forme. J'ai aimé Cicéron autrefois, je l'ai même imité, mais je suis devenu homme, et mon goût s'est modifié. Les fêtes asiatiques ont cessé de me plaire, je préfère les banquets attiques."[18]

Le terme "attique" appliqué au mouvement anticicéronien de Sénèque et de Tacite ou au mouvement correspondant des XVIe et XVIIe siècles semble un peu obscur et nécessite quelque explication. Le style artificiel, pour ne pas dire affecté, qui prévalut à ces deux époques, semble à l'esprit moderne plus éloigné de la concision de Démosthène que de l'élégance de Cicéron lui-même. Cependant, le terme fut constamment employé pendant les deux périodes, et la critique de nos jours ne l'a point rejeté. En fait, il explique la nature du mouvement qui se fit dans la prose entre 1575 et 1675 dans la mesure où il exprime un mépris de l'ornement inutile et du formalisme creux et la recherche de l'expression précise et brève.

Dans d'autres lettres, Lipse indique ses goûts d'une façon plus nette. Ses adversaires avaient signalé aux maîtres la détestable influence de son style sur la jeunesse:

> "Si c'est là leur crainte, écrit-il, il [mon style] doit avoir un charme et une séduction étranges. En vérité, le sentiment qu'ils expriment là leur prouve bien (j'en appelle à lui comme témoin) qu'il y a quelque chose de rapide et de vivant dans mon style, bien qu'il soit érudit, qu'ils raillent du bout des lèvres plutôt que du fond du cœur. Nous les connaissons, ces êtres méprisables qui se raccrochent à leur précepte étroit: 'Hoc exordium, haec narratio est: hic allegoria, hic metaphora,' et jurent qu'ils sont les interprètes éminents de Cicéron, oui, et cicéroniens eux-mêmes. En vertu de quoi? Parce que leurs écrits manquent de vie et d'énergie [*elumbis* et *exsanguis*], qu'ils sont apathiques par l'expression, le sentiment et le rythme, si froids en un mot qu'ils glaceraient jusqu'à leurs neiges allemandes. Et ce qu'il y a de plus amusant, c'est que ce n'est pas Cicéron qu'ils voudraient nous voir soutenir, mais leur Mélanchton, un homme que je m'en voudrais de mépriser, si ce n'est à cause de sa religion, mais qui, parmi les maîtres

[18] *Ep. Misc.*, II.10, dans *Opera*, II, 75. [Croll recurs to this statement in *APS*, III (pp. 70-71).]

de l'éloquence, ou même parmi les meilleurs de ses défenseurs, n'a droit à aucune place."[19]

Ailleurs, c'est un critique français, Henri Estienne probablement, qui attire les foudres de Lipse:

"Dans quel siècle vivons-nous, pour qu'un fatras nonchalant et languissant y soit apprécié! Et c'est en cela qu'ils se croient cicéroniens? Puisse en vérité mon style avoir quelque chose de piquant et d'érudit qui sorte de l'ordinaire; qu'il montre quelque sentiment, et pas seulement l'éclat, mais encore la chaleur du génie."[20]

Ces remarques caractérisent parfaitement la nature de la réaction anticicéronienne de la fin du XVIe siècle. La force d'expression, plutôt qu'une beauté sensuelle et extérieure, l'attention portée sur tous les détails, plutôt qu'une diffusion, et une dispersion de l'intérêt pour un effet d'ensemble—une concision mordante, plutôt qu'une recherche cérémonieuse—la pensée sérieuse de l'individu rendue avec toute la chaleur de sa conception première dans l'esprit, de préférence aux idées plus vastes, plus nobles et plus générales qui appartiennent à toute une portion de l'humanité: voilà ce qu'a cherché le mouvement anticicéronien, et les paroles de Lipse que nous avons rapportées prouvent que ce fut aussi son idéal. Si, en insistant comme elles le font sur les mots "érudit" et "concis," elles montrent bien quelles tendances dangereuses le mouvement contenait à l'état latent, elles n'en sont que plus intéressantes. En un mot, le mouvement anticicéronien fut une protestation contre une manière conventionnelle et vide dans la rhétorique. Il paraît quelquefois même être une protestation contre toute espèce de style conventionnel; si nous lisons ses manifestes en pensant à l'histoire des siècles qui viendront, il nous semble parfois entendre les premiers mots de la théorie du style individuel, qui a laissé si peu de place à l'étude de la rhétorique dans les programmes modernes. Mais, si le mouvement anticicéronien eut bien pour effet de préparer le monde à cette théorie, ce serait une grave erreur de voir là le but de ce mouvement. Montaigne, il est vrai, la prévoyait, mais les intuitions des hommes de génie sont rarement comprises de leur génération, et les chefs de la révolte contre Cicéron ne purent ni

[19] *Ep. ad Belgas*, III.28, dans *Opera*, II, 486.
[20] *Ep. ad Germanos et Gallos*, 15, dans *Opera*, II, 332. [Cf. *APL*, II (pp. 176-177).]

ne voulurent en général tirer les conclusions logiques de leur enseignement. Ils changent de modèle, mais non point de méthode. Ils visaient à la personnalité, à l'originalité d'expression, mais, à leur sens, ce but n'est nullement incompatible avec la ferme croyance à la doctrine de l'imitation. Lipse, et il est peut-être le seul, a nettement formulé cette opinion, et, après avoir longuement réfléchi, il fit connaître sa méthode d'application dans son traité intitulé *Epistolica Institutio.*

Cette œuvre commence par établir que l'imitation, "cette harmonieuse conformité de notre discours avec celui des anciens," harmonie manifestée par le style, est le seul moyen d'atteindre à la perfection en rhétorique; et l'auteur expose alors un plan d'imitation qui remplacerait la méthode exclusive de l'étroite école cicéronienne. Il faut citer le passage presque en entier. Se demandant quels auteurs doivent être imités et dans quelles circonstances, Lipse dit:

"En premier lieu, il serait à désirer qu'il nous restât une suffisante abondance de textes [anciens] pour que le procès puisse être jugé en toute équité. Nous avons peu d'auteurs anciens, qui osera nier qu'il soit bon de les lire tous? Quelques Italiens l'ont fait récemment et restreint la liberté de l'éloquence en lui assignant comme limites le texte de Cicéron. Hommes difficiles et stupides, qui ne vont pas seulement à l'encontre des opinions des anciens maîtres, mais à l'encontre de l'expérience et de la raison. Croyez fermement avec moi qu'il vous faut tout lire et tout imiter, pas en même temps cependant, ni à la même période de votre vie. Une distinction s'impose entre les âges, qu'il est peut-être bon que je définisse.

"Il y a une première imitation, celle de la jeunesse; une imitation pour la jeunesse plus avancée [crescens] et une autre pour les adultes. Pendant la première période, l'hérésie italienne me satisfera; durant ce laps de temps, on devra non seulement beaucoup lire Cicéron, mais Cicéron uniquement. Pourquoi? Eh bien! afin que la langue dans son ensemble puisse se mouler sur un modèle défini et sur un style oratoire uniforme. Je ne sais si mon opinion resterait la même au cas où les œuvres de Calvus, de Cœlius, de Brutus, de César et d'autres encore parmi les orateurs classiques existeraient encore. Mais, dans les conditions actuelles, qui nous a enseigné nos périodes, nos constructions et nos rythmes et l'art d'en-chaîner le discours, si ce n'est Cicéron? C'est à son école donc, à mon avis, que la jeunesse doit faire ses débuts. Comme un peintre qui, ayant entrepris un portrait, trace d'abord les con-tours avant de rechercher les couleurs convenant à chaque partie, mon imitateur, après avoir trouvé les grandes lignes de son style, ira chercher, de divers côtés, les couleurs. S'il ne fait pas ainsi (crois-moi maintenant, jeune homme, ou tu seras bien obligé de me croire plus tard), il arrivera à un style mal composé, qui aura pris différentes formes dans différents auteurs et ne sera jamais stable, je vois le fait se produire tous les jours, et je n'ignore point les causes de cette erreur.[21] Que Cicéron donc occupe la première place, et qu'il l'occupe seul.

"Dans l'imitation de l'adolescence, j'introduirai cependant d'autres modèles, mais successivement, afin que vous n'avan-ciez pas par bonds, mais par degrés, pour ainsi dire. Aussi, si vous m'en croyez, vous vous tournerez d'abord vers ceux qui s'écartent le moins de Cicéron, et qui, par la richesse, l'har-monie et l'abondance de leur diction rapellent le plus cet heureux et facile génie. Tel est surtout Fabius, ou encore, Quinte-Curce, Velleius Paterculus, César; ils auraient tous ressemblé davantage à Cicéron, si un autre ordre de sujets ne les avaient retenus et dirigés. Pendant cette période, lisez-les donc, mais superficiellement, lisez Plaute et Térence, au con-traire, avec grand soin. Chez qui trouvera-t-on mieux le terme propre? Chez qui cette élégance attique de la phrase? C'est dans la même catégorie que je rangerai aussi Pline, le concis, le fin, le raffiné Pline, bien qu'il se montre par instants, et d'une façon qui n'est point déplaisante, prolixe et pas assez viril. Et je lui adjoindrai un moderne, plus grand cependant que les modernes,[22] le fameux Ange Politien, Toscan,[23] qui, malgré

[21] Il se peut que Lipse pense à Montaigne. Dans son style, comme dans celui de Burton et (dans une certaine mesure) de Browne, on voit le résultat d'un indi-vidualisme voulu et le mépris des tournures, des locutions, des phrases et des pé-riodes classiques conventionnelles. Pour eux, l'antiquité ne sert plus à former leur art, mais à l'enrichir de connaissances, à l'orner de nobles détails, à le broder d'allusions. Ils sont libérés des lois de l'imitation servile et cela leur donne un nouveau et précieux privilège. Ils considèrent les classiques en romantiques pour ainsi dire; ils sentent leur charme, leur éloignement comme aucun humaniste con-sciencieux n'aurait voulu le faire.

[22] Pointe typique qui illustre les *argutiae* que Lipse condamne sans conviction chez Politien à la ligne suivante.

[23] Ange Politien fut l'un des premiers anticicéroniens. "Condamnez-vous Tite-

quelque recherche et quelque affectation, semble égaler les
anciens eux-mêmes dans l'art de l'épître.

"Que cette période préparatoire couvre deux années pendant
lesquelles les jeunes écrivains doivent être retenus dans leur
recherche du style par la *toga pura* de la jeunesse, et alors, je
leur donnerai pleine liberté d'errer çà et là parmi toutes les
sortes d'écrivains, qu'ils lisent, qu'ils voient, qu'ils cueillent
toutes les fleurs dans tous les jardins pour orner la couronne
de l'éloquence. Mais je leur recommande surtout Salluste,
Sénèque, Tacite et d'autres écrivains aussi concis, aussi péné-
trants, pour que leur abondance se trouve fauchée, comme par
un fer tranchant, et que leur discours devienne fort, précis et
véritablement viril.

"J'en ai fini maintenant avec cette première partie; à moins
que je n'ajoute, avec un semblant de légèreté, qu'il sera bon
de lire et de relire Cicéron, tous les jours, dans la soirée
surtout, et, si l'on en a l'occasion, au moment même de s'en-
dormir. L'esprit, je ne sais trop pourquoi, saisit, retient et
s'assimile mieux à cette heure tranquille. Essayez, et d'un avis
insignifiant vous tirerez le plus grand profit."[24]

Bien que le but où tend ce plan d'études progressif soit commun
à tous les anticicéroniens, l'invention du plan lui-même appartient

---

Live, Salluste, Quintilien, Sénèque et Pline parce que ce sont des barbares," de-
mande-t-il à Scala dans une lettre en 1493. Voir *Epistolarum Libri XII*, v.1, dans
Omnium Angeli Politiani Operum (Paris, 1519), fol. 40v.

[24] *Ep. Inst.*, Ch. XI, dans *Opera*, II, 538-539. [See *Muret*, n.66.] Le dernier
paragraphe semble être inspiré par un scrupule très particulier à Lipse: la crainte
de nuire à une vérité en défendant une autre. Il pense peut-être à ses élèves im-
prudents qui se moquaient tout haut de Cicéron; d'un autre côté, le passage peut
être une imitation de l'enthousiasme cicéronien, il rappelle le *Ciceronianus* d'Érasme.
L'*Ep. Inst.* est condensé dans deux chapitres des *Discoveries* de Jonson [accord-
ing to F. E. Schelling in his ed. of Jonson's *Discoveries* (London, 1892) and
Maurice Castelain in his ed. of it (Paris, 1906); Castelain prints extracts from
Lipsius' Latin and points out parallel passages (pp. 110-116). Jonson may well
have known the Lipsian original but his borrowings were derived through John
Hoskyns, *Direccons for Speech and Style*: see H. H. Hudson, ed., *Directions for
Speech and Style* (Princeton, 1935) and L. B. Osborn, *The Life, Letters, and
Writings of John Hoskyns* (New Haven, 1937). See also Dunn, "Lipsius and the Art
of Letter-Writing," *SR*, III; Trimpi, pp. 62-75; *Ben Jonson*, ed. C. H. Herford and
P. and E. M. Simpson, 11 vols. (Oxford, 1925-52), VIII, 629-633 and XI, 275-278];
quand on lisait les lettres de Lipse dans quelques écoles anglaises au XVIIe siècle,
on se servait quelquefois du traité comme ouvrage de rhétorique. Voir "Scholars
and Scholarship, 1600-1660," *Cambridge History of English Literature* (New
York, 1932), VI, 357, par le professeur Foster Watson et, du même, *The English*

à Lipse, et son extrême confiance dans sa réussite vient probablement de ce que lui-même l'a suivi. Comme l'élève auquel il pense, il a commencé par être un cicéronien sincère, bien que sa période d'apprentissage se soit étendue au delà de la limite qu'il prescrit à ses disciples; puis, par des essais faits à l'aventure, il est petit à petit parvenu à se libérer des modèles affectés de sa jeunesse, jusqu'à ce qu'enfin, dans le style "concis et pénétrant" qu'aimaient Tacite et Sénèque, il eût trouvé "son but et son repos." Il n'est pas étrange qu'il se soit imaginé que d'autres après lui pourraient acquérir un style aussi expressif, aussi vivant que le sien, en suivant la même méthode, et réussir, comme lui, à garder tous les charmes de la nouveauté, sans quitter pour cela la voie sûre de l'imitation.

Nous n'avons point besoin de faire remarquer, cependant, que l'esprit moderne découvre dans ce plan une fâcheuse complexité et prévoit les dangers qui résulteraient de son succès. Car il paraît impliquer l'union idéale des deux grands principes de tout art littéraire —la convention et l'originalité—et supposer que cette union, le but et le désespoir de tous les artistes, puisse s'effectuer au moyen de purs artifices. Or, nous pouvons comprendre ce qu'il y a d'absolument conventionnel dans le système cicéronien d'imitation et tolérer les restrictions qu'il impose, parce que la théorie en est au moins simple et normale; nous pouvons aisément excuser l'insuffisance du style du XVIIIe siècle, parce que nous comprenons, et, jusqu'à un certain point nous approuvons, son conventionalisme plus ou moins libéral; quant à la doctrine moderne du style individuel, de celui qui appartient en propre à un homme, elle gagne immédiatement notre sympathie et nos suffrages. Mais que dire d'un système qui prétend unir les extrêmes de ces tendances dans une méthode pratique, combiner l'imitation imposée à la chaleur et l'originalité du génie? Car, le but de Lipse n'est pas moins ambitieux. Il prescrit les modes de l'expression individuelle, une routine qui assure l'originalité, un système pour produire la nouveauté. Son plan d'imitation prend pour base l'hypothèse que l'ardeur et la vivacité du génie sont dans le domaine de la rhétorique et peuvent s'enseigner avec le même succès que les figures du style cicéronien.

Nous voyons clairement maintenant qu'un tel système, dans sa donnée même, contient une contradiction, et nous pouvons, sans

---

Grammar Schools to 1660: Their Curriculum and Practice (Cambridge, 1908), p. 415. [Cf. Trimpi, pp. 62-75; for Jonson's classical adaptations, see *APL*, n.15.]

crainte de nous tromper, prédire (après la lettre) ce qui résultera de son application rigoureuse; nous obtiendrons ou bien cette sécheresse qui suit toujours l'effort fait pour trop resserrer l'expression, ou un succès passager dans le genre emphatique et exagéré. Mais, la génération de Lipse ne pouvait pas se voir avec des yeux des modernes, elle se trouvait à mi-chemin entre le moyen âge et le monde moderne, elle cherchait en aveugle son chemin vers la liberté et l'originalité de la pensée. Elle avait eu un aperçu des vastes champs qui s'ouvraient devant la raison humaine émancipée; mais, d'un autre côté, elle n'en était pas encore arrivée à une philosophie d'indépendance sur laquelle elle eût pu fonder sa confiance dans la validité de ses perceptions intellectuelles. Elle aspirait vaguement (pour continuer ici l'image de Lipse) à errer librement dans les champs ensoleillés de la nature, mais elle ne savait pas encore que sa robe et sa toque médiévales ne convenaient guère à de pareils exercices juvéniles. En somme, l'époque du mouvement anticicéronien fut celle qui précéda Descartes, l'époque de la philosophie de Bacon, période qui semble, à de certains moments, avoir comblé le gouffre qui nous sépare du moyen âge et paraît à d'autres bien plus lointaine, bien plus médiévale que l'âge si simple des premières années de la Renaissance.

✦ III ✦

L'Application Des Théories De Lipse

La théorie de Lipse, qui veut que tous les auteurs classiques soient imités, créera, naturellement, une grande variété de style chez les différents imitateurs. Même parmi les écrivains des premiers temps de l'Empire qu'il recommande à l'imitation des adultes, le choix est vaste, et un admirateur de Sénèque, par exemple, n'écrira pas comme celui qui a pris Tacite pour modèle. Nous ne nous proposons pas de discuter ici les différences entre ces deux auteurs, qui furent les principaux modèles de l'école anticicéronienne; mais la preuve de l'influence de l'un ou de l'autre peut approximativement s'établir en comparant leurs diverses tendances en ce qui concerne la qualité de clarté.

Il est évident que la subtilité et l'extrême concision dans toutes les formes littéraires risquent d'amener l'obscurité; Sénèque obvie à cet inconvénient par un effort volontaire vers la clarté. Dans ses critiques, il insiste sans cesse sur la nécessité de la clarté, et, quoiqu'il méprise ces allongements, cette diffusion de la phrase par laquelle l'orateur réussit à flatter l'intelligence de la foule, il a grand soin de composer et de présenter son aphorisme le plus succinct de telle façon qu'un auditeur attentif et intelligent le comprenne au premier abord. Tacite, au contraire, augmente plutôt l'obscurité d'un discours naturellement compact et extrêmement expressif. Il aime à enchevêtrer les paradoxes et étudie toutes les ressources de l'ellipse; le fait que l'obscurité de l'école de prose espagnole dite "conceptiste" est généralement attribuée à la mauvaise influence de ce "prince des ténèbres"[25] montre quelle fut, au XVIIe siècle, sa réputation sous ce rapport.

Lipse n'ignorait pas les dangers qui résultent de la recherche d'un style "concis et pénétrant," car, dans l'*Epistolica Institutio,* s'il place au premier rang la qualité de concision, il y ajoute quatre qualités qui en corrigent le défaut, à savoir la netteté, la simplicité, la grâce et la justesse d'expression.[26] L'influence de Sénèque apparaît là, comme aussi dans la formule fort commode qu'il inventa pour le style, "Concision et clarté."[27]

Son style montre l'union de ces deux qualités; il est expressif, nerveux, elliptique et précis, mais, comme dans Sénèque, la phrase est nettement esquissée, les ellipses se comprennent facilement, et les "pointes" sont rendues claires par la forme sous laquelle elles se présentent; si, par exemple, il y a antithèse dans la pensée, cette antithèse se retrouve aussi dans l'expression. L'influence de Tacite

[25] C'est ainsi que Dominique Bouhours, *La Manière de Bien Penser dans les Ouvrages d'Esprit* (Amsterdam, 1688) le dépeint en parlant de son imitateur Balthazar Gracián. [The fourth dialogue says a good deal about obscurity, and Tacitus and Gracián, but does not use this phrase. Tacitus' style is also discussed in a passage in the third dialogue. John Oldmixon "Englished" the work as *The Arts of Logick and Rhetorick* (London, 1728).]

[26] "La seconde vertu est la justesse d'expression, mise à dessein immédiatement après la concision, parce que la première se trouve grandement menacée par cette dernière." *Ep. Inst.,* Ch. VIII, dans *Opera,* II, 536. [Trimpi (pp. 248-249) abbreviates this part of Croll's essay and (pp. 62-68) summarizes Lipsius' discussion of the main characteristics of epistolary style—brevity, perspicuity, simplicity, graceful charm (*venustatem*), and appropriateness (*decentiam*). Trimpi observes (p. 258, n.13) that the Lipsian characteristics of style are nearly those described as the virtues of Stoic style by Diogenes Laertius in his "Life of Zeno," VII. 59: "There are five excellences of speech—pure Greek, lucidity, conciseness, appropriateness, distinction" (*Diogenes Laertius,* Loeb, ed., trans. R. D. Hicks, London, 1925).]

[27] *Ep. Inst.,* Ch. VIII, dans *Opera,* II, 537: "Écrivez donc, si vous pouvez, clairement et avec concision, n'oubliant jamais que cette dernière qualité est louable, la première indispensable." [For a fuller extract from this passage, translated into English, see Trimpi, p. 64.]

se remarque dans certaines locutions, mais, dans l'ensemble, son style imite clairement celui de Sénèque.

Au point de vue technique, les caractères de ce style sont plus exactement les suivants:

1º La concision. Par là nous entendons ses phrases courtes, ses locutions brèves, où, constamment, il nous faut compléter les ellipses, et l'habitude qu'il a d'éviter volontairement, et avec quelque affectation, les détours polis des préfaces, des apologues et des exordes cicéroniens.[28]

2º L'omission, chaque fois qu'il le peut, des conjonctions et des transitions. Ce caractère est presque nécessairement celui du style haché, fait de phrases courtes, et, au contraire, ne se rencontre pas dans le style périodique; Macaulay, par exemple, possède ce trait en commun avec Lipse, bien qu'il soit absolument différent pour ce qui est du caractère suivant.

3º Lipse évite les phrases qui se répondent, il évite le parallélisme, la similitude et tous les autres procédés de la "concinnité" cicéronienne. Il cherche plutôt à rompre le rythme en arrêtant brusquement ses phrases, manquant ainsi, comme des critiques hostiles l'ont dit, à ce que l'oreille attendait de lui.

4º Il fait un emploi fréquent des parenthèses et des tournures concises; si nous rapprochons ces deux traits, c'est que ce sont là deux procédés pour couper la longue période cicéronienne et stimuler l'esprit en trompant l'oreille. Les parenthèses de Lipse sont fameuses, et c'est un des signes qui permettent de reconnaître les auteurs qui l'ont imité.[29]

5º Lipse s'exerce aux pointes ou "acumina," c'est-à-dire aux pensées subtiles (généralement très brèves et très serrées et présentées sous forme d'antithèse), qui veulent défier la vivacité d'esprit du lecteur.

[28] Une manière brève de commencer et de terminer les lettres, les préfaces, etc., est la marque d'un esprit anticicéronien. Lipse écrit à Montaigne qu'ils n'aiment ni l'un ni l'autre faire autrement, et la préface de Wotton à ses *Elements of Architecture* (1624) est un excellent exemple de cette raideur voulue. Voir la lettre de Lipse, plus bas et la note.

[29] Chez l'évêque Hall, par exemple. Voir la remarque faite par un des amis de Hall, prédicateur célèbre à Londres, Thomas Adams, dans *The Sermons of Thomas Adams*, ed. John Brown (Cambridge, 1909), p. 197: "He was no talkative fellow: that to every short question returns answer able to fill a volume; with as many parentheses in one sentence as would serve Lipsius all his life." [An article by Croll on Adams is extant among his unpublished papers in Princeton Library.]

6° Il aime les métaphores.[30] Voilà un trait caractéristique de la prose du XVIIe siècle, et qui la distingue de celle du XVIe, qui préférait la comparaison plus claire et plus diffuse. Ce goût a d'abord marqué le style des chefs du mouvement anticicéronien, Montaigne, Bacon, Lipse et les concettistes espagnols, et, dans les théories de ces derniers, il a joué un rôle très important.

Les passages des lettres et des traités de Lipse que nous avons déjà cités et traduits illustrent toutes ces qualités; mais nous pouvons y ajouter ici deux courts extraits, dans la langue originale, d'une lettre sur les voyages à l'étranger que Lipse écrivit a un jeune noble [Philippus Lanoyus]. Le premier l'avertit des vices des nations étrangères et est cité en grande partie parce qu'il illustre le choix des figures subtiles et érudites, de préférence aux images simples, réalistes et jolies des cicéroniens, parce qu'il montre, pour parler en termes de prose anglaise, l'image à la façon de Bacon employée plutôt que celle de Sidney:

"Tu haec fuge, et imprimis vera et interna animorum vitia, quorum ubique larga et obvia seges, e qua ne quas spicas improvide colligas, magna mihi pro te cura, imo metus. Admittimus enim nescio quo modo et combibimus facile peregrinas illas culpas; sive quia novitate aliqua blandiuntur, sive quia specie virtutum. Atque ut venena vinis admixta, medicorum scito, perniciter et perniciose penetrant: sic peccata haec adsita virtuti. Fere enim ita fit: ut in qua gente vitia certa increbuere, mores jam vocentur, nec in veniam modo veniant, sed laudem. Adde, quod natura ipsa proniores nos ad mala imitanda. Ut pictor, levi manu, et volante penicillo, rugas, verrucas, naevos in facie exprimit, haud tam facile ipsam:

[30] Cette qualité, il est vrai, est moins remarquable chez Lipse que chez les autres anticicéroniens, sans doute à cause de son désir de clarté. Dans le passage que nous citons plus bas, la comparaison est plus fréquente que la métaphore, mais le goût nouveau qui s'était développé pour la figure concise se voit dans un passage de l'*Ep. Inst.* cité plus haut et aussi dans ce qui suit (déjà cité en partie). Remarquer aussi l'extrême concision et le piquant du style de Lipse: "Quid, quod nec Schemata, et ornatus illos floridæ orationis tango? nam visum mihi pertenuia haec et Scholastica esse, *quae didicisse oporteat magis quam discere*: aut alio certe doctore discere, neque Aquila, ut in proverbio est, captat muscas. Ergo politica et graviora illa dogmata explicares, dicet alius: et conveniebat Aulae, cui scribis. Haud negaverim istud, illud non suscipio. Quia etsi talium monitorum uberrima et pulcherrima hic seges; tamen falcem meam nunc non sentiet, et satis atque abunde messuisse arbitror in POLITICORUM libris, qui exstant." *Commentario in Plinii Panegyricum*, "Ad lectorem," dans *Opera*, IV, 297.

sic probitatem laboriose imitamur, nullo negotio maculas illas animorum."

Plus loin, l'humeur sententieuse de Polonius reparaît, et le style offre presque toute la concision mordante des essais de Bacon:

"Cres mihi esto inter Cretas. Nec viam tibi tamen ad fraudes praeco absit, sed ut medici, venena quaedam venenis pello, in salutem tuam non in noxam. Ad minutas et innocentes quasdam simulatiunculas te voco: nec ad alienas insidias, sed ad animi tui opportuna tegumenta. In Italia tota tria haec mihi serva. Frons tibi aperta, lingua parca, mens clausa.[31] Comis et communis vultus adversus omnes sit, animus externo nulli pateat: et velut in theca clausum eum habeas, dum redeas ad notos animos et vere amicos. Epicharmeae sapientiae ille nervus hic valeat, nulli fidere. Nisi facis: non unus Ulysses Ajacem te circumveniet; et dolorem nobis debes, illis risum."[32]

Ces derniers mots sont un bon exemple de pointes sous forme d'antithèse, à la manière de Sénèque.

✦ IV ✦

Sa Place dans l'Histoire Littéraire

Il est évident, d'après les plaisanteries de ses adversaires "de imitatione Lipsiana," que les idées nouvelles de Lipse sur la rhétorique eurent une grande popularité. Nous avons vu comment, jeune encore, il était devenu le chef d'une école de rhétorique et se plaignait déjà du zèle maladroit de ses disciples. Bientôt on le regarda comme l'homme dont les erreurs avaient, pendant sa vie

[31] Cela rappelle, non seulement Polonius, mais aussi la maxime de Sir Henry Wotton (*Life and Letters*, ed. Logan Pearsall Smith, Oxford, 1907, I, 109) pour les ambassadeurs envoyés en Italie: "The thoughts close and the countenance loose."

[32] *Ep. Misc.*, I.22, dans *Opera*, II, 21-22. La lettre fut traduit en anglais sous le titre *A Direction for Travailers*, par Sir John Stradling (1594). Un court passage extrait de la traduction du *De Constantia*, par Stradling (*Tvvo Bookes of Constancie*, London, 1595, p. 19), montre non seulement la concision pénétrante du style de Lipse, mais aussi la tournure d'esprit rationaliste et sceptique qui le rapproche de Montaigne: "If fire should happen to be kindled in this cittie, we should have a generall out-cry: the lame and almost the blind would hasten to help quench it. What think you? For their countries sake? Aske them and you shall see, it was, because the losse would have redounded to al, or at the least, the feare thereof. So falleth it out in this case. Publike evils doe moove and disquiet many men, not for that the harme toucheth a great number, but because themselves are of that number."

31

même, servi de base aux doctrines d'une secte,[33] et la raillerie ne perd rien de son sel pour n'être qu'une répétition de la campagne autrefois menée contre Sénèque. Quel fondement y avait-il exactement aux plaintes de Lipse et aux attaques de ses ennemis, et jusqu'où s'étendait en réalité la secte lipsienne, nous ne pouvons maintenant le dire; elle pouvait se composer seulement des élèves qui avaient reçu l'enseignement du maître à Leyde et ailleurs, ou, d'un autre côté, comprendre toute l'école anticicéronienne, puisque Lipse en était le chef reconnu et enseignait sans cesse ses doctrines dans sa correspondance. Mais, quel qu'ait été le champ de son influence personnelle—c'est un point sur lequel nous reviendrons tout à l'heure—il est certain que, dans la critique littéraire de son siècle, il occupe une plus grande place qu'aucun autre maître de rhétorique. La controverse dont son nom fut le centre embrasse une période d'au moins soixante-quinze ans, s'étendant de la grande époque de la Renaissance à celle de la prose classique française, période qui se divise en deux parties distinctes correspondant à deux phases du progrès de l'opinion en rhétorique. Durant sa vie, et pendant les dix années qui suivirent sa mort, on attaque Lipse comme innovateur, comme hérétique littéraire, on l'accuse de nier les traditions les plus sacrées de l'humanisme orthodoxe, et on peut remarquer, comme une curiosité littéraire, que, alors qu'il était encore professeur dans une université protestante, ses appuis étaient surtout dans les pays du midi et que les attaques dirigées contre lui étaient envenimées par un sentiment de haine contre le catholicisme.

La première de ces deux périodes de controverse est marquée par les écrits de Joseph Scaliger et du plus jeune des Estienne. Dès 1586, Henri Estienne consacra un gros volume aux principes de l'humaniste hollandais;[34] cette œuvre déçoit celui qui étudie la théorie de la rhétorique; le peu de critique littéraire qu'on y trouve est une critique de texte, sans grand intérêt, et, dans la majeure partie de ses cinq cent soixante pages, des questions de trahisons et de conspirations politiques et religieuses se mêlent d'une manière

---

[33] Voir, par exemple, la préface des *Lettres Diverses de Monsieur de Balzac* (Paris, 1663), sig. a5v. Dans sa "Dissertation, ou Responses à Quelques Questions," dans *Socrate Chrestien . . . et Autre Œuvres* (Paris, 1661), pp. 352, 355, Balzac prétend que Lipse avait corrompu un nombre infini de jeunes gens préférant Sénèque à Cicéron, mais il ajoute qu'il l'excuse, car, en plaidant la cause de Sénèque, il plaidait la sienne aussi. [Cf. *APS*, III (p. 71).]

[34] Le titre (abrégé) est *De Lipsii Latinitate . . . nec Lipsiomini, nec Lipsiocolacis; multoque minus Lipsiomastigis. Libertas volo sit Latinitate, sed Licentia nolo detur illi* (Frankfort, 1595).

inexplicable à la discussion des tendances de Lipse en rhétorique. Des influences perfides, venues d'Espagne et d'Italie, travaillent étrangement pour le style "sallustien," comme il l'appelle quelquefois, et contre le protestantisme: personne ne pouvait sans doute comprendre ce que tout cela voulait dire.

Les commentaires de Scaliger offrent beaucoup plus d'intérêt. On trouve dans Norden une description très exacte, étant donné son hostilité, du style de Lipse, tirée du poème latin *De stilo et charactere*. En voici la traduction:

"D'autres sont choqués de ce genre de style uni et égal qu'ont cultivé César et Cicéron et apprécient la manière compacte et serrée des pointes, qui vont sautillant, plutôt qu'elles ne marchent, et n'offrent à la fin à l'attention impatiente du lecteur qu'une chose qu'il lui faut interpréter, plutôt que lire."[35]

Ainsi s'expriment les adversaires contemporains de Lipse,[36] conservateurs qui défendent la tradition cicéronienne contre les attaques

[35] *Silva Variorum Carminum*, No. 14, dans *Poemata Omnia* (Leyden, 1615), p. 20. Consulter Norden, *Die Antike Kunstprosa*, II, 776, n.2. [Trimpi translates this epigram from *Poemata Omnia* (Berlin, 1864), p. 21, as follows (p. 49): "The uniform plainness, which Caesar and Cicero once cultivated, offends others, who are pleased by 'points' bound tight in the joints, which leap, rather than walk, through rough places (*Quae per salebras saltitant, non ambulant*) and, while the expectation of the reader hangs, need more to be understood than read."] On trouve cette remarque brève sur Lipse, *male scribit*, dans Joseph Juste Scaliger, *Scaligerana* (Cologne, 1667), p. 142. [Scaliger admired Lipsius' ed. of Tacitus (*Scaligerana*, Cologne, 1695, p. 243), but he was outspokenly harsh in condemning the Lipsian books on the miracles: *Lipsius crepitum edit, admirantur omnes* (p. 153). Cf. "Muret," n.67.]

[36] Il y a dans le même ton un "Jugement d'un homme célèbre sur la latinité de Lipse" cité par Balzac, *Œuvres* (Paris, 1665), II, 608: "Si l'on désirait écrire en latin de vieux mots à demi morts se présentaient ramassés chez Ennius et Pacuvius; les périodes, devenues de courtes phrases, allèrent sautillant, et un discours maigre, sec, délabré, privé d'énergie et d'abondance [copia], coupé de pointes [punctilium] et d'allusions, ou de parenthèses et de questions courtes et piquantes produisaient un effet de nausée et répugnaient." [The passage cited by Balzac occurs in Daniel Heinsius' funeral oration on Joseph Scaliger. Heinsius states that though Lipsius urged his students not to imitate him or his models, they did so and, instead of his eloquence, achieved mannered roughness and awkward archaisms: "If anyone wished to write in Latin, dead words were fetched from as far back as Pacuvius and Ennius; sentences hopped along; a lean and jejune speech, juiceless and meagre, broken by some short phrases and plays on words, or by abrupt clauses and short questions, occasioned nausea and disgust." Such was the literary crisis faced by Scaliger when he succeeded Lipsius at the University of Leyden. (Trans. G. W. Robinson in his *Autobiography of Joseph Scaliger*, Cambridge, Mass., 1927, pp. 62-83).] Dans ma discussion, j'ai laissé de côté certains traits du style de Lipse, tels que l'emploi d'un vocabulaire non classique ou impur, qui n'eurent aucun effet sur les langues vivantes des différents pays.

d'un innovateur et répètent les phrases mêmes par lesquelles les anciens cicéroniens Quintilien, Fronton, Aulu-Gelle avaient montré leur mépris des deux Sénèque et de leurs imitateurs.

Pendant les vingt dernières années de la vie de Lipse et pendant les vingt années qui suivirent sa mort, le ton de la critique reste le même, mais, à la fin du premier quart du XVIIe siècle, une période nouvelle s'ouvre dans l'histoire de la prose, période où la critique française devait jouer le plus grand rôle. Descartes, Balzac et les Pères jésuites Nicolas Caussin et François Vavasseur sont les théoriciens de la rhétorique à l'époque de Richelieu et de la fonda-tion de l'Académie française. Lipse est encore au premier plan, le point de mire de la critique, et le mouvement qu'il a dirigé et personnifié est toujours la cause des débats; mais la nature des attaques a radicalement changé. Le cicéronianisme est mort, et, à l'exception de quelques maîtres en province, personne ne préconise plus la doctrine de l'imitation exclusive; on reconnaît partout que Tacite et Sénèque ont été sauvés de l'oubli et du mépris où on les avait autrefois tenus et qu'un nouveau style, fondé sur l'imitation de ces maîtres, non seulement rivalise avec le style imité de Cicéron, mais l'a déjà supplanté dans la faveur publique; on signale ses erreurs; les dangers qui le menacent—l'obscurité et l'extravagance— sont mis en lumière par de nombreux exemples tirés surtout des écrivains espagnols, mais on reconnaît les fautes du genre cicé-ronien avec presque autant de franchise. Il est en somme clair qu'un style unique ne pourra plus jamais faire seul autorité. Le succès du mouvement anticicéronien a détruit l'unité de but qui caractérisait les premiers humanistes, et, si ceux qui les suivirent visaient à corriger et à purifier le goût littéraire, il leur fallait, pour réussir, trouver un principe plus large que l'admiration et l'imitation d'un auteur donné ou d'une école donnée. On prit donc désormais l'habitude d'énumérer les différents types de prose qui avaient prévalu dans l'antiquité et ont aussi, par imitation, prévalu dans les temps modernes; d'indiquer les dangers qui menaçaient chacun d'eux, et, finalement, de préconiser—excellent conseil—l'imitation des qualités plutôt que des défauts. Cette conclusion peut paraître faible et boiteuse, mais c'était en réalité une immense modification apportée à la doctrine d'imitation et un grand pas fait en avant vers l'indépendance da la raison et du goût.

Telle est, par exemple, la méthode du Père Nicolas Caussin, le maître jésuite, qui réussit à grouper autour de sa chaire de rhétorique à Clermont des nobles, des prêtres et des grandes dames de la cour de Louis XIII. Dans son long traité *Eloquentiae Sacrae et Humanae Parallela Libri XVI*, il n'énumère pas moins de dix espèces de styles, l'ampoulé, le scolastique, etc., et, en dernier lieu, le style qui se distingue par une concision pénétrante et des expressions subtiles et mordantes. Parlant de celles-ci, il dit:

"Si je condamnais ce style en tous points, je montrerais que je raisonne mal en ce qui concerne l'éloquence. Je n'ai ni l'intention, ni le dessein de porter accusation contre ces héros: Sénèque, Salluste, Pline, Tacite, et d'autres encore, qui ont adopté cette manière, non seulement avec enthousiasme, mais en arrivant à de fort heureux résultats; je veux simplement démontrer que ce style, que chacun convoite, n'est approprié ni à tous les talents, ni à tous les sujets, ni à tous les temps [voilà la modération où en est réduit un cicéronien] et que, si on s'obstine à l'affecter, ce style sera probablement défiguré par mainte faute de goût [ineptiis] d'une espèce puérile."[37]

Caussin est cicéronien dans le sens où le terme se comprend à son époque. Le fond de son livre, qui est écrit avec charme, est une attaque contre les "Anti-Cicérones," comme il les appelle, et la défense de ce qu'il y a de meilleur dans le style de Cicéron. Mais il ne se contente pas de faire soigneusement le départ entre les mérites et les erreurs de Sénèque et de Tacite, il excuse aussi ce qu'il y a de diffus et de vide chez son héros, ce qui en a fait un objet de ridicule, et va jusqu'à s'efforcer de démontrer que Cicéron, en ses plus beaux endroits, possède précisément les qualités dont les partisans de Sénèque sont si fiers. Il cite ainsi, dans ses discours, des exemples de ces "acumina" ou pointes qui distinguent l'école anticicéronienne, le fameux "Tu ipsam victoriam Caesar vicisti," entre autres. Si bien qu'en somme, le Cicéron qu'il adore n'est pas tout Cicéron, mais l'orateur des *Philippiques*, et il met à côté de son nom, pour qu'on le révère encore davantage, le nom de Démosthène.

Tout cela, et mainte autre chose dans son livre, indique bien quel changement s'est opéré dans l'opinion au point de vue de la rhétorique dans le premier tiers du siècle.

[37] (Louvain, 1609), II, xiv, p. 73. [Ch. xiv is entitled *De Acuta Styli Brevitate, Sententiisque Abruptis et Suspiciosis;* Ch. xv, *Subjiciuntur Quaedam Laudatorum Acumina Exempla*; and Ch. xvi, *De Erroribus Abruptis Styli, et Frigide Acuti.* Croll also treats Caussin in *APS*, n.44 and *Muret*, n.25.]

Ce fut cette période qui vit le commencement du règne de la raison et des règles du goût, d'où sortit l'art classique en France. Il est naturellement impossible de décrire ici les changements successifs que subit l'opinion au sujet de la rhétorique: c'est un drame trop long et aux personnages et aux incidents multiples et divers; nous désirons seulement montrer qu'il y eut une étape préliminaire dans le changement graduel né du mouvement anticicéronien, en partie à cause de la réaction et de l'opposition, en partie aussi parce que les forces lancées par le mouvement lui-même ont continué d'agir et se sont developpées. Ce mouvement, par conséquent, et les événements qui l'ont immédiatement suivi sont bien les anneaux de la chaîne qui relie la prose de la Renaissance à celle de la période classique.

Balzac est le plus grand prosateur du temps, et ses opinions, bien qu'identiques à celles de Caussin dans la plupart des cas, marquent plus exactement le progrès de la pensée. Comme la majeure partie des prosateurs de son temps, Balzac avait reçu l'enseignement anticicéronien de Lipse, de Montaigne et de Bacon; dans sa jeunesse, il se pénétra surtout du style attique ou "moderne" de Sénèque et de Tacite, et l'on a toujours beaucoup critiqué sa langue, parce qu'il se livre trop aisément aux pointes ou recherches d'esprit.[38] En effet, dans la préface à l'édition de 1658 de ses Lettres, écrite par un ami, on raconte que, jeune, Balzac avait rencontré Lipse à Metz, et que le vieux savant lui avait assuré qu'il n'avait rien à lui apprendre, car il s'était déjà rendu maître des principes de style que lui-même avait prêchés toute sa vie.[39] Plus tard, il ne

[38] Les goûts littéraires de Lipse pendant la première partie de sa carrière sont exposés exactement, par un certain Frère André, dans un opuscule publié à la fin de la première partie des Lettres de Phyllarque à Ariste par Jean Goulu (Paris, 1628); il fut aussi publié par François Ogier, à propos de son Apologie pour M. de Balzac, un peu plus tard. [For details, see Émile Roy's dissertation, De Joan. Lud. Guezio Balzacio contra Dom. Joan. Gulonium Disputante (Paris, 1892).] Le but de ce travail est de montrer Balzac plagiaire, et cent dix passages de ses œuvres environ sont rapprochés des passages qui sont censés les avoir inspirés. Il y en a trente-cinq de Sénèque, quinze de Tacite, onze de Plutarque, neuf de Cicéron, une vingtaine ou davantage de divers auteurs latins, neuf des Meditations et Characters de l'évêque Joseph Hall et deux des Essays de Bacon. L'Apologie d'Ogier est intéressante, particulièrement à cause de son bel éloge de la mélancolie (pp. 234-240) qui causa tant de souffrances à Balzac, mais servit aussi de nourriture à son génie. "C'est de cette humeur que deviennent tous les hommes à mesure qu'ils acquièrent de l'expérience et de la sagesse." Voilà un trait qui le rapproche encore de Lipse et de Burton, de Montaigne et de Sir Thomas Browne. L'étude de la mélancolie au XVIIe siècle éclairerait grandement quelques phases obscures de son histoire littéraire.

[39] Il doit y avoir une erreur ici, car Balzac n'était qu'un enfant quand Lipse

renia point l'enseignement de sa jeunesse, et quand la pratique eut rendu évidentes les erreurs de la méthode de Lipse, il resta "attique," et dans ses derniers écrits il condamne avec l'ardeur des premiers réformateurs l'asiaticisme vide et fleuri qui ne s'adresse qu'à l'oreille. Il croyait que l'erreur de Lipse avait été de choisir des modèles médiocres, non pas de s'être trompé sur le style, et il essaya de corriger les mauvais résultats obtenus en recherchant le meilleur "attique" partout où il put le trouver dans Sénèque et dans Tacite (en tant du moins qu'on peut en cela les prendre pour guides), dans les derniers et plus sévères discours de Cicéron, les *Philippiques* par exemple, et surtout dans les discours de Démosthène, où la veine attique est la plus pure. C'est-à-dire qu'il s'en tient toujours aux méthodes d'imitation des humanistes et que, comme Lipse, il recommande l'imitation de plusieurs types, plutôt que le choix des auteurs aboutissant à l'étude d'une école ou d'une période particulière: Balzac remet à la raison critique le soin de faire ce choix.

Ce programme correspond, dans son ensemble, à celui d'autres écrivains de la période de transition qui s'étend entre le mouvement anticicéronien et le XVIIIe siècle, époque à laquelle on arriva à une doctrine stable. C'est en réalité une nouvelle preuve du désir de trouver un modèle de pureté qui s'était fait jour aux premiers temps de l'humanisme et qui apparaît maintenant sous une forme plus libérale et plus rationnelle. Caussin raisonne comme Balzac, nous venons de le voir, quand il conseille d'imiter ce qu'il y a de meilleur plutôt que de plus mauvais dans les auteurs, leurs qualités plutôt que leurs défauts. Vavasseur offre presque le même programme, mais le cicéronianisme, chez lui comme chez Caussin, est réactionnaire à l'excès, sans doute parce qu'en leur qualité de prédicateurs, ils regardent le discours comme la forme typique d'expression. En tous cas, ils ne surent pas voir combien le style attique, sous sa forme la plus sévère, convenait à l'expression de cette morale de l'héroïsme qui était devenue partie intégrante de l'idéal du XVIIe siècle.

Francis Bacon serait peut-être arrivé à une position comparable à celle de Balzac. Après avoir joué un rôle important dans le mouvement anticicéronien, à la fois par un passage fameux de son

---

mourut. Mais le fait qu'on raconte cette histoire montre que Balzac était considéré comme le produit du mouvement anticicéronien.

Progrès de la science et par ses propres imitations de Tacite et de Sénèque, il vit aussi les fautes de ce nouveau style tel qu'on le pratiquait souvent, et ajouta, en 1622, un passage peu connu à son édition latine du *Progrès de la science*, où il expose ces fautes dans les termes ordinaires.[40] Il ne dit pas en quoi son expérience personnelle a modifié ses théories en rhétorique, mais il est probable qu'il en était arrivé au principe d'imitation et de choix raisonnés que ses contemporains formulèrent un peu plus tard.

Nulle autre méthode, en effet, n'était possible à une époque où l'on croyait encore à l'imitation. Mais, d'un autre côté, cette doctrine de l'imitation elle-même se trouvait menacée et affaiblie par la forme nouvelle qu'elle prenait. Car, un goût qui est assez raffiné pour pouvoir distinguer les qualités et les défauts des différents modèles classiques sans qu'aucune autorité, aucune méthode le guide, affirmera bientôt son indépendance et commencera à chercher une autorité dans la simple réalité des choses et dans les lois naturelles de la pensée.

C'est chez Descartes que nous trouvons les premiers indices de cette nouvelle phase; dans l'histoire de la pensée moderne, c'est sur sa philosophie que repose l'indépendance du jugement et de la raison humaine, et nous avons heureusement un aperçu de la façon dont il eût appliqué sa philosophie à l'art de la prose. Une lettre

[40] Bacon, *De Augmentis Scientiarum*, dans *Works*, ed. Spedding, Ellis, and Heath (London, 1868), I, 452. [The "famous passage" describing the first vanity of learning as Ciceronian imitation occurs in *The Advancement of Learning*, ed. William Aldis Wright, 5th ed. (Oxford, 1957), I.iv.2, pp. 28-30 and in *Works*, III, 282-284. The paragraph added in *De Augmentis* occurs *ibid.*, I, 452, beginning *Paulo sanius est aliud styli genus* and is paraphrased in III, 285, n.1. In Gilbert Wats's translation, *Of the Advancement and Proficiencie of Learning or the Partitions of Sciences* (Oxford, 1640), p. 29, the passage is as follows:

Litle better is that kind of stile (yet neither is that altogether exempt from vanity) which neer about the same time succeeded this *Copy* and *superfluity of speech*. The labour here is altogether, *That words may be aculeate, sentences concise, and the whole contexture of the speech and discourse, rather rounding into it selfe, than spread and dilated*: So that it comes to passe by this Artifice, that every passage seemes more witty and waighty than indeed it is. Such a stile as this we finde more excessively in *Seneca*; more moderately in *Tacitus* and *Plinius Secundus*; and of late it hath bin very pleasing unto the eares of our time. And this kind of expression hath found such acceptance with meaner capacities, as to be a dignity and ornament to Learning; neverthelesse, by the more exact judgements, it hath bin deservedly dispised, and may be set down *as a distemper of Learning*, seeing it is nothing else but a hunting after words, and fine placing of them.

Cf. Williamson, *Senecan Amble*, p. 29 and Chs. III-IV, esp. pp. 112-120; *Muret*, n.54; and the translation (Croll's own?) in *APL*, IV, par. 3.]

où il loue fort le style de Balzac indique clairement ses opinions. Comme beaucoup d'autres auteurs de son temps, il décrit les genres littéraires qui dominent; il y a d'abord le style imité de Cicéron où "un sujet ennuyeux, longuement exposé, déçoit l'esprit attentif." Puis il y a le style imité de Sénèque opposé à celui de Cicéron et dont Descartes parle avec plus de sympathie, tout en signalant ses erreurs, car si "les phrases les plus pleines de sens et de nobles réflexions plaisent par leur richesse aux esprits cultivés, trop souvent aussi elles fatiguent par leur style trop serré, qui tend à l'obscurité."

Il passe alors au style sec et sans ornement, au style des concettis et des pointes, avec ses "fantaisies poétiques, ses raisonnements faux et ses pointes puériles," et son admiration de Balzac est grande, parce que, d'un côté, il a su éviter la diffusion de Cicéron et que de l'autre "la grandeur et la dignité des sentences . . . n'est point ravalée par l'indigence des mots."[41]

Ce qui fait l'intérêt principal de cette lettre, c'est que Descartes, dédaignant pour ainsi dire une opinion surannée, n'attribue pas à ces styles nouveaux les noms classiques que nous leur connaissons. Il ne fait mention d'aucun modèle classique et les Grecs et les Romains n'apparaissent que comme les corrupteurs de la pureté de l'éloquence à l'âge héroïque. Des phrases, qui seront plus tard dites et redites, s'entendent ici pour la première fois, ou plutôt s'y entendent pour la première fois avec le sens que nous leur donnons maintenant: "la langue du peuple corrigée par l'usage," "des pensées élevées rendues en des termes familiers," "une heureuse harmonie entre les choses et le style," "l'élégance naturelle du discours." Mais pas un mot n'est dit de l'imitation, pas une allusion n'y est faite. La théorie de Descartes, autant qu'on en peut juger par cette lettre, paraît être qu'un bon écrivain devrait chercher à puiser dans la langue ordinaire des hommes "corrigée par l'usage" les éléments de beauté qui s'y trouvent et s'efforcer de les combiner de façon à se rapprocher le plus possible de la beauté idéale du style, beauté naturelle et simple qui, avant d'être corrompue par la rhétorique des sophistes de l'Antiquité, existait, pense-t-il à l'origine, à un âge d'or.

Descartes, naturellement, est en avance sur son temps; avec cette prescience de l'esprit philosophique, il prévoit—en partie au moins—ce qui se produira. La doctrine de l'imitation n'est pas encore morte, et il est intéressant de voir le père Bouhours, à la fin du siècle presque, lutter encore contre Tacite et Sénèque en

---

[41] *Lettres de Monsieur Descartes* (Paris, 1657), no. 100, pp. 572-573.

défendant le nom de Cicéron et essayer de montrer ce qu'on devrait imiter et ce qu'on devrait laisser de côté chez ces auteurs, tandis qu'au commencement du XVIIIe siècle, Shaftesbury, en Angleterre, se moque de ses compatriotes et de leur imitation servile du style de Sénèque.[42]

Nous ne pouvons pas nous étendre davantage sur les progrès de cette tendance. Il nous suffit de faire remarquer ici que la critique des trente ou quarante premières années du siècle révèle dans le style, et d'une façon presque universelle, une tendance attique, inspirée de l'école anticicéronienne antique, que cette tendance ouvre une ère nouvelle à la prose des différents peuples, et finalement qu'on regarde Lipse comme la figure la plus en vue de ce mouvement, et comme celui qui le fit triompher.

Il n'en fut pas, naturellement, l'unique promoteur; le mouvement était trop général pour n'avoir qu'une seule source; il aurait pu naître spontanément des besoins intellectuels du siècle, sans l'enseignement de Lipse. Cependant, plus on l'étudie, plus on se rend compte de l'importance du rôle qu'y joua le maître; le fait qu'il fut le premier en date de ses chefs après Montaigne ne peut être négligé, sa théorie bien définie du style et sa méthode extra-ordinairement claire d'enseignement aidèrent certainement au succès de la prose nouvelle; la publication de ses éditions des anti-cicéroniens de l'antiquité fut plus importante encore, et, sans aucun doute, son fameux *Tacite*, qui parut alors que Bacon n'était qu'un écolier et que Montaigne n'avait encore rien publié, alors que la grande école des historiens espagnols ne faisait que commencer ses travaux, doit compter parmi les forces maîtresses qui donnèrent l'impulsion au mouvement.

Ajoutons à tout ceci que Lipse exerça, par sa correspondance, une influence que l'on peut considérer comme remarquable, même à une époque où la propagande littéraire se faisait surtout par les lettres. J'ai parlé précédemment de la difficulté qu'il y avait à déterminer les limites de la secte lipsienne, mais il n'est pas difficile de trouver les noms des chefs de la réforme anticicéronienne dans

[42] L'influence de Saint-Évremond compte pour une grande part dans l'admiration qu'on a continué à avoir pour l'imitation de Sénèque ou des anticicéroniens, dans la seconde moitié du siècle, au moins en Angleterre où elle survécut plus longtemps qu'en France. Voir Auguste Bourgoin, *Les Maîtres de la Critique au XVIIe Siècle* (Paris, 1889), pp. 79-85, 112-116. Une renaissance importante de l'influence de Montaigne en Angleterre semble être due à la présence de Saint-Évremond. [Cf. Pierre Villey, "Montaigne en Angleterre," *Revue des Deux Mondes*, XVII (Sept. 1, 1913), 115-150.]

les différents centres littéraires de l'Europe. En Angleterre, Bacon, l'évêque Hall et Sir Henry Wotton sont les grands noms; en France, Montaigne surpasse tous les autres; en Espagne, Quevedo et Gracián, les maîtres du "conceptismo" en prose, ont eu l'imprudence de pousser le mouvement à l'extrême, et l'ont, par la suite, fait universellement condamner. Je me propose en terminant d'apporter ici les preuves que j'ai pu recueillir de l'influence de Lipse sur ces trois écoles anticicéroniennes, en ce qui concerne la prose de chaque pays.

Il y a très peu à dire sur l'Angleterre, bien que l'action de Lipse, comme philosophe et comme rhétoricien, paraisse y avoir été aussi forte qu'en France. Si Bacon n'était point le plus discret des hommes quand il s'agit de ses obligations envers les autres savants, nous apprendrions peut-être qu'il doit le choix de ses modèles en prose aux opinions connues par l'un de ces enchaînements de correspondance qui répandaient si vite les idées à son époque. Il est fort probable aussi que, par l'intermédiaire du "grand Van Does," l'ami intime de Lipse qui vint deux fois en Angleterre comme envoyé des états belligérants, les voyageurs anglais cherchaient à voir à Leyde le célèbre érudit. Mais, parmi les lettres de Lipse, pas une n'intéresse l'Angleterre, et nous ne connaissons à Lipse, parmi les hommes qui se sont distingués dans le mouvement littéraire de son temps, aucune relation chez les Anglais, si ce n'est l'évêque Hall, qui exprime certainement l'estime qu'il a pour lui en homme qui l'a connu. Hall fit deux fois le voyage des Pays-Bas, et, la première fois, en 1605, prit une part active dans certaines discussions avec les partisans des Jésuites à Spa.[43]

Lipse, au contraire, entretenait une correspondance régulière avec les beaux esprits espagnols, alors même qu'il était professeur d'une université protestante; toutes ses lettres montrent, d'une façon fort intéressante, qu'il répandait activement ses nouveaux principes littéraires et que les cercles espagnols partageaient de tout cœur son admiration pour Tacite et Sénèque. Mais nous nous occuperons seulement ici d'une série de lettres qui forment, pour ainsi dire, un

[43] Il y a une lettre de Lipse (*Ep. Misc.*, II. 96, dans *Opera*, II, 107-108) à Lancelot Brown, un médecin, sur William Paddy (plus tard Sir William Paddy, médicin du roi Jacques) que Brown avait envoyé à Lipse. Lipse accueillit le jeune homme et, quand il le renvoya, il était devenu "de notre troupeau" et se faisait remarquer en ce qu'il avait "notre nuance de goût littéraire particulière." [*Sum natura in omnes benignus, tum maxime in nostri gregis homines, et qui commendant se colore isto litterarum.*] Paddy fut reçu docteur à Leyde en 1589.

anneau dans la chaîne de témoignages qui relient l'art espagnol du "conceptismo" au mouvement anticicéronien.

Francisco Quevedo, le jeune auteur burlesque qui, dans ses œuvres sérieuses, chercha à être le Sénèque de l'Espagne—le Sénèque chrétien de la réaction catholique—avait commencé une étude sur les Vestales, lorsqu'il reçut le *De Vesta et Vestalibus* de Lipse. Il écrivit immédiatement au vieux savant (ceci se passait en 1604, Quevedo avait vingt-quatre ans et Lipse cinquante-sept), avouant qu'une grande partie de son travail était inutile maintenant, mais proposant de refaire son livre sur un plan nouveau et demandant à Lipse l'autorisation de soumettre le manuscrit à son appréciation. Lipse repondit, et Quevedo envoya une seconde lettre qui ne montre pas seulement la nature des idées qu'échangeaient les deux hommes, mais est aussi un exemple frappant de ce genre "concis et subtil," tout fait d' "acumina" ou pointes, et que Lipse enseignait à ses disciples. La lettre de Lipse, dit-il, l'avait guéri d'une maladie:

> "Nunc verbis virtutem inesse credo, non a Magia, sed a tua doctrina: et ideo quae olim scripsisti lego. Quae scribis opto pro futuris laboribus tibi a Deo vitam, et ab aliis mihi. . . . Seneca noster te totum habet, et non aliter totum Senecam habere possumus. Felix ille qui tuo labore ante ultimum solem mundi iterum vivus *volitabit per ora virum*.[44] Bellis ferrea vestra tempora videntur, sed tuis scriptis aurata secula emulantur. Credo et Marte non Minervae facta; sed tu facis. Quid de mea Hispania non querula voce referam? Vos belli praeda estis. Nos otii, et ignorantiae. Ibi miles noster, opesque consumuntur. Hic nos consumimur: et desunt qui verba faciant, non qui dent."

Dans sa réponse, Lipse lui donne l'accolade qui l'arme chevalier de l'ordre nouveau "Quel charme, quel esprit dans vos lettres," dit-il! "Elles m'ont fait doublement plaisir, et, à vous dire vrai, me rappellent cette Espagne des temps anciens, la mère de génies comme le vôtre."

Lipse mourut moins de deux ans après, mais les lettres qui

---

[44] Ernest Mérimée, dans sa traduction, ne voit pas la signification du mot *ante*, et il se trompe aussi sur le sens de la phrase précédente où Quevedo fait allusion à l'édition de Sénèque, que l'on attendait de Lipse.

restent montrent qu'il avait déjà conquis un ascendant considérable
sur l'esprit de ce jeune disciple, ascendant qui n'était rien moins,
dit le biographe de Quevedo, qu' "une sorte de direction à la fois
philosophique et littéraire, exercée de loin par le grand humaniste."
Et M. Mérimée ajoute que l'œuvre de Quevedo prouve combien
l'influence de Lipse fut réelle.[45]

L'amitié qui unit Lipse et Montaigne ne fut pas celle d'un
maître pour son élève, mais celle de deux égaux. La supériorité
que l'âge et le génie pouvaient donner à Montaigne était com-
pensée par l'autorité qu'avait Lipse comme érudit, et aussi par le
fait que ce dernier était déjà célèbre quand Montaigne commença
à écrire; peut-être même la balance pencherait-elle du côté de
Lipse, car Mlle. de Gournay assure que c'est la main de Lipse qui
"ait ouvert par Escrit public, des portes de la louange" aux *Essais*
de son père intellectuel.[46] Quoi qu'il en soit, les deux amis furent
attirés l'un vers l'autre par la similitude de leur goût littéraire et
par une sympathie naturelle, et ils trouvèrent l'un chez l'autre le
secours dont ils avaient besoin. Si Lipse tient de Montaigne l'habitude de parler à la première personne, et de vivre dans une nouvelle
intimité avec son lecteur, c'est probablement à Lipse, d'un autre
côté, que Montaigne doit son admiration de la morale stoïcienne
et son plaisir toujours croissant à imiter le style de Sénèque. Les
travaux de M. Villey[47] ont révélé l'étendue exacte de la dette de
Montaigne, tandis que les lettres de Lipse montrent les raisons de
leur sympathie intellectuelle. Dans la plus ancienne des lettres que
nous possédions (1588), il dit qu'il connaît l'amour de Montaigne

[45] Je dois la connaissance de cette correspondance au livre de E. Mérimée,
Essai sur la Vie et les Œuvres de Francisco de Quevedo (Paris, 1886), ouvrage
de grande valeur. Les lettres de Quevedo se trouvent dans *Sylloge Epistolarum
a Viris Illustribus Scriptarum*, ed. Petrus Burmannus, 5 vols. (Leyden, 1727),
Ep. 835-836, II, 162-164. [The quotation is from the second letter. Lipsius' reply
to the first, as Burmann notes, is *Ep. Misc.*, v.55, in *Opera*, II, 243; see also, as
Mérimée notes (p. 18), *Vincentii Marineri Valentini Opera Omnia Poetica et
Oratoria* (Tournon, 1633), pp. 340, 404. See Croll's parallel account in *Muret*,
III (pp. 126-127).]

[46] Voir sa préface aux *Essais* (Paris, 1635), sig. iiiʳ. [The preface first appeared
in the 1595 ed. of *Les Essais*, which Marie de Jars de Gournay supervised; it was
withdrawn from the 1598 ed. and reinstated, with amendments, in later eds.]

[47] Villey, *Les Sources*, I, 177-183, 404, 406, 415; II, 65-66, 298-299, 400, 525-
526. Sur les relations personelles des deux hommes, voir Paul Bonnefon, *Montaigne et ses Amis* (Paris, 1898), II, 178-180, 185n.; et aussi Amiel, *Un Publiciste*,
p. 94. M. Villey a montré que Montaigne lisait les ouvrages de Lipse à mesure
qu'ils paraissaient et n'y fit pas moins de cinquante-huit emprunts de diverse
nature.

pour Sénèque et son mépris d'un style fleuri et creux, qui ne saurait véritablement instruire.[48]

Il est inutile de nous attarder à rechercher lequel des deux amis montra la route à l'autre, car ils obéissaient en réalité tous les deux à l'influence de leur époque. Leur rationalisme, leur curiosité mêlée d'incertitude, la préoccupation que leur causent les problèmes moraux, leur amour de l'isolement stoïcien, leur désir étrange, mais sincère de concilier la soumission au dogme et le doute philosophique étaient le résultat de cette évolution de la pensée qui était en train de transformer la Renaissance pour en faire le monde moderne; leur tendance anticicéronienne n'était au fond qu'une manière d'exprimer cette évolution en termes de rhétorique. C'est pourquoi il est inutile d'insister sur l'antériorité qu'on pourrait réclamer pour Lipse sur les autres chefs de ce mouvement; la question: qui, le premier, fit telle ou telle chose, est impossible à résoudre en pareil cas, et d'une façon générale absurde, car, dans un organisme vivant, le point de départ de tout mouvement est impossible à découvrir. Le fait vraiment important, c'est que Lipse incarne son époque; son goût pour un certain genre de latinité fut partagé par bon nombre de ses contemporains les plus originaux, il devint universel pendant la première moitié du XVIIe siècle, et, s'alliant de diverses manières à d'autres tendances, à d'autres habitudes du siècle, produisit dans les différents pays les genres de prose qui caractérisent l'époque, tandis qu'il imprimait au grand courant de la prose du XVIIe siècle une certaine direction.

[48] *Ep. Misc.*, ii. 41, dans *Opera*, ii, 86-87. Le 30 septembre, il écrit (*Ep. Misc.*, ii. 55): "J'avoue qu'il n'y a point d'homme en Europe avec qui je me rencontre plus souvent qu'avec vous."

Foreword to Essay Two

This famous essay is more indebted to classical scholarship than any other of Croll's articles, and especially to G. L. Hendrickson's work (as Croll fully acknowledged), but its universal acclaim is deserved. Not only has it saved many scholars much work, but, with more than Senecan perspicuity, it has served to relate ancient theories of style to Renaissance prose in a way which perhaps no other essay has yet rivaled. It provides the indispensable background for the earlier Lipsius essay and for the later more detailed studies of the other principal figures. Had Croll been content with short-cuts, he would have confined himself to Seneca and the other Silver Latin writers who, by his own admission, were the effective models for Lipsius and his collaborators. The first half of this essay, however, is a comparison of the Renaissance attempt to domesticate the *genus humile* with the history of this genre in Greek rhetoric. By showing the philosophical basis of the essay style in Plato, and the logical (as opposed to rhetorical) bias of the first two books of Aristotle's *Rhetoric*, Croll demonstrated the part which Greek precedents played in Renaissance theory, although European civilization was then predominantly anti-Greek. His account of the *genus humile* in Rome explains its late naturalization there—after Cicero—and emphasizes the scientific exploration of human nature to be found in Stoic writing: its interest in searching the crannies of an interior, subjective reality. In so doing, Croll recognized the great variety of individual forms which the *genus humile* was thereby likely to take, and confesses that the philosophical essay style was never really a plain style; though its rhetoric was more subtle and less ornate than the oratorical style, it nevertheless retained many aural qualities, even while aiming at the exact representation of thought. He also made a point of refuting the standard opinion of such scholars as W. C. Summers that sententious prose was generally the mark of a decadent age.[1]

[1] W. C. Summers, ed., *Select Letters of Seneca* (London, 1921), p. xvii; the whole introduction is a valuable analysis of Senecan style. See also Merchant, D'Alton, etc., as cited in *Lipse*, n.11.

Since this essay was written, there has been considerable discussion of Roman Atticism, and Cicero's relation to it. E. Castorina holds that Cicero himself began writing under Attic influence, and, after a middle period of hostility toward an unembellished oratory, ended his career by thinking of himself as the true Attic.[2] This theory has not been wholly accepted, but it suggests that the distinctions between Attic and Asian styles are harder to make than Croll allowed. (Williamson has shown, for example, that Erasmus distinguished between Gorgias and Isocrates in a way Croll did not.) A. Desmouliez, following Norden, claims that Attic style in Rome was part of an archaizing movement, connected with a trend to establish early Greek models in various arts, and that Cicero thought of himself as upholding the evolutionary principle in oratory which the Atticists, with their preference for Lisias and Thucydides over Demosthenes, ignored.[3] Classical scholars are at least agreed on the existence of more than one kind of Atticism in ancient Rome, and S. F. Bonner has concluded that the subject is not closed.[4] Croll's discussion over-simplifies the issue, and by minimizing the archaic element in Atticism he has traced a more regular history of the philosophical style than in fact exists. His conclusions for the seventeenth century, however, remain unaffected, unless it could be shown that "Attic" was then a complicated term, not merely a name for the *genus humile*. Croll understood clearly that Senecanism was a cult before it became a popular style, but his emphasis tends to fall as a rule on the progressiveness of the movement.

[2] *L'Atticismo nell'Evoluzione del Pensiero di Cicerone* (Catania, 1952).

[3] "Sur la Polémique de Cicéron et des Atticistes," *Revue des Études Latines*, XXX (1952), 168-185.

[4] "Roman Oratory," in *Fifty Years of Classical Scholarship*, ed. M. Platnauer (Oxford, 1954), pp. 363-368. The standard essay on Roman Atticism is U. v. Wilamowitz-Möllendorf, "Asianismus und Atticismus," *Hermes*, XXXV (1900), 1-52; see also P. Giuffrida, "Significati e Limiti del Neo-Atticismo," *Maia*, VII (1955), 83-124, an essay which describes the controversy as philosophical rather than stylistic; and José Guillén, "Cicerón y el Genuino Aticismo," *Arbor*, XXXI (1955), 427-457, which lists the principles of Atticism which Cicero praised. Roman historical style, which is closely related to the subject, has been discussed by A. D. Leeman, "Le Genre et le Style Historique à Rome: Théorie et Pratique," *RÉL*, XXXIII (1955), 183-208. Leeman distinguishes three kinds of Atticism.

An important article by Mlle. A. Guillemin has tended to confirm Croll's view of Seneca's style, especially in its emphasis on subtler forms of imitation, which were not committed to reproducing verbatim the characteristics of an original model, but above all she has indicated the great extent to which Seneca was influenced by the new theory of the sublime, and the *Treatise on the Sublime* in particular.[5] The sublime, Mlle. Guillemin asserts, was essentially the epideictic style which Cicero treated so inadequately; it was not hostile to other features of Senecan theory—clarity, the rejection of Asiatic *flores*, etc.—and neither did Seneca reject "abundance," although his was a copiousness which differed greatly from Cicero's. The significance of enlarging the range of effects possible in the Senecan manner is that one is helped to explain the enormous differences among the Senecan performances in the early seventeenth century. Croll himself was obviously puzzled by these variations, writing (in this essay) of the "monstrous births"—metaphysical sermons—engendered by the copulation of the philosophical style with oratorical magnificence; later he was to posit a "baroque" strain running through the three forms of Senecanism—Stoic (curt), libertine (loose), and political (Tacitean)—and finally was to label all the forms as subspecies of the baroque. In other words, he had an increasing sense of a much larger amount of embellishment and verbal wit in Senecan style than he had at first been prepared to admit.

His difficulty probably arose from his failure to make sufficient allowance for the differences between the sixteenth and seventeenth centuries, and he continued to write about the theorists of the plain style after the Restoration as if they had the same principles as Lipsius; to a certain extent he was right, but of course they were the excesses of the Senecan style which the plain stylists berated. Even in his treatment of the sixteenth century there is a dilemma.

[5] "Sénèque Directeur d'Âmes: Les Théories Littéraires," *RÉL*, XXXII (1954), 250-274. Tacitus' concern for psychological accuracy, which Croll saw as intrinsic to the Attic style, has recently been made the subject of an interesting essay by J. Cousin, "Rhétorique et Psychologie chez Tacite: Un Aspect de la 'Deinôsis,'" *RÉL*, XXIX (1951), 228-247.

Croll recognized that Senecan style, though it aimed at rendering the movements of the mind exactly and without ornament, was in fact a "highly imaginative portrayal" of the writers' relations with truth, and was thus perforce highly rhetorical. Yet he also recognized in the statements about clarity and concision an effort to achieve a plain style; he was the first to perceive that Bacon had his reservations about florid Senecanism, but could speak also of Lipsius, Bacon, Balzac, and Browne as having a "normal" style; he noted "concettismo" as a "rhetoric of thought" arising directly out of Senecan theory, and yet stressed the antirhetorical aims of the movement. One is struck first with the justice of all these observations, and the bravery with which he suppressed none of the evidence. But, knowing what we now do, one must argue that some factor of genuine plainness eluded him, and that his theory about "the modern spirit of progress," born with the Senecan style, did not help him to find it.

Perry Miller and W. J. Ong have made out an overwhelming case for the part which Ramism played in the ultimate triumph of a plain style,[6] and, with some reservations from Williamson, Richard Foster Jones has demonstrated that science reformed all *flosculi*, Senecan or Ciceronian, and did much to insure a style which would describe an exterior rather than an interior reality.[7] That these two influences, coming into their own during the seventeenth century, did much to bring about a reaction against Senecanism can hardly be disputed. However, even Ong does not deny Rosemond Tuve's thesis[8] that Ramism, by strengthening the hold of dialectic over imagery, encouraged the strong lines of metaphysical poetry. And if poetry, why not

[6] Perry Miller, *The New England Mind: The Seventeenth Century* (Cambridge, Mass., 1954), esp. pp. 300-362; W. J. Ong, *Ramus, Method, and the Decay of the Dialogue* (Cambridge, Mass., 1958), passim, but esp. pp. 212-213, 283-288. For an important critique of studies of Ramus's influence on seventeenth-century prose style, see Jackson I. Cope, *The Metaphoric Structure of* Paradise Lost (Baltimore, 1962), pp. 27-49.

[7] "Science and English Prose Style in the Third Quarter of the Seventeenth Century"; "The Attack on Pulpit Eloquence in the Restoration"; "Science and Language in England of the Mid-Seventeenth Century," all in *The Seventeenth Century* (Stanford, 1951), pp. 75-160.

[8] *Elizabethan and Metaphysical Imagery* (Chicago, 1947), esp. pp. 331-353.

48

the metaphysical sermon also, though Perry Miller has said roundly that it would have been impossible to be a Ramist and preach like John Donne? Moreover, by 1650 the Ramist New England divines were left defending their flowers of speech against the attacks of their plainer Anglican brethren. It seems clear, therefore, that Ramism, even though it slighted rhetoric, made a definite place for it as appliqué work (to use Ong's term), and that its tendency towards plainness had to be reinforced from another quarter; the forces, whatever they were, and they certainly included science, were strong enough to change the dominant Anglican mode from metaphysical to plain preaching. Reaction to Laudian excesses, in style as in politics, probably accounts for some of it, social pressures for more. Latitudinarian sermons were not at first especially plain, as W. Fraser Mitchell has shown,[9] but the simplicity of spirit and word of men like John Hales and George Herbert, harking back to a moderate Anglicanism which existed before Jacobean politics, was in the long run the greatest influence for plainness in England.[10] As Croll was well aware, and as Mitchell has made even clearer, the patristic reading of the high Anglicans was largely responsible for their marked deviation from a Senecan norm, but there was in existence from the Reformation, and gathering strength as the revolt against enthusiasm proceeded, a belief in the pure and simple milk of the Word, shared by many Puritans and some Anglicans alike. The manifesto for such plainness can be heard in Jewel's famous sermon against pulpit rhetoric. For all the sympathy many churchmen felt for Seneca's morals, his rhetoric was pagan and held in special esteem by the sceptics, official believers though they were. Such plainness

[9] *English Pulpit Oratory from Andrewes to Tillotson* (New York, 1962), pp. 276-307.
[10] On this tradition see John Tulloch, *Rational Theology and Christian Philosophy* (London, 1874), I, 1-75, and Richard Foster Jones, "The Moral Sense of Simplicity," in *Studies in Honor of Frederick W. Shipley* (St. Louis, 1942), pp. 265-287. On the plain style in journalism and politics during the first half of the century, see Hugh Macdonald, "Another Aspect of Seventeenth-Century Prose," *RES*, XIX (1943), 33-43. Trimpi gives a full account of the plain style and considers its philosophical commitments, moral and aesthetic implications, and chief exponents.

owes nothing to an idea of progress, and little to the motives which Croll ascribed to the initiators of the Anti-Ciceronian program. But even in enumerating these reservations about Croll's thesis, one is aware how his work makes it possible to arrive at them. Without this essay on Attic prose we should be much further away than we are now from an understanding of seventeenth-century style.

JOHN M. WALLACE
THE JOHNS HOPKINS UNIVERSITY

"Attic Prose" in the Seventeenth Century*

EDITED BY JOHN M. WALLACE

✧ I ✧

TWO TERMS present themselves to the literary historian seeking a name for the new kind of style that came into general use in Latin and all the vernacular languages at the end of the sixteenth century.[1] "Anti-Ciceronian prose" has the merit of indicating the character of the controversy out of which the new tendency emerged victorious: it connects the successful movement led by Lipsius, Montaigne, and Bacon with the frustrated efforts of Erasmus, Budé, and Pico early in the sixteenth century. But it is open to several objections. In the first place, it indicates only revolt, suggests only destructive purposes in a movement that had a definite rhetorical program. Secondly, it may be taken as describing a hostility to Cicero himself, in the opinions of the new leaders, instead of to his sixteenth-century "apes," whereas in fact the supreme *rhetorical* excellence of Cicero was constantly affirmed by them, as it was by the ancient Anti-Ciceronians whom they imitated.[2] And thirdly, it was not the term usually employed in

---

* Originally published in *Studies in Philology*, XVIII (April 1921), 79-128.

[1] The present paper is part of a more extended study [projected by Croll as an independent volume] with the same title, the object of which is to show that the successful Anti-Ciceronian movement inaugurated by Muret, Lipsius, Montaigne, and Bacon, in the last quarter of the sixteenth century, gave a new direction to European prose style and determined its characteristic forms throughout the seventeenth century. For the history of this movement and the description of the forms of style which it created, the reader must be referred to the other parts of this study.

Various discussions of the Ciceronian movement of the Renaissance are familiar, and in all of these the earlier phases of the opposition to it—led by Erasmus, Pico, and others—receive due attention. On the other hand, the decisive Anti-Ciceronian movement of the last quarter of the century has heretofore received but cursory mention, as by Norden, pp. 778-779, Sandys, pp. 145-173, and Izora Scott, pp. 106-111—all cited in *Lipse*, n.9.

[All bracketed editorial additions to Croll's notes in this paper were written by J. Max Patrick. J.M.W.]

[2] Montaigne, "Des Livres," *Essais*, II.x, ed. J.-V. Le Clerc (Paris, 1865), II, 124,

contemporary controversy, and was never used except by enemies of the new movement. The only name by which its leaders and friends were willing to describe the new style during the century of its triumph, from 1575 to 1700, was "Attic."

For these reasons "Attic" is the preferable term, and should take its place in literary history as the name of the dominant tendency in seventeenth-century prose style in contrast with that of the sixteenth century. To use it at the present time, however, for this purpose, without a full and clear explanation of the meaning attached to it could only cause positive misunderstanding or utter confusion. For it is a word that has suffered vicissitudes. In current and uncritical literary writing of the last two centuries it has often been employed to designate a style conformed to the conversational customs of a well-trained and sophisticated society—the society of Paris in the eighteenth century rather than of Athens in the age of Pericles. This meaning, it is true, was imposed by a later age than the seventeenth century and might safely be disregarded, the more safely, indeed, because it does not correspond to any of the more important meanings recognized as sound by the best students of antiquity. But unhappily in the usage of classical scholars themselves the word does not now carry a single and definite meaning; and the most recent researches tend to add complexity rather than clearness to its history. For the truth is that it was never a formalized word of rhetorical theory in ancient criticism, such as can be used for definition; it always tended to be a nickname of compliment or eulogy, and was subject to the variations of meaning that we may observe in many similar words of the modern critical vocabulary. There was a disposition, it is true, to associate it in Roman criticism with one of the two great "characters of style" of which we will

---

is franker than any other of the leaders in expressing a dislike of Cicero. Yet he admires his *eloquence*. "There is no real excellence in him," he says, "unless his eloquence itself is so perfect that it might be called a real and substantive excellence." Of course part of the point of this is, however, in the implied doubt of the value of pure eloquence, in itself; for no Ciceronian would think of doubting it. [Croll's "quotation" appears to be a conflation of two passages on Cicero, the one as documented above, the other in "Considération sur Cicéron," *Essais*, I.xxxix (xl in modern eds.), ed. Le Clerc, I, 358: "Fy de l'eloquence qui nous laisse envie de soy, non de choses! si ce n'est qu'on die celle de Cicéron, estant en si extreme perfection, se donne corps elle-mesme." This passage is quoted in (Croll's own?) English trans., *APL*, III (p. 178); cf. *Muret*, n.10. The attitudes of Muret and Montaigne toward Cicero are compared by W. H. Alexander in "The Sieur de Montaigne and Cicero," *UTQ*, IX (1939-1940), 222-230.]

speak presently. But on the other hand it might denominate a *quality* of style, vaguely associated with Athens in the time of its glory, which neither of the "characters" could afford to neglect and which might appear equally well in either. Or again it could be used in its exact geographical sense, of any author who lived at Athens, without reference to either the quality or the character of his style.

All the trees in this forest have again been studied close up by recent scholars; and we are now no more competent to give a comprehensive definition of "Attic" than the ancients themselves were. Evidently any one who wants to use the term at the present time for the purpose of identification must explain what he means by it. If this involved an attempt to discuss the many questions still in controversy among the classicists, or to adjust the relations of the various ancient meanings of the word that have been mentioned, it would be too pretentious an undertaking for one who is not a trained classicist. But we are not concerned here with any of these thorny problems. Our business is to understand "Attic" as the seventeenth-century critics did; and they at least had a clear idea of what they meant by it, and used it to define the stylistic purposes of their own age. It meant in their critical vocabulary one of two kinds of characters of style made familiar to them in modern and vernacular use by the imitation of antiquity since the beginning of the Renaissance, and corresponding, as they saw, roughly but definitely enough with the two leading "characters," or *genera dicendi*, distinguished by ancient criticism.[3] This limitation of meaning will serve as a clue to guide us through all complexities.

Classical scholars may not, therefore, feel highly rewarded by the present survey, and it is not in their interest that it is undertaken. Yet it may have some value even for them. For the word "Attic" had a lively, contemporary interest in the seventeenth century that it has never had since, and was used by men whose own writings were, by intention at least, direct continuations of ancient Latin literature. Their knowledge was limited in its range as compared with that of the most accomplished modern classicists; but as far as it went it was both sounder and more vivid than that of any later generation. It is possible that their use of the term we are considering will help to simplify a problem which has been greatly confused by the investigation of details; and it is certain that it is truer to

[3] Of course in the matured theory there are *three* characters. See explanation below on pp. 59-61 and 77-82.

ancient usage than that which has been current in popular criticism since the eighteenth century.

✧ II ✧

The seventeenth century, then, regarded the history of ancient prose style chiefly as a story of relations and conflicts between two modes of style, which—for the sake of the utmost simplification— we may characterize at once (in modern terms) as the oratorical style and the essay style, and may describe by the kind of ornament most used in each. The oratorical style was distinguished by the use of the *schemata verborum*, or "schemes," as we may call them, which are chiefly similarities or repetitions of sound used as purely sensuous devices to give pleasure or aid the attention. The essay style is characterized by the absence of these figures, or their use in such subtle variation that they cannot easily be distinguished, and, on the other hand, by the use of metaphor, aphorism, antithesis, paradox, and the other figures which, in one classification, are known as the *figurae sententiae*, the figures of wit or thought.[4] But of course such characterizations are mere caricature, and serve only as convenient labels. The form and history of the two styles must be fully considered.

The first is of earlier origin: it is the style in which prose first came to be recognized as a proper object of artistic cultivation among the Greeks. According to the sketchy and untrustworthy reports of ancient literary historians, Gorgias was its "inventor"; but this may mean no more than that he first formulated and systematized for teaching purposes the "schemes" which serve to ornament it, and especially the three most important of these, which still go by his name in rhetorical theory: and it is almost certain that even these figures originated long before Gorgias' time, in certain liturgical or legal customs of the primitive Greek community.[5] The next state in its history is associated with the name of

---

[4] The division of the figures into *schemata verborum* and *figurae sententiae* is here adopted because it represents the opposition of styles that we are concerned with. There were, of course, other classifications in antiquity, based on other principles.

[5] They are 1) *Isocolon*, approximate equality of *length* between members of a period; 2) *Parison*, similarity of *form* between such equal members as in the position of nouns, verbs, adjectives, etc.; 3) *Paramoion*, likeness of sound between words thus similarly placed. Descriptions of them may be found in Richard Volkmann, *Rhetorik der Griechen und Römer*, in *Handbuch der Klassischen Alter-tums-Wissenschaft*, ed. I. von Müller, 3rd ed. (Munich, 1901), II, iii, 40-49; Friedrich Landmann, *Der Euphuismus, sein Wesen, seine Quelle, seine Geschichte*

54

Isocrates, a disciple of Gorgias, to whom is always attributed the elaboration of the form of the rhythmic "period" and the subordination to this, in their proper artistic relation to it, of the Gorgian schemes. Isocrates was the most important of all that class of teachers to whom Socrates and Plato have given a much worse reputation than they deserve. The sophistic scheme of education included a great use of oratory because it was founded on a study of politics; the individual man was conceived as a kind of mirror reflecting the character and interests of his town or state, and his literary education was wholly determined by the customs of the forum and the public uses of rhetoric.[6]

In spite of all opposition from the philosophers this type of education spread generally throughout the Greek world, in the colonies perhaps even more widely than in the home cities, and was disseminated in the Hellenistic period throughout the greater part of the Mediterranean world. And with it, of course, went the "sophistic" rhetoric everywhere, now exfoliating in *cultus* and flamboyancy under the influence of provincial tastes, now degenerating into a merely puerile and academic employment of the schemes, or again assuming the normal grandeur of its proportions and the purity of its design, but preserving through all variations the essential features of its form as they had been perfected by Isocrates. In fact the conventionalized oratory of the sophistic schools must be considered not only the most conspicuous contribution of the Greeks to the prose style of Europe, but also the standard and normal form of their own prose, of which all other forms are variations, and to which it always returned as to the true rhetorical point of departure. Nor did it perish with the passing of classical Greek culture. It lived again in the Roman rhetoric which culminated in the oratory of Cicero, and survived, to enjoy still longer and stranger destinies, in the teaching of the Christian schools of the Middle Ages.[6a]

(Giessen, 1881); Clarence Griffin Child, *John Lyly and Euphuism* (Erlangen, 1894); Croll, *Sources*, printed in full below; or better in a number of the medieval treatises collected in Karl F. von Halm, ed., *Rhetores Latini Minores* (Leipzig, 1863), of which see index. They may be briefly described as the chief figures by which oratorical concinnity is effected.

[6] Edward M. Cope in the introd. to *Plato's Gorgias Literally Translated* (London, 1883) gives a clear statement of the character of sophistic education. [See H. M. Hubbell, *The Influence of Isocrates on Cicero, Dionysius, and Aristides* (New Haven, 1913); T. K. Whipple, "Isocrates and Euphuism," *MLR*, xi (1916), 15-27, 129-135; Williamson, *Senecan Amble*, pp. 20-37 and passim.]

[6a] [M. B. Ogle, "Some Aspects of Medieval Latin Style," *Speculum*, i (1926),

The form of Isocratean rhetoric need not detain us long here; we are concerned with it only in its relation with the style that arose in opposition to it, and the only point that it is necessary to emphasize here is the sensuous character of its appeal to its audience. Its "round composition" and the "even falling of its clauses" do not always satisfy the inward ear of the solitary reader. Heard solely by the reflective mind, it is an empty, a frigid, or an artificial style. But it is not meant for such a hearing. It is addressed first, like music, to the physical ear; and the figures with which its large and open design are decorated have been devised with a reference to the attentive powers and the aural susceptibilities of large audiences, consisting of people of moderate intelligence, and met amid all the usual distractions of public assemblage—as Cicero says, *in sole et pulvere.*

In their appropriate place they are the legitimate resource of a great popular art, and their fitness for their ends is vindicated by the fact that they reappear whenever the necessary conditions of popular eloquence are satisfied. But it is evident that their literary adaptability is strictly limited. They offer nothing that is pleasing to an intellect intent upon the discovery of reality; and a people like the Greeks, in whom philosophic curiosity was quite as strong an incentive to literary art as the love of sensuous forms, would not long resist the temptation to ridicule or parody them, and to study modes of expression deliberately contrasted with them. The beginning of the history of the essay style among them follows hard, as we should expect, upon that of the oratorical, in the lifetime indeed of the reputed founder of the latter.

170-189; Charles Sears Baldwin, *Medieval Rhetoric and Poetic to 1400* (New York, 1928) and *Renaissance Literary Theory and Practice: Classicism in the Rhetoric and Poetic of Italy, France, and England 1400-1600* (New York, 1939); Lee S. Hultzén, "Aristotle's *Rhetoric* in England to 1600," Cornell Univ. Diss., 1932; Richard P. McKeon, "Rhetoric in the Middle Ages," *Speculum,* xvii (1943), 1-32; J. W. H. Atkins, *English Literary Criticism: The Medieval Phase* (New York, 1943); Ernst R. Curtius, *European Literature and the Latin Middle Ages,* trans. W. R. Trask, Bollingen Series xxxvi (New York, 1953) from *Europäische Literatur und Lateinisches Mittelalter* (Berne, 1948); Wilbur S. Howell, "English Backgrounds of Rhetoric," *History of Speech Education in America* (New York, 1954), pp. 3-47, and the earlier chapters of his *Logic and Rhetoric in England, 1500-1700* (Princeton, 1956)—but see Walter J. Ong, *RN,* ix (Winter 1956), 206-211; Ong's concern, here and elsewhere, is with the special problem of the impact of Ramus on logic and rhetoric during the Renaissance; see his *Ramus, Method, and the Decay of Dialogue* (Cambridge, Mass., 1958); but see also R. J. Schoeck, *New Scholasticism,* xxxiv (1960), 537-545.]

In his dialogue named for the orator, Plato relates a conversation that is supposed to occur on a visit of Gorgias to Athens in about the year 405, when Gorgias was perhaps eighty years of age. Socrates had been invited to meet him at dinner and hear him deliver a new oration that he had prepared. Socrates avoided the proffered entertainment, probably with some malice; but, either by accident or design, met the dinner party on its way home, and was again invited to hear an oration by the master—this time at Callicles' house. Socrates went with the party, but asked whether Gorgias would not consent to converse with him instead of speaking to him. In the long conversation that followed, the philosopher succeeded by his unequalled dialectic art in making Gorgias and one of his disciples acknowledge that the true aim of education is not the art of persuasion, but how to see and like the truth, how to know right from wrong and love it; and gave an original turn to the whole theory of style by showing that it is at best a kind of cookery which makes things palatable whether they are good for us or not, whereas the study of morality is like medicine, which puts the soul in a state of health and keeps it there.

In this dialogue of Plato's, and in the *Phaedrus*, which treats the same theme, are laid the foundations of a new interpretation of the functions of rhetoric, wholly different from those of oratory, and of the practice of a style appropriate to these functions. But it is not fair to say that Plato and Socrates foresaw such an outcome of their controversy with the sophists, or would have been pleased by it if they had done so. Cicero complained that it was Socrates who first instituted the opposition between philosophy and oratory which, as he properly observed, is fatal to the highest development of the latter; and this statement seems to represent the attitude of Socrates in the *Gorgias* with substantial correctness. The purport of his argument is almost certainly that in the public life of a sound commonwealth, and, with still more reason, in the private activities of its citizens, there would be no use of an art of rhetoric of any kind. The Protestant, or Puritan, divorce of spirit and sense is apparent in his treatment of the subject, and he has apparently not thought of the possibility that a new theory of style could be erected on the foundation of his opposition to oratory and its forms.

History shows, however, that when you put rhetoric out at the door it comes in at the window, and the inevitable next step in the development of the ideas of Socrates and Plato was their systemization with reference to an art of prose composition. Aristotle effected this in the first two books of his *Rhetoric*, which have served as the starting point of all subsequent theories of style that have called themselves "modern." This book was a wholly new thing in the world; for the theory of rhetoric was here worked out for the first time, not on the basis of the susceptibilities of audiences, and the aural effect of language, but on the basis of the processes of reasoning and in strict relations with the science of logic. Speaking roughly, we may say that the *Rhetoric* treats for the first time the art of writing, as opposed to the art of speaking.[7]

This statement will have to be very carefully guarded, however; for there is an astonishing inconsistency in the work, which it will be useful to consider here for a moment. After treating style in the first two books as dependent upon the forms of thought, Aristotle discusses, in the third book, which is about style, a form which is not distinguishable from the Isocratean oratorical style, except that he lays an emphasis perhaps on shorter periods and treats the oratorical figures very simply. The explanation is probably to be found in the fact that the two parts were composed for different purposes at different times. The first is the work of a philosopher seeking to explain the part that rhetoric is observed to play in the life of man, and is not meant to have anything to do with the practice of the art; the second is a purely objective description of the form of style which he saw in actual use, the only describable, conventionalized form then in existence.[8] Of course this explanation does not get rid of the essential inconsistency of his two modes of treatment. Nothing can do that; for it is involved in Aristotle's theory, and we encounter here for the first time a phenomenon that meets us at every point in the later history of the intimate or essay style, namely, the slipperiness of all rhetorical theory when it tries to establish itself on anything other than the sensuous character of language and the social conventions that give it opportunity and effect. When it aspires to be the art of presenting things or thought in their essential character and their true lineaments, rhetoric at once begins to lose its identity and be dissolved into one or another

[7] For the relation between the ideas of Plato and those of the *Rhetoric* see Cope, *Gorgias*, pp. xxv-xxviii, and G. L. Hendrickson, "The Origin and Meaning of the Ancient Characters of Style," *AJP*, xxvi (1905), 249-252.

[8] On the inconsistency spoken of see Hendrickson, "The Origin," p. 251, n.2, and pp. 252-255. Norden, *Die Antike Kunstprosa*, i, 125-126, speaks of inconsistencies of the same kind between the *Rhetoric* and other works of Aristotle.

of the sciences. It is an art, in short, and every art is a social convention.

But we need go no further into this subject at present; what concerns us is that Aristotle's *Rhetoric* exactly represents the state of unstable equilibrium which had necessarily followed Plato's attack upon oratory. A new use of prose style had now attained general recognition as a form of art—in brief the use of style for the purposes of philosophy and as closely related to the art of dialectic; and on the basis of this new conception of the purpose of prose discourse Aristotle had erected the theory of the art of rhetoric. But in the meantime the older, traditional, oratorical customs had not yielded to the vigor of Plato's attack, but on the contrary were as flourishing as ever, and were universally recognized, even by Aristotle, as displaying the form of style which, in a purely rhetorical sense, is the ideal and abstract best. In other words, theory and the tradition of practice were in conflict, and Aristotle had done nothing to reconcile them.

The recognition of this difficulty was what determined the next step in the development of Greek rhetorical theory. The followers of Aristotle resolved it in a purely empirical way by recognizing a division of prose style into two distinct characters or genera, which henceforward played the leading role in all the rhetorical criticism of antiquity. At a later stage in the development a third "character" was added and appears in all Latin criticism; but in the most recent and much the best treatment of the subject this addition is considered as a makeshift which tends to confuse the principle on which the original division was based.[9] We shall have to speak of it in its place; but the main facts of modern stylistic history, as of the ancient, are best represented by a consideration of the two characters which first make their appearance in Theophrastus and are more clearly defined in later successors of Aristotle.

The first was known as the *genus grande* or *nobile*. It was the rhetorical style of the Gorgian tradition, and the adjectives used to describe it indicate the character it was originally supposed to have. When it was practiced independently of the social and political conditions upon which it depends for its greatest success, its

[9] In all that concerns the history of the three characters of style and the relations between the *genus grande* and the *genus humile* in ancient theory, I follow the convincing article by Hendrickson cited in the preceding notes, and its companion, "The Peripatetic Mean of Style and the Three Stylistic Characters," *AJP*, xxv (1904), 125-146.

elaborate form and ornamental figures, studied merely for their own charm, gave it a character of *cultus,* or empty ornateness; and it was so portrayed at certain periods by its opponents. But the true nature of the *genus grande* is to be broad and general in its scope, large and open in design, strong, energetic, vehement. Tacitus ridicules its degenerate practitioners as minstrels or dancers, in allusion to the musical beauty of their rhythms;[10] but Cicero in more than one passage compares the true orator with the tragic actor, in allusion to the breadth and passion of his portrayal of life.[11]

The newer style, which had appeared in opposition to this, was known as the *genus humile* or *submissum* (*demissum*), but its quality is better indicated by the more descriptive appellations often given to it, or to branches or varieties of it: *lene, subtile,* insinuating, flexible, subtle. A style of this general character would naturally have many particular forms. It might, for instance, become a deliberately rude, formless, negligent style—*décousu,* as Montaigne says of his own—in order to express contempt for *cultus,* or even for rhetoric itself, and a love of "honest" simplicity; on the other hand, it might emulate the colloquial ease and *mondanité* of good conversation, in intended contrast with the vulgar pomp of public oratory, and be distinguished as elegant, graceful, *nitidus;* or again it might declare its superiority to popular tastes, as in the hands of the Stoics, by affecting a scornful and significant brevity of utterance. All of these and other species of the genus were recognized by the ancients as actually existing, or as having existed at different times and places, and were distinguished by appropriate terms.[12] But the genus as a whole is properly characterized by its origin in

---

[10] *Dialogus de Oratoribus,* XXVI: *Plerique jactant cantari saltarique commentarios suos.* It is interesting that the reformers of style in the Renaissance compared the corrupt medieval form of the *genus grande* to minstrels' elocution. See my introduction to Lyly's *Euphues,* section V, glossed "Passage from Wilson's *Rhetoric.*"

[11] For example, in *Brutus,* LV.203: *Grandis et, ut ita dicam, tragicus orator.*

[12] See, for instance, the classification by Demetrius, *De Elocutione:* graceful, plain, and arid; all of these being species which, in a different classification from Demetrius', would form parts of the *genus humile.* [For Demetrius' main passages on the plain style, see the Loeb ed., *On Style,* trans. W. R. Roberts (Cambridge, Mass., 1953), 190-222; also his observations on epistolary style, 223-239.] See also Diogenes Laertius, "Life of Zeno" [VII.59, quoted in *Lipse,* n.2], and Quintilian, *Institutio Oratoria,* XII.x.20-26. [Trimpi treats the *genus humile* at length, using Demetrius' statements and Cicero's account of the Attic orator "as the norm for the plain style in classical prose" (p. 8).]

philosophy. Its function is to express individual variances of experience in contrast with the general and communal ideas which the open design of the oratorical style is so well adapted to contain. Its idiom is that of conversation or is adapted from it, in order that it may flow into and fill up all the nooks and crannies of reality and reproduce its exact image to attentive observation.[13]

As to its specific rhetorical forms nothing needs to be said here; they will be considered fully elsewhere. But a general point must be urged which is often, or usually, ignored by admirers of a *genus humile*, and even by those who practice it, though the neglect of it is a prolific source of aberration both in theory and practice. And this is the point that its rhetorical forms are modifications, adaptations of those of the oratorical style. The ancients were very slow to recognize any kind of literary customs other than oral ones; and even in the genres that were obviously meant for silent reading, such as the letter, the form of the style was controlled by the ear. This is a sound principle at all times, and for all kinds of style, and its operation cannot be escaped even though it is forgotten or denied. There is only one rhetoric, the art of the beauty of spoken sounds. In oratory this beauty displays itself in its most obvious, explicit, exfoliated forms; in the *genus humile* in much more delicate, implicit, or mingled ones. But the forms are ultimately the same, and whatever beauty of style we find in the most subtle and intimate kinds of discourse could be explained—if there were critics skillful and minute enough—in terms of oratorical effect.

The history of Greek and Roman style is chiefly the story of the relations of the *genus grande* and the *genus humile*. Theoretically the two kinds are not hostile or exclusive of each other; Cicero is always anxiously insisting that they are both necessary in their proper places and relations to the oratory that he dreamed of as the perfection of literary art. But in fact they almost always proved to be rivals; and different schools, even long and important literary periods, distinguish themselves by their preference for one of them, their dislike of the other.

[13] Quintilian's metaphor (*Inst. Or.*, XII.x.37) is beautiful. Advising the Romans to cultivate the grand style rather than the "Attic," he says: "Greek keels, even the little ones, know well their ports; let ours usually travel under fuller sails, with a stronger breeze swelling our canvas. . . . They have the art of threading their way through the shallows; I would seek somewhat deeper waters, where my bark may be in no danger of foundering."

✧ III ✧

It proved to be so again during the formative period of modern prose style. The literary movement which is the subject of the present discussion was a successful attempt to substitute the philosophical *genus humile* for the oratorical *genus grande* in the general practice of authors and the general favor of readers.

Both the customs and the spirit of sixteenth-century life demanded literary expression in oratorical forms. It was a period of social unity, or at least of social unities. Brittle, temporary, illusory, these unities were; yet they were effective and brilliant while they lasted, and created the congregational and social customs which are favorable to a spoken literature. Even the religious controversy, so destructive of European society in the long run, had the opposite effect at first. For it consolidated large masses of people in devotion to a common cause, and gathered them together in popular assemblies which listened with a new motive for attention to discourses in the traditional forms of popular oration.

More important than all partisan loyalties, however, was the new feeling of national unity which made itself felt almost everywhere during this century. Whatever divisive forces were latent in the religious controversy were controlled and subordinated by centripetal tendencies in the political world; and the bitterest sectarian foes were compelled to share, with at least a semblance of concord and common loyalty, in the dazzling social and public life that centered in the courts of princes and in the cities that swarmed about them and took them as their models of conduct and manners. We hear remarkably little, during this period, of solitary and contemplative existences, of local characters, or of the self-dependent individualism of the country house. Everyone was present, either in fact or in idea, at court, and the most striking opportunities for literary distinction were offered at the constant gatherings, public or semi-public, more or less formal, which attended its various ceremonies and progresses and procedures. The occasions for the public display of stylistic art in the presence of the sovereign or one of his (or her) greater satellites were many: in the minor circles of courtiers and ladies-in-waiting they were innumerable. We should doubtless be greatly astonished, if we were able to recover a complete picture of the court life of the time, to observe how many of the uses of books like *Il Cortegiano*, Guevara's *Libro Aureo*, the

62

Arcadia, and *Euphues* were oral rather than literary. It is probable that these books—and there is no reason why we should not add Ariosto's and Spenser's epics—were habitually read aloud in assemblies of which we can now form but a faint picture in our minds, and were indeed composed chiefly with a view to such performance. When we add that solitary reading with the eye was only beginning to be a customary form of entertainment, we are prepared to understand why the literary education of the Renaissance was almost wholly conducted by means of the practice of oratory.

The various forms of prose style that resulted from this training need not be distinguished here. They were as various, of course, as the elements of the literary tradition in which the Renaissance was living. They were partly (indeed chiefly) medieval, partly classical, partly popular or folk forms. But it is enough for our present purpose to observe that all of them, by whatever channels they had come to the culture of the sixteenth century, had their ultimate origin in the Gorgian, or Isocratean type of oratory that we have been discussing in the preceding section. That this is true of the style taught by the orthodox humanists is well known: their aim was to teach their pupils to "write Cicero." But it is also true of the many kinds of style due to the survival of medieval educational customs and social modes: the forms of preaching style, for instance, that were prevalent until after the middle of the century, both in Latin and the vernacular; the style employed in letters composed for social display or amusement; the aureate style affected by those accustomed to Renaissance courtly ceremony, as in the show speeches of knights in tournaments, or in begging or complimentary addresses to sovereigns; and the literary *cultismo* practiced in many moral treatises and romances, as by Guevara, Sidney, and Lyly. However unclassical all these may be in their effect upon our ears and taste, they have one character in common: they are all arrived at by the elaboration of the "schemes," or figures of sound, that have been described as the chief ornaments of the Isocratean oratory. And that is all that is necessary in order to fix them in their place in the one great European tradition of oratorical style.

Against the literary tyranny of this tradition, and more particularly against its sixteenth-century efflorescence, the representatives of the modern spirit of progress were in revolt during the last quarter of the century. The temporary unities of the Renaissance were evidently breaking up; and the literary customs that had flowered upon them responded immediately to the tokens of their decay. The historian versed in the poetry of this period can detect the coming of the severer air of the seventeenth century in the new distaste that declares itself everywhere for the copious and flowing style of Ariosto and Spenser, and the "tedious uniformity" of Petrarchanism: the student of prose style is made aware of it at an even earlier date by the eager malice with which some of the new leaders recognize the artificiality of the oratorical customs of their time.

It was Muret, it seems, that remarkable prophet of seventeenth-century ideas, who first tossed this straw into the wind. In one of the latest and boldest of his academic discourses he asserts that the reasons for the practice of oratory in the time of his rhetorical predecessors, Bembo and Sadoleto, are no longer of any effect in the present age, because the real concerns of political life, and even the most important legal questions, are no longer decided in the public audience chambers of the senates and courts, but in the private cabinets of ministers of state and in the intimacy of conversation.[14] It was a cynical observation, perhaps, but a true one, justifying Machiavelli's wonderful realism at last, and foretelling the Richelieus, Bacons, and Cecils of a later generation.

Like his fellows in the new rationalism Muret arrived at his ideas by the first-hand study of facts. But he was like them too in that he desired to support his case by classical authority. The source of the passage just alluded to seems to be the discussion at the opening of the *Rhetoric* in which Aristotle explains that the justification of oratory is to be found in the imperfection and weakness of judgment characteristic of an uneducated public, incapable of distinguishing truth from error by the tedious processes of reason. Aristotle was perhaps the only ancient author whose authority was great enough to stand against that of Cicero on a question of this kind, and this famous statement in the *Rhetoric* was eagerly seized on by the anti-oratorical critics of the seventeenth century: its echoes are heard from Muret and Bacon to Pascal and Arnauld. But the same idea came to the Anti-Ciceronian leaders from other ancient sources; and it is to be observed that they find a more specific appropriateness to the circumstances of their own time in the magnificent de-

---

[14] Oration of 1582, introducing his course on the *Epistolae ad Atticum*, in *Orationes* (Leipzig, 1838), II, 140-151; see also his double oration of 1580, defending himself for the public teaching of Tacitus, which had made him the object of open attack and secret intrigue, II, 108-131.

scription of the decline of Roman oratory during the Empire which
Tacitus puts into the mouth of Maternus in his *Dialogue*.[15] This
passage played a great part in forming Muret's ideas; but the first
clear intimation of its vital relation to modern life is found in
Montaigne's essay on "The Vanity of Words" (I.51). After some
introductory words suggested by the *Gorgias* of Plato, and the
passage of Aristotle already mentioned, Montaigne goes on to say
that oratory has flourished most in states where "the vulgar, the
ignorant, or the populace have had all power, as in Rhodes, Athens,
and Rome," and in periods of turmoil and civil strife, as at Rome
during the Republic; "even as a rank, free, and untamed soil," he
continues, "beareth the rankest and strongest weeds."

> Whereby it seemeth that those commonweals which depend of
> an absolute monarch have less need of it than others. For that
> foolishness and facility which is found in the common multi-
> tude, and which doth subject the same to be managed, per-
> suaded, and led by the ears by the sweet-alluring and sense-
> entrancing sound of this harmony, without duly weighing,
> knowing, or considering the truth of things by the force of
> reason: this facility and easy yielding, I say, is not so easily
> found in one only ruler, and it is more easy to safeguard him
> from the impression of this poison by good institution and
> sound counsel.

Is he looking back toward the Roman Empire or forward to the
regime of absolutism beginning to be established in his own time?
One cannot tell. In the literature of the period that was then beginning, these two historical phenomena are always presenting
themselves side by side. For example, in a passage of Étienne
Pasquier, plainly suggested by the same discourse in Tacitus'
dialogue: "Tels fanfares sont propres en une Democratie, à un
orateur du tout voué et ententif à la surprise du peuple par doux
traits et emmiellement de sa Rhétorique. Ce qui ne se présenta onc-
ques entre nous."[16]

[15] Chs. XXXVI-XLI. Hippolyte Rigault, Ch. I of *Histoire de la Querelle des Anciens et des Modernes*, in *Œuvres Complètes* (Paris, 1859), I, 1-17 has made an
admirable use of this dialogue as one of the starting-points in antiquity of the
modern idea of progress. An interesting paper might be written on the effect of the
Anti-Ciceronian agitation on the growth of this idea.

[16] "Lettres," I.2 in *Œuvres* (Amsterdam, 1723), II, 5 (1st letter in *Œuvres
Choisies*, ed. Léon Feugère, 2 vols. [Paris, 1849]). [As quoted by Croll, the passage
contained minor errors which we have corrected, making it coincide with the

Political motives, however, were not the ones that weighed most with the Anti-Ciceronian leaders. Their scientific interests and above all their universal preoccupation with moral questions played a still greater part in determining their rhetorical program. The old claims of philosophy to precedence over formal rhetoric, long ago asserted by Plato, are revived by them in much the old terms, and the only justification they will admit for the study of style is that it may assist in the attainment of the knowledge of oneself and of nature. "The art of writing and the art of managing one's life are one and the same thing" is the motto of Montaigne and all his followers. "As for me," writes Lipsius to Montaigne in 1588, "I mightily scorn all those external and polite kinds of studies, whether philosophical or literary, and indeed every kind of knowledge that is not directed by prudence and judgment to the end of teaching the conduct of life."[17] Bacon deprecates the harsh treatment of rhetoric by Plato and labors its justification in *The Advancement of Learning*; but he treats it as a subordinate part of dialectic or logic, as Aristotle does, and in certain portions of its subject-matter as identical with moral or political philosophy.[18] La Mothe le Vayer is more express and clear than any of his predecessors. They have all praised the new genres, the letter and the essay; but he professes at the beginning of his discussion of rhetoric to treat of written style alone, *la*

---

text in Estienne Pasquier, *Choix de Lettres sur la Littérature, la Langue, et la Traduction*, ed. D. Thickett (Geneva, 1956), p. 78. Pasquier's pointing to Henri III's unsound policies is shown in Th. Glaser, "Deux Discours Manuscrits d'Estienne Pasquier," *Revue de la Renaissance*, VIII (1907), 1-28.] Andreas Schott develops at length the relations between the decline of oratory and the political conditions at the fall of the Republic, in the prefatory letter (to Lipsius) of his edition of the elder Seneca (Geneva, 1613).

[17] *Ep. Misc.*, II.41 in *Opera Omnia* (Antwerp, 1637), II, 86.

[18] *Of the Advancement of Learning*, in *Works* (1868), III, 409-411, ed. Wright, II.xviii.1-5 (cf. *De Augmentis Scientiarum*, VI.iii): "For although in true value it is inferior to wisdom . . . yet with people it is the more mighty." Its function is to "contract a confederacy between the Reason and Imagination against the Affections"; and again: "Logic handleth reason exact and in truth, and Rhetoric handleth it as it is planted in popular opinions and manners." The chief defect that he notes in the study of rhetoric is that too little attention has been paid to the study of *private* modes of discourse. In this art orators are likely to be defective, "whilst by the observing their well-graced forms of speech they leese the volubility [i.e. lose the subtlety or flexibility] of application." He then proceeds to supply this defect in part by making a collection of aphorisms and antitheses on the moral and political life of man, which he greatly extended in the *De Augmentis*, observing that whether this belongs to politics (prudential wisdom) or to rhetoric is a question of no importance.

rhétorique des livres, a style to be read, not heard: all that has to do with speaking he repudiates.[19]

This is the general attitude of the leaders of opinion in the first half of the century. In the second half it is not changed, but, on the contrary, is more clearly defined. Pierre Bayle speaks of the *faux éclat* of oratory. "Ces Messieurs-là [les orateurs] ne se soucient guere d'éclairer l'esprit . . . ils vont droit au coeur, et non pas droit à l'entendement: ils tâchent d'exciter l'amour, la haine, la colere."[20] Bayle displays the scorn and intolerance that have always been characteristic of the scientific rationalist; but with proper deductions his opinions may be taken as characteristic of the age of La Bruyère, Arnauld, Fénelon, and Malebranche, of the Port-Royal community and the Royal Society of London. The temporary success of Puritanism and Quietism, the rapid progress of scientific method, and the diffusion of Cartesian ideas, all in their different ways helped to create a taste for a bare and level prose style adapted merely to the exact portrayal of things as they are. The severest theorists indeed can hardly be brought to recognize a difference between logic and rhetoric; while even the most liberal would exclude the characteristic beauties of oratorical form from the legitimate resources of literary art. Persuasion is indeed the object of rhetoric. But the legitimate means of attaining this end, they constantly assert, is not by the sensuous appeal of oratorical rhythm, but, on the contrary, by portraying in one's style exactly those athletic movements of the mind by which it arrives at a sense of reality and the true knowledge of itself and the world.[21] Fénelon is the harshest critic of Isocrates

[19] *Considérations sur l'Éloquence Françoise de ce Temps* (1638), in *Œuvres* (Dresden, 1756-1759), II, i, 193-195. He also has a treatise *Sur la Composition, et sur la Lecture des Livres* (II, i, 319-391). Whether a work had ever been written before on this subject I cannot say.

[20] *Œuvres Diverses* (The Hague, 1727), III, 178, col. 1. Cf. I, 644-645 on the "Faux Raisonnement de Cicéron" and his *Dictionnaire,* s.v. "Pitiscus."

[21] Antoine Arnauld, *La Logique ou l'Art de Penser,* ed. L. Barré (Paris, 1874), Part III, Ch. 20, p. 284: "la principale [partie de l'éloquence] consiste à concevoir fortement les choses, et à les exprimer en sorte qu'on en porte dans l'esprit des auditeurs une image vive et lumineuse, qui ne présente pas seulement ces choses toutes nues, mais aussi les mouvements avec lesquels on les conçoit." Cf. Fénelon, *Dialogues sur l'Éloquence,* "Second Dialogue, Pour Atteindre son But, l'Orateur Doit *Prouver, Peindre,* et *Toucher,*" *Œuvres,* ed. Louis Aimé Martin (Paris, 1870), II, 668-679. And again: "La vive peinture des choses est comme l'âme de l'éloquence." [Wilbur S. Howell relates the rhetorical theories of Arnauld and Fénelon in the Introd. to his trans. of Fénelon's *Dialogues on Eloquence* (Princeton, 1951); I. von Kunow discusses ideas on style in "Sprach und Literarkritik bei Antoine Arnauld," *Romanische Forschungen,* XXXIX (1921), 67-200.]

and his school—he was aware that this included Bossuet—that the century produced;[22] and Malebranche proposed to correct the too-imaginative prose of the age of Montaigne and Bacon by applying to it its own rationalistic criticism with a rigor that Montaigne and Bacon never dreamed of.[23]

In short, though this was the period when the Isocratean model was revived by Bossuet, the critics were all on the side of the severer style, and most of them were either hostile or indifferent to oratory in all its forms. The doctrine of the *genus humile* was taught everywhere.

Up to this point we have not mentioned the word "Attic," which is the object of the discussion. We have considered only the two great modes of style, the grand and the familiar, and the relation of the ancient rivalry between them to the theory of modern Anti-Ciceronianism. This, however, is the proper approach to our subject. For in the controversies of the Anti-Ciceronians "Attic style"

[22] See a passage near the beginning of the first dialogue, and a more interesting one near the end of the second (*Œuvres*, II, 658, 675-679), in which Fénelon seems to apprehend not only the connection between Bossuet and Isocrates, but the Isocratean character of medieval Latin preaching style. [Gonzague Truc gives a good general account of French pulpit oratory from the Middle Ages in *Nos Orateurs Sacrés* (Paris, 1950); See also E. C. Dargan, *A History of Preaching* (New York, 1905-1912); C. H. E. Smyth, *The Art of Preaching: A Practical Survey of Preaching in the Church of England 747-1939* (London, 1939); H. Caplan, "Classical Rhetoric and the Medieval Theory of Preaching," *Classical Philology*, XXVII (1933), 73-96; J. M. Neale, *Medieval Preachers and Medieval Preaching* (London, 1856); G. R. Owst, *Literature and Pulpit in Medieval England*, 2nd ed. (Oxford, 1961) and *Preaching in Medieval England* (Cambridge, 1926); H. Caplan and H. H. King, "Latin Tractates on Preaching: A Book List," *Harvard Theological Review*, XLII (1949), 185-206, and "French Tractates on Preaching: A Book List," *Quarterly Journal of Speech*, XXXVI (1950), 296-325; Joseph Vianey, "L'Éloquence de Bossuet dans sa Prédication à la Cour," *Revue des Cours et Conférences*, XXX, v-x (Feb. 15-Apr. 30, 1929): in the first of these articles Vianey shows how Bossuet adjusted his arguments and subjects to the needs of a courtly, *libertin* audience; the third treats the means—clarity, vivacity, anecdotes, emotional passages—used to attract and keep attention; the fourth appraises Bossuet's style, including sentence architecture, increased use of short sentences and maxims, etc. See the excellent bibliography in J. W. Blench, *Preaching in England in the Late Fifteenth and Sixteenth Centuries* (Oxford, 1964). See also *Muret*, n.48.]

[23] See the passages of *La Recherche de la Vérité* cited in n.66, below. [István Sőtér, in his *La Doctrine Stylistique des Rhétoriques du XVIIe Siècle* (Budapest, 1937), distinguishes three stages in the art of expression: triumphant Ciceronianism; then a period dominated by simplicity, *bienséance*, and moderation; finally a stage characterized by the new issues of *je ne sais quoi* and *esprit*. Jean Cousin attributes French classicism to the influence of ancient rhetoric and Stoic philosophy in "Rhétorique Latine et Classicisme Français," *Revue des Cours et Conférences*, XXXIV, i-ii (Feb. 28-July 30, 1933). For related studies see *A Critical Bibliography of French Literature*, ed. David C. Cabeen and Jules Brody, Vol. III, *The Seventeenth Century*, ed. Nathan Edelman (Syracuse, 1961), pp. 281-284.]

means to all intents and purposes the *genus humile* or *subtile*,
"Asiatic" describes the florid, oratorical style of Cicero's early
orations or any style ancient or modern distinguished by the same
copious periodic form and the Gorgian figures that attend upon it.
"Attic" is always associated with philosophy and the *ars bene vi-
vendi*, "Asiatic" with the *cultus* of conventional oratory. This is not
the usual modern method of relating the two terms. Probably the
fault now most commonly associated with Asianism is one to which
the Anti-Ciceronians of the seventeenth century were themselves
peculiarly liable when they used the characteristic forms of their art
for oratorical purposes. We think of the tumor, the exaggerated
emphasis, the monstrous abuse of metaphor in the preaching of
the first half of the century in all the European countries; or of
qualities dangerously related to these in the non-oratorical prose
writings of Donne, Gracián, Malvezzi, and other masters of the
"conceit"; or even of tendencies of the same kind that we may
observe in writers so normal as Lipsius, Bacon, Balzac, and Browne.
There is a kind of Asianism, in short, that arises from a constant effort
to speak with point and significance, as well as from an excessive
use of the ornate figures of sound, from too much love of expressiveness as well as from the cult of form; and inasmuch as this vice
was more familiar to the reformers at the end of the century than
the other, and was the one that was in immediate need of correction at that time, it has taken its place in our traditions as typical
Asianism. But the Anti-Ciceronians were not aware that they were
falling into error through an excess of their own qualities; they
called themselves "Attic" because they avoided certain traits of
style which they disliked, and did not observe that they sometimes
ceased to be Attic through avoiding and disliking them too much.
It is true therefore that their use of the terms was a one-sided and
inadequate interpretation of their meaning in ancient criticism.[24]
But on the other hand, it is fair to remark that so is the present use,
and indeed that the seventeenth century was far more nearly in

[24] In antiquity, however, there was much the same variation of usage as that
described in the text. The opponents of Cicero always tended to identify Asianism
with the oratorical *cultus*, just as the modern Anti-Ciceronians did; but of course
the prevalent doctrine was that there are two ways of becoming Asian; *aut nimio
cultu aut nimio tumore*; either by studying too zealously the *orationis cultus* (as
Bembo, Lyly, and many sixteenth-century writers did) or by exaggerating the
sententiarum venustas (as Montaigne and Lipsius did, and Browne in the seventeenth century). See Hendrickson, "The Origin," p. 287, where the appropriate
passages from Diomedes, Cicero, and St. Augustine are cited.

accord with the ancient ideas of the character of Attic prose than we are. Through the influence of eighteenth-century tastes we have come to associate it with the laws of taste and good form imposed by a slightly frivolous, or at least not very intellectual, social custom; and have lost sight of the fact that it had its original in philosophy rather than in the manners of "the world," and preserved its philosophical associations in antiquity through all its transmutations. This fact the Anti-Ciceronians of the seventeenth century never forgot. It was the basis of their distinction between Attic and Asian prose.

The evidence on this point is clear and decisive, and begins with the earliest phases of the sixteenth-century Ciceronian controversy. Erasmus, however, is the only witness that we shall need to cite from the first period. Throughout the *Ciceronianus* "Attic" denotes opposition to the copiousness of Cicero, and fondness for a scientific or philosophical brevity, marked by the same tendency toward ingenuity and point which accompanied the *genus humile* in ancient times. Speaking of the humanist Lazare de Baïf, one of the interlocutors says: "He prefers to be pointed [*argutus*], it seems, Attic rather than Ciceronian."[25] William Grocyn "was always inclined to the epistolary pointedness, loving laconism and appropriateness of style;[26] in this genre certainly one would call him nothing but Attic; indeed he aimed at nothing else, and when he read any writings of Cicero would say that he could not endure his fulness of expression."[27] Linacre, again, "surpasses an Attic in the repression of his feelings . . . ; he has studied to be unlike Cicero."[28] Scaliger, answering Erasmus, bullies and berates him for calling Cicero "redundant and Asiatic."[29] Improperly of course; for Erasmus is using these opprobrious words only in echoing Cicero's own criticism of his earlier orations, and is careful to point out the

[25] Desiderius Erasmus, *Opera Omnia* (Leyden, 1703-1706), I, col. 1012A.

[26] *Proprietatem sermonis*: on the technical meaning of this term in the theory of the *genus humile* see below, pp. 88-90.

[27] Erasmus, I, cols. 1012D-E.

[28] Erasmus (I, col. 989F), paraphrasing Horace's description of the brief style that tends to obscurity, calls it Atticism, though Horace has nothing to suggest this. [Cf. G. L. Hendrickson, "Horace, *Sermones*, i.4, A Protest and a Program," *AJP*, XXI (1900), 121ff. and "Satura—the Genesis of a Literary Form," *CP*, VI (1911), 129ff.; M. A. Grant and G. C. Fiske, "Cicero's *Orator* and Horace's *Ars Poetica*," *Harvard Studies in Classical Philology*, XXXV (1924), 26-34.]

[29] Julius Caesar Scaliger, *Pro M. Tullio Cicerone, contra Desiderium Erasmum Roterdamum, Oratio I* (Toulouse, 1620), p. 12, and elsewhere, in *Adversus Desiderium Erasmum Orationes Duae* (Toulouse, 1621).

variety of styles in his works. Still Cicero is prevailingly a copious and ornate orator. Controversy is never nice and discriminating; and Cicero continues "Asian" to the end of Anti-Ciceronian history. Lipsius, for example, writes in 1586; "I love Cicero; I even used to imitate him; but I have become a man, and my tastes have changed. Asiatic feasts have ceased to please me; I prefer the Attic."[30]

"Attic," however, by this time was beginning to be more fully defined, and all its ancient associations re-awakened in defence of it. Erik van der Putten (or Puteanus), evidently a follower of Lipsius, publishes a rhetoric of "Laconism," in which he marshals an array of "brief" ancient writers, Thucydides, Cato, Tacitus, especially, who are properly called Attics, he says, because they are so reticent, so incisive, so significant. But this term is inadequate to express their true glory; they may better, he thinks, be called the Spartans.[31] Later Balzac in the Preface to his *Socrate Chrestien* (1652), makes the same distinction. "Que si nostre zèle ne peut s'arrester dans nostre cœur: Qu'il en sorte à la bonne heure! Mais qu'il se retranche dans le stile de Lacedemone: Pour le moins dans l'Atticisme: Au pis aller, qu'il ne se desborde pas par ces Harangues Asiatiques, où il faut prendre trois fois haleine pour arriver à la fin d'une periode." Further on he is more exact, and speaks of the "Attiques de Rome, qui contrefaisoient Brutus, et n'imitèrent pas Ciceron," meaning Seneca and his school.[32]

Great progress in critical discrimination and historical knowledge has evidently been made since the sixteenth century. This progress continues in a later generation; and the clearest witness of all is Père Bouhours. He has the prose of the century in perspective: its faults and dangers are vividly before his mind, and

---

[30] *Ep. Misc.* II.10, in *Opera*, II, 75 [cited in French translation by Croll in *Lipse*, II (pp. 20-21)].

[31] *De Laconismo* (Louvain, 1609). In 1607 Lipsius was succeeded in the chair of rhetoric at Louvain by Van der Putten; he was one of the disciples who caused contemporaries to speak of Lipsius in the terms that Quintilian used of Seneca, as "the man upon whose faults a sect was founded." Ideas adapt themselves to the size of the minds they find a lodging in, and it is not Lipsius' fault altogether that *concettismo* of one kind or another makes its appearance so soon in the style of his followers. Van der Putten thinks (pp. 78-79) that there is too much *copia* in Demosthenes and the other Attic orators!

[32] Guez de Balzac, *Œuvres*, ed. Louis Moreau (Paris, 1854), II, 14, 16. [Cf. *Lipse*, IV, par. 1, nn.33 and 36; Williamson, *Senecan Amble*, pp. 349-350; Gaston Guillaumie, *Jean-Louis Guez de Balzac et la Prose Française* (Paris, 1927); Ferdinand Brunot, *Histoire de la Langue Française des Origines à 1900*, Vols. III-V (Paris, 1927-1939).]

he sees that they are immediately connected with the imitation of the ancient models of the acute and subtle *genus humile,* Tacitus, Lucan, Seneca: yet, he says, I am still an Attic in my tastes; and what he means by that is exactly shown in a passage from an earlier work, every sentence of which is important for our purpose. He is speaking of the French language, and says that what he admires most in it is "that it is clear without being too diffuse [*étendue*]. (There is perhaps nothing that is less to my taste than the Asiatic style.) It takes pleasure in conveying a great deal of meaning in a few words. Brevity is pleasing to it, and it is for this reason that it cannot endure periods that are too long, epithets that are not necessary, pure synonyms that add nothing to the meaning, and serve only to fill out the cadence [*nombre*]. . . . The first care of our language is to content the mind [*esprit*] and not to tickle the ear. It has more regard to good sense than to beautiful cadence. I tell you once again, nothing is more natural to it than a reasonable brevity."[33] The form of the opposition between "Attic" and "Asian" in the seventeenth-century mind is more exactly expressed in the various phrases and turns of this passage than in any other that we shall be likely to find.

✧ IV ✧

The aim of the literary historian is the utmost simplification that is consistent with the actual variety of the facts he deals with; and in the preceding pages we have been trying to make our generalization broad enough to include all the significant facts of seventeenth-century prose style. But on the other hand, the uniformity of any large set of phenomena is only interesting in relation with their diversity. The *genus humile* had a history in antiquity running through seven or eight centuries, and during that period developed various phases of theory and various forms of style, most of which were known to the leaders of Anti-Ciceronianism and played their different parts in the drama of rhetorical controversy in the seventeenth century. To distinguish these phases, and the character and extent of the influence that each of them had in the

---

[33] Dominique Bouhours, *Les Entretiens d'Ariste et d'Eugène* (Amsterdam, 1671), p. 69. [The ed. by René Radouant (Paris, 1920) contains three of the six *entretiens* and treats relevant scholarship. Alexander F. B. Clark surveys Bouhours' influence on English writers and critics on pp. 262-274 of *Boileau and the French Classical Critics in England, 1660-1830* (Paris, 1925), with a useful bibliography; see *Muret*, n.26.]

period we are studying, is no less important than to observe the general tendency that is common to them all; and this will be the purpose of all the rest of our discussion.

The earlier Greek phases of this history—the only ones that we have considered up to this point—were of minor importance in determining the actual forms that prose style took in the seventeenth century; and if we only wanted to know what models it could imitate we might confine our attention to the Stoic school of rhetoric that triumphed over Ciceronian oratory in the first century of the Roman Empire. But, on the other hand, the critics whose business it was to defend and explain it were well acquainted with its purer sources in the classical period of Greek culture; and they very often, one might say usually, defended or concealed their real use of the inferior "Atticism" of Seneca and Tacitus by claiming the sanction of greater names than these. Unless we can interpret the disingenuousness of men laboring under the imputation of literary heresy we shall constantly be puzzled in reading their manifestoes. Three names associated with three phases of the history of *genus humile* in the classical Greek period occur with some frequency in their writings, those of Plato (or Socrates), Aristotle, and Demosthenes; and in the present section we will take up briefly each of these phases, with reference to its place in seventeenth-century prose criticism—reserving for the proper point the explanation of the paradox of describing the style of Demosthenes as a phase of the *genus humile*.

(a) Plato

Of the first not much needs to be said. The nature of the controversy recorded in the *Gorgias* and *Phaedrus* was of course known to the Anti-Ciceronian leaders; and they knew perfectly well, moreover, that the Isocratean, or Gorgian rhetoric was of essentially the same kind as the Ciceronian rhetoric taught by the orthodox humanists of the sixteenth century. It would have been strange if they had not used the name of Plato in propagating their new taste for a philosophical and intimate prose, or had not detected the similarity of the aims of their opponents to those of the ancient sophistic rhetoricians. It was in fact their occasional practice to apply to these teachers and their seventeenth-century successors the old name of "sophists."[34]

[34] See Balzac, "Paraphrase ou la Grande Éloquence," *Œuvres*, I, 278-289; the

There was an additional motive, however, for the revival of this ancient controversy, which will strike the modern reader as a curiosity of literary history. The new "Attics" were nine-tenths Stoic in their morals, as they were in their rhetoric. But Stoicism was stigmatized as heresy—especially when it called itself "Christian"—at every distributing center of Catholic orthodoxy; at Rome itself it was under constant surveillance. In these circumstances the name of Socrates was a convenient disguise, partly because it was not hard to wrench his philosophy into a Stoic form, and partly because his conduct at his trial and the manner of his death had long given him a place among those who had fallen as martyrs of the struggle against conventional sentimentality. Quevedo occasioned no surprise when he linked the names of Socrates, Cato, and Job in his Stoic hagiology;[35] and Balzac's title *Le Socrate Chrestien* could easily be read in its real sense of *le stoique chrétien*.

For these reasons, then, we occasionally meet with the names of Plato and Socrates in the propaganda of the new school. But as far as the form of its style was concerned the earliest masters of Attic had but little influence upon it. In the first half of the century it is almost safe to say that they had none. In the second, on the other hand, there were several ambitious revivals of Hellenism, both in England and France, and the name of Plato is often heard as that of a writer and a model to be imitated. Thus the Chevalier de Méré proposes a purely Greek literary program: Plato in prose and Homer in verse are the preferred models, and next to these (since one must do lip service, at least, to oratory) Demosthenes.[36]

---

works of Naudé, passim [and, handwritten in a copy of this essay presented to T. M. Parrott, now in Princeton University Library, Croll adds:] also Muret, Oration of the Year 1572. [For a summary of French knowledge of Plato in the seventeenth century, see Thérèse Goyet, "Présence de Platon dans le Classicisme Français" in Association Guillaume Budé, Congrès de Tours et Poitiers, 3-9 septembre, 1953, *Actes du Congrès* (Paris, 1954), pp. 364-371; also Ferdinand Gohin, *La Fontaine: Études et Recherches* (Paris, 1937), pp. 19-62.]

[35] See Mérimée, *Essai sur . . . Quevedo*, pp. 283-287. [Cf. *Lipse*, n.45.]

[36] The "Atticisme mondain" of Antoine Gombaud, Chevalier de Méré is very exactly described and placed in its true relations by Fortunat Strowski, *Histoire du Sentiment Religieux en France au XVIIIe Siècle: Pascal et son Temps*, 3 vols. (Paris, 1907), ii, 248-269, iii, 179-187. [Croll was considerably influenced by the work of Strowski whose treatment of Stoicism in Vol. i is partly superseded by Julien-Eymard d'Angers, "Le Stoïcisme en France dans la Première Moitié du XVIIe Siècle. Les Origines (1575-1616)," *Études Franciscains* (1951), no. ii, 287-297, 389-410 (1952), no. iii, 5-20, 133-154. D'Angers and M. H. Guervin list other studies on French Stoicism of the same period in XVIIIe Siècle: *Bulletin de la Société d'Étude du XVIIIe Siècle*, xix (1953), 241-243; xxi-xxii (1954), 510; xxix (1955), 353, n.2. See also works listed in *Lipse*, n.2.]

But there is some disingenuousness in this and similar professions. The actual style of de Méré does not differ in kind from that of St. Évremond, for example, which was formed in the "libertine" school of the first half of the century and "corrected" by the new *mondanité* of the second. Like other representative critics of his century, de Méré calls himself an Attic; but he had already discovered the eighteenth-century formula in which Atticism is identified with the "agreeable" style of *l'honnête homme*; and this is a style very different from Plato's.

With less emphasis the same statement can be made of the style of Fénelon in his *Dialogues*. Though it superficially resembles the model it imitates, its Platonism is but a thin disguise of the romantic and Christian poetry that we are familiar with in his other prose writings. Indeed there is but one prose style of the seventeenth century that will stand a comparison, either in kind or quality, with that of Plato: the prose style of the *Lettres Provinciales*; and Pascal is neither deceived nor disingenuous about the sources of this. He acknowledges that it has been formed by the imitation of the same Stoic models that were in favor in the first half of the century.[37]

The most important part played by Plato was to perpetuate the idea of an "Attic" style, with new and somewhat different associations, in the second half of the century, at a time when the Latin models of such a style, heretofore in favor, had begun to be discredited.

(b) Aristotle

The part played by Aristotle was much greater. Of course neither his *Rhetoric* nor any other of his surviving works could serve as a model for stylistic imitation, as the works of Plato could. Yet it is probably correct to say that certain forms of seventeenth-century prose style are chiefly due to the attempt to apply directly, in practice, ideas concerning the relation between logic and rhetoric

---

[37] "La manière d'écrire d'Epictète, de Montaigne, et de Salomon de Tultie [that is, of Pascal himself in the *Lettres Provinciales*], est le plus d'usage," etc. Blaise Pascal, *Pensées*, ed. Léon Brunschvicg (Paris, 1904), I, 30. See also Pascal's *Entretien sur Epictète et Montaigne*. [Presumably Croll refers here to the *Entretien de Pascal avec M. de Sacy*. See Joseph Bédier, "Établissement d'un Texte Critique de l'Entretien de Pascal avec M. de Saci" in his *Études Critiques* (Paris, 1903), pp. 21-80. But P. L. Couchoud argues convincingly that the conversation never occurred and that Sacy's secretary, Nicolas Fontaine, composed the dialogue by recasting an *Étude sur Epictète et Montaigne* by Pascal, Sacy's acknowledgment of receiving it, and Pascal's letter in reply ("L'Entretien de Pascal avec M. de Saci a-t-il eu Lieu?" *Mercure de France*, CCCXI, Feb. 1, 1951, 216-228.)]

gathered from the first two books of the *Rhetoric*. This is probably true of styles so different in their associations as that recommended by the Royal Society of London and often used by its scientific contributors and that imposed upon the writers of the Port Royal Community by their teachers. Both of these are characterized by a deliberate plainness which Aristotle would have been far from recommending for literary use; but they both seem to rest finally on Aristotle's resolution of the forms of rhetorical persuasion into forms of syllogistic reasoning.

The importance of his influence upon the forms of style was as nothing, however, when compared with that of his influence on the *theory* of the Attic school. The advocates of a style suited to philosophical thought needed a classical authority for their support as unquestionable and orthodox as that of Cicero, and Aristotle's *Rhetoric* provided them with what they needed. The rhetorical aphorisms and discussions in Seneca's letters expressed their ideas, it is true, in popular and telling ways. They served the purposes of Attics who did not need to profess any great amount of classical learning or any profound knowledge of rhetorical theory. But Muret, Bacon, Hobbes, and the teachers of Port Royal—the men whose task was to lay the philosophical foundations of seventeenth-century style—were all Aristotelian at first hand, while many others, Lipsius, Descartes, and so on, obtained their ideas from the same source, though perhaps less directly. To show adequately the relation of each of these philosophers to the *Rhetoric* would be a task far beyond our present limits; but at least it may be taken for granted that seventeenth-century Anti-Ciceronianism, like all other historical movements of protest against the excessive study of rhetorical form, derives its *ultimate* authority from the first two books of that work.[38] Even its third book proved useful. For its descrip-

[38] Muret's dependence upon Aristotle has been mentioned on an earlier page. One of the characteristic expressions of his irony was his choice of the *Rhetoric* instead of a Ciceronian subject for his course in 1576-1577, when he had been badgered into a temporary renunciation of the new antirhetorical studies of the rationalists. See Charles Dejob, *Marc-Antoine Muret* (Paris, 1881), pp. 293-296. Dejob fails to interpret Muret's career in an intelligible fashion because he does not understand the "Attic" movement and its intellectual implications.

Aristotelianism manifests itself clearly in the subordinate relation of rhetoric to dialectics and ethics in Bacon's *Advancement* and in the Port-Royal Treatises. On this point see Paul Jacquinet, *Francisci Baconi de Re Litteraria Judicia* (Paris, 1863), pp. 48-51. [See also Williamson's chapter on "Bacon and Stoic Rhetoric," *Senecan Amble*, pp. 150-185; K. R. Wallace, *Francis Bacon on Communication and Rhetoric* (Chapel Hill, 1943); R. S. Crane, *Wit and Rhetoric in the Renaissance* (New York, 1937); and Howell, *Logic and Rhetoric*.]

tion of the usual Isocratean oratorical forms was taken for what it was, a mere conventional recognition of existing customs; whereas its highly original treatment of Enthymemes was often employed for guidance in the art of forming aphorisms and *antitheta* in which the seventeenth century arrived at absolute perfection, and its treatment of the metaphor was often appealed to by the new Attics in defence of their favorite figure.[39] It is somewhat astonishing to find Aristotle quoted in justification of the devices of style by which *concettismo* achieves its dubious effect of power; but *concettismo* is, in fact, implicit in any "rhetoric of thought," such as Aristotle's was.

(c) Demosthenes

The third phase of Greek influence, namely that of Attic oratory, requires a larger discussion; for it involves the re-opening of the subject of the *genera dicendi*. Hitherto we have considered only two genera, or "characters," and this, as we have said, appears to have been the original form of the classification. The *genus humile* arose in opposition to oratory, as the appropriate language of intimate philosophical discussion; and the Gorgian kind of rhetoric which was then regarded as the only, or at least the typical, form of oratorical style, then properly assumed the name of the *genus grande* in contrast with it. But a kind of oratory arose at Athens during the fourth century which was not open to the charges brought against the Gorgian rhetoric by Socrates and Plato, which, on the contrary, had some of the same qualities that the masters of

[39] The raptures of the *concettisti* in praise of metaphor may be studied in Baltasar Gracián, *Agudeza y Arte de Ingenio*, in *Obras* (Madrid, 1674), I, *passim* [*Arte de Ingenio*, 1st ed. Madrid, 1642; see the ed. of Madrid, 1944]; in Cardinal Sforza-Pallavicino, *Trattato dello Stile e del Dialogo*, Ch. VII, in *Opere* (Milan, 1834), II, 594-597 ("si chiama reina delle figure") [*Trattato del Dialogo e dello Stile*, 1st ed. (Rome, 1646)]; and in Emmanuele Tesauro, *Il Cannochiale Aristotelico* (Bologna, 1693), Ch. VII, p. 179 ("il piu pellegrino e mirabile . . . parte dell'umano intelletto") [1st ed. 1654]. But Dominique Bouhours, the determined corrector of *concettismo*, is not less an admirer. See *La Manière de Bien Penser dans les Ouvrages d'Esprit* (Amsterdam, 1688), pp. 16-17. The whole theory of *concettismo* is derived from Aristotle, *Rhetoric*, especially II.xxii-xxiv (on enthymemes) and III.ii.8-15 (on metaphors). This point has been admirably brought out in the old work by Giovanni Ferri, *De l'Éloquence et des Orateurs Anciens et Modernes* (Paris, 1789), pp. 228-233, the only discussion I know of in which the preëminence of prose over poetry in any proper consideration of the seventeenth-century conceit is observed. [For a discussion of doctrines about conceits, with apt quotations from Gracián, Tesauro, Sforza-Pallavicino, Pierfrancesco Minozzi, Giulio Marzot, and modern theorists, see Joseph Mazzeo, *Renaissance and Seventeenth-Century Studies* (New York, 1964), Chs. II, III.]

the *genus humile* arrogated to themselves, an oratory disdainful of the symmetries and melodious cadences of the Isocratean model and professing to make its effect by the direct portrayal of the mind of the speaker and of the circumstances by which he has been aroused to vehement feeling. This later type of oratory was of course familiar to the post-Aristotelian theorists who adopted the bipartite division; but so strong was the tradition of the earlier type of oratory that they took no account of it in their theory. They merely wished to represent the dichotomy of style in its original and most striking form. When, however, the oratory of Lysias and Demosthenes and their school had at last taken so firm a place in the tradition that they could no longer be disregarded in the doctrine of the genera, a curious situation presented itself. For now a mode of style had to be recognized which was allied in its rhetorical form and procedure with the *genus humile*, yet was unmistakedly grander than the *genus grande* and had the same uses. Nothing but disorder could result from such an anomaly; and in fact the adjustment that was finally made was little better than a confused and illogical working arrangement. The "Attic" oratory of Demosthenes usurped the title of the *genus grande*; the *genus humile* remained undisturbed in its old functions and character; and a third genus was added to take care of the Isocratean oratory, and was given the name of the *genus medium* (*modicum, temperatum*, etc.), though this name does not appropriately represent either the historical or the formal relation of the Isocratean style to the other two. In the time of Cicero it had become customary to define the character of the three genera more fully by a reference to the effect of each upon the audience. The *genus humile* is best adapted to teaching or telling its hearers something; the *genus medium* delights them or gives them pleasure; the *genus grande* rouses them and excites them to action.[40]

It is true that this explanation of the development of the tripartite classification is not so clearly documented as we should like to have it. It is only probable. But it is the result of what seems the best investigation of the subject, and it at least *explains*. We may now add that the treatment of the three styles in the seventeenth century tends to confirm it, because it shows a similar solution of the prob-

[40] This interpretation of the relation of the three characters follows that of Hendrickson; see n.7 and n.9 above.

lem by men placed in a situation strikingly like that of the ancient theorists.

The aim of the founders of seventeenth-century prose style was to domesticate a *genus humile*. The movement inaugurated by the Anti-Ciceronian leaders, Bacon, Montaigne, Lipsius, was like that of Plato and Socrates and their followers in that it was meant to make and legalize a breach between oratory and philosophy, and to establish in general use a style meant to express reality more acutely and intimately than oratory can hope to do. And the form of oratory which was present to their eyes in the usage of their own age was, as we have seen, the same Isocratean form that the founders of the ancient *genus humile* had before them. But the seventeenth century could not sacrifice its love of grandeur and nobility to its love of philosophic truth any more than the Athens of the fourth century could. It was, indeed, an age that for peculiar reasons, affected solemnity, a kind of somber magnificence, in all the forms of its artistic expression. It was the immediate heir to the Renaissance, for one thing, and came naturally by a taste for pomp and grandiosity; but, furthermore, the peculiar political and religious temper of the time, especially as it came under Catholic and Anglo-Catholic influence, tended to strengthen these inclinations and to give them a special character. "Persuade the King in greatness," said Bacon in the confidence of his private journal; and the words might be taken as an index of the temper in which some of the most representative art of his age was produced. It was the age of the Baroque in sculpture and architecture; of the intense and profound Catholicism of El Greco; of the conscious Romanization of moral ideals; of the dogma and ceremony of absolutism; and of the elaboration, in sermon and essay, of a somber liturgy of Death.

Such an age could not be satisfied with the intimate and dialectic uses of prose alone. It needed them and made the most of them; but its rhetorical preceptors must also hold up before it the image of a great and noble oratory, greater and nobler even than the Ciceronian, but as free from Cicero's "Asianism," as "Attic," as their own philosophical essay style. They need not actually achieve this style, it is true, in their own practice; but even though it should prove to be far beyond its powers, the seventeenth century demanded the contemplation of such a model as the ideal form to "persuade" it in greatness.[41] The name of Demosthenes therefore appears in the writings of the Anti-Ciceronian rhetoricians from the beginning of the century to the end as the symbol of the *genus grande* in the Attic manner. Bacon, in a letter written in the name of Essex, says that if one must study oratory, Demosthenes (not Cicero) is the model to be imitated.[42] Fénelon, opposing the Isocrateanism of preaching style—which had been revived in the eloquence of Bossuet and his followers—eloquently proclaims the superiority of the greater Attic orator.[43] And between these two great critics there are many that utter the same sentiment. But it was Balzac who made the name of Demosthenes his trade-mark or heraldic device. The sum and substance of his writings on the subject of style is that he aims to produce a union of Attic quality with the grand manner of a "heroic" oratory, to combine the virtue of Brutus' style, as he says in one place, with that of Cicero's, the naturalism, that is, of the one with the eloquence of the other. For the purposes of this program the authors who served as the models of his own style—Seneca, Tacitus, and Tertullian—were ill-adapted, and he publicly repudiated them—with a disingenuousness which was justified perhaps by a lofty purpose—as inferior and debased Attics, professing to find the only model of the true heroic style in Demosthenes, or perhaps in the late "Attic" orations of Cicero against Antony.[44]

Balzac took all this program with a grand seriousness worthy of it. It expressed a genuine will toward *la grande éloquence*. But

[41] Compare with this phrase of Bacon's one of Balzac's, wholly characteristic of him. In his later works, he says, he has written most on political themes, and his aim in these productions has been to express himself "de ce qu'il y a de plus magnifique et de plus pompeux en la vie active."

[42] *The Letters and the Life of Francis Bacon*, ed. James Spedding (London, 1861-1866), II, 25: "Of orators . . . it shall be Demosthenes, both for the argument he handles, and for that his eloquence is more proper for a statesman than Cicero's."

[43] *Œuvres*, II, 668. See n.21. [Georges Duhain compares Fénelon's translation of Demosthenes with other French renderings in *Jacques de Tourreil, Traducteur de Démosthène* (Paris, 1910).]

[44] Balzac, "Avant-Propos," *Socrate Chrestien*, in *Œuvres* (1854), II, 15-16, and *Paraphrase, ou la Grande Éloquence*, I, 284-289; also the attack of an enemy [Frère André] in Jean Goulu's *Lettres de Phyllarque à Ariste*, and François Ogier's answer in his *Apologie pour M. de Balzac*. [See *Lipse*, n.38. In the original publication, the following two sentences were misplaced at the end of the preceding note:] Lipsius, in his *Judicium super Seneca ejusque Scriptis*, prefixed to his ed. of Seneca, 1605, 1652, etc., anticipates Balzac's theory. See also the same use of Demosthenes' name and credit in Nicolas Caussin's chapter entitled *Anticicerones* in his *Eloquentiae Sacrae et Humanae Parallela Libri XVI*, II.xvii (Paris, 1619), pp. 79-80. [Cf. *Muret*, n.25.]

judged by his practice, or that of any one else of his time, it has as much significance as a flare of trumpets or a pyrotechnic display. The kind of Attic practiced in the seventeenth century could not combine with the magnificence of oratory to advantage, and the bizarre effects so common in the sermons and panegyrics of the first half of the century are the monstrous births that proceeded from the unnatural union between them. The taste of the age was not equal to the Athenian feat of being simple and grand at once; and when Bossuet turned from his early studies in Attic ingenuity and point to the reform of oratorical style, it was not the example of Demosthenes or Lysias that served his turn, but the old conventional oratorical model of Isocrates, and the medieval preachers.

The professed study of Demosthenes' oratory, in short, had but little practical effect upon seventeenth-century prose; and the same thing is true of all other Hellenistic programs of style in France and England during the period of Balzac and the generation that immediately followed him. Some of them were important as indicating new turns of thought and a widening of literary horizons; but none of them and not all of them taken together had a decisive influence on the form of vernacular style, or provided models that could be effectively imitated. Concerning the first half of the seventeenth century and the generation that preceded it a much stronger statement than this must be made. The truth about this period can only be expressed by saying that it was anti-Greek. The study of Hellenistic culture had become associated with the ornamental learning, the flowery science, of the humanists. "The wisdom of the Greeks," said Bacon, "was rhetorical; it expended itself upon words, and had little to do with the search after truth." This statement has a strange sound in modern ears; and in fact Bacon would have expressed the opinion of his age better if he had made it more carefully. We could not object if he had said that the Greeks were *speculative* and rhetorical; and the age of Bacon, Montaigne, and Descartes was equally averse to disinterested speculation and disinterested rhetorical beauty. The new rationalists were incapable, in short, of understanding the value of Greek culture; and even though they had been able to form a juster estimate of it, they would still have rejected it merely on the practical ground that it was too remote, too ancient, conveyed in a language too foreign to their own. It is thus that we are to explain the bravado of Burton and Descartes, and several other great scholars of the time, who professed that they knew no Greek or had forgotten what little they had been taught.[45]

The culture of the period from 1575 to 1650 is almost wholly Latinistic; and we must seek for the models on which it chiefly formed its style in the forms of Latin prose which it considered Attic.

✧ V ✧

The history of Latin prose style during the classical period displays the same constant tendency to a rivalry and opposition between two great characters of style that prevailed in Greece; and indeed from the time that the facts begin to be clear enough for exact historical statement this rivalry is conducted under the direct influence of Greek theory and largely in imitation of it. But there was a difference, due to a difference in the characters of the two races, which manifests itself especially in the associations that attached themselves to the *genus humile*. In Greece, as we have seen, this "character" of style originated in philosophy and arose, later than the other, out of a protest against the emptiness and unreality of oratory. In Rome, on the other hand, it had its roots in the very beginnings of Roman life, and was originally the expression of the practical and *un*philosophical nature of the Roman

[45] Montaigne's reason for not reading Greek is characteristic of the period: "I am not satisfied with a half understanding" ("Des Livres," in *Essais*, II.x, ed. Le Clerc, II.115); see also "De l'Institution des Enfants," I, 233. [Croll probably had in mind "De l'Héllénisme au XVIIe Siècle," pp. i-lvi in *De l'Héllénisme de Fénelon* (Paris, 1897), by Léon Boulvé, who argues against the strong case for Greek influence made by Émile Egger, *L'Héllénisme en France* (Paris, 1869). Roy C. Knight is more thorough and brings the subject up to date in "La Grèce dans la Littérature Française au XVIIe Siècle," pp. 13-138 in his *Racine et la Grèce* (Paris, 1950); he counters Egger by emphasizing the superficiality of much in French Hellenism and by showing how modernization colored imitation of Greek models. Henri Peyre probably exaggerates the debt to antiquity in *L'Influence des Littératures Antiques sur la Littérature Française Moderne* (New Haven, 1941), pp. 36-46. See also R. R. Bolgar, *The Classical Heritage and its Beneficiaries* (Cambridge, 1954). Frank L. Schoell, "L'Héllénisme Français en Angleterre à la Fin de la Renaissance," *Revue de Littérature Comparée*, V (1925), 193-238 surveys Greek learning in England under Elizabeth I and James I.] On the Latinization of culture in this age see an excellent passage by Désiré Nisard, *Histoire de la Littérature Française* (Paris, 1883), I, 435-437; Ferdinand Brunetière, *L'Évolution des Genres* (Paris, 1890), p. 53; J. E. Spingarn, *A History of Literary Criticism in the Renaissance*, 2nd ed. (New York, 1908), p. 186. [See also H. Brown, "Classical Tradition in English Literature," *Harvard Studies and Notes in Philol. and Lit.*, XVIII (1935); Sandys, *A History of Classical Scholarship;* Douglas Bush, *Classical Influences in Renaissance Literature* (Cambridge, Mass., 1952); Bolgar, *The Classical Heritage and its Beneficiaries.*]

people. In its first phases it was certainly not a literary style at all, or at least owed nothing to formal rhetorical method; and the beauties that were later seen or imagined in it were merely the natural expressions of the soldierly and rustic character of the early Roman gentlemen, the accidental effects of art that sometimes arise spontaneously from a Spartan or Puritan contempt of art.

So at least we may suppose. Almost nothing remains to show what it actually was, and we cannot say with assurance how much of the character attributed to it was due to the philosophic theories of the days when Roman thought had already been profoundly affected by the Stoicism of later Greek culture. Probably there is general truth in the idea then prevalent that there had been a severe early Roman prose expressive of the national character; and whether there was or was not the belief in it had its effects upon the later prose, and the *genus humile* at Rome took from it associations of virility and sturdy practical purpose, associations with primitive and archaic forms of virtue, which always made it something different from its Greek counterpart even after Roman culture had been generally Hellenized. To these associations the *genus humile* owed part of its great success during the Empire, largely because they transported the men of that age to a different world from their own; and it had the same value once again in the seventeenth century to those who were reviving at that time "Roman" and Stoic conceptions of literary style. But even in a somewhat simpler and more classical period than either of these, in the pre-Augustan age of Cicero and Brutus, the *genus humile* was already supposed to have a peculiarly Roman and primitive character. In the style of the *Commentaries* of Caesar, as manly and efficient, men have always said, as his legionaries themselves, it was believed that the national genius still survived, though Caesar had in fact studied rhetoric assiduously in the schools; and in Brutus' treatise *De Virtute*—whose non-survival was the occasion of many Stoic tears in the seventeenth century—we might be able to behold an image of the early Roman through all the sophistication of a philosophical and rhetorical theory.[46]

We cannot in fact tell when or how the native tendencies of Latin style blended with foreign influences, or what forms of na-

---

[46] Norden *identifies* Roman "Atticism" with the archaizing movement. With all deference to his authority, the reader is compelled to feel he has made his point only *as regards the second century*, and has introduced new confusion into the history of the term "Attic."

tional prose they might have produced if they had been left to exfoliate in their own manner. What we do know is that Roman rhetoric became outwardly well Hellenized during the last century of the Republic, that the theory of the rhetorical genera was established in the same form that it had then come to have in Greek practice, and that henceforward the history of the *genus humile* in Latin prose—like that of its rival, the grand oratorical style of Cicero—has to be written chiefly in terms of Greek rhetorical theory. The Greek *genus humile* was not now, however, what it had been in the time of Aristotle; during the two centuries that had intervened it had undergone important changes in its technique and had acquired new associations, all of which are exactly reproduced in the Latin style that represents it. We must turn back to the point where we left off the account of its development and consider these changes.

We have seen that Aristotle first developed into a system the theory of style as it is determined by the processes of thought and that in the generations immediately after him a place was found in rhetorical teaching for a kind of style, known as the *genus humile*, founded upon this way of looking at rhetorical phenomena. We have now to observe that the great increase in the interest in philosophical studies in Greek communities during the third and second centuries was the cause of an increased attention to this *genus humile* and of interesting developments in its theory and practice, and that the occasions for the proper and healthy use of the more popular oratorical style were at the same time greatly reduced as a result of changed political conditions in the Greek world. Whether this change is to be regarded as a beneficent consequence of the restoration of order by absolute authority, as the Romans of the first century and most seventeenth-century observers considered it to be, or was, on the other hand, a lamentable indication of the decay of character that follows the loss of liberty, as Milton, for instance, undoubtedly thought it was, we will not stop to inquire. It is the fact alone that concerns us, and we will proceed at once to specialize it still further by noting that its importance did not consist so much in the spread of philosophical interest in general, as in the remarkable diffusion of the principles of the Stoic sect. This does not mean necessarily that Stoicism was in itself the most important philosophy of the age—though that also may be true—but only that it had clearer and more systematic theories than the other sects with regard to the form of a philosophical style, and was able to speak, at least on most points, as the general rhetorical representative of them all.

Aristotle describes two essential virtues of style: *clearness* and *appropriateness*. But his method of treating the theory of rhetoric in the first two books implies another of almost equal importance, namely, *brevity*; and in his immediate followers this virtue assumes actually a coordinate place with the other two in the description of the *genus humile*. Upon his analysis, modified in this way, the Stoic rhetoric depends; and the three qualities—clearness, brevity, and appropriateness—appear and reappear in it, usually in the order named, and with only such additions and subtractions as always occur in a traditional formula. Each of them, however, is interpreted in a particular way and takes on a special meaning in the Stoic system.[47] We will consider the three in order, and what they meant in Stoic practice.

(a) Clearness

Aristotle places clearness first. The Stoics often—though not always—give it the same titular position. But, whether they do so or not, it is never first in their affections. There were two features of Stoic thought that tended to reduce this virtue to a subordinate rank, or even to give a positive value to its opposite. Clearness is evidently the first merit of an exposition of objective reality, as in the statement of the facts and laws of natural science; Aristotle occasionally had such exposition in his mind, and, partly on his authority, there have been in modern times several attempts to erect the theory of style on the foundation of mere scientific clearness. But the kind of truth that the Stoics chiefly had in mind was

[47] The clearest statements of the form of Stoic style in antiquity are in Diogenes Laertius, "Life of Zeno," VII.59 [See *Lipse*, n.26]; Cicero, *De Oratore*, especially II.xxxviii.159 and III.xviii.65-66 (which Zielinski, with some exaggeration, describes as an exposition of Stoic theory), and Quintilian, *Inst. Or.*, XII.x.10ff. In the modern period, Lipsius' treatise on style, *Epistolica Institutio*, and La Mothe le Vayer's *Considérations sur l'Éloquence Françoise* [n. 19 above] rest directly on ancient Stoic authority. The clearest recent statement is by Hendrickson, "The Origin," pp. 257-261, 272, 284.

It should be said that in Diogenes Laertius another virtue, purity of language as determined by the usage of good society, precedes these three. This, however, proved so foreign to other ideals of the Stoic school that it was often omitted, and when it appears and is made prominent, as it is in the Roman Stoics of the second century, it is interpreted in such a way that it falls into virtual coincidence with the quality of appropriateness. Its history in the seventeenth century would make an interesting chapter, but must be omitted here.

moral and inward. It was a reality not visible to the eye, but veiled from common observation; hidden in a shrine toward which one might win his way, through a jostling, noisy mob of illusory appearances, by a series of partial initiations. This kind of reality can never be quite portrayed, of course, because ultimate knowledge of the mystery of truth is never attained. But it is at least possible to depict the effort of the athletic and disciplined mind in its progress toward the unattainable goal. And this effort of the mind was the characteristic theme of the Stoics, and the object of their rhetorical art. Though by the rigor of their theory they were bound to a cold passionless objectivity, they really aimed at a highly imaginative portrayal of their relations with truth; and even those who professed to strive for clearness, and in fact did so, could not resist the temptation to convey the ardor of their souls in brevities, suppressions, and contortions of style which are in fact inconsistent with a primary devotion to the virtue of perspicuity.

In the second place, the Stoic sage was always, by his own account, a foreigner in the world. His outward fortunes were bound up in every conceivable way with powers and conventions which were alien to his soul; and the form in which the problem of life presented itself to him was how to reconcile his inward detachment and independence with his necessary outward conformity to the world, or even with the desire—which he usually professed—to be of service to it. Obscurity, therefore, might be useful to him in two ways. Sometimes it was a necessary safeguard of the dangerous truths he had to utter; sometimes it was a subtle mockery of the puerile orthodoxies of society.

Clearness is a virtue, then, to which the Stoics pay lip service, which they more honor in the breach than the observance; and its value in the criticism of their prose consists chiefly in the fact that it enables us to distinguish two classes of writers among them. One consists of those who studiously defy it for the reasons just mentioned. Tacitus—*le prince des ténèbres*—Persius, and Tertullian are of this class, and their imitators in the seventeenth century, Donne (in his letters), Gracián, Bacon, Malvezzi, etc., may easily be distinguished by their cult of significant darkness. The other is of those who studiously cultivate clearness, not for its own merits, but as a wise corrective to the other qualities of Stoic prose, brevity and appropriateness, which they love better. Seneca and the seventeenth-century writers who directly imitate him, such as Lipsius and Bishop Hall, and Montaigne and Browne in some of their writings, are representative of this class.

(b) Brevity

Aristotle's second virtue is brevity, and this the Stoics liked so well that they sometimes actually put it first, in the place of clearness.[48] It is a quality that is almost necessarily involved in the attempt to portray exactly the immediate motions of the mind. In the history of all the epochs and schools of writing it is found that those which have aimed at the expression of individual experience have tended to break up the long musical periods of public discourse into short, incisive members, connected with each other by only the slightest of ligatures, each one carrying a stronger emphasis, conveying a sharper meaning than it would have if it were more strictly subordinated to the general effect of a whole period. Such a style is a protest against easy knowledge and the complacent acceptance of appearances. It was of course a style loved by the Stoics. But there was a feature of their discipline which gave a particular value to the virtue of brevity; for they made greater use than any of the other sects of the art of condensing their experience into "golden sayings," *dicta*, maxims, aphorisms, *sententiae*. Chrysippus, working perhaps on hints received from Pythagoras, gave directions for the manufacture of *sententiae*, and the use of them in moral discipline, directions which are familiar to modern readers through Bacon's reproduction and expansion of them in his *De Augmentis*, unhappily without due credit given to his predecessor.[49] It is not enough to say of Stoic style that it tends toward brevity. In its most characteristic forms it tends toward the *sententia*, which is as properly to be called its ideal form as the rhythmic cumulative period is that of the Ciceronian style.

[48] So, for instance, Lipsius, *Ep. Inst.*, Ch. VII, in *Opera*, II, 536: *Prima illa, prima mihi sermonis virtus est.*

[49] VI.iii, in *Works*, I, 674ff. [corresponding to *The Advancement of Learning* (ed. Wright), II.xviii.1-9; cf. Aristotle, *Top.* I.12ff., *Rhet.* I.vi.7] La Mothe le Vayer is more candid: see his *Considérations sur l'Éloquence Françoise* in *Œuvres*, II, Part 1, p. 196, etc. The source is Chrysippus as reported by Plutarch in his "Controversies of the Stoics" [i.e. "The Contradictions of the Stoic Philosophers," pp. 865ff. in Plutarch's *Morals*, trans. Philemon Holland (London, 1657)], but Aristotle's analysis of the enthymeme also contributed to the discussions of Bacon and La Mothe le Vayer. [Cf. n.39 above and *Muret*, n.33.]

(c) Appropriateness

The quality of appropriateness is not so easy to deal with, for it has been the subject of puzzled discussion, and has assumed a Protean variety of forms. Yet it is of the utmost importance in the interpretation of Stoic style. Aristotle does not clearly enough define what he means by it, but it is evident that he thinks chiefly of appropriateness to the character of the audience addressed and the nature of the occasion: a style should adapt itself to the social requirements of discourse, and not be, for instance, either too lofty or too mean for the kind of audience contemplated. Through the recognition of this virtue of style, it seems, he is able to introduce into his *Rhetoric* the description of the Isocratean model of oratory which occupies his third book.[50] But in this use of the word there was an obvious danger to the Stoics; for it might be used as an open door for the entrance of those modes of popular and sensuous appeal which they deprecated in public oratory and carefully excluded from their own private discourses. They gave to the quality of appropriateness, therefore, a meaning more suitable to the theory of a style which was to concern itself intimately with experience.

The statement of it by Lipsius will serve to present their view briefly.[51] Appropriateness, he says, has two aspects, appropriateness to thing and to person. The former we will consider first for a moment. It is evident that taken in its strict sense appropriateness to the thing has nothing to do with rhetoric. If (as Lipsius defines it) "everything is said for the sake of the argument" (or subject), and "the vesture of sentence and phrase exactly fits the body of the thing described," thought and discourse are exactly identical, and there is only one science of both, which we may call logic or dialectic, or what-not. The proper outcome of the doctrine of "appropriateness of the thing" is such a mathematical style as was contemplated by Bayle and some seventeenth-century Cartesians, a style admirable of course for scientific exposition, but limited to uses in which art has no opportunity. In short this phase of the Stoic doctrine of style exactly illustrates the instability of an anti-oratorical theory of style, which we have already noted in other connections. But, as we have also observed, practice never squares

---

[50] See Hendrickson, "The Peripatetic Mean," pp. 135-136 and "The Origin," p. 254.

[51] *Epist. Inst.*, Ch. x in *Opera*, II, 537.

exactly with a theory; and insistence upon the more literal truth of language has often served as a wholesome corrective or a partisan challenge in periods sated with the conventional ornaments of style.

Secondly, there is appropriateness to person; and this, says Lipsius, has two phases: appropriateness to the person or persons addressed, and appropriateness to the speaker or writer himself. In the former phase it may be taken as justifying the study of the abstract rhetorical beauties of oratory. So Aristotle seems to take it. But the Stoics lay all the emphasis on the other phase, namely, the exact interpretation in one's expression of the mode of one's thought; or rather they identify the two phases, the proper and effective mode of impressing one's hearers being, in fact, to render one's own experience in the encounter with reality as exactly, as vividly, as possible. And here we must return to what was said a moment ago concerning the character of Stoic morality, in order to show how this interpretation of appropriateness brings into play the rhetorical artifices which are characteristic of the Stoic style and were often so overdone in the periods that we are chiefly concerned with. If truth and reality were easily come at and declared themselves in the same unmistakable terms to all inquiring minds, their expression in language would be a comparatively simple task. The style appropriate to the thing would be almost the same as that appropriate to the mind of the speaker. But it is not so, of course. The secrets of nature are made known only to attentive and collected minds, prepared by a long preliminary training in habits of exclusion and rejection; and even to them but partially, and in moments of rare illumination. A style appropriate to the mind of the speaker, therefore, is one that portrays the process of acquiring the truth rather than the secure possession of it, and expresses ideas not only with clearness and brevity, but also with the ardor in which they were first conceived. It is no more a bare, unadorned, unimaginative style than the oratorical style is; it aims, just as oratory does, to move and please, as well as to teach, but is distinguished from oratory by the fact that it owes its persuasive power to a vivid and acute portrayal of individual experience rather than to the histrionic and sensuous expression of general ideas.

The figures it uses, therefore, are not the "schemes," or figures of sound, which characterize oratory, but the figures of wit, the rhetorical means, that is, of conveying thought persuasively. Antithesis is one of the chief of these, not however as a figure of sound, which it may be, but as a means of expressing striking and unforeseen relations between the objects of thought. Closely connected with this is the study of "points," or *argutiae*; for the effect of points or turns of wit is found to be due nearly always to an open or veiled antithesis. These two, antithesis and point, are the chief means employed in the art of aphoristic condensation, which, as we have seen, is the normal form of Stoic rhetoric. Of equal importance with these, and of greater literary value, is the metaphor. If Aristotle first expounded the uses of this figure, the Stoics of the late Greek period, and especially those of the Roman Empire, may have the credit of having first shown fully in practice its marvelous expressive powers. It is the greatest of the figures by which literature may interpret the exact realities of experience; and is as much the characteristic possession of the essay style as the musical phrase is of the oratorical.[52]

It has been necessary to enter into these details concerning the Stoic rhetorical technique because all subsequent practice of the *genus humile* was affected by it; in the Stoics of the late Greek period, of the first and second centuries of the Roman Empire, and of the seventeenth century we encounter the same traits of style.

We return now to the history of the *genus humile* at Rome.

How much progress the opponents of the Ciceronian type of oratory had made during the last century of the Republic in domesticating the devices of Stoic rhetoric which have just been described we cannot say with definiteness, because the remains of the literary activity of the circles of the Scipios and Laelius, and of Brutus and Pollio, are singularly few and fragmentary. It may be that the example of Cato and the image of the primitive Roman gentleman preserved a simpler and plainer character in their prose, and made them chary of adopting too freely methods of expression which had the double taint of foreign culture and philosophic sophistication. We cannot say with certainty. But we know that in its theory and general outlines the Stoic rhetoric was approved and imitated by them. Cicero's testimony makes this sure. For he calls the kind of rhetoric which was usually (but without his approval) set in contrast with his own almost indifferently by the names *genus humile* or *stilus Stoicus*, and the terms in which he describes it in his rhetorical treatises show that it had the same general features that the *genus humile* had assumed in Greece during the third and

[52] See n.39.

second centuries: its brevity, its significant abruptness, its tendency
to sententiousness, and its preference of the "figures of thought"
to the "figures of sound."

This form of style had, as we have seen, all the advantage of
being associated in men's minds with the native Roman tradition.
It was the "ancient" style in contrast with the Ciceronian model,
which bore the imputation of Asianism and novelty. Why, we may
well inquire, was it so slow in winning its way to a position of
pre-eminence in Roman letters? When we read in Cicero's writings
the names of the authors who represented it in his own time and the
century before him we cannot fail to see that they are both more
numerous and vastly more respectable and Roman than those of
their literary opponents. Indeed if the name of Cicero himself is
eliminated from the history of the grand style, a comparatively
small number of important names remains to it. Yet this is unquestionably the style that won the greater successes during the pre-
Augustan age and even in the Augustan Age itself, whereas the
Stoic style did not attain its proper triumph until a later generation
and after it had submitted itself to the process of regularization and
conventionalization in the schools of declamation.

The explanation may be found in the uncompromising haughti-
ness of its pretensions during the earlier periods. It was *intransi-
geant* in two senses, both as Stoic and as "ancient Roman." Cicero's
great success was due to his sympathy with popular tastes; and his
own confidence and joy in the rightness of the rhetorical appeal
which the people loved saves him from the imputation of insincerity.
The Stoics, on the other hand, may have suffered from an excess
of scruple. Their unwillingness to confess the aid of rhetoric or to
study their characteristic modes of expression in the systematic and
deliberate way in which they were later studied in the schools of
declamation may have cost them their chance to be heard either
in their own time or by later generations.

These are mere speculations concerning an interesting fact. What
is clear and certain is that Stoic style entered on a new and brilliant
phase of its history with the foundation of the "schools of declamation," which first made their influence felt during the Augustan
Age, and later came to control the style of almost all Roman
literature for more than two centuries.

If there is a common misunderstanding in the mind of the general
reader of the character of the training in the schools of declamation,

the blame must be imputed to the scholars who have written on the subject. The fault commonly attributed to the teachers in these schools is too great a fondness for rhetorical artifice and the love of it for its own sake; and this is a sound indictment. But without the critical specifications that might be expected to accompany it in the statements of scholars it is more misleading than helpful; for it might more justly be brought against the masters of the style that the new schools repudiated and supplanted than against those that accepted their training and practiced according to their precepts. A reader, for instance, who accepted the careless, denunciatory language of most modern historians on this subject—rather than their actual meaning—would suppose that Seneca wrote with more rhetorical exuberance and display than Cicero, that Tacitus' style reflected a less exact image of the actual world than that of Livy, and that Juvenal and Persius are characterized by an habitual use of the flaccid ornaments of conventional rhetoric![53] It is necessary, therefore, to point out that the purpose of the schools of declamation was to train their pupils in the practice of the *genus humile*—*de re hominis magis quam de verbis agitantis*. Their pretension was realism; their program the cultivation of all the means of individual expression at the expense of conventional beauty. It is true that they studied for this purpose the figures and devices that had been conventionalized by the rhetoricians of the Stoic schools of Greece; they even practiced them with a more conscious art and found in them new resources for purely literary and rhetorical pleasure. But these figures and devices were metaphor, antithesis, paradox and "point"—the appropriate means for the literary expression of ingenious thought and acute realism.

The name by which these schools were known has doubtless done much to create a prejudice against them; but the general custom of denunciation is due in a still greater degree to the fact that the period in which their influence culminated and produced its greatest results is conventionally treated as a period of literary decadence. That there was a general depreciation of moral values in the public and social life of the age of Nero and Domitian no one will deny; and it is probable that the literature of such an age reflects some of its evil conditions even in the character of works which are designed to correct them. But there is often an undue

[53] Gaston Boissier's *Cicero and his Friends,* trans. Adnah David Jones (New York, 1897) is very misleading in this way.

readiness to distribute the honors of degeneracy; and it is fair to recall that in great measure the literature of the Silver Age was a literature of protest. The first fruits of the schools of declamation came to maturity during the Augustan Age, in the writings of Ovid; and in the constant stylistic trickery, combined with the soft delicacy of sentiment and the absence of ideas that characterize these exercises in poetry there are grounds for the expectation of a literary decline. But the characteristic products of the next century are not at all in that vein. On the contrary they are nearly all the new births of a union between the forms of style taught in the schools of declamation—Stoic, as we have seen, in their origin, but not necessarily so in their application—and a genuine and powerful movement of Stoic philosophy, which derived its impetus from a revolt of the best ideas of the age against the corruption prevalent in society. The style of the schools of declamation gained a new value, a new meaning, from this happy alliance. In the writings of Seneca, Tacitus, Lucan, and Juvenal it served to recall the ideas of an age of Rome that seemed almost as primitive then as the Middle Ages do to us now, and reaped the advantages of that association with early native forms of prose which the Stoic style had always enjoyed. To this association, indeed, it partly owed its tremendous success. But on the other hand it might claim at the same time the honors of a "modern" style in a sense that that term has enjoyed in almost all periods; for its expressive and piquant forms lent themselves admirably to the needs of the new rationalists and their independent criticism of contemporary society.

✧ VI ✧

In the previous sections of this paper we have seen that "Attic prose" in the seventeenth century denoted the *genus humile*, or philosophical essay style, in contrast with the Ciceronian type of oratory; and have discussed the influence of the earlier Greek theorists and exemplars of this genus upon it. We have now to observe that the forms of the *genus humile* that were of practical use to it as models for its own imitation were the Roman forms whose history has been outlined in the preceding section.

This statement must be made still more specific, however. The prose that actually determined the forms of its style was that Stoic prose of the first century of the Empire—along with some later prose of the same school—which was alembicated in the schools of declamation. The traditions of the Republic on which "Silver-Age Latinity" rested, to which it always referred, were valuable, it is true, to the seventeenth century, and it is for that reason that they have been considered so carefully here. The example of Brutus, for instance, was of incalculable advantage to it both in morals and rhetoric when it wished to describe in the clearest and purest terms the ideal to which it aspired, or to express most unequivocally the motives of its opposition to an oratory of pure display; and we have seen that Balzac spoke of "the style of Brutus" as if it were a familiar form that could be studied at large in existing documents. The example of Caesar again served their purposes in the same way. That he did not actually belong to a particular school of philosophy or style made no difference. For his conduct and that of his legionaries were regarded as the counterparts in practice of the heroic virtue which Epictetus and Seneca portray in its moral and inward effects;[54] and his style, virile and *soldatesque*, like his life, would have been taken by Montaigne and Bacon as the model of their own, in preference to that of Seneca or Tacitus, if they had not been compelled by the spirit of their age to be rhetoricians *malgré soi.*[55]

But seventeenth-century writers could not imitate Brutus or Caesar or Cato in their own style. The explicit and inartificial candor of the Republic was the quality that some of them loved best, but none of them could emulate it in their own manners, because they were living in a different kind of an age and were wholly conscious of the difference. They felt sincerely, almost instinctively indeed, that they were living in a period of decline. There had been a culmination of energy and confidence in the sixteenth century; but the external unities of the Renaissance were dissolving, and the most striking phenomenon of the new age was the division

[54] In a sea letter to his father, the sailor-son of Sir Thomas Browne (*Works*, ed. Simon Wilkin [London, 1846], I, 143) is naïvely delighted with the spirit of the old Caesarian legions as portrayed in Lucan's *Pharsalia*: "This temper would have served [us] well," he says, "and had probably concluded the warre in our first fight with the Dutch."

[55] Daniello Bartoli ("Dello Stile," *Dell' Uomo di Lettere*, in *Opere* [Venice, 1716], III, 101), describing the "modern" style (a name often given to the new "Attic"), says "Its beauty does not rob it of its strength. It can make the same boast that Caesar's soldiers did, who were able *etiam unguentati bene pugnare.*" Bacon's Secretary names Caesar with Seneca and Tacitus as his master's favorite authors. Montaigne's almost poetic praises of him are well known.

between their outward and inward interests and allegiances which revealed itself to its wisest minds. As in the first century, authorities and orthodoxies were establishing themselves in the corporate political and spiritual life of the age which derived their sanction from its weaknesses rather than from its strength; and these the "good man," the "sage," felt himself bound to support or obey because they were the only safeguards against the evils which the divisions and corrupt tendencies of the time would bring in their train if they were left free to work out their natural results. But his true devotion was given elsewhere; his true ideals were not embodied in the external forms and symbols of the age; his real standards could not be made manifest by signs which would be visible to the crowd.[56] In such an age the true literary modes are those that serve the purposes of criticism, protest, individual intelligence. The *ideal* form of style to which it refers is of course the "natural" style which expresses naïvely the candor of the soul. But in fact the style it demands for its self-expression is one that has been wrought upon with subtle art to reveal the secret experiences of arduous and solitary minds, to express, even in the intricacies and subtleties of its form, the difficulties of a soul exploring unfamiliar truth by the unaided exercise of its own faculties.

It was not only its social and political state, however, that turned its literary tastes in the direction of the inferior Atticism of the Empire. An explanation that lies nearer the surface of things is found in the state of its artistic culture, the character of its literary tastes as determined by its historical position. It was still in the Renaissance, or at least was its immediate successor, and it had not yet cast away the love of rhetorical ornament for its own sake which had descended to the Renaissance from the Middle Ages. Its purpose indeed was to escape from this tradition, to represent things as they are, to be as little ornate and rhetorical as possible; but it could not express even this purpose except by means of artifice, mannerism, device. It was still somewhat "Gothic" in spite of itself; and the rhetoric elaborated in the schools of declamation offered it exactly the opportunity it needed to indulge what was

[56] This view is more rigorously asserted in Fulke Greville's neglected prose classic *A Letter to an Honourable Lady* than almost anywhere else (in *Works*, ed. A. B. Grosart, 4 vols., 1870, esp. Ch. III ff.). But it is implied in the voluntary retirement of Montaigne and Charron, Lipsius and Balzac, Greville and Browne, to mention only a few of the philosophical solitaries of the age.

most traditional, most unclassical in its tastes under the protection of classical authority.

For these, and doubtless for many other, reasons there was a revival of Silver-Age literature in the seventeenth century, or in the period from 1575 to 1675 which we are treating here as the seventeenth century. Many of the isolated facts which are included in this general statement and justify it have been noted of course by literary history. But the disingenuous or merely traditional orthodoxy which runs through the age has partly veiled the actualities of its taste and practice from the eyes of modern students. And it is partly at least for this reason that the period (1575-1675) between the Renaissance, properly so-called, and the neo-Classical age has never been clearly differentiated in literary history, although in the other arts, in sculpture, painting, and architecture, its character has been recognized and described. We shall not understand the seventeenth century, we shall not know the exact meaning of the eighteenth century, until we have come to realize more clearly than we now do that a century intervened between the eighteenth and the sixteenth in which Lucan had a more effective influence on the ideas and the style of poetry than Virgil did; in which Seneca was more loved and much more effectively imitated in prose style than Cicero had been in the previous generations; in which Tacitus almost completely displaced Livy as the model of historical and political writing; in which Martial was preferred to Catullus, and Juvenal and Persius were more useful to the satirists than Horace; in which Tertullian, the Christian representative of the Stoic style of the Empire—*notre Sénèque*, as he was called—exercised a stronger power of attraction over the most representative minds than St. Augustine, who is the Cicero and the Ciceronian of patristic Latin.

These are the great names. But the movement of imitation and rehabilitation extended the broad mantle of its charity over minor works which have not at any other time been well regarded by the modern world. Velleius Paterculus' odd mixture of anecdote and aphorism[57] and Pliny's unpleasing *Panegyric to Trajan*[58] played their

---

[57] In Trajano Boccalini's *I Ragguagli di Parnaso e Pietra del Paragone Politico*, I.23, ed. Giuseppe Rua (Bari, 1910), pp. 67-75, Velleius Paterculus carries Lipsius' works to Apollo to receive immortality, and leads the author himself into the presence, between "Seneca the moralist" and "Tacitus the politician." There is an allusion here to Lipsius' *Commentary* on Paterculus. Gracián the *concettisto* finds in Paterculus a storehouse of examples of his loved *Agudeza*.

[58] Dom Jean Goulu, the translator of Epictetus, published a long eulogy and

several parts, and not unimportant ones, in seventeenth-century prose history; and it would be possible to add interesting details concerning the taste of this period for other minor authors of the first century. But space must be reserved even in so general a survey for the mention of two Greek writers, by no means minor, who were at Rome during the period of Seneca and Tacitus and display in different ways the spirit of the Roman culture of their time. Plutarch's *Morals* and Epictetus' *Discourses*, known chiefly in translation, exercised an enormous influence upon the moral ideas, and only a little less upon the literary ideas, of the generation from Montaigne to Pascal.

The zeal of this revival was not more remarkable than its success. It is probably true that no other modern period has so thoroughly domesticated in its own literary productions the thought and the style of a period of antiquity; and the title of the Silver Age of modern literature as applied to the period of European literature beginning about 1575 would have considerably more in its favor than nicknames given by this method of nomenclature usually have.

To prove the soundness of assertions sweeping over so wide an area as this would of course be impossible within the limits of a single paper; and even the evidence concerning prose style, which is all that we are concerned with here, would only be convincing through its cumulative effect in a series of chapters. There is no more than room here to gather together a few of the passages in which the dependence of the age upon first-century models is most broadly depicted.

François Vavasseur, the French Jesuit rhetorician of chief authority in the middle of the century, may almost be said to have devoted his literary career to the exposition of the Silver-Age proclivities of his time and an attack upon them. His admirable treatise on the Epigram is meant to show, among other things, the superior excellence of Catullus over Martial, and that on the *Novum Dicendi Genus* is an accurate and sweeping description of the preference of the age for the Latin authors of the Decadence.[59] All this is echoed, but less clearly and with less candor, in the later opinions of Balzac,

---

analysis of the "Panegyric to Trajan." Lipsius made a commentary on it, and analyses and imitations of it were common in Italy and Spain. For an English imitation see Wotton's "A Panegyrick to King Charles." [See *Lipse*, n.17.]

[59] François Vavasseur, *Oratio Tertia Pro Vetere Generi Dicendi Contra Novum* (1636), in *Opera Omnia* (Amsterdam, 1709), pp. 201-209. [*Muret*, n.25.]

who probably learned more from Vavasseur than his critics have confessed. But Balzac is torn between his romantic tastes and his classical judgment; and the perspective is better preserved in two critics of the latter half of the century. In describing the taste of Priolo, the historian, for the ancient Anti-Ciceronians of the first century, Bayle allows himself to enlarge his theme into a discussion of the contrast between the three Augustans, Cicero, Livy, and Virgil, who have an eloquence of the same general kind, he says, and Seneca, Pliny, Tacitus, and Lucan, whose style he describes in striking terms of denunciation, and adds: "The French begin to be sick of the same distemper." One questions, after reading what he says of Mlle. de Gournai and Montaigne, and other writers of the earlier part of the century, whether he does not mean the word *begin* ironically.[60] Father Bouhours, at least, has no doubt of the cause of the distempers which have appeared for a century in French style. In his various critical writings he constantly draws a parallel between a certain class of ancient authors, in which Seneca, Tacitus, Lucan, and Tertullian are the chief names, and the authors of the century past. At different places he includes on the modern side of the parallel Montaigne, Lipsius, Balzac, the *concettisti* of Spain and Italy, especially Gracián and Malvezzi, and a great array of other writers of the seventeenth century. And in his best-known work he represents Philanthe, the voice of the common tastes of his time, as saying that he finds his opinions beginning to change: he does not despair of some day coming to prefer Virgil to Lucan, Cicero to Seneca.[61]

Poets and prose-writers are mingled in these citations indiscriminately; and in this respect they correctly represent the criticism of the time, which usually makes no distinction between them in discussions of style. There is no lack of witnesses, however, who are concerned wholly with questions of prose; rather there is an embarrassment of riches. We need not cite the polemics of Muret and

[60] Pierre Bayle, *The Dictionary* (London, 1737), IV, 778, s.v. "Priolo," n.L. See also the articles on Balzac, Goulu, and Javersac.

[61] Bouhours, *La Manière* (1688), end of 3rd Dialogue, p. 336. Cf. p. 388: "plus capable de préférer les pointes de Sénèque au bon sens de Cicéron, et le clinquant du Tasse à l'or de Virgile." [Alexander F. B. Clark, pp. 262-274 (see n.33), treats Bouhours' influence on English writers. There are useful bibliographical references in V. M. Hamm, "Father Dominic Bouhours and Neo-Classical Criticism," in *Jesuit Thinkers of the Renaissance: Essays Presented to John F. McCormick, S.J.* (Milwaukee, 1939), pp. 63-65. Bouhours' estimate of Gracián is explored in Adolphe Coster, "Balthasar Gracián (1601-1658)," *Revue Hispanique*, XXIX (1913), 666-685.]

Lipsius, who were engaged in a deliberate attempt to rehabilitate Seneca, Tacitus, and the whole school of Silver-Age Latinity, or of Montaigne, who was just as consciously the propagandist of the influence of Plutarch and Seneca. For these are controversialists whose testimony is prejudiced. The comments of later writers who have observed the current of their times serves our purpose better. In the Latin translation of his *Advancement of Learning*, published nearly twenty years after the English version, Bacon added a significant passage to his famous denunciation of Ciceronianism, which has wholly escaped the attention of critics. Here he describes another *styli genus*, characterized by conciseness, sententiousness, pointedness, which is likely to follow in time upon a period of oratorical luxury. Such a style is found, he says, in Seneca, Tacitus, and the younger Pliny, "and began not so long ago to prove itself adapted to the ears of our own time."[62] If this passage had not been concealed in Latin it would have had a greater influence upon our reading of the seventeenth-century prose. It is admirably confirmed by what Father Caussin said in France in 1619: he describes the new form of style in the same way, mentions the same ancient models, adding Sallust to the list, and says it is the style that *everyone now covets*.[63]

From the middle of the century an interesting array of parallels in ancient, Biblical, and seventeenth-century literature drawn up by the libertine scholar Gabriel Naudé must suffice. Naudé puts Seneca and Plutarch in the first rank of his preference, as a Montanist should; and with them Epictetus and Aristotle; the Wisdom of Solomon he thinks has the same value; and the chief modern authors of like quality are Montaigne, Charron, and Du Vair.[64]

After 1650 the knowledge of what has been happening in prose grows steadily clearer; the defects and errors of the first half of the century are under correction, but it is generally recognized that the same models are still preferred, the same "Attic" tendency prevails. Perhaps the most interesting comment of all, because of the genius of its author, is the fragment of Pascal's, cited on a former page, in which he asserts that the spirit of the time has all been favorable to

---

[62] Quoted in full in *Lipse*, n.40.

[63] Caussin, *Eloquentiae*, II.xiv-xvi, ed. 1619, pp. 73-78.

[64] *Bibliographica Politica*, p. 25 in *Grotii et Aliorum Dissertationes* (Amsterdam, 1645). See also his *Syntagma de Studio Liberali* (Rimini, 1633), pp. 55-56 et passim [and James V. Rice, *Gabriel Naudé 1600-1653*, Johns Hopkins Studies in Romance Lit. and La., Vol. xxv (Baltimore, 1939)].

an intimate style, which portrays things in their familiar form and as they are known at first hand, and that the style of Epictetus, Montaigne, and Louis de Montalte (that is of Pascal himself in the *Lettres*) is of this kind.[65] Pascal, it is true, derives his Stoicism, and the intimate style appropriate to it, partly from the Greek spring of Epictetus, but even he was more influenced by the style of his French translation, says Strowski, than by the original; and, as we have had occasion to observe, the Latin sources of neo-Attic were those that availed most for the uses of the seventeenth century. Malebranche, looking back over its history and criticizing it from the angle of a "mathematical" Cartesian, sees three great literary influences, all of the same kind, that have constantly been in operation. Tertullian, Seneca, and Montaigne are the members of this interesting trio; all of them, as he says, enemies of clear thinking and pure reason, because they have more fancy than judgment and dress the truth in colors of imagination.[66]

Finally, in the last year of the century, Shaftesbury sums up the history of Senecan imitation in his *Characteristics*. He describes accurately the form of the familiar essay in the manner in which Seneca had written it, and says: "This is the manner of writing so much admired and imitated in our age, that we have scarce the idea of any other model. . . . All runs to the same tune and beats exactly one and the same measure."[67]

It may be expected by the reader that in order to round off our argument we shall give illustrations of the use of the word "Attic" in the seventeenth century as applied specifically to the style of Seneca and Tacitus and their contemporaries. Many passages could be cited, of course, in which this attribution is implied; but those in which it is expressly stated would not be very numerous. For the age was aware, as our own is, that "Attic" had certain associations which made it seem inappropriate to authors so fond of rhetorical artifice as the Stoics of the first century were, even though it recognized that their philosophical and intimate manner gave them a general right to this appellation when they are contrasted with the

---

[65] See n.37.

[66] *La Recherche de la Vérité*, II.iii. Ch. 3 [the best modern ed. is in Vols. I-III of Nicholas Malebranche, *Œuvres Complètes* (Paris, 1958-   ), ed. Geneviève Rodis-Lewis], in *Malebranch's Search after Truth*, trans. Richard Sault (London, 1694), I, 411, chapter entitled "Of the Force of the Imagination of Certain Authors: Of Tertullian"; the next two chapters discuss Seneca and Montaigne.

[67] *Miscellaneous Reflections*, Miscellany I, Ch. 3, in *Characteristics*, ed. J. M. Robertson (London, 1900), II, 171. Cf. the first chapter also.

Ciceronian and Isocratean kind of orators. "Attic" in short named in their use a *genus dicendi* that was very general in its character and very inclusive, and they were reluctant, just as the ancients were, to apply it to particular schools of writers. But this need not greatly trouble us. It is not so important for our purpose to defend our use of the term "Attic" as it is to indicate the relation between ancient forms of style and those prevalent in the seventeenth century. And this relation is exactly expressed by saying, first, that "Attic" meant in the seventeenth century the *genus humile*, and secondly, that the form in which the ancient *genus humile* was actually imitated in its own practice was the form in which it appeared in the prose and poetry of the Silver Age of Latin literature, and especially in the prose of Seneca and Tacitus. The term "Attic" is, in truth, not wholly satisfactory; but it is the only one that seems to be available to describe the dominant tendency of the seventeenth-century style, and was also the only one generally used for the purpose in the seventeenth century itself.

Foreword to Essay Three

When Croll's essay on Marc-Antoine Muret appeared in 1924 its import was revolutionary. For centuries scholars had regarded his prose as an exemplar of Ciceronianism; they associated him with Julius Caesar Scaliger, in whose household he once resided, as an opponent of Erasmus and a persecutor of Ramus. But Croll, while conceding that Muret had begun as a model Ciceronian, demonstrated that he had led the reaction against it. More truly even than Montaigne, Muret led the way to Anti-Ciceronianism for Justus Lipsius, Quevedo, and Bacon. Croll not only demonstrated this forgotten, never well-understood truth; he had to explain how the misconception arose and prevailed. To correct it, he placed Muret accurately in the intellectual history of his time.

Even today, Muret's literary career is not well known: he left a few short volumes of Latin orations and epistles; and the usual tribute paid to him in biographical dictionaries is seldom more than a few lines. In contrast to the lofty stature which he enjoyed during his lifetime, he has almost dwindled from sight. Modern critical and historical attention focuses on authors who wrote and published more extensively than he did. His contribution was largely oral, and it was composed in Latin. Because he chose not to write in the vernacular, even the great lectures which he delivered as Professor at Rome are now neglected. Perhaps the very fact that he ended his career in that city has something to do with this oversight, for the modern student is likely to forget, in the light of the earlier glories of northern Italian humanism, that it was with the Counter-Reformation that Rome finally came into its day, a day in which, Croll points out, Muret played a particularly important part.

Much of the little which we are likely to know of Muret is associated with his earlier years in France before his conviction, at Paris and Toulouse, for alleged heresy and sodomy, and before he rebuilt the ruins of his career in the Italian climate. After summing up the rhetorical situation in twenty or more pages, Croll turns to Muret himself. The summary he accomplishes with great excellence, especially for a generation that has forgotten (or grown out of sympathy with) rhetorical theory, which, he points out, "expressed itself in a congeries of similar dogmas in all the chief subjects of sixteenth-century learning." We tend to forget that rhetoric was the central doctrine about which the edifice of sixteenth-century learning was constructed, and we think of it as mere organization or as a collection of figures of speech or, what is worse, as a burden of dry-as-dust exercises. To the Renaissance mind it was the stuff of life itself, and not the least merit of Croll's articles on prose style is that they interrelate controversies over rhetoric with political, religious, and social issues.

The analysis which Croll makes of Muret's prose is a somewhat cursory one; but even a hasty comparison of Muret's earlier pieces anthologized in the two volumes of *Scripta Selecta* (Leipzig, 1871, reprinted by Teubner in 1887) with the later ones, which were not published there, indicates that Croll's principles are correct. Muret's style clearly changes. But, as Croll observes, that fact somehow escaped the attention of the classical scholars best able to perceive it—though their failure was in part due to the unrepresentative nature of the pieces in *Scripta Selecta*.

It would be convenient to date Muret's change, his disillusionment about Ciceronianism, with his conversion from Protestantism to Roman Catholicism; but Croll, who is a stickler for accuracy in such matters, denies this notion. He shows that earlier there was evidence of what was to take place and that later, after Muret had adopted the "Attic" style, there are still instances in which he is highly Ciceronian, especially the lecture delivered in 1575, which he composed on orders from authority. But while these qualifications need to be made, on the whole Muret's course is clear enough, once Croll points it out, and we can easily trace his growing attention to Seneca, Tacitus, and Pliny and see him become the earliest leader of the Anti-Ciceronian movement. Thus Croll reversed an accepted academic opinion (based mainly on lack of attention) concerning Muret.

Croll also makes clear that Muret himself did not always know where he was headed. It would be too much to ask for the clarity of our historical perspective from a sixteenth-century writer; moreover, the philosophical implications of Anti-Ciceronianism, its Stoicism and tendency toward scepticism—Croll prefers the term "libertinism"— were by no means clear to Muret. It was in the works of his follower, Lipsius, that Stoicism appeared in clear outline; and in those of Montaigne the scepticism was unmistakable. Nevertheless, in literary history and in the history of ideas Muret's position is paramount, although no one of the twentieth century before Croll recognized so much. His eminence was, of course, recognized in his own day. Thus Croll's essay rehabilitates Muret, who had become a minor figure, and attempts to regain for him major status. At the same time Croll provides a summary of the development of "Attic" prose, which, as a piece with his other essays, constitutes the authoritative work on the subject to this day. The tribute paid by Williamson in *The Senecan Amble* remains a valid one: "For a proper understanding of the [Anti-Ciceronian] movement in general, the various studies of 'Attic Prose' by Morris W. Croll are indispensable."

One or two minor matters of considerable interest are also pursued in the essay. For example, Croll does not regard Muret simply as an advocate for the *genus humile*, as a writer who produced his greatest work in the epideictic rhetoric despite his recognition that henceforth deliberative rhetoric was to be vastly more important. Croll also traces to him the beginnings of a style that found virtues in obscurity.

ROBERT O. EVANS
UNIVERSITY OF KENTUCKY

Muret and the History of "Attic Prose"*

EDITED BY J. MAX PATRICK AND ROBERT O. EVANS

✧ I ✧

Introduction

IT IS doubtful whether any other great literary reputation of the Renaissance has survived in so ambiguous and confused a state as that of Marc-Antoine Muret, recognized in his own time and ever since as the best writer of Latin prose in the second half of the sixteenth century. The most important event in the history of literary ideas during that period was the controversy concerning the imitation of Cicero, and in that controversy and the various conflicts connected with it Muret was more or less engaged at all periods of his career. Yet modern literary history tells us nothing intelligible of his part in it; or, to speak more exactly, it records two conflicting statements. On the one hand, he appears as the associate of Bembo, Sadoleto, Longueil in the stricter sect of the Ciceronians, a more accomplished, and not less devoted, imitator of the master. This is certainly the commoner view among those who have any acquaintance with his name; for generations he has been held up to the admiration even of school-children as the modern Cicero.[1] How confusing it is then to find that he also holds a conspicuous place in the sketches—few and inadequate—of the move-

---

* Reprinted by permission of the Modern Language Association from *PMLA*, XXXIX, 2 (1924), 254-309. Although publication of this essay took place after "Attic Prose: Lipsius, Montaigne, Bacon" reached print, Croll indicates in the first footnote of that article that it was "meant to follow one with the title *Marc-Antoine Muret and Attic Prose* in a current number (1923) of *PMLA*"; accordingly the essay on Muret is here restored to the position originally intended for it.

Originally the introductory section of the essay was not numbered and the following sections here numbered II, III, etc. were numbered I, II, etc.

The footnote numbers used below correspond to those in the original publication except for a few minor rectifications.

[1] See the quotations from German teachers prefixed to Antonius Muretus, *Scripta Selecta*, Teubner ed., 2 vols. (Leipzig, 1887); S. Reinach, *Cornélie, ou le Latin sans Pleurs* (Paris, 1914), Preface.

ment of opposition that finally triumphed at the end of his century over the great rhetorical scheme of education! From his letters and orations one or two passages have been cited which outdo the sarcasm of Erasmus' *Ciceronianus* and display a latitude of classical taste which even a modern critic cannot regard without dubiety.[2]

It is clear that this is a case requiring some particular explanation; the evidence will not tell a consistent story without careful interpretation. But when we turn to the scholars who have attempted a picture of Muret's career, we find neither agreement among them nor any single explanation that carries conviction to the mind of the reader. Mark Pattison, in a readable but superficial review of the subject, decides that he is one of those true Ciceronians who succeed in being like their master by not imitating him.[3] Yet this interesting conclusion will not stand the test of the most obvious facts in the case; for it is evident that in some of his orations he deliberately does imitate Cicero, while in others he is just as deliberately *not* imitating him, but self-consciously reproducing a style directly opposed to his. Charles Dejob, Muret's only careful biographer, has indeed marshalled all the facts of his life with admirable care, and provided the materials for their interpretation.[4] But he has placed himself too near his subject to see it in its historical relations, and his only explanation of the variations of opinion and purpose that appear in Muret's intellectual career is found in the extreme mobility of his temperament. This is an explanation that might indeed satisfy a reader's curiosity; but it would leave him with no further interest in the career of Muret.

It is a curious, not to say a disgraceful, fact that an author whose reputation depends—whether justly or unjustly—almost solely on the excellence of his prose form has not yet been placed in an intelligible relation with the progress of modern style. But the fault does not lie chiefly with the critics who have written about him. It lies in the failure of modern literary history to recognize the importance and the true character of the literary movement in which the explanation of Muret's career is involved—the movement of opposition to the Ciceronian dogma which swept everything before it in the last quarter of the sixteenth century and established the

[2] Quoted by Izora Scott. Cf. *Lipse*, n.9.

[3] *Essays by the late Mark Pattison.* 2 vols. (Oxford, 1889), I, 124-131.

[4] *Marc-Antoine Muret* (1881) [see *Lipse*, n.10]. Upon this accurate and useful work I have depended almost wholly for the facts of Muret's life.

forms of prose style both in Latin and in the vernacular tongues that prevailed throughout Europe in the seventeenth century. The modern scholar finds peculiar difficulties in the study of this subject, the most baffling of them all perhaps being his inability to pass in thought back and forth from the facts of Latin to the facts of vernacular style as easily as men of the age of Montaigne and Bacon were wont to do. But these difficulties explain rather than excuse his failure to recognize a phase of the history of prose style which must be understood before the transition from the Renaissance prose of the sixteenth century to the so-called classical style of the end of the seventeenth can be intelligibly described. Hitherto the opposition of Bacon, Lipsius and Montaigne to the imitators of Cicero has been but casually and perfunctorily described as a negative movement, designed to correct the extravagances of humanism and to complete the correction of taste begun by Erasmus fifty years earlier. It was in fact a movement of progress and discovery, which brought prose style into living connection with the intellectual movement of the period from 1570 to 1660 and with the parallel tendencies of the same period in the other arts, the sculpture and architecture of Bernini, the painting of Tintoretto and El Greco, the poetry of Donne and Marino, of Ben Jonson and Corneille.[5]

It is in connection with this later Anti-Ciceronianism that Muret's literary opinions are to be interpreted; and there are therefore two good reasons for studying them anew. The first is that by this means we may get such a view of a great intellectual and literary movement as may be had only in the period when its purposes are beginning to formulate themselves clearly. The second is that we may do belated justice to a critic and artist whose real aims and merits have been obscured by contemporary prejudice and the ignorance of later ages.

What is necessary to the accomplishment of these purposes is not a knowledge of new facts in Muret's career. Those that we have already at our command are enough. We only need to restudy them in their relation with the larger body of facts that belong to the life

---

[5] In "Attic Prose in the Seventeenth Century," I discussed the theory of this Anti-Ciceronian movement of 1575-1660, and especially its relations to its classical models and authorities. An object of the present study is to show its relations with the *movement of ideas* in its age. "Attic Prose: Lipsius, Montaigne, Bacon" carries the history into the generation following Muret. "Juste Lipse et le Mouvement Anticicéronien" now calls for revision at several points.

of the age in which Muret lived, with the history of the movement of ideas in a period when an old generation had not yet quite passed away, and a new one had not yet quite learned what its mind was to be. That is to say, we are compelled to look pretty widely round about our subject before we can look intelligently at it.

✧ II ✧

Ciceronianism and Anti-Ciceronianism

The history of thought in the sixteenth century, seen in its simplest outlines, is the story of the relations between two tendencies, both of which at the times of their sharpest opposition took the form of well-defined and self-conscious movements. The first was the tendency to give free, or freer, play in the knowledges that were then most critically placed, to the spirit of sceptical enquiry which had been the characteristic and novel part of Petrarch's message to the modern world, which had been indeed the only strictly new thing in it. It was in short the growth of scientific and positive rationalism, and we need define it no more exactly than this, for we recognize it at once as the movement which by its further developments in the seventeenth century has created what we call the "modern" world.

The other is not so easy to describe exactly or to estimate justly; first, because it is *not* what we call "modern," and, secondly, because, like all movements of conservatism, it mingled in more intimate and intricate ways with the various special interests of its age than the radicalism that opposed it, and presents to the historical student cross-lights and contradictions which it is much harder for him to pattern or arrange. We may sum it up perhaps as the tendency to summarize and systematize the gained knowledge of the world, both that which had been inherited from the medieval past and that which had been added to this by the Renaissance, and to express this by means of formulistic methods or abstracts which would serve the practical purposes of general education. More briefly described, it was the tendency to study the *forms* of knowledge, as the Middle Ages had done, rather than the facts of nature and history. But if it was conservative and often reactionary, it was also eminently literary and classical, and was the friend of the beauties and symmetries of Renaissance art. Ciceronian imitation was, as we shall see, the representative of all that was best and worst in it. This is a very inadequate description, it is true; but it will be more convenient to adjourn further discussion of it to the point where we find it in sharpest conflict with the various radical movements which it attempted—successfully for a time—to check or divert. Its real character can be made clearer at that point.

Meanwhile it is necessary, for our present purpose, to sketch the progress of the rationalistic tendency in the various fields of knowledge in which it showed most vitality during the century; and this need not be so elaborate an undertaking as it would seem; for we can conveniently take as our guides the "strong wits" of the seventeenth century. These bolder positivists of a later day, when the victory of their cause had already been won, were fond of making out catalogues or calendars of their heroes in the preceding century, and these lists, with other hints from their works, will serve to show us at least where to make the emphasis strongest, since it is precisely their view of the sixteenth-century conflict that we are most interested in.[6]

[6] The best studies of the Libertine movement will be found in F. Strowski, *Histoire du Sentiment Religieux*, Vol. I; François T. Perrens, *Les Libertins en France au XVIIe Siècle*, 2nd ed. (Paris, 1899); J. Roger Charbonnel, *La Pensée Italienne au XVIe Siècle et le Courant Libertin* (Paris, 1919). [See also the treatment of *libertins* in Henri Busson, *La Pensée Religieuse Française de Charron à Pascal* (Paris, 1933); Ch. II in Louis I. Bredvold, *The Intellectual Milieu of John Dryden* (Ann Arbor, 1934); René Pintard's detailed and indispensable *Le Libertinage Érudit dans la Première Moitié du XVIIe Siècle* (Paris, 1943) and Henri Gouhier's review of it and other books by Pintard in *Revue Philosophique de la France et de l'Étranger*, CXXXIV (1944), 56-60; Antoine Adam, *Histoire de la Littérature Française au XVIIe Siècle*. I. *L'Époque d'Henri IV et de Louis XIII* (Paris, 1948), pp. 285-329; Julien-Eymard d'Angers, *L'Apologétique en France de 1580 à 1670* (Paris, 1954), pp. 11-28; and R. H. Popkin, "The Sceptical Crisis and the Rise of Modern Philosophy," *Review of Metaphysics*, VII (1953-54), 132-151, 307-322, 499-510.] The roots of this movement in pure philosophy lie too deep for our present purpose but may be studied in Charbonnel, [Pintard, and Popkin]. Muret's real interest was in *popular* philosophy and *practical* culture. It should be added here that all the "strong wits" were not professed libertines. In the best of them—Montaigne, Lipsius, Sir Thomas Browne, etc.—scepticism and stoicism intermingle in always varying relations. Such catalogues as I speak of in the text will be found in Lipsius' *Institutio Epistolica* and often in his letters, and often in Gabriel Naudé, *Bibliographia Politica*, p. 25, and *Syntagma de Studio Liberali*, pp. 77-80, both published in *Grotii et Aliorum Dissertationes* (Amsterdam, 1645). Compare the famous gallery of portraits in a room in Guy Patin's Paris house, described by him in a letter of Dec. 1, 1650; see pp. 159-160, and n.46 below.

Accounts of the rise of rationalism during the sixteenth century and after will be found in the introduction to Villey [*Lipse*, n.4], and in Nisard's *Histoire* [*APS*, n.45], especially I, 428ff. and II, 66-70, which seem to me to give a better account of the relation of ideas to letters in the period than any of the later works. [Both are utilized in, and partly superseded by, Henri Busson, *Les Sources et le*

Politian's was the earliest name that had a current value among them, if we exclude those of certain sceptical philosophers whose works were too difficult to be known to the public at large or paraded for propaganda. Why they should have preferred Politian to Petrarch himself or to any other of Petrarch's successors during the fifteenth century we need not stop to inquire. He was slightly nearer to them in time, for one thing; his activities had been more public and conspicuous than those of any other fifteenth-century humanist of their type; and his militant opposition to the two "superstitions" of orthodox humanism, Platonism and Ciceronianism, justified the admiration of philosophers like Lipsius and Naudé.[6a]

His name, however, was overshadowed by that of Erasmus, who was generally considered by the seventeenth-century rationalists, from Montaigne and Bacon to Halifax and La Bruyère, as the greatest teacher and patron of their own method of acute realism. To limit the range of Erasmus' influence to a single subject of inquiry, or even to two or three subjects, would be a serious error. For the essence of his liberalism was his equal respect and enthusiasm for all kinds of learning; and the reason for his peculiar enjoyment of learned society in England was that there he could still observe the Renaissance in its first phase of unlimited and hopeful curiosity, scarcely touched as yet by the formalizing, the rhetorical, influences which he was combating with all his industry and wit on the Continent. Indeed it was Erasmus' spirit and temper rather than any of his particular doctrines that made him the hero of rationalism. For he had in perfection the manner that is constantly encountered in later protagonists of that school and was often studiously cultivated by the strong wits of the seventeenth century—a satirical and purposeful gaiety that was meant to reveal by contrast the pedantry of his opponents.

Développement du Rationalisme dans la Littérature Française de la Renaissance, 1533-1601 (Paris, 1922). See also René Bray's comprehensive *La Formation de la Doctrine Classique en France* (Paris, 1927, repr. 1951); R. Michéa, "Les Variations de la Raison au XVIIe Siècle: Essai sur la Valeur du Langage Employé en Histoire Littéraire," *RPFE*, cxxvi (1938), 183-201; Joseph E. Fidao-Justiniani, *Discours sur la Raison Classique* (Paris, 1937)—though all of these are chiefly concerned with the seventeenth century.

Croll parallels his account of the progress of rationalism in *APL* pp. 195ff.]

[6a] [For the views of Politian (Angelo Poliziano), see his correspondence with Paolo Cortesi in Izora Scott's introd. to the trans. of Erasmus' *Ciceronianus* in *Controversies*, pp. 14-22; J. W. H. Atkins, *English Literary Criticism*: *The Renascence* (London, 1955), pp. 8-34.]

Yet we should have but a faulty idea of the character of his influence if we failed to note that his successors during the century that followed his death looked to him chiefly for instruction in a particular subject of knowledge, and that not one of the subjects that modern scholars oftenest associate with his name. Moral philosophy was the dominant interest of the sixteenth century, and even in the seventeenth it was more important than the new scientific studies; it was virtually the exclusive theme of Lipsius, the founder of Neo-Stoicism, and of Montaigne, the teacher of philosophical libertinism; and it may be for this reason alone that these philosophers read a moral significance in almost every conspicuous phase of Erasmus' activity, even where we should not suspect that they would find it. His vast collections of the adages and apothegms of the ancients were chiefly of use to them in the discovery of a realistic method in the study of human nature; his especial diligence in the reading of Seneca and Plutarch's *Morals* had an effect—how much we cannot say—in determining the most characteristic tastes of Lipsius and Montaigne and a host of their contemporaries; his dislike of oratory, his preference of the more intimate modes of discourse, meant to them primarily a new emphasis on the inner and individual life of men in contrast with the plausible and public forms of their social existence; and, finally, his discourse on the method of writing familiar epistles helped to reveal to them the chief instrument of moral instruction and casuistical discipline through which the seventeenth century was to practice the "heroic virtue" of self-dependence. Whether his own century estimated him more justly and correctly than later ones have done we need not stop to inquire; but we must at least recognize that Erasmus has more profoundly affected the modern world by teaching a rationalistic method in the study of morals than by any other part of his varied labors.

Budé and Vives were perhaps the two humanists of his own time who best understood Erasmus' spirit. In the interests of both of them, however, the subject of political and social science, which had been subordinate in Erasmus' mind to private morals, occupied a high, or even the highest, position; and their names may therefore be conveniently used to introduce another important phase of the development of sixteenth-century rationalism. The most conspicuous names in the reform of political study in the sixteenth century are of course those of Machiavelli and his disciple Guicciardini. In

113

a later generation than their own their acute and sceptical method, reinforced by a new study of Tacitus, was to prove the chief instrument of one of the most radical movements in the history of modern rationalism. But it was both too bold and too difficult to produce this effect at once, and it was not perhaps until Lipsius had made Tacitus familiar by his famous 1575 edition that the period of its great success really began.

Meanwhile, during the earlier generations of sixteenth-century scholarship the cause of progress in political science was chiefly associated with the outcome of the struggle—so typical in every way of the conflict of ideas in the Renaissance—between the approved medieval method of the Barthollist Commentators and the effort of some of the greatest and bravest scholars of the century to show that the Institutes of the Roman Law are really historical documents, to be studied in the light of particular conditions of life in the Roman republic. The actors in this drama who were most admired by the positivists of the seventeenth century were Frenchmen of three successive generations, Guillaume Budé, Jacques Cujas, and the French-Swiss, François Hotman; and even in Muret's time the pre-eminence of the first two was so well recognized that the new historical study of Law was spoken of as the French method.[7] It is true that Alciati deserved at least an equal place in their esteem for his service to their cause. But they were accustomed to choose their heroes with as much attention to their temperaments as to the value of their ideas; and in both Budé and Cujas they recognized the quick mobility of mind, the venturesome satirical

[7] [At the end of this section, in n.16, Croll provided information which is more pertinent at this point. He explains that wherever possible he used the Teubner volume of Muret's *Scripta Selecta* (see n.1 above), and he adds, "For material not there included, I refer to the two volumes of Orations, Letters, and Poems, published at Leipzig in 1629, *juxta editionem postremam Ingoldstadianam.*" Presumably these volumes were another imprint of the ed. published by M. J. Rhenii, *Volumina Duo Orationum cum Tribus Libris Epistolarum. Item Hymni et Poemata et Alia Ejusdem . . . quae in Ultima Ingoldstadiana Editione Habentur* (Leipzig, 1628). Croll continues, "The publication of Muret's works after his death seems to have been in the hands of German Jesuits. Unfortunately the modern edition of Muret's collected works, ed. by Frotscher [*sic*] has not been available." *M. Antonii Mureti Opera Omnia*, ed. C. H. Frotsher (Leipzig, 1834) is nevertheless cited in the originally published n.7, where he also refers to the "1629" ed. In the footnotes below we retain Croll's refs. to the 1629 ed.]

See a letter addressed to Muret in 1578 by the German "Nation" at Padua (1629 ed., Ep. lxxv; ed. Frotsher, II, 212); also a letter dated 1564 from Martinus Belliviceius, a former colleague at Padua (1629 ed., I, Ep. i, 45).

wit that have always been dear to the intellectual radical. Were they not also, like most of their successors, Northerners?

Morals and politics—*sapientia* and *prudentia*—were the subjects of thought in which the cause of rationalism made most progress during the sixteenth century. This would have been so, if there had been no other reason, merely because private and public morality were the chief subjects of interest, even to scholars, during that century. But a second fact of almost equal importance was that these subjects could be pursued with little danger of interference from the established authorities of the intellectual world. They were near the circumference of the intellectual system, no more than its outer defences, and the attacks of the radical modernist spirit of the age could be tolerated more easily at these points than when they were directed closer to the citadel of orthodoxy itself. And this Pierre de la Ramée found out to his grief when he promulgated to the world his new—or, as he said, his old—logic, which, he declared, had not been invented by Plato, or by Aristotle, or by Petrus Ramus, but by nature herself. He was challenging, or could be made to seem to be challenging, the authority of Aristotle. The authorities of the Sorbonne, representing all the orthodoxies, rallied to the defence of a fading tradition, rejoicing perhaps that at last the issue was thus sharply drawn. They had the temporary success which those who hold power may always enjoy, and the convenient death of Ramus among the crowd of undistinguished slain on St. Bartholomew's Eve may have seemed to his friends and enemies alike a symbol of the failure of the movement for free thought in the Renaissance.

To us, of course, that event seems rather the signal of the beginning of its triumph. For in the year 1572 Montaigne was already contemplating his philosophic retirement from the world—the symbol of a new age; Lipsius had returned from his visit to Rome with the new program of positive radicalism born full-armed in the moment of his meeting with Muret; and Bacon was beginning his studies at Cambridge. Within two generations of that date rationalism had won all its decisive victories—in moral philosophy, politics, and the natural sciences; an acrid and virile realism had displaced the fluent eloquence of the sixteenth century in all the arts; and the beginning of the modern age of reason waited only for the unifying influence of the Cartesian philosophy.

Seen from the vantage point of a modern historical student, this victory seems of course inevitable; it must have seemed certain to an intelligent spectator even in the last decade of the sixteenth century. But at any earlier period it was far from certain; and during the middle and the third quarter of the century the forces that stood in the way of radicalism and progress enjoyed more powerful and intelligent support than ever before and recovered the ascendancy of which Erasmus' singular influence had at least seemed to deprive them for a time. During this period the leaders of orthodox humanistic opinion in both Protestant and Catholic circles, Ascham, Melanchthon, and Sturm in the North, the organizers of the new Catholic education in the South, were first of all practical men, more interested in training pupils who should worthily represent the political and religious causes to which they themselves were so devoted than in promoting the triumph of pure reason or disinterested scholarship. The liberalizing influence of Erasmus, Budé, Vives, and Cujas was not lost upon these leaders; they were more intelligent and humane conservatives than the orthodox scholars of Erasmus' own generation. But the use they made of their broader wisdom was to reason more broadly and wisely for a policy of reaction which was hostile to all the purposes of Erasmus, to formulate a more humane program of imitative and formal education, which doubtless had its immediate usefulness, but was fatal for the time to the progress in positive knowledge which the rationalists of the Renaissance believed that the modern world could achieve.

It would be easy—but not wise—to dismiss this conservative movement as an aberration in the history of modern education. A movement which has entered into history *cannot* be dismissed; and to do justice to this one we have to observe carefully a distinction of great importance in Renaissance culture. If we mean by the Renaissance the beginning of the modern mastery of fact, the progress of positive and sceptical modes of reasoning in the thought of Petrarch, Erasmus, Montaigne, and Descartes, of course the movement we are considering was a counter-Renaissance, a surrender of the disinterested purposes of the Revival of Learning to the immediate educational needs of an age. But the Renaissance was also a revival of *letters*, an attempt to create cultured habits in the minds of modern men by contact with the literary forms of ancient art; and of this part of its tradition Ascham and Sturm and the more orthodox party among the Jesuit teachers professed honestly and truly to be the devoted representatives, while their opponents, the radicals, they constantly and correctly asserted to be its enemies. (It must be observed that the later history of the rationalist movement exactly bears them out in this contention: from Montaigne to Descartes there is an anticlassical tendency in this movement, which shows itself most clearly in the scorn of Greek studies which is characteristic of it. It may justly be regarded, in this respect, as a counter-Renaissance.) In their view the Renaissance, the rapid advance in learning, that is, of the past hundred years—for it is necessary to remind ourselves that the word *Renaissance*, with its implications of sudden and utter change, is a modern coinage—had brought with it a serious public peril, the peril of the disorganization of educational programs and a consequent failure in the task which to these conservatives seemed most important, namely, the diffusion of the new culture among the laity of the upper classes. The free range of intellectual curiosity, the unlimited extension of what we should call the "elective system" in learning, was doubtless a safe enough process as far as the class of professional scholars was concerned. But education is not for them. It is for the ordinary sensual human beings who have the means of paying for it, and in the sixteenth century it needed to be brought especially, so these conservatives argued, within reach of the desires and tastes of a class of nobles and gentlemen who were still lingering, for the greater part, in the gross ignorance and provinciality of the fifteenth century. The way to win such a class, they said, was not to address their minds to the exact truth of reason or the immediate study of things as they are. The truth of nature is too diffuse and various for their needs; it is dull and inornate; and it does not act directly and quickly enough upon the barbarism of inherited manners and customs. The only education that would meet their needs—and this is more or less true of any class that must acquire a culture alien to it—was one that would give them a palpable design, a single and sensuous pattern, which might finally teach them—when they had learned to conform their speech, their manners, their external lives to it—the method of apprehending the truth itself. Surely, said Thomas Wilson the English rhetorician, if we learn the gesture of the ancients, we shall not fail at last to have minds like theirs too.[8] Yes, literature, they thought, had to be the staple subject,

---

[8] *The Arte of Rhetorique, 1560,* ed. G. H. Mair (Oxford, 1909), p. 5. [The Scholars' Facsimiles and Reprints series provides the 1553 text, ed. Robert Hood

practically the unique subject, of education for their time; literature, too, in the easy and teachable form of oratory.[9]

It was a reasonable enough argument. There was nothing in it that was not humane and intelligent; and as a general or abstract theory of education we dare not treat it with contempt unless we are prepared to put out of court the only principles upon which a classical education can be defended. The judgment of history upon its proponents in the sixteenth century must depend solely upon whether it decides that they had read the character of their age correctly. If it was indeed an age that had reached such a maturity in the positive sciences that it could afford to pause and consider a balancing of its accounts; or, on the other hand, if it was so weak and immature that it could not hope to advance by its own inventive power but must rest content with the imitation and revival of a more glorious past; in either of these cases a study of the external forms and conventions of culture was what was required. But if, on the contrary, it was an age full of new and unbreathed energies, on the eve of great discoveries and expansions, and capable of coping with the ancients themselves in the criticism of life, then of course the reactionary teachers cannot escape the condemnation due to those who misread the signs of their times. And the modern world is not slow to render its judgment. Had the sixteenth-century rhetoricians succeeded in their purposes the progress of the seventeenth century in natural science and the study of life would have been postponed we cannot tell how long, and the Cartesian philosophy would never have been born in the womb of Time. If their success had been permanent they would have done for the culture of the upper classes of European society in succeeding centuries

---

Bowers (Gainesville, Fla., 1962). Russell H. Wagner's Cornell dissertation, "Thomas Wilson's *Arte of Rhetorique*," 1928, has not been printed. For a good short account, see Howell, *Logic and Rhetoric*, pp. 98-110.]

[9] The following words of a rhetorician to a philosopher are worthy of being pondered by all who are interested in education: "Now, what you write about ideas I am very loth to question, seeing that you are a learned man and have great reputation. But how can you think that there is an idea of style innate in your mind? As for me, I can only declare that I saw no form of style, no image of discourse in my mind until I had formed one there by attentively reading the ancients for many years and by practising long. Before I did this, I used to look into my mind and seek as from a mirror some shape from which I could fashion what I wished. But there was no image there. And when I tried to write, I was borne along at random without law or principle of judgment. None of those things that you mention, no idea, no image, guided me." (Pietro Bembo to Pico della Mirandola, Rome, Calends of January, 1513.)

what the philosophers of China had already done centuries before for the culture of *their* aristocratic patrons.

And even that does not tell the whole truth. The sixteenth century was in a state of rapid and confused transition—at least this was so in the northern countries—from medieval to modern civilization. It had, strictly speaking, no definable character of its own, and but one thing is clear about it, that it could not rest where it was. It must go forward or back, and whatever in its culture and ideas did not impel it towards the future was sure to strengthen its links with its past. The advocates of a program of pause and recollection in such an age were sure to promote other results than those they had in view. However humane and intelligent their own culture might be, they were doomed to witness the revival in their pupils and imitators of ancient habits of superstition justifying themselves by modern pretensions, of the old medieval indolences disguised by the great classical names of the Renaissance. And this was in fact a phenomenon that was generally observed by the teachers of the more progressive policy. When Bacon and Montaigne, for example, looked about them and took stock of the learning of the sixteenth century they remarked with justice that almost every impulse of the new age had been re-conformed to a medieval habit or formula. The new study of Plato had only produced a new, a more frivolous, Platonism; the enlarged knowledge of Aristotle's method had given new vigor to the old Aristotelianism of the Universities; the new investigations of the history of Roman Law had enriched the orthodox Barthollism of the schools with a few specious ornaments; the more critical reading of the science of Pliny and Plutarch had had no other visible effect than to re-establish medieval pseudo-science in a new position of literary respectability; the revival of the pure Latinity of the best ages had issued in the new authoritarianism of the Ciceronian cult. They might be pardoned if they believed that another hierarchy of orthodoxies had arisen out of the ashes of the Renaissance.

Ciceronianism, then, was not an isolated phenomenon, a mere aberration of Renaissance taste; it was the representative in rhetorical theory of a tendency which expressed itself in a congeries of similar dogmas in all the chief subjects of sixteenth-century learning. To show this relation has of course been the object of the preceding survey. And we must now observe that it was much the most conspicuous of all these dogmas of orthodoxy, and was chosen more frequently than any of the others to appear in the controversial arena as their common champion.

The explanation of this fact is not difficult. In the first place, merely because it was a *rhetorical* doctrine, Ciceronianism ideally represented the aims and interests of the conservative orthodoxies. For rhetoric was the form of learning toward which they all consciously or unconsciously aspired. The method that characterized them all, Barthollist, Platonist, Aristotelian, was in a broad sense the method of rhetoric, in the sense, that is, that they all tended toward the study of the *forms* of their various sciences rather than toward the direct observation of the facts; they all busied themselves, as their opponents constantly affirmed, with words rather than with things. Well, there is, as we have observed, a great deal to be said, at least educationally, for the study of forms. But it was only the Ciceronian who could profess this doctrine with perfect confidence and consistency; for his was the only learning— unless it be music—which is directed solely toward the art of expression through a conventional form, and the model he offered for the imitation of his pupils was admittedly the most perfect single instrument of education that the world has in its possession. It is not surprising that the principle on which educational conservation rested in that period expressed itself in the words of a rhetorician and Ciceronian. "Ye know not what hurt ye do to learning," says Roger Ascham, with a boldness that may still make one stare, "that care not for words, but for matter."[10]

A second reason, but a little less important than this, for the pre-eminence of Ciceronianism is to be found in the love of authority and a single standard of reference which still flourished in the medieval mind of the sixteenth century. All of the orthodoxies, it is true, drew their profit from this inherited habit of mind; but none of them in the same degree as the Ciceronian cult, because it alone

---

[10] *The Whole Works of Roger Ascham*, ed. J. A. Giles, 3 vols. in 4 (London, 1864-65), III, 211. [Trimpi, p. vii, notes how, "in the most general terms, the emphasis shifted from expression to content," from this "Ciceronian comment of Ascham," which he quotes, "to Bacon's Senecan reversal of the proposition when he lamented that 'Men began to hunt more after words than matter.'" Cf. Trimpi, p. 33. On Ascham see Lawrence V. Ryan, *Roger Ascham* (Stanford, 1963), esp. pp. 259-279.] The rhetorical tendency of *all* learning is admirably illustrated in the introductory discourse of Lorenzo Valla's *De Latinae Linguae Elegantia* (Paris, 1541). "Who," he asks, "are the men who have been great philosophers, orators, jurists, in short, great authors? Why, only those who have striven to speak well. . . . If we will only strive heroically enough, the Roman speech, and along with it every branch of learning, will revive and flourish in its old splendor."

could claim the full sanction of the Renaissance. The authority of Aristotle in philosophy, the authority of Rome in religion had suffered in various ways because they were evidently survivals of a medieval mode of thought that had now for a considerable time been subject to attack and suspicion. They were, even in the least damaging view of them, habitual and routinary. Ciceronianism alone could offer the freshness and charm of modernity combined with unity and simplicity of doctrine.

It is hard for us of the present day to understand the customs of an age in which a rhetorical doctrine made common cause with philosophical and religious orthodoxies, sharing the benefits of their sanctions, and lending them in turn the support of its literary prestige. That this was in fact, however, the relation between Ciceronianism and the other dogmas of learning in the sixteenth century is proved by all the evidence that is necessary. The reader of the correspondence of Lipsius, for instance, will find it impossible to explain in any other way the curious air of mystery and danger in which the Belgian scholar envelops his Anti-Ciceronian, or "Attic," principles. Though he had been converted to these principles before 1570 he did not dare to profess them openly until after 1585.[11] And if we desire a specific illustration of the kind of dangers he dreaded, we need look no further than the indictments drawn up against Ramus by the doctors of the Sorbonne, in which the rhetorical doctrine of his *Ciceronianus* marches *pari passu* with his Anti-Aristotelian logic and his ecclesiastical heresy. The Jesuit teacher quoted by a modern historian, in fact, merely stated a common opinion more incautiously than most when he said that the authority of Cicero in rhetoric, of Aristotle in science, and of Rome in religion would stand or fall together,[12] and of the same substance is Ascham's constant plea that the radical opponents of Ciceronian imitation are undermining the defences of the semi-Protestant establishment of Henry and Elizabeth.

It is just as clear, on the other hand, that Anti-Ciceronianism

[11] See *Lipse*, II, pp. 15-17. Even in the 1580's, Lipsius' two letters to Montaigne show caution and concealment.

[12] "As in the study of theology we follow the divine Thomas Aquinas, and in philosophy Aristotle, so in the humanities Cicero must be regarded as our peculiar and pre-eminent leader. . . . But some, misguided by a willful and self-formed taste, have gone astray, preferring a style totally different from that of Cicero; such an erratic course is quite at variance with the genius of our institutions and hostile to the spirit of prompt obedience" (quoted by W. S. Monroe, *Comenius and the Beginning of Educational Reform*, New York, 1900, pp. 7-8).

was associated with the radical and rationalistic tendency in whatever fields of controversy it manifested itself, though there are not here the same signs of concerted *action*—there seldom are in a radical movement—that one may observe among the defenders of the traditional dogmas. The names of the scholars most frequently mentioned in the preceding pages have been chosen, without reference to their rhetorical opinions, as those of the positivist teachers who made the strongest impression on the minds of their successors. It is interesting, therefore, to find that they were all Anti-Ciceronian in theory and practice, and that nearly all of them took some part in the agitation against the Ciceronian dogma. This statement needs no defence in the case of Erasmus. His *Ciceronianus* was almost the Bible of the later movement; for it not only showed the method which was to be employed by all subsequent leaders in the attack upon orthodox style; it was also a model of the easy and fearless competence in the criticism of the ancients which it was their duty to oppose to the deferential purism of the Ciceronian.

Vives and Ramus played a somewhat important role of course in the rhetorical conflict; but the broad scheme of education outlined by the first, founded expressly on the subordination of rhetoric to less academic subjects, was well known to the leaders of liberalism,[18] and the excellent and temperate treatise of the second, named like Erasmus' dialogue, exerted a steady influence throughout the last quarter of the century.

[18] Best described in his *De Tradendis Disciplinis*, 1531. [See the translation by Foster Watson, *Vives: On Education* (Cambridge, 1913) and his ed. of *Vives and the Renascence Education of Women* (New York, 1912); Trimpi, Ch. II; Atkins, *English Literary Criticism: The Renascence*, pp. 35-65; and *Joannis Ludovici Vivis Opera Omnia* (Valencia, 1782), especially *De Ratione Dicendi* (1533) in Vol. II. Montaigne's debt to Vives is discussed by William F. Smith in "Vives and Montaigne as Educators," *Hispania*, XXIX (1946), 483-493.

The "treatise of the second" mentioned later in the same sentence is probably Petrus Ramus (Pierre de La Ramée), *Dialecticae Libri Duo, A. Talaei Praelectionibus Illustrati* (1560); an ed. by Roland MacIlmaine was published in London in 1574 and one with a commentary by George Downame in 1669. See Frank Pierrepont Graves, *Peter Ramus and the Educational Reformation of the Sixteenth Century* (New York, 1912); René Radouant, "L'Union de l'Éloquence et de la Philosophie au Temps de Ramus," *Revue de l'Histoire Littéraire de la France*, XXXI (1924), 161-192; Norman E. Nelson, *Peter Ramus and the Confusion of Logic, Rhetoric, and Poetry*, University of Michigan Contributions in Modern Philology, No. 2 (Ann Arbor, 1947); Pierre Albert Duhamel, "The Logic and Rhetoric of Peter Ramus," *MP*, XLVI (Feb. 1949), 163-171; Wilbur S. Howell, "Ramus and English Rhetoric: 1574-1681," *QLS*, XXXVII (1951), 299-310, and his *Logic and Rhetoric*, pp. 146-281; Walter J. Ong, S.J., "Hobbes and Talon's Ramist Rhetoric in English," *Transactions of the Cambridge Bibliographical Society*, I (1949-1953), 260-269.]

The "French" school of legal studies and Roman jurisprudence does not occupy a large place in modern histories of sixteenth-century literature, because modern historians are disposed to divide the fields of learning very sharply, and especially to treat science and letters as distinct provinces of human culture. In this respect, however, the sixteenth century itself differed from them, and it is a habit of thought which we shall have to correct if we are to understand the important role that was played by unliterary scholars like Cujas and Budé in the history of modern prose style. It may have been chiefly because they were so realistic and positive in their intellectual purposes that these scholars showed themselves hostile to the rhetorical formalism of the Ciceronian school: they were Anti-Ciceronian, that is, for the same reason that Erasmus and Ramus were. But there was also a reason peculiar to them, which is worthy of a moment's consideration because it opens up a curious and almost unexplored region of literary history. The historical studies of these legalists made them acquainted with some of the most curious forms of written language that the records of the past have to show—the law French of the Middle Ages, for instance, and the special forms it took in England, the legal medieval Latin, more despised by Renaissance Latinists than any other style of the Gothic ages, and, finally, the primitive ancient Latin of the laws of the Twelve Tables. By contrast with the impoverished and regularized Latin of their Ciceronian schoolmasters, there was a rich feast for their fancy, their curious, erudite humor, in the language of these ancient documents—not only in its novel old words, though they took a keen pleasure in these, but also in its licentious, wandering sentence form, phrase added upon phrase in delightful disregard of the rules of classical form. Anti-Ciceronianism thus had a special character and a peculiar charm for these antiquarian scholars, because it meant to them, not a more liberal classicism, or the substitution of one kind of classical model for another, but rather the freedom of individual fancy from academic control; in their own prose they expressed their tastes with exuberant license; and before the end of the century their writings, especially their letters, were being used as models of that "libertine" type of Anti-Ciceronian prose which is at present so much in need of a historian.[14]

[14] The excellent work of Louis Clément, *Henri Estienne et son Œuvre Française* (Paris, 1898, 1899) has a brief discussion of the influence of law Latin on the French and neo-Latin vocabulary, and the ideas on this subject derived by Estienne

And there is another chapter in this story of the connection between literature and the law. In their study of early Roman institutions the masters of historical jurisprudence were of course compelled to study Plautus; and of this necessity they made a literary opportunity. A taste for this author became known as one of their characteristic eccentricities, and finally a kind of shibboleth by which their followers claimed the right of initiation both into the new legal method and into the school of extreme Anti-Ciceronianism. His antique and "rustic" vocabulary was one of the sources from which Muret, Henri Estienne, and Lipsius enriched the modern Latin which the Ciceronians had so impoverished; and he takes his place beside Rabelais and Plutarch and Montaigne among the heroes and models preferred by many writers of libertine prose in the seventeenth century—for example, Gabriel Naudé and Robert Burton.[15]

The scholars whose opinions we have been considering were primarily moralists, social philosophers, legalists, or logicians; not one of them was a professed rhetorician. To explain their common interest in a rhetorical controversy we need not suppose anything resembling a deliberate agreement among them, or even a transmission of ideas from one to another. There is a golden chain wherein the sciences (like the virtues) "linked are y-fere," and they

---

from Guillaume Budé. Concerning Cujas' influence in the movement for freer vocabulary, see below. Budé's *Forensia* (1544), his *Notes on the Pandects*, and his *De Studio Litterarum* (1532) will have to be studied carefully by anyone who should wish to consider the subject.

[15] The following will be useful in the investigation of Plautus' part in the Anti-Ciceronian triumph: Henri Estienne, *De Plauti Latinitate*, appended to his *De Latinitate Falso Suspecta*, 1576; Lipsius, *Quaestiones Epistolicae*, 1577, introd. epistle [also v. 26: "*Idem in hoc scribendi genere est, necessario potest, quam pulchro. At in verbis fui, quam debui, antiquior. Jam enim is sermo aures meas tetigit. Et Plautum, inquiunt, potius sapit quam Ciceronem. Utinam verum dicerent! nam hoc volui.*" See also *Lipse*, II, esp. pp. 16-17, 23-25. Trimpi, pp. 66, 74-75, quotes praise of Plautan style from Lipsius' *Epistolica Institutio* and letters, and, p. 65, cites the high estimates of Plautus held by Jonson and Varro]; Sir Thomas Browne's letter addressed *Amico Opus Arduum Meditanti*, in his *Works*, ed. S. Wilkin (London, 1836), IV, 291-293; Gabriel Naudé, *Syntagma de Studio Liberali* [*APS*, n.64]; Balzac, letter (in Latin) in his *Epp. Sel.*, published with Vavasseur's *De Ludicra Dictione* (Leipzig, 1722). [The influence of Plautus, chiefly but not exclusively in drama, is treated in Marie Delcourt, *La Traduction des Comiques Anciens en France avant Molière* (Paris, 1934). For the influence of the Latin sentence on sixteenth-century style, see Charles Bruneau, "La Phrase des Traducteurs au XVIe Siècle," in *Mélanges . . . Henri Chamard* (Paris, 1951), pp. 275-294.]

are quick to feel anywhere the presence of a spirit hostile or friendly to their mutual purposes. In the sixteenth century, rhetoric was the *nodus* in which their interests were all knit up. As the Ciceronian doctrine was the representative of all the educational orthodoxies, so the opposition to it was the form in which a liberal and rationalizing spirit in any of the sciences could most effectively express itself.

It has been necessary to treat these two great tendencies in sixteenth-century thought at so much length because without a clear understanding of them and especially without a clear understanding of their connection with the rhetorical controversy, it is impossible to interpret Muret's career intelligently. Through failure to grasp the true implications of Ciceronian and Anti-Ciceronian doctrine, it has been possible, as we have seen, to represent the variations of his opinion and practice as the mere whims of a volatile temperament. But in fact the history of his ideas is a steadily unfolding drama of consistent change. Beginning a Ciceronian, establishing in his youth a European reputation which led his patrons to regard him as the probable successor of Bembo, he diverged from this expected course, in the face of much opposition, by a series of steps which can be accurately distinguished, until in middle age he had become a declared Anti-Ciceronian and a pioneer in the development of the rhetorical and intellectual program of the triumphant Anti-Ciceronianism (or "Atticism") of the seventeenth century. His later life was spent in confirming, defining, extending this program. It was a progress, like that of his age, from conventionality to intellectual realism; and his position in it was at the front, often far in front, not among the slowly increasing numbers of the rank and file.

The story of this progress is written in all of his publications and academic labors, and even in some of the events of his career in the world; but it is written most conspicuously and clearly in the long series of orations which he delivered year after year in introducing the courses of reading in ancient literature through which he conducted his pupils; and upon these, interpreted by other evidence, we may safely depend in tracing the interesting course of his intellectual adventures.[16]

16 See n.7 above.

✧ III ✧

Muret's Progress

At the age of twenty-five years, Marc-Antoine Muret was widely known both in poetry and prose as a better master of Augustan Latinity than any other member of the rising generation of humanists; and his tastes and associations seemed already to have committed him irrevocably to the Renaissance program of rhetorical education. He had been adopted as the intellectual "son" of Scaliger, Erasmus' bitterest literary antagonist; he was supposed to have taken an active part in the persecution from which Ramus was now beginning to suffer; and the fame of his own oratorical style had already signalized him, even beyond the bounds of his own country, as the Ciceronian of the future. In short his intellectual career seemed to be unalterably determined, when, at the age of twenty-eight, disaster overtook him and he began anew in a different scene. He was convicted at Paris and Toulouse of Protestant heresy and of sodomy; he was burned in effigy by public order at the latter city; and he fled from France to begin his career over again in the new Italy that was rising out of the moral and material catastrophes of the previous generation—the Italy of the Counter-Reformation.

We will not discuss the effects of this disaster upon his character and opinions. It may have confirmed in his mind a tendency toward the Machiavellianism of his later political doctrines; for his personal sufferings were in some ways characteristic of the general disturbances which occasioned so wide a diffusion of Machiavellian principles in the later sixteenth century. But biographers are, on the whole, too prone to read the inward life of their heroes in terms of manifest events of their external experience. The crisis in Muret's affairs does not coincide in time with the critical point in the change of his literary teachings and practice that we are to trace in the following pages. It neither caused nor hastened this change, as far as we can see; and it is possible that it tended rather to retard it.

After some weeks of curious and dangerous adventure in the north of Italy, he secured, with surprising ease, from the Venetian Senate, the appointment to the vacant professorship of eloquence at the University of Padua, and preluded his first courses of reading (in 1554 and 1555) with orations *De Laudibus Literarum* . . .

adversus quosdam earum Vituperatores, which have often been cited in evidence of his blameless Ciceronianism. That he was Ciceronian at this time they do in fact abundantly demonstrate. Their perfect elegance of phrase, the conventional beauty of their cadence, could be illustrated by the quotation of one or two of the elaborate periods in which they are composed; but to display adequately their poverty of ideas, the suave emptiness of complimentary paragraph after paragraph—so strangely different from the incisive utterance of the later Muret—would demand a larger space than we have at our command.[17] The young scholar, in short, had elected to begin his new career by being what his employers unquestionably intended him to be, the successor of Bembo in the Ciceronian tradition; and all of his public acts during the four years of his incumbency serve to make clear this deliberate choice of vocation.[18] The works he published at Manutius' press to justify his new academic honors were either Augustan or impeccably orthodox: one on Catullus, one on Terence; and he let it be known that his public readings would be from Cicero's works in every alternate year as long as he held his professorship.[19]

Is it possible to imagine that Muret was guilty of an elaborate deception during these four Venetian years? Had he already broken definitely in his own intelligence with the literary orthodoxy which he was publicly defending? Was his desire to re-establish his ruined reputation so strong that he was willing to conform, either in bitter irony or in pure cowardice, with the opinions of a Senate which had lately forbidden the reading of Erasmus and Budé in its university and conferred the title of *Ciceronianus* as the crown of literary achievement? There are two considerations that might lend

---

[17] Muret, *Scripta*, I, Orat. i, ii; 1629 ed., I, Orat. ii, iii. The following is a period from the 1555 oration:

A quibus ego quoniam ita dissentio, ut ex omnibus, qui se aliquid docere profitentur, horum vel gravissimum munus esse contendam, neque ullos esse, qui aut laborum plus perferant, aut majores in republica pariant fructus, doctrinae denique a nullo hominum genere majorem aut copiam requiri aut varietatem arbitrer: constitui hodierno die, Patres amplissimi vosqui caeteri viri ornatissimi, eam mihi ad dicendum materiam sumere, et nobilissimam studiorum partem, quantum id quidem in me positum erit, a contemptu atque ab intolerabili ineruditorum hominum insolentia vindicare.

[The fourth last word was erroneously printed in 1924 as *eruditorum.*]

[18] Pietro Bembo, who had died seven years before, had been official historiographer of Venice.

[19] Dejob (Ch. VI) has strangely distorted the meaning of Muret's Venetian utterances in a mistaken effort to find a consistency in his career. The only consistency to be found is a progressive change.

color to so unlikely a conjecture. One is the fact that when we find him, settled once more—after an interval of a few years, it is true—in a different kind of situation, he has already gone far from his first opinions. The other is that during his last year and a half in France he had already attempted to establish himself as a teacher of jurisprudence according to the new method of Cujas, and had been hailed by Douaren as a brilliant novice in its mysteries.[20] A man could not consistently be both a Ciceronian rhetorician and a disciple of Cujas! We will have occasion to consider the meaning of both of these facts at a later point. Neither of them however, must be taken as indicating insincerity in Muret's Venetian professorship. It was never his way to truck and huckster in the affairs of the mind; he was capable of an exquisite diplomacy in the accomplishment of his intellectual purposes; but his temperament was too lively and eager to let him conceal them for any great length of time. Indeed it would be possible, if it were worth while, to point out, even in these Venetian orations, the first faint beginnings of his later opinions.

Events happened, however, immediately after this which made him more susceptible to new ideas or encouraged a change which may have already begun, by removing him from the scene on which he had so unhappily committed himself to the policy of reaction. Enemies of Muret asserted, some years after his death, that the cause of his departure from Venice was his continued practice of the vice that had driven him out of France.[21] This is all obscure; and what we know is only that he was taken into the employment of the magnificent Hippolito II, Cardinal d'Este, during the year 1558, and went to reside in his Ferrarese palace. During the next five years he traveled once at least to Rome with his employer and accompanied him in 1561, in the capacity of official orator, on an embassy to his native country, whence he had fled seven years before, an outlawed Huguenot and libertine. Finally in 1563, by the appointment of Pope Pius IV, he became professor at the University of Rome—professor, we note, not of rhetoric this time, but of moral philosophy—and began the course of teaching and

[20] Dejob, pp. 48-50.

[21] See *Scaligerana* II [p. 267 in the alphabetized ed. (Cologne, 1695)]; also an unpublished biography of Muret by Guillaume Colletet, used by Dejob, p. 47. [Presumably this was one of the "Vies des Poètes François" which Colletet left in manuscript. See item 2682 in *A Critical Bibliography of French Literature*, III, ed. Cabeen and Brody.]

public discourse which was to occupy him without interruption until his retirement in the eighties. The salary of his post was small; but this was a matter of little importance, as his fellow-scholars enviously observed, because he enjoyed, during almost all of this period, the material luxuries and artistic splendors of Hippolito's palace at Tivoli.

His transplantation meant that Muret had at last reached the center and source of European Catholic culture during the period of the Counter-Reformation. After the disasters which she had suffered during the preceding generation, the city of Rome was undergoing a process of material transformation which exactly corresponds to the change that was taking place in her relation to the culture of Southern Europe. Before her misfortunes she had been the beneficiary of the arts and learning of the Renaissance; but she had not been the original source or teacher of them. Painters, sculptors, poets, and scholars had sometimes brought their various works to adorn the papal city; but the schools in which they had learned to produce them were elsewhere. And this condition was almost a necessary consequence of the non-Christian character of the Renaissance arts as they were practiced at the beginning of the sixteenth century. An art of Latin prose, for instance, which excluded the mention of the Christian titles and offices as one of the conditions of its excellence could not, openly at least, acknowledge the inspiration of the Holy See. But the Reformation had given a check to the cult of Paganism by making everyone vividly aware of it. The secular glories of the high Renaissance could never be renewed; the arts that should adorn the new age must be animated by the spirit of the Catholic revival; their motives and sanctions must proceed from a re-Christianized papacy, as the opportunity for the practice of them proceeded chiefly from the need of restoring the damaged splendors of the papal court.[22]

[22] The best description of the effect of the Catholic revival upon the arts is in Marcel Reymond, *De Michel-Ange à Tiepolo* (Paris, 1912), Chs. I–II. [A vast literature has grown up since 1924 on this matter: the view that seventeenth-century art is essentially related to the Counter-Reformation is implicit throughout Émile Mâle's *L'Art Religieux après le Concile de Trente* (Paris, 1932). For a time scholars tended to identify baroque art with the Counter-Reformation: this view is explicit in Werner Weisbach, *Der Barock als Kunst der Gegenreformation* (Berlin, 1921); see also the section on religious painting in his *Französische Malerei des XVII Jahrhunderts im Rahmen von Kultur und Gesellschaft* (Berlin, 1932). However, the difficulty of restricting the baroque to post-Tridentine Roman Catholicism, excluding Protestants such as Agrippa d'Aubigné, is causing modifications in this view and emphasis on the intimate connection between the

That the culture of the Counter-Reformation must be Christian and Roman was a point of common agreement among the leaders of Catholic policy. But this does not mean that there was unity of literary doctrine or educational program among them. On the contrary, the conflict between the formal classicism of the Renaissance and the "modern," or positivistic tendency of sixteenth-century thought is displayed just as clearly in the Catholic education of this period as in that of the northern countries; and indeed there is no body of writings in which it may be so advantageously studied as in those which proceeded from various representatives of Jesuit education. This is a point which needs to be insisted upon because the history of the literary tendencies of the succeeding century has been confused by the failure to give it the attention it deserves. A number of critics have attempted to show that the authority of the Jesuit teachers was chiefly thrown into the scales on the side of classical purism and the Ciceronian dogma;[23] and there is a huge array of facts and names to be cited in support of their contention. But, on the other hand, an equal weight of evidence has been urged by others in favor of the opinion that the Anti-Ciceronian movement, and particularly the *concettismo* that was one of its offshoots, owed their success to the influence of teachers of the same order.[24] The truth of the matter is that there was no more unity of intellectual purpose among the Jesuits than there was among the Protestant humanists of the North, and it would be as absurd to look for a common tendency among their various educational programs as to try to present a synoptic view of the doctrines of Roger Ascham and Francis Bacon. There was a faction among them, as

---

baroque and the general Christian ethos: see, for example, Imbrie Buffum, *Studies in the Baroque from Montaigne to Rotrou* (New Haven, 1957), pp. 134-135. See also Croll's "The Baroque Style in Prose" and the works listed in connection with it.

Recent studies incline to withdraw the term *baroque* to the later part of the period once covered by that term and to classify its earlier part as *mannerism*. See N. Pevsner, "The Architecture of Mannerism," *The Mint*, ed. G. Grigson (London, 1946); I. L. Zupnik, "The 'Aesthetics' of the Early Mannerists," *Art Bulletin*, xxxv (Dec. 1953), 302-306; W. Friedländer, *Mannerism and Anti-Mannerism in Italian Painting* (New York, 1957); Roy Daniells, *Milton, Mannerism and Baroque* (Toronto, 1963), especially Index, s.v. Counter-Reformation.]

[23] So, for instance, Norden, *Die Antike Kunstprosa*, ii, 779, n.1, where many Jesuit rhetoricians are cited; and B. Borinski, *Gracian und die Hofliteratur in Deutschland* (Halle a S., 1894), p. 54.

[24] See Arturo Graf, "Il Fenomeno del Secentismo," in *Nuova Antologia*, cxix (Sept.-Oct. 1905), 372ff. Graf himself thinks that Jesuitism had little to do with the *secentismo*.

there was in the North, that was devotedly attached to the conservative doctrine of classical imitation; and another that had felt the rationalistic impulses of the time and was groping its way toward the positivistic formula of the seventeenth century: *de re magis quam de verbis*. That the weight of official sanction was always on the side of literary orthodoxy is shown by a great variety of evidence. But, as in other societies, forces were openly at work in literary Jesuitry quite different from those that were officially acknowledged; and the historian of the positivistic movement in prose style has to observe that new phases of this movement constantly come to light within the Order or under its patronage: it is enough here to mention the rhetorical doctrines of Lipsius, Quevedo, and Gracián. In the first half of the seventeenth century, Father Caussin and Father Vavasseur represent that alliance of literary orthodoxy with authoritarianism in politics and religion which was approved by high Jesuit policy;[25] but, on the other hand, Father Bouhours, though he was the professed reformer of the vices of *concettismo* in the following generation, is just as clearly Anti-Ciceronian, or "Attic," as they are conservative and Augustan.[26]

When Muret arrived in Rome in 1563 the conflict of intellectual forces had not yet declared itself there. The teaching in the University and the other educational institutions controlled by the Papacy had been reformed in the sense that it had been brought into harmony with the new moral seriousness of the Counter-Reformation; but it showed no disposition to reform itself in any other sense. The new Jesuit discipline, which was already imposing

[25] See Caussin, *Eloquentiae . . . Parallela* [*Lipse*, n.37 and *APS*, n.44], which is largely an attempt to correct the prevailing Anti-Ciceronianism of the seventeenth century, and Vavasseur, *De Novo Dicendi Genere* [for the proper title, see *APS*, n.59], an oration of 1636, devoted, like Vavasseur's other rhetorical works, to the same purposes. Both writers had a considerable part in correcting the errors of *secentismo* and establishing the dominion of "good taste," though their use of the Latin language has concealed their true importance from most modern critics. [On *good taste* or *goût*, see Charles H. Wright, *French Classicism* (Cambridge, Mass., 1920), Ch. VIII; Bray, as in n.6; Elbert B. O. Borgerhoff, *The Freedom of French Classicism* (Princeton, 1950).]

[26] See the passage from Bouhours, *Les Entretiens*, quoted in the last paragraph of *APS*, III (p. 72); also the quotation from a Louvain Jesuit, Erik van der Putten, in the paragraph preceding this. [Bouhours' significance in the history of *goût* is discussed with bibliographical references by Victor M. Hamm in "Father Dominic Bouhours and Neo-Classical Criticism," in *Jesuit Thinkers of the Renaissance: Essays Presented to John F. McCormick, S.J.* (Milwaukee, 1939), pp. 63-75. Georges Doncieux, *Un Jésuite Homme de Lettres au XVIIe Siècle: le Père Bouhours* (Paris, 1886) is still worth consulting.]

itself upon the life of the University, displayed all the familiar signs of intellectual conservatism and academic orthodoxy. During the twenty years of his professorship it was to be Muret's mission to give voice to the new intellectual tendencies of the age at the very center of Catholic education and under the protection of Popes and Cardinals. He was not only a man of mobile intelligence, quick to adapt itself to new perceptions; he also had the active and challenging disposition which leads men to give immediate effect to their ideas in the world about them. The successive steps in the evolution of his own thinking are exactly indicated, therefore, by the controversies in which he was involved; and the history of his activity at Rome during the two decades from 1563 to 1583 is a kind of microcosm in which we can study the rise of positivistic culture in Europe from apparent defeat at the middle of the century to an almost universal triumph at the end.

He was appointed professor of moral philosophy, not of literature; and in the three public lectures with which he inaugurated his courses in 1563-1565 he made clear the deliberateness of his breach with his rhetorical past by discoursing on "the praises," the "necessity" of *philosophia moralis*, and the "lauds of justice." The pattern of his style, it is true, is still moderately Ciceronian; in his exordiums he still displays the suavity and copiousness of the epideictic oration; nor is there anything original or challenging in the ideas he expresses. These are productions made to order, with the deliberate purpose of illustrating the moral gravity and elevation that Pope Pius and his Cardinals wish the world to look for in the new art of the Counter-Reformation. Their only significance in Muret's intellectual development is to be found in their subject.[27]

Immediately after his series of readings on the *Nicomachean Ethics* was completed, however, Muret announced another deliberate change in his intellectual pursuits which might convict him of the volatility which his biographer so readily invokes at hard places in his career, were it not apparent that it was the result of a process of change which had been going on slowly in his mind for a number of years. Muret, as we have already seen, had made an experiment in the teaching of jurisprudence and Roman law during his last years in France, and had rashly attached himself to the new school of Cujas and Douaren. There is even some slight

[27] Muret, *Scripta*, I, Orat. iv-vi; 1629 ed., I, Orat. vii-ix.

evidence to show that he maintained an interest in this suspected subject and in the study of Plautus, which often accompanied it, by discussions in an intimate circle during the years of his professorship at Venice.[28] It is not easy to relate this discordant note to the smooth harmony of his other intellectual interests at this period; and he himself apparently made no attempt to resolve the discord. We can only infer, therefore, that he was unaware at this time of the significance which he afterward came to see in the rationalistic jurisprudence of Andrea Alciati and Jacques Cujas. It appealed to his lively temperament because it was novel and exciting; it appealed to his love of adventure because it was slightly dangerous; but he had evidently not yet observed the connection between the new jurisprudence and the radical movement of the age in moral and political philosophy (perhaps no one had yet seen it quite clearly); and, in particular, he had not discovered a necessary relation between it and the literary tendencies of his day, which after all were his chief interest.

Since his Venetian days, however, his ideas had been undergoing a steady, and partly unconscious, development, and his fortunate encounter with certain works of Alciati and Budé soon after his settlement at Rome had the effect upon his mind of a revelation. The scales fell from his eyes, he says; he awoke to the full consciousness of his former ignorance; and the way he was henceforth to travel lay clear before him. The exact date of this illumination is not clear. But in 1567 he threw down his gauntlet. He announced the Pandects [the abridgement, in fifty books, of the opinions, writings, decisions of ancient Roman jurists] as the subject of his course, and in an initial discourse, composed, we observe, in a wholly new and Anti-Ciceronian manner, rashly asserted that he would henceforth teach no other subject but jurisprudence. He recalls now with pride his youthful adventure in this direction, which in the interval he had been willing to forget, and asserts that his audience is well aware of the causes that have detained him now for so long in the "softer studies" of rhetoric and moral philosophy. (Of course he implies that it was the will of his superiors; but does he not acknowledge that his own enlightenment has been recent?) These other pursuits, he says, have been the wanderings of Ulysses to the caves of the Sirens and the land of the lotus leaf. He has now returned to rugged Ithaca, enriched, it is true, by his adventures,

---

[28] See Belliviceius' letter, cited in n.7.

but resolved never again to wander from the country of his intellectual birth.[29]

The importance of this conversion, so defiantly announced, is not to be measured by the value of Muret's contribution to the science of Roman law; both he and his critics declare that this is very slight. When his eyes were unsealed, the vision revealed to him was not of new facts in legal history, but of the new spirit in which, as he dimly foresaw, the pursuit of letters and learning would be conducted in the age that was then beginning. The terms in which he compares his old studies with his new one are such as we constantly hear from the "strong wits" of the next generation; and, though he returned before ten years had passed to the subject of moral philosophy which he had been appointed to teach, it is clear that from the moment he detected a significant relation between *sapientia* (private wisdom) and *prudentia* (public or worldly wisdom), on the one hand, and *jurisprudentia*, on the other, he became a conscious forerunner and founder of the seventeenth-century positivistic learning.

The bad Latinity of the Barthollist legal commentaries—*illas mixobarbaras cantiones*, as Muret himself calls them—was notorious; and it had even created a general supposition that the study of style and the study of law were disjunct and irreconcilable. It was incumbent upon a man of Muret's literary reputation to show that this was a pernicious heresy. The necessary union of science and art, then, may be more or less correctly stated as the subject of all his four academic discourses of 1567, 1569, and 1571.[30] This was an interesting and important doctrine, with all the charm of novelty in the sixteenth century. But what is still more significant in these discourses is that Muret is here gradually revealing in public what he was more frankly admitting in private, that his literary tastes and theories themselves had accommodated themselves to his new zeal for political science and jurisprudence.

[29] 1629 ed., I, Orat. xv: "On the History of his Intellectual Pursuits and the Necessity of Uniting Eloquence and the Other Subjects of Study with Jurisprudence."

[30] 1629 ed., I, Orat. xv-xviii. These orations and the oration of November, 1565 (described below) are the most significant for the history of Muret's ideas, being written in an un-Ciceronian style with a spirit and zest which he had not displayed before. Their omission from *Scripta Selecta*, by which he is now chiefly known, gives a disproportionate value to the perfunctory orations of 1564 and March, 1565, and the commanded discourse of 1575 on "The Excellence of Literary Studies."

This change had, it is true, occurred before his public profession of law. After the three "public" discourses of 1564 and 1565, in which he spoke officially, as we have seen, for the court of Rome, he had delivered another in November of the latter year to a smaller, essentially a "private," audience of his pupils in introducing a second term of readings in Aristotle's *Ethics*; and to any of his hearers who were intelligent enough to understand what Muret meant, the contrast with the epideictic orations which had immediately preceded it must have greatly heightened the effect of this remarkable deliverance.[31] He not only describes admirably the alliance of moral philosophy and political science (*sapientia* and *prudentia*), which was to become, partly through the mediation of his disciples, the educational formula of seventeenth-century rationalism; he also shows what were to be the ideals of the new kind of style which was to accompany this educational program, and even illustrates the methods by which many of his successors in the next age were to teach themselves and others the practice of it. After describing *prudentia* ("policy," as Bacon calls it; political science, as we might say; though perhaps the recent term *Realpolitik* would be more exact) he goes on to say that "we acquire from nature, or at least may easily learn, certain maxims or sentences concerning good and evil, things to be desired and things to be avoided: of which sort are: 'the social laws that bind men together must be observed'; 'justice must be observed'; 'we must abstain from injuring others'; 'to repel force with force is both law and righteousness'; and others of the like sort, which are the rudiments, or as it were the seeds, of the arts necessary to life. From these rudiments springs at last the art that is schoolmistress of life—*prudentia*." The passage is founded wholly upon Aristotle, partly on the *Ethics*, but partly also upon the discussion of the use of "positions," or commonplaces, in the *Rhetoric*, which served as authority for the cultivation of the fixed form of the aphorism, or *pensée*, in the seventeenth century.[32] Who

---

[31] 1629 ed., I, Orat. x, "On the Knowledge of Oneself and on All the Faculties of the Human Mind."

[32] It could be said without much exaggeration that the whole subject matter of Bks. I-II of Aristotle's *Rhetoric* is propositions (κοιναὶ προτάσεις), or Commonplaces; for propositions are the elements of logic or dialectic; and Aristotle's purpose is to establish rhetoric in an intimate, insoluble connection with dialectic. It is for this reason that his treatise was taken as the foundation of Anti-Ciceronian theory in the seventeenth century. On this point see *APS*, pp. 75-77. The passages on which Muret particularly depends, in the passage quoted are I, Ch. 3, sect. 8-9, and perhaps II, Ch. 21 (on the maxim or γνώμη). [The reference here seems

can fail to think of the famous passage in the *Advancement of Learning* in which Bacon, using Aristotle as his monitor, advises the study of the "colours of good and evil" and of *antitheta rerum*, as a great aid in that "politic part of eloquence in *private* speech" which he opposes to the "well-graced forms of speech" of "the greatest orators," and professes that he is indifferent whether this new kind of literary practice ought to be considered a branch of "policy" or of rhetoric?[33]

The style itself of this oration of 1565—its broken period; its deliberate rhetorical roughness, every phrase a thought; its original metaphors, themselves thoughts—what is it but the pure Baconian positivism in rhetoric? A reader familiar with his earlier orations might suppose that Muret is here speaking merely as a *savant* indifferent to the effect of his style, except that a moment later he calls attention, in a challenging manner, to his *quotidiana verba*, his *inornatum dicendi genus*, and appeals, in his peroration, to those, if there be any, who can be captivated by an exact treatment of things "arduous and remote from a vulgar comprehension," who can find a pleasure in discourse that it not grand and *sublimis*, but concerned with matters of daily use and adapted to the needs of real life.

It is clear that in 1565 Muret had already renounced the *genus sublime* and the *genus ornatum* (or *medium*) of ancient rhetorical theory; his literary formulas were already those of the *genus humile*. The effect of his public espousal of the law in 1567 was to commit him more definitely in the same sense; and in his oration of 1569, on the method of teaching law, we find him more "Attic" than he has ever dared to show himself before. The style he now proposes as a corrective to the barbarism of the legalists has the three qualities

---

particularly to be to *Rhetoric*, II.20-21; cf. the discussion of virtue and practical wisdom in *Nicomachean Ethics*, VI.13.]

[33] Bacon, *Works* (1867), III, 411; *Advancement*, ed. Wright, II.xviii.5; in the corresponding passage in *De Augmentis*, VI.iii (*Works*, I, 673ff.) the discussion is extended by the addition of fifty pages meant to supplement Aristotle's *Rhetoric*, I.vi-vii. [Cf. *APS*, nn.18 and 49.] See also *De Aug.* VIII.i-ii (*Works*, I, 746ff.) on Civil Knowledge Touching Negotiation or Business; in the corresponding section of *Advancement* (ed. Wright, II.xxiii.1 ff.; *Works*, III, 445ff.), Bacon employs an extraordinary number of English names to describe what in Latin versions are called *axiomata*, *aphorisma*, or *sententiae*: sentences politic, axioms, aphorisms, precepts, positions (Cf. Aristotle's *Topics*, I.2, I.21, and elsewhere [in *Rhetoric*, II.xxiii he enumerates 28 topics]; all of these English terms and their Latin equivalents are in effect renderings either of Aristotle's κοιναὶ προτάσεις or of his γνῶμαι. Of course almost all of Bacon's own works illustrate the method of writing by aphorisms or "commonplaces."

of the Stoic rhetoric; first, the purity of idiom that can be studied in the conversation of cultivated people; secondly, terseness; thirdly, aptness or expressiveness. The dishes he eats from, he says, need not be of gold; they need not be adorned with jewels and emblems. (He alludes here, in his new metaphorical manner, to the richness of oratory.) He can eat of earthen vessels, provided the viands are fine; but these vessels must be well rubbed (*tersa*), clean (*nitida*), trim in appearance.[34]

Two years later, in 1571, he has made still further progress, spurred on clearly by opposition. He had resolved, he says,[35] to begin his course of legal readings without a prefatory discourse; his friends and patrons protest, however, against so violent a break with custom, and he has yielded on the main point. "But," he says, "that I should take as my theme something, however remote from and alien to our subject, something popular and plausible, in which to display merely verve and copiousness of style (*vim ac copiam dicendi*)—that they should have leave to obtain this of me, I could not obtain leave of myself to grant them. Hardly could I persuade myself to do this when I was young and devoted myself to the rhetorical studies that justify such things. If I should show myself anxious *now* to frise and rouge my style after the manner of boys and sophists, I could hardly escape the reprehension of serious and resolved men." "I mean to discourse, therefore," he continues, "not in the oratorical manner, but in a scholastic, domestic (*umbratili*), and composed manner of our own, not meant to excite but to teach, not planned to catch the clamors of applause, but rather to win the respect of silence and attention."—These are the terms constantly employed by students of Attic in the seventeenth century, and are derived by them from the same critics in antiquity.

In the preceding section of this paper, a connection was traced between the new study of jurisprudence and the Anti-Ciceronian cult of unfamiliar, new or old words.[36] There is evidence to prove that in this phase of the movement Muret played the part of a mediator between the scholarly legalists and the taste of the general public. The fondness he indulged for Plautus is made manifest in his letters and *Variae Lectiones* of all periods; that this was long cherished as a heretical hobby of his unacademic hours is also clear.

[34] 1629 ed., I, Orat. xvii.
[35] 1629 ed., I, Orat. xviii.
[36] See above, II, paragraph following ref. to n.13.

When he cites Plautus therefore in the same breath with Cicero, Caesar, and Terence as masters of Latinity in his revolutionary oration of 1569, he is fully aware of the meaning of his words; and we are not surprised at the fact that the first step taken by Lipsius after his conversion from Ciceronianism by Muret (in 1568) was a public profession of his pleasure in the rustic words and the ingenuous style of the old comedian.[37] But we are able to connect Muret's fondness for Plautus directly with his devotion to Cujas and his interest in jurisprudence. There is a letter,[38] from a former colleague at Padua, implying that in a circle of his friends there his project for an edition of Plautus and his study of Cujas' method had been discussed side by side, as if they were closely related; and there is a passage in his *Variae Lectiones* (XI, 17) concerning Cujas himself, in which Muret expresses his delight at the old words with which the legalist has enlivened his pages, and congratulates him on his effort to correct by this means the tendency of Ciceronian purism to impoverish the vocabulary of modern Latin. As Dejob has pointed out,[39] the word *pauperare*, used here by Muret, occurs only in Plautus.

Muret's adhesion to the new rationalistic program of studies did not involve in his own mind a renunciation of his old interest in literature; on the contrary he regarded it as a movement of rhetorical as well as intellectual progress. But the opponents of modernism could not or would not see it in that light. He was under constant pressure to return to the teaching of the subject with which the world even yet persists in associating his name; and when a lectureship in rhetoric fell vacant in 1572[40] he was urged to accept the appointment, without, however, as it would appear, giving up his professorship in philosophy. He yielded on the advice of his patrons and announced as the subject of his first course of reading, Cicero's *Tusculans*, and as the topic of his initial discourse, "the Method of Arriving at Distinction in Eloquence." It seemed a victory for the reactionaries, but if they indulged the hope of his return to orthodoxy on the strength of these promises they had not made sufficient

[37] In the Preface to his *Epistolicae Quaestiones*, 1577. On the significance of this see *Lipse*, II, par. 7.
[38] 1629 ed., I, Ep. xlv.322-323.
[39] 1629 ed., I, 242.
[40] Through the honorable dismissal of an old Professor, Caesareo Cosentino, whose noonhour lectures had long been the scene of notable undergraduate disorder.

allowance for the ironies that Muret was capable of.[41] For this discourse proved to be not only a diatribe against the Ciceronians, but the most telling attack yet delivered upon the conventional academic method of rhetorical teachings.[42]

The general tenor of his remarks on this occasion will not surprise any one who has read the orations in 1565, 1569, and 1571; but the discourse is epoch-making in the history of modern style because here the greatest rhetorician of the second half of the century for the first time openly arrays himself by the side of Erasmus and Ramus; and it is full of interest to the careful student of Muret's career because it shows his advance in several respects toward the complete Atticism of the seventeenth century. In the first place, it contains the first intimations of the leaning toward utter individualism in style, and even toward the "libertinism" of Montaigne, which Muret often displays throughout the rest of his career, though his orthodox past usually holds him back from a free expression of it. "It is no better than an eloquence of Picts and parrots," he says, "to echo and reverberate words you have already heard, nor ever to say anything that is really and peculiarly your own." Muret never rejected in terms the Renaissance doctrine of Imitation; probably he never determined clearly whether he had broken with it in fact; but such words as these show how little hold it retained upon his affections or his imagination. In the second place, he made clearer than before the connection between his literary ideas and his enthusiasm for *prudentia,* or political philosophy. The ancient teachers of style, he says, were masters of the history of institution and laws, were skilled students in the art of government, and prided themselves in the name—not of rhetoricians or sophists—but of politicians (*politici*).

Thirdly—to complete the picture of this striking work—Muret here places the study of rhetoric firmly upon the foundation of Aristotle's treatise, where it was to rest during the century of "Attic" prose which was to follow. Aristotle's *Rhetoric* is a difficult work to

[41] A letter written to a former pupil, Francisco Bentio, indicates the spirit in which Muret went at his new task. After relating the circumstances of his appointment, he says that the additional money has prevailed with him. He will return for a time to those *congerrones* of his youth, Horace and Cicero—*et mihi quodammodo repuerascere videbor.* He adds that those who had expected to hear him continue his exposition of the Pandects are raising a tumult (*Scripta*, II, 65).

[42] *Scripta*, I, Orat. vii; 1629 ed., I, Orat. xxi.

interpret historically; the modern historian finds inconsistencies in it that are hard to explain. But Muret and his successors disregarded these; to them the work meant one thing, an inexpugnable authority, equal in magnitude to that of Cicero himself, to which they could appeal in their effort to divorce prose-writing from the customs of epideictic oratory and wed it to philosophy and science. It is so that Muret interprets the work in this oration. Its teaching is, he says, that rhetoric is "a something that arises (or floats up) out of the mixture of dialectic and politics,"[43] and he cites the passages in which the study of it is brought into connection with the processes of reasoning and feeling and with the proper methods of carrying on a demonstration. Muret, then, derives his *theory* of style here from the first two books of the *Rhetoric*; his doctrines concerning *practice* are drawn from the same work. But here he picks his way carefully, disregarding, as the seventeenth-century "Attics" did, Aristotle's full treatment of the conventional style of oratory in Book III and basing his doctrine on the connection between dialectic and rhetoric elaborated in Books I and II and Chapter 17 of Book III. "As the dialectician," says Muret, "uses two instruments of proof, the syllogism and induction; so the orator, the twin and true comparative of the dialectician,—his exact similitude in a dissimilar *genre*—has two also, each of which corresponds to one of these: the enthymeme, which corresponds to the syllogism, and the *exemplum*, which corresponds to induction. . . . Without a copious supply of enthymemes and *exempla* adapted to every subject matter no one can support the name of an eloquent writer." In these passages is foreshadowed a new method of rhetorical training founded on the use of the *Index Rerum* and the Common-place book, the method of "colours," "positions," and *pensées*, practised by countless seventeenth-century writers, and learned by them, partly from Aristotle, partly from the prose writers of the Roman Silver Age.

The delivery of this public discourse determined Muret's intellectual and literary position unalterably. During the decade of active life that remained to him he was only to carry out toward their logical conclusions the principles he had now arrived at. But before we continue the story of this progress, we must notice a phase of his literary career which has done more than anything else to shadow his reputation and confuse the judgment of posterity

---

[43] See Aristotle, *Rhetoric*, I.ii.7 and I.iv.5. Bacon frequently refers to this doctrine of Aristotle's [e.g., *Advancement*, ed. Wright, II.xviii.5].

concerning his service to modern literature. His position at Rome was more than that of a professor. He was also the official orator of the Roman court; and, as it happened, his activities in this function attained their greatest fame during the years 1571-1572, just at the time, that is, when he was making clear his final emancipation from the rhetorical formalism of the Renaissance. During these years he was called on by his patrons to use the art for which he was famous throughout Christendom in the adornment of three great occasions of public ceremonial: the celebration of the victory of Lepanto in the church of *Ara Coeli*, the funeral of Pope Pius V in St. Peter's in the Vatican, and the reception, probably in the Vatican palace, of an envoy-extraordinary sent by the king of France to lay his fidelity at the feet of the new Pope, Gregory XIII. Muret responded exuberantly to these opportunities to celebrate the glories of reformed Catholicism; and on the third occasion even went out of his way—it would seem—to glorify the massacre of St. Bartholomew's Eve in the most ornate and fulsome rhetoric that the odious art of panegyric could provide him with.[44]

The moral aspect of these performances does not interest us here. Our only concern with them is to show their right relation with the intellectual and literary tendencies that we have been studying and their curious effects upon Muret's literary reputation. Both in their form and in their substance they appear to be in direct conflict with the positivistic movement on which Muret was now embarked. Inasmuch as they are in the oratorical genre, and in a peculiarly inflated and grandiose variety of it, they are hard to reconcile with the professions of one who was teaching the form of an intimate and philosophical *genus humile*; and they have in fact tended to confirm his reputation as a Ciceronian in the minds of those who can conceive of only one type of oratory. Inasmuch as they are apologies of absolution and persecution, they seem to run counter to the liberal stream of modern thought. With the sceptical liberalism of the eighteenth century, which developed out of the "libertinism" of the seventeenth century, they are in fact at complete variance. But we are interested here only in Muret's relation to his immediate successors, the "strong wits" of the seventeenth century; and the orations we are speaking of are in both respects, that is, both in the character of their ideas and in the character of their

---

[44] 1629 ed., I, Orat. xxii (Jan. 1572 Old Style, 1573 N.S.). The others mentioned are Orats. xix-xx (Dec. 1571 and May 1572).

style, representative of one of the most important tendencies of that school.

Almost all of the liberal and sceptical thinkers of the seventeenth century were believers in external conformity. Montaigne and Bacon, Browne and Balzac, for instance, supported the religious and political orthodoxies of their time, though their inward convictions and principles were almost wholly independent of them; and they were all advocates of absolutism in the administration of public affairs. These philosophers, it is true, also believed in a policy of toleration, and most of them played some part in promoting the growth of this modern principle in the mind of the seventeenth century. But there was another mode of thought on this subject, directly opposed to theirs, and on the whole more characteristic of the positivistic movement of ideas in their time. The "strong wits" of the century had in a special degree the weakness characteristic of their kind in all ages, namely, an undue contempt for the conventional sentiments and tender prejudices of the minds that they considered commonplace. They were convinced realists, and applied the principle of "thorough" as firmly in their political and social philosophy as Strafford and Richelieu did in the political practice of two kingdoms. The heroic thinker, the heroic statesman, was in their opinion he who was willing to march rough-shod over the feelings of the weaker part of mankind, or the scruples of his own mind, straight toward a clear-seen goal; and if persecution was necessary to the accomplishment of his ends and the advancement of civilization—well, persecution is justified by the incompetency of mankind in all great matters and large programs.[45]

Muret's eulogy of St. Bartholomew's could give no offense to thinkers of this kind; on the contrary, when it was taken in connection with the rumors of his secret "atheism" which circulated underground in the seventeenth century, it might especially qualify

[45] Concerning this phase of libertine thought, see Paul-Alex Janet, *Histoire de la Science Politique* (Paris, 1872), Bk. III, Ch. II, "L'École de Machiavel"; Charbonnel, Ch. IV, pp. 389-437; Perrens does not deal much with political ideas; see n.6. Fra Paolo [Paolo Emilio or Paulus Aemilius of Verona, author of *De Rebus Gestis Francorum* (1517?)], Lipsius, Gaspar Scioppius [see n.59, below], Naudé, and Gracián are good representatives. Bacon, in spite of what is said of him above, was strikingly Machiavellian, and Descartes somewhat less so. [On political thought see John William Allen, *A History of Political Thought in the Sixteenth Century* (London, 1928); Pierre Mesnard, *L'Essor de la Philosophie Politique au XVIe Siècle* (Paris, 1936); Henri Sée, *Les Idées Politiques en France au XVIIe Siècle* (Paris, 1923). See also the essays on Machiavelli in Joseph A. Mazzeo, *Renaissance and Seventeenth-Century Studies* (New York, 1964).]

him for their admiration. There can be no doubt, for instance, that it won him his place among the *libri homines* of the past venerated by Gabriel Naudé, Guy Patin, François de La Mothe le Vayer and the circles of learned libertines that gathered about them in the middle of the seventeenth century; and it is not improbable that the praise of St. Bartholomew's, which was one of their favorite themes of discourse, was suggested to them by this very work of Muret's. It may not be possible to prove that Lipsius took his notorious formula *Ure et seca* from the same source; but it is certain that the idea it expresses sprang from the general complex of ideas that he derived from his master.[46]

As regards the form in which Muret expressed these dangerous doctrines, it is to be observed, in the first place, that the positivists of the seventeenth century by no means rejected the use of public oratory. On the contrary, though they acknowledged a secret or open contempt for its necessary insincerity, they constantly recommended the study and practice of it as an important instrument in controlling the affairs of the world.[47] The style, however, that they employed was not of the Ciceronian form, but of a form exactly opposed to that, namely a condensed style full of points and aphorisms for which they often professed to find the model in Demosthenes' orations, but which they in fact derived from the study of Roman prose of the first century, and especially from Pliny's *Panegyric to Trajan*. It was a style developed, in fact, from the practice

[46] Janet, pp. 95-98; Charbonnel, pp. 53, 58, 617-620; Naudé, *Considérations Politiques sur les Coups d'État* (1639), III, 379-392. [La Mothe, Naudé, and Patin are incisively treated by Pintard and others listed in n.6 above. See also Julien-Eymard d'Angers, "Stoïcisme et Libertinage dans l'Œuvre de François La Mothe le Vayer," *Revue des Sciences Humaines*, LXXV (1954), 259-284; Jean Grenier, "Le Sceptique Masqué: La Mothe le Vayer," *Table Ronde*, XXII (Oct. 1949), 1504-1513; Florence Wichelgren's more conventional, *La Mothe le Vayer, sa Vie et son Œuvre* (Paris, 1934); and the evaluative introduction and critical bibliography in Ernest Tisserand's ed. of La Mothe's *Deux Dialogues Faits à l'Imitation des Anciens* (Paris, 1922); also R. H. Popkin, "Theological and Religious Skepticism," *Christian Scholar*, XXXIX (1956), 150-158. Selections from Patin's works are topically arranged in *Guy Patin*, ed. Pierre Pic (Paris, 1911); the treatment of his ideas is broader than the title suggests in Francis R. Packard, *Guy Patin and the Medical Profession in Paris in the Seventeenth Century* (New York, 1925). Cf. *Lipse*, I, par. 2, and *APS*, n.64. See also Josephine De Poer, "Men's Literary Circles in Paris, 1610-1660," *PMLA*, LIII (Sept. 1938), 730-780.]

[47] Bacon's opinion is exactly representative. Concerning "that science which we call Rhetoric, or Art of Eloquence," he writes, "For although . . . it is inferior to wisdom . . . yet with people it is the more mighty" (*APS*, n.18). See also his letter to Fulke Greville (signed with Essex's name and cited in *APS*, n.42), advising him about his studies.

of the Stoic *genus humile* of antiquity, but vitiated, as this style is likely to be when it is used for purposes of public oratory, by the tumor which Cicero recognized as one form of Asianism. The style of Muret in the three orations we are considering is exactly in this form; and it is strange indeed that none of the competent classicists who have written of Muret's style should have pointed out its complete contrast with the oratory of his Ciceronian period.[48] How far it is true that these orations set the model of style for the panegyrics of the seventy-five years following—until Bossuet returned to the normal Isocratean model of oratory—it is impossible to say until the history of this form shall have been adequately studied. At least they have the same traits that prevailed throughout that period; they are certainly among the earliest examples of the art of panegyric in which these traits are displayed; and they derive them from the imitation of the same work that was so minutely studied in the succeeding generations, Pliny's *Panegyric*.

We return to the study of the academic orations in which the course of Muret's intellectual development is so clearly depicted. After the discourse on style, delivered in 1572 from a chair of rhetoric, there could be no turning back; he had reached the climax of a long development. But the process of change in his opinions had by no means ceased, and his services to the rising generation were to be even greater in the ten years of activity that remained to him than any that he had yet performed. If we are able to record them more briefly than the former steps in his career, this will only

[48] A single sentence will illustrate: "O Catherine, Queen-mother, most blessed of women, who, after she had by her admirable foresight and anxious care preserved for so many years his kingdom for her son, her son for his kingdom, at last beheld this son effectively a king." (O felicissimam mulierem Catharinam regis matrem, quae cum tot annos admirabili prudentia parique sollicitudine regnum filio, filium regno conservasset, tum demum secure regnatem filium adspexit.) [Croll cites the Teubner ed. I, 197, erroneously for this passage; it occurs in the Jacobus Thomasius ed. of the Orations (Venice, 1751), I, 160: Orat. xxii.] The sentence shows exactly the truth of the paradox that a style planned to express acuteness and subtlety of thought falls into a tumor and violence far worse than Ciceronian emptiness when it is used for the purposes of oratory. The vices of sermon style in the reign of Louis XIII and in seventeenth-century England are to be accounted for in this way. [Jacques Truchet makes an excellent survey of sacred eloquence, with bibliography, pp. 309-329 in "Aspects Divers des Questions Religieuses au XVIIe Siècle," a special issue (No. xxix, Oct. 1955) of *XVIIe Siècle: Bulletin de la Société d'Étude du XVIIe Siècle*. See also Eugène Griselle, *Le Ton de la Prédication avant Bourdaloue* (Paris, 1906); Paul Jacquinet, *Des Prédicateurs du XVIIe Siècle avant Bossuet* (Paris, 1863); *Panegyrics of the Saints, from the French of Bossuet and Bourdaloue*, ed. D. O'Mahoney (London, 1924); works listed in *APS*, nn. 22, 58; *Lipse*, n.17.]

be because their significance is more easily understood in the light of what has already been said.

The defect of the Anti-Ciceronian movement before 1575 was its failure to offer a program of literary imitation in exchange for the one that it attacked. Erasmus himself had failed in this respect; and the reaction toward Ciceronianism noticeable in the third quarter of the century among men like Ascham and Melanchthon, who were the natural inheritors of Erasmus' ideas, was due to the feeling that he had led them out of Egypt into an educational wilderness—and left them there. Abstractly considered—if such questions ever could be abstractly considered—his reference of the choice of models to free individual taste and reason had everything in its favor; the time might even come when it would be a practical method of education. But actually, said Bembo and Ascham, it asked too much of men living in the sixteenth century. Whatever the theory of education might be, such men, they argued, must hold to the practice of imitation in their effort to learn the classical mode of thought; imitation, moreover, of prescribed models and by a defined method. And history has proved that they were right. For it was not until it had learned to suggest other models for imitation in place of Cicero and Isocrates, as it did in the last quarter of the sixteenth century, that the Anti-Ciceronian movement became a positive force and began its career of triumph.

What these models must be seems clear enough to the historian, who can look both before and after the event. For the range of choice was limited. Greek models of the classical period were out of the question because Greek education had so far proved impracticable for any but a small band of *savants,* and was declining rather than gathering power; and in Latin the poverty of the pre-Augustan ages in literary prose and the marks of approaching decay and medievalism in most of the literature produced after 200 A.D. were facts too evident to be overlooked. The only escape from the superstitious purism of Augustan imitation was in the literature of the first century of the empire, in the poetry of Lucan and Juvenal and Persius, and especially in the splendid prose of Seneca, Tacitus, and the younger Pliny, or in the Greek prose classics of the same period which had been made available by translation, Plutarch and Epictetus. Both philosophically and rhetorically, we can now see how admirably adapted this literature was to the needs of the seventeenth century; but the facts of a situation are never

145

so clear to those who are involved in all its actual complexities as they are to the historian; and the duties of a prophet and leader were made more difficult in this case by the fact that the Latin writers of the first century were imputed dangerous to good Latinity, good morals, and good political philosophy. It required both the clearsightedness of a prophet and the courage of a warrior to proclaim a rehabilitation of the Silver Age in the third quarter of the sixteenth century.[49]

The honor of effecting, or at least initiating, such a program must be divided between Montaigne and Muret, who were arriving, at the same time, but by different processes, at the same conclusions. There was neither correspondence nor co-operation, however, between them;[50] and though Montaigne's ideas had vastly greater results in the course of time on the general opinion of the world, Muret's immediate influence upon the learned classes was greater, and the conspicuousness of the post in which he challenged and suffered attack may justify us in attributing to him a higher degree of courage. The gradual discovery and proclamation of this literary program was the work of his last decade. During this time he forgot his vow to jurisprudence; and indeed it is now clear that that stirring episode in his career, important as it was in the development of his ideas, was a following after false fires. He had long been seeking a formula to express his new intellectual needs, and the reformed study of law had for a time seemed to be the true center of all his desires. But it proved to be too special a theme for his peculiarly impatient mind; and it was not until he embraced the cause of Silver-Age literature that he found the single and significant word to express at the same time his political, his moral, and his literary philosophy.

It remains for us only to trace rapidly the course of this last development of his thought, by which he earns the title of the chief founder of the theory of Attic prose in the seventeenth century.

The first post-Augustan author to attract him was naturally the younger Seneca. But he could not proceed at once with the development of his true intellectual purposes after his declaration of opinion in 1572. The requirements of his new rhetorical post had

[49] For a fuller statement of the relations between seventeenth-century and first-century literature, see *APS*, VI.

[50] The fact that Muret was Montaigne's house tutor for a time, when Montaigne was a boy, probably has no especial relevance.

to be acknowledged. In 1573 he delivered a purely ceremonial oration for some important anniversary day of the University, on the theme—commanded, as he is careful to say, by the authorities—of the excellence of literary studies. Then he begins the reading of Plato's *Republic* during the winter term of 1573-1574, protesting against the opposition that is being made to his program, and renewing his praise of Aristotle's rhetorical principles. All this he continues in the spring term of 1574,[51] and his plan was to pursue the study of Plato in the following winter; but the authorities—whose reasons for their conduct it is not becoming in us, he says, to inquire into—have ordered him to devote the year to Cicero alone. His characteristic revenge is to renew his Anti-Ciceronian pledges and cite the authority of Cato beside that of Aristotle; and it is in the prelude oration of this course that we first detect the influence of Seneca clearly. For the first time the terms in which he describes the Anti-Ciceronian style are drawn from that author—though he does not mention his name—and his style betrays the influence of Seneca's brief antithetical sentences. *Vera et solida eloquentia,* he says, *non tantum in verbis posita est, sed in rebus.*[52] In the following year he gives a course in the *De Providentia,* preluded with a discourse in which he begs his auditors not to let their minds be poisoned by the reproaches they constantly hear directed against this author.

A word of explanation concerning these reproaches is necessary. Seneca was one of the ancients who needed least to be interpreted by the humanists of the Renaissance. His works had come down through the Middle Ages almost unimpaired and constantly studied; and in the fifteenth and sixteenth centuries the employment of them by teachers for the practical purpose of moral instruction continued without interruption. Probably it is in these facts that we are to find one of the reasons for his hard treatment by the rhetorical humanists. His long popularity had given him an air of medieval vulgarity; and his moral usefulness made the supposed defects of his Latinity peculiarly dangerous. It was a literary prejudice, therefore, that he had to overcome in order to take his place as the model and mentor of the new generation, and the chief significance of

---

[51] See the orations for these courses, 1629 ed., II, Orats. iv-v (not in *Scripta*).
[52] 1629 ed., II, Orat. vi, *Ingressurus Explanare M. T. Ciceronis Libros De Officiis.* [Montaigne paraphrases this statement in his essay "Considération sur Cicéron."]

Muret's oration about him is that it portrays him as a master of eloquence and wisdom alike, and an exemplar of that new style to which Muret was inviting his pupils—*ad graves et serias res bonis et lectis verbis explicandas.*[53]

In this oration Muret gives no hint of a purpose of rehabilitating the authors of the Silver Age, or even of a preference for any of them as such. But in the autumn of the same year this purpose has evidently taken definite form in his mind. He has elected to study the Thirteenth Satire of Juvenal, and in the first words of his discourse throws out a challenge to those who disapprove of the study of the authors of his age. He begins the discussion of this prejudice with a sketch of the history of culture since the beginning of the Renaissance—perhaps one of the earliest attempts to place the Renaissance in its historical relations.[54] The first effect, he shows, of the Renaissance was to create an indiscriminate classical erudition, in which the more obscure and difficult authors were even preferred, because of their novelty and the neglect of the Middle Ages. Then followed the generations of the Bembos and Sadoletos,[55] by whom the hands of the clock are set as far wrong in one direction as they had been before in the other. For now "no prose authors are allowed except Cicero and his contemporaries; all poets are dubbed barbarous save Virgil, Catullus, Lucretius, and three or four others"; and the whole effort of teachers is spent in proving that "silly orations may be made by using no words but Cicero's, bad verses of none but Virgil's." Writers of modern Latin, who have never heard a Roman speak, have become so infatuated that they prefer their own writings to the Latin of Silius Italicus, Lucan, and Seneca. They dare to despise Ovid, next to Virgil the best of Latin poets; and one of them has translated his works into the vernacular for his pupils' use, for fear their Latinity might suffer contamination

[53] 1629 ed., II, Orat. iii (misdated 1585).

[54] 1629 ed., II, Orat. xii; *Scripta*, I, Orat. xi. A similar sketch, possibly influenced by Muret's, will be found in Bacon's *Advancement* (ed. Wright, I.iv.2): this account of "the first distemper of learning, when men study words and not matter," is Bacon's sketch of the causes of Ciceronianism in the sixteenth century; he supplements it interestingly in *De Augmentis*, I, noting the rise of the Anti-Ciceronian movement and the imitation of Seneca and Tacitus since 1600 [for the text, see *Lipse*, n.40]. A similar and longer account occurs in John Barclay's *Satyricon* (Leyden, 1674), 90-95. Of course the late term "Renaissance" does not appear in Muret, Bacon, or Barclay.

[55] [Cardinal Jacopo Sadoleto.]

148

from his.[56] In fact, says Muret, in a fine frenzy raging, the cooks and mule-drivers of any of these ancients could write better Latin than a modern Latin rhetorician.

Muret, in short, has made another clear step forward in the formulation of his ideas. Though he may still choose the names of Ciceronians to point his scorn, the object of his attack is now the theory of Augustanism *in toto*—and that in a public oration. How much further he could go, how much franker he could be, when he was less hampered by conventional necessities, is shown by a long essay in one of the later series of his *Variae Lectiones*,[57] in which he reports a conversation with a young friend. Here Muret admits that he himself had once believed that only the Augustans should be imitated. But at a later time, when he had considered the matter more fully, he came to see how presumptuous it would be in him to pass judgment on the style of writers like Seneca, Valerius Maximus, Quintilian, Pliny, Tacitus, Vellius Paterculus, Firmianus Lactantius, and others of that kind who had lived so near to the time when Latin flourished at its best, and had been considered excellent writers at that time. Certainly, he says, none of the ancients ever accused them of writing faulty Latin. In this list he hardly extends his charity beyond the limits of the Silver Age (as it came to be called in the generation following Muret). But a little further on in the same essay he takes a flight which has caused his commentators and admirers the greatest concern. He describes the method of teaching and practicing style which was later to be taken up and much more fully developed by Lipsius in his treatise on style in letter writing.[58] His plan is, he says, to derive the general form of his style from Cicero, Caesar, Terence, and others of the best kind; but then also to imitate and adapt whatever beauties he can find that other writers have excelled in; and he will look for these beauties, he adds, not only in the authors of the Silver Age, but even in

[56] This association of Ovid with the writers of the Silver Age is interesting; in the seventeenth century Ovid and Sallust were generally recognized as the only Augustans who displayed the traits of style of the succeeding century and were therefore worthy to rank with Tacitus, Seneca, and Lucan as models of "Attic" style.

[57] xv.2; in *Scripta*, Ch. LVIII.

[58] *Epistolica Institutio*, esp. the concluding chapter [see n.66 below and *Lipse*, II, second paragraph following n.20]. Barclay (*Satyricon*, pp. 96-97) gives a similar method of teaching as his own. In fact, it may be considered the typical Anti-Ciceronian method.

Tertullian, Saint Jerome, Saint Augustine, or Saint Ambrose, and, yes, even in Apuleius, Sidonius Apollinaris, and Cassiodorus. There was nothing here to cause disturbance of mind to the Stoic or Libertine writers of the first half of the seventeenth century; for Tertullian at least became almost as great a favorite of a number of them as Seneca and Tacitus themselves. But commentators who were resolved at any cost to retain the authority of Muret on the side of orthodoxy were guilty of strange contortions in the attempt to rob these words of their sting. It was argued, for instance, that Muret put in this passage in order to have an excuse if he should by mistake have used any words or phrases that were not Ciceronian; and a comparatively recent commentator has been found to accept this explanation as correct.[59]

Another work of post-Augustan rehabilitation remained for him to perform, the most difficult and dangerous, but also the most congenial to his tastes and temperament. When he first contemplated the teaching of Tacitus, we cannot exactly determine; for he seems to have entered into a kind of truce with the orthodox party after his readings in Seneca and Juvenal, and the subjects of his courses during the next four years (1576-1579) were Aristotle, Virgil, and Sallust. But the fact that Lipsius applied himself to the editing of Tacitus immediately after his momentous visit to Muret in 1568 is not without significance; and a careful study of the orations of the period from 1576 to 1580 makes it clear that he was veiling with an appearance of conformity the preliminaries of a more startling offensive moment than any that he had yet attempted. His aim in all of these discourses is evidently to relate as closely as possible the several subjects he is now interested in: dialectic, history and politics (*prudentia*), and rhetoric, and to try to organize them into a definite program or curriculum of positivism. This purpose is apparent, for instance, in his Sallust discourse; and in the two orations of 1576, on the subject of Aristotle's *Rhetoric*, he has worked out much more fully than he did in 1572-1573 his conception of the uses of the *genus humile*, founded on the doctrines of that treatise. For the first time, too, he has here expressed or hinted the prophetic opinion that obscurity may be a virtue of style.

When he finally announced that his winter term subject for

[59] David Ruhnken, quoted in *Scripta*, II, 203, n.3. It was Gaspar Scioppius, in his *De Stilo Historico*, p. 64, who originally expressed the idea; see also his *De Rhetoricam Exercitationum Generibus* (1660).

1580-1581 would be the first book of the *Annals* of Tacitus, the storm he must have anticipated broke upon his head. The opposition from the authorities which he had met at every step in his progress from Ciceronianism to "Atticism" now became more acute. His overture-oration was a general and moderate defence of Tacitus; but it evidently roused his opponents to new energy, and there are hints that disorders in his classroom were fomented by their machinations. Muret was never diverted from his intellectual ends by persecution, though he was capable of Machiavellian policy in the pursuit of them; and on this occasion he returned to the defence of Tacitus in a second oration which is distinguished among all his productions by the originality of its thought and the energy of its style, and must be considered his most important contribution to the history of modern thought.[60]

Its abrupt beginning, "Those who have been attempting to debar me from the interpretation of Tacitus have brought five particular charges against him," was itself a challenge to the Ciceronian taste for copious and mellifluous exordiums; and he proceeds to consider the five objections in a discourse in which, for the first time probably in the Latin of a modern author, the pointed brevity, the studied asymmetry of Tacitus' own style are successfully imitated. It is unnecessary to follow his argument *seriatim*; but in answering the charges against his new hero he makes some observations so significant in the history of the ideas and the literary style of the succeeding century that they should be rescued from the obscurity in which they have been allowed to remain.

The most serious of all the scandals that attached themselves to the cult of Tacitus during the period from 1575 to 1650 was the alleged use of his writings as a manual of Machiavellian policy, especially by the supporters of the regime of absolutism in church

---

[60] This oration (ed. Leipzig, 1629, Orat. xiv) is dated November 4, 1580 (the day following his first Tacitus oration, ii, xiii, in ed. Leipzig, 1629) in the early, and hence also in the modern editions; but for a number of reasons it seems to me likely that it was delivered in March, 1581, at the opening of a second term of reading in the *Annals*, probably in the Second Book. In November, 1581, he continued with the Third Book, thus completing a *triennium* in one author: his favorite method, as he had recorded. As regards the disorders in his classroom, Norden attributes them to Jesuit instigation; but Norden has falsely read the Jesuit literary doctrine as uniformly Augustan and Ciceronian; see above, pp. 6-7 [*sic*: Croll seems to refer to the pages of his original manuscripts, for no such pages occur in the 1924 publication. Presumably he has in mind pp. 130-131 and n.23, above.] At this time Muret's most intimate friends and some of his favorite former pupils were important members of the Order.

and state. The parallel that was constantly drawn during this period between the affairs of the Roman Empire as described by Tacitus[61] and the contemporary affairs of European states[61] was as constantly (and justly) denounced by the lovers of liberty as an insidious corrupting influence in political thought. Well, Muret meets the charge with an astonishing frankness in a passage which must be quoted at length as an illustration of modes of thought that were to become extremely common in another generation.

In the first place [he says] it must be observed that there are very few republics to-day; there is almost no nation but hangs upon the beck and nod of one man, obeys one man, is ruled by one man: therefore in this respect at least the state of things in our time is more like that of Rome under the Emperors than when the people had the power. And the more like their history is to ours, the more things we may find to study in it that we can apply to our uses, and adapt to our own life and customs. Although by the blessing of God we have no Tiberiuses, Caligulas, and Neros, yet it is profitable for us to know how good and prudent men managed their lives under them, how and how far they tolerated and dissimulated their vices; how, on the one hand, by avoiding an unseasonable frankness they saved their own lives when they would have served no public end by bringing them into danger, and on the other hand showed that baseness was not pleasing to them by not praising things in the conduct of princes which a good man cannot praise, but which he can cover up or pass by in silence. Those who do not know how to connive at such things not only bring themselves into danger, but often make princes themselves worse. For many men, if they believe that their vices are concealed and unknown, gradually get out of them of their own accord, for fear they will be detected, and *become* good from thinking that they are *considered* good.[62] These same men, however, if they see that their baseness is recognized, their reputation fixed, will openly live up to what they know is openly said of them, and become indifferent to a bad reputation because they despair of a good one.[63] And again, a man

---

[61] E.g. in the essays of Bacon, Gracián, and Virgilio Malvezzi [1595?-1653?, author of discourses on Tacitus].

[62] An excellent Tacitean "point": *Dum se bonos haberi putant, boni fiunt.*

[63] Eidem si turpitudinem suam palam esse videant, jam famae securi, quae

(of the present time) will the better bear the fewer and lesser vices of his own princes, when he has observed how the good and brave men of a former day endured worse and more numerous ones.

This is a language quite familiar to students of Bacon, Malvezzi, Gracián, Naudé, and many other strong wits and Machiavellians of the seventeenth century.

In all of these authors, moreover, the love of Tacitus' singular wisdom is attended by a love of his significant darkness of utterance; for the *prince des tenèbres*, as they called him in the seventeenth century, was the chief model of the use of the conceit in prose. Muret deals as boldly and prophetically with this aspect of his author's reputation as with the other. On the subject of the "debased Latinity" of the Silver Age he had already made himself clear enough, and the only notable addition here is a statement to the effect that the lower limit of good Latinity is the reign of Hadrian. But in answering the charge of obscurity and harshness brought against Tacitus, he stirs the ground about the roots of seventeenth-century style; the peculiar merits and also some of the faults of the prose of Bacon, Donne, Greville, Browne, of Quevedo and Gracián, of Balzac and La Bruyère, and even of Pascal, are foretold in the novel and dangerous ideas he here expresses. After saying that the Greeks recognized his obscurity as one of the virtues of Thucydides, he goes on:—

> For although a bare and clear style gives pleasure, still in certain special kinds of writing *obscurity* will win praise sometimes. By diverting discourse from common and vulgar modes of expression, it wins a dignity and majesty even out of strangeness (*peregrinitas*) and grips the reader's attention.[64] It acts as a veil, to exclude the view of the vulgar. Thus those who enter the dark crypt of a temple feel a kind of awful solemnity sweep in upon their souls. *Asperity* of style, again, has almost

---

palam dici vident, palam quoque faciunt, et famam dum bonam desperant, malam negligunt.

[64] The idea of a style meant for readers, as contrasted with hearers, was new and anticipates Attic theory of the seventeenth century. See *APS*, n.19. [Williamson (*Senecan Amble*, pp. 122-123), notes how the passage here quoted by Croll "found its way into late seventeenth-century English from the work of La Mothe le Vayer."]

the same property as bitterness in wine: which is thought to be
a sign that the wine will bear its age well.

In short, Muret has stated admirably in this oration all the chief
causes of the popularity which Tacitus was now beginning to
enjoy. He has left little to say; and in his third Tacitean discourse,
in November 1581, he devotes himself to the praise of three other
Post-Augustans: Plutarch, chiefly, and Seneca and Pliny, thus
practically completing his task of the rehabilitation of the prose of
the Silver Age.[65]

One other task, however, he had still to perform in the service of
the new Attic prose: the discovery of the genre in which it best
displays its peculiar merits. The discourse in which he introduced his
students to a reading in Cicero's *Epistolae ad Atticum* is chiefly an
argument to show that the only practical use that can now be made
of rhetorical skill is in the writing of letters. He sketches again, as he
had done once before, the history of culture in the Renaissance,
and shows that though the Ciceronians had attained to excellent
eloquence (though partial) there is no modern author "to whom
simply and unexceptionably one can give the praise of *writing* Latin
well." He commends, however, two writers of epistles, Giovanni
Casa, and his friend Paulus Manutius [Paolo Manuzio], and then
proceeds, after an invocation to his young hearers' love of dangerous truth, to show that the practical uses of oratory have ceased
in the present state of society. For the decision of great affairs is no
longer made in open senates or even in open law courts, but in the
cabinets of single men (of course he means princes and their
ministers). Of the three uses of oratory described by Aristotle,
therefore, but one now remains, the epideictic: school disputations,
sermons, panegyrics, and funeral orations. On the other hand, the
writer who nowadays may hope to be admitted to the intimacy of
princes and a part in the serious and great business of the world is
one who has learned to write with charm and wisdom letters exactly
adapted to the facts of the case, the character of the persons involved, and the actual state of society (*ad res, ad personas, ad
tempora*).[66]

[65] On Bacon and Tacitus see my article: "Lipsius, Montaigne, Bacon" [i.e. *APL*,
IV, (a)].

[66] *Scripta*, I, Orat. xvii; 1629 ed., II, Orat. xvi. See also his letter concerning the
collection and publication of his own letters (1629 ed., I, Ep. I.i; *Scripta*, II, Ep.
1). Those who may wish to study the new literary significance of the letter at the

Muret's work was now complete. He had traveled all the way from sixteenth-century rhetorical culture to the naturalism of Montaigne, Lipsius, and Bacon; and in his latest discourses had illustrated a new art of prose, as somber in mood, as heightened in emphasis, as the new sculpture, painting, and architecture devised in his time to express the spirit of the Counter-Reformation. And now, in the last act of his career, his withdrawal from the public scene, he was to show once more how sensitively he felt the spirit of the changing age in which he lived. One of the most striking signs of the spiritual transformation of Europe in the period from 1575 to 1650 was the voluntary withdrawal of so many of its representative men from the affairs of the world, to seek unity of mind and moral self-dependence in a contemplative retirement, either philosophical or religious. The external activities of the Renaissance had lost the power to satisfy their minds; it was an inward weakness that demanded their attention. To the list of these students of wisdom must perhaps be added the name of Muret. In or about the year 1573 he had taken holy orders, and the latter years of his life were lived in complete sobriety and with an attention to the duties of Christian observance which—there is every reason to believe—reflected the true state of his mind. Finally in 1584 he requested and obtained his release from academic duties, refused a professorship urged upon him by Bologna, and spent the few remaining months of his life in domestic retirement with a nephew, the son of a brother

---

beginning of the seventeenth century will find interesting points in the following: Lipsius, *Institutio Epistolica* in his *Opera Omnia*, 4 vols. (Wesel, 1675), II, esp. 1083-86 [Croll refers to this work as *Epistolica Institutio* when he describes and quotes from it in *Lipse*, II, p. 23; it was written in 1590 and was appended to *Justi Lipsi Epistolarum Selectarum* (Antwerp, 1605); previous citations made by Croll were usually from *Opera Omnia* (Antwerp, 1637), II; cf. *Lipse*, nn. 24, 26, 27, 30]; Étienne Pasquier, "Lettres," I.1, citing Erasmus, Budé, and Politian as models, and x.12, citing Cyprian, Jerome, and (chiefly) Seneca, in *Œuvres* (Amsterdam, 1723), II; a very interesting letter by Donne in *Life and Letters of John Donne*, ed. Edmund Gosse (London, 1899), I, 122-123, and another extraordinary one, I, 168; Joseph Hall, *Epistles in Six Decads* (London, 1608), epistle dedicatory to Prince Henry; Bacon's intended dedication to Prince Henry of the 1612 ed. of his *Essays* (Bacon's *Letters and Life*, ed. Spedding, IV, 340). In all of these the novelty of the letter as a literary genre is insisted on or implied. As an intimate and "moral" form, like the essay, it was in fact new, and was associated in all minds with the "Attic" tendency. See a passage in Victor Fournel's *De Malherbe à Bossuet* (Paris, 1885), p. 54. [See also Dunn, "Lipsius and the Art of Letter Writing"; Jean Robertson, *The Art of Letter Writing* (Liverpool, 1942); Katherine Gee Hornbeak, *The Complete Letter-Writer in English, 1568-1800* (Smith College Studies in Modern Languages, xv, nos. 3-4); Trimpi, Ch. III, "The Epistolary Tradition"; Williamson, *Senecan Amble*, pp. 136ff.]

who had died some years before, and in so strict an intimacy with several Jesuit friends that an opinion—probably false—became current that he himself had joined their order.

One of his aims in seeking quiet and leisure was undoubtedly to contribute some lasting work of erudition to the cause for which he had spent so much active energy as a teacher. He in fact completed his Latin translation of the first two books of Aristotle's *Rhetoric*; but his commentary on all the works of Seneca was interrupted by his death in June 1585, and the glory of domesticating the Stoic philosopher in the seventeenth century remained to Lipsius, Muret's greatest disciple.

✧ IV ✧

Muret's Reputation

A number of leaders of European culture in the post-Renaissance period, the period, that is, from 1575 to 1660, have been restored of late years to the honors due to them: Lipsius, for instance, as the founder of Neo-Stoicism in thought and style; Donne as the voice of a new age in poetry; Donne, Quevedo, and Gracián as masters of a new art of prose style; El Greco and Bernini in the other arts. That Marc-Antoine Muret has not taken his proper place in the history of this period is partly due, no doubt, to the fact that he was primarily an oral teacher. He left no very substantial and extended works as monuments of his doctrines, and a great deal of his influence passed into the works of others without being expressly recorded as his. There are several other important reasons, however, for the confusion and misapprehension that early settled down upon Muret's reputation, and have finally left him in modern times the mere shadow of a name as a rhetorician and the champion of the cause of Augustan purism which he spent most of his life attacking! Without some attention to these special circumstances we can hardly have a clear conception of his career.

His position in the world was unfavorable, not indeed to the dissemination of his doctrines, but to the open recognition of his influence. In the century of the Reformation, when sectarian partisanship colored all intellectual opinion, in the part of this century, moreover, when the leadership in humanism was rapidly passing from the South to the North and both sections had become aware of this new condition, a professorship at Rome and the open patronage of Cardinal d'Este and Pope Gregory were not points of vantage for a disinterested teacher of new ideas. Muret, moreover, suffered in Protestant countries, and, especially, in France, the peculiar suspicion and dislike that fall to the lot of the renegade. There is some doubt, it is true, whether he was actually—as it was charged in the indictment that drove him out of France—a Huguenot; but he had been a house pupil of the elder Scaliger; his associates, it seems, had been chiefly of that sect; and it is clear that the malice of the younger Scaliger in some public utterances concerning him are due to the memory of these early experiences. Even Lipsius, who was professor at the Calvinistic University of Leyden when he visited Muret at Rome, and remained in that position for ten years afterwards, during all that time carefully veiled much of what he learned from Muret. Only in letters, did he reveal the full change of his opinions and the cause of it.

Muret was unquestionably a *literary* renegade, and the literary world has never yet recovered from the confusions and obstinate perversions of opinion concerning him into which it fell, even during his lifetime, as a result of the change of his ideas during the years from 1558 to 1568. A few men of his own age, a good many men twenty or thirty years younger than he, made the same change, some of them much more abruptly than he; but none had to execute the dangerous *volte-face* on so exposed an eminence or after so express a commitment; and the world could never quite learn that the successor of the tradition of Bembo had become an Anti-Ciceronian and the rehabilitator of Seneca and Tacitus. In Germany and the Netherlands, particularly, it appears that his rhetorical reputation kept growing after he had cut its taproot, partly because the "new learning" that he had espoused was slower to be understood there, partly through a deliberate unwillingness to renounce a model of pure style which had already found its way into the schools. There were amusing efforts to conceal or even to deny that Saul also was among the prophets of a new style. Joseph Juste Scaliger was no less than disingenuous in his admiration for Muret's early Ciceronian prose and his disregard of all the prose of his maturer years; for he at least must clearly have understood the significance of Muret's change of literary opinions.[67] And one hardly

[67] There is no way of explaining the younger Scaliger's various opinions about Muret except by assuming a constant interplay of malice and intelligent admiration in his mind. Thus he says that Muret could write excellent prose style (it is clear

knows what to make of the argument by which Gaspar Scioppius (echoed by other Germans) attempted to find in his Anti-Augustan tirades a subtle expression of Ciceronian orthodoxy.[68] Curious but not unjust return of the extravagance of an ironist upon his own head! In Germany and England, at all events, the youthful Muret won the victory over the mature man, and his early Ciceronianisms kept their place in the educational curriculum of many schools, it is said, until the end of the eighteenth century—a fact exactly paralleled in the study of Cicero himself in the sixteenth century, when the first two orations were regularly studied in England and Germany as the best models for imitation, though Cicero in his mature years regretted their style as too Asian.[69]

Even in Anti-Ciceronian quarters Muret met the kind of ill-luck that often attends the man who changes. It is frequently seen in politics, science, and all kinds of affairs that the originators of programs and policies lose the credit of their achievements merely because men hate to associate themselves with a name blown upon by violent controversy; the policy lives while its author is repudiated. Muret's radicalism in thought and letters was made the mark of obloquy by the reactionary party at Rome, because the European reputation he had won by his early Ciceronian style could so easily be turned against him; the contest became confused with other than literary kinds of partisanship; violent and irrelevant prejudices were aroused; and on the whole men found it safer to avoid Muret's name than to explain their indebtedness to him. An illustration of how his reputation was obscured a generation after his death may be seen in Boccalini's, *I Ragguagli di Parnaso*,[70] where Lipsius is presented to Apollo for the honors of literary immortality by Velleius Paterculus and attended by "Seneca the moralist" and "Tacitus

---

that he means *Ciceronian* excellence), if only he had not chosen sometimes to write in different modes; yet there are sayings in the *Scaligerana* that show how well he understood Muret's later stylistic aims and how much he admired his later style; e.g. in *Scaligerana* (The Hague, 1668), II, 235-236: *Muretus optime percepit mentem Aristotelis in Rhetoricis*, and *Quid elegantius ejus oratione de Tacito aliis?* [For other sayings see "Muret," in the alphabetized ed. (Cologne, 1695), where the quoted passages occur on pp. 276-278. Cf. *Lipse*, n.35.]

[68] See above, n.59.

[69] Another interesting parallel in the criticism of Lipsius:—C. Nisard, himself a Ciceronian of the old school, commends the style of Lipsius' first work, *Variae Lectiones*, as the best he ever wrote (*Le Triumvirate Littéraire*, p. 7: see *Lipse*, n.1). Having been converted by Muret soon after its publication, Lipsius always looked on it as a youthful error.

[70] (Milan, 1614), I, 23. [See *APS*, n.57.]

the politician," one riding on either hand. Here the whole program of realistic studies and late Latin rehabilitation is transferred from the master to the disciple who learned it of him.

The most important cause, however, of the depression of Muret's reputation was the character of his opinions. In the rapid development of rationalistic thought that went on during the last quarter of the sixteenth century, two strains soon made themselves apparent: a general movement of scepticism, or, as it was more commonly called, libertinism, and a revival of the Stoic morality of the ancients. The former of these is probably to be regarded as the more important in the history of modern thought: it was in the form of libertinism that the rationalist movement first attained to full consciousness of itself in the last quarter of the sixteenth century; this was the form, too, in which it finally triumphed and produced the philosophic liberalism of the eighteenth century. But by the end of the sixteenth century it had already begun to be clear that libertinism was in advance of its age. Its anarchical, or centrifugal, tendencies had at that time to be corrected by the strengthening and unifying moral discipline of Stoicism; and the philosophers who best represent normal rationalism in the period from 1575 to 1660 are men, like Montaigne and Browne, who are both Sceptics and Stoics. Muret's opinions, on the other hand, were formed too early to include the Stoic element of the new intellectual amalgam; and he is to be looked upon chiefly as a precursor of libertine doctrines in thought and letters. It is true, of course, that he was not conscious of a dichotomy which had not yet revealed itself plainly; and how he would have been affected if he could have seen later developments of libertinism we cannot say. But his temperament constantly led him into extravagance of statement in his running fight against intellectual orthodoxy and commonplaceness, and some of his opinions, often exaggerated and distorted by oral tradition, made him too much a favorite of the "strong wits" of a later generation.

Illustrations of this phase of his reputation are numerous. We have already seen that the praise of St. Bartholomew's became a favorite paradox of radicals like Naudé and La Mothe le Vayer in the middle of the seventeenth century, and there is reason to believe that Muret's notorious oration of 1572 suggested this method of startling "plebeian intelligences." How little the praise of persecution had to do with sectarian partisanship or religious prejudice is shown by the fact that Muret was also spoken of sometimes (quite unjustly) as an "atheist." He was regarded, says Imperiali, in his *Musée Historique*, as one of those Italians, like Paolo Giovio and Della Casa, who never opened their breviaries and were therefore attacked by those "little minds that love to hang a quarrel on the point of a needle";[71] and this opinion at last gained such currency that he was one of the many writers to whom was attributed late in the seventeenth century the authorship of the mysterious work, *De Tribus Impostoribus* (that is to say, Moses, Jesus, and Mahomet): one of the highest honors that libertinism could bestow.[72] The most valuable evidence, however, concerning the libertine tendency in Muret's opinions, recognized by men who were familiar with them, is to be found in the fact that his portrait was among those gathered by Guy Patin to adorn the interesting room in his Paris house in which a company of strong wits sometimes held their convivial synods.[73] Other sixteenth-century worthies honored in this carefully chosen collection were Erasmus, Montaigne, Charron, Justus Lipsius, and "enfin François Rabelais." It is a kind of genealogy of positivism from 1500 to 1600.

In his temperament as well as in his doctrines Muret showed his kinship with the philosophers of the libertine tendency; and with some consideration of this point we may fitly close the present consideration of his career.—Certain traits of character and temper are common to sceptical rationalists of all periods. Curiosity about new ideas, for example, and readiness to adopt new opinions, an individual turn of wit and a constant tendency toward satire—these are traits just as conspicuous in scholars like Petrarch, Politian, and Erasmus as they are in their successors, the libertines of the later Renaissance. In the latter, however, they are attended by others peculiar to their own age. For reasons that need not be specified, these later rationalists felt themselves even more hostile to the accepted commonplaces of their time than it is the usual lot of the radical intellectualist to be; and their sense of estrangement betrayed itself frequently in excess, or even violence, of statement; sometimes in pride, sometimes in exasperation, they allowed themselves to abound, even extravagantly, in their own peculiar sense. Many *libres penseurs*, like Naudé, were secretly delighted with the

[71] Quoted by Charbonnel, p. 102.

[72] Erasmus, Rabelais, Aretino, Machiavelli, Bruno, Hobbes were among others similarly honored (Charbonnel, p. 696).

[73] See Guy Patin's letter to Falconet, Dec. 2, 1650. [Presumably Croll had in mind Patin's *Lettres*, ed. J. H. Reveillé-Parise, 3 vols., Paris, 1846.]

name of atheists, when it was thrown at them by horrified weaklings; and even a meditative philosopher like Browne allowed his doctrines of tolerance to cover a multitude of startling paradoxes. Some hardy adventurers, like Donne and Gracián, guarded their speculations from the apprehension of vulgar wits behind a veil of obscurity; while many others, like Estienne and Burton, expressed their protest against convention by an affectation of eccentricity. In fact, for every classical virtue of the Renaissance the strong wits of the seventeenth century discovered a counter-virtue of romantic individualism and violence.

Muret was temperamentally of the new school and was among the first who displayed its virtues and vices in their conduct. To speak more exactly, he gradually discovered the temper appropriate to the new positivism as he gradually discovered its program. Enough has already been said of his eulogy of absolutism and persecution. It may be—it doubtless is—true that the famous orations on these subjects were prompted by a sudden and sincere conversion to the doctrine of authoritarianism. But the excess with which he charged his guns on this occasion was none the less symptomatic of a new violence of intellectual temper. And this was but one of many occasions on which he invited danger. Challenged to defend his championship of later Latin authors, he encouraged his pupils to study Tertullian, Apuleius, and Cassiodorus. The opposition to his teaching of Tacitus in 1580 struck from his mind— like flint on steel—a sketch of the rapid decline of freedom and public counsel in the politics of the sixteenth century. When he was charged with corrupting the purity of Latin style, he retorted with an all-but-public acknowledgement of the doom that hung over the modern use of the ancient tongue.

A display of extravagance and violence of opinion may doubtless be accounted for in various ways. It may be the expression, for instance, of normal joy in the noise of combat; it may be the vehicle of a healthy sense of humor; it may be a somewhat provincial way of showing confidence and ardor in one's cause. And in one or another of these ways we can usually explain the excesses and oddities of the earlier humanists of all parties, of men like Rabelais, Erasmus, Budé, and the elder Scaliger, for instance. Their exuberance of wit may be regarded, on the whole, as a sign of mental well-being. But their successors in the last period of the Renaissance were not conscious of mental well-being, but of the contrary, and their extravagances are the signs of an inward exasperation, an inward dis-ease, seeking an opportunity to vent itself upon some external object. To appease their own sense of maladjustment they wreak their pain upon dull intelligences that know nothing of the agues that shake the mind. The Rabelaisian humors of Henri Estienne and Robert Burton are not an overflow of high spirits, but the symptoms of an unappeasable restlessness of soul; the raillery of Lipsius and the paradoxes of Donne are the guiled shore to a most dangerous sea of melancholy. Melancholy, in fact, was the root of the bitter wisdom of the seventeenth century; and Muret showed himself to be of the spiritual company of Montaigne, Donne, Browne, and Balzac (not to say of Pascal himself) when he voluntarily withdrew to a contemplative retreat in the midst of an active career.[74] His death within a year after he had taken this step of course suggests that his physical condition may have been the cause of it. But even though this may be true, the earlier moves by which he had gradually submitted his mind to the spiritual direction of his Jesuit friends show that he was aware of the same inward weakness that drove so many of his intellectual kindred into solitude and philosophy. The sense of strength and unity of mind which men of the high Renaissance had been able to enjoy without effort, by mere conformity with the world, or in unreflective industry, had now to be studied in the quietness of thought and a rigorous discipline of self-examination.

[74] Observe the interesting characterization of him by Bernays (*Lipse*, n.3), quoted by Dejob, p. 400n.: "Muret was a complete virtuoso in the art of smiling; his patronizing compliments, his contempt, his frivolity, and, in his later years, his melancholy also, express themselves in the smile, and conceal themselves behind it; but just because he is always smiling, he never laughs. [On the theme of retirement see Maren-Sofie Røstvig, *The Happy Man: Studies in the Metamorphoses of a Classical Ideal, 1600-1700* (Oslo and Oxford, 1954).]

Foreword to Essay Four

"Attic Prose: Lipsius, Montaigne, Bacon" marks a stage in the development of Professor Croll's ideas about prose styles in the sixteenth and seventeenth centuries. In this article he clarified, summarized, and furthered the theories presented in earlier essays, advancing his concept that a style both reflects and in part conditions its age, and making more precise his history and definition of the Anti-Ciceronian or "Attic" movement, especially its philosophic base in a Neo-Stoicism which he preferred to call libertinism. In his judgment, the revolt against the prescriptive and proscriptive emphases of the so-called Ciceronians began with Montaigne but did not become a force until Muret's conversion to Atticism and Lipsius' development and spread of its practice and principles.

It is well to remember that Cicero was master of varied styles used for different purposes and that the "Ciceronianism" of the late Middle Ages and Renaissance deviated from its alleged model; similarly, the "Aristotelianism" that Bacon and Milton attacked distorted Aristotle's own teachings.

It is also wise to remember that although Croll refers to Anti-Ciceronian or "Attic" style, he meant not one but at least two styles, one loose and informal, the other terse. Both were reactions against the artificialities and rigidities of sixteenth-century emphases on words and forms; their common goal was maximal expressivity; in each, content and the mind in the process of thinking took precedence over conventional form and the rigidities of genre and tradition.

One respect in which this article marked a stage in the development of Croll's ideas is that in the penultimate paragraph he remarks upon "a tendency which . . . manifests itself everywhere as the peculiar mark of the genius of the seventeenth century," a tendency for which "there is unfortunately no convenient name in English." He rejects "metaphysical" as being even less happy as a term to describe the kinds of prose in which this tendency appears than it is as a description of the related kinds of poetry. Having granted that "It may be known as the 'prose of imaginative conceit' in order that

163

we may keep in line with the terms of current criticism," he admitted a temptation "to make the bold innovation of calling it 'the baroque style' in prose, for no other term will so exactly describe its characteristic qualities." According to Professor René Wellek, it was he who first, in a Princeton seminar, suggested that Croll use "Baroque" instead of "Attic" for this style in prose. It was, of course, neither of these two scholars who invented the idea of transferring the terminology of art to literature. As early as the eighteenth century that game was being played—by critics of Spenser, for example; and in the twentieth century Spengler filled his *Decline of the West* with such phrases as the "Titian style of the madrigal." Nor was Croll the first to apply *baroque* to literature. Certainly Oskar Walzel preceded him with the general usage in his article "Shakespeares Dramatische Baukunst," *Jahrbuch der Shakespearegesellschaft*, LII (1916), 3-35. Walzel was adopting the criteria of Heinrich Wöfflin (*Kunstgeschichte Grundbegriffe*, Munich, 1915) to literary matters, and René Wellek in "The Concept of Baroque in Literary Scholarship," originally published in *JAAC*, V (1946), 77-109, and reprinted, with updating, in his *Concepts of Criticism* (New Haven, 1963), seems ready to credit Walzel with having introduced the term with respect to an English writer, though he adds that, as far as he knows, Friedrich Brie's *Englische Rokokoepik* (1927) was the first attempt of this sort. But Valdemar Vedel's pioneer article, "Den Digteriscke Barokstil om Kring aar 1600," *Edda* (Christiana), II (1914), 17-40, should not be overlooked. Parallel to the style of painters like Rubens, Vedel perceives a poetic baroque style in English and French literature between 1550 and 1650. However, credit for the peculiar application of the word *baroque* to Attic style belongs to Croll's adoption of Wellek's suggestion. Whether or not it is a satisfactory term has been debated, but it has had wide currency and will probably persist, though it is now being partially replaced by *mannerist*. (See the fuller discussion in Croll's "The Baroque Style in Prose," in the foreword and notes to that essay, and in *Muret*, n.22.)

Too much emphasis should not be placed on mere terminology.

What deserve attention are the main theses of this article: for example, that the central idea of Anti-Ciceronianism was the adaptation of style to the differences of men and times, and that the "new" style not only paralleled but also imitated the Anti-Ciceronianism of the first century A.D., both in its character and in its relation to the oratorical prose which preceded it.

J. Max Patrick and Robert O. Evans

Attic Prose: Lipsius, Montaigne, Bacon*

EDITED BY J. MAX PATRICK AND ROBERT O. EVANS

❖ I ❖

THE decade beginning just before 1570 is clearly indicated as the time at which the Anti-Ciceronian, or "Attic," movement first arrived at a program and became conscious of its connection with a general change of intellectual interests that was coming over the world. It was the beginning of a century in which, in spite of many oppositions, at first from a dying generation, and later from a generation just coming to birth, it was to dictate the prevailing form of prose style in all the countries of Europe. In the career of Muret, for instance, we are able to mark with definiteness the late sixties and the early seventies as the time when he first arrived at a complete sense of his own meaning and mission; the succeeding years of his life were spent in working out the philosophical implications of the Anti-Ciceronian rhetoric in moral and political science.[1]

It was not only Muret's conversion, however, that made this the decisive moment in the history of the movement. Muret was then too old to make the world clearly aware of his changed intentions: his record was confusing. Moreover, other men of his generation, almost equally authoritative, had taken the opposite direction to his. In the North particularly, whence it seemed that new impulses must come, in the great Protestant countries of Germany and England, the leading humanists, Ascham and Car, Sturm, Melanchthon, and Camerarius were all Ciceronian, mildly and moderately so, it is true, since Erasmus had spoken, but still definitely in the tradition of rhetorical education and eminently puristic in their theory of style. The situation was not clear, and the world

---

* Originally published in *Schelling Anniversary Papers by his Former Students*. New York: The Century Co., 1923, pp. 117-150.

[1] The present essay is meant to follow one with the title "Marc-Antoine Muret and Attic Prose," which appears in a current number (1923) of *PMLA*. [The title was changed; the text was apparently revised, and publication was deferred to 1924.] In that essay I have tried to show the relations of the Anti-Ciceronian movement to the thought of the sixteenth and seventeenth centuries. As regards the relations between this movement and its models in antiquity, see *APS*, above.

might be going in either direction for all one could tell. It depended on what the *young* men would say, what formulas they would adopt, what challenges they would respond to; and it is chiefly because of what was thought and said by two men who were both comparatively young at that time that we are able to date the beginning of the Anti-Ciceronian period at approximately 1570.

These two men were Joest Lips (better known as Justus Lipsius) and Montaigne. In 1567 Montaigne was thirty-four years old but not yet an author or a philosopher; Lipsius was twenty years old and had already published. We will consider the latter first.

✧ II ✧

JUSTUS LIPSIUS

His Discovery of the Stoic Model

There is no scholar of the Renaissance concerning whom the opinion of scholars has undergone so radical a change in recent years as Justus Lipsius, of Leyden and Louvain. His association, from 1586 onward, with the Jesuits of Louvain won him the hatred and abuse of Protestant partisans in the Northern countries; on the other hand, the more orthodox of his own party regarded him with constant suspicion and refrained from acknowledging their real intellectual indebtedness to him because it was believed that he had imbibed from his Stoic masters in antiquity doctrines dangerous to the faith of a Christian; and, finally, the shadow of academic disapproval always rested upon his literary doctrines, even during the period when they were enjoying almost unrivaled success in the actual practice of the world. For these and other reasons his name appears much oftener in the seventeenth century in hostile than in friendly allusion, though it was recognized that he deserved his place beside Scaliger and Casaubon in the intellectual triumvirate of his time; and modern scholars were content until a few years ago to accept the judgment of his contemporary foes at their face value. It was sometimes recalled, with facile humor, that there was a Lepidus in the Roman triumvirate; and it was the custom to hold him up to scorn as a typical linguistic pedant insensible to the philosophy and literature of the ancient authors whom he edited. These were strange judgments to be passed on the philosopher who has now come to be known as "the founder of seventeenth-century

Neo-Stoicism" and the writer who must finally take an almost equal place with Montaigne and Bacon among the founders of the prose style of the seventeenth century.[2]

The stages in Lipsius' development as a philosopher can be clearly discerned. His history properly began, when he was twenty-one years old, with his visit to Muret at Rome in 1568, though at that time he had already won considerable reputation as a linguist and rhetorician. The first result of this encounter was his quick—if we may believe him, his *instantaneous*—conversion from a purely literary and rhetorical learning to a realistic—or, as we should say, a positivistic—study of politics. He began at once the intense and rapid labors which bore fruit, after only seven years, in his famous edition of Tacitus (1575), and a little later in the important compilation known as *Six Books of Politics*.[3] These works won him a reputation as a "politician," or student of *prudentia*, which was never equalled or corrected, at least in Italy, by the fame of his later work. The *Politics* unfortunately won him also the hatred of most scholars of the North by its advocacy of the policy of "fire and sword" in dealing with heresy, though a careful student of his mind will be convinced that his ruthlessness, like the orthodoxy of Montaigne and Browne, was founded in scepticism and not in bigotry.

These first works do not, however, represent his matured interests. They reflect directly the influence of Muret, just as we may discover in all the first part of his career the mobility of mind, the physical restlessness, the extravagance of wit veiling an inward dissatisfaction, which are observable in his master. The time of his full self discovery may be fixed with some certainty at the point of his career when he severed his connection with the Protestant University at Leyden and deliberately chose a life of quiet and retirement as teacher in his own Louvain college. There was an interval in which he was received as an honored guest at several German courts and universities and was offered more than one brilliant and conspicuous position of public activity. He deliberately chose to

---

[2] I have used again, in this section, some of the materials more fully elaborated in *Lipse*. An excellent and full study of Lipsius' philosophical doctrine and its influence will be found in Zanta, *La Renaissance du Stoïcisme au XVIe Siècle.* See also Strowski, *Histoire du Sentiment Religieux . . . Pascal et son Temps*, I, [and the works cited in *Lipse*, n.2 and *APS*, n.36].

[3] [*Politicorum, sive Civilis Doctrinae Libri Sex*, begun as early as 1583, published 1589; trans. into French by Simon Goulart as *Les Politiques* (Geneva, 1613). See Saunders, p. 27.]

retire to the house on a quiet side street of Louvain not far from the college, where he spent the rest of his life in the placid orderliness that he describes in his letters, teaching a small number of chosen students, walking in the country with his Scotch dog Mops, and cultivating his tulips.

In the *De Constantia*, his first work of Stoic philosophy, he attributes his choice of retirement and his study of "apathy" to the trouble of his time and the varied spectacle of human suffering that he has witnessed in the devastated towns and country regions of the Netherlands. But the roots of seventeenth-century Stoicism lie much deeper than the events of a generation. Once started by Muret in the way of a naturalistic study of public and private morality, Lipsius could never have rested until he had attained the formula of spiritual recollection and cure which his age required. Having found this, he had found himself at last, and the rest of his life was devoted to Seneca and the doctrines of Stoic *sapientia*.[4]

The progress of his literary ideas was like that of his philosophy and seems always to have kept a step in advance of it. Like Muret, he blundered into the wrong track at the beginning of his career—the back-track of Ciceronianism. In 1569, having scarcely finished his studies at Louvain, he published a volume of precocious learning containing three books of *Variae Lectiones*.[5] It is dedicated to the mighty Cardinal Granvelle—so high does he dare to aspire already—in copious Ciceronian periods, indistinguishable from many other examples of the same style produced by the rhetorical humanists of the sixteenth century. But his conversion was early, instantaneous, and thorough. Muret had gradually divined the new program of studies, had worked out their relations one to another, had discovered their appropriate rhetorical medium; Lipsius' task was merely to understand the meaning of his message, to develop the implications in it which Muret himself had not dared to reveal, and to devote the energy and fire of his youth to its propagation. It was in 1568, only a year after his Ciceronian debut, that he met

---

[4] Of course his *Manuductionis ad Stoicam Philosophicam* (1604), written as a preparation for his ed. of Seneca (1605), had a greater influence upon the better instructed part of the public, but the *De Constantia* (1584), reached a *larger* audience everywhere. [On the former, see Saunders, Ch. III; on the latter, *Lipse*, n.4.]

[5] [The date erroneously given by Croll, "1567," has been rectified. Cf. *Lipse*, n.10a.]

Muret in Cardinal Hippolito d'Este's palace at Tivoli, and a few days later wrote to him as a disciple to a master. Muret has found the true way of study: nothing more *Attic* has ever met Lipsius' eyes than the letter he has just received from him. A year later Muret wrote, admitting him, as it were, to the mysteries. At Tivoli, he said, it is true that we live in all the delights of the senses—a truly Phaeacian life—but there are none who delight in the same studies that you and I enjoy. There is something of the strange secrecy and sense of danger in this correspondence that is often to be noted as characteristic of the Anti-Ciceronian movement; and it is not unlikely that Muret's description of the sensual life of Tivoli alludes in a veiled style to the rhetorical, purely literary tastes of the patrons whom he was serving, contrasting them with his own enthusiasm for the virile and "modern" studies which he did not dare to profess openly.[6]

Lipsius' resolve is taken at once. Political and moral science, not rhetoric; Attic style, not Ciceronian, shall be the objects of his effort. And he begins to work on an edition of Tacitus. But how shall he make the transition decently from the opinions that the public still thinks he holds to those he has actually espoused? It was an embarrassing situation for a young man who had already attained reputation as a stylist; and we can follow—not without enlightenment—the steps of his cautious preparation. First he publishes nothing of any import for eight years after the date of his first work; and then he comes out, in a new preface, in 1577, with the astonishing statement that Plautus' old style has more savor for him than Cicero's.[7] The quaint and ancient words, the piquant realism of this author made him a favorite of Anti-Ciceronians from Cujas to Guy Patin; he was tonic to minds suffering from the lassitude of a long season of purism. But Lipsius is careful to give the air of a whimsical and ingenuous weakness to his preference, and in the same tone he continues to speak of the style he uses in this new work, the *Quaestiones Epistolicae*. While he professes that his sub-

[6] See an account of this correspondence, with references, in "M.-A. Muret and Attic Prose," *PMLA*, as above. [Apparently this account was deleted before the article was published under its revised title.]

[7] [Errors in the original of this sentence ("seven years" and "1574") have been corrected. Eight years after the appearance of *Variae Lectiones* in 1569, *Quaestiones Epistolicae* was published (Antwerp, 1577). The passage mentioned is quoted in *Lipse*, n.11.]

ject compels him here to employ a style more pointed and significant than he has heretofore employed, he seeks a justification for his new manner in the *Letters* of Cicero.

The disingenuousness of all this is apparent when we consider that his Tacitus had already been printed[8] when these words were written. The true account of the style he employs in the *Quaestiones* is contained in a letter to a friend, and the words are worth quoting as one of the best descriptions of the new Attic. "I am afraid," he says, "of what you will think of this work [the *Quaestiones*]. For this is a different kind of writing from my earlier style, without showiness, without luxuriance, without the Tullian concinnities; condensed everywhere, and I know not whether of too studied a brevity. But this is what captivates me now. They celebrate Timanthes the painter because there was always something more to be understood in his works than was actually painted. I should like this in my style."[9] Both the terms of criticism in this passage and the style in which it is written come from Seneca.

Of course the air of mystery could not long be maintained after the appearance of his Tacitus in 1575. It is true that he continued to write to his literary intimates, even to Montaigne, as if he and they had been initiated into an esoteric cult, a secret order of taste and ideas, which involved them in opinions contrary to those they were bound to profess in public and odious to vulgar and orthodox intelligences.[10] But this curious attitude continued to be characteristic of certain phases of the Anti-Ciceronian movement during at least two generations. The world soon became aware, through his voluminous and international correspondence, that Lipsius was a man with a philosophical and literary mission. Almost immediately after the appearance of the Tacitus he let it be known that he would

---

8 [Corrected from Croll's original, "Tacitus must already have been in the press." In 1575, when his ed. of Tacitus was published, Lipsius also wrote commentaries on Plautus' comedies, *Antiquae Lectiones*. In them (vii.8) he cautiously grants that Tacitus is better than ordinary writers (*Tacitus scriptor haud paullo melior quam vulgus*) and that he will not deny his liking for the elegant wit and urbanity of Plautus (ii,1: *Negare nolo: amo Plauti elegantes et urbanos sales*). Cf. Saunders, p. 15.]

9 [For the Latin wording, see *Lipse*, n.11.]

10 *Epp. Misc.*, ii.87. [We have not identified the edition referred to: numbering varies. A letter beginning *Scripsi ad te ante menses*, addressed to Montaigne and dated 1588, and containing a reference to the work on Tacitus occurs as ii.45 in *Justi Lipsi Epistolarum Centuriae Duae* (Paris, 1601), along with two other letters to Montaigne expressive of intellectual sympathy (ii.59 and 96). In *Eppistolarum Selectarum Centuria Miscellanea* (Antwerp, 1611-1614), these letters are numbered ii.41, 55, and 92.]

devote the rest of his life to preparing an edition of Seneca.[11] This resolve he faithfully carried out, and the great work did not appear until 1605, the year before his death. It was then already world-famous, however, and almost immediately attained a currency such as few works of learning have enjoyed. It was the chief instrument of the extraordinary diffusion of Seneca's influence throughout the seventeenth century and was so closely identified with the study of the Stoic philosopher that people sometimes spoke of "Lipsius" when they meant the works of Seneca. There seems to have been doubt during the years following his death whether his influence was to be of more use to the imitators of Tacitus or to the imitators of Seneca. But there can be none in the mind of a modern student who studies the works of the many writers who derive from him. He and Montaigne are the chief sources of the Senecan literary mode, and his own style is obviously formed by a slight exaggeration of Seneca's point and brevity, and unfortunately a great exaggeration of his play upon words.

In the course of twenty-five years of preparation for his Seneca, Lipsius' program of studies gradually enlarged and at the same time defined itself. He found himself involved, like Muret, in the enterprise of rehabilitating the Latin masters of the Silver Age, but with the difference that his interests were almost wholly limited to prose writers—he is like Bacon, Browne, Balzac, Pascal, and many other literary masters of the seventeenth century in this respect—and that he was much clearer in his literary purposes than Muret. What these purposes were is described in a passage from a Latin eulogy composed by a Mechlin judge, a literary disciple of Lipsius, immediately after his death. The reader will perhaps be rewarded for his patience in enduring Rivius' style for a few sentences—somewhat mitigated in translation, it is true—for the sake of the information he conveys, and also because the passage will show that a certain kind of Asianism arises, as Cicero observed, from an exaggeration of the very qualities called Attic. Gaugericus Rivius is

---

[11] [*L. Annaei Seneca Philosophi Opera, Quae Exstant Omnia . . . Emendata et Scholiis Illustrata* (1605); trans. Thomas Lodge, *Workes of Seneca* (1614; rev. 1620); used as a basis for Roger L'Estrange, *Seneca's Morals* (1678), especially "Of Seneca's Writings" (extracted from Lipsius), appended to the preface. The source of Lipsius' announced intention to edit Seneca is not given by Croll, but among his lecture notes preserved in Princeton Library, he states concerning Lipsius (again without source), "In a letter to a Spanish humanist he wrote *Dederam Tacitum, prudentiae (tuo quoque judicio) patrem; debui certe volui, et Senecam, sapientiae fontem.*"]

plainly one of those disciples of Lipsius, often mentioned in contemporary criticism, who imitated only the faults of his master.

Declaring, Rivius says, that he existed for the good of the State, not the State for *his* good, he [Lipsius] decided at the beginning to save the lives of his own kind by his labors, to recover health to the sick by his ministrations, to restore their original possessions to those who had been unjustly despoiled, and to liberate them from their chains. It was for this purpose that he visited all the prisons and took note of Seneca, the tragic poet, Velleius Paterculus, the famous Pliny, that once-celebrated panegyrist of Trajan, and many others besides, wearing the chains and the dress of prisoners, living there in mud and ordure, branded with the red-hot iron, shaven, half-dead. In the same wretched gang he saw also Valerius Maximus, so unlike himself, so unlike his name.

 . . . And two prisoners were particularly noteworthy as having been unjustly condemned—L. A. Seneca and G. Cornelius Tacitus. These men, who had held consular rank, he beheld crawling out of I know not what *barathrum*, what cave of Polyphemus, or rather what cavern peopled with tigers and panthers. . . . To Lipsius, who took pity on them and demanded to know why men who had served the public good as citizens had been thrown into chains, why they were bound who had attached all humanity in bonds to themselves by their services, and ought to be held in the hands and in the hearts of princes; why they lay darkened in filth who had cast a light beyond the limits of the world, beyond nature—the dazzling light of *prudentia* and *sapientia*; to Lipsius, inquiring thus. . . . [The period continues to much greater length.][12]

Rivius' words are valuable as indicating the full scope and deliberateness of Lipsius' innovations. They help us to understand, for instance, why several minor contemporaries of Tacitus and Seneca enjoyed so much more favor in the seventeenth century than they have done since: why Valerius Maximus is so often quoted by Montaigne, Jonson, and Browne, Velleius Paterculus by the concettisti in prose, and the younger Pliny by panegyrists and students of "point." But they also reveal the fact that Lipsius limited his

[12] Rivius' discourse appeared in a volume issued by Moretus in 1607, the year after Lipsius' death. [See *Lipse*, n.16.]

174

charity to authors of this school and century. Though his classicism is deliberately not Augustan, it is a true classicism, and he carefully avoids the dangerous mistake which Muret did not sufficiently guard his followers against, and which the "libertine" prosaists of the seventeenth century were frequently to make, of frolicking anew in the semi-barbarism of the "low Latin" style.

His Place in Seventeenth-Century Culture

Of course Lipsius was not the sole founder of the Stoical philosophy of the seventeenth century or even of the Senecan imitation which accompanied it in prose literature. Du Vair, Montaigne, and Charron had all discovered the path of renunciation and self-dependent morals before him or without his aid. But the clearness and exclusiveness of his program, his international authority as a humanist, and his use of the new prose model in the authoritative Latin language gave the impetus to the Stoic philosophy and style which carried them into every part of Europe and almost every lettered circle of society. He soon had many followers among professed scholars at the universities who dared to brave the imputation of heterodoxy. But the greatest success of his program (though he himself always wrote in the ancient tongue) was won in the more open fields of the vernacular languages and the popular philosophy of laymen. Most conspicuous among his professed disciples was Francisco Quevedo, the young Spanish nobleman who had already won a brilliant reputation in burlesque fiction. There was a correspondence between the two men during Lipsius' last years in which Quevedo hailed Lipsius as the hierophant of a new mystery in terms that recall the letter that Lipsius had written to Muret forty years before. To Lipsius he owes the discovery of the way that he will henceforth follow throughout his life.[13] His writings soon showed what he meant; for he became the consistent and enthusiastic exponent of Christian Stoicism in many works of philosophy in Spanish and Latin, in which Job, Socrates, Cato, and Seneca appear as the saints and heroes of one dispensation. When one reads the bold and extravagant pages in which he equalizes pagan and Hebraic models of morality, one easily understands why Lipsius himself narrowly escaped the Index, and why he felt it necessary to destroy his dissertation called *Thraseas* in defence of the right of suicide, which had won, even though unpublished, a

[13] See *Lipse*, IV, n.45, and the three paragraphs preceding ref. to n.45.

dangerous notoriety. Quevedo's discipleship was complete, for he adopted not only Lipsius' philosophy but also his literary style and his devotion to the masters of Silver-Age Latinity. "Mi Seneca, mi Lucano, mi Juvenali," he exclaims, in a kind of rapture. It was a literary program which gained peculiar plausibility in Spain from the fact that Seneca and Lucan had been natives of that country. The somber dignity of the Spanish character was believed to be as friendly to Stoic ideals of conduct as the Spanish love of "emphasis" was to the significant rhetoric of the first century.

The impression made by Lipsius upon England was almost as great, however. His dialogue *Of Constancy* was translated and published in 1593 by Sir John Stradling, a minor author who had a part also in disseminating the taste for Martial and the epigram in this decade.[14] Jonson studied the political, the rhetorical, and the Stoic writings of Lipsius and may have learned from them some of the admiration for the two Senecas which is displayed in his prose and poetry alike, and some of the Stoic philosophy which he expounds—or translates—so admirably in many a passage of his verse.[15] A Senecanism more obsequious to Jacobean defects of taste is revealed in Bishop Hall's *Epistles* and *Meditations*. It is hard to believe that these works have not been directly influenced by the Belgian scholar, who Hall met in person, encountered in sectarian controversy, and mentioned frequently in his writings. Lipsius' influence at least appears far and wide in many other English moral writings of the century, and it is recorded that his letters were sometimes used as Latin texts in English schools.

These are remarkable instances of Lipsius' authority; yet the knowledge of its range and power must chiefly be won, for reasons that have been explained, from the vigorous opposition it aroused. The attacks made by his opponents during his lifetime are of little value to the historian, because of the religious prejudices that

[14] *Lipse*, n.4.

[15] The facts are recorded in the eds. of *Discoveries* by Schelling and Castelain. [See *Lipse*, n.24 for subsequent scholarship that shows that Jonson received Lipsian ideas through Hoskyns.] See a series of articles, in various periodicals, by Professor Briggs on Jonson's classical adaptations. [William D. Briggs, "Note on the Sources of Ben Jonson's *Discoveries*," *MLN*, xxiii (Feb. 1908), 43-46; "Studies in Ben Jonson," *Anglia*, xxxvii (1913), 463-493; xxxviii (1914), 101-120; xxxix (1916), 16-44, 209-251, 303-318; "Source-Material for Jonson's *Epigrams Forest*," *CP*, xi, 2 (April 1916); and "Source-Material for Jonson's *Underwoods* and Miscellaneous Poems," *MP*, xv (1917). See also J. E. Spingarn, "The Sources of Jonson's *Discoveries*," *MP*, ii (1905); and Trimpi, esp. pp. 60-75.]

mingle with and obscure their literary purposes. Henri Estienne, who was himself an Anti-Ciceronian—though more nearly akin to Montaigne than to Lipsius—published in his old age a long and fantastic book *De Lipsii Latinitate*.[16] But he has so entangled the literary doctrines of Lipsius with the intrigues of Spain and the Ligue and the supposed alliance of the Catholic powers with the Turk that no modern reader can hope or care to discover his exact meanings. Scaliger is a better critic and has left the first intelligent description of the new Senecan style by an opponent.[17] But he was the official voice of Protestant literary orthodoxy, and his appointment to the chair of rhetoric at Leyden vacated by Lipsius was probably meant to have both sectarian and rhetorical significance.

Two decades later the cause of correct classicism in style rests in different hands, the hands of the Jesuit rhetoricians who have taken charge of the literary education of the French court and society. To rally the taste of their time to pure Augustanism is the task of Father Caussin and Father Vavasseur, and the tendencies they are hopelessly struggling against are chiefly those that were set going by Lipsius and his school.[18] It is still so in the middle of the century, when Balzac is the arbiter of taste; Montaigne and Lipsius are the protagonists of the tradition from which he seeks—in vain—to disengage himself. And even a generation later, Bouhours attributes both good and bad elements in the prevailing modes of style to Lipsius' teaching.[19] It is remarkable that a model set in Latin writing by a philologist should have had so much power in determining the form of prose style in several of the living languages. But the explanation is clear: Lipsius provided the model of a Stoic style.

[16] [See *Lipse*, n.34.]

[17] In *Poemata Omnia* and in *Scaligerana*, under "Lipsius," the brief dictum, *male scribit*; see *Lipse*, n.35.

[18] Caussin, as in *Lipse*, IV, par. 6 and n.37; cf. *APS*, n.44 and *Muret*, n.25. Vavasseur's third oration (cited in *APS*, n.59) was in favor of the old style and opposed the new. This *novum genus* was the Anti-Ciceronian, the post-Augustan, which had become almost universal in his time.

[19] Bouhours, *La Manière* (Paris, 1687), passim; see the copious index. [In *Lipse*, n.25 and *APS*, nn.39, 61, Croll cites the Amsterdam, 1688 ed.; cf. *Muret*, n.26.] There is some discussion of Bouhours' criticism in my essay "Attic Prose" [i.e. pp. 71-72, 98; cf. *Muret*, p. 98].

MONTAIGNE

The Founder of Libertine Style

There is a striking similarity between the moral experience of Montaigne at the time of his retirement and that through which Lipsius passed more gradually in arriving at the ultimate form of his thought. He too was touched with the melancholy of the late Renaissance. His confessed aim in his retirement was to study it and come to terms with it, and the method of his study in the first phase of his philosophical development was purely Stoic. The essays which we can prove to have been written during the first five or six years after his retirement are as like in tone and spirit to the Stoical treatises of Lipsius as the writings of two authors working independently are ever likely to be. The essay on *Solitude*, for instance, is a kind of companion piece or complement to Lipsius' dialogue on *Constancy*.

Rhetorically, too, Montaigne effected his escape from humanistic orthodoxy through the Stoic doorway; and he asserted his freedom with more boldness and promptitude, perhaps actually became conscious of it at an earlier date, than Lipsius. He is in no doubt, even in the earliest of his Essays, about his distaste for Cicero's style, and indeed is the only Anti-Ciceronian who dares to express his independence with perfect frankness. "Fie upon that eloquence," he says, when speaking of Cicero, "that makes us in love with itself, and not with the thing."[20] The very beauty of Cicero's language, the faultlessness of his oratorical rhythm, is the defect he finds in him, just as Erasmus had found him too perfect. "He will sometimes," he admits, "confound his numbers; but it is seldom." "As for me, I like a cadence that falleth shorter, cut like Iambics." He may make his opposition more particular and varied in his later writings; he cannot make it more clear and positive than it is in the period between 1572 and 1576.

But he has not yet attained the characteristic independence of his matured opinions. Like Lipsius', his opposition to Cicero's sole authority is that of a school. The terms of his polemic are all Stoic

---

[20] "A Consideration upon Cicero," *Essays*, I.xxxix (xl in most modern eds.). [The main comments of Montaigne on Cicero occur in I.xxxix and II.x; on rhetoric otherwise, in I.xxv and li. The other quotations in this paragraph appear to be Croll's own translations, based on I.xxxix. Cf. *APS*, nn.2, 45; *Muret*, n.10.]

terms; the books that he reads, he says, in words that are almost identical with a later phrase of Lipsius, are only those that will make him "more *wise* and *sufficient*, not more worthy or eloquent";[21] and the authors who have won away his admiration from "the master of those who speak" are also those in whom he has studied the Stoic philosophy which meets his moral need at this time: Seneca and, in a less degree, Lucan. The "soldatesque" style of Caesar, it is true, also commands his special admiration; for what is it but the language of a great Stoic in action; but he is after all a writer, that is to say, a rhetorician, and as a model for his own imitation Seneca alone could serve his turn. Upon this model, in fact, his style was formed in his early writing, and the general character it took at that time was never radically changed, as he himself observed, even though his theory of style and his tastes passed through more than one phase of development in succeeding years. Étienne Pasquier described him as *un autre Sénèque de notre langue*, Père François Garasse as *un Sénèque en désordre*, and the careful analysis of his style by many modern critics has but confirmed these judgments of an earlier day. His style, says Sainte-Beuve, is "a tissue of metaphors," and, as regards the other conspicuous trait of a Senecan style, Pasquier has truly said of his book that it is "un vrai séminaire de belles et notables sentences."[22]

If Montaigne had advanced no further in the development of his moral and rhetorical theory than the stage he had reached in 1576, he would not have become the pioneer in a new phase of modern thought. His talent, his inimitable skill would of course have made his writings more familiar to the world than those of Muret and Lipsius, but he would still have occupied a place similar to theirs and about equal to it in the history of the rationalist movement of the age.

Doubtless his freedom from the obligations of a professional con-

[21] *Essays*, I.xxxix.

[22] [Croll failed to document the sources of these quotations. In *The Happy Beast in French Thought of the Seventeenth Century* (Baltimore, 1933), George Boas gives an account of the attack on Montaigne and Montaigne's follower, Pasquier, by Garasse and others. See also Pierre Villey, *Montaigne devant la Postérité* (Paris, 1935), and Alan M. Boase, *The Fortunes of Montaigne: A History of the Essays in France, 1580-1669* (London, 1935) and its excellent bibliography. In *The Influence of Montaigne* (New York, 1908), Grace Norton gathers comments on Montaigne and allusions to him in French and English. See also Floyd Gray, *Le Style de Montaigne* (Paris, 1958) and the excellent dissertation by Camilla Hill Hays, *Montaigne, Lecteur et Imitateur de Sénèque* (Poitiers, 1938).]

sistency was a cause that his influence was not bounded by these limitations; some would prefer to say that it was merely an effect of the native superiority of genius to any circumstances whatever, and perhaps the truest statement of all would be that his preference of an unrelated freedom to the embarrassments of a defined career was in and of itself the decisive manifestation of his genius, including all the rest as its natural consequence. At all events, he passed beyond the limits of the "new kind of learning," even at the time when Muret and Lipsius were still seeking its exact academic formulae and definitions. By the time his first volume appeared, in 1580, he had already renounced systematic stoicism—though he never moved out of the zone of intellectual and literary interests into which his stoic study had introduced him—and had found his way to the main highway of modern thought, which leads directly from Petrarch and Erasmus to the liberal scepticism of the eighteenth century. He had discovered that the progress of rationalism meant much more than a change of orthodoxies, meant nothing less in fact than the full exercise of curiosity and the free play of individual differences.[23]

A change of literary tastes kept pace with this philosophic development. Students of Montaigne's *Essais* have discovered that the publication of Amyot's translations of Plutarch's works, and particularly of *Les Œuvres Morales et Meslées* in 1572, had a decisive effect in this respect upon all his later work.[24] The full meaning of the extraordinary delight he always took thenceforth in the reading of this work cannot be discussed here: we need only observe that it was quite as much an effect as a cause of the progress that was going on in his literary opinions. In an addition to his last volume, in the edition of 1588, he said that of all the authors he knew Plutarch was the one who "best mingled art with nature,"[25] and

[23] The change of Montaigne from Stoicism to Libertinism is well treated in Fortunat Strowski, *Montaigne* (Paris, 1906; rev. 1931) and also in his *Histoire du Sentiment Religieux . . . Pascal et son Temps*, I, 28-58. Villey's *Les Sources* provides the exact details necessary. [See also Victor Giraud, *Maîtres d'Autrefois et d'Aujourd'hui* (Paris, 1912), pp. 1-54 (discusses Villey); the criticisms of Villey and Strowski in Arthur Armaingaud, "Montaigne, Socrate et Épicure," *Nouvelle Revue*, 4th S., XLII (1919), 97-104, 215-224, 309-318; Busson, *Sources*, pp. 434-459; and the works listed in *APS*, n.36 and *Muret*, n.6.]

[24] [Joseph de Zangroniz, *Montaigne, Amyot and Saliat; Étude sur les Sources des Essais* (Paris, 1906); Pierre Villey, "Amyot et Montaigne," *Revue d'Histoire Littéraire de la France*, XIV (1907), 713-727; Grace Norton, *Le Plutarque de Montaigne* (New York, 1906).]

[25] III.vi, "Des Coches," near the beginning. [In "Des Livres," (II.x), Montaigne

the phrase exactly describes the literary ideal toward which he was tending throughout his career. He was always in quest of the natural man in himself, the free individual self who should be the ultimate judge of the opinions of all the sects and schools; and as the natural complement of this philosophic enquiry he was always feeling his way at the same time toward a theory of style which should allow the greatest possible scope to the expression of differences of individual character, or, in other words, the greatest possible naturalness of style that is consistent with the artificial limits necessarily imposed upon all literary composition. We can observe through all the stages of his development a steady approximation to such a theory, but in the latest editions of his *Essais* he has worked out its formulae with surprising definiteness and has become, both as teacher and model, the initiator of a particular tendency within the general bounds of the Anti-Ciceronian movement which is destined to have even greater consequences in literary history than the Stoic model of style described by Lipsius. To this tendency we are justified in giving the name "Libertine"—though the term is new in *literary* criticism—because it not only indicates the connection between the kind of prose style which it produces and the philosophy to which it is related but also exactly describes the character of this prose style itself.

The freedom of Montaigne's literary opinions was partly due, as we have already observed, to his deliberate choice of a career free from official responsibilities: he became a "man writing for men." But it was also due in large measure to the fact that he was the first of the Anti-Ciceronian leaders to use a vernacular language in his writings, and this is so great a point of difference that it cannot be passed over in a discussion of seventeenth-century prose style.

Latin and the Vernacular Tongues 1575-1625

The last quarter of the sixteenth century was the period when the literary claims and pretensions of Latin and the modern languages were almost evenly balanced, when it was easiest to pass from one to the other without a change of subject matter or style. Before that

---

groups Plutarch with Seneca and Pliny as advocating that each writer follow his own bent, not otherwise prescribing a *Hoc Age*; in his essay in Defence of Seneca and Plutarch (II.xxxii) he states that his book "is merely framed of their spoils"; in "Des Livres," he says that they served him to "range his opinions and dress their conditions." "Their instruction is the prime and cream of philosophy, and presented in a plain, unaffected, and pertinent fashion."]

time there had been a fairly clear, though by no means a deliberate, differentiation of their uses. The chief artistic use of the vernacular in the sixteenth century had been to express the surviving medievalism of the culture of that age. It was the language, for instance, of what had been perhaps the most general medium of medieval literary expression, the sermon; it was the language of a multitude of romantically retold tales of both antiquities, in which the fading ideals and customs of chivalry were adapted to an age of courtiers; it was the language of courtly ceremonial and show; it was the medium in which the medieval book of etiquette and universal instruction enjoyed a brief revival. It reflected, in brief, the customs of a courtly life which had not been modified in its essential features by the intellectual effort of the Renaissance. On the other hand, whatever was really new and forward looking in the Renaissance found its prose expression in the ancient tongue. Some humanists, it is true, foresaw the modern uses of their mother languages: Bembo, DuBellay, Ascham, for instance. Yet their writings are not representative of the usual vernacular prose of their time; and there is little distortion in the statement that in 1550 all serious, modern thought was expressed in Latin; all that was traditional, or merely popular, in its character tended to find its way into vernacular prose.

One hundred years after that date the progress of modernism had reversed these relations in most respects. The usual language of serious criticism, and even of philosophy, had become English, French, or Italian; and, what is more important, the *subject* of literary criticism had become chiefly the vernacular languages and their usages; Latin was already the language of a dead literature, whose chief value was to enrich the native styles with romantic allusion, heroic images, and far-echoing rhythms.

In these observations there is of course nothing new, and the purpose of reviving them here is to call attention to a fact which scholarship has not yet clearly enough taken account of, that between the two *termini* that have just been mentioned there was a most interesting period in which the two languages, or the two kinds of languages, the ancient and the vernacular, were present in the minds of most well-educated people in relations of almost exact balance and equality, and there were no real differences whatever between the uses of the one and the other. This period, which extended over about two generations, one before the turn of the century, one after, was the hinge on which the great change turned, a quiet revolution, effected unconsciously in the main, it would seem, and participated in by many who would have regretted it if they had known what they were doing, but of vastly more importance than most of the changes which have been the subject of literary controversy. This period should be more carefully studied by literary historians with reference to the history of the modern languages than it has yet been, and there are two comments on it which are directly suggested by the study of "Attic" prose.[26]

The first has to do with the effect of the equalization of the languages upon the vernacular literatures and is to the effect that out of this passing state of equilibrium emerged a standard form of literary prose in every modern language, upon which all later forms are founded and out of which they have developed without radical or revolutionary change.

Italian, English, and French prose of the preceding periods has various merits which antiquarians love to point out for the reproof or exhortation of writers of the present day. But none of it is quite *standard* prose. Some of it is too popular and crude and violent. Some of it is too highly wrought and fantastically mannered. And a third kind, the smallest class, though pure and correct, is too poverty-stricken, thin, and limited in its expressive resources. The explanation of this fact of course is that, as we have just observed, men of ideas reserved all the serious, progressive, and modern uses of their intellects for expression in Latin; they felt that the spoken languages had not been sufficiently conventionalized to carry the definite meanings and logical processes of continued exposition. It was good for *concrete* uses alone. And as long as this sort of differentiation continued in force there could not be a standard prose style in either Latin or the various vernaculars, for a standard form of prose is determined by the *general* thought of the age which it expresses, its collective wisdom and experience; it is neither remotely and professionally intellectual, on the one hand, nor a simple record of facts and sensations, on the other; its function is rather to relate the varied phenomena of the external life of each period to its dominant ideas and the general philosophic trend of its mind. It is clear that no such style could make its appearance in an age when the intellect spoke one language, the senses another.

[26] Many interesting points concerning the relation of the vernacular languages and Latin in the sixteenth century are brought out by Clément in *Henri Estienne et son Œuvre Française* (Paris, 1888), pp. 197-304 and elsewhere.

On the other hand, when these two languages had become virtually interchangeable in the minds of a great many writers, as they were, for example, in the minds of Montaigne and Bacon, when one and the other came with equal ease and idiomatic freedom from their pens, it made little difference in fact which one they used, for each would have some of the characteristic quality of the other. A writer in Latin would show the colloquial and concrete qualities of his speech in his own language; a writer in French or English would derive from his Latin the rhetorical firmness, the exact use of abstraction, the logical process which the learned language imposes.

This is the phenomenon that we observe in fact in the period of Montaigne and Bacon. These are the first writers in the vernacular languages who employ a style which renders the process of thought and portrays the picturesque actuality of life with equal effect and constantly relates the one to the other, and it is in this sense that we may justify the statement that the Anti-Ciceronian leaders— Montaigne, Charron, Pasquier in France, Bacon, Hall, Jonson, Wotton in England—are the actual founders of modern prose style in their respective languages. In the works of these authors, and in none of those that precede them, we can find a style in the popular language which is at once firm, uniform, and level enough to be called a style and also adaptable enough to adjust itself to the changing life of the modern world—a style which may grow and change in later generations without losing its recognizable features.

The second comment to be made in this connection is that the character of the Anti-Ciceronian movement in prose style—whether we consider its fundamental principles or the models it proposed for imitation—was eminently favorable to the process of leveling and approximation, the virtual blending, in fact, of Latin and vernacular style that was going on during this period. Ciceronian purism had tended to keep the two kinds of speech apart from one another. Not that the Ciceronians had been unfavorable to the study of prose style in the vernacular. Bembo and Ascham, on the contrary, had studied the subject carefully. But their purism in Latin style begot a corresponding temper in their treatment of the native languages, and they mistakenly attempted to shut up Italian, French, and English within the inadequate limits of the literary vocabulary which they had acquired at the beginning of the sixteenth century. Misled by the lack of a proper historical sense which was characteristic of their school, they pretended that the vernacular tongues had already attained their full maturity and were ready to be standardized in grammars, dictionaries, and rhetorics. The central idea of the Anti-Ciceronian movement, on the other hand, was that style should be adapted to the differences of men and times. The great modern principle of unending change and development was implicit in its rhetorical theory, and many of its leaders expressed their new-found joy in freedom by indulging in strange caprices of vocabulary. English and French are suddenly deformed by a riot of freakish Latinisms, on the one hand, and expanded at the same time by new and piquant discoveries in the expressiveness of colloquial speech. The Latin of humanist and scholar of course loses its remoteness by the same process and begins to bristle with strange words picked up from Plautus, or Greek, or medieval Latin, or the living languages.

To discuss the interesting results in the style of seventeenth-century prose that followed this general prevalence of the hedge-breaking custom would require a separate essay, perhaps a volume. We must proceed here merely to point out that there was a more specific way in which Anti-Ciceronianism aided the process of leveling and the transference of the qualities of Latin prose to the various vernaculars, namely, through the character of its preferred Latin models. The Ciceronian style cannot be reproduced in English, or indeed in any modern language. The ligatures of its comprehensive period are not found in the syntax of an uninflected tongue, and the artifices necessary to supply their function must produce either fantastic distortion or insufferable bombast. This is true after all the experiments of four centuries in quest of formal beauty. Certainly in the sixteenth century no modern speech had developed an art of prose adequate to the imitation of so difficult a model, and the best that any of them could do was to reproduce the oratorical style of medieval Latin, in which only the ornaments and the simpler elements of the form of the Ciceronian pattern are employed for the purpose of formal beauty. That these could indeed be transferred with some success into vernacular forms and style had been proved in Spain and England, and even in Italy and France; but it was evident that none of the varieties of *estilo culto* developed by this process was adequate to serve as a vehicle for the advancing thought of the new age or to portray the actualities of any real world. No oratorical prose, indeed, whether based on the pure Ciceronian, or on the derived medieval, pattern, could serve for this purpose. As long as these were the preferred models a normal form of French or English prose could not appear.

But Seneca is easy. There is nothing in his syntax that could prove a bar to the expression of the ideas of a keen-minded critic of the end of the sixteenth century concerning the moral experience of his times or himself; on the contrary, the brevity of his constructions, the resolved and analytic character of his sentences, would provide such a writer with a mold exactly adapted to the character of his mind and the state of his language. Tacitus, of course, is harder reading; but the kind of difficulty that he offers would prove to be no more than a welcome stimulus and challenge to the trained wits of rationalists like Lipsius, Bacon, Malvezzi, Gracián, and Balzac. In brief, ancient Anti-Ciceronianism worked in a *resolved* style, and the perfect success with which its manner was transferred to French, Italian, Spanish, and English style during the early seventeenth century is proof of its fitness to serve as the model on which a standard modern prose could be formed.

Finally, it is to be observed that the equilibrium between the languages determines the sources from which the student of the Anti-Ciceronian movement must draw his knowledge of contemporary opinion. He must learn to disregard linguistic boundary lines. He must use the Latin discussions of contemporary and ancient Latin style, discussions in Latin of contemporary vernacular style (and these are frequent until the middle of the seventeenth century), and of course more and more as time goes on, discussions of vernacular tendencies in the vernacular; and he must learn that all of these are of equal value. It has already been seen that the beginnings of the movement were in humanistic Latin prose, in the works of Erasmus, Muret, Lipsius; and naturally the theory and criticism of it are found in the same place. But it is somewhat surprising to discover that, a whole generation after the balances have tipped in favor of the literary use of the vernacular, criticism of the vernacular tendencies in prose style continues to appear in Latin. Descartes, for instance, writes to Balzac in Latin an illuminating letter concerning the French style of the time, and Bacon was certainly thinking of English, French, and Italian style in the paragraph concerning recent prose which he added to his Latin translation of the *Advancement of Learning* in 1622.[27] The student

[27] See *Lipse*, IV (p. 38 and n.).

must learn, in short, that as far as style is concerned there was no difference in the mind of this period between Latin prose, on the one hand, and English, French, Italian, or Spanish, on the other: Lipsius writes to Montaigne of his style, after reading his first volume of *Essais*, in similar terms to those he had used in writing at an earlier date to Muret of his new manner of writing.[28]

Nor are these facts valuable only as indicating a method of study. They are of first-rate importance in the history of the movement itself as showing that in the minds of most of its leaders it was in the classical and not in the popular tradition. On this point there can be no question. Even when the custom of writing prose in the native languages had become very common, as it did during the decades 1590-1610, most of those who fell in with the new tendency felt that they were following in the train of Politian, Erasmus, and Muret, and ultimately of Seneca and Tacitus. They thought of their vernacular style as having come over to them from the Latin of the humanists or as directly derived from the Latin style of antiquity; and they seem usually to have been unaware of any relation, either of opposition or evolution, with the vernacular prose of the preceding age.[29]

The only very important exception to this general rule is to be found in the critical utterances of Montaigne and of certain writers, like Étienne Pasquier, for instance, who were directly influenced by him. Montaigne was well read in the vernacular literature of the sixteenth century and even of an earlier period, and he was too humane a critic of life to pass by the true mirrors of his age without studying his own features in them too, even though his grand enthusiasms are all for certain of the ancients. His criticisms, it is

---

[28] Lipsius to Montaigne, 1588, *Ep. Misc.*, II.41, in *Opera Omnia* (Antwerp, 1637), II. 86. [For a translation of what Lipsius wrote to Montaigne, see p. 66.] See also the correspondence between Mlle. de Gournay and Lipsius in which the lady writes in French, the savant in Latin; yet the style is of the same mold. Concerning this correspondence see Paul Bonnefon, *Montaigne et ses Amis* (Paris, 1898), II, 334-352.

[29] [E.g. Ascham in a Latin epistle sent to Bishop Stephen Gardiner with a copy of *Toxophilus* (1545) says that in contrast with the artistic license prevalent in vernacular prose, he has "taken pains to depart far and differ from almost the entire rout of English authors. . . . For indeed they have a sufficiency of neither dialectic for reasoning nor rhetoric for the embellishment of style; and thus in our vulgar tongue they strive to be, not familiar and appropriate, but rather outlandish and strange" (Ascham, *Works*, ed. Giles, I, 79; cf. Ryan, *Ascham*, p. 60). It should be remembered that Cicero was neither unknown nor uninfluential in the Middle Ages and, on the other hand, that relatively little sixteenth-century English prose is truly Ciceronian.]

true, are too few and inexplicit to be satisfying, but they tend to show that he regarded the ornate prose and poetry of the past age with something of the same contempt that he felt for Bembo and other Ciceronianizing Latinists. We wish that he had been more definite in telling us why he scorned Guevara's famous *Golden Book*,[30] but we may be reasonably certain that the poverty of their content and the richness of their stylistic ornament were equal causes of his distaste. We should like to be certain too that he is thinking of the Spanish prosaists and the style of Guevara and Mexia[31] when he speaks of "l'affectation et la recherche des fantastiques élévations espagnoles et petrarchistes,"[32] for the association of Petrarchanism in verse and the *estilo culto* of Guevara and Lyly in prose as two similar manifestations of the medieval love of rhetoric would be exactly what we should expect in an Anti-Ciceronian and rationalist like Montaigne. But the passage as a whole does not permit us to say with *certainty* that he was thinking of Spanish *prose*, and we must be content to know that he did actually dislike both these kinds of vernacular writing. The *franche naïveté* of Froissart was, on the other hand, wholly to his taste, and if he seems not to understand the real importance of Rabelais he at least enjoyed him.[33]

✧ IV ✧

BACON

(a) *Bacon and Tacitus*

There is only one other author of nearly equal importance with Lipsius and Montaigne in the history of the establishment of the Attic tradition—Francis Bacon. He was not quite the first professed Anti-Ciceronian in England. Thomas Nashe and Gabriel Harvey

[30] "Des Destries." [Croll refers to Antonio de Guevara's *Libro Aureo* as adapted by John Bouchier, Baron Berners, from the French version of René Bertaut and entitled *The Golden Boke of Marcus Aurelius* (1534; ed. J. M. G. Olivares, Berlin, 1916); for Guevara's possible influence on Montaigne, see Louis Clément, "Antoine de Guevara, ses Lecteurs et ses Imitateurs Français au XVIe Siècle," *RHL*, VII (1900), 590-602 and VIII (1901), 214-233.]

[31] [Pedro Mexia or Mejía whose *Silva* influenced Montaigne. See G. L. Michaut, "The Spanish Sources of Certain Sixteenth Century Writers," *MLN*, XLIII (1928), 157-163, and Janet Girvan (Scott) Espiner, "Quelques Érudits Français du XVIe Siècle et l'Espagne," *RLC*, xx (1940-1946), 203-209, for the influence of both Guevara and Mexia.]

[32] II.x, "Des Livres."

[33] See Villey, *Sources*, I, 204.

undertook a vigorous attack during the nineties against both Ciceronian Latin and the ornate vernacular style of Lyly and his school,
each of them seeking an escape from formalism through the
method of extravagance and licentious freedom of style, and there
are interesting similarities between their efforts and those of some
Continental "libertines" of the same period. But neither of these
writers had philosophy or authority enough to lead his age, and their
attack on tradition was soon lost sight of in the great success of
Bacon's more imposing offensive movement.

As a historian, Bacon offers useful aid to the student of prose
style. In a passage in the *Advancement of Learning* (most of which
was probably written some years before its publication in 1605),
he has sketched the history of the Ciceronian cult and described
the causes that produced it. He is perhaps following a faulty sketch
in one of Muret's orations (delivered at Rome in 1575, in introducing a course in Juvenal), but his account is so much more
complete and correct that it may be considered the first attempt to
place the Renaissance in historical perspective.[34] (Should we add
that his success is a sign that the Renaissance has already passed or
is passing? Perhaps so.) Ciceronianism is his illustration of that
distemper of learning "when words are valued more than matter";
its origin, he finds, was in the excessive zeal of the scholars of the
sixteenth century for an exact knowledge of the words of antiquity,
and he attributes this in turn—acutely enough but not altogether
correctly—to the controversial needs created by the Reformation,
and the search for authority among the Fathers of the Church. He
quotes a joke from Erasmus' *Ciceronianus*, names as leading
Ciceronians since Erasmus' time Ascham and Car, the Protestant
German humanist Sturm, and the "Portugal bishop Osorius" (the
latest exemplar of the pure cult), describes their style with his usual
analytic skill, and closes with the striking statement, which perhaps
is due to hints in Erasmus' dialogue, that if he should have to
choose between the "weight" of the scholastic philosophers and the
"copie" of the rhetorical humanists he would take the former.

The words of this passage are probably familiar to most literary
scholars, but this is not true of the supplement to it which Bacon
added when his work was translated into Latin and published as
De Augmentis Scientiarum in 1622. The new passage provides a

[34] [*Advancement*, ed. Wright, I.iv.2; *Lipse*, n.40; Croll discusses Muret's oration
in *Muret*, III (pp. 148-149).]

fairly exact measure of the amount of water that has run under the bridge in three or four decades of literary history, and has an additional interest as an illustration of a new kind of curiosity, in the men of this generation, which enables them to turn upon themselves and recognize their own changes of taste and temper. Their perception of historical perspectives has made them more observant of change and progress in their own world; a new intelligence is emerging from the methods of sceptical inquiry taught by Petrarch, Erasmus, and Montaigne. In translation, Bacon's words are as follows:

Somewhat sounder is another form of style,—yet neither is it innocent of some vain shows,—which is likely to follow in time upon this copious and luxuriant oratorical manner. It consists wholly in this: that the words be sharp and pointed; sentences concised; a style in short that may be called "turned" rather than fused. Whence it happens that everything dealt with by this kind of art seems rather ingenious than lofty. *Such a style is found in Seneca very freely used, in Tacitus and the younger Pliny more moderately; and it is beginning to suit the ears of our age as never before.* And indeed it is pleasant to subtle and low-ranging minds (for by means of it they conciliate the honor due to letters); however better-trained judgments disapprove it; and it may be looked upon as a distemper of learning, in as far as it is accompanied by a taste for mere words and their concinnity.[35]

This passage tells admirably what the Anti-Ciceronian movement is and how it arose. It describes the form of the new style and provides a motive for its rapid diffusion at the beginning of the seventeenth century. Not only this, however; it also establishes the parallel between this contemporary Anti-Ciceronianism and that of the first century, both in the character of its style and in its relation to the oratorical prose of the preceding century. The only point we miss is that Bacon does not clearly say that the new tendency is due to actual imitation of the ancients; and this defect is easily accounted for by Bacon's unwillingness to admit the effective survival of the principle of imitation and authority either in himself or his age; it is of a piece with the unfortunate, and sometimes mean,

[35] [*De Aug.* I, *Works* (1868), I, 452; see *Lipse*, n.40 for Wats' strikingly different translation of this passage.]

reticence he displays concerning his own great obligations to intellectual masters of the ancient and modern worlds.

And in fact, notwithstanding the apparent cool detachment of his criticism, Bacon knows very well that he is here describing his own style. He has left sufficient evidence in his own utterances of the truth of his secretary's statement that Tacitus, Caesar, and Seneca were his favorite authors, and that the order of his preference was that in which these three names are here mentioned. Nor have the critics required the aid of such statements; the resemblance of Bacon's style to that of his masters has often been observed by them. The praise he bestows on Seneca's style, says one of them, *ad ipsum Verulamium haud immerito detorqueri possit*. He was attracted to Seneca and Tacitus, this writer continues, by kinship of talent; and it was in the assiduous reading of these authors that he cultivated his taste for a style of acute and condensed brevity, ornamented, at the same time, with the riches of rhetoric and an almost poetic splendor of words.[36]

How are we to account then for the derogatory, or at least balancing, tone of the passage we have just quoted? Properly interpreted, it may serve as an aid to a more exact description of Bacon's tastes and the character of his literary influence than has yet been attempted, or to a correction of some misconceptions concerning them. It has been the custom to place Seneca first among Bacon's models and favorites, but this is an error. When his words are carefully examined, it is apparent that what he says in discommendation of the style "freely used" by Seneca is all directed toward "vain shows" and verbal ornament, the same fault of undue love of concinnity, in short, which was a cause of the revolt against Cicero's form of rhetoric. This is somewhat puzzling, especially in view of the fact that Seneca himself had made current among Anti-Ciceronian critics the phrases they habitually used to express their contempt for the sensuous beauty of the balanced Ciceronian phrase: *non ornamentum virile concinnitas*, and so forth. But the reader of Seneca can reconcile the contradiction. For that very literary and rhetorical essayist customarily framed his *antitheses* and *argutiae* in a balanced form, different indeed from that of the copious oratorical style, but yet capable of becoming almost as transparently artificial. At its best an excellent literary form for the insinuation of subtle

---

[36] See Paul Jacquinet, *Francisci Baconi de Re Litteraria Judicia* (Paris, 1863), pp. 98ff.

shades of thought and fine distinctions, at its worst it is indeed no more than "mere words and their concinnity." And it must be added that Bacon has in mind the imitators of Seneca more than Seneca himself: almost certainly Lipsius' Latinity; probably the English style of Bishop Hall's *Epistles* and other moral writings; perhaps also the Senecan manner of a number of English essayists who had written since his own first volume of 1597. All these writers had shown how easily the imitation of Seneca could descend to verbal ingenuity or mere pun on occasions when the idea was not worthy of the artifice bestowed upon it.

The faults of Tacitus and his imitators were clear enough to seventeenth-century critics, but they did not run in this direction. Obscurity, enigma, contortion are not qualities of style that comport with concinnity and the study of the abstract charm of words. Evidently Bacon is drawing a vertical line of distinction down through the area of Anti-Ciceronianism in addition to the other transverse line that divides it as a whole from the Ciceronian types of prose; and when this is observed and confirmed by a reference to the qualities of his own style, his literary comments and judgments throughout his works become more consistent. It becomes clear that he has not expressed anywhere a positive approval of Seneca's subject matter or style, though he refers to his letters as a model for the new essay form and cites his father as skilful in antitheses.[37] But on the contrary he has praised Tacitus in a private letter to Sir Fulke Greville, as the first of historians, and again, in the *Temporis Partus Masculus*, with the characteristic emphasis of his laconic style: "Many like the moral doctrines of Aristotle and Plato; but of Tacitus it may be said that he utters the very morals of life itself."[38] The former of these passages is worthy of a careful consideration. He says that history is of most use for those who wish to know only humanity, and continues: "For poets, I can commend none, being resolved to be ever a stranger to them. Of orators, if I must choose any, it shall be Demosthenes, both for the

[37] ["as a model"—in the cancelled dedication to Prince Henry intended for the 2nd ed. of the Essays. The citation of the "father" (more probably, uncle), Lucius Annaeus Seneca is in *De Aug.* VI.iii just before the examples of antitheses (*Works*, I, 688).]

[38] *Aristotelis et Platonis moralis plerique mirantur; sed Tacitus magis vivas morum observationes spirat* (*Works*, III, 538). [Croll's misquotation, *admirant* instead of *mirantur*, has been corrected.]

argument he handles, and for that his eloquence is more proper for a statesman than Cicero's. Of all stories, I think Tacitus simply the best; Livy very good; Thucydides above any of the writers of Greek matters."[39] In every respect this is a characteristic Anti-Ciceronian utterance: in its rejection of poetry from useful studies, in its preference of Tacitus to Livy (along with which goes a liking for Thucydides), and in its contemptuous treatment of oratory, partly veiled by the exaltation of Demosthenes above Cicero. Finally, it is to be noted that the extraordinary enthusiasm of the writer for history—which virtually means politics when connected with the influence of Tacitus—associates him with a particular phase of the Anti-Ciceronian complex which had already declared itself in the programs of Muret and Lipsius. It is true that at about the same time that Bacon was writing these words he must also have been writing the passage in an early section of the *Advancement of Learning* in which he speaks without qualification of Cicero as the first, or second, of orators, Livy as the first of historians, Virgil and Varro as first in their kinds of all those known to men.[40] But the apparent conflict only gives us the opportunity to note a fact that every student of one subject must take account of: that the Anti-Ciceronian critics, even the boldest of them, always keep an Augustan and Ciceronian orthodoxy in reserve; and even Montaigne will admit that if an abstract literary excellence, independent of the practical and moral uses of the works in which it is displayed, be the basis of one's judgment, the Augustan Age and the ages that resemble it are on a higher plane than any others. It is sometimes necessary to surprise them in the more confidential tone of letters and casual notes in order to discover the full range of their heterodoxy.

In Bacon's case, the frequency of his quotation from Tacitus may be accepted as evidence of his preference of that author to all others, for an acquaintance with Tacitus was not in that age to be taken for granted, nor was the citation of his difficult phrases a literary convention, as was that of the Senecan "sentences." On

[39] I accept the attribution of this letter to the hand of Bacon suggested by James Spedding, *The Letters and the Life of Francis Bacon* (London, 1861-1874), II, 2-6 [the quoted passage is in II, 25], though it was sent in the name of Essex. It seems to me impossible that Essex should have been so familiar with the new trend of thought and studies in the nineties as the writer shows himself to be.

[40] *Advancement*, ed. Wright, I.ii.8.

the contrary, it was the mark of an individual taste or a peculiar initiation.[41] Bacon's influence, like his own prose style, can best be explained in terms of his admiration and imitation of Tacitus, and the point has had to be elaborated at some length for the reason that it has a special bearing upon the development of seventeenth-century English style. The other models of Anti-Ciceronian prose were already known to Englishmen: Hall and the letter writers were familiarizing them with the Senecan manner of Lipsius, and the intimate whimsical vein of Montaigne was beginning to be domesticated in their own prose. From these sources they could learn most of what Anti-Ciceronianism had to teach concerning the expression of acute wit by ingenious rhetoric. But the desire for wit and ingenuity was only one phase of seventeenth-century taste. Combined with it was a desire for ceremonious dignity, an ideal of deliberate and grave demeanor, which was partly, no doubt, an inheritance from the courtly past but was modified and indeed largely created by the profound moral experience which the new age was undergoing. A prose style that should adequately express this age must contrive, therefore, to mingle elements that in any other period would appear oddly contrasted. It must be at once ingenious and lofty, intense yet also profound, acute, realistic, revealing, but at the same time somewhat grave and mysterious. It must have in short that curious sublimity which is felt in the painting of El Greco, in the sermons and letters of Donne, and in certain sculptures of Bernini.

Seneca—its favorite author—might *suggest* the ideal manner;

[41] [The conventional view is expressed by Henry Savile whose final note to the *Life of Agricola* in his translation of Tacitus, *The Ende of Nero and Beginning of Galba. Fower Bookes of the Histories of Cornelius Tacitus* (Oxford, 1591) refers to "that Heresie of Style begun by *Seneca, Quintillian*, the *Plinies*, and *Tacitus*." It is noteworthy that Savile links Seneca and Tacitus, for Williamson, partly in criticism of Croll, argues that Tacitus' style "offers more likeness than difference when compared with 'Seneca's own style—disconnected, pointed, antithetic, metaphorical and piquant'" (*Senecan Amble*, p. 187, quoting J. W. Duff, *A Literary History of Rome in the Silver Age* [London, 1927], p. 108). Cf. Williamson, pp. 82-83, 113-115, 127, 187-190, and passim for refinements on Croll's ideas, especially those about Bacon, Seneca, and Tacitus.

Croll's remarks should not obscure the fact that Tacitus was popular in the first half of the seventeenth century (cf. Williamson, p. 191), because of his mastery of statecraft and court wisdom, his poignant significance of utterance, his moral sententiousness, and his individualism. Tacitus' popularity was a European phenomenon which began about 1575 with Lipsius' ed. of his works and Diego Hurtado de Mendoza's account of the War of Granada, which imitated the historian's style and method.]

but he was too superficial, too familiar, to furnish a complete model
of it. Lucan's nodosity and rhetorical pomp served better as a guide
to the poets; and Tacitus, if he had not been too difficult (and
indeed too novel, for he had not been widely read in the sixteenth
century) would have been the usual exemplar of English prose
style. Bacon's great service to English prose was that he naturalized
a style in which ingenious obscurity and acute significance are the
appropriate garb of the mysteries of empire, and by means of his
example the Tacitean strain became familiar to many English
writers who were not sufficiently trained in Tacitus himself to
imitate his style directly.[42]

(b) *Science and Seventeenth-Century Prose*

Besides domesticating the style of Tacitus in English prose,
Bacon aided in various technical ways which cannot be described
here in the formulation of a new rhetorical program.[43] But of course
his greatest service to the prose movement of his time was not
directly and expressly a literary one. It is to be found in his contributions to the great intellectual movement of which Anti-Ciceronianism is but the rhetorical and literary expression.

The progress of rationalism during the sixteenth century had
been rapid, and it had been increasingly so as the century drew to
an end. But the complete triumph which it was to obtain was still
adjourned by a partial lack of co-operation among its leaders in
the various fields of intellectual endeavor. Many of them were
specialists, of course, who failed to understand as clearly as the
defenders of orthodoxy in the universities and courts did how closely
their various subjects were related to one another in the general
interests of progress. Cujas and Alciati, for instance, were jurists;
Ramus' studies ranged widely, but he impressed himself on his age

---

[42] On the sublimity of Tacitus, see an interesting passage in François de La
Mothe le Vayer, *Jugemens sur les Anciens et Principaux Historiens Grecs et
Latins* in his *Œuvres* (1685), III, 208: "Son genre d'écrire grave (etc.)." [Cf.
Muret, III (pp. 153-154 and n.64).]

[43] To avoid repetition I have omitted several points concerning Bacon's rhetorical theory which are more or less developed in *Muret* [II, par. 5 and the second
paragraph following n.9; III, par. 7; nn. 33, 43, 47, 54, 61, 65, 66 and, by implication,
passim]. Most important of these perhaps is Bacon's constant dependence upon
Aristotle's *Rhetoric*—often a peculiar sign of Anti-Ciceronian intention. There is
need of a thorough and complete study of Bacon's rhetorical writings [the need
is largely satisfied by Wallace, Crane, and Howell, cited in *APS*, n.38 and *Lipse*,
n.9. The account of the progress of rationalism which follows in the present
essay is paralleled in *Muret*, II; for relevant bibliography, see *Muret*, n.6].

as a logician; Montaigne was a moralist pure and simple; and though Muret and Lipsius were both fully aware of the revolutionary implications in their methods of study, they were daunted by the formidable front of orthodoxy. Intellectually free, they were involved in practical relations with the powers of conservatism which compelled them to protect themselves by disingenuous compromises and a shocking Machiavellianism. Of course their hesitations and concealments were only the usual marks of all movements of radicalism and innovation; a forward tendency never presents as solid a front as the established system that it is bound to conflict with, because its aims are partly concealed in the future and no one can tell how the various elements that co-operate in it will relate and adjust themselves in the final settlement. But reformers had more than the usual reasons for fear and vacillation in the sixteenth century because the orthodoxies of all kinds, religious, political, intellectual, and literary, were more than usually aware at that time of the community of their interests and more effectively united in self-defense. What was needed at the end of the century was such an appraisement of the situation as would give an equal consciousness of their common aims, and equal clearness of purpose, to the champions of the more progressive and positive modes of thought.

This was the most important part of the task undertaken by Bacon in the *Advancement of Learning* and the *Novum Organum*. It is now generally recognized that the materials of which these works were made were most of them old and familiar; many of them had even been worked up by his predecessors into almost the form in which Bacon used them. Aristotelianism, medieval scholasticism, Barthollism, Platonism, Ciceronianism, Euphuism, and whatever other shadowy phantoms of reality had haunted the Renaissance, had already been severally exposed to the criticism of reason. But Bacon gathered them all together within the limits of a single survey and covered them all over with one narrow *hic jacet*. After that they were as pallid and ridiculous as ghosts astray in the open daylight; they could no longer frighten anyone.

But that was not all that he did for the new rationalism. He put the vigorous new natural sciences of his age at the center of all his projects for the progress of knowledge. The program of education announced by Muret and elaborated by Lipsius included only the two branches of moral philosophy (the *sapientia,* or private morality, of the ancient Stoics and Peripatetics, and the *prudentia*, or worldly wisdom, which they studied in Tacitus, Machiavelli, and other ancient and modern politicians), with the rhetoric appropriate to them. The effect of Bacon's writings was to put natural science in a definite place in this program—not the first place, it is true, because the century that began with Montaigne and ended with La Bruyère and Halifax was above all else the century of moral philosophy—but yet in a recognized position of authority, from which it could exercise a constant influence upon the moral researches of the age by clarifying, illustrating, defining their method of procedure. This modification had such important literary effects that it must not be passed over here with a mere mention.

The method introduced by Lipsius and Montaigne in the study of the moral situation of their time was in fact the method of science. It does not appear that these philosophers thought of it in that way or were in any profound way affected by the scientific studies that preceded Bacon's work: their intellectual houses were without windows, or had very narrow ones. But they were compelled by the impulse of their positivistic purposes to adopt the same method of experiment and induction in their own subjects that has since produced such astounding results in natural science. These philosophers were in revolt, not only against the medieval forms of thought, as they are often said to have been, but also against the aims of the Renaissance itself as they had chiefly displayed themselves hitherto. For the effort of their own century had been devoted, exactly like that of the more remote past, chiefly to the rearing of conspicuous philosophic constructions which had no foundations in immediate observation or experience. "Men have despised," said Bacon, "to be conversant in ordinary and common matters . . . ; but contrariwise they have compounded sciences chiefly of a certain resplendent or lustrous matter, chosen to give glory either to the subtility of disputations or to the eloquence of discourses."[44] They themselves took the humbler task of searching these glorious Houses of Pride to their sandy foundations. Nor did they pretend to raise other constructions in their stead, except only such modest shelters as would serve their immediate moral needs. To be conversant in ordinary and common matters was their only boast. To distinguish the facts of moral experience with critical and

[44] *Advancement of Learning*, in *Works* (1868), III, 418 [ed. Wright, II.xx.2. Croll's misquotation, "either to give glory to the subtlety" has been corrected].

inquiring eyes, to record their observations with the acuteness and exactness of the new literary style they had devised for this purpose, this was an intellectual exercise well adapted to their subtle wits; and it was a task moreover that afforded them the thrill of novel adventure. In short, the intellectual program of the seventeenth century was the scientific work of moral observation and delineation, and Montaigne's avowal of his purpose to portray for the first time exactly what the thing is that goes by the name of a man is echoed at the other end of the century with only a slight difference of tone, in La Bruyère's truly scientific program, "the *description* of man."

Bacon therefore did not have to teach the method of science to the moralists of his age, for they had already learned it. But the new studies in natural history which Bacon helped to make popular were of great aid to them in their own work, because it trained them, and of course their audiences too, in the habit of exact observation, sharp definition, and clear classification which were necessary for their purpose. Bacon himself provides an excellent illustration of scientific method in the realm of moral observation; for the aphorisms, *Antitheta*, "topics," "colours of good and evil," etc., from which, as from a spinner's bobbin,[45] he says, he unwound the thread of his essays, are pieces of scientific apparatus used in a moralist's workshop. They are the notes he has taken at the moment when the experiment was on and observation was keenest and then allocated, by a rough and ready scheme of classification, among certain headings and subheadings which will make them available for future reference. To enumerate the works of seventeenth-century morality that were composed by this method would be tedious: Descartes' *Meditations*, Wotton's *Aphorisms of Education*, and countless other works display the method even in their form; and it is but slightly veiled by a more elaborate manner in Browne's *Religio Medici*; Pascal, La Bruyère, Temple, and Halifax all employed it.

To distinguish rhetorical from intellectual process in the writings of professed naturalists is to divide between the bark and the tree; whatever the motions of their minds, they will betray themselves in their style. But some of the results of the addition of science to the intellectual program may be traced most clearly in the history of prose style. They are chiefly of two opposite kinds, which finally

[45] [The misprint, *bottom* for *bobbin*, has been corrected.]

came into open conflict in the second half of the century. At first the natural sciences tended to give greater imaginative range and freedom to the new Attic prose. We may observe this phenomenon most clearly in the writings of certain professed men of science who became literary men and stylists through an interesting blending in their thought of the ideas of Bacon and Montaigne, students of medicine especially, like Sir Thomas Browne and Robert Burton or the Parisian doctor Guy Patin, who bring into new and curious relations the results of their physical explorations of man's nature and the moral speculations of their time. Essentially moralists, as all men of their age were, they were able to add to the common stock of ideas and images a wealth of curious detail derived from their professional pursuits and their knowledge of unfamiliar facts. The courageous scepticism of the new kind of morality and the rhetorical audacity that accompanied it appealed equally to their tastes, and they contributed in their turn out of their mastery of physiological research to the effects of curiosity and novelty on which so much of the success of the new prose depended. In two writers in whom we may fairly describe the union of scientific and moral interest as perfect and equal, in Sir Thomas Browne and Pascal, we may observe at their highest development the powers of intellectual imagination which might be born of this union.

As the century advanced, however, it became apparent that science was not to remain on the side of poetry and the imagination; on the contrary, it allied itself more and more closely with the movement for clarity and common sense which was gathering strength from so many different sources. A well-known pronunciamento of the Royal Society in England expressly dissociated the literary aims of that scientific body from the rhetoric of Bacon and aligned them with the new taste for a plain and clear style. At the same time, in France, the influence of Descartes was gradually making itself felt even among those who were not at all willing to accept his philosophy: *imagination* began to be a word of derision; Malebranche taught an almost geometrical use of reason as a corrective of its evil influence; the teachers of Port Royal found in logic the way to a Christian plainness and purity of style; and the quality that distinguishes the style of La Bruyère, and even the nobler language of Pascal, is a strictly scientific precision rather than those occasional, and as it were accidental, triumphs of revelation which are effected by an ambitious imagination or a roving fancy.

✧ V ✧

Conclusion

Muret, Lipsius, Montaigne, and Bacon, though the period of their collective activity covers three quarters of a century, belong to a single generation in the development of Renaissance culture, the generation in which modern rationalism definitely declared itself as the doctrine of the future, and the new, the Anti-Ciceronian, form of prose style assumed its place in the world of letters. But Muret belongs at the beginning of this generation; he is partly the pioneer, partly the founder of its intellectual program. The three philosophers we have considered in the preceding pages lived in the full flower of its career, when its conflict with the forces of the past was virtually over. Rationalism had now won its victory, and displayed that tendency to divide into various schools or phases which always appears when a general idea mingles with the several elements of a varied intellectual life and takes different color from each of them.

In this phase of its history Attic prose divides into three main forms, or perhaps we should call them merely tendencies toward distinct forms, which displayed themselves more conspicuously in the generation that followed, and even can be distinguished, though less clearly, in the "classical" prose which developed in a succeeding generation out of seventeenth-century Attic. Lipsius, Montaigne, and Bacon each represents one of these three forms or tendencies, and the discussion of their ideas has perhaps made clear what they are. A specific statement will serve, however, to make more definite what has already been said of them.

First in order of importance is a tendency due to the prevalence of Stoic philosophy. The prose in which this tendency is manifest can best be known as prose of the Stoic model. "Senecan prose" would be more definite, but it would sometimes include too much, and on the other hand it would fail to indicate the full scope of Stoic imitation. Lipsius is as clearly the founder of this style as he is of the Neo-Stoic philosophy which usually accompanied it in the first half of the century.

To the student of events beyond the limits of the seventeenth

200

century, a tendency in style associated with the sceptical or "libertine" thought of that century and especially with the influence of Montaigne, would seem worthy of the first place in order of importance. This we can only call "libertine" prose, whether we consider its philosophical implications or its rhetorical theories and form. The groundwork of this style is the Senecan pattern, which is so much more apparent in the Stoic model; but it aims at freedom, and chooses several other writers, ancient and modern, as the models by which it seeks, through the method of imitation, to escape from the method of imitation. Rabelais is the chief of these. Montaigne adds the taste for Plutarch's essays; and the form of Montaigne's own style, from 1600 onward, mingles with that of Rabelais' in almost equal proportions in the prevailing forms of libertine style in the seventeenth century.

Next to these in the favor of the age was the prose of "politicians" and students of "prudential wisdom": Bacon, Malvezzi, Gracián, Grotius, and a host of others, who get their rhetorical and often their political ideas chiefly from Tacitus.

To these three major forms must be added a tendency which cannot be separated from any of them but manifests itself everywhere as the peculiar mark of the genius of the seventeenth century, a tendency observable in writers as normal as Bacon, Browne, and Balzac, but apparent in its full efflorescence in the letters of Donne, the essays of Gracián and Malvezzi and many of their fellow countrymen, the histories of Pierre Mathieu, and many similar works. For this tendency there is unfortunately no convenient name in English. "Metaphysical" is even a less happy term to describe the kinds of prose in which it appears than the related kinds of poetry, and there seems to be no possibility of making a practicable adjective or noun in English from the continental terms *concettismo*, etc. It may be known as the "prose of imaginative conceit" in order that we may keep in line with the terms of current criticism. But I am tempted to make the bold innovation of calling it "the baroque style" in prose, for no other term will so exactly describe its characteristic qualities.

In the three forms enumerated above (with due regard to the *concettistic* tendency in each of them) may be ranged all the Attic prose of the century from 1575 to 1675, and that is to say all its characteristic prose, except the writings of one or two great individualists who escape the influence of their time; and it is upon

THE ANTI-CICERONIAN MOVEMENT

the lines laid down in this classification that the further study of seventeenth-century prose style must be conducted. What is now necessary is a thorough survey of Stoic prose, libertine prose, and Tacitean prose separately, each treated with reference to its philosophical theory, its preferred models in antiquity and modern times, its relation to the culture of the age, and its rhetorical forms. Only the outlines of such a survey can be suggested, of course, in the study of individual authors—even of such representative and influential leaders as Muret, Lipsius, Montaigne, and Bacon.

Foreword to Essay Five

Croll's abandonment of his earlier term "Attic," with its associations of simplicity and plain brevity, for the controversial title "baroque" indicates an even greater commitment than before to the idea of the "self-conscious modernism" of the Renaissance.[1] After the previous essays, there is some disingenuousness in using a word connected with the greatest decorative period Europe has known to describe a movement which professed to be antirhetorical. "Baroque," however, contains for Croll exactly the suggestions he wanted of

[1] René Wellek, "The Concept of Baroque in Literary Scholarship," cited in the Foreword to *APL*, should be consulted for a basic bibliography of works on the baroque. See also W. Stechow, "The Baroque: A Critical Summary," *JAAC*, xiv (1955), 171-174, and "Definitions of the Baroque in the Visual Arts," *JAAC*, v (1946), 109-115; William Halewood, "The Uses of the Term 'Baroque' in Modern English Literary Criticism," Diss. Univ. Minnesota, *DA*, xx (1959), 2290; Bernard C. Heyl, "Meanings of Baroque," *JAAC*, xix (1961), 275-287. General studies of the problem, all having a bibliographical value, may be found in the first chapter of Giuliano Pellegrini, *Barocco Inglese* (Florence, 1953), and the ever-increasing number of works by Helmut A. Hatzfeld: "A Critical Survey of Recent Baroque Theories," *Boletín del Instituto Caro y Cuervo*, v (1948), 1-33; "A Clarification of the Baroque Problem in the Romance Literatures," *CL*, i (1949), 113-139; *Literature through Art* (New York, 1952); "The Baroque from the Viewpoint of the Literary Historian," *JAAC*, xiv (1955), 156-164; "Italia, Spagna e Francia nello Sviluppo della Letteratura Barocca," *Lettere Italiane*, ix (1957), i-29; *Der Gegenwärtige Stand der Romanistischen Barockforschung*, Bayerische Akademie der Wissenschaften, Philosophische-historische Klasse: Sitzungberichte, iv (Munich, 1961); also R. A. Sayce, "The Use of the Term Baroque in French Literary History," *CL*, x (1958), 246-253; Roy Daniells, "Baroque Form in English Literature," *UTQ*, xiv (1944-45), 393-408, and *Milton, Mannerism and Baroque* (Toronto, 1963); Gustav R. Hocke, *Manierismus in der Literatur* (Hamburg, 1959); Paul Meissner, *Die Geisteswissenschaftlichen Grundlagen des Englischen Literaturbarocks* (Munich, 1934); Part iii of James V. Mirollo, *The Poet of the Marvelous, Giambattista Marino* (New York, 1963); Lowry Nelson, Jr., *Baroque Lyric Poetry* (New Haven, 1961); Harold M. Priest, *Renaissance and Baroque Lyrics* (Evanston, 1962); Frank J. Warnke, *European Metaphysical Poetry* (New Haven, 1961); also the Baroque issue of *Cahiers du Sud*, xlii (1955); *La Critica Stilistica e il Barocco Letterario: Atti del Secondo Congresso Internazionale di Studi Italiani* (Florence, 1958); and *Rettoria e Barocco: Atti del III Congresso Internazionale di Studi Umanistica*, ed. Enrico Castello (Rome, 1955). From among the applications of the term to prose, the following may be mentioned: R. A. Sayce, "Baroque Elements in Montaigne," *French Studies*, viii (1954), 1-16; Imbrie Buffum, *Studies in the Baroque from Montaigne to Rotrou* (New Haven, 1957); Helmut A. Hatzfeld, "Per una Definizione dello Stile di Montaigne," *Convivium*, n.s. i (1964), 284-290; Sister Julie Maggioni, *The Pensées of Pascal: A Study in Baroque Style*, Catholic University Studies in Romance Languages and Literatures, Vol. xxxix (Washington, D.C., 1950). "Baroque" as a literary term is so involved in defining itself and so committed to metaphorical descriptions of literary qualities and analogies between the arts that its value is highly questionable.

the human mind struggling bravely with resistant masses of thought, and producing in the effort masterpieces of asymmetric design. It has proved impossible to write about the curt and the loose styles without employing Croll's distinctions, but Williamson has found the "desire for speed of communication, for returns on one's time" sufficiently explains much Senecan brevity, without invoking the craving for expressiveness which Croll sees everywhere in baroque style.

With twice the space available it would be difficult to do justice to Williamson's revisions of Croll's work. Fundamentally, they consist in making more complicated the overlapping of styles which Croll described firmly as Euphuistic, Senecan, Tacitean, libertine, and so on. Croll's own division of styles was basically twofold: on the one hand were the styles which specialized in patterns of sound (*schemata verborum*), and which were distinguished by rigid parallelism, paromoion, and jingles of every kind—even Cicero must be included in this group, as well as Isocrates, Lyly, and many patristic writers; on the other hand were the new expressive writers whose schemes were the figures of thought or wit, and whose styles as a whole were marked by deliberate asymmetry. Williamson returned to the three ancient categories of style, which he defined structurally as the circular (Ciceronian), the antithetic (Euphuistic), and the loose (Senecan), and he has shown conclusively that all these styles share different qualities with each other: that Gorgian patterns are common in Seneca, that Bacon's prose is often Euphuistic, that terse Asian and Stoic styles are hard to tell from all but the plainest Attic, and that antithetic constructions can be used to display either thought or sound. The use to which the schemes are put, not their mere presence or absence, is to Williamson of primary importance. Croll's division of the Anti-Ciceronian style into its curt, loose, and obscure forms Williamson alters so as to make curt the norm, from which writers moved either towards a Tacitean truncatedness (and Lipsius belongs here), or towards the loose, which is not essentially a brief style at all. These realignments have resulted in a demonstration that Croll, especially in this essay, overemphasized asymmetry as the mark of Senecanism (though it would be true of Tacitean imitation), and have revealed many cases of disguised symmetry which Croll overlooked. One may still accept Croll's description of a curt period as "a series of imaginative moments occurring in a logical pause or suspension," but one has to relinquish the notion of the unpremeditated nature of Senecan style, even in its looser form, although the latter generally aimed at effects which appear unpremeditated.

If Williamson has noted, however, that Croll's analyses of style are more subtle than those the seventeenth century often recognized, the same comment can be made of Williamson's. His book remains indispensable to serious students, less so to readers who want only the ground rules. For these Croll is still an excellent cicerone to the first half of the century, but an untrustworthy guide to the second half, when the "natural" style was one which increasingly buttressed its spontaneity with logic, in which second thoughts were always preferable to first thoughts, and Sprat's style could be praised for being "as polite and as fast as marble." For the earlier period, Croll's "baroque" has been triumphantly vindicated by Jonas Barish's *Ben Jonson and the Language of Prose Comedy*, which is the most important study of Jacobean prose style to appear since Williamson's; the second chapter in particular needs to be read in conjunction with Croll's essay. Not only has Barish added "baroque" techniques to Croll's list—such as the disturbing of logical word order, separating grammatically-related words, coupling incongruous elements in parallel forms—but he has shown with many examples how these techniques were used dramatically to portray states of mind like anger, distraction, simple-mindedness, indignation, and ceremonial foppishness. The roughness of Jonson's style, Barish suggests, was painstakingly achieved, and served not to express the doubts and introspections of Jonson himself (who would have denied he had them), but as a means of representing the follies of the world in its language. An objective use of the baroque Croll did not envisage. By successfully proving the use of baroque style as linguistic satire, and by documenting its devices so thoroughly, Barish has freed the baroque from some of Croll's moorings, while justifying, in one important case, Croll's insistence on the asymmetry of its design.

Barish's study of the witty use of baroque style, in a writer famous for the strength of his judgment, is a reminder that concepts of wit and decorum now enter all discussions of seventeenth-century literature. Croll himself was the first to point out how carefully the Anti-Ciceronians veiled their heterodoxy, and he regarded Royal Society prose as a plainer variety of Senecanism dictated solely by decorum. Wit, on the contrary, was always a means of amplification which delighted in ingenious comparisons and antitheses, and was extremely compatible therefore with the hidden symmetries and bold asymmetry of baroque style. If Croll may be said to have underplayed the controlling power of these artistic canons, in the interests of his thesis concerning the humane importance of the Anti-Ciceronian movement, he did expose with a new clarity the prevalence of Stoic and libertine tendencies in the seventeenth century. When he explained how the Renaissance could be classical and modern at the same time, prose from Muret to the Royal Society acquired a sharper outline and a more rational history.

JOHN M. WALLACE
THE JOHNS HOPKINS UNIVERSITY

The Baroque Style in Prose*

EDITED BY JOHN M. WALLACE

✧ I ✧

Introduction

IN THE latter years of the sixteenth century a change declared itself in the purposes and forms of the arts of Western Europe for which it is hard to find a satisfactory name. One would like to describe it, because of some interesting parallels with a later movement, as the first modern manifestation of the Romantic Spirit; and it did, in fact, arise out of a revolt against the classicism of the high Renaissance. But the terms "romantic" and "classical" are both perplexing and unphilosophical; and their use should not be extended. It would be much clearer and more exact to describe the change in question as a radical effort to adapt traditional modes and forms of expression to the uses of a self-conscious modernism; and the style that it produced was actually called in several of the arts—notably in architecture and prose-writing—the "modern" or "new" style. But the term that most conveniently describes it is "baroque." This term, which was at first used only in architecture, has lately been extended to cover the facts that present themselves at the same time in sculpture and in painting; and it may now properly be used to describe, or at least to name, the characteristic modes of expression in all the arts during a certain period—the period, that is, between the high Renaissance and the eighteenth century; a period that begins in the last quarter of the sixteenth century, reaches a culmination at about 1630, and thenceforward gradually modifies its character under new influences.

Expressiveness rather than formal beauty was the pretension of the new movement, as it is of every movement that calls itself modern. It disdained complacency, suavity, copiousness, emptiness, ease, and in avoiding these qualities sometimes obtained effects of

* From *Studies in English Philology: A Miscellany in Honor of Frederick Klaeber*, ed. Kemp Malone and Martin B. Ruud (Minneapolis: University of Minnesota Press, copyright 1929; renewed 1957 by Kemp Malone).

contortion or obscurity, which it was not always willing to regard as faults. It preferred the forms that express the energy and labor of minds seeking the truth, not without dust and heat, to the forms that express a contented sense of the enjoyment and possession of it. In a single word, the motions of souls, not their states of rest, had become the themes of art.

The meaning of these antitheses may be easily illustrated in the history of Venetian painting, which passes, in a period not longer than one generation, from the self-contained and relatively symmetrical designs of Titian, through the swirls of Tintoretto, to the contorted and aspiring lines that make the paintings of El Greco so restless and exciting. Poetry moves in the same way at about the same time; and we could metaphorically apply the terms by which we distinguish El Greco from Titian to the contrast between the rhythms of Spenser and the Petrarchans, on one hand, and the rhythms of Donne, on the other, between the style of Ariosto and the style of Tasso. In the sculptures of Bernini (in his portrait busts as well as in his more famous and theatrical compositions) we may again observe how ideas of motion take the place of ideas of rest; and the operation of this principle is constantly to be observed also in the school of architecture associated with the same artist's name. In the façade of a Baroque church, says Geoffrey Scott, "a movement, which in the midst of a Bramantesque design would be destructive and repugnant, is turned to account and made the basis of a more dramatic, but not less satisfying treatment, the motive of which is not peace, but energy."[1]

And finally the change that takes place in the prose style of the same period—the change, that is, from Ciceronian to Anti-Ciceronian forms and ideas—is exactly parallel with those that were occurring in the other arts, and is perhaps more useful to the student of the baroque impulse than any of the others, because it was more self-conscious, more definitely theorized by its leaders, and more clearly described by its friends and foes. In some previous studies I have considered the triumph of the Anti-Ciceronian movement at considerable length; but I have been concerned chiefly with the theory of the new style; and my critics have complained, justly, that I have been too difficult, or even abstract. In the present study I hope to correct this defect. Its purpose is to describe the *form* of Anti-Ciceronian, or baroque, prose.

[1] *The Architecture of Humanism* (London, 1914), p. 225.

There are of course several elements of prose technique: diction, or the choice of words; the choice of figures; the principle of balance or rhythm; the form of the period, or sentence; and in a full description of baroque prose all of these elements would have to be considered. The last-mentioned of them—the form of the period—is, however, the most important and the determinant of the others; and this alone is to be the subject of discussion in the following pages.

The Anti-Ciceronian period was sometimes described in the seventeenth century as an "exploded" period; and this metaphor is very apt if it is taken as describing solely its outward appearance, the mere fact of its form. For example, here is a period from Sir Henry Wotton, a typical expression of the political craft of the age:

> Men must beware of running down steep hills with weighty bodies; they once in motion, *suo feruntur pondere*; steps are not then voluntary.[2]

The members of this period stand farther apart one from another than they would in a Ciceronian sentence; there are no syntactic connectives between them whatever; and semicolons or colons are necessary to its proper punctuation. In fact, it has the appearance of having been disrupted by an explosion within.

The metaphor would be false, however, if it should be taken as describing the manner in which this form has been arrived at. For it would mean that the writer first shaped a round and complete oratorical period in his mind and then partly undid his work. And this, of course, does not happen. Wotton gave this passage its form, not by demolishing a Ciceronian period, but by omitting several of the steps by which roundness and smoothness of composition might have been attained. He has deliberately avoided the processes of mental revision in order to express his idea when it is nearer the point of its origin in his mind.

We must stop for a moment on the word *deliberately*. The negligence of the Anti-Ciceronian masters, their disdain of revision, their dependence upon casual and emergent devices of construction, might sometimes be mistaken for mere indifference to art or contempt of form; and it is, in fact, true that Montaigne and Burton, even Pascal and Browne, are sometimes led by a dislike of formality

---

[2] "Table Talk," in *Life and Letters*, ed. Logan Pearsall Smith (Oxford, 1907), II, 500.

into too licentious a freedom. Yet even their extravagances are purposive, and express a creed that is at the same time philosophical and artistic. Their purpose was to portray, not a thought, but a mind thinking, or, in Pascal's words, *la peinture de la pensée*. They knew that an idea separated from the act of experiencing it is not the idea that was experienced. The ardor of its conception in the mind is a necessary part of its truth; and unless it can be conveyed to another mind in something of the form of its occurrence, either it has changed into some other idea or it has ceased to be an idea, to have any existence whatever except a verbal one. It was the latter fate that happened to it, they believed, in the Ciceronian periods of sixteenth-century Latin rhetoricians. The successive processes of revision to which these periods had been submitted had removed them from reality by just so many steps. For themselves, they preferred to present the truth of experience in a less concocted form, and deliberately chose as the moment of expression that in which the idea first clearly objectifies itself in the mind, in which, therefore, each of its parts still preserves its own peculiar emphasis and an independent vigor of its own—in brief, the moment in which truth is still *imagined*.

The form of a prose period conceived in such a theory of style will differ in every feature from that of the conventional period of an oratorical, or Ciceronian, style; but its most conspicuous difference will appear in the way it connects its members or clauses one with another. In the period quoted above from Wotton the members are syntactically wholly free; there are no ligatures whatever between one and another. But there is another type of Anti-Ciceronian period, in which the ordinary marks of logical succession—conjunctions, pronouns, etc.—are usually present, but are of such a kind or are used in such a way as to bind the members together in a characteristically loose and casual manner. The difference between the two types thus described may seem somewhat unimportant; and it is true that they run into each other and cannot always be sharply distinguished. The most representative Anti-Ciceronians, like Montaigne and Browne, use them both and intermingle them. But at their extremes they are not only distinguishable; they serve to distinguish different types, or schools, of seventeenth-century style. They derive from different models, belong to different traditions, and sometimes define the philosophical affiliations of the authors who prefer them.

210

They will be considered here separately; the first we will call, by a well-known seventeenth-century name, the *période coupée*, or, in an English equivalent, the "curt period" (so also the *stile coupé*, or the "curt style"); the other by the name of the "loose period" (and the "loose style"); though several other appropriate titles suggest themselves in each case.[3]

✧ II ✧

Stile Coupé

(a)

One example of the *période coupée* has already been given. Here are others:

Pour moy, qui ne demande qu'à devenir plus sage, non plus sçavant ou eloquent, ces ordonnances logiciennes et aristoteliques ne sont pas à propos; je veulx qu'on commence par le dernier poinct: i'entends assez que c'est que Mort et Volupté; qu'on ne s'amuse pas à les anatomizer. (Montaigne)

'Tis not worth the reading, I yield it, I desire thee not to lose time in perusing so vain a subject, I should be peradventure loth myself to read him or thee so writing, 'tis not *operae pretium*. (Burton)

No armor can *defend* a fearful heart. It will kill itself, within. (Feltham)

Oui; mais il faut parier; cela n'est pas volontaire, vous êtes embarqués. (Pascal)

L'éloquence continue ennuie.
Les princes et les rois jouent quelquefois; ils ne sont pas toujours sur leurs trônes, ils s'y ennuient: la grandeur a besoin d'être quittée pour être sentie. (Pascal)

The world that I regard is myself; it is the microcosm of my own frame that I cast mine eye on: for the other, I use it but like my globe, and turn it round sometimes for my recreation. (Browne)

---

[3] For example, the *stile coupé* was sometimes called *stile serré* ("serried style"), and Francis Thompson has used this term in describing a kind of period common in Browne. For synonyms of "loose style" see section III of this paper.

211

Il y a des hommes qui attendent à être dévots et religieux que tout le monde se déclare impie et libertin: ce sera alors le parti du vulgaire, ils sauront s'en dégager. (La Bruyère)[4]

In all of these passages, as in the period quoted from Wotton, there are no two main members that are syntactically connected. But it is apparent also that the characteristic style that they have in common contains several other features besides this.

In the first place, each member is as short as the most alert intelligence would have it. The period consists, as some of its admirers were wont to say, of the nerves and muscles of speech alone; it is as hard-bitten, as free of soft or superfluous flesh, as "one of Caesar's soldiers."[5]

Second, there is a characteristic order, or mode of progression, in a curt period that may be regarded either as a necessary consequence of its omission of connectives or as the causes and explanation of this. We may describe it best by observing that the first member is likely to be a self-contained and complete statement of the whole idea of the period. It is so because writers in this style like to avoid prearrangements and preparations; they begin, as Montaigne puts it, at *le dernier poinct*, the point aimed at. The first member therefore exhausts the mere fact of the idea; logically there is nothing more to say. But it does not exhaust its imaginative truth or the energy of its conception. It is followed, therefore, by other members, each with a new tone or emphasis, each expressing a new apprehension of the truth expressed in the first. We may describe the progress of a curt period, therefore, as a series of imaginative moments occurring in a logical pause or suspension. Or—to be less obscure—we may compare it with successive flashes of a jewel or prism as it is turned about on its axis and takes the light in different ways.

[4] References are as follows: Montaigne, "Des Livres," *Essais* II.x, ed. J.-V. Le Clerc (Paris, 1865), II, 122; Robert Burton, "To the Reader," *The Anatomy of Melancholy*, ed. A. R. Shilleto (London, 1893), p. 24; Owen Felltham, "Of Fear and Cowardice," *Resolves* I.71 (London, 1677), p. 110; Pascal, *Pensées*, ed. Léon Brunschvicg (Paris, 1904), II, 146 (section VII in 1670 Port-Royal ed.); *Pensées*, II, 269 (section XXI in Port-Royal ed.); Sir Thomas Browne, *Religio Medici*, Part II, section 11, in *Works*, ed. Simon Wilkin (London, 1846), II, 110; La Bruyère, "Des Esprits Forts," *Œuvres*, ed. G. Servois (Paris, 1865), II, 239. These editions have been used for subsequent quotations from the authors' works.

[5] The phrase comes from a midseventeenth-century work on prose style, and is there applied to *il dir moderno*: Daniello Bartoli, "Dello Stile," *Dell' Uomo di Lettere*, in *Opere* (Venice, 1716), III, 101.

It is true, of course, that in a series of propositions there will always be some logical process; the truth stated will undergo some development or change. For example, in the sentence from Montaigne at the beginning of this section, the later members add something to the idea; and in the quotation from Pascal's *Pensées sur l'Éloquence*, given below it, the thought suddenly enlarges in the final member. Yet the method of advance is not logical; the form does not express it. Each member, in its main intention, is a separate act of imaginative realization.

In the third place, one of the characteristics of the curt style is deliberate asymmetry of the members of a period; and it is this trait that especially betrays the modernistic character of the style. The chief mark of a conventional, or "classical," art, like that of the sixteenth century, is an approximation to evenness in the size and form of the balanced parts of a design; the mark of a modernistic art, like that of the seventeenth, and the nineteenth and twentieth, centuries, is the desire to achieve an effect of balance or rhythm among parts that are obviously not alike—the love of "some strangeness in the proportions."

In a prose style asymmetry may be produced by varying the length of the members within a period. For example, part of the effect of a sentence from Bishop Hall is due to a variation in this respect among members which nevertheless produce the effect of balance or rhythmic design.

> What if they [crosses and adversities] be unpleasant? They are physic: it is enough, if they be wholesome.[6]

But the desired effect is more characteristically produced by conspicuous differences of form, either with or without differences of length. For instance, a characteristic method of the seventeenth century was to begin a succession of members with different kinds of subject words. In the sentence quoted from Wotton the first two members have personal subjects, the third the impersonal "steps"; in the quotation from Pascal the opposite change is made.

> Mais il faut parier; cela n'est pas volontaire, vous êtes embarqués.

[6] Joseph Hall, *Heaven upon Earth*, XIII, in *Works* (Oxford, 1837), VI, 20. Note how exactly this reproduces a movement characteristic of Seneca: *Quid tua, uter* [Caesar or Pompey] *vincat? Potest melior vincere: non potest pejor esse qui vicerit.*

In both of these periods, moreover, each of the three members has a distinct and individual turn of phrase, meant to be different from the others. Again, in the period of La Bruyère quoted at the beginning of this section, each new member involves a shift of the mind to a new subject. (Observe also the asymmetry of the members in point of length.)

Sometimes, again, asymmetry is produced by a change from literal to metaphoric statement, or by the reverse, or by a change from one metaphor to another, as in the last example quoted from Pascal, where the metaphor of one embarked upon a ship abruptly takes the place of that of a man engaged in a bet. Or there may be a leap from the concrete to the abstract form; and this is an eminently characteristic feature of the *stile coupé* because this style is always tending toward the aphorism, or *pensée*, as its ideal form. The second passage quoted from Pascal illustrates this in a striking way. It is evident that in the first three members—all concrete, about kings and princes—the author's mind is turning toward a general truth, which emerges complete and abstract in the last member: *la grandeur a besoin d'être quittée pour être sentie.*

The curt style, then, is not characterized only by the trait from which it takes its name, its omission of connectives. It has the four marks that have been described: first, studied brevity of members; second, the hovering, imaginative order; third, asymmetry; and fourth, the omission of the ordinary syntactic ligatures. None of these should, of course, be thought of separately from the others. Each of them is related to the rest and more or less involves them; and when they are all taken together they constitute a definite rhetoric, which was employed during the period from 1575 to 1675 with as clear a knowledge of its tradition and its proper models as the sixteenth-century Ciceronians had of the history of the rhetoric that they preferred.

In brief, it is a Senecan style; and, although the imitation of Seneca never quite shook off the imputation of literary heresy that had been put upon it by the Augustan purism of the preceding age, and certain amusing cautions and reservations were therefore felt to be necessary, yet nearly all of the theorists of the new style succeeded in expressing their devotion to their real master in one way or another. Moreover, they were well aware that the characteristic traits of Seneca's style were not his alone, but had been elaborated before him in the Stoic schools of the Hellenistic period; and all the earlier practitioners of the *stile coupé*, Montaigne (in his first phase), Lipsius, Hall, Charron, etc., write not only as literary Senecans, but rather more as philosophical Stoics.

Senecanism and Stoicism are, then, the primary implications of *stile coupé*. It must be observed, however, that a style once established in general use may cast away the associations in which it originated; and this is what happened in the history of the curt style. Montaigne, for instance, confessed that he had so thoroughly learned Seneca's way of writing that he could not wholly change it even when his ideas and tastes had changed and he had come to prefer other masters. And the same thing is to be observed in many writers of the latter part of the century: St. Évremond, Halifax, and La Bruyère, for instance. Though these writers are all definitely anti-Stoic and anti-Senecan, all of them show that they had learned the curt style too well ever to unlearn it or to avoid its characteristic forms; and there was no great exaggeration in Shaftesbury's complaint, at the very end of the century, that no other movement of style than Seneca's—what he calls the "Senecan amble"—had been heard in prose for a hundred years past.

(b)

The curt or serried style depends for its full effect upon the union of the several formal traits that have been described in the preceding section. We have assumed hitherto that these traits are as rigorous and unalterable as if they were prescribed by a rule; and in the examples cited there have been no significant departures from any of them. But of course slight variations are common even in passages that produce the effect of *stile coupé*; and some searching is necessary to discover examples as pure as those that have been cited. This is so evidently true that it would need no illustration except for the fact that certain kinds of period eminently characteristic of seventeenth-century prose arise from a partial violation of the "rules" laid down. Two of these may be briefly described.

(A) In a number of writers (Browne, Felltham, and South, for example) we often find a period of two members connected by *and*, *or*, or *nor*, which evidently has the character of *stile coupé* because the conjunction has no logical *plus* force whatever. It merely connects two efforts of the imagination to realize the same idea; two as-it-were synchronous statements of it. The following from Browne will be recognized as characteristic of him:

215

'Tis true, there is an edge in all firm belief, and with an easy metaphor we may say, the sword of faith.

Again:

Therefore I perceive a man may be twice a child, before the days of dotage; and stand in need of Æson's bath before three-score.[7]

Often, too, in a period consisting of a larger number of members the last two are connected by an *and* or the like. But this case can be illustrated in connection with the one that immediately follows.

(B) The rule that the successive members of a *période coupée* are of different and often opposed forms, are asymmetrical instead of symmetrical, is sometimes partly violated inasmuch as these members begin with the same word or form of words, for example, with the same pronoun subject, symmetry, parallelism, and some regularity of rhythm thus introducing themselves into a style that is designed primarily and chiefly to express a dislike of these frivolities. It is to be observed, however, that the members that begin with this suggestion of oratorical pattern usually break it in the words that follow. Except for their beginnings they are as asymmetrical as we expect them to be, and reveal that constant novelty and unexpectedness that is so characteristic of the "baroque" in all the arts.

One illustration is to be found in the style of the "character" writings that enjoyed so great a popularity in the seventeenth century. The frequent recurrence of the same subject word, usually *he* or *they*, is the mannerism of this style, and is sometimes carried over into other kinds of prose in the latter part of the century, as, for instance, in writings of La Bruyère that are not included within the limits of the "character" genre,[8] and in passages of Dryden. It is indeed so conspicuous a mannerism that it may serve to conceal what is after all the more significant feature of the "character" style, namely, the constant variation and contrast of form in members that begin in this formulistic manner.

The style of the "character," however, is that of a highly specialized genre; and the form of the period with reiterated introductory formula can be shown in its more typical character in other kinds of

[7] *Religio Medici*, 1.10 and 1.42, in *Works*, II, 14, 61.
[8] For instance, in the famous passage "De l'Homme," 128, in *Œuvres*, II, 61, describing the beast-like life of the peasants of France.

prose, as, for example, in a passage from Browne describing the Christian Stoicism of his age:

> Let not the twelve but the two tables be thy law: let Pythagoras be thy remembrancer, not thy textuary and final instructer: and learn the vanity of the world, rather from Solomon than Phocylydes.[9]

Browne touches lightly on these repetitions, and uses them not too frequently. Balzac uses them characteristically and significantly. A paragraph from his *Entretiens* may be quoted both in illustration of this fact and for the interest of its subject matter:

> Nous demeurasmes d'accord que l'Autheur qui veut imiter Seneque commence par tout et finit par tout. Son Discours n'est pas un corps entier: c'est un corps en pieces; ce sont des membres couppez; et quoy que les parties soient proches les unes des autres, elles ne laissent pas d'estre separées. Non seulement il n'y a point de nerfs qui les joignent; il n'y a pas mesme de cordes ou d'aiguillettes qui les attachent ensemble: tant cet Autheur est ennemy de toutes sortes de liaisons, soit de la Nature, soit de l'Art: tant il s'esloigne de ces bons exemples que vous imitez si parfaitement.[10]

The passage illustrates exactly Balzac's position in the prose development of the seventeenth century. Montaigne is indeed—in spite of his strictures upon him—his master. He aims, like Montaigne, at the philosophic ease and naturalness of the *genus humile*; he has his taste for aphorism, his taste for metaphor; he is full of "points," and loves to make them show; in short, he is "baroque." But by several means, and chiefly by the kinds of repetition illustrated in this passage (*c'est . . . ce sont; il n'y a point . . . il n'y a pas mesme; tant . . . tant*), he succeeds in introducing that effect of art, of form, of rhythm, for which Descartes and so many other of his contemporaries admired him. He combines in short the "wit" of the seventeenth century with at least the appearance of being "a regular writer," which came, in the forties and fifties, to be regarded in France as highly desirable. In his political writings, and especially in

---

[9] *Christian Morals*, section XXI, *Works*, IV, 107. The period occurs in the midst of a paragraph in which each main member of each period begins with a verb in the imperative mood.

[10] No. XVIII, "De Montaigne et de ses Escrits," in *Œuvres*, ed. L. Moreau (Paris, 1854), II, 402-403.

THE ANTI-CICERONIAN MOVEMENT

Le Prince, his iterated opening formula becomes too evident a mannerism, and on page after page one reads periods of the same form: two or three members beginning alike and a final member much longer and more elaborate than the preceding that may or may not begin in the same way. The effect is extremely rhetorical.

(c)

Finally, we have to observe that the typical *période coupée* need not be so short as the examples of it cited at the beginning of the present section. On the contrary, it may continue, without connectives and with all its highly accentuated peculiarities of form, to the length of five or six members. Seneca offered many models for this protracted aphoristic manner, as in the following passage from the *Naturales Quaestiones* (vii.31):

There are mysteries that are not unveiled the first day: Eleusis keepeth back something for those who come again to ask her. Nature telleth not all her secrets at once. We think we have been initiated: we are still waiting in her vestibule. Those secret treasures do not lie open promiscuously to every one: they are kept close and reserved in an inner shrine.

Similar in form is this six-member period from Browne's *Religio Medici*:

To see ourselves again, we need not look for Plato's year: every man is not only himself; there have been many Diogeneses, and as many Timons, though but few of that name; men are lived over again; the world is now as it was in ages past; there was none then, but there hath been some one since, that parallels him, and is, as it were, his revived self.[11]

What has been said in a previous section of the characteristic mode of progression in *stile coupé* is strikingly illustrated in such passages as these. Logically they do not move. At the end they are saying exactly what they were at the beginning. Their advance is wholly in the direction of a more vivid imaginative realization; a metaphor revolves, as it were, displaying its different facets; a series of metaphors flash their lights; or a chain of "points" and

[11] I.6, in *Works*, II, 11. Felltham uses this manner with too much self-consciousness. See, for instance, a passage on the terse style (*Resolves*, I.20) beginning "They that speak to *children*, assume a pretty lisping."

218

paradoxes reveals the energy of a single apprehension in the writer's mind. In the latter part of the seventeenth century a number of critics satirize this peculiarity of the Senecan form. Father Bouhours, for instance, observed that with all its pretensions to brevity and significance this style makes less progress in five or six successive statements than a Ciceronian period will often make in one long and comprehensive construction. The criticism is, of course, sound if the only mode of progression is the logical one; but in fact there is a progress of imaginative apprehension, a revolving and upward motion of the mind as it rises in energy, and views the same point from new levels; and this spiral movement is characteristic of baroque prose.

✧ III ✧

The Loose Style

(a)

In the preceding pages we have been illustrating a kind of period in which the members are in most cases syntactically disjunct, and we have seen that in this style the members are characteristically short. It is necessary now to illustrate the other type of Anti-Ciceronian style spoken of at the beginning, in which the members are usually connected by syntactic ligatures, and in which, therefore, both the members and the period as a whole may be, and in fact usually are, as long as in the Ciceronian style, or even longer.

It is more difficult to find an appropriate name for this kind of style than for the other. The "trailing" or "linked" style would describe a relation between the members of the period that is frequent and indeed characteristic, but is perhaps too specific a name. "Libertine" indicates exactly both the form of the style and the philosophical associations that it often implies; but it is wiser to avoid these implications in a purely descriptive treatment. There is but one term that is exact and covers the ground: the term "loose period" or "loose style"; and it is this that we will usually employ. In applying this term, however, the reader must be on his guard against a use of it that slipped into many rhetorical treatises of the nineteenth century. In these works the "loose sentence" was defined as one that has its main clause near the beginning; and an antithetical term "periodic sentence"—an improper one—was

219

devised to name the opposite arrangement. "Loose period" is used here without reference to this confusing distinction.

In order to show its meaning we must proceed by means of examples; and we will take first a sentence—if, indeed, we can call it a sentence—in which Bacon contrasts the "Magistral" method of writing works of learning with the method of "Probation" appropriate to "induced knowledge," "the later whereof [he says] seemeth to be *via deserta et interclusa*."

> For as knowledges are now delivered, there is a kind of contract of error between the deliverer and the receiver: for he that delivereth knowledge desireth to deliver it in such form as may be best believed, and not as may be best examined; and he that receiveth knowledge desireth rather present satisfaction than expectant inquiry; and so rather not to doubt than not to err: glory making the author not to lay open his weakness, and sloth making the disciple not to know his strength.[12]

The passage is fortunate because it states the philosophy in which Anti-Ciceronian prose has its origin and motive. But our present business is with its form; and in order to illustrate this we will place beside it another passage from another author.

> Elle [l'Imagination] ne peut rendre sages les fous; mais elle les rend heureux, à l'envi de la raison qui ne peut rendre ses amis que misérables, l'une les couvrant de gloire, l'autre de honte.[13]

There is a striking similarity in the way these two periods proceed. In each case an antithesis is stated in the opening members; then the member in which the second part of the antithesis is stated puts out a dependent member. The symmetrical development announced at the beginning is thus interrupted and cannot be resumed. The period must find a way out, a syntactic way of carrying on and completing the idea it carries. In both cases the situation is met in the same way, by a concluding member having the form of an absolute-participle construction, in which the antithetical idea of the whole is sharply, aphoristically resumed.

---

[12] *Of the Advancement of Learning*, Bk. II, in *Works*, ed. Spedding, Ellis, and Heath (London, 1868), III, 403-404; ed. Wright, XVII.3.

[13] Pascal, *Pensées*, II, 3 (section XXV in 1670 Port-Royal ed.). There should, rhetorically speaking, be semicolons after *raison* and *misérables*.

The two passages, in short, are written as if they were meant to illustrate in style what Bacon calls "the method of induced knowledge"; either they have no predetermined plan or they violate it at will; their progression adapts itself to the movements of a mind discovering truth as it goes, thinking while it writes. At the same time, and for the same reason, they illustrate the character of the style that we call "baroque." See, for instance, how symmetry is first made and then broken, as it is in so many baroque designs in painting and architecture; how there is constant swift adaptation of form to the emergencies that arise in an energetic and unpremeditated forward movement; and observe, further, that these signs of spontaneity and improvisation occur in passages loaded with as heavy a content as rhetoric ever has to carry. That is to say, they combine the effect of great mass with the effect of rapid motion; and there is no better formula than this to describe the ideal of the baroque design in all the arts.

But these generalizations are beyond our present purpose. We are to study the loose period first, as we did the curt period, by observing the character of its syntactic links. In the two sentences quoted there are, with a single exception, but two modes of connection employed. The first is by co-ordinating conjunctions, the conjunctions, that is, that allow the mind to move straight on from the point it has reached. They do not necessarily refer back to any particular point in the preceding member; nor do they commit the following member to a predetermined form. In other words, they are the loose conjunctions, and disjoin the members they join as widely as possible. *And*, *but*, and *for* are the ones employed in the two sentences; and these are of course the necessary and universal ones. Other favorites of the loose style are *whereas, nor* (= *and not*), and the correlatives *though . . . yet, as . . . so*. Second, each of the two periods contains a member with an absolute-participle construction. In the loose style many members have this form, and not only (as in the two periods quoted) at the ends of periods, but elsewhere. Sir Thomas Browne often has them early in a period, as some passages to be cited in another connection will show. This is a phenomenon easily explained. For the absolute construction is the one that commits itself least and lends itself best to the solution of difficulties that arise in the course of a spontaneous and unpremeditated progress. It may state either a cause, or a consequence, or a mere attendant circumstance; it may be concessive or justificatory;

it may be a summary of the preceding or a supplement to it; it may express an idea related to the whole of the period in which it occurs, or one related only to the last preceding member.

The co-ordinating conjunctions and the absolute-participle construction indicate, then, the character of the loose period. Like the *stile coupé*, it is meant to portray the natural, or thinking, order; and it expresses even better than the curt period the Anti-Ciceronian prejudice against formality of procedure and the rhetoric of the schools. For the omission of connectives in the *stile coupé* implies, as we have seen, a very definite kind of rhetorical form, which was practiced in direct imitation of classical models, and usually retained the associations that it had won in the Stoic schools of antiquity. The associations of the loose style, on the other hand, are all with the more skeptical phases of seventeenth-century thought—with what was then usually called "Libertinism"; and it appears characteristically in writers who are professed opponents of determined and rigorous philosophic attitudes. It is the style of Bacon and of Montaigne (after he has found himself), of La Mothe le Vayer, and of Sir Thomas Browne. It appears always in the letters of Donne; it appears in Pascal's *Pensées*; and, in the latter part of the century, when Libertinism had positively won the favor of the world away from Stoicism, it enjoyed a self-conscious revival, under the influence of Montaigne, in the writings of St. Évremond, Halifax, and Temple. Indeed, it is evident that, although the Senecan *stile coupé* attracted more critical attention throughout the century, its greatest achievements in prose were rather in the loose or Libertine manner. But it must also be said that most of the sceptics of the century had undergone a strong Senecan influence; and the styles of Montaigne, Browne, Pascal, and Halifax, for instance, can only be described as displaying in varying ways a mingling of Stoic and Libertine traits.

(b)

Besides the two syntactic forms that have been mentioned—the co-ordinating conjunctions and the absolute construction—there are no others that lend themselves by their nature to the loose style, except the parenthesis, which we need not illustrate here. But it must not be supposed that it tends to exclude other modes of connection. On the contrary, it obtains its characteristic effects from the syntactic forms that are logically more strict and binding, such as the

222

relative pronouns and the subordinating conjunctions, by using them in a way peculiar to itself. That is to say, it uses them as the necessary logical means of advancing the idea, but relaxes at will the tight construction which they seem to impose; so that they have exactly the same effect as the loose connections previously described and must be punctuated in the same way. In other words, the parts that they connect are no more closely knit together than it chooses they shall be; and the reader of the most characteristic seventeenth-century prose soon learns to give a greater independence and autonomy to subordinate members than he would dare to do in reading any other.

The method may be shown by a single long sentence from Sir Thomas Browne:

> I could never perceive any rational consequence from those many texts which prohibit the children of Israel to pollute themselves with the temples of the heathens; we being all Christians, and not divided by such detested impieties *as* might profane our prayers, or the place wherein we make them; *or that* a resolved conscience may not adore her Creator any where, *especially* in places devoted to his service; *where*, if their devotions offend him, mine may please him; if theirs profane it, mine may hallow it.[14]

The period begins with a statement complete in itself, which does not syntactically imply anything to follow it; an absolute participle carries on, in the second member. Thereafter the connectives are chiefly subordinating conjunctions. Observe particularly the use of *as, or that*, and *where*: how slight these ligatures are in view of the length and mass of the members they must carry. They are frail and small hinges for the weights that turn on them; and the period abounds and expands in nonchalant disregard of their tight, frail logic.

This example displays the principle; but of course a single passage can illustrate only a few grammatical forms. Some of those used with a characteristic looseness in English prose of the seventeenth century are: relative clauses beginning with *which*, or with *whereto, wherein,* etc.; participial constructions of the kind scornfully called "dangling" by the grammarians; words in a merely ap-

[14] *Religio Medici*, i.3, in *Works*, ii, 4. Italics are mine.

positional relation with some noun or pronoun preceding, yet constituting a semi-independent member of a period; and of course such subordinating conjunctions as are illustrated above. It is unnecessary to illustrate these various cases.

(c)

The connections of a period cannot be considered separately from the order of the connected members; and, in fact, it is the desired order of development that determines the character of the connections rather than the reverse. In the oratorical period the arrangement of the members is "round" or "circular," in the sense that they are all so placed with reference to a central or climactic member that they point forward or back to it and give it its appropriate emphasis. This order is what is meant by the names *periodos*, *circuitus*, and "round composition," by which the oratorical period has been variously called; and it is the chief object of the many revisions to which its form is submitted.

The loose period does not try for this form, but rather seeks to avoid it. Its purpose is to express, as far as may be, the order in which an idea presents itself when it is first experienced. It begins, therefore, without premeditation, stating its idea in the first form that occurs; the second member is determined by the situation in which the mind finds itself after the first has been spoken; and so on throughout the period, each member being an emergency of the situation. The period—in theory, at least—is not made; it becomes. It completes itself and takes on form in the course of the motion of mind which it expresses. Montaigne, in short, exactly described the theory of the loose style when he said: "J'ecris volontiers sans project; le premier trait produit le second."

The figure of a circle, therefore, is not a possible description of the form of a loose period; it requires rather the metaphor of a chain, whose links join end to end. The "linked" or "trailing" period is, in fact, as we have observed, an appropriate name for it. But there is a special case for which this term might better be reserved, unless we should choose to invent a more specific one, such as "end-linking," or "terminal linking," to describe it. It is when a member depends, not upon the general idea, or the main word, of the preceding member, but upon its final word or phrase alone. And this is, in fact, a frequent, even a characteristic, kind of linking in certain authors, notably Sir Thomas Browne and his imitators. The sentence last quoted offers two or three illustrations of it: the connective words *as*, *especially*, and *where* all refer to the immediately preceding words or phrases; and in another period by the same author there is one very conspicuous and characteristic instance.

As there were many reformers, so likewise many reformations; every country proceeding in a particular way and method, according as their national interest, together with their constitution and clime, inclined them: some angrily and with extremity; others calmly and with mediocrity, not rending, but easily dividing, the community, and leaving an honest possibility of a reconciliation;—*which*, though peaceable spirits do desire, and may conceive that revolution of time and the mercies of God may effect, yet that judgment that shall consider the present antipathies between the two extremes,—their contrarieties in condition, affection, and opinion,—may with the same hopes, expect a union in the poles of heaven.[15]

Here the word *which* introduces a new development of the idea, running to as much as five lines of print; yet syntactically it refers only to the last preceding word *reconciliation*. The whole long passage has been quoted, however, not for this reason alone, but because it illustrates so perfectly all that has been said of the order and connection of the loose period. It begins, characteristically, with a sharply formulated complete statement, implying nothing of what is to follow. Its next move is achieved by means of an absolute-participle construction.[16] This buds off a couple of appositional members; one of these budding again two new members by means of dangling participles. Then a *which* picks up the trail, and at once the sentence becomes involved in the complex, and apparently tight, organization of a *though . . . yet* construction. Nevertheless it still moves freely, digressing as it will, extricates itself from the complex form by a kind of anacoluthon (in the *yet* clause), broadening its scope, and gathering new confluents, till it ends, like a river, in an opening view.

The period, that is, moves straight onward everywhere from the point it has reached; and its construction shows ideally what we

[15] *Religio Medici*, I.4, in *Works*, II, 5.
[16] Observe that the period from Browne quoted on p. 223 begins with movements of the same kind.

mean by the linked or trailing order. It is Browne's peculiar mastery of this construction that gives his writing constantly the effect of being, not the result of a meditation, but an actual meditation in process. He writes like a philosophical scientist making notes of his observation as it occurs. We see his pen move and stop as he thinks. To write thus, and at the same time to create beauty of cadence in the phrases and rhythm in the design—and so Browne constantly does—is to achieve a triumph in what Montaigne called "the art of being natural"; it is the eloquence, described by Pascal, that mocks at formal eloquence.

(d)

The period just quoted serves to introduce a final point concerning the form of the loose period. We have already observed that the second half of this period, beginning with *which*, has a complex suspended syntax apparently like that of the typical oratorical sentence. The Anti-Ciceronian writer usually avoids such forms, it is true; most of his sentences are punctuated by colons and semi-colons. But, of course, he will often find himself involved in a suspended construction from which he cannot escape. It remains to show that even in these cases he still proceeds in the Anti-Ciceronian manner, and succeeds in following, in spite of the syntactic formalities to which he commits himself, his own emergent and experimental order. Indeed, it is to be observed that the characteristic quality of the loose style may appear more clearly in such difficult forms than in others. For baroque art always displays itself best when it works in heavy masses and resistant materials; and out of the struggle between a fixed pattern and an energetic forward movement often arrives at those strong and expressive disproportions in which it delights.

We shall return to Browne in a moment in illustration of the point, but we shall take up a simpler case first. In a well-known sentence, Pascal, bringing out the force of imagination, draws a picture of a venerable magistrate seated in church, ready to listen to a worthy sermon. *Le voilà prêt à l'ouïr avec un respect exemplaire.*

Que le prédicateur vienne à paraître, que la nature lui ait donné une voix enrouée et un tour de visage bizarre, que son barbier l'ait mal rasé, si le hasard l'a encore barbouillé de surcroît, quelque grandes vérités qu'il annonce, je parie la perte de la gravité de notre sénateur.[17]

Unquestionably a faulty sentence by all the school-rules! It begins without foreseeing its end, and has to shift the reader's glance from the preacher to the magistrate in the midst of its progress by whatever means it can. Observe the abruptness of the form of the member *quelque grandes vérités*. Observe the sudden appearance of the first person in the last member. Yet the critic who would condemn its rhetorical form would have also to declare that there is no art in those vivid dramatic narratives that so often appear in the conversation of animated talkers; for this period moves in an order very common in such conversation.[18]

In this passage the free and Anti-Ciceronian character of the movement is chiefly due to its dramatic vividness and speed. It follows the order of life. Sometimes, however, we can see plainly that it is the mystical speculation of the seventeenth century that changes the regular form of the period and shapes it to its own ends. Sir Thomas Browne provides many interesting illustrations, as, for instance, in the period quoted in the preceding section, and in the following:

> I would gladly know how Moses, with an actual fire, cal-cined or burnt the golden calf into powder: for that mystical metal of gold, whose solary and celestial nature I admire, exposed unto the violence of fire, grows only hot, and liquefies, but consumeth not; so when the consumable and volatile pieces of our bodies shall be refined into a more impregnable and fixed temper, like gold, though they suffer from the action of flames, they shall never perish, but lie immortal in the arms of fire.[19]

With the first half of this long construction we are not now concerned. In its second half, however, beginning with *so when*, we see one of those complex movements that have led some critics to speak of Browne as—of all things!—a Ciceronian. It is in fact

[17] *Pensées*, II, 4-5 (section xxv in Port-Royal ed.).

[18] It may be said that Pascal's *Pensées* should not be cited in illustration of prose form because they were written without revision and without thought of publication. But a good deal of characteristic prose of the time was so written, and the effect at which Bacon, Burton, Browne, and many others aimed was of prose written in that way.

[19] *Religio Medici*, I.50, in *Works*, II, 73.

the opposite of that. A Ciceronian period closes in at the end; it reaches its height of expansion and emphasis at the middle or just beyond, and ends composedly. Browne's sentence, on the contrary, opens constantly outward; its motions become more animated and vigorous as it proceeds; and it ends, as his sentences are likely to do, in a vision of vast space or time, losing itself in an *altitudo*, a hint of infinity. As, in a previously quoted period, everything led up to the phrase, "a union in the poles of heaven," so in this everything leads up to the concluding phrase, "but lie immortal in the arms of fire." And as we study the form of the structure we can even observe where this ending revealed itself, or, at least, how it was prepared. The phrase "like gold" is the key to the form of the whole. After a slow expository member, this phrase, so strikingly wrenched from its logical position, breaks the established and expected rhythm, and is a signal of more agitated movement, of an ascending effort of imaginative realization that continues to the end. In a different medium, the period closely parallels the technique of an El Greco composition, where broken and tortuous lines in the body of the design prepare the eye for curves that leap upward beyond the limits of the canvas.

The forms that the loose period may assume are infinite, and it would be merely pedantic to attempt a classification of them. In one of the passages quoted we have seen the dramatic sense of reality triumphing over rhetorical formalism; in another, the form of a mystical exaltation. For the purpose of description—not classification—it will be convenient to observe still a third way in which a loose period may escape from the formal commitments of elaborate syntax. It is illustrated in a passage in Montaigne's essay "Des Livres," praising the simple and uncritical kind of history that he likes so much. In the course of the period he mentions *le bon Froissard* as an example, and proceeds so far (six lines of print) in a description of his method that he cannot get back to his general idea by means of his original syntactic form, or at least cannot do so without very artificial devices. He completes the sentence where it is; but completes his idea in a pair of curt (*coupés*) sentences separated by a colon from the preceding: "c'est la matiere de l'histoire nue et informe; chascun en peult faire son proufit autant qu'il a d'entendement."[20] This is a method often used by Anti-Cicero-

---

[20] *Essais*, II.x, ed. Le Clerc, II, 127.

nians to extricate themselves from the coils of a situation in which they have become involved by following the "natural" order. A better example of it is to be seen in a passage from Pascal's essay on "Imagination," from which another passage has already been cited.

> Le plus grand philosophe du monde, sur une planche plus large qu'il ne faut, s'il y a au-dessous un précipice, quoique sa raison le convainque de sa sûreté, son imagination prévaudra. Plusieurs n'en sauraient soutenir la pensée sans pâlir et suer.[21]

Nothing could better illustrate the "order of nature"; writing, that is, in the exact order in which the matter presents itself. It begins by naming the subject, *le plus grand philosophe*, without foreseeing the syntax by which it is to continue. Then it throws in the elements of the situation, using any syntax that suggests itself at the moment, proceeding with perfect dramatic sequence, but wholly without logical sequence, until at last the sentence has lost touch with its stated subject. Accordingly, this subject is merely left hanging, and a new one, *son imagination*, takes its place. It is a violent, or rather a nonchalant, anacoluthon. The sentence has then, after a fashion, completed itself. But there is an uneasy feeling in the mind. After all, *le plus grand philosophe* has done nothing; both form and idea are incomplete. Pascal adds another member (for, whatever the punctuation, the *plusieurs* sentence is a member of the period), which completely meets the situation, though a grammatical purist may well object that the antecedent of *plusieurs* was in the singular number.

Pascal is usually spoken of as a "classical" writer; but the term means nothing as applied to him except that he is a writer of tried artistic soundness. He is, in fact, as modernistic, as bold a breaker of the rules and forms of rhetoric, as his master Montaigne, though he is also a much more careful artist. *La vraie éloquence*, he said, *se moque de l'éloquence*.

(e)

Two kinds of style have been analyzed in the preceding pages: the concise, serried, abrupt *stile coupé*, and the informal, meditative, and "natural" loose style. It is necessary to repeat—once more —that in the best writers these two styles do not appear separately

[21] *Pensées*, II, 5.

in passages of any length, and that in most of them they intermingle in relations far too complex for description. They represent two sides of the seventeenth-century mind: its sententiousness, its penetrating wit, its Stoic intensity, on the one hand, and its dislike of formalism, its roving and self-exploring curiosity, in brief, its sceptical tendency, on the other. And these two habits of mind are generally not separated one from the other; nor are they even always exactly distinguishable. Indeed, as they begin to separate or to be opposed to each other in the second half of the century we are aware of the approach of a new age and a new spirit. The seventeenth century, as we are here considering it, is equally and at once Stoic and Libertine; and the prose that is most characteristic of it expresses these two sides of its mind in easy and natural relations one with the other.

✧ IV ✧

The Punctuation of the Seventeenth-Century Period

The "long sentence" of the Anti-Ciceronian age has received a remarkable amount of attention ever since it began to be corrected and go out of use; and there have been two conflicting views concerning it. The older doctrine—not yet quite extinct—was that the long sentences of Montaigne, Bacon, Browne, and Taylor were sentences of the same kind as those of Cicero and his sixteenth-century imitators; only they were badly and crudely made, monstrosities due to some wave of ignorance that submerged the syntactic area of the seventeenth-century mind. Their true character, it was thought, would be shown by substituting commas for their semicolons and colons; for then we should see that they are quaint failures in the attempt to achieve sentence unity.

The other view is the opposite of this, namely, that we should put periods in the place of many of its semicolons and colons. We should then see that what look like long sentences are really brief and aphoristic ones. The contemporary punctuation of our authors is again to be corrected, but now in a different sense. This is the view urged by Faguet in writing of Montaigne, and by Sir Edmund Gosse concerning the prose of Browne and Taylor.

This later view is useful in correcting some of the errors of the earlier one. But, in fact, one of them is just as false as the other; and both of them illustrate the difficulties experienced by minds

230

trained solely in the logical and grammatical aspects of language in interpreting the forms of style that prevailed before the eighteenth century. In order to understand the punctuation of the seventeenth century we have to consider the relation between the grammatical term *sentence* and the rhetorical term *period*.

The things named by these terms are identical. *Period* names the rhetorical, or oral, aspect of the same thing that is called in grammar a *sentence* and in theory the same act of composition that produces a perfectly logical grammatical unit would produce at the same time a perfectly rhythmical pattern of sound. But, in fact, no utterance ever fulfils both of these functions perfectly, and either one or the other of them is always foremost in a writer's mind. One or the other is foremost also in every theory of literary education; and the historian may sometimes distinguish literary periods by the relative emphasis they put upon grammatical and rhetorical considerations. In general we may say, though there may be exceptions, that before the eighteenth century rhetoric occupied much more attention than grammar in the minds of teachers and their pupils. It was so, for instance, in the Middle Ages, as is clear from their manuals of study and the curricula of their schools. It was still true in the sixteenth century; and the most striking characteristic of the literary prose of that century, both in Latin and in the vernacular tongues, was its devotion to the conventional and formal patterns of school-rhetoric.

The laws of grammatical form, it is true, were not at all disturbed or strained at this time by the predominance of rhetorical motives. There was no difficulty whatever in saying what these rhetoricians had to say in perfect accordance with logical syntax because they had, in fact, so little to say that only the most elementary syntax was necessary for its purposes. Furthermore, the rhetorical forms they liked were so symmetrical, so obvious, that they almost imposed a regular syntax by their own form.

But a new situation arose when the leaders of seventeenth-century rationalism—Lipsius, Montaigne, Bacon—became the teachers of style. The ambition of these writers was to conduct an experimental investigation of the moral realities of their time, and to achieve a style appropriate to the expression of their discoveries and of the mental effort by which they were conducted. The content of style became, as it were, suddenly greater and more difficult; and the stylistic formalities of the preceding age were unable to bear the burden. An immense rhetorical complexity and license took the place of the simplicity and purism of the sixteenth century; and, since the age had not yet learned to think much about grammatical propriety, the rules of syntax were made to bear the expenses of the new freedom. In the examples of seventeenth-century prose that have been discussed in the preceding pages some of the results are apparent. The syntactic connections of a sentence become loose and casual; great strains are imposed upon tenuous, frail links; parentheses are abused; digression become licentious; anacoluthon is frequent and passes unnoticed; even the limits of sentences are not clearly marked, and it is sometimes difficult to say where one begins and another ends.

Evidently the process of disintegration could not go on forever. A stylistic reform was inevitable, and it must take the direction of a new formalism or "correctness." The direction that it actually took was determined by the Cartesian philosophy, or at least by the same time spirit in which the Cartesian philosophy had its origin. The intellect, that is to say, became the arbiter of form, the dictator of artistic practice as of philosophical inquiry. The sources of error, in the view of the Cartesians, are imagination and dependence upon sense impressions. Its correctives are found in what they call "reason" (which here means "intellect"), and an exact distinction of categories.

To this mode of thought we are to trace almost all the features of modern literary education and criticism, or at least of what we should have called modern a generation ago: the study of the precise meaning of words; the reference to dictionaries as literary authorities; the study of the sentence as a logical unit alone; the careful circumscription of its limits and the gradual reduction of its length; the disappearance of semicolons and colons; the attempt to reduce grammar to an exact science; the idea that forms of speech are always either correct or incorrect; the complete subjection of the laws of motion and expression in style to the laws of logic and standardization—in short, the triumph, during two centuries, of grammatical over rhetorical ideas.

This is not the place to consider what we have gained or lost by this literary philosophy, or whether the precision we have aimed at has compensated us for the powers of expression and the flexibility of motion that we have lost; we have only to say that we must not apply the ideas we have learned from it to the explanation of seventeenth-century style. In brief, we must not measure the customs of the age of semicolons and colons by the customs of the age of commas and periods. The only possible punctuation of seventeenth-century prose is that which it used itself. We might sometimes reveal its grammar more clearly by repunctuating it with commas or periods, but we should certainly destroy its rhetoric.

PART II

The Sources of the Euphuistic Rhetoric

Essay Six. The Sources of the Euphuistic Rhetoric

Foreword to Essay Six

This introductory essay has been a standard reference in Renaissance studies for half a century, and although it has needed updating in a number of particulars, it still stands on very solid merits.

Its main thesis, that the important roots of the Euphuistic style are to be found in medieval rhetoric, remains unchallenged. William Ringler's cogent argument in favor of the Latin prose of John Rainolds as "The Immediate Source of Euphuism" (*PMLA*, LIII [1938], 678-686), explains, in part, the chronological difficulty of several men's writing in the same complex manner at about the same time; insofar as it does not overstate its case, it supplements Croll's thesis and provides a strong link between medieval schematic prose and the development of Euphuism; and it suggests a complete model, containing both the schematic patterns and the learned humanistic element, for the prose of *Euphues*. It may well be that other intermediaries besides Rainolds will be uncovered and adduced; at best these now seem likely only to strengthen the mid-sixteenth-century linkage. What is important, *pace* C. S. Lewis' treatment in his *Oxford History* volume on the sixteenth century, is that we do know the sources of Euphuism, and what is more important is that we are thereby able to know something of both the aims and the methods of the Euphuistic writers. More needs to be done, to be sure, with such writers in pseudo-Ciceronian style as Henri Estienne—author of *De Latinitate Falso Suspecta* (Geneva, 1576), of *Pseudo-Cicero* (1577), and of *Nizoliodidasculus* (1578)—and of connections between the contemporary neo-Latin styles and the vernacular.

Two gaps in Croll's approach and coverage in this essay must be noted. First, in it he says nothing about the *cursus* and its influence on English prose style. However, he rectified this omission in 1919 in "The Cadence of English Oratorical Prose." Second, he does not give sufficiently full indication of the impact of translations, particularly during the sixteenth century, upon English prose style (though he discusses a few individual translations, such as that of Guevara);

237

a useful starting point is provided by Samuel K. Workman, *Fifteenth-Century Translation as an Influence on English Prose*, Princeton Studies in English, xviii (1940), and by F. O. Matthiessen, *Translation: an Elizabethan Art* (Cambridge, Mass., 1931). In the parallel field of translation into French, Basil Munteano's "Port-Royal et le Stylistique de la Traduction" (*Association Internationale des Études Françaises: Cahiers*, viii [1956], 151-172) deserves mention because it reveals how seventeenth-century "free translators" relied on ancient and patristic theory and practice. See also Charles Bruneau, "La Phrase des Traducteurs au XVIe Siècle," *Mélanges . . . Henri Chamard* (Paris, 1951), pp. 275-284.

Also neglected by Croll is Leonard Cox, whose *Arte or Craft of Rhetoryke* was written about 1530. Although it manifests little of the interest in style that was characteristic of the later Sherry and Wilson (and of course Lyly), Cox's work is important in that it shows how well before Wilson's time and in fact quite early in the Tudor period there was a gradually evolving system of literary criticism. More, indeed, needs to be done with shifts in fashion, with the changing tastes and vogues of Elizabethan prose: such an approach explains in part Webbe's praise and Sidney's censure of Euphuistic style (with Nashe halfway between the two: he outgrew the style). The fifth chapter of G. K. Hunter's *John Lyly: The Humanist as Courtier* (Cambridge, Mass., 1962) is an admirable introduction to the problem of Lyly and Elizabethan fashion.

Croll's essay is printed in full below. His co-editor, Harry Clemons, prepared the text of Lyly, but Croll was responsible for the remaining contents of the volume, including the footnotes and a short Preface. In the latter he explains that he could not write a conventional résumé about *Euphues* and its author "without seeming to accept a view of the history of Euphuistic style which seemed to me to place it in wrong historical relations. . . . The Introduction therefore is addressed chiefly to scholars." Croll's researches for the notes "resulted in the discovery of a few new sources": Alciati's book of emblems, Lupton's

A Thousand Notable Things (1579), and the prose works of Gascoigne, especially the *Entertainments*: "these must be accounted among the most important models of the Euphuistic style." These additions to our knowledge bring out Lyly's fondness for handy compendia: "His classical knowledge is not that of the real humanist; his classical curiosity is strictly limited by the requirements of the current literary mode of which he is a delightful exemplar." Croll also showed originality in his treatment of proverb lore. The footnotes reveal how Lyly used Heywood's gatherings, Erasmus' adages, and many proverbs of his own finding; Lyly imitates their form and style. These observations led Croll to comment that the extent of the part played by this process of imitation in the prose style of the sixteenth and seventeenth centuries "will only appear when the subject has been studied more carefully."

Two of the footnotes written by Croll merit quotation here because they concern prose style. According to one, "Lyly need not be suspected of insincerity in apologizing for the plainness of his style. In the first place, his aim in the first part of his work is moral edification: he is as serious as Elyot or Ascham. And in the second place, he was accustomed to a rhetoric more fantastic than his own in very grave and reverend authors, for example in Augustine and Cyprian." According to the other footnote, "Proverbs are likely to occur in *Euphues* in clusters," for "this way of using them was a convention in sixteenth-century style. . . . The part played by proverbs in sixteenth- and seventeenth-century literature . . . needs treatment." Such comments reveal the threefold greatness of Croll's scholarship: he rectifies the researches and criticisms made by his predecessors, adds new information and insights, and points the way to further discoveries.

As one re-reads Croll's introduction to *Euphues* across the distance of nearly half a century, holding in mind the more recent work of European scholars such as Atkins, Curtius, Lewis, and Hunter, and of such American scholars as T. W. and C. S. Baldwin, D. L. Clark, Howell, Ringler, McLuhan, and Ong, one finds this essay still germane to the studies of every graduate student in English and one realizes that there is not a Renaissance or rhetoric scholar who will not reap good harvest from a reading of it. In the corpus of Croll's works it stands among the best; and that is to praise it highly.

R. J. Schoeck and J. Max Patrick

The Sources of the Euphuistic Rhetoric*

EDITED BY R. J. SCHOECK AND J. MAX PATRICK

✧ I ✧

What is Euphuism?

THE form of the Euphuistic rhetoric was finally defined, after much debate, by Landmann in a well-known paper, and has since been made familiar by Child's excellent résumé of the controversy, by Bond's edition of Lyly's works, and by Feuillerat's recent volume.[1] It is impossible and unnecessary to repeat the details of these descriptions here. The object of the present discussion is to re-open the question of the ultimate origins of the Euphuistic rhetoric; and for this purpose what is most needed is a general statement which will serve to isolate the essential and typical character of the style in question.

Such a statement cannot well be made, even now, without the danger of arousing controversy. But the simplest and safest form of the definition is that Euphuism is a style characterized

Euphuism
defined

by the figures known in ancient and medieval rhetoric as *schemes* (*schemata*), and more specifically by the word schemes (*schemata verborum*), in contrast with those known as *tropes*; that is to say, in effect, by the figures of sound, or vocal ornament.[2] The most important of these figures are three which

---

*Originally printed as the Introduction to *Euphues: The Anatomy of Wit; Euphues and his England*, by John Lyly, ed. Morris William Croll and Harry Clemons (London: Routledge and Sons, Ltd. and New York: E. P. Dutton and Co., 1916), pp. xv-lxiv.

[1] Landmann, *Der Euphuismus*; Child, *John Lyly*; R. W. Bond, *The Complete Works of John Lyly*, 3 vols. (Oxford, 1902), I, 120-134; Albert Feuillerat, *John Lyly, Contribution à l'Histoire de la Renaissance en Angleterre* (Cambridge, 1910), pp. 411-475.

[2] It is not strictly correct to speak of the schemes as being all figures of sound, since in some classifications a small group of figures (rhetorical question singly or in series, apostrophe, etc.) are included as a subdivision with the title "schemes of thought or wit"; but these are sometimes differently classified and sometimes

can be used, and in Euphuism are often and characteristically used, in combination in the same form of words: first, isocolon, or equality of members (successive phrases or clauses of about the same *length*); secondly, parison, or equality of sound (successive or corresponding members of the same *form*, so that word corresponds to word, adjective to adjective, noun to noun, verb to verb, etc.); thirdly, paromoion, similarity of sound between words or syllables, usually occurring between words in the same positions in parisonic members, and having the form either of *alliteration*, similarity at the beginning, or *homoioteleuton* (*similiter cadentes* or *desinentes*), similarity at the end, or, as often in Euphuism, of both of these at once. Other *schemata* are also frequently and characteristically used, such as simple *word repetition*, and *polyptoton* (the repetition of the same stem two or more times within the same clause or sentence, each time with a different inflectional ending); but these need not be detailed. The essential feature of the style—to repeat— is a vocal, or oral, pattern, and all its other characteristics, such as the use of antithesis, and the constant use of simile, are only means by which the Euphuist effects his various devices of sound design.

Such a characterization of Euphuism may not, it is true, pass unchallenged. It may be said, for instance, that it is not supported by the contemporary critics of Lyly, who invariably emphasize his similes from the natural history of myth and tradition, beasts, stones, and herbs. But these criticisms are directed at that feature of Lyly's work which was peculiar, or nearly so, to him, and owe their point to this fact. The style which we call Euphuism was, as everyone now recognizes, a very common form of style in the sixteenth century, and it is only in modern times that it has been given a name which associates it particularly with Lyly. The critics had usually no intention of finding fault with this style, because they really admired and in various degrees practiced it. They were ridiculing a particular mode which had become associated with it through the popularity of Lyly's novel. In the definition suggested above, however, Euphuism is taken as the name of the general tendency rather than of the

An objection considered

---

not included among the figures of rhetoric. The real figures of thought or wit are the tropes (metaphor, metonomy, allegory, and so on); and the true distinction between these and the schemes is that the tropes are devices for adorning one's idea, or illustrating it, while the schemes are ornaments of one's speech or manner of utterance. The simplest description of the figures will be found in Volkmann, *Rhetorik*, II, iii, 40-49.

particular form of it which appears in *Euphues*. It is unfortunate that it ever received its name from Lyly's book, and it would be very desirable to substitute a more general title, but the association is perhaps too long-standing to be broken up. As far as the purpose of the present inquiry is concerned, there is at least an advantage in excluding the nature similes from view; for their sources have already been carefully studied. Their form, it is admitted, comes from the *exempla* of the medieval sermon, and their substance partly from the same source, partly from the medieval bestiary from which the preachers also drew, and partly from Pliny.

On the other hand, it may be said, or rather it has often been said, that the characteristic feature of Euphuism is the constant use of antithesis.[3] But this statement is a prolific mother of errors—if it is not itself an error. Antithesis is the worst possible figure to use for purposes of charac-

A second objection

terization, because it may, according to the way it is used, look in one or the other of two opposite directions. It may be a figure of words, or sound, on the one hand, and a figure of thought (*figura sententiae*), on the other.[4] In the latter use, it is one of the most important *differentia* by which we recognize the style of the Anti-Ciceronian movement which arose at the end of the sixteenth century in reaction from the various forms of ornate, formal style in the preceding age, such as Euphuism itself, Ciceronian imitation, and so on. Without or with similarity of sound between the opposed words or members, it distinguishes the style of Bacon, who usually avoids balance in its use, and the style of Sir Thomas Browne, who likes just so much symmetry of form as will serve to point his artful and rhythmical departures from it, and the style of Montaigne in his latest period. In Lyly's use of it, on the other hand, antithesis is purely a "scheme," that is, a figure of the arrangement of words for an effect of sound. It is not meant to reveal new and striking relations between things; and it is as different as possible, for instance, from such a use of it as in Bacon's saying that "revenge is a kind of wild justice." This contrast will, of course, be admitted by everyone; and it is a pity to use as the test of style a figure which may lead to the identification—and, alas, still does lead to it—of styles so different in kind as that of Browne and that of Lyly.

But whatever differences of definition may still remain to be

---

[3] See Child's summary of the history of Euphuistic criticism.
[4] This is recognized by Volkmann, p. 46.

resolved, there is nothing to add to Landmann's *description*. That chapter of the study may be considered ended. The same thing cannot be said of the history of the sources of the Euphuistic style. That chapter is apparently only beginning. In attempting a reconsideration of what has heretofore been said on the subject, it seemed the wisest course to begin with the removal of some technical difficulties; but we must now approach the problem from another side, namely, through a general view of the historical position of the book *Euphues* and its author.

✧ II ✧

Humanism in Lyly's Day

M. Feuillerat has done a great deal in his recent work on Lyly toward placing *Euphues*—and particularly its first part, the *Anatomy of Wit*—in its proper relation to the literary movements of its day. Lyly's fame from his own time up to the present moment has rested chiefly on his work as a dramatist of the court and a forerunner of those novelists who dally nicely with the psychology of love. And rightly so: not only because the greater part of his life was spent in the effort to adorn and entertain the court of an ungrateful queen, but also because he was pre-eminently fitted by nature for this kind of labor. It was with far different prospects and ambitions, however, that he commenced his career; and M. Feuillerat has even been able to show that the change in the direction of his literary pursuits is connected with certain definite events in his life.[5]

A change in Lyly's literary career

The *Anatomy of Wit* was printed about Christmas-time in the year 1578. Its sequel, *Euphues and his England*, appeared in the spring of 1580; and in this work Lyly already shows a consciousness of the adventitious charm which had attracted readers to the first part, and professes himself, at the expense of all consistency, an expounder of the science of love. It is between these dates that the events just alluded to probably took place. We cannot exactly date the begin-

The history of it

[5] Most of the biographical facts in the following pages are derived from M. Feuillerat's admirable study of Lyly's life. This acknowledgment is made in lieu of many specific references which would otherwise be necessary. [Some further details are added in G. K. Hunter, *John Lyly: The Humanist as Courtier* (Cambridge, Mass., 1962); Hunter will provide fuller documentation when he publishes his Clarendon Press edition of Lyly's works.]

ning of his service in Oxford's train, it is true;[6] but the terms in which he dedicates the new work put it beyond all doubt that he was already on terms of intimacy with Burleigh's Italianized son-in-law, in whose veins flowed some of the maddest blood that was stirring even in those hot days; and he may by this time have transferred his residence from the sober precincts of the Savoy Hospital to the Earl of Oxford's London house, where we know that he had steady employment of various kinds for a number of years following. It was in this circle that he found out for better or for worse the career that was open to such talents as his. His refined taste, his feeling for elegance and grace, his delicate lyrical gift, his wit, his moderate learning—"it is not deep, but it will suffice"—and even his lack of profound or strong feeling, all his qualities, in short, adapted him to the task of clothing Elizabeth's court in the chic and brittle literary adornments which a gay society always admires.

The change indeed was inevitable. But it could not have been anticipated by his earlier friends and patrons, and to some of them it must have been disappointing. For when the young Lyly came up to London from the University, in search of a poor man's opportunities, every circumstance of ancestry, education, and patronage was guiding him in a different direction. His grandfather was, we now know, the Hellenist and grammarian William Lyly, the friend of Erasmus and Colet, a pioneer of humanism.[7] His uncle, George Lyly, inherited the thirst for learning, and under the protection of Reginald Pole built himself a reputation as antiquarian, historian, and geographer.[8] His father,

His beginnings

---

6 [Add Josephine Waters Bennett, "Oxford and *Endimion*," *PMLA*, LVII (1942), 354-369; and Hunter, *Lyly*, Chs. I-III. On Lyly and the Italian sources, see V. M. Jeffrey, *John Lyly and the Italian Renaissance* (Paris, 1929), and the more general but more recent studies by Napoleone Orsini, *Studii sul Rinascimento Italiano in Inghilterra* (Florence, 1937), and by Mario Praz, *The Flaming Heart* (New York, 1958).]

7 [William Lily (Lilius or Lylly), ca. 1468-1522, attended Magdalen College, Oxford. He became high master of St. Paul's School and the author of a Latin syntax (1513) which was largely utilized for the compilation of the *Institutio Compendiaria Totius Grammaticae*, later erroneously known as Lily's Latin grammar. For his biography see Hunter, *Lyly*, and C. S. Emden, *A Biographical Register of the University of Oxford*, II, 1147. On Lily's grammar, see C. G. Allen, "The Sources of 'Lily's Latin Grammar': A Review of the Facts and Some Further Suggestions," *The Library*, Ser. v, IX (1954), 85-100.]

8 [George Lily contributed an account of his father William to the *Descriptio Britanniae* of Paolo Giovio (Paulus Jovius): Emden, *Register*, II, 1147; Hunter, *Lyly*, p. 352.]

Peter Lyly, a younger son of the grammarian, was prebendary and registrar at Canterbury under the learned Parker, and though he himself attained no distinction as an author, it would seem that he committed to his son the duty of perpetuating the traditions of a "family of scholars." For at the age of fifteen John was sent to Magdalen College, where his grandfather and his uncle had gone before him; and, what is more, he went with the patronage of Burleigh. With such a history behind him he could look forward to a grave career. His undergraduate record may indeed reveal to the historian some omens of his final destiny, but his lapses from sobriety were not serious enough to forfeit the favor of his great patron, and when he came to London nearly all his connections were within the circle of influence which had its center at the Lord Treasurer's house.

In this circle Lyly found himself beset by intellectual and moral ideals, not only different from those of his later associates, but often in direct rivalry with them. The coteries of Leicester, Oxford, and Sidney, which depended immediately upon Elizabeth's court, represented the Renaissance in all its worldly pride and pomp. Their culture was courtly, aristo-cratic, and in part exotic, and their life often mirrored that of the small Italian despots and their trains. But at Burleigh's house life and thought moved in an austerer air, and severer standards were maintained, both in scholarship and in morals. Burleigh himself had been Greek lecturer at St. John's, Cambridge—the college of Cheke and Ascham—and had married Cheke's sister;[9] while his second wife, Mildred Coke, was famous even beyond England as one of the learned ladies of the Renaissance. Her household must have had all the gravity, though perhaps not all the graciousness, which has been recorded by a grateful son of the home life of her sister, the wife of Nathaniel Bacon. These two houses were, in fact, the chief London centers of the humanistic movement; and the love of pure learning had descended to them, through a second generation of scholars, from the cell of Colet and the country house of Sir Thomas More. Here, even more than at Oxford, Lyly must have felt the weight of his grandfather's name; and here he began

At first a humanist

---

[9] See J. B. Mullinger, *The University of Cambridge from the Royal Injunctions of 1535 to the Accession of Charles I* (Cambridge, 1884); and *D.N.B.* [For Burleigh, add Conyers Read, *Mr. Secretary Cecil and Queen Elizabeth* (New York, 1955), and Mark H. Curtis, *Oxford and Cambridge in Transition, 1558-1642* (Oxford, 1959).]

his literary career, not as a dependent of courtiers, but as the successor of Ascham, to whom the task of carrying the discipline of humanism to a new generation had fallen as by natural choice.

The humanistic movement had not passed through the eventful half-century since his grandfather's death, however, without suffering some change of character. It had definitely allied
The humanism of his day itself, for one thing, with a certain religious and political tendency. Colet, More, and William Lyly had for the most part pursued learning in a spirit of disinterested idealism, and even when they engaged in party strife their scholarship remained, as it were, a neutral territory, in which their minds moved with greater freedom and had a broader range than in the controversies of the hour. Of Cheke, Wilson, and Ascham, on the other hand, it is not unfair to say that they gave up to party what was meant for mankind: they devoted their learning to the cause of the Protestant Reformation. Their first aim in education was to train up defenders of the Elizabethan settlement, and to maintain that sound native sentiment of morality which they regarded as the best bulwark against foreign ideals of conduct and methods of thought.[10]

They unquestionably gained vigor and effectiveness from this alliance with the movement of their time. They succeeded, as the more exclusive humanists always failed to do, in having something to say, in giving well-trained expression
Its literary and rhetorical aims to a living national spirit; and, what is still better, they succeeded in doing this in the native speech. But, on the other hand, the scope of their learning and of their educational program was inevitably narrowed in the pursuit of practical aims. And this does not only mean that their strong bias brought them into conflict, especially under Burleigh's inspiration, with some manifestations of the Renaissance spirit in Elizabethan literature. Their scholarship itself suffered in the same way that continental scholarship for similar reasons was suffering. The noble attempt of earlier humanists, such as Grocyn, Linacre, More, to naturalize all of the learning of antiquity, including the

[10] [On Thomas Elyot, an important bridge between the Colet-More circle and that of Wilson and Ascham, see Stanford E. Lehmberg, *Sir Thomas Elyot: Tudor Humanist* (Austin, Texas, 1960), and the qualifying reviews of it in *RN*, XIV (1961), 178-181, and *Manuscripta*, VI (1962), 110-112; and also John M. Major, *Sir Thomas Elyot and Renaissance Humanism* (Lincoln, Nebraska, 1964).]

sciences and speculative philosophy,[11] and more particularly their effort to naturalize the classical temper and habit of life, could not be reconciled with the need of immediate practical success which was felt so strongly by Melanchthon, Sturm, and Ascham. Perhaps it really was too ambitious a program in view of the actual state of European culture. Minds that were still medieval below the surface probably needed to approach the intellectual freedom and curiosity of antiquity by some single well-defined avenue. At all events it is true that in the educational scheme of the later humanists literary culture assumed the almost exclusive rights which it has maintained in orthodox education ever since. And not only this. Literary culture itself came to consist chiefly in rhetorical excellence, to be attained through the study of the ancients; and the exclusive theory of Ciceronian imitation,[12] which had been so effectively ridiculed by Erasmus and Ramus, resumed its sway, though in a somewhat less rigorous form, in the teaching of Melanchthon, Sturm, and Ascham.[13] It is true that the proper aim of classical scholarship was always kept in sight, namely, the enfranchisement of modern wits through contact with ancient ones; but the theory of Ascham and Wilson, as of all those who held the doctrine of "imitation," was that those who had attained the speech and gesture of the ancients by hard practice could not fail to resemble them in some degree in thought.[14] "Ye know not what hurt ye do to learning," exclaims Ascham, "that care not for words, but for matter,"—anticipating the very terms of the famous attack of Francis Bacon on him and his fellow-Ciceronians.[15]

[11] [Among the early humanists, the sciences and speculative philosophy were in the main excluded—see P. O. Kristeller, *Studies in Renaissance Thought and Letters* (Rome, 1955)—and Linacre and More are unusual for their strong interest in science. For a general discussion of the situation of humanism in England, see Douglas Bush, *The Renaissance and English Humanism* (Toronto, 1939).]

[12] [For a convenient summary of the complex story of Ciceronian imitation see C. S. Baldwin, *Renaissance Literary Theory and Practice* (New York, 1939), pp. 44ff. and R. R. Bolgar, *The Classical Heritage and its Beneficiaries* (Cambridge, 1954); both of these are based on the scholarship of Remigio Sabbadini, *Storia del Ciceronianismo e di Altri Questioni nell' Età della Rinascenza* (Turin, 1885), and *Ciceronianus*, trans. Izora Scott (Columbia Univ. Contributions to Education, Albany, N.Y., 1908). See also n.58 below, and *Lipse*, n.9.]

[13] As regards a similar development in Italian humanism, see W. H. Woodward, *Vittorino da Feltre and other Humanist Educators* (Cambridge, 1897), pp. 210ff.

[14] Thomas Wilson, *The Arte of Rhetorique, 1560*, ed. G. H. Mair (Oxford, 1909), p. 5.

[15] *The Whole Works of Roger Ascham*, ed. J. A. Giles, 3 vols. in 4 (London, 1864-1865), III, 211 (*Scholemaster*, II, "Imitatio"). Cf. *Of the Advancement of Learning*, ed. William Aldis Wright (Oxford, 1957), I.iv.3: "the first distemper

In its content and the general character of its ideas, the *Anatomy of Wit* exactly represents this later phase of humanism. It appeared,

Euphues and the Schole- master

as Robynson's translation of *Utopia* had done a quarter of a century earlier, and as Ascham's *Scholemaster* had recently done, with a dedication to Lord Burleigh; and this fact alone would suffice to stamp it as a work in which learning and sound religion, pedagogy and moral earnestness, should be found consorting together. And this external circumstance is only a sign of a real and intimate relation between this book and the *Scholemaster*. Its hero—or rather the barely-personified type chosen to illustrate its teaching—derives not only his name, but also his attributes, from a well-known passage in which Ascham attempted to interpret to his British public the Greek ideal of a harmoniously developed human excellence. The passage is well known, both in Plato and Ascham; but it has not been pointed out that an important change takes place in the character of Euphues in the process of translation.

And what is most notable is that nothing is said of Euphues' rank in society. He has the graces of mind and body in a just balance, "excellence in learning . . . joined with a comely per-

The bourgeois character of both

sonage"; but the absence of gentle blood from the catalogue of his equipment is the most significant point in the description. His great gifts are not meant for the service of his own ambition or to add glory to a Prince's name, but for a nobler end. "How can a comely body be better employed than to serve the fairest exercise of God's greatest gift? and that is learning."[16] Indeed, whenever Ascham speaks of the nobles and courtiers of his age he sounds a note of warning, or even of reproof. His book is inspired throughout by a bourgeois ideal: learning is a greater ornament than birth; and the best servants of the common good are the men sprung from the middle class of the professions and the humbler gentry, like

---

of learning, when men study words and not matter." [For a full study of Ascham, see Lawrence V. Ryan, *Roger Ascham* (Stanford, 1963), esp. Ch. XI on *The Scholemaster*.]

[16] Ed. Giles, pp. 105-107; *The English Works of Roger Ascham*, ed. W. Aldis Wright (Cambridge, 1904), pp. 194-195. See "Note to Title-Page" below [i.e. in the 1916 ed. of *Euphues*. It explains that the Greek word from which Euphues derives "means in Plato, 'well endowed with natural gifts, both physical and intellectual.' But Lyly may have gone no further than Ascham's *Scholemaster*, for the name and character of his hero." Quotations from Wright's ed., pp. 194-195 follow.]

More, Colet, Linacre, Burleigh, and Ascham himself, who attain influence by their intellectual powers. This point is of some importance in connection with Lyly. The *Euphues* is often, indeed usually, spoken of as a manual of courtly culture, and its *estilo culto* as a model of courtly speech. Yet the bourgeois motif runs through the book, in a form only slightly different from that in which it is heard in the *Scholemaster*. It is true that Lyly wavers between two ideals that were inviting him, the humanistic and the courtly; and he makes Eubulus say to the hero: "Thy birth doth show the express and lively image of gentle blood."[17] But there is no hint of this in the set description of Euphues at the beginning and the only addition to the Plato-Ascham model is the circumstance that Euphues owes to Fortune an "increase of his possessions,"[18] which is, of course, only a heightening of the bourgeois theme, suggested perhaps by the wealth of such men as Burleigh and Bacon, and by Lyly's own taste for elegant worldliness. The statement that *Euphues* is a Book of Courtesy must be accompanied, therefore, by the modification that it is not meant for courtiers, but for "gentlemen" in the somewhat vague sense that that term had already acquired, and for worthy young men, in general, who had obtained a good education and had useful connections. The point may not be of very great importance, since gentlemen of the upper middle class were apt to derive their manners finally from the court; yet it is interesting to note that, whereas the style of the *Anatomy of Wit* is associated in some way not yet exactly defined with a Spanish style known as *oratio aulica*, its subject matter and social animus are due to other influences than those of courtiers and "society."

Moreover, the whole teaching and tenor of the book show that it is an offshoot of the *Scholemaster*. The name of the first part—*The Anatomy of Wit*—has perhaps created false expectations in some readers; but of course "anatomy" is used here in the same disparaging sense as in the contemporary titles *Anatomy of Abuses* and *Anatomy of Absurdities*.[19] Throughout the book *wit* is identified with the wanton and

Their morality

---

[17] Ed. Giles, p. 14.
[18] Ed. Giles, p. 10. [On the general problem of bourgeois culture, see Louis B. Wright, *Middle-Class Culture in Elizabethan England* (Chapel Hill, 1935).]
[19] [According to the "Note to Title-Page," *anatomy* had already been used in English book titles, but Lyly's use of it may account for its frequency in subsequent titles. Cf. N. Frye, *The Anatomy of Criticism* (Princeton, 1957), esp. pp. 311-312.]

secular curiosity of the Renaissance, and is often used in antithesis with *wisdom*, which stands for the indissoluble union of virtue, learning, and religion in the service of the national cause.[20] The aim of the *Anatomy*, in short, as of the *Scholemaster,* is to rally the scholarship of the national party against the Italianizing influences which were so busy in the letters and life of the court; and this purpose is not as yet clouded by the conflict which makes itself apparent in *Euphues and his England.*

✧ III ✧

The Problem Stated

The question of the relation between the *style* of *Euphues* and the rhetorical teaching of the later school of humanists cannot be

Their relations as regards style

so easily answered. That there is, in this respect as well as in the nature of their ideas, a certain *general* connection, may be taken for granted. The narrowing of the humanist effort toward the single path of literary study had brought about a great revival of rhetoric, and this revival had its part in creating the taste for ornate style of which Euphuism is one of the results. Perhaps the relation may be still more exactly stated, and in the summary of our final conclusions it must be fully taken into account. But it is not this general relation which we are to consider at this point. The question we wish to ask is the more definite one: Is the exact *form* of the Euphuistic rhetoric due to the same influences that formed the moral nature of Euphues? Are the "schemes," or "Gorgianic figures," which constitute, as we have already said, the most characteristic feature of Euphuism, and which run through so large a body of sixteenth-century prose in the vernacular, found there as a result of the humanistic training in the imitation of the ancients? It is the

[20] See *Wit* in the "Note to Title-Page" [which states that "wit" as used by Ascham in the passage which suggested the subtitle, *The Anatomy of Wit*, "means simply talent for studies, intellectual capacity . . . the usual meaning in the sixteenth century. Lyly often places it, however, in antithesis with *wisdom*, much as he contrasts *lust* and *love*. A new turn is thus given the word (which it also displays in other writers); it becomes almost equivalent to worldly curiosity and an unholy desire of knowledge—the lust of the mind—and stands for the dangerous and insidious tendencies of the Renaissance in their conflict with the severer religious ideas of the Reformation." On *Wit*, see also Mazzeo, *Renaissance and Seventeenth-Century Studies*, Chs. II and III, and Mirollo, *The Poet of the Marvelous, Giambattista Marino*, entries listed in the Index s.v. *Wit*.]

answer to this question which is the object of the present discussion.

The critics are now unanimously of the opinion that the answer must be in the affirmative. In the paper from which all recent study

The theory of classical imitation

dates, Landmann expressed the belief, though he offered almost no proof, that Euphuism is a humanistic product, and that the figures which he first described accurately were used in imitation of the ancient orators. Child, Bond, and Wendelstein followed him in this respect, though both Child and Wendelstein[21] showed a disposition to push the inquiry into broader fields. Both of these authors cited examples which, if properly interpreted, might have raised some doubts concerning Landmann's conclusion. But in the meantime appeared Norden's wonderfully useful book, in which a long chapter was devoted to the question we are considering.[22] Norden accepts the opinion that Guevara and Lyly write practically the same style; and in a long argument, full of contemporary citation, he tries to prove that Guevara was a humanist, as of course Ascham was, that Ascham and other humanists of the sixteenth century were particularly devoted to the study of two ancient writers, Cicero and Isocrates, that from both of these orators, but more especially from the latter, they derived their use of the schemes, and finally that Guevara's style and Lyly's is the result of practice in such imitation. The weight of Norden's authority has settled the question for all subsequent critics, and in the last important work,

[21] Ludwig Wendelstein, *Beitrag zur Vorgeschichte des Euphuismus* (Halle, 1902), p. 67. [Cf. George Parks, "Before Euphues" in *J. Q. Adams Memorial Studies* (Washington, 1948), pp. 475-493.]

[22] Norden, *Die Antike Kunstprosa*, II, 773-809. [Cf. Walter N. King, "John Lyly and Elizabethan Rhetoric," *SP*, LII (1955), 149-161. In this important article the function of the euphuistic style in Lyly's narrative prose is discussed, with the conclusion that "in *inventio* and *dispositio* Lyly is not the example *par excellence* of the Elizabethan writer who relies on the topics only for sources of amplification. . . . Duhamel is justified in maintaining that Lyly *is* overly interested in *elocutio*. His style too often gets in the way of his argument, with the result that the gold, such as it is, of the latter is offset by the glister that is not always gold of the former. As regards *inventio* and *dispositio*, Lyly suggests the writer who follows the middle of the road, leaning now toward logic, now towards amplification, as characterization and dramatic exigencies dictate. . . . Lyly is an innovator. For Lyly is adapting the rhetorical set-piece to narrative purposes, reducing it from a thing-in-itself to a functional part of a larger whole." See also n.64 below and *Lipse*, n.9. See the brilliant discussion of Invention in Grahame Castor, *Pléiade Poetics: A Study in Sixteenth-Century Thought and Terminology* (Cambridge, 1964), esp. Chs. VIII-XII. On *dispositio* and *elocutio*, see Chs. II-III in J. W. Blench, *Preaching in England in the late Fifteenth and Sixteenth Centuries* (Oxford, 1964).]

Feuillerat's authoritative study of Lyly's life and writings, his conclusion is accepted and indeed more positively stated, with an emphasis on Isocrates' influence even stronger than Norden's.[23]

This is a formidable array of authority, and it must be admitted that it is supported by arguments which have an appearance of solidity. Yet there are obvious objections. Appearances at least are against the opinion of the scholars, and it is safe to say that the ordinary reader, versed in Renaissance history, but unversed in the terms of the controversy, would reject the theory of classical imitation. For he would point out, in the first place, that the spirit of *estilo culto* in the sixteenth century is the reverse of classical. He would say that if it is due to the teaching of the humanists, then the humanists misunderstood the nature of that they worked in; and he would add that his experience had assured him that they did not ordinarily misinterpret the spirit of the classics. But, in the second place, such a reader might very well object that the actual form in which the schemata appear in *estilo culto* does not even suggest the way in which they appear in the ancients; that although they are present in both Isocrates and Cicero, they appear there in a minor relation to other features of their style, and with a wholly different effect upon the total result. In Cicero the cumulative and comprehensive period is the normal unit of expression, and the members of the period have a noble and varied rhythm; whereas in Lyly there is no periodicity, and the members are usually short and sharp. And in Isocrates the particular figures used by Lyly appear with comparative infrequency and are always used with a careful study of variety in form and rhythm which is in sharp contrast with Lyly's study of uniformity and exactness.

These are merely first impressions, it is true, the views of the casual reader, and they would perhaps be modified in some degree by consideration of certain facts which cannot be mentioned at the moment. Yet they are strong enough to raise a real doubt concerning the soundness of Norden's theory. They justify a reopening of the question and a search for other possible sources and models of the Euphuistic style and the related styles of the sixteenth century.

The obvious objection to it

Other sources must be sought

[23] See also T. K. Whipple, "Isocrates and Euphuism," *MLR*, XI (1916), 15-27, 129-135, and King, "John Lyly and Elizabethan Rhetoric."

Other influences have in fact been suggested as having operated to aid and abet that of the classical orators. Some writers, for instance, have mentioned the parallelism of the Psalms, and the prophetic books of the Old Testament, but this suggestion may be dismissed without consideration, though writers were often willing after the event to support their use of schemes by sacred authority. Much more interesting, however, is the use of Gorgianic forms in the late and provincial Latinity of the Church Fathers—and in the Greek and Latin romance writers contemporary with them,—which is due, as Norden has shown, to a variety of influences.[24] It is hardly necessary to illustrate the great revival of early Christian theology in the sixteenth century: More lectures on St. Augustine in London; Ascham reads Cyprian with the Princess Elizabeth; the school curricula show these authors side by side with Xenophon, Cicero, and Sallust; and although there is a steady, thin stream of opposition to the early legalists of the church by some of the most enlightened spirits of the Renaissance, from Colet to Milton, yet on the whole the tendency of the age brought them into an extraordinary popularity.[25] To deny that they exerted a great influence on prose style would be to fly in the face of all the evidence. That they played a certain part in promoting the use of the Gorgianic figures, just as the revival of Cicero and Isocrates did, is perfectly clear.

It does not follow, however, that either the Church Fathers or the classical orators played the most important part in producing this result. For there is a third explanation which does not seem to have occurred to the minds of those who have given their attention to this subject, yet which lies closer at hand than either of the others. It is to be found in the great body of medieval literature in Latin which descended to the period of the Renaissance, and the immense influence

The Church Fathers

Medieval Latin prose

---

[24] The form of the style of Apuleius, for instance, is hardly distinguishable in some of his works from that of Cyprian. *The Greek Romances in Elizabethan Prose Fiction*, by Samuel L. Wolff (New York, 1912), draws attention to a source which must be further investigated. It would seem, however, that the Greek romances served as a model for *estilo culto* in Sidney alone, if at all.

[25] [*Legalists*, a term usually reserved for the canonists, who were of a much later period, is a curious word to use for the Church Fathers. On the general point of their popularity, see P. Polman, *L'Élément Historique dans la Controverse Religieuse du XVIe Siècle* (Gembloux, 1932); for the medieval period, B. Smalley, *The Study of the Bible in the Middle Ages*, 2nd ed. (Oxford, 1952); and for the English Renaissance, Rosemond Tuve, *A Reading of George Herbert* (Chicago, 1952).]

which the medieval tradition exercised upon the sixteenth century, in matters of style as well as in thought. This is the element in the history of the Euphuistic style which I wish to emphasize, and to estimate as exactly as may be. Great difficulties, it is true, attend the student who would thread the maze of medieval Latin prose, and uncertainty is bound to wait upon his conclusions. Even the history of its monuments has only been written in part, and the description of its rhetorical forms has not even been attempted. It is a *selva oscura* in which one finds no guide.[26] This fact explains clearly enough the neglect of it by students of sixteenth-century style, and at the same time it justifies a modest claim for the present discussion. In the existing state of our knowledge no conclusions can be considered final or satisfactory; but at least the lines which future investigation of Euphuism must follow may be indicated.

✧ IV ✧

Medieval Latin Prose

The study of rhetoric in the Middle Ages began at an early date to divide into two branches. The first was the method of study formulated in the rhetorical schools of the Empire, founded on the imitation of the Roman and Greek orators, and handed down, with inevitable changes, to the monastic schools of all Europe. At first, of course, the ancient tradition was represented with a fair degree of fullness: the well-rounded method of Cicero and Quintilian had worthy interpreters among a certain class of teachers; on the other hand the Anti-Ciceronianism of Seneca and Tacitus found advocates in other schools of the Empire; while in still others the rhetoric taught by the Greek sophists returned with renewed vigor from certain provincial centers where it had been adopted by leaders of Christian thought. But when instruction passed over into the monastic schools, both the method and the subject matter of the ordinary training in oratorical style were gradually narrowed and defined. The classical method of imitation of authors was replaced by the method of precept, definition, and example; Church Fathers and the Scriptures replaced the classical authors to a great extent as the sources of illustrative citations;

Two kinds of medieval rhetorical training

---

[26] [There are now some guides: see *APS*, n.6a.]

and the more solid and serious parts of rhetoric, dealing with invention, the disposition of materials, and so on, dropped out of use. This branch of rhetoric, therefore, was reduced in most schools to the study of the figures of speech; and the typical textbook or manual consists merely of a list of the schemes and tropes with one or two examples of each.[27]

The forms of prose in which the results of such monastic training are apparent are those in which the church addressed itself to its popular audience in the tone of warning, exhortation, and appeal. The sermon is certainly the most important of these: the Lives of Saints are usually most closely allied to the sermon; and the Treatise of Devotion or Edification is generally not very different for it too is often meant to be read aloud. A heightened rhetoric of the same type appears also in some chronicles, especially in the speeches, and in passages where the narrative is raised to a high emotional level. In short, the monastic rhetoric, as we may call it, betrays its origin in oratory, and its peculiar fitness for public discourse on elevated themes.

1. The oratorical

The other branch of rhetorical study, in which the figures of speech played only a minor part, is not less important. The *ars dictandi*—to give it the name it assumed at the end of the eleventh century—began as an art of formal and official letter-writing, but its important function was to control the style of the official documents and the ceremonial forms of church and state. The secretarial offices of the Papacy and the Empire were the centers from which its influence emanated; and there was no phase of public life in the Middle Ages which it did not adorn and in some degree direct; it was the school, it is now believed, in which medieval law was bred and brought to maturity; it presided over the organization of the liturgy and the style of its prayers; it prescribed the form of proclamations, bulls, decrees; it directed the stately observances of princely courts. Indeed there is no form of art which expresses so fully the institutional life of the Middle Ages as the ceremonial

2. The ceremonial or secretarial

---

[27] The chief sources from which information has been drawn in this and the following paragraphs are Norden, pp. 659-731; P. Abelson, *The Seven Liberal Arts: A Study in Medieval Culture* (New York, 1906), esp. Ch. v; Dietrich Reichling, *Das Doctrinale des Alexander de Villa Dei*. Monumenta Germaniae Paedagogica, XII (Berlin, 1893), Einleitung; *Rhetores Latini Minores*, ed. Karl F. von Halm (Leipzig, 1863); Karl Hirsche, *Prolegomena zu einer Neuen Ausgabe der Imitatio Christi* (Berlin, 1873), I, 89-264.

Latin prose of church and state, and none, unless it be architecture, which expressed it in a nobler and worthier way.[28] It has its representatives, too, in certain forms of sixteenth-century English prose which are worthy of their Latin prototypes.

But we are concerned here with the *ars dictandi* only as it affected the history of the other kind of rhetorical training. It rapidly rose in

Impover-
ishment
of the
former

importance and dignity after the new foundation of the Empire by Charlemagne, assuming finally most of the rights and privileges, and sometimes even claiming the use of the name, of *ars rhetorica* in the trivium.[29] And as it grew in dignity it enriched its content by assimilating the noblest parts of the rhetoric of the ancients. The school rhetoric of schemes and tropes on the other hand, tended to become more arid and trivial as it isolated itself from the other features of an ancient orator's training. Its impoverishment was due in part, of course, to the widening gap between the ancient and the medieval world, but probably in a still greater degree to the aggrandizement of the *ars dictandi* at its expense.

It must not be supposed, however, that there was a real rivalry or competition between the two. They were both parts of the education

Results
of this

of the medieval clerk, and the effect of the immensely important development of the dictator's function[30] was rather to reduce the rhetoric of figures to an earlier period and a humbler station in the curriculum than to exclude it. Indeed it may have had the result of making the training in schemes and tropes more general and elective. For when such training lost ground in the higher education, it was apparently magnified in a corresponding degree in the elementary stages, where it had already had a part in the schools of the Empire.[31] The great grammars of the

[28] See Ludwig Rockinger, "Über die *Ars Dictandi* und die *Summae Dictaminis* in Italien," *Sitzungsberichte der Historische Klasse der Akademie der Wissenschaften zu München*, I (1861), 98-151 [and his standard edition of *dictamen* texts in *Briefsteller und Formelbucher des Eilften bis Vierzehnten Jahrhunderts*, Quellen und Erörterungen zur Bayerischen und Deutschen Geschichte, IX:1 (Munich, 1863; repr. 2 vols., New York, 1961)]; and the sketch and bibliography in L. J. Paetow, *The Arts Course at Medieval Universities with Special Reference to Grammar and Rhetoric* (Champaign, Ill., 1910). [Cf. R. J. Schoeck, "Rhetoric and Law in Sixteenth-Century England," *SP*, L (1953), 110-127.]

[29] [On rhetorical training in Charlemagne's court, and the importance of Alcuin, see L. Wallach, *Alcuin and Charlemagne* (Ithaca, N.Y., 1959).]

[30] [I.e. the function of one who dictates.]

[31] [See A. Gwynn, *Roman Education from Cicero to Quintilian* (Oxford, 1926); C. N. Cochrane, *Christianity and Classical Culture* (New York, 1944); and H.-I.

early Middle Ages, Donatus and Priscian, each contained a section on the figures, and the *Doctrinale* of Alexander de Villa Dei, which in some places superseded these old books from the thirteenth century onward, offered the same instruction in versified form.[32] What is true of these important books is also true of nearly all the minor grammars, and it is clear that the figures did not suffer from neglect by losing the name of rhetoric.

So much needed to be said in order to account for the forms of Latin prose that are involved in the history of Euphuism. When the story of medieval style comes to be written, it will have

Examples of the oratorical style

to proceed systematically along such lines as these, that is, by a careful study of the methods of rhetorical training. But the subject cannot be followed farther here. All that can be done is to illustrate the results of the universal study of the figures of speech by gathering a few examples of the kinds of prose in which they appear. The difficulty arises only from embarrassment of riches; but there is no need for nice selection, because the countless examples offer but little variation, as regards the points of style with which we are concerned, except such as are due to individual choice. The examples we select are from the forms of prose discourse mentioned in a previous paragraph, the sermon, the *vita sancti*, the book of devotion, and the chronicle; and they are all chosen from works which were either written in England or very well known there.

The earliest is from Bede's sermon on the Annunciation. (Some of the simpler forms of *paromoion*, or sound correspondence, are indicated by markings.)

Nec se tamen de singularitate meriti excellentioris singulariter extollit, sed potius suae conditionis ac divinae dignationis in omnibus memor, famularum se Christi consortio humiliter adjungit, famulatum Christo devota quod jubetur impendit.[33]

Marrou, *Histoire de l'Éducation dans l'Antiquité* (Paris, 1950), esp. 268ff. On twelfth-century use of Priscian and Donatus, see C. H. Haskins, *The Renaissance of the Twelfth Century* (Cambridge, Mass., 1927), pp. 129ff. and G. Paré, A. Brunet, P. Tremblay, *La Renaissance du XIIe Siècle* (Paris, 1933), pp. 151-152.]

[32] See the collection *Grammatici Latini*, ed. H. Keil, 7 vols. (Leipzig, 1857-1880), which contains Priscian in I and II and Donatus in IV.

[33] Bede, "Homilae Genuinae," in *Opera Omnia*, ed. J. A. Giles, 12 vols. (1843-1844), repr. in J. P. Migne, ed. *Patrologia Latina*, XC-XCV (Paris, 1844-), XCIV,

Almost immediately following:

Cujus vocem mentemque nos, fratres charissimi, pro modulo nostro sequentes, famulos esse nos Christi in cunctis actibus nostris motibusque recol*amus*, ejus semper obsequiis omnia corporis nostri membra mancipetur, ad ejus implendam voluntatem totum mentis nostrae dirig*amus* intuitum.[34]

The author of the earliest Latin life of St. Guthlac was a certain Felix, who was an inmate of an English monastic house, possibly Croyland, at the same time that Bede was living at Jarrow. The following sentences are from his *prologus*:

(1) Quapropter admoneo te, Lector, ut aliena non reprehendas, ne ab aliis quasi alienus reprehendaris.[35]

(2) Quoniam igitur exegisti a me, ut de vita Sancti Guthlaci vel conversatione tibi scriberem, *que*madmod*um* coeper*it*, *qui*dve ante proposit*um* fuer*it*, vel *qu*alem vitae termin*um* habuer*it*, . . . addendi minuendique modum vitans eadem orthodemia depinxi; ad hujus utilitatis commodum hunc codicellum fieri ratus sum, ut ill*is*, *qui*

---

col. 14B. As to the figures of sound, note, first, that the first, third, and fourth members are bound together by transverse homoioteleuton (*-iter* (*-etur* . . . *-it*); secondly that within the first member there is transverse alliteration, within the second transverse homoioteleuton, between the third and fourth transverse alliteration; and thirdly that combining with these at several places is the figure sometimes called *figura etymologica*, sometimes *polyptoton*, namely, that form of repetition in which the same stem occurs twice or more, but each time with a different ending or in different inflectional form.

[The literature on the medieval sermon is now rather large; convenient summaries of scholarship on the *ars praedicandi* and the practice of the medieval sermon occur in Louis Mourin, *Six Sermons Français Inédits de Jean Gerson* (Paris, 1946), esp. pp. 583ff.; and W. O. Ross, ed., *Middle English Sermons*, *EETS*, CCIX (Oxford, 1940). Still standard is Th.-M. Charland, *Artes Praedicandi: Contribution à l'Histoire de la Rhétorique au Moyen Âge*, Publications de l'Institut d'Études Mediévales d'Ottawa, VII (Paris, 1936); and still foundational are the studies of Owst and Caplan listed by Ross and by James J. Murphy in his excellent bibliography of the *ars praedicandi* and its place among the arts of discourse: "The Medieval Arts of Discourse: An Introductory Bibliography," *Speech Monographs*, XXIX (1962), 71ff. See also *CBEL*, V, 318 and Ryan, *Ascham*, p. 362, n.109, and the Bibliography in Blench, *Preaching in England*.]

[34] Ibid., col. 14c. This is chosen to illustrate the less obvious use of the figures. Note, first, isocolon (the four members have 23, 24, 22, 24 syllables respectively); secondly, the rhyme (*-amus*); thirdly, the polyptoton in *nostro . . . nostris . . . nostri . . . nostrae*; etc.

[35] *Das Angelsächsische Prosa-Leben des Heilige Guthlac*, ed. Paul Gonser, Anglistische Forschungen, XXVII (Heidelberg, 1909), 102. Two cases of polyptoton crossing each other.

sciu*nt* memoriam tanti viri, nota revocandi fia*t*, h*is* vero, *qui* ignora*nt*, velut latae panseniae indicium innotesca*t*.[36]

In his narrative Felix is much more turgid:

(1) Sic (sc. *Deus*) . . . Guthlacum de tumide aestuantis sae-culi gurgite, de obliqu*is* mortal*is* saeculi anfract*ibus*, de atr*is* vergent*is* mund*i* fauc*ibus* ad perpetuam beatitud*inis* militia*m*, ad rect*i* itin*eris* calle*m*, ad ver*i* lum*inis* pros-pect*um* perduxit.[37]

(2) Quod ubi qu*i* intererant prospex*erunt*, statim tremefact*i* stupentes stet*erunt*, adeo ut vix fari potui*ssent*, vix mira-culum intueri aud*erent*, et vix ipsi quid ag*erent* no*ssent*.[38]

The next examples are from chronicles; the first two from Jocelyn of Brakelond, in the thirteenth century:

(1) Et ita omnia complanari fecit, quod infra annum ubi stet*erat* nobile edificium vidimus fab*as* pullul*are*, et ubi jacu*erant* dolia vini, urtic*as* abund*are*.[39]

(2) Vidit et alium cum eo militem, Gilbertum de Cerivilla, non solum quantum ad apparentiam gradu dignitatis in-feriorem, sed et ab humeris supra statura minorem. . . . Et jam totus desper*ans*, et rationem in impetum con-vert*ens*, impugn*antis*, non defend*entis*, assumpsit officium. Qui dum fortiter percussit, fortius percussus est, et dum viriliter impugnabat, virilius impugnabat, virilius im-pugnabatur. Quid multa? Victus occubuit.[40]

Capgrave, in the fifteenth century, conducts his narrative usually on a low level of fact and record, where only simple forms of the figures are appropriate; but in dedications he rises higher, as is usual indeed in other authors:

[36] Ibid., pp. 102-103. In the last part occurs a phenomenon which, I think, is not noted by writers on medieval rhyme-prose, though it is very common, namely, transverse rhyme, i.e. rhyme between alternate members (*-ny* . . . *-t* . . . *nt* . . . *-t*). Observe that rhyme-prose does not simply rhyme, but also involves other sound correspondences within the rhyming members. [See n.78 below.]

[37] Ibid., p. 59. Note the exact correspondence of final sounds, word by word, in successive numbers, and also the "syllabic antithesis" (intentional variation of vowels) in *-am* . . . *-em* . . . *-um*, near the end.

[38] Ibid., p. 13. Here, beside other figures, is enclosed rhyme, at the end (and also "syllabic antithesis"); *-issent* . . . *ērent* . . . *-ērent* . . . *-ossent*.

[39] *Chronica Jocelini de Brakelonda*, ed. J. G. Rokewode, Camden Society, XIII (London, 1840), p. 23.

[40] Ibid., p. 52.

Hunc libellum . . . ubi laudes eorum qui nomen vestrum sortiuntur ex veterum libris collegi, quatenus vos, qui hoc *nomine* laure*amini*, virtutem quoque *nomin*is imit*emini*.[41]

The style of many books of devotion may be represented by some selections from the *Imitatio Christi*, in the first of which I have ventured to represent the divisions into which the sentence falls with regard to the figures of sound by printing them in a form resembling a stanza of verse:

(1) Quod idcirco cum electis tuis dispensanter agis: ut
        veraciter agnoscant
                et
        patenter experiantur
    quantum infirmitatis ex se ipsis habeant,
                et
        quid bonitatis et gratiae ex te consequantur;
            quia
    ex semet ipsis frigidi duri et indevoti:
    ex te autem ferventes alacres et devoti
                      esse merentur.
Quis enim
    ad fontem suavitatis humiliter accedens
        non modicum suavitatis inde reportat?
Aut quis
    juxta copiosum ignem stans
        non parum caloris inde percipit?
Et tu
    fons es semper plenus
      et superabundans:
  ignit jugiter ardens,
    et numquam deficiens.[42]

(2) Etenim licet tanto *desiderio* tam specialum devotorum tuorum non ardeo, tamen de gratia tua illius magis in-

[41] John Capgrave, *Liber de Illustribus Henricis*, ed. F. C. Hingeston (P.R.O., *Rerum Britannicarum Medii Aevi Scriptores*, no. 7, 1858), p. 2.

[42] The point to be observed here is the alternating rhyme (*a b a b*) spoken of in a note just above. The arrangement in lines is made (except at the end) for the purpose of illustrating this. It must be understood that the arrangement does not imply a belief in the metrical character of the prose; it has no such character. The passage is from Book IV, Ch. 4.

polyptoton

flammati *desiderii desiderium* habeo orans et *desiderans*, omnium talium fervidorum amatorum tuorum participem me fieri ac eorum sancto consortio annumerari.[43]

Now in the choice of these passages no attempt has been made to find those which particularly resemble Euphuism in the exact

Varieties in the schematic medieval style

form of the *schemata* used. Such passages could be found by a careful selection. But they would not fairly represent the medieval Latin use of the *schemata*, and this is all that I aim to do here. Nor indeed can any selection of short passages accomplish this purpose as well as could be desired. For in medieval Latin, as in all other forms of style characterized by the schemes, variety is studied: a passage characterized by one of the schemes is followed by one in which a different one is used; or if the same schemes are continued they are combined in a different pattern. By far the most prevalent figures, however, are those which are most characteristic of Euphuism, namely, *parison* with the various kinds of *paromoion*. Nor is there variety within a composition alone. Different authors have their characteristic patterns, their favorite schemes, their own ways of combining them, alternating, and varying them, their preferences in rhythm, clause length, and periodic structure. There is the same variety, in short, in all these respects that there is between all the sixteenth-century ornate rhetoricians, between Guevara and Lyly, for instance, between North and Lyly, between Lyly and Sidney.

It cannot be denied that there is a similarity between the medieval rhetorical style and the usual form of *estilo culto* in the sixteenth

Two objections

century. Two difficulties present themselves however, when we attempt to establish a historical connection between the two things on the basis of similarity of form.

First, there is a difficulty due to the history of the schematic style. The source of the medieval use of the schemes is in the Gorgianic

[43] Book IV, Ch. 14. This is a patterned web of sound. (1) The polyptoton on the stem *desider-*; (2) the repetition at the end of the pattern *-tum -orum -orum* which had occurred near the beginning; (3) the repetition of final *o* at fairly regular intervals in the first part (*desiderio . . . ardeo . . . habeo*); (4) the gathering up in the last words of these two sound patterns (*-orum* and *-o*); (5) the homoioteleuton in the final words of the last two members (*me fieri . . . -merari*).

1. The schemes are also classical

school of ancient Greece, of which Isocrates was the inheritor and the chief ornament. From him the Gorgianic rhetoric passed on to the sophists' schools of the decadent period, and was thence diffused to Imperial Rome and the founders of Christian eloquence, Ambrose, Augustine, Cyprian; and it was by way of the latter, the Church Fathers, especially through the mediation of Gregory the Great, that it proceeded to its great medieval destinies. It may be argued therefore, with some appearance of truth, that on the one hand it makes little difference whether we call the Euphuistic rhetoric classical or medieval, since whatever its immediate source may be its ultimate source is the school of Gorgias, and on the other hand that the problem is insoluble after all, since we have no instruments of precision delicate enough to mark the distinction between classical and medieval influence. But these inferences would not be justified by the facts. For the medieval oratory is in fact as unlike the Greek of Isocrates or the Latin of the Church Fathers as Western Gothic is unlike Romanesque, or Romanesque unlike the pure architecture of Athens or Rome. It is different in spirit, as everything medieval is different from everything classical. But it is also different in form, so different from Isocrates that the similarity cannot be detected except by minute analysis, and unlike the style of the Church Fathers (to which it is more closely related) in certain definite particulars.

The dissimilarity can best be explained by a reference to what has already been said of the method of medieval rhetorical study.

Yet they are used in one way in the classics

In the training of the Greek orator the study of the figures was a part—a small part—of an elaborate system of stylistic education. The word schemes therefore occur, when they occur at all, in their speeches and writings, with comparative infrequency, and always in a subordinate relation to other elements in their composition, especially rhythmic design and periodic structure, which they are meant to reinforce and illustrate. This is true even of Gorgias, who has more use of schemes than his followers and a less elaborate period; while it is eminently true of Isocrates. Indeed in the case of the latter writer, the alleged model of Euphuism, it was commonly recognized by Renaissance critics that the only one of the schemes which can be called characteristic of him is isocolon, or equal members, and that this is used by him for the sake of rhythmic effect. Parison and the various forms of paromoion he uses in the same moderation in which they appear in much good modern speaking, and always in simple forms rather than ingenious or complex ones.

In the Middle Ages, on the other hand, the results of an almost exclusive training in the figures are apparent. The schemes have

And in a different way in the Middle Ages

become the main, often the only, resource for the adornment and heightening of discourse. Every other feature of style has become subordinate to them. Their use is no longer to mark and emphasize rhythm: on the contrary, rhythm arises incidentally from the use of isocolon, parison, and paromoion, and takes its pattern from the laws of these *schemata*. The period is only a certain complete design of verbal and oral device. In short, the figures give the style its pattern and structure; and it need hardly be added that in the characteristic works from which we have been quoting, Bede's sermons, the *Imitatio*, and so on, they appear, not occasionally, but in sentence after sentence, paragraph after paragraph.

But not only are the schemes very much more frequent in medieval prose than in classical. They are also used in different

And they are of different forms

ways. The schematic ornament is constantly made more obvious in one of two ways. Either a single figure is repeated over and over in a succession of short members, with something of the effect of a magic incantation (parison with homoioteleuton being the commonest form for this purpose), or else different schemes or different forms of the same one are woven together in a complicated pattern within a period or paragraph. Both of these methods of elaboration are illustrated also in Euphuism and its related forms, but the latter is especially important in connection with our present subject of inquiry. It is abundantly illustrated even in the few illustrations quoted in the preceding pages. We have seen, for instance, in a single sentence of Bede, a very remarkable combination of transverse alliteration, transverse homoioteleuton, and paronomasia, each of these schemes occurring more than once, and one crossing or including another; in Felix, homoioteleuton used, not in the final words alone of parisonic members, but in all the words, and this not once but two or three times in the same sentence; in Thomas à

Kempis a pattern of transverse parison with transverse paromoion which equals in complexity some of the more difficult forms of stanzaic structure in verse; and so on. In all the authors quoted there appears, moreover, in combination with the figures already mentioned, that form of repetition in which the same stem occurs two or more times, each time with a different inflectional ending, the scheme known as polyptoton.[44]

Of course it need not be said that nothing even suggesting such a use of the "Gorgianic" figures can be found in any classical author.

Schematic rhetoric in the Church Fathers

To distinguish between the medieval rhetoric and that of Augustine, Cyprian, and other Church Fathers is a somewhat more difficult task and one from which we are debarred here by limitations of space. It can only be said in general that, while the schemes are used much more profusely by the patristic writers than by any classical author, they give no signs of the exclusive medieval method of study, but on the contrary constant signs of intelligent imitation of the ancients, and in particular that these writers prefer the simpler of the two methods of schematic elaboration described above, namely, the use of parison and homoioteleuton in a row of phrases or clauses, while the more *characteristic* medieval method is the complication of figures within a period. This difference, however, is less marked in Cyprian than in Augustine and Ambrose; and it must be said that if we had to depend on internal evidence alone, or on the style of single authors, it would be hard to distinguish the influence of medieval rhetoric on the *estilo culto* from that of Cyprian and his immediate imitators, or, we may add, from that of Apuleius, which Cyprian's so markedly resembles. When all of the authors of *estilo culto* and all the Church Fathers are taken together, however, the case is very clear.

The second objection that may be urged to some of the examples of medieval style which have been quoted, and to many which might

---

[44] A note is required on this figure. It is one of the commonest schemes in medieval Latin; but some writers use it a great deal, others rarely. So also in *estilo culto*. Lyly uses it seldom, though he produces a similar effect by repeating a word several times in different parts of his sentences or period, each time with a peculiar difference of context—as, for instance, if it be a noun, with a different preposition each time, or preceded by a different verb. Guevara and Sidney, on the other hand, are very fond of it. In Sidney, for instance, *beauty . . . beauties . . . beautiful, likely . . . likeliest.*

2. Rime-prose should be excluded

be cited for the same purpose, is that they illustrate a very peculiar type of prose which should not be used in the discussion, namely, the medieval rime-prose, of which so much has been said, and so little said wisely. There are two answers to this objection. The first is that rimed Latin prose is nothing but a form of the medieval schematic prose style with a special attention to parison and homoioteleuton. It is prose, not poetry; and Norden has proved that its origin is in the prose use of the schemes.[45]

The answers to this objection

The second answer, still more to the purpose, is that, whatever its history may be, rime-prose is very important in the discussion of the forms of style that appear in Euphuism. For it is not only rimed prose. Along with its rime (the character of which will be spoken of in a moment) it uses constantly all of the other figures of sound which appear in the schematic prose of medieval Latin and sixteenth-century Spanish and English. This point does not need elaboration; it has already been illustrated in the specimens of medieval Latin prose quoted above.[46] But there is an observation to be made here which is of the very first importance to the student of Euphuism, though it has to do with a detail of style. In the rimed Latin prose there is a constant occurrence, not accidental or careless, but conscious and planned, of so-called rimes, in which there is correspondence of the final sound, but non-correspondence, intentional contrast, between the sounds which would have to correspond to make true rime. A typical case is where the unaccented final syllables are alike, but the preceding syllable, bearing the accent, has in each case a different vowel. Thus: *habere, audire, amare*. But it is enough if the final *sounds* correspond; the rest of the final *syllable* may differ. For instance, in the example quoted by Norden from Hroswitha: *extorsi . . . cremari*. A final consonant may

---

[45] *Die Antike Kunstprosa*, II, 760-763. "I am satisfied to have shown that it is a thousand-year-long development from Gorgias, and the traces of its origin are found in it everywhere." But also, of course, the traces of the medieval schematic mind. There is no reason, in short, for drawing any distinction between rime-prose in the form in which it most commonly occurs, and the other forms of prose due to the monastic oratorical training. As we shall see below, rime-prose is a form which has special significance in connection with sixteenth-century style. [The standard treatment, Karl Polheim, *Die Lateinische Reimprosa* (Berlin, 1925).]

[46] See nn.33-43.

THE SOURCES OF THE EUPHUISTIC RHETORIC

even be the only trait of likeness, the vowel of the final syllable being intentionally different in each case, as in a sentence quoted above from Felix: *militiam . . . callem . . . prospectum*. Commenting on this usage, Norden wonders just when such correspondences of sound came to be considered rime or homoioteleuton, since they were never regarded as such by the ancient rhetoricians.

Now such correspondences are a common and characteristic feature of Euphuism, again not by accident, but by intention. The

Syllabic antith- esis

examples are many: *nature . . . nurture, lover . . . liver, travail . . . trouble, hapless . . . hopeless*, and so on. Child discusses the figure, while limiting it too narrowly, under the name *annomination*,[47] and Land-

mann and Weymouth more exactly describe it as *syllabic antithesis*. But it has not been noticed that Wilson[48] refers to it when he says that "like endings" are made more attractive when "letters are altered," and in his examples of "like endings" gives *cart . . . court, labour . . . honour, living . . . hanging*. Norden might well have extended his query concerning this figure and asked how it happened that Lyly, Guevara, North, and so many other sixteenth-century writers came by it if the source of their rhetoric is indeed the imitation of antiquity. In fact, its occurrence is in itself a convincing evidence that *estilo culto* derived its form, in part at least, from medieval Latin prose, for this characteristic feature of it could not have come from the classics, from the Church Fathers, from Apuleius, or from the Greek romances.

✧ V ✧

Humanistic Criticism of the Schemata

The foregoing survey has made it apparent, I think, that there is a striking resemblance between the oratorical prose of the Middle

---

[47] *John Lyly and Euphuism*, p. 54. Child quotes from G. P. March, *Lectures on the English Language* (1861), p. 567, the statement that this figure "can hardly be distinguished from Euphuism," meaning that it is the characteristic feature of the style.

[48] *Arte of Rhetorique*, ed. Mair, p. 202. [Of Wilson's examples, only *cart/court* is an example of strict syllabic antithesis; of the examples of Euphuism cited, only one (*travail/trouble*) is not. Wilson's appear to be accidental occurrences, but in Euphuism they are clearly intentional. There is a discussion of Croll on Wilson in Williamson, *Senecan Amble*, pp. 61-67, 76-83. See n. 78 below.]

Ages and the Euphuistic type of prose. The questions of origins must ultimately be decided by such comparisons of form. But there are several kinds of external evidence bearing on this subject which must not be disregarded. The first of these is found in the testimonies of contemporary critics who discuss the schematic rhetoric and the forms of prose in which it appears. It is one of the many merits of Norden's work that it has revealed the remarkable soundness of Renaissance criticism wherever questions of style are involved. He has declared himself the champion of the humanists as against many modern scholars who are disposed to hold them lightly; and it must be said that he has made good his contention that they are better to be trusted as guides through the maze of Renaissance prose than any recent historians of the subject, and that they are usually better critics, too, of *ancient* prose than we. Everyone who has to treat these subjects must acknowledge that he has revealed new sources of knowledge. In the particular case before us, however, it would seem that he himself has misrepresented the critics whom he values, as the result of his zeal for a theory which he has adopted too hastily. The passages he cites from the humanists seem, it is true, to support his belief in the classical origin of Euphuism and its related styles. But if space permitted their close examination, it would appear that they are either irrelevant, inconclusive, or to be interpreted in a different sense from that which Norden gives them. There are certainly other passages, overlooked by Norden, which militate against his theory.

Norden's argument from humanistic criticism

Our first point, then, is that the testimonies of humanistic critics, in so far as they are significant at all—many of them we will not understand until we know more of medieval prose style—indicate both a dislike of the schematic rhetoric and a disposition to associate it with anticlassical tendencies and tastes.

Not justified by the facts

For instance, not one only, but many humanists refer to the most familiar kinds of schemes as characteristic of the style of preachers, and especially of medieval preachers. Thus, Wilson, writing of the custom of abusing "similar endings," says: "I heard a preacher deliting much in this kind of composition, who used so often to end his sentences with words like unto that which went before, that in

The schemata are usually associated

268

with
sermon-
style

my judgment there was not a dozen sentences in his whole sermon, but they ended all in Rime for the most part."[49] Indeed the use of this figure is constantly qualified as *de more fratrum*—as, for instance, by an anonymous rhetorician of the fifteenth century quoted by Norden,[50] and in the following significant passage from Coluccio Salutati in a letter to the bishop of Florence. He is praising a sermon of his correspondent, in which, he says, everything is pleasing, but especially that "it does not trifle with that artificial rhythm; there is none of that equality of syllables, which is not wont to happen without exact counting; there are none of those clausules which end or fall alike. For this is reprehended by our Cicero as nothing else than a puerile thing which is far from decent in serious matters or when used by men of gravity. Blessed be God that we now see one sermon in which this ferment has not been at work, which can be read without a tune or an effeminate prattle of consonance (*sine concentu et effeminata consonantiae cantilena*)."[51]

In these passages the popular sermon is the object of the humanists' odium. Elsewhere, however, other forms of schematic style

The
schematic
style
usually
contrasted
with the
classical

are compared with a pure prose in imitation of the ancients. And the terms of the comparison are always the same: the latter is serious, weighty, dignified; the other is vain and entertaining. Vives uses it when he compares the *oratio aulica*, that is, the style of Guevara, which he characterizes as *deliciosa, lasciva, ludibunda*, with the true form of a *gravis et sancta oratio*.[52]

Wilson takes up the theme, ridiculing what he calls "Minstrels' elocution," which in lieu of "weightiness and gravitie of words," has nothing to offer but "wantonness of invention."[53] It is notable, moreover, that Wilson, as we shall see in a moment, does not mention the true classics in his elaborate discussion of the figure of like endings; while in writing of "equal members" he says: "Isocrates passeth in this behalfe, who is thought to write altogether in nomber [that is, rhythmically], keeping just proportion in framing of his sentence."[54] By the figure of "equal members" he means approximate balance in the *length* of clauses (not in their form),

[49] *Arte of Rhetorique*, p. 168.   [50] *Antike Kunstprosa*, II, 765, *n*.
[51] Ibid.
[52] Ibid., II, 794, referring to Vives, *De Ratione Scribendi* (1532), p. 114. [See n.74 below.]
[53] *Arte of Rhetorique*, p. 203.   [54] Ibid., p. 204.

for the sake of rhythmical effect, and he disconnects it, as his examples show, from the more obvious schemes which are characteristic of medieval and Euphuistic prose. The significance of the passage is that a typical humanist shows a clear knowledge of what is really characteristic of Isocrates, distinguishes it from the other schemes, and praises the former, while he condemns the abuses which have arisen in the use of the latter.

The objection may arise here that in some of the criticisms just quoted the critics use only the term "like ending" or its equivalent. It may be said that they are excluding the other schemes, or even that they are not thinking of anything but rime-prose. In the first place, concerning rime-prose, it has been shown above what figures are included in it. And, in the second place, the figure called *similiter cadentes* (or *desinentes*) does not, in the common use of the time, include only rime, even when it is scornfully alluded to under that name. It is the practice of rhetoricians, from Bede onward,[55] to treat under this caption all correspondences of sound between words occurring in similar positions in parallel phrases or clauses. The passage from Salutati clearly shows, for instance, that he has in mind the general use of the schemes by medieval preachers, though Norden applies his words only to the rimed sermon; and the examples framed by Wilson to illustrate the figure of like endings show how much he includes in it. Some of these are as follows: "Where learning is loved, there labour is esteemed: but when sloth is thought solace, there rudeness taketh place"; "A King is honoured that is a King indeed"; "He is a meeter man to drive the cart than to serve the court"; "Through labour cometh honour, through idle living followeth hanging." Here of course are parison, repetition, alliteration, simple and transverse, and syllable antithesis—all Euphuistic traits—as well as like endings. After remarking, perhaps with allusion to the *Diall of Princes*, which had appeared three years before,[56] that "divers in this our time delite much in this kind of writing,"

The content of the phrase "like endings"

[55] Bede, "De Schematis et Tropis Sacrae Scripturae Liber," in Migne, *Patrologia Latina*, xc (1862), cols. 175-186. [See under *Homoeoteleuton*, cols. 178-179. In Halm, *Rhetores*, pp. 607-618.] Bede gives examples from Gregory and says that this is the figure which Jerome called *concinnas rhetorum declamationes*. [Cf. the discussion of Bede in Howell, *Logic and Rhetoric*, 116ff.]

[56] That is, before 1560. The 1553 ed. of the work is much shorter, and does not contain some of the most important parts.

Wilson goes on to sketch the history of "this kind of writing"; and the whole passage must be quoted at greater length than it has already been, because it supports in a remarkable way the contention that the associations of the Lylyan forms were chiefly medieval in contemporary thought:

"S. Augustine had a goodly gift in this behalfe, and yet some thinkes he forgot measure, and used overmuch this kind of figure. Notwithstanding, the people were such where he lived that they tooke muche delite in rimed sentences, and in Orations made ballade wise. Yea, thei were so nice and so waiward to please, that except the preacher from time to time could rime out his sermon, they would not long abide the hearing. . . . So that for the flowing

Passage from Wilson's *Rhetoric*
stile and full sentence, crept in Minstrels elocution, talking matters altogether in rime, and for waightinesse and gravitie of wordes, succeding notthing els but wantonnesse of invention. Tullie was forsaken, with Livie, Caesar, and other: Apuleius, Ausonius, with

such Minstrell makers were altogether followed. And I thinke the Popes heretofore (seeing the peoples folie to bee such) made all our Himnes and Anthemes in rime, that with the singing of men, playing of Orgaines, ringing of Belles, and Riming of Himnes and Sequences, the poore ignorant might think the harmonie to be heavenly, and verely believe that the Angels of God made not a better noyce in heaven. I speak thus much of these ii. figures, not that I thinke folie to use them (for they are pleasant and praise worthy) but my talke is to this ende, that they should neither onely nor chiefly be used, as I know some in this our time, do overmuch use them in their writings. And overmuch (as all men knowe) was never good yet."[57]

Of course this passage is a little obscured by the Protestant digression concerning the liturgical use of the parisonic figures;

Its significance
but it is clear that Wilson attributes the common use of these figures to the imitation of the Church Fathers and their contemporary masters of late Latinity, that

he regards it as a departure from true classicism, and that the associations of these figures in his mind are all medieval and non-humanistic.[58]

---

[57] *Arte of Rhetorique*, pp. 202-204.
[58] We may quote, as in the same tone as Wilson's criticism, the discussion of the style of St. Ambrose by one of the speakers in the dialogue *Ciceronianus*, by

Not quite so clear as Wilson's, yet of the same effect, are the testimonies of two other English humanists of a little later date: Thomas Drant and Gabriel Harvey. In the preface to his translations from Horace (publ. in 1566) Drant laments the difficulty of finding readers for "lettered and clerkly makings"; "and no doubt," he continues, "the cause that books of learning seem so hard is, because such and such a scull of amorous pamphlets have so preoccupied the eyes and ears of men, that a multitude believe there is no other style or phrase else worth gramercy." He describes the "wanton tricks of lovers" which form the subject matter of these romantic tales, and at the same time parodies their style, which, in contrast with a clerkly style, is "easy to be understanded and easy to be endited."[59] The passage must be written with reference to the recent successes of Painter and Fenton, who seem first to have used the schematic style in the *novello*, though less elaborately than Pettie and Lyly afterward did; for the parody is an imitation of the style that later came to be known as Euphuistic.

There is something more than mere abuse in Harvey's railing at Lyly's style; and though his *Advertisement for Pap-hatchet* was provoked by Lyly's part in the Martin Marprelate controversy, he makes it clear that his strictures are meant for the Euphuizing Lyly. After parodying Eu-

Thomas Drant

Gabriel Harvey

Erasmus: *membris incisis comparibus numerosus ac modulatus suum quoddam dicendi genus habet aliis inimitabile, sed a Tulliano genere diversissimum (Opera,* Leyden, 1703-1706, I, 1008): ("Made rhythmic and measured by short members of equal length, his style has something peculiar to himself, inimitable by others, but most unlike the Ciceronian style.") This is a typical humanist way of apologizing for the barbarism of the Latinity of the fathers of the church.

In a famous interview with two Cardinals, Petrarch was loaded with compliments. He was very much disturbed and embarrassed by the consciousness that these would finally lead to an offer of employment. Though he was resolved to maintain his freedom, he saw no method of procedure open to him, until he learned that the offer was that of literary service in the Papal Chancery. Then his mind was set at ease. For he could show without difficulty that his kind of prose would be unintelligible to readers accustomed to the monkish style, "too aspiring," as he ironically put it, "for the humility of the Apostolic Seat." (*Lettere delle cose familiari,* Book XIII, Letter v [in *Epistolae de rebus familiaribus et variae,* ed. F. Fracassetti (Florence, 1892), II, 229-230 (226-233), but not in A. F. Johnson's *Epistolae Selectae*]). It is probable that the style he alludes to— the style which, as he says, he had had to unlearn when he grew up—was the familiar medieval rhetoric of schemes, especially since he boasts that his own writing is not meant to appeal to the *ears.* "I cannot cater to itching wits or pampered ears" (ibid.).

[59] Quoted by Wendelstein, p. 21n. [Drant's prefaces are reprinted by O. L. Jiriczek in *Shakespeare Jahrbuch,* XLVII (1911), 42-68 and (1919), 126.]

phues for a few sentences, he says: "Gentlemen, I have given you a taste of his sugar-loaf, that weeneth Sidney's dainties, Ascham's comfits, Cheek's succats, Smith's conserves, and More's junkets nothing comparable to his pap." Here Lyly's style is opposed to that of five leading humanists in contempt, but no definite indications of the nature of the contrast are given. Immediately after, however, he says: "The finest wits prefer the loosest period in M. Ascham or Sir Philip Sidney before the tricksiest page in Euphues or Pap-hatchet." Here the true contrast between a classical style and a schematic one is drawn. And the same contrast is more fully brought out in a following passage: "As for a fine or neat period, in the dainty and pithy vein of Isocrates or Xenophon, marry that were a periwig of a Siren, or a wing of the very bird of Arabia, an inestimable relique. . . . It is for Cheek or Ascham to stand leveling of colons, or squaring of periods, by measure and number; his pen is like a spigot, and the wine-press a dullard to his ink-press."[60] Here, it is true, he is writing of Nash, or at least of the pamphlet style, not of the Euphuist; but the words are worth quoting because they characterize the style of Isocrates and the efforts of his imitators in the correct terms; in the terms used by Wilson and by all intelligent critics. It is inconceivable that a critic who recognizes that periodicity and rhythm are the master qualities of Isocrates' prose should fail to draw the same contrast between it and the style of *Euphues*.

✧ VI ✧

The Uses of the Schemata in the Sixteenth Century

In the following pages some further illustrations of how the humanists felt about *estilo culto* will occur. But we proceed to consider a second kind of external evidence concerning its history. This is to be obtained by observing the associations which the Euphuistic rhetoric had in sixteenth-century minds, as they are shown by the kinds of writing in which it appears.

Both Feuillerat and Wendelstein[61] have devoted a good deal of attention to the history of Euphuism in the earlier part of the

[60] "A New Letter of Notable Contents" and "Pierces Supererogation," partly printed in G. Gregory Smith, *Elizabethan Critical Essays* (2 vols., 1904), II, 273-277.
[61] As cited in n.1 and n.21 above.

Supposed humanistic use of Euphuistic figures

century. But they have both started with the theory that the tendency toward Euphuism is humanistic. Wendelstein, it is true, has extended his search very widely, and arrived at much more readable conclusions, but Feuillerat limits his quest for the figures to three humanists—Fisher, More, and Elyot. Now John Fisher, Bishop of Rochester, yields him the most significant results, and indeed we may say that the only examples cited by him which are really characteristic of the Euphuistic tendency come from this writer. But Fisher is not a humanist in the writings which we have from his pen. He had his part in the revival of culture in England, but his own culture and his own style, however admirable they are, are essentially medieval. There is no test fine enough to discover any real change between the earlier fifteenth-century sermon and tractate and those which the Bishop of Rochester wrote for the Lady Margaret and the court of Henry the Eighth. So far as the citations of Feuillerat prove anything they prove the medieval origin of Euphuism.

Not often found in More or Elyot

But More and Elyot are humanists in a different sense, and if the passages quoted from these authors were really Euphuistic and really representative of their authors, they would have an important bearing on the question of origins. It must be said, however, that they are neither the one nor the other. Occurring among a mass of passages from the authors, they may easily pass as having a general similarity with the rest. But if they are carefully separated from this association it will be found that they are not conspicuously schematic at all,—this is especially true of those which are written in the humanistic spirit,—and, further, if they are traced back to the works from which they are taken, and examined in their context, they lose all the significance which is attributed to them. For they occur there at wide intervals, just as they occur in almost any author who thinks of style. They are by no means representative, and it is hardly too much to say that the passages quoted by the investigators are the only conspicuous instances to be found in the works which they have examined. Indeed in the case of Elyot, the citation of a few uses of the *schemata* must be resented as a libel against the memory of a scholar who thoroughly understood the *phrasis* of Greek oratory and tried to reproduce its effect in English. To assume that he was a classicist so ignorant and inexpert that when he tried to imitate the ancients he fell unconsciously into the same devices that characterize popular preaching, is to show one-self ignorant of the real accuracy and intelligence of classical schol-arship in that age. A careful study of any leading humanist will convince one that their knowledge is not to be treated so lightly.

Humanists, however, did not always write with a humanistic intention. They were citizens as well as scholars, and they could descend on occasion from the Olympian heights to speak the familiar dialect of their even-Christians. In order to understand the meaning of any traits of style that may be observed in their works this fact must be kept in mind, and the nature of the subject matter and the general tone of the discourse in which they occur must be carefully considered. Sir Thomas More is on fire with one kind of enthusiasm when he is writing his *Dialogue of Comfort*, and with quite another when he is translating the life of Pico; he has different models of composition before his mind when he is com-posing his *Richard III* and his *Utopia*. And it would not be at all surprising to find that the former of each of these pairs of works is stylistically more medieval than the latter. This is in fact what we do find, if it be granted that the *schemata* are chiefly medieval survivals in the sixteenth century. For Wendelstein has remarked (pp. 8-9) that the figures appear in greater number in the religious works that he has examined than in the *Pico*, and the same difference exists, we may remark, between the *Richard III* and the *Utopia*.[62]

And least in their most hu-manistic writings

[62] [Croll expresses himself rather confusingly in this paragraph, and his rather special uses of "medieval" and "humanistic" may distract a reader from his essential point—that the number of *schemata* in *Richard III* and the *Dialogue of Comfort* is significantly greater than in *Utopia* and the translation of the life of Pico. If it be granted, as Croll has previously been contending, that in most medieval schools the more serious parts of rhetoric dropped out of use, and study of oratorical style reduced to study of figures of speech (cf. above, section IV, second paragraph) or, in the words of this paragraph, that the *schemata* are chiefly "medieval survivals in the sixteenth century," then it follows that in this one stylistic respect (greater use of *schemata*), *Richard III* and the *Dialogue of Comfort* are more medieval than the other two works. In other respects, of course, there are many medieval elements in *Utopia* and non-medieval ones in *Richard III*.

[But Croll makes a fuller point about the humanistic aspect. He claims, in this context, that *Utopia* and the life of Pico are written from Olympian heights and that *Richard III* and the *Dialogue* are written in a more "familiar dialect" and on a less exalted level. In the light of the section on Renaissance Humanism in this essay and the points made in *APL*, it is evident that in tone, subject matter, and models, he finds More's *Utopia* and Pico closer to the highest kind of classicism, and thus more "humanistic" than are the *Dialogue* and *Richard III*. (On Croll's further development of "classical-humanistic" and "Ciceronian," see *APL*.)

But there is little enough of elaborate schematizing in any of More's works. The case is not the same, however, with Ascham, and it is chiefly with reference to him that the above remarks have been made. Both in the *Toxophilus* and in the *Scholemaster* there are passages that are very markedly Euphuistic in the use of figure, *much* more so than any in Elyot or More, and so much so that they cannot be excluded from a place in the line of Euphuistic development. The point that we are now making, however, is that these passages are not to be regarded necessarily as examples of his humanistic ideals in style. For it is easy to draw a line between the passages in which Ascham is writing, on the one hand, in the grave classical manner (as, for instance, at the close of the *Scholemaster*, and in some letters to Cecil[63]), and those in which he writes, on the other hand, in the light, popular vein so well suited to his genius (as in most of the *Toxophilus*), in the tone of the anxious Protestant moralist (as in the passage of the *Scholemaster* which he entitles, "Horsemen be wiser in knowledge of a good colt, than schoolmasters be in knowledge of a good wit"[64]), or in the manner appropriate to courtly

The same distinction to be observed in the case of Ascham

[That More had classical models at hand, especially Tacitus, for his *Richard III*, as R. S. Sylvester demonstrates, and that there is a great deal that is not medieval in that work, does not seriously weaken Croll's terminology; for Tacitus was the first strong influence in the Anti-Ciceronian movement, and Croll is taking the traditional view that the Ciceronian purists were more "classical" or "humanistic" than those writers who, like Lipsius, Muret, and Bacon looked to Tacitus, Seneca, and other Silver Age authors as models. See Richard S. Sylvester, ed., *The History of King Richard III*, Vol. 2 in The Yale Edition of *The Complete Works of St. Thomas More* (New Haven, 1963), pp. lxxxii ff.]

[63] For instance, letter CLXV in Ascham, ed. Giles, I, 349-355. Anyone who wishes to see what the imitation of the classics really produced in English should study this letter. I do not know of any other attempt to reproduce Cicero which is so successful. A single sentence will illustrate the difference between balance as carried out on the Ciceronian model and the same thing in Euphuistic form: "Which sentences I heard very gladly then, and felt them soon after myself to be true." [For an edition, see Albert M. Hayes, "The English Letters of Roger Ascham" (Princeton Univ. diss., 1934).]

[64] *Scholemaster*, Bk. I, in Ascham, ed. Giles, III, 104. [Cf. Ryan, *Ascham*, pp. 279-384: Ascham admired "the so-called 'Gorgianic figures'"; his main classical model was not Cicero but Isocrates. In passages quoted, Ascham uses *isocolon*, *parison*, and *paramoion*, "figures which occur in varying degree in nearly all classical writers of prose," which Ascham had inherited from the ancients and through the works of the Church Fathers and the pulpit oratory of medieval and Tudor preachers. In n.59 (p. 337), Ryan observes that Norden first argued that Isocrates exerted the main influence of euphuism's development and that Croll and T. K. Whipple took issue with this view. "Whipple believed that the influence of Isocrates 'ran counter to the tendency which culminated in *Euphues*. Isocrates

observance (as in the dedication of *Toxophilus* to Henry VIII). It
will be found that the passages in which he dallies nicely with words
in a Euphuistic manner are chiefly of the latter classes.

Yet there does remain in Ascham's letters, especially in his Latin
letters to Sturm, and in certain passages of the *Scholemaster*, a body
of writing in which he uses with conscious preciosity
the figures of parison and paromoion, and plainly does
so in imitation of classical models. It is possible indeed
to draw a distinction between the form of style which
results from such imitation and that which results
from the use of *schemata* elsewhere in his writing. An
ear trained in both the classical and the medieval use
of the schemes will not fail to observe the difference.

But
Ascham
has the
schemes
in much
greater
number

But this point need not be pressed. It must be frankly acknowledged that it was possible for a student of classical oratory by
choosing particular models and laying a particular emphasis on
certain traits—not the most important ones—in those models, to
arrive at a style which would have the use of the *schemata* as its
chief mark and signature. This is in fact what Ascham was doing
in the latter part of his career, when his attention was chiefly given
to literary style. He was studying Cicero and Isocrates constantly;
and one direction that his study was taking is indicated by the fact
that he corresponded with Sturm concerning the antitheta in
Cicero's notorious oration *Pro Quinctio*.[65] One direction only it is

explains the difference between Ascham and Lyly—but not the similarities.' Croll
went further and argued that the well-known medieval development of Gorgianic
and other schemes beyond their use in classical oratory led directly to the peculiar
stylistic features of euphuism. In 1938 William Ringler lent Croll support by
offering as the direct link between medieval practice and euphuism the highly
schematic orations delivered . . . by John Rainolds." (Whipple, "Isocrates and
Euphuism," *MLR*, XI [1916], 15-27, 129-135; Ringler, "The Immediate Source
of Euphuism," *PMLA*, LIII [1938], 678-686.) Ryan concludes (p. 284) that
though one cannot without qualification call Ascham an immediate begetter of
euphuism, "the force of his example undoubtedly lent authority to stylistic
experimentation and may even have led to some of the schematic, though not
the metaphorical, excesses of Lyly and his followers."]

[65] Ascham, ed. Giles, II, letter XCIX (written in 1568). [Ryan (p. 337, n.57)
notes that Gorgianic figures would have been familiar to Ascham from early
grammatical training as well as from pulpit oratory. "In the *Barbarismus*, a standard text in the schools, Donatus treats them among the sixteen figures of words
(*schemata lexeos*) belonging to the grammarian. . . . Ascham's familiarity with
such patristic authors as Sts. Augustine, Cyprian, and Basil . . . would have
exposed him further to the figures. Finally, throughout his correspondence he had
shown exceptionally keen interest in Cicero's rather Gorgianic *Pro Quinctio* and
in the *Gorgias* itself."]

true; for it cannot be too often repeated that these Ciceronians knew their Cicero better than any scholars of the seventeenth or eighteenth century. If Sturm wrote with affection of the balances of sound in Cicero he also wrote a treatise concerning his periods, and even another on those prose rhythms which later scholars, until a recent date, declared to be the birth of disordered fancy in the critics who had observed them. Yet it is not to be denied that he and Ascham liked the frailer beauties of oratory too, and, as men of their time, exaggerated the beauties they liked.

I do not wish to minimize the importance of these considerations; but their importance must not be exaggerated either. The force of the argument which Norden has built up on the strength of the facts we have mentioned might be considerably weakened by asking why it was that men who understood the real beauty of Cicero and Isocrates could yet be so beguiled by their faults or their lesser graces. It would then appear that their tastes at least were medieval, whatever their models were, and that their love of the figures was due to a tradition they could not escape from. But even a weightier reply to Norden is that Ascham, the only humanist who makes much use of the Euphuistic figures, comes far too late to effect any important result in the movement that we are studying. His rhetorical ideas took form after the publication of *Toxophilus*, and appear in writings which did not see the light until the seventies. But even though this were not so we must still look for causes that were operating long before *Toxophilus* was published. If Euphuism is a product of classical influence then we must learn of the humanist activity early in the reign of Henry the Eighth that produced it. We must prove that Berners and Bryan in their translations of Guevara were under classical influence, or if they derived their style as well as their substance from Guevara, that Guevara himself formed his style as Ascham sometimes formed his. Nay, we must prove that all the popular, controversial, and sermon uses of the well-known figures, the figures which were indeed current everywhere, were due to the revival of Isocrates.

There is a last point. If it is true that the Euphuistic figures are characteristic of the humanists, why do they not appear in their Latin style, and why do not the critics who hold this opinion try to establish it by showing that the imitation of Isocrates and Cicero produces the same result

Consideration of this fact

The use of schemata

278

in the
Latin of
the leading
humanists

in the language in which it is so much easier to imitate them? It does not do so except in some letters of Ascham. Petrarch, Erasmus, Bembo, Melanchthon, Vives, the humanists *par excellence*, always avoid them. Is it not true that the avoidance of them is the very mark of a classical taste in Latin?

In short, the gaudery of Euphuism plays a small part in the rhetoric of the humanists; and it is only when we have excluded

Non-hu-
manistic
uses

them from view that we can begin to answer the important question: In what kinds of writing are the *schemata* frequent, appropriate, and characteristic? This question is not without its complications. But I think that it can be simplified by observing that there are two main lines of tendency in the vernacular use of the schematic style, if we exclude its specialized use in Guevara, Berners, North, Pettie, and Lyly. One of these has been clearly established by students of the subject, the other has not yet been pointed out.

The first is the use of this style in the sermon and in related works of piety or devotion. In Hugh Latimer and Thomas Lever, who best represent the Protestant pulpit of this age, the use of the schemes is of quite a different order of interest from that which is found in the works of More and Elyot. But even here a distinction must be

1. The
sermon

observed. For, although Wendelstein and others have extracted many cases of the figures of alliteration, homoioteleuton, and word repetition from Latimer, it must be said that they are not used by this orator in the way that is significant for the history of Euphuism. In this respect Latimer's sermons must be classified with the numerous and voluminous works of economico-theological controversy which have also been drawn upon for examples of Euphuistic figure. It is true that the schemes are extremely common in these works, and that they reflect only those uses which range on a lower artistic level. Their purpose is almost wholly to heighten the effectiveness of a rattling invective, or to wing the shafts of ridicule; they lack both the elaborateness of form and the dignity of use that we must look for in the sources of Euphuism. They ape, in fact, those successions of brief members, all in the same form, which characterize the medieval schematic style when it is written *submisse*, not *granditer*, to use a distinction which medieval rhetoric carefully observed.[66]

[66] [*Submisse* was the opposite of ornate, and *granditer* a more sublime style.

To find an exact equivalent of the more dignified Latin style we must turn to other orators than Latimer, and especially to Thomas

Thomas
Lever

Lever. To show the significance of Lever's style it is not enough to quote brief phrases or sentences; for the characteristic of the medieval rhetoric, as of Euphuism, is not, as we have already seen, the occasional appearance of the schemes, but their constant use in patterned forms. When Lever is read in long passages it is apparent that he reproduces in English the effect of the rimed Latin prose, in which rime is never regular and long-continued, but only appears in a succession of phrases and then disappears—just as it does in Lever. And in Lever, as in Latin, the other schemes always accompany homoioteleuton in rime-prose.[67]

Barely second in interest to Lever is Bishop Jewel—not in his controversial works, but in his sermons. The *schemata* which Jewel

Bishop
Jewel

prefers are not those which Lever likes best, the transverse forms of sound repetition, rime, and so on, but others which are equally important in the history of Euphuism. He is fond of word repetition, especially at the beginnings and ends of successive parallel clauses or sentences—indeed the commonest form of parison in him is the form in which most of the words of a clause are repeated in the next clause, but particular ones, which thus obtain special emphasis, are different,—of

---

It was a Ciceronian distinction—*eloquens qui poterit parva submisse, modica temperate, magna granditer dicere (De Optimo Genere Oratore)*—reinforced by Quintilian (x, 2, 22; xII, 10, 58) and by Augustine (*Confessions*, I, 9). See Erich Auerbach, "Sermo Humilis," in *Literatursprache und Publikum in der Lateinischen Spätantike und im Mittelalter* (Bern, 1958), 25ff.]

[67] The exact effect of rime-prose is produced in the following from a Sermon made in the Shrouds [i.e., the Crypt] in St. Paul's [Thomas Lever, in *English Reprints*, ed. Edward Arber (London, 1871), p. 22]: "Yea, but what mercyes of God have we refused, or what threatenynge of God have we here in England not regarded: whyche have forsaken the Pope, abolyshed idolatrye and supersticion, receyved goddes word so gladly, reformed all thynges accordinglye therto so spedily, and have all thinges most nere the order of the primitive churche universallye? Alas, good brethren, as trulye as al is not golde that glystereth, so is it not vertue and honesty, but very vice and hipocrisie, wherof England at this day dothe moste glorye." In a different pattern: "Everye covetouse man is proude, thynkynge hymselfe more worthy a pounde, than a nother man a penye, more fitte to have chaunge of sylkes and velvettes, than other to have bare frise cloth, and more conveniente for hym to have aboundance of diverse dilicates for hys daintye toth, than for other to have plenty of biefes and muttons for theyr hongry bellyes: and finally that he is more worthye to have gorgeouse houses to take his pleasure in, in bankettynge, than laborynge men to have poore cotages to take rest in, in slepynge" (pp. 23-24).

the figure of climax or gradation, and of a succession of questions, each followed by its answer.[68]

But there is a second use of the *schemata* in the sixteenth century which may prove to be more important than their sermon use. This is their oratorical use in various ways connected with the formalities and ceremonies of court and state.

2. Courtly oratory

I say "oratorical," for the *official* prose, as in proclamations, state letters, and so on, is in a different style, namely that described above as having its origin in the *ars dictatoria*. But wherever we have ornate public discourse for the purpose of persuading or pleasing or denouncing, and connected with a great occasion of public life, we are likely to find that characteristic style that we are looking for. And first we find it in Chronicles, as in Grafton's;[69] and again in works cast in the oratorical mold, whether actually spoken or not, of which a remarkable example is James

---

[68] For instance from the sermon on Romans xii.16-18 (John Jewel, *Works*, ed. J. Ayre, Parker Society, xxiv [Cambridge, 1847], p. 1094): "Thus, good brethren, humility preserveth the church of God: humility upholdeth all good commonweals. Pride it is that scattereth the church of God: pride overthroweth all good commonweals. There was never yet pride in any city without dissension, nor dissension that continued without destruction of the whole commonweal. . . . In the city of Rome, which was called the lady of the whole world, there were two that took upon them the governance of the empire, Julius Caesar and Pompey. Julius Caesar was a man of so haughty courage that he could abide no peer: Pompey was of such an high mind that he could suffer no man to be his equal. . . . Rome, that sometime was the wealthiest city in the world, and called therefore the lady of the whole world, fell to division; and therefore was she overthrown, and utterly destroyed. The Grecians, which were a people of greatest force, fell to dissension; and therefore was their whole estate pulled down, and cast flat to the ground." Climax, or gradation, is illustrated in the third sentence of this passage. [Jewel's *Oratio contra Rhetoricam*, ca. 1548, has been translated and commented on by Hoyt H. Hudson in *QJS*, xiv (1928), 374-392.]

[69] The following quotations are all from speeches: 1. "He can be no sanctuary man that hath neither discretion to desire it nor malice to deserve it" (Richard Grafton, Continuation, 1543, of Hardyng's Chronicle: ed. Henry Ellis, *The Chronicle of John Hardyng*, London, 1812, p. 486). 2. "And when you determined to besiege the town of Neuse, you thought yourself in a great doubt whether you should lo*se* more at home by your ab*sence* . . . or el*se* gain more in Germany by your *power* and *presence*" (Grafton, *A Chronicle at Large* (1569), ed. Henry Ellis, London, 1809, ii, 47). 3. "But if God will it so ordain that you and my master join in a league and amity, I dare both *say* and *swear* that the fine *steel* never *cleaved* faster to the adamant *stone* than he will *stick* and *clasp* with you, both in *wealth* and *wo*, in pro*sperity* and adver*sity*." (Ibid., p. 54.) 4. "A *peace* both as hon*orable* and as prof*itable* to you as a *peascod*, and not so *wholesome* as a *pomegranate*." (Ibid., p. 56.) The oratorical use of the figures here is in direct line with medieval tradition. [In 3 there is even greater richness: note am*ity*, s*tone*.]

Harrison's *Exhortation to the Scots* to accept the terms of composition offered them by the Lord Protector Somerset in 1547, a work which is "Euphuistic" throughout;[70] in dedications and addresses of books constantly, as in the dedication of *Toxophilus* and in a number quoted by Wendelstein (in this use the Euphuistic figures are almost universal); and finally in a number of uses connected with court shows and entertainments. In the last of these classes belong certain passages in Goldingham's masque in honor of the Queen, performed on the 21st of August 1578;[71] the challenges and retorts of the opposing champions in the great tournament commemorated in a sonnet by Sidney, when four of Elizabeth's knights met a large band of the French followers of the Duc d'Anjou;[72] and many compli-

[70] "These be thei whiche professyng knowledge, abuse the ignoraunce of the nobilitie and commonaltie, to the destruccion of bothe: havyng peace in their mouthes, and all rancor and vengeance in their hartes: pretendyng religion, perswade rebellion: preachyng obedience, procure al disobedience: semyng to forsake all thyng, possesse all thyng: callyng themselfes spirituall, are in deede moste carnall: and reputed heddes of the Churche, bee the onely shame and slaunder of the Churche." "An Exhortation to the Scotts," in *The Complaynt of Scotlande*, ed. James A. H. Murray, *EETS*, ES 17, 18 (London, 1872) p. 209. I have used the colon here to indicate *rhetorical* structure.

[71] Masque Performed before the Queen, Aug. 21, 1578, in the publications of the Roxburghe Club, vol. 40. This is quoted by Wendelstein, p. 28.

[72] The speakers who represent the different challengers had their speeches written for them by different persons, perhaps by the challengers themselves. At least the variation in style seems to show this. Query: did Sidney write those which are addressed to the Queen by a young boy on behalf of all the challengers? They are very schematic, but in the Arcadian manner, not the Euphuistic. Most Ephuistic are those spoken for Sir Thomas Perot and Master Cooke, and for Master Ratcliffe. The following is from the former: "Despair, no not despair (most high and mighty Princess), could so congeal the frozen knight in the air, but that Desire (ah sweet Desire) inforced him to behold the sun on the earth; whereon as he was gazing with twinkling eye (for who can behold such beams steadfastly?), he began to dissolve into drops, melting with such delight that he seemed to prefer the lingering of a certain death before the lasting of an uncertain life. . . . [Later one of their pages, disguised as an angel, speaks to the Queen:] The sun in the highest delighteth in the shadow which is shortest, and nourisheth the tree whose root groweth deepest, not whose top springeth loftiest. . . . Sir knights, if in besieging the sun, ye understood what you have undertaken, ye would not destroy a common blessing for a private benefit. Will you subdue the sun? Who shall rest in the shadow where the weary take breath, the disquiet rest, and all comfort? Will you bereave all men of those glistering and gladsome beams? What shall then prosper in the shining but you will then climb it by the rays? O rare exhalations! Brothers you may be to Desire, but sons ye are to ill-hap, which think you cannot sink deep enough into the sea unless you take your fall from the sun. Desist, you knights, desist, sith it is impossible to resist: content yourself with the sun's indifferent succor, suffer the juniper shrub to grow by the lofty oak, and claim no prerogative where the sun grants no privilege." Henry Goldwell, *A Brief Declaration of the Shows, Devices* [etc.], London, 1581 (repr. in John Nichols, *The Progresses and Public Processions of Queen Elizabeth*, 4 vols. [London, 1788-1821], II, 133-134). The date of composition of *Shows and De-*

mentary addresses and masques presented to the Queen on her various progresses through the towns and to the castles of her subjects, as, for example, those that George Gascoigne wrote and spoke on the occasion of her visits to the town of Kenilworth and the town of Woodstock in 1575.[73]

But, it may be asked, what have these two classes of works to do with each other? How does it happen that a style which appears

Courtly
culture
still
medieval

in the sermon, the great type of medieval discourse, also appears in connection with the ceremonies and observances of a great and cultivated court of the Renaissance? And the answer must be that the one is not more medieval than the other. If Ascham in addressing King Henry in praise of the bow, or Elizabeth's knights in challenging their foreign foes, or Gascoigne in praising his sovereign lady in an allegory, if all of these use a style that is medieval in form, there is nothing surprising in the fact, for the occasions that inspire them all are essentially medieval. If Bishop Antonio de Guevara writes a similar style (calling it *oratio aulica*), why should we wonder, when we know that his subject matter, his thought, and his sources of information are as medieval as his

---

vices was later than the appearance of the first part of *Euphues*; but that their style was in an established tradition is shown by the quotations in the following note.

[73] "Well, worthy Queen, and my most gracious Sovereign, it hath been written in authority and observed by experience, that thunder oftentimes bruiseth the bones, without blemishing of the flesh; or (as some have held opinion) that hath been seen to break the sword, without hurt to the scabbard. The which as yet is a rare and strange adventure: so in my judgment that deserveth to be deeply considered; and being once well weighed it requireth also to be well remembered. . . . And this allegorical exposition of thunder have I prettily picked out of mine own youthful pranks. . . . He hath bruised my bones with the scourge of repentance, though my body bear the show of a wanton and wavering worldling. And he hath broken the blade of my heady will, though the scabbard of my wishing remain whole and at liberty. But . . . I am compelled to take comfort in one other observation which we find in worldly occurrents: for we see that one self-same sunshine doth both harden the clay and dissolve the wax, whereby I am encouraged to gather that as God (by his wrath justly conceived) hath strucken me, so (by his mercy pitifully inclined) he may, when it pleaseth him, graciously recomfort me, and the same sun which shineth in his justice to correct stubborn offenders, may also glister in his grace to forgive the penitent sinner." The account of the entertainments at Woodstock, 1575, in Nichols, *Progresses*, II, 19-21. The style here seems to me more like Euphues than that of any other work that preceded Lyly's, more so even than Pettie's. See also the *Tale of Hametes*, told also by Gascoigne, immediately following; *The Princely Pleasures at Kenilworth Castle*, 1575, in same volume, especially a speech of Sylvanus, p. 81; and in Vol. II of the same work, an old shepherd's speech in *The Speeches at Bissam*.

style?[74] In fact courtly and medieval are not contrasted terms, as applied to the culture of Spain and England in the sixteenth century; and *per contra* the culture of the new humanism and the culture of "high" society are not identical, but often contrasted and sometimes hostile. It is true that humanism often found its home at the courts of the Renaissance princes; yet the older streams of civilization also ran along there in much its old way, scarcely mingling its waters with those of the new tributary.[75]

A second question, different from this, but related to it, is this: If the rhetorical forms of Euphuism and Guevarism are those long familiar in Latin prose, what was it that gave them their new life?

Cause of the revival of the schemata

What new charm did they take on in the sixteenth century that made them seem the appropriate forms of *estilo culto*? We might answer that the love for all forms of ornateness, characteristic of the Renaissance, would alone have served to revive the *schemata*. But the true explanation of the phenomenon is certainly that now for the first time these figures appeared in an artistic and elaborate use in the vernacular. The novelty consists, not in the figures themselves, but in the fact that they are sounded on a new instrument, and that an art which had been the possession of clerks

---

[74] The introduction of the *Libro Aureo* is borrowed from Dares and Dictys, as Norden tells us in n.2 on p. 792; and all the humanists quoted in this same note by Norden complain that Guevara did not draw his learning from classical authors. In spite of this showing, Norden tries to prove, unsuccessfully, it seems to me, that Guevara was a humanistic scholar. [See n.52 above.]

[75] A careful investigation of the meaning of the phrase *oratio aulica* in the Renaissance and the Middle Ages would probably illustrate the point raised in the above paragraph. For it could be shown, I think, that it is associated with the chanceries, or official secretarial bureaux, of the Popes and Emperors, and therefore indicates the same form of style from which Petrarch celebrated his narrow escape in a letter quoted above, and which so many humanists rejoice to have unlearned, after being taught to use it in their youth. This is evidently what it means when applied to Guevara himself, who is its chief exponent in the vernacular; for on the title pages of his works it is connected with his employment as historiographer and court preacher to the Emperor Charles. In a passage from Miraeus quoted by Norden (p. 793), concerning Guevara, *aulici* are contrasted as a matter of course with *eruditi*, the latter term being used of course in the humanist sense. The famous *Libro Aureo* is essentially a medieval book, as regards plan, content, and purport, as will appear from Child's comparison of it with the French original of Michel's *Ayenbite of Inwit* by Frère Lorens: "Old and new, the books of both are books royal, books for the king, mirrors of the world. From one into the other the set homily and tractate pass—not the form only in the set discourse, but the Simon-pure theological homily itself" (p. 122). Child does not, I think, mean that the one directly influenced the other, but only that they drew from similar medieval stores.

alone becomes the property of men and women of the world. In the history of fashions there are episodes much stranger than this.

It has been pointed out by Child and others that the Euphuistic figures do not disappear from English literature immediately after

The seven-teenth century

the passing of the courtly fashion; that they continue in fact to adorn a considerable body of early seventeenth-century prose; and it is customary to treat these later occurrences as examples of the persistent influence of Lyly. But if the opinion here advanced is correct, they are rather to be regarded as independent survivals of the long monkish tradition of style, owing little or nothing to the courtly use of the preceding age, but testifying remarkably to the power of a convention which had endured for so many ages. The examples heretofore suggested tend to support this view, for they have been brought from sermons and works of religious edification, in which the medieval tone survives; and the two illustrations which we have to add to these are of the same character. The first is Thomas Heywood's *Hierarchie of the Blessed Angels*,[76] the second the Sermons of Thomas Adams.[77]

[76] "As *fire* cannot be long smother*ed*, but it will find *vent*; nor the sun be so e*clipsed* and *clouded*, but it will soon work itself into its own glory and splendor; so the omnipotency of the great Creator cannot so darken*ed*, either by the *stupidity* of the ignorant, or the malicious ob*stinacy* of the seeming-wise, but even out of their voluntary *blindness* it will extract its own *brightness*." Th. Heywood, *Hierarchie of the Blessed Angels* (London, 1635), Book IV (prose), p. 218. The work is dedicated to Queen Henrietta Maria.

[77] Adams' sermons represent in a remarkable way the transition from sixteenth-century schematic prose to the "new style" of the Jacobean age. Beginning with the gay ornaments of Latimer and the medieval preachers, as in the *City of Peace* and *Politic Hunting*, he gradually emerges into a new world of thought and style under the influence of Bacon and Donne, until in *England's Sickness*, for example, he echoes the solemn tones of Thomas Browne. (In his friend Bishop Hall a similar melting of old into new may be seen by the student of style.) As examples of the earlier style: "But if they that fly from God by contempt shall thus speed, what shall become of them that fly upon God by contumacy?" *Politic Hunting* in *The Works of Thomas Adams*, 3 vols. (Edinburgh, 1861-1862), I, 4. "But as a man may be Crassus in his purse, yet no Cassius in his pots; so, on the contrary, another may be, as it is said of Job, poor to a proverb, yet be withal as voluptuous as Esau. Men have *talem dentem, Qualem mentem*—such an appetite as they have affection. . . . The poor man that loves delicate cheer shall not be wealthy; and the rich man that loves it shall not be healthy." (Ibid., p. 5.) "Sometimes the sun's heat working upon a muddy and baneful object breeds horrid serpents." "Thus when the sun is hottest the springs are coldest." "It is written of the Tracian flint that it burns with water and is quenched with oil." In the last three (from *The Forest of Thorns, Works*, II, 476ff.) he is perhaps imitating Lyly, but in the others merely the tradition of preaching gives him his figures.

✧ VII ✧

The Uses of the Schemata in Middle-English Prose

A third kind of evidence tending to prove the close connection between Euphuism and the medieval rhetoric is found in the fact that the Euphuistic figures appeared in the vernacular tongues before humanism had begun to affect the culture of Europe. The fact is not new, for a few medieval uses have already been pointed out in previous studies of Euphuism. What remains, therefore, is to prove that these medieval occurrences are much more common than has been supposed, and to show their real significance.

The *schemata* occur constantly in Anglo-Saxon and early English literature, but only in their simplest forms, never used conspicuously or artfully. The vernacular was felt to be too crude to bear the ornaments associated with the ancient tongue; and they are first employed with regular and conscious art at the time when modern poetry was born,—in the fourteenth century.[78] A marked similarity to Euphuism has been noted in the use of the figures in the *Ayenbite of Inwyt*,[79] and a treatise has been devoted to the "Euphuistic tendency" in Richard Rolle.[80] To these may be added some occurrences which have been cited from Caxton's *Charles the Grete*.[81] Beyond this nothing has been done, to my knowledge, with the history of the *schemata* in Middle English; yet these are but a few examples of a practice which, as future investigations will certainly show, was extremely common in the prose of the fourteenth and fifteenth centuries. The *schemata* are as freely and as artfully used, for instance, by Rolle's followers[82] and by the contemporary

Some of the medieval occurrences

---

[78] [For analysis of syllabic antithesis (there called alliterative assonance) in certain early fourteenth-century English verses, see R. J. Schoeck, "Alliterative Assonance in Harley MS 2253," *English Studies*, XXXII (1951), 68-70; but the suggestions there offered concerning sources need to be revised. See n.36 above.]

[79] Child, *John Lyly and Euphuism*, pp. 120-122.

[80] J. P. Schneider, *The Prose-style of Richard Rolle of Hampole with Special Reference to its Euphuistic Tendencies* (Baltimore, 1906).

[81] Wendelstein, *Vorgeschichte des Euphuismus*, p. 4.

[82] (1) "Many forsoth that with me have spoken, like wer to scorpions, for with there hede flater and thai have fagyd, and with thare tayl bakbytand and thai have smyttyn." Richard Misyn, *The Fire of Love* (1435) (*EETS*, 106, p. 22) —a translation of Rolle's *Incendium Amoris*.

(2) "And ilke a day when thou mysdose þan he repro*fes be*, and whene þou repent*is* þe þan he forgy*ffes the*, and when þou *erris* þan he amend*is* þe, and when þou dred*is* be þan he ler*is* the" (etc.) *Mirror of St. Edmund* (trans. of a Latin original), in C. Horstmann, *Yorkshire Writers: Richard Rolle of Hampole and his Followers* (London, 1895), p. 221.

mystic Walter Hilton[83] as by Rolle himself; they appear in a more highly developed and graceful form in the *Mirrour of the Blessed Lyf of Jesu Christ*, a work translated before 1410 by an English monk from the Latin of Bonaventura;[84] and a remarkable example, very enlightening for the history of Euphuism, will be found in Atkynson's translation of the *Imitatio Christi*, made at the end of the fifteenth century.[85] Only a little search would be needed to add to the number of such works, and it is safe to say that the *schemata* are characteristic of the style of the ecclesiastical English literature of the fifteenth century. And indeed there is no reason why we should not add to these pre-Renaissance works many sixteenth-century writings produced under medieval inspiration. Who, for instance, will imagine that the style of Fisher's sermons, or Latimer's or Lever's, or of Grafton's *Chronicles*, has been affected in a considerable degree by humanistic influence? For the sake of clearness, however, we will limit our attention to the medieval examples.

The similarity to Euphuism in the style of several of these older writings has, as we have just seen, already been observed by various critics. It is the more remarkable that its significance has never been properly understood. Feuillerat, for instance, waives the discussion of Rolle's style, which, as he admits, "has all the characteristics of Lyly's style," with the remark: "Cela est inutile pour ma démonstration. Ce serait, en outre, rattacher l'euphuisme à un

These due to medieval Latin

---

(3) See, in the same volume, *The Privity of the Passion* (trans. from Bonaventura), p. 199. [On the popularity of Richard Rolle and other fourteenth-century English mystics during the sixteenth century see Hope Emily Allen, *Writings Ascribed to Richard Rolle, Hermit of Hampole, and Materials for his Biography* (New York, 1927), esp. Ch. 1; and E. P. Goldschmidt, *Medieval Texts and their First Appearance in Print* (London: Bibliographical Society, 1943).]

[83] In Hilton's works the figures are more simply used, usually without as much elaboration as in the examples in the preceding note; but see a quotation from him just below.

[84] "Arise up therfore now al my ioye, and comforte me with thy ageyn comynge, whom thou so discomfortest, through thyn awaie passynge." *The Mirrour of the Blessed Lyf of Jesu Christ*, ed. Lawrence F. Powell (London, 1908), p. 263. "Sothely, I trowe that with soverayne mervaile here hertes melted into likynge sorwe and sorowful likynge" (p. 259). In this work there is the characteristic combination of alliteration and similar endings that is found in *Euphues*. On p. 284 there is a good example of successive clauses ending in similar sounds, as in the rhymed Latin prose.

[85] *The Earliest English Translation of the First Three Books of the* De Imitatione Christi, ed. J. K. Ingram, *EETS*, ES 63 (London, 1893). There are many attempts in this work to produce complicated figures something like those of the original, but they usually result only in awkwardness: "O thou servyce, worthy alwey to be desyr*ed* and hals*ed* wherby *al*mighty God *is* gotten, and *e*verlasting ioy and glad*nes* gotten" (p. 207, III, xi).

mouvement de style avec lequel il n'a historiquement aucune relation."[86] If Feuillerat means only that Rolle's use of the figures in
English is not directly a cause of their use in the English of the
sixteenth century, he is perhaps right. But when it is remembered
that all the cases of schematic prose in Middle English are only the
occasional overflows of a stream of Latin prose style which runs
on with almost unabated volume into the sixteenth century itself,
it is not so clear that they are phenomena of a different order from
Euphuism. It is a curious fact that the scholars who have observed
them have treated them as if they were phenomena peculiar to the
vernacular and originating there. None of them, not even Professor
Child, who has laid most emphasis on the medieval occurrences,
has seen that they are due to the attempt to render the current
Latin style. This fact scarcely needs to be proved, but if evidence
were needed it could easily be found by comparing some of the
passages mentioned with their known Latin originals, and observing how closely they correspond in form. A sentence from Walter
Hilton will show both how close the imitation could be and how
much it could resemble Euphues in style: "*Altiora te ne quesieris,
et fortiora te ne scrutatus fueris,* that is for to saye, hygh thynges that
are above thy wi*tte* and thy *reason seke not,* and greate thynges
that are above thy myg*ht* ran*sake not.*"[87] From Atkynson: "These
desyre rather by *p*omp and *p*ryde to be great in the worl*d* than by
mekenesse and charyte to be in favoure with Go*d*, and therefore
they vanysshe in theyr thoughtis and desyres as the smoke that ever
the more it ascend*eth* the more it *f*ad*eth* and *f*ayl*eth.*"[88] We have
here, under no influence but monkish Latin, a style that is more
like the Euphuistic model than that of many passages quoted from
sixteenth-century predecessors of Euphuism.[89]

---

[86] *John Lyly,* p. 451n.
[87] *Epistle on Mixed Life,* conclusion, in Horstmann, *Yorkshire Writers,* p. 292.
[88] Bk. I, Ch. 3; ed. Ingram, p. 156.
[89] I have little doubt that medieval French would offer examples as interesting
as the English. The French original of the *Ayenbite* has the figures in greater pro-
fusion than the translation, and the preacher Gerson provides the following phrase,
in which there are both transverse alliteration and transverse assonance: "les faiz
d'ung bon prince qui fut gracieulx a regarder, vigoureux a guerroyer." (Charles
Aubertin, *Histoire de la Langue et de la Littérature Française au Moyen Âge*
[Paris, 1876-1878], II, 367.) [In addition to studies of Gerson as preacher, see
further: A. Hamon, *Un Grand Rhétoriqueur Poitevin: Jean Bouchet (1476-1557),*
(Paris, 1901); W. F. Patterson, *Three Centuries of French Poetical Theory* (Ann
Arbor, 1935). The vogue for elaborate speech was shared by such French "rhétori-
queurs en vers" as Marot and Lemaire de Belges, as well as by the "prosateurs."]

The kinds of evidence which we have suggested so far could be supplemented by one of a different sort, namely, that which could be
Sixteenth-century study of Isocrates
derived from a careful consideration of the actual knowledge and use of the writings of Isocrates— which the critics place easily first among the models of Euphuistic rhetoric. It could be shown that in the first half of the century, when the Euphuistic tendency was establishing itself firmly, the study of this author was limited to a very small circle of humanists, and that it was not until Euphuism was at its very height that he was taught to any such extent as to affect the main currents of English style. Indeed, as regards his place in the school curricula, the evidence on this point has already been produced by the chief authority in the subject.[90] How is it possible, we may well ask, that the humanistic study of a single Greek author, in days when humanism was still struggling for a firm foothold, could have been the chief cause of a tendency almost universal in English style? But this subject must be left to future investigation.[91] Nothing remains for us to do here but to state the general conclusions which are to be drawn from the evidence presented.

❖ VIII ❖

Summary and Conclusion

In the first place it must be said again that no single influence caused the prevalence of the Euphuistic figures in the sixteenth
Feuillerat's analysis
century. This is recognized by all. Feuillerat is very emphatic in saying that Euphuism "is due to the imitation of the ancient literatures," and in particular that Isocrates "seems to be the author who caused the adoption of these figures by English stylists." But he also observes that the influence of Isocrates was reinforced by that of all the "authors, Greek or Latin, who had cultivated artistic style" (he is apparently thinking here only of the authors of classical antiquity);

---

[90] "Indeed, from a consideration of all the facts, it seems clear that the study of Greek in any way bearing directly on school practice had no stronghold . . . before the return of the English refugees . . . after the Marian persecution." Foster Watson, *English Grammar-Schools* (1908), p. 490. See the earliest records for the prescription of Isocrates, in the same work, p. 491.

[91] It has been carefully studied by T. K. Whipple in "Isocrates and Euphuism," *MLR*, XI (1916), 15-27, and 129-135.

he recognizes the part played by the study of rhetoric in manuals (though here again he expressly limits his view to the contemporary and the classical); and he assigns a certain role, herein following Child, to the national English poetry.[92]

Now the history of Euphuism is certainly quite as complex as Feuillerat represents it. It is true that I would analyze and define the elements that enter into it in a different way, and I think that he has left out of account, as Norden and all other critics have done, the most important part of the history of the aureate style. But whatever changes in the analysis we may make, we must still recognize that Euphuism was due to an interplay of forces of the same kind that Feuillerat describes; and the difference between his explanation and that which we propose consists largely in the order in which these forces are taken and the relations between them. The difference, however, is of such a kind that it would place Euphuism in a new historical perspective.

History of Euphuism complex

And first as regards the cause of the taste for ornate prose. Feuillerat is clear on this point. He says that it was due to "the fascination which the classical languages exercised on the men of the Renaissance."[93] But this explanation will not serve. The phenomenon was caused by the concurrence of the same elements in the taste of the Renaissance that give the character of ornateness to nearly all of its art, the same mixture of the classical, the medieval, and the courtly in the culture of the age that makes the *Orlando Furioso*, for instance, and the *Faerie Queene* so fantastic and so unclassical. And of the causes that apply particularly to prose style, the first place must be given, not to the imitation of the classics, but to the novelty of literary prose in the vernacular, and the need of adapting the familiar speech to unaccustomed uses of art and beauty. Indeed, the humanistic imitation of the classics, if we could isolate it from the other forces of the time, and as it were extract its essence, would appear the one strong influence working for purity and simplicity. To attribute the love of a fanciful ornateness to this cause is to fall into the common error of identifying the Renaissance with the revival of antiquity.

1. Cause of the love of ornate rhetoric

[92] *John Lyly*, pp. 469-470.   [93] *John Lyly*, p. 460.

Secondly, as regards the *process* by which Euphuism was evolved, there is a similar objection to Feuillerat's theory. The humanistic method of learning to write by imitation of authors
2. Process of fabrication of Euphuism had a part in it, but only the minor part. Here and there we can find independent-minded writers, like Ascham and perhaps his exalted pupil, who could extract clauses from Isocrates, Cicero, or Saint Cyprian and imitate them in English. But such experiment had little effect upon the general movement. The laboratory in which the simples of Euphuism were extracted from their sources and compounded in a conventional form for general conveyance was the universal study of the art of rhetoric. In estimating the importance of this study we must not think only of the new manuals in the vernacular, which have been made familiar by modern reprints. Much the greater number of textbooks were in Latin and are unknown to the present day; and even the multiplicity of manuals gives but a poor idea of the actual prevalence of rhetorical training in schools and universities, and under the private tuition of all kinds of teachers, from the most enlightened humanist to the most benighted scholiast. The old art, in short, lost none of the dignity it had long enjoyed in the *trivium*, but, on the other hand, greatly increased its popularity. Some of the remarkable favor in which rhetoric was held during the Renaissance was of course due to the revival of classical learning: the later humanistic theory of education through the study of form greatly stimulated the interest in style. But it does not follow that even when the impulse came from this side the method was that of the humanists; and in fact we can see by the manuals which remain that it was usually the traditional method of figures and formulas, definitions aided by examples handed down from old books, or invented by the teacher.[94]

Thirdly, if the theory here advanced is accepted, the *sources* from which rhetoric drew its favorite figures must be placed in a

[94] After the necessary training in the elements, through grammars and "colloquies," the introduction to rhetoric was achieved by means of manuals of the "figures," such as Susenbrotus. Sherry's work is entitled: *A Treatise of Schemes and Tropes*. See *CHEL*, III, 488. [See generally Howell, *Logic and Rhetoric*, 109ff. On school-rhetoric in England, see T. W. Baldwin, *William Shakespere's Small Latine and Lesse Greeke* (1956); and on Susenbrotus, see Joseph X. Brennan, "Joannes Susenbrotus, A Forgotten Humanist," *PMLA*, LXXV (Dec. 1960), 485-496.]

3. Whence did it derive the schemata?

different order from that which is now customary. In individual cases the imitation of the classical orators produced such figures as appear in Euphuism, but even in these cases they merely confirmed a tendency already well established. And in general the effect of classical imitation, in the Renaissance as in the Middle Ages, was to discourage or limit the use of the *schemata* rather than to promote it. The Greek and Latin romances and their English translations perhaps had an effect when *estilo culto* came to be used in fiction,[95] and there was certainly a constant effect upon ecclesiastical usage from the study of the Church Fathers, though its extent is very hard to determine because the forms it produces are often like those of medieval rhetoric. But the real and effective cause of Euphuism is not, let us repeat, imitation of any kind. It is tradition—the force of the long and uninterrupted custom of the immediate past.

The medieval tradition was somewhat broken, it is true, by the Reformation on one hand and humanism on the other. But the interruption was not nearly so sudden or complete as is commonly supposed; and there is no difficulty in tracing the channels through which the forms of medieval style could descend to the sixteenth century. It is constantly being forgotten that the reading of the first generation of humanists, Colet, More, and so on, was necessarily in medieval books, except for a few works that they could get from abroad; that education in England was still monastic in the youth of Ascham, Wilson, and North; and that up to the year 1538 the only libraries in England were those maintained by the religious orders at their various institutions,—of which Oxford colleges were the most important.[96]

The channels of medieval influence
1. Medieval books

[95] See above, n.23.

[96] See R. H. Benson, *The Dissolution of the Religious Houses*, in *CHEL*, III, Ch. 3; and W. H. Woodward, *CHEL*, III, Ch. 19. [On the effects of the Dissolution, see M. D. Knowles, *Religious Houses*, III. For English Libraries before 1700, see the work edited by F. Wormald and C. E. Wright (London: Athlone Press, 1958), reviewed by R. J. Schoeck in *SCN*, XIX (Autumn 1961), 42-43. At least one other kind of library was maintained before 1538: the libraries in the Inns of Court, of which Lincoln's Inn library goes back to the mid-fifteenth century—see R. J. Schoeck, "The Libraries of Common Lawyers in Renaissance England," *Manuscripta*, VI (1962), 155-167. The point is of importance here because of the role of the lawyers in Renaissance rhetoric: see idem, "Rhetoric and Law in Sixteenth-Century England," *SP*, L (1953), 110-127.]

Even the later Protestant humanists must have been trained in churchly literature in their youth; and when we consider that the earlier leaders in the new culture were all Catholics, some of them peculiarly devout Catholics, and a few of them martyrs to their faith, we may be certain that they were constant readers of devotional Catholic works, and especially of the works of piety, Saints' Lives and contemplative treatises, which were produced in increasing number during the latter part of the fifteenth century.[97] And in such works as these they would see the medieval rhetoric of schemes in its full flower; for the churchly literature preserves its old forms in spite of the Renaissance.

The first channel, then, through which the medieval world kept up its communication with the sixteenth century was the reading of medieval books. But even though all the books had been lost, the force of custom would have sufficed to carry over the old forms of style into the new age. The public disputation and oration in Latin were, throughout the century, the chief forms of rhetorical exercise, just as they had always been; and it is simply inconceivable that any important change in the style of these performances occurred during the quarter-century that followed the suppression of the monasteries.[98] Where shall one look for the machinery by which such a change could have been brought about? All education was in a disorganized, almost desperate, condition during this period; and it is a notorious fact that Protestantism did not succeed in finding an effective substitute for the old monastic discipline until Elizabeth's reign was well advanced. Indeed we are not left to conjecture as regards the style of Latin oratory at this time. There is a sermon preached, during the reign of Edward VI, by the young academic orator who was to become Bishop Jewel, in which the form is the usual rhyme-prose of the Middle Ages, with all the ornamental figures that accompany that style.[99]

2. Force of custom

[97] [On Saints' Lives generally, see H. Delehaye, *The Legends of the Saints*, ed. R. J. Schoeck (University of Notre Dame Press, 1961), and on the popularity of religious literature during the period of printing, see the following: Goldschmidt, *Medieval Texts*; H. S. Bennett, *English Books and Readers* (Cambridge, 1952); and Helen C. White, *Tudor Books of Private Devotion* (Madison, Wis., 1951).]

[98] [The disputation continues into the seventeenth century: see Wm. T. Costello, *The Scholastic Curriculum at Early XVIIth-Century Cambridge* (Cambridge, Mass., 1958)—with the qualifications indicated in *New Scholasticism*, XXXIII (1959), 387-390.]

[99] *Works*, Parker Soc. ed., pp. 950ff. [Cf. Ringler, "The Immediate Source of Euphuism," which argues for the direct and primary influence of Rainolds.]

To the survival of old books and the force of custom we must add a third influence working even more effectively for the transmission of the old figures of speech: namely, the continuance in common use of the old rhetorical manuals and the writing of new ones in imitation of them. Wilson's rhetoric must not be taken as characteristic of the books regularly used, for he is a humanist and shares the humanist dislike for the figures we are now interested in. And besides his book was too advanced for use in schools or even in colleges. Sherry's *Treatise of Schemes and Tropes* (1555) in English represents much more nearly the scope of the ordinary instruction; and the usual Latin rhetorics, the *Figurae* of Mosellanus and the *Epitome Troporum* of Susenbrotus, show by their titles just what they included. These were all comparatively recent books, but if we could learn of the manuals and textbooks that were actually used by all the schools, as well as those that were talked about and officially recognized, we should probably find that they were often the same that had been recognized as orthodox for centuries; for there is a curious tendency in education to adhere to old forms of practice long after they have become antiquated by the progress of thought in the world outside of school. The books in which Latin grammar was taught show this tendency even more clearly than the rhetorics do. We know by almost countless references that the textbooks in general use in Shakespeare's boyhood were "Donet," Priscian, and the *Doctrinale* of Alexander, the medieval favorites; and we have already seen that all these books gave instruction in the *schemata*.[100]

3. Survival of medieval manuals of rhetoric

And in this connection there is still another point to be noted. It must be remembered that in England and in Spain the Renaissance trod more closely upon the heels of the Middle Ages than in France and Italy. The fourteenth and fifteenth centuries had made deep inroads into medievalism in the latter countries, and had gradually assimilated the new classicism. In the countries farther from the center, on the other hand, the ground had not been cleared before the new seed was sown. The new learning[101]

Closeness of the Renaissance to the Middle

---

[100] This tendency is illustrated in our own, or the last-preceding, age, by the fact that the accepted rhetorical teacher, at least in America, until thirty or forty years ago [i.e. about 1880] was Hugh Blair, the exponent of the style of Addison.

Ages in made a late and abrupt appearance, and found many
England old forms of learning, many popular, traditional, and
national feelings and tastes, not only still intact, but
flourishing with new vigor under the enlivening influence of the
general stir and excitement of the age. It is probably for this reason
that *estilo culto* assumed particular forms in Spain and England,
which it did not take in France and Italy.

The sum of our argument, then, is that Euphuism is not the
product of humanistic imitation of the ancients, that it is, on the
other hand, a survival of the "rhetoric of the schools."
Con- The *schemata* of medieval Latin, revivified by being
clusion translated into the popular speech, enjoyed a brief new
career of glory, to fall into their final disgrace and desuetude before
the conquering advance of naturalism and modern thought at the
end of the sixteenth century. The humanists often tried to check
their course, or confine their use within the limits of good taste; but
they failed of their purpose, first, because the study of rhetoric,
which they advocated as the best approach to the classical mind,
often proved to be in effect merely a school for the practice of the
schemata, and, secondly, because the authors whom they imitated
might be used to sanction the same figures. It was left for a new
school of Anti-Ciceronian style, of which Montaigne, Lipsius,
Bacon, and the Spanish prose-concettists were the chief exemplars,
to put an end at the same time, both to the superstitious imitation of
Cicero and to the rhetoric of schemes and vocal devices which had
run a triumphant course, in spite of all opposition, through two
thousand years of literary history.

101 [That the phrase "the new learning" during the sixteenth century seems to
have meant the new religious ideas from Germany rather than humanistic ideas
has been well argued by Allan G. Chester in *Studies in the Renaissance*, II (1955),
139-147.]

Part III

Oratorical Cadence and Verse Rhythm

Foreword to Essay Seven

The subject of prose rhythm is as old as literary criticism or prosodical analysis, and historical references to it are likely to begin with Plato's nebulous remarks on "smooth flowing." Aristotle, Quintilian, and Longinus deal briefly with the subject, as part of their discussions of periodic style, and Cicero was certainly familiar with it (*De Oratore*, III). A distinction between prose rhythm and that of poetry has been attributed to Aristotle; that is, it has been maintained that he reserved the word *rhythm* for prose and the word *meter* for poetry, but the distinction is unclear (and certainly the state of Aristotelian texts does not encourage reliance upon it). In modern times no such classification exists, and much of what has been said of prose rhythm has been contained in books on poetry. Croll himself was interested in both aspects of rhythm, and the one must necessarily take into account the other.

The study of prose rhythm as it occurs in the English language has been dated, by John Hubert Scott in his essay *Rhythmic Prose* (University of Iowa Studies, III, 1, 1925), from the appearance in 1838 of Edwin Guest's *A History of English Rhythms* (2 vols.). But one could as well begin with Joshua Steele's *Prosodia Rationalis* (1775, complete edition 1779), which deals extensively with prose rhythm, though it is not listed under that subject heading in *CBEL*. In fact *CBEL* lists some 270 books on prosody under the subject heading "Prosody and Prose Rhythm" and about 34 more on prose rhythm itself. Many of those in the first category deal, more or less, with the topic. The monumental history of the subject is George Saintsbury's *A History of English Prose Rhythm* (1912), though its treatment has usually been considered controversial.

Scott further divides the subject into two major schools: 1) the timers or meterers, a classification under which he mentions Sidney Lanier, R. M. Alden, T. S. Omond, William Thomson, etc. (all primarily concerned with verse); and 2) the pattern makers or clausulists, the *cursus* school, including Theodor Zielinski, A. C. Clark, John Shelly, and Croll himself, the entire school traceable,

299

he claims, to Cicero. Of this group Croll is certainly the giant. However, the arbitrary nature of such grouping is easily demonstrable, for Croll's unpublished essay *The Rhythm of English Verse* (which follows) clearly associates him with the timers. Croll was well versed in all aspects of prosodical analysis and could make a significant contribution using either method. His approach to prose rhythm is essentially scholarly and dispassionate; he did not engage in the subject for polemical purposes but rather to further knowledge, though admittedly his original stimulus arose from the writings of other scholars with whom he disagreed. As a timer in the essay *The Rhythm of English Verse* he seems to have been more committed emotionally, perhaps because he felt himself on the defensive, than as a clausulist in the "Cadence" essay. On the whole his analyses furnish an exemplum of sweet reasonableness and in that respect differ greatly from the argumentative approach of many analysts, particularly William Thomson.

Major contributions of the "Cadence" essay, in addition to a newer and fuller study of the particular subject matter, are twofold. First, Croll liberalizes the classical *cursus* patterns, admitting, as Scott says (p. 21), "a very considerable number of new arrangements of stressed syllables with unstressed" and at the same time contributing a new analysis of trochaic cadence. Such liberalization, if it is valid—Croll's work certainly indicates that it is—greatly increases the utility of the entire method. Croll himself refers to much work remaining to be done, and the fact that interest in the subject has declined since his day is probably a result of the difficulty of analysis itself and, perhaps, changing fashions in graduate study (particularly in the United States). Second, Croll makes a very important discovery when he demonstrates that *cursus* effects need not take place only in terminal positions; that is, at the ends of *commata*.

It is not possible to foresee what result *cursus* studies might someday have on revisions of the *Book of Common Prayer*, particularly the American version, which can be changed in general convention. It seems that revisionists have only a sketchy understanding of the attempts made by the original composers of the *Book of Common*

Prayer to preserve *cursus*, for sound aesthetic reasons, though the actual Latin *cursus* patterns themselves were seldom exactly imitated. Should a comprehensive study of *cursus*, rooted in Croll's work, ever be completed, it would doubtless affect the entire question of revision. And, it is also unknown whether certain portions of the *Authorized Version* would find stronger justification after a *cursus* study had been made.

Finally, Croll's essay, while it by no means exhausts the subject, is the most definitive treatment yet made. It stands as a beginning for further study and also as a monument to classical, humanistic education.*

ROBERT O. EVANS

UNIVERSITY OF KENTUCKY

* I am indebted to Mrs. Carolyn Davis Scott for editorial assistance, and to the University of Kentucky Research Fund for typing expenses.

The Cadence of
English Oratorical Prose*

EDITED BY ROBERT O. EVANS

✧ CHAPTER ONE ✧

INTRODUCTORY

IN APRIL 1912 an article, "Rhythmical Prose in Latin and English," appeared in the *Church Quarterly Review* by Mr. J. Shelly, the object of which was to prove that the *cursus*, or system of rhythmical clause endings employed in the composition of the Latin prayers of the Church during the best periods of liturgical art, had been reproduced in the translation of them in the English *Book of Common Prayer.* For this purpose Shelly scanned the endings of all the clauses that he considered final in all the collects of the Prayer Book, and gave a special consideration, as there is good reason for doing, to the Sunday collects. His conclusion was, that of the 187 endings in all the collects, 94, or about 50 per cent are in the three forms of the *cursus*, and that, of the 148 endings in the Sunday collects, 80, or 54 per cent, are in these forms.

It will not be necessary here to repeat the story of the development of the study of cadence in prose during the last fifty years, through the various stages which have finally led to Shelly's suggestion. It is interestingly told in a number of accessible places.[1]

---

* Originally published in *Studies in Philology*, XVI (January, 1919), 1-55.

[1] The clearest and most convenient summary of the facts concerning the classical *clausulae* is in Louis Laurand, *Études sur le Style des Discours de Cicéron* (Paris, 1907 [repr. 3 vols., 1930-1936], where a good bibliography of the researches of Havet, Zielinski, Meyer, and others will be found. It contains a sketch also of the medieval *cursus*. [There is a more up-to-date bibliography of writings on the Latin Accentual Cursus by Laurand, "Bibliographie du *cursus*," in *Revue des Études Latines*, VI (1928), 73-79. See also his "Le Cursus dans la Liturgie de l'Office Divin," *Bibliothèque de l'École de Chartes*, XLIII (Paris, 1881).] Still fundamental for this subject is the work of L. Rockinger, "Briefsteller und Formelbücher des Elften bis Viersehnten Jahrhunderts," *Quellen und Erörterungen zur Bayerischen und Deutschen Geschichte*, IX (Munich, 1863; repr. 1960). The grammarians collected by Charles Thurot, "Notices et Extrais de Divers Manuscrits Latins pour Servir à l'Histoire des Doctrines Grammaticales au Moyen Âge," *Notices et*

But for the convenience of readers to whom the subject is un-familiar, the three cadences mentioned in the preceding paragraph may be described at once.

The first is PLANUS, of which there are two forms: PLANUS-1: / ᴗ ᴗ / ᴗ or (according to the notation which I will use throughout this paper) 5-2; in which there are accents on the fifth and second syllables, counting from the *end* of the phrase. Examples: *poten-tiam suam*, and *virtute succure* (4 Sun. in Adv.); *help and defend us* (3 Sun. after Ep.). This corresponds to, and descends from, Cicero's cretic-trochee ‿ ᴗ ‿ ‿ ᴗ as in *audeant arte, causa sublată*. PLANUS-2: / ᴗ ᴗ ᴗ / ᴗ or 6-2, as in *terrena moderaris* (2 Sun. after Ep.), *supplications of thy people* (ibid.), *written for our learning*, etc. This corresponds either to Cicero's cretic-trochee with resolution of the first long into two shorts, or to his beloved peon-trochee, as in *esse videantur*.

The second is TARDUS: / ᴗ ᴗ / ᴗ ᴗ or 6-3, as in *peccata praepe-diunt, propitiationis acceleret* (4 Sun. in Adv.), and *governed and sanctified* (2 Good Fri. collect), *[vo]cation and ministry* (ibid.).

Extraits des Manuscrits de la Bibliothèque Impériale et Autres Bibliothèques, XIII (Paris, 1868), are essential. N. Valois, in his study of the rhythm of the Pontifical Bulls, "Étude sur le Rhythme des Bulles Pontificales," *Bibliothèque de l'École des Chartes*, XLII (1881), 161-198, 257-272, first applied the rule to texts. E. Va-candard, "Le Cursus: son Origine, son Histoire, son Emploi dans la Liturgie," *Revue des Questions Historiques*, N.S. XXXIV (1905), 59-102, is best in its field. The researches of Wilhelm Meyer in *Gesammelte Abhandlungen zur Mittellatein-ischen Rhythmik* (Berlin, 1905) have enlarged our knowledge. There are bibliog-raphies in Laurand and A. C. Clark's pamphlet, *The Cursus in Medieval and Vulgar Latin* (Oxford, 1910); [and *CBEL*, I, 23-24 and V, 8. Vacandard's biblio-graphical footnote on "différentes collections" in which the material is to be found is worth adding here: Gabrieli, "L'Epistole di Cola di Rienzo e l'Epistolo-grafia Medievale," *Archiva della Reale Società Romana di Storia Patria*, XI (1888), 381-479; Duchesne, "Note sur l'Origine du Cursus," *Bibliothèque de l'École des Chartes*, L (1889), 161; L. Couture, "Le Cursus du Rhythme Prosaique, du IIIe Siècle de la Renaissance," *Compte Rendu du Congrès International des Catho-liques*, V: "Sciences Historiques" (Paris, 1891), p. 103 (cf. *Rev. des Quest. Hist.*, XXVI, 1892, 253-261); L. Havet, *La Prose Métrique de Symmaque et les Origines Métriques du Cursus* (Paris, 1892); P. Lejay on Havet's book, *Rev. d'Hist. et de Litt.* (Mar. 6, 1893), 186; M. Meyer, "Die Rhythmische Lateinische Prosa und L. Havet...," *Göttingische Gelehrte Anzeigen*, I (1893), 1-23; Dom Mocquereau, "Le Cursus et la Psalmodie," *Paléographie Musicale* (Solesmes and Paris: Picard), IV, 27; P. Bainvel, "La Métrique et la Prose Rhythmique," *Études* (May, 1893); Dahin, "Nos 'Oremus,' Paroles et Chant," *Revue du Chant Grégorien* (Grenoble, Feb.ff., 1895); Grospellier, "Le Rhythme des Oraisons," *Rev. du Ch. Grég.* (Feb.ff., 1897); E. de Jonge, "Les Théories Récentes sur la Prose Métrique en Latin," *Musée Belge*, VI (1902), nn.2, 3, and "Les Clausules de Saint Cyprien," *ibid.*, VI, 344-363; Angelo de Santi, *Il Cursus nella Storia Litteraria e nella Liturgia* (Rome, 1903). See also n.65, below].

This represents Cicero's dicretic $\_ \smile \_\_ \smile \_$ as in the phrases *cerno rempublicam* and *vincla perfregerat*.

The third is VELOX: $/\smile\smile\diagdown\ \smile/\smile$ or $\overset{.}{7}\text{-}\overset{.}{4}\text{-}\overset{.}{2}$, as in the phrases *misericorditer liberemur* (Sept.), and *punished for our offences* (ibid.). This corresponds to Cicero's cretic-ditrochee $\_\smile\_\_\_\smile\_\smile$ as in *gaudeat servitute*. Some explanations of its form will occur later.

A fourth form, the TRISPONDAIC, must be mentioned, though it is not included by Shelly and must not be used in estimating the value of his report. It is, in its briefest form $\_ \smile \smile \_\_ \smile \smile \_\smile$ or $\overset{.}{9}\text{-}\overset{.}{6}\text{-}\overset{.}{4}\text{-}\overset{.}{2}$, though the medieval theorists permit a further prolongation of the sequence of trochees. It is really *velox* plus one or more additional trochees: a three-syllable period followed by three or more two-syllable periods. Examples: *errantium corda resipiscant* (7 Latin Good Fri. collect, 3 in the English Prayer Book); *profitable to our salvation* (15 Sun. after Tr.), *pass to our joyful resurrection* (Easter Evening), *such good things as pass man's understanding* (6 Sun. after Tr.), and *in the midst of so many and great dangers* (4 Sun. after Ep.), where the accent on 4 is almost suppressed.[2]

That the idea developed by Shelly must have occurred to a number of other scholars at about the same time is proved by the reception given to his paper. It immediately became the starting-point of a considerable number of learned or semi-popular discussions, in most of which the original limits of the investigation were largely and hastily extended. Professor Clark at once accepted the results of Shelly's studies and sought to find the same phenomena in a varied body of English prose.[3] Mr. Oliver Elton was still bolder in conjecture and experiment.[4] Other students, while admitting the occurrence of the forms described by Shelly, attempted to disconnect them with the Latin *cursus*.[5]

[2] The *trispondaic* is not mentioned by any of the writers on English cadence, though it is described by the medieval theorists (see Maître Guillaume, MS Sorbonne 1519, in Thurot, pp. 485ff.); Vacandard, as above, pp. 72ff., seems to me to misinterpret the medieval documents. That there was a *dispondaic* ending except preceded by a dactyl needs better evidence than he produces. The *trispondaic* will be found a favorite form in Gibbon.

[3] Albert C. Clark, *Prose-Rhythm in English* (Oxford, 1913).

[4] Oliver Elton, "English Prose Numbers," *Essays and Studies by Members of the English Association*, 4th Ser. (Oxford, 1913); rept. in *A Sheaf of Papers* (Liverpool, 1922).

[5] See a series of very radical papers, apparently interrupted by the war, by P.

All of this indicates clearly the opportuneness of Shelly's suggestion. But in their eagerness to explore the new realms which it opened to their imagination, these scholars have failed to apply the methods of sceptical inquiry to the suggestion itself. Shelly's report of his investigation has never been publicly tested, and this in spite of the fact that it was not accompanied by the specifications which scholars would desire. There is no question of his candor or intelligence; but the problems involved require a considerable experience in such studies; and their proper treatment demands an accumulation of repellent detail which Mr. Shelly could not ask his audience of laymen (largely clergymen they happen to be in this case) to be patient with.

In the first chapter of this paper I will try to test his conclusions by a re-examination of the Sunday collects, and I hope to be able also to mark some of the limits and boundaries in the study of cadence which are in need of more exact definition. In later chapters, I will offer some new suggestions concerning the form and occurrence of the conventional oratorical cadences in English.

I

According to medieval theory, the *cursus* was used at the ends of the *commata, cola,* and *periodus* (or *conclusio*), the parts, large or small, of which a rhetorical period is constructed. In other words it was a conventional way of giving a beautiful flow at the end of a rhetorical unit. In practice, I will try to show, it was not used only in the final positions. But for the present we need not consider this point, for Shelly has naturally followed the medieval theory and studied only the ends of the clauses. In attempting, however, to determine what he considers clauses, and where the cadences are therefore to be expected to occur, we encounter the most serious obstacle to an exact judgment of his results. This difficulty must be explained.

He counts 148 clauses in the Sunday collects, and we turn to them to learn how he arrives at this figure. There are two obvious

---

Fijn van Draat ["The Cursus in Old English Poetry," *Anglia*, xxxviii (1914), 377-404; "Voluptas Aurium," *Englische Studien*, xlviii (1914), 394-428; *Rhythm in English Prose*, Heidelberg (1910)], in which he tries not only to trace the cadences to Anglo-Saxon poetry, but also to reconstruct the rhythmical theory of that poetry. [After the publication of Croll's essay appeared van Draat's "The Place of the Adverb. A Study of Rhythm," *Neophilologus*, xvi (1917).]

ways of counting. One is to include in the number all rhetorical divisions of a period (all the Sunday collects consist of a single period; that is, a single articulated sentence), however short, all the *commata* and *cola*, that is, which according to Latin rule might have *cursus* endings. To put the thing more simply, we might, according to this method, look for a cadence wherever the sense allows or requires a considerable pause. We cannot say exactly how many such places occur in the Sunday collects, because the "phrasing" of an English period is not so definite as in Latin, or at least so regular.[6] But the number is not less than 180, and might be ten more than that. The only other natural process is to count those divisions of a prayer which are indicated by semicolons in the authorized editions. There is much to be said for this method, because the semicolons mark important divisions in the subject matter and the syntax and the *cursus* forms are at least as likely to occur there as elsewhere.[7] But this cannot be Shelly's method, for according to it there are actually 113, not 148 endings.[8]

It is impossible to say exactly how Shelly has reached his definite figure. It seems probable that he has used the semicolons as his main guide, but has often chosen to break a long clause into two or three clauses, on the testimony of his own ears, or perhaps of the customary manner of recitation in English churches. But this is a dangerous procedure when one's object is to prove the existence of objective phenomena of rhythm. For experience will show that it is very easy (within certain limits) to make such divisions where one desires to have them occur, and there will be a great temptation to have them occur where the cadences themselves occur, if one has these sounding in his ears. At all events his use of these methods, sound or unsound, makes it impossible to apply an exact test to his results.

We can make a rough one, however, by using either of the two methods just discussed; that is, either by counting all the rhetorical

[6] See Ch. Three, par. 1, below, for a full discussion of the theory of "phrasing" and the form of the period.

[7] On the structure of the collects see E. M. Goulburn, *The Collects of the Day* (London, 1880), Bk. 1, Ch. 3.

[8] If the concluding formulae ("to whom," "through whose meditation," "through," etc.) are counted, the number would be 167, but these are obviously not meant to be rhythmical in the English translation. It must be added that the semicolon is not absolutely a definite indication of structural division, because sometimes the two parts (*protasis* and *apodosis*) are so closely connected syntactically that a comma is used. But this makes no practical difficulty.

pauses as places for cadence, or by counting only the pauses marked by semicolons. If the percentage of cadenced endings as compared with the whole number of endings is in either case approximately the same as Shelly's percentage, his results will be confirmed. There would be advantages in each method; but I choose the latter, the method of counting the pauses marked by semicolons, because it eliminates the necessity of doubtful decisions.

The result, it must be said, is not favorable to Shelly's conclusions. Of the 113 endings occurring at the places described only 43, or 38 per cent of the whole number, are in the three forms, according to the strictest possible interpretation of the requirements of these forms; only 45, or 40 per cent, according to the freest interpretation of them.[9] Between either of these figures and Shelly's 54 per cent there is a difference that cannot be disregarded, and it does not appear that Shelly has meant to include in his figure any of the possible variations from the Latin forms which we shall presently discuss. In as far then as the test we have used indicates the value of his results, it must be taken as showing that he has sometimes yielded to the temptation which besets an experimenter in English rhythm of the forcing of accents and the partial and subjective decision of questions of pronunciation.[10]

II

Before concluding the criticism of Shelly's paper a question must be asked which has not been raised by Shelly himself or by any of his successors, though it bears directly on the thesis which he maintains. It is the question whether the same clause endings are cadenced in English and in Latin, and the same uncadenced; and

[9] The first doubtful case is: *To rise again for our justification* (1 Sun. after Easter), where the last word forms a *planus* if we may admit that a whole cadence may fall within one word; but the rules for division of words in medieval usage would forbid this; the custom of the ancients did not favor it; and the English ear rejects it as foreign to the character of cadenced endings. *Action and honor* is not the same rhythmically as *justification*. The second is: *prayers of thy humble servants* (10 Sun. after Tr.) where the doubt is due to the uncertainty of the pronunciation of *prayers*. It is probably to be considered as one syllable, making this ending a regular *velox*. [In Milton's *Paradise Lost*, the word *prayers* is often monosyllabic.]

[10] In description Shelly shows caution and criticism, but in scanning it must be said that he betrays the weakness spoken of in the text. He scans a *single province of the Roman Empire* and *to the Latin language* as examples of planus-2 (6-2); and *when in difficulties* and *the force of genius* (from Newman) as planus-2 and *tardus*, respectively. *Rising with the occasion* (Newman), obviously a *velox*, he scans as *tardus*, accenting *with* and treating *occasion* as four syllables.

whether, further, the same cadence occurs at corresponding places. That is: does *velox* appear for *velox*, *tardus* for *tardus*, etc., or not?

The answer is that there is no such correspondence. Indeed the disagreement is so striking that it will be well to illustrate it in some detail.

In the first place, the cadences occur in English where there are none in Latin and *vice versa*. For example, although the great majority of the Latin prayers are written with close attention to the rules of the *cursus*, including those which provide for variety by the use of different cadences in neighboring clauses, there are a few, as, for instance, the collects for the 7 and 11 Suns. after Tr., in which almost none but simple *planus* cadences occur, and those perhaps accidentally, or as the result of a fixed habit. These prayers are chiefly from the Sacramentary of Gelasius, though I do not know what significance there may be in this fact; and in all of them there are marked effects of balance and rhyme, which serve, in the absence of the *cursus*, to provide the *voluptas aurium* which public prayers should give. In the English translation the *cursus* forms are just as common in these prayers as in others.

In the second place, there is no relation between the *form* of the Latin ending at a given place and the form of the corresponding English ending. If there is *planus* in the one there may be *velox* or *tardus* (if anything) in the other; and so on. The collect for the 11 Sun. after Tr. is a case in which there is agreement in both main clauses, but this is one of the prayers just mentioned in which only the inconspicuous *planus* appears. To this we may add the second collect for Good Friday, though we have hitherto been confining our attention to the Sunday collects. Here *tardus* occurs in the first clause and *velox* in the second in both Latin and English. Except in these two prayers an agreement even in a single clause is an exceptional phenomenon, and in the English prayers in which the *cursus* forms are most conspicuous it happens that there is no agreement with the Latin original (see for instance Whitsunday and the 4 Sun. after Tr.).

The significance of these facts is too clear to be missed. The translators did not set themselves the task of copying the forms before them in a given prayer, as the uninformed reader of Shelly might suppose. And when this fact is taken in conjunction with those that we have previously noted, namely, the relatively small number of English endings that display the *exact cursus* forms, as compared with the number counted by Shelly, it becomes evident that we must change the idea of the relation between the English and the Latin rhythmic procedure that has been formed heretofore by all the readers of Shelly's paper. Instead of deliberate and systematic imitation, we must suppose general, purely aural, and in some degree unconscious influence. Instead of working by clearly-understood methods and formulated rules, as the authors of the Latin did, the translators were controlled merely by the desire to produce an effect in general like that of the Latin. Whether they knew of the Latin rules, or were aware that there were rules, we cannot positively say; in view of the fact that the teaching of the rules had, according to all the best evidence, been neglected or wholly abandoned in the secretarial offices of both church and state since about the beginning of the fourteenth century,[11] it is probable that Cranmer and his associates were not familiar with them. But however that may be, their practice seems to show that they were less anxious to imitate exactly at this point or that, than to produce prayers that would lend themselves to the traditional mode of intonation and attain the traditional oratorical effect.

Their procedure could be exactly illustrated by a comparison with their method in reproducing the other rhetorical features of the Latin prayers. These works are singularly rich in rhyme, alliteration, balance, and the other figures of sound which form the chief adornments of medieval Latin prose and are used there with more complexity and involution than in any other prose. The echoes of them in the English Prayer Book will provide the interesting subject of some future investigation, and it will prove to have important relations to the subject of rhythm itself. All that can be said here is that the translators have never failed to observe the artifices of their predecessors, have done all that their language and the conditions of their task permitted them in reproducing their effect in English, but have avoided the pedantry of exact imitation. It is exactly so in their study of rhythmic effect. They have seen that to write cadence for cadence would involve the sacrifice of beauty of phrase. They have allowed the English phrase to develop its own beauty, to perfect the oratorical form toward which we can see it slowly growing in the earlier translations. But in doing so they have also—perhaps unconsciously—tended to guide it toward one of the

[11] See Valois, "Le Rhythme des Bulles Pontificales."

forms of final cadence to which their ears were habituated by their lifelong use of the Latin liturgy.[12]

Of course a wholly different conclusion may be drawn from the corrections and criticisms of Shelly's article which we have found necessary. They may be regarded as throwing serious doubt upon the alleged Latin influence *in toto*. They need not however have this effect. The occurrence of three (or four) forms of cadence in 40 per cent of all the endings is not an accidental phenomenon. If, for example, we should limit the study of Cicero's clausules to the three forms he liked best (and this would be the equivalent of Shelly's method), we should find that he cadences only 44 per cent of his endings; and if we should add his use of the form which corresponds to Shelly's fourth form (*planus*-2), the percentage would still be only 46.[13] But it must also be remembered that these results have been obtained by limiting ourselves strictly to Shelly's method of observation. The purpose of the two following chapters of this paper will be to show that he has limited too narrowly the area in which we may properly look for the influence of the *cursus* in the Collects, in the first place in his study of the *forms* of English cadence, and in the second place in his ideas concerning the places where cadence may occur. If the arguments to be adduced there are sound, it will be necessary to disregard Shelly's figures and attempt a new estimate of the extent of the Latin influence on a different basis. It must be remembered, however, that however high the percentage of cadenced endings may be found to be, it will not be so high as in the Latin collects. Cadencing was regularized and prescribed in certain forms of medieval Latin prose, and it was therefore much more frequent and pervasive than in any classical Latin, or any English, prose.

[12] Some examples profitable for study will be found in the collects for Innocent's Day, the 4 Sun. after Easter, and the prayer in the service for the Churching of Women. The last will be found in J. H. Blunt's *Annotated Book of Common Prayer* (a book which should have been mentioned earlier as invaluable to the student of our subject), II (London, 1866), p. 306. [Page references to Blunt are usually accurate for the later editions.]

[13] These figures are founded upon those of Theodor Zielinski, "Der Rhythmus der Römischen Kuntsprosa und seine Psychologische Grundlagen," *Archiv für die Gesammte Psychologie*, VII (1906).

CHAPTER TWO

ENGLISH VARIATIONS OF THE CURSUS FORMS

The remarks just made concerning the *modus operandi* of the translators were suggested by observing the places of the *occurrence* of cadences. But their importance cannot be limited to that part of our subject. Once admit that the influence of the Latin *cursus* was of the general and aural character that has been described, and the theory of the *forms* the cadences would assume when transferred to English is radically affected. If the translators did not know the chancelry rules, as seems probable, or, knowing them, chose to observe them only in so far as they made for the general effect of euphony and ceremony that they desired, why should they have been more pedantic in following their exact forms than in observing their places? Why should they not relax the rigidity of these forms if their ears were satisfied that their essential beauties could be transferred in this way, perhaps only in this way, into their own language?

Shelly has not admitted such a possibility. He has worked, as all who have followed him have done, on the assumption of a mechanical transfer to the collects (and hence to other English prose) of the exact metrical forms of the originals. It is a new step, therefore, in the development of the theory of cadence that is here suggested—one that will of course introduce some confusion and uncertainty into a subject that is now at least definite, but may also place it finally on a foundation at once broader and firmer. At least it is a radical step and must not be taken without due consideration. In presenting the arguments in favor of it, the collects will still furnish us with most of our examples; but the discussion will gradually extend itself to other pieces of cadenced English prose.

There are three variations of the regular Latin forms which would be most likely to appear with frequency if the translators worked in the free way we have described. I will describe and illustrate these three before giving the reasons for considering them equivalent to the Latin forms.

1. The ending *velox* would easily become 8-4-2 in English, and would not lose its essential character in so doing. Some examples are:—*carry us through all temptations* (4 Sun. after Ep.); *defended by thy mighty power* (5 Sun. after Ep.); *partakers of his resurrection* (Sun. before Easter); *the weakness of our mortal na-*

ture (1 Sun. after Tr.); *declarest thy almighty power* (11 Sun. after Tr.); *continually to be given* (17 Sun. after Tr.).

2. *Velox* again could be modified by the addition of a light syllable at the end, the form thus becoming 8-5-3 instead of 7-4-2, or 9-5-3 instead of 8-4-2. This is a very common ending:—*defend us from all adversities* (Tr. Sun.); *serve thee in all godly quietness* (5 Sun. after Tr.); *return into the way of righteousness* (3 Sun. after Easter); *always prevent and follow us*[14] (17 Sun. after Tr.); *visit us in great humility* (1 Sun. in Adv.); *the example of his great humility* (Sun. before Easter); *our defence against all our enemies* (3 Sun. in Lent); *protection of thy good providence* (2 Sun. after Tr.); *hearts of the disobedient* (3 Sun. in Adv.).

3. *Tardus* would often become 7-3 instead of 6-3. This is in fact the commoner form, I believe, in elevated prose; and certainly some of the most beautiful phrases in the Prayer Book owe their character to it. Examples are:—*several necessities* (All Cond. of Men); *dangers and adversities* (Collect in the Litany); *free from all adversities* (22 Sun. after Tr.); *acknowledging our wretchedness* (Ash Wed.); *ordered by thy governance* (5 Sun. after Tr.); *never-failing providence* (8 Sun. after Tr.).

Clark has included two of these three forms (2 and 3) in his consideration of English cadences;[15] but he has done so on the ground of their regular occurrence in the medieval *cursus*, which he assumes without giving the evidence. Neither the theory nor the practice of medieval Latin, in fact, recognizes either of them; and if their occurrence in English is to be ascribed to the imitation of the Latin rhythms, it must be only because we admit that such imitation in English has been of the free and adaptive kind described above. That is, to include them among the cadence forms is to recognize a principle of freedom in the English laws of cadence which is wholly contrary to the Latin laws, and which may perhaps be extended to other variations besides these three.

What are the reasons then for accepting this principle; that is, for expecting the three variations, and perhaps still others, to appear in English as equivalents of the regular Latin forms? There are two, both derived from differences between the two languages:

---

[14] The validity of this example depends upon the strength given to the syllable *al-*.

[15] *Prose-Rhythm*, p. 6.

the first from a difference in the character of their words, the second from a difference in their metrical character and customs.

I. English is far less polysyllabic than Latin. It had been so even in its classical Anglo-Saxon form, in the period when Anglo-Saxon was enjoying its highest courtly and literary cultivation; and with the loss of inflections which attended its rapid decline before and after the Norman Conquest, its words of course became still shorter. It was then in the same relation in this respect to its more ancient form that modern Greek is to the literary Greek of the classical age, or that the spoken Latin of the periods when it was merging into the modern vernaculars was to the Latin of the age of Augustus. In this state it was incapable of receiving the *cursus*. But in this state it did not, as we know, long remain. Even in Anglo-Saxon times the importation of Latin words, chiefly names of things ecclesiastical, had already begun, and this process of enrichment and alteration of the English vocabulary continued steadily through all the centuries that followed. The causes that contributed to it have often been described. But perhaps the liturgical vocabulary of the church has a greater share in it than historians of the language have observed. It might appear, on exact investigation, that the Latin words which first came into the language between the Conquest and the middle of the fourteenth century were in great number the words familiarized by the constant public repetition of the prayers; and it is certainly true that the ever-increasing importation of such words from the middle of the fourteenth century onward to the middle of the sixteenth was in some degree due to the early efforts in the translation of the liturgy, and in great degree to the steady stream of translation of devotional works written in a semi-liturgical style which was characteristic of this period. These facts, of course, have an important bearing on the subject of cadence, and would account for the success of the sixteenth-century translators in transferring the effect of the *cursus* into the Prayer Book.

The only point to be made here, however, is the more general one that in as far as this process of Latinization of the vocabulary had gone on it was possible to have the cadences in English—and no further. Native English was not of a character to lend itself to them, and it had become still more foreign to them during the period of its decline. It is true that in any language and under any condition of its development it is possible to produce forms that will exactly fill the metrical schemes of the *cursus*. But anyone who has studied the *cursus* in medieval Latin must be aware that its effects are not produced merely by exact metrical forms. The rules of the medieval theorists show that the relation between the fall of the accents and the number of syllables in the words on which they fall is of the essence of its beauty, and is part of the actual form of the cadences themselves.

This point may first be illustrated by a rather full consideration of *velox*. This form is very inadequately represented by the formula 7-4-2, $\_ \cup \cup \_ \cup \_ \cup$; for it is of its essence that the accent on 4 shall be subordinate to that on 2, and the characteristic case of it is that in which it ends in a four- or five-syllable word, with the main accent on the penult, and hence (according to Latin rule) a subordinate accent on the second syllable preceding. Thus: *et ad implenda quae viderint, convalescant* (1 Sun. after Ep.); *misericorditer liberemur* (Sept. Sun.). So characteristic is this form that there are but three or four exceptions to it in the Sunday collects. In fact the rules for the *cursus* are uniformly stated by medieval theorists in terms of the length of the words used in it. *Velox* is said to consist of a four-syllable word with the accent on the penult preceded by a word of three or more syllables with an accent on the ante-penult, though a writer of one period may admit that two words of two syllables each may take the place of the last word;[16] and another of different date may include also a three-syllable word with accent on the penult preceded by a monosyllable, and even other forms.[17] But in all kinds of prose which have been examined these varieties are infrequent.

In order to produce exactly the Latin effect, therefore, English would have had to have taken over a large number of such words from the Latin; that is, four- or five-syllable words; and, further, it would have had to have preserved the accents where they were in Latin, or at least to have kept the Latin law that a minor or secondary accent falls on the second syllable before the main accent. But there are not a great many such words in English, partly because in taking long words from the Latin we have so modified and clipped their endings that they are no longer accented on the penult, as in *comparative*, partly because the tendency to

[16] So, for example, a *Summa Dictaminis* of Saxon origin reproduced in part in Rockinger, pp. 209-346 (p. 213).

[17] See *Summa Dictaminum magistri Ludolphi* (Ludolph of Hildesheim), also in Rockinger.

recessive accent in English has produced the same result, as in *difficulty, ordinary*, etc., and partly because the law of the fall of the minor accents, just mentioned, is not observed in English, and we have such pronunciations as *justification, simplification*, etc. And, moreover, it is to be observed that there were not so many of them in the middle of the sixteenth century as there are now. Not many can be gathered from the Prayer Book itself: *confirmation, mediation, resurrection, supplications, regeneration, satisfaction, circumcision, advantageous*, and a few others, nearly all words in *-ion* or else words that are not likely to occur at the ends of phrases.[18]

In order to produce the exact form of the second part of Latin *velox*, therefore, the translators had to resort to one of two combinations of word length both of which were comparatively rare in Latin, though as we have seen they were recognized by some theorists. The first is a three-syllable paroxytone word preceded by a monosyllable bearing a minor accent. Nearly all the *veloxes* in the Latin collects that do not come in the first case show this form: *propitius, et agendi* (9 Sun. after Tr.); *oratio non praesumit* (12 Sun. after Tr.); etc. Instances of this combination are not uncommon in English, are relatively more frequent than in Latin; and the point for us to notice is that here again English is chiefly dependent upon the Latin words in its vocabulary, for the native phrase will not often go in this undulant meter. Some examples are: *lose not the thing eternal* (4 Sun. after Tr.); *keeping of thy commandments* (1 Sun. after Tr.); *increase in us true religion* (7 Sun. after Tr.); *by our frailty we have committed* (24 Sun. after Tr.).

The other word combination recognized in Latin is that in which the second part of the cadence consists of two two-syllable words. This is less frequent than either of the others in Latin. But it is important for English because it lends itself to the needs of a language that is not rich in polysyllables. It is relatively frequent in the Prayer Book, and still more so in some later prose, especially Gibbon's. It is important, therefore, to remark that like the other combinations just mentioned it is dependent upon the Latinization of our vocabulary. This is apparent as soon as we recall, once more, that the accent on 4 in *velox* is subordinate. Not any combination

---

[18] A very small number of native words also have the proper form: *everlasting, understanding*, etc.

of two-syllable words therefore will produce the necessary effect, but only certain two-word *phrases*; and nearly all such phrases will prove to consist of a noun preceded by an adjective. The Latin origin of most phrases of this kind suitable for use in the *velox* cadence may be illustrated from the following examples: *renewed by thy Holy Spirit* (Sun. after Christmas); *sending to them the light of thy Holy Spirit* (Whit.); *rejoice in his holy comfort* (ibid.); *look upon the hearty desires of thy humble servants* (3 Sun. in Lent); *the prayers of thy humble servants* (10 Sun. after Tr.); *the wills of thy faithful people* (25 Sun. after Tr.). It is true that the word *holy* is not a Latin word, but all of the phrases in these cadences owe their existence and their form to liturgical Latin, and to the efforts of 150 years in the translation of its copious and conventional style into English.[19]

It is not to be denied of course that English may produce a correct and beautiful *velox* cadence by short words of its own, as in *thy people which call upon thee* (1 Sun. after Ep.), and perhaps in *evermore by thy help and goodness* (16 Sun. after Tr.). But the cases are rare and do not affect the general validity of the point we have been urging. This point is merely that the Latinization of the English vocabulary had not proceeded far enough in the middle of the sixteenth century—perhaps has not yet proceeded far enough—to make the *exact* reproduction of the metrical forms of the *cursus* easy or natural. The length of the argument is perhaps out of proportion to the difficulty of establishing the point. But in the course of it the opportunity has arisen to make clear some necessary features of cadence which have been almost wholly obscured in English discussions of the subject. And the facts we have been examining will yield, moreover, another argument which serves our purpose more directly. For they show, not only that it is difficult to reproduce the exact Latin forms in English, but also

[19] A study of the development in style from the earliest primers and service books in English up to the Prayer Book of 1549 is much to be desired. [For such a study, the following are useful: C. C. Butterworth, *The Literary Lineage of the King James Bible* (Philadelphia, 1941) and *The English Primers (1529-1545): their Publication and Connection with the English Bible* (Philadelphia, 1953); J. Holland, *The Psalmists of Britain*, 2 vols. (London, 1843); H. B. Swete, *Church Services and Service Books before the Reformation* (London, 1905); E. Brightman and K. D. Mackenzie, "The History of the Book of Common Prayer down to 1662," in *Liturgy and Worship*, ed. W. K. L. Clarke (London, 1932)—(includes a useful bibliography); W. T. Brooke, *Old English Psalmody . . . 1557-1660* (London, 1916)—a short history; B. Wigan, *The Book of Common Prayer, 1549-1649 . . . a Guide . . .* (London, 1949).]

that the exact reproduction of their *form* will not always produce their *effect*, that this effect may, on the contrary, sometimes be better produced by variations of the forms.

Two examples will serve for illustration. The Latin rule of accenting every other syllable (counting backward from the main accent) serves to give a definite character and value to the secondary accent in a four-syllable paroxytone word, as in *dependentes*, for instance; upon it, indeed, the character of Latin *velox* depends. English not only has no such rule but is much less attentive to subordinate accent within a word. Thus *resurrection* and *meditation* may easily be pronounced without any accent on the first syllable, or with so little that the characteristic undulation of Latin would not be felt; and that this is true is shown by the fact that an accented syllable immediately preceding usually draws all accent away from them. If, however, a long run of unaccented syllables precede such a word, the accent on its first syllable is inevitably somewhat strengthened. For this reason, then, it seems not unreasonable to conclude that the ending 8-4-2 will sometimes better represent the true form of Latin *velox*, as, for instance, in the phrase *partakers of thy resurrection*, than 7-4-2 will.

Again: In the case of the two-word phrases ending a *velox*, as *mortal nature, faithful servants*, etc., there is a departure from the exact Latin effect, but in the opposite direction from that just mentioned. That is, there is here a tendency to put too strong an accent on the adjective and hence to give too much importance to the minor accent of the cadence. And the same remark applies often to phrases consisting of a monosyllable plus a trisyllable. This effect will not be produced, however, if the last accent of the cadence is followed by *two* unaccented syllables instead of by one, because the lengthening of this unaccented part of the period has the effect of strengthening its accent, and the minor accent of the preceding period is thus relatively reduced. *Defend us from all adversities, our defence against all our enemies*, and *serve thee in all godly quietness* are better reproductions of *velox* than phrases of the form 7-4-2 would be in their places.

So far our discussion has been limited to the case of the *velox* cadence. The same points may be more briefly illustrated by *tardus*. We have described this cadence as 6-3, or $/\smile\smile/\smile\smile$; but to make this statement without taking into account also the forms of the *words* used in achieving this arrangement of accents is an uncritical procedure. For in fact the two periods of this ending are not equal, as the metrical notation might be taken to indicate. A certain slight difference might, it is true, be taken as implied in this notation, since it is recognized in all metrical theory that final syllables have a tendency to be light and short unless supported by rime or otherwise.

But in the present case that is not all. In medieval usage this difference was heightened by the kind of words used in the cadence, In both theory and practice it always ends in a three- or four-syllable word: most theorists say, a four-syllable word, saving themselves by adding that a three-syllable word proparoxytone preceded by a one-syllable word unaccented is equivalent to a four-syllable word proparoxytone,[20] as in *non possumus, sit libera.* In practice, we find that at least three-quarters of the *tardus* cadences end in a four-syllable word, as, in the collects, *mortalis infirmitas* (1 Sun. after Tr.), *habere perpetuum* (2 Sun. after Tr.), *defensionis auxilium* (3 Sun. after Tr.); and of the others nearly all end in a monosyllable plus a trisyllable, as in *esse non possumus* (9 Sun. after Tr.) *amare quod praecipis* (14 Sun. after Tr.), *mundet et muniat* (16 Sun. after Tr.). The result of these restrictions of form is that a pause occurs within the first period of *tardus* (some authors call it a cesura), but none within the second, and the first period is therefore longer to the ear than the second.[21]

Now English is embarrassed in trying to render this effect by the same comparative lack of long native words that has been noted above, and though it may achieve the result through the use of its Latinistic vocabulary it cannot do so often. It follows that *tardus* must either be rare in English—so rare as not to appear a characteristic form of English cadence—or else must often change its metrical form in order to maintain the inequality between its two periods which is a necessary part of its effect. In fact *tardus* in the form 6-3 is very infrequent in the Prayer Book,[22] and also, I

[20] See the same treatises cited above for *velox.*

[21] We need not go further back than medieval Latin for our purposes; but it is interesting to observe that in Cicero 86 per cent of the dicretic clausules (the predecessors of *tardus*) end in a three-, four-, or five-syllable word, 43 per cent in a four-syllable word. Zielinski indicates his sense of the greater weight of the first period by analyzing this clausule as a cretic plus a trochee and a half ("Der Rhythmus," p. 129).

[22] Among the 45 cadenced endings which I have counted (accepting Shelly's restrictions as to form and occurrence), only 6 are in this form.

think, in other cadenced prose. On the other hand, the form 7-3 is one of the commonest, as it is one of the most beautiful, of English endings, and must be regarded as usually a better equivalent for the Latin than 6-3.[23]

II. We have been considering the effects of differences of vocabulary upon the relation between Latin and English cadence. A second reason, equally strong, for expecting a modification or relaxation of the forms of the *cursus* when transferred to English is to be found in the difference between the metrical usages and traditions of the two languages, the difference between a strictly regulated metrical or numerical custom and a free custom in which only accent is strictly regarded.

Whatever their popular poetry may have been, the classical languages submitted themselves from an early date to a discipline which imposed an exact weight and value upon each syllable of a word and a line. The "foot" was established as the metrical unit, and the time relations of its parts as carefully fixed as are those of a bar of music, the thesis receiving as strict attention as the arsis. English of course has never been so rigorous. It has always tended to rob the unaccented syllables of importance in order to pay more abundantly to the accented. And in particular it has usually permitted itself some freedom in the number of syllables following or preceding the one that has the beat. This is obviously the case in our native forms of verse, the alliterative long line, and its degenerate form of later centuries, of the ballad verse (if this is really a native form), and of all popular song measures. But it is also true, though in a less degree, of the naturalized romance forms which have been used by our most learned poets. None of these poets, not even Milton, has succeeded in regularizing his verse as regards the number of its syllables, the rules of elision, etc., to the same extent that classical verse was regularized,[24] and whenever this result has been even approximated, a strong reaction has set in after a short time toward the freer native method.

In view of these familiar facts, what would be the likely procedure of the translators of the collects? If they knew the Latin rules and were pedantically determined to observe them, of course they might subordinate effect to exact form and by considerable

---

[23] For examples (*acknowledging our wretchedness, dangers and adversities,* etc.), see above, Ch. Two, par. 3, item 3.

[24] [But much of the work done on Milton's verse since 1919 has tended to show far more regularizing than was commonly supposed when Croll wrote.]

effort find phrases that would scan by the Latin rules. But if they were guided only by such aural influences as we have been supposing, and by their trained sense of oratorical effect, they would be likely to observe the accents of the Latin *cursus* forms, but would be likely to take the same freedom with the unaccented syllables that English poetry always tends to take. They would adhere to the Latin number of unaccented syllables just in as far as they would have to do so in order to maintain the accents in their proper relation to each other (this relation being determined by the ear alone), and they would adhere to it no further than this.

But we may state the relation somewhat more precisely. For what we have just said is equivalent to saying that the tendency of English will be to *increase* the number of syllables at certain places. The syllable-counting custom of medieval Latin gives a definite inalterable value to each unaccented syllable of a metrical unit; and a slight difference between the number of such syllables in one part of a cadence and another, between the two of the first period of *velox*, for instance, and the one of each of its other periods, may be depended upon to produce an effect and establish a desired relation between the parts. In English, on the other hand, so slight a difference might easily fail to produce its effect in certain circumstances, and this would be especially the case in the prose cadences, where the two (or three) periods of a cadence are of different lengths, and its effect depends upon this difference. There would thus be a tendency in English to secure a clearer recognition of the relation between the accents by increasing the difference of the intervals between them. Thus, to take our examples from the three variations we are considering in this chapter, the cadence 8-4-2 would mark more clearly than 7-4-2 the fact that *velox* consists of a longer period followed by shorter ones, and the form 7-3 would often be the only one that would correctly represent the relation between the periods of *tardus*.

It is hardly necessary, however, to resort to *a priori* argument to make the point. The difference in the metrical practice of the two languages has resulted in such actual differences in the enunciation of unaccented syllables that numerical comparison of them is often misleading. *Venire, legere, possumus, fortiter* have three syllables each in all circumstances, and are always to be represented in musical notation, by a quarter-note plus two eighth-notes; but *heavenly, glorious, interests, evening*, even *company*, may be either a quarter plus two-eighths or a quarter plus one-eighth, according to circumstances. Latin *fur* is always one syllable, *flore* always two; but *power, flower, fine, prayer, ever, even, dear, common, higher* [*heaven*], are sometimes one syllable and sometimes two syllables. Poetry regulates this freedom by its pattern, and can impose a full three-syllable value on *glorious, every,* and the like by its own laws. But prose is not capable of such arbitrary prescription, and these words will seldom be felt as having the same value as three-syllable words in Latin, *flower, prayer,* etc., as equivalent to a Latin two-syllable word. It follows that English cadence can never be properly described by a numerical system, and that it can never produce the same effect as the Latin cadence unless it is allowed a certain freedom in its use of unaccented syllables.

We have now considered at length the three variations from the regular forms of the *cursus* which occur most frequently in English use, with the reasons which lead us to regard them as English equivalents of the regular forms. It may seem that more space has been devoted to these forms than is due to their importance, especially in view of the fact that one scholar has already included two of them among the English cadences without considering it necessary to argue the question at all. The purpose of the discussion, however, has been not only to establish these forms—though they are very important in themselves—but also to use them as the best tests of a principle which, once clearly recognized, may be more widely extended. If we are willing to admit the principle that English metrical custom tends to blur and relax the metrical forms of the cadences and to retain only their characteristic movements, we may carry its applications considerably beyond the point which we have now reached. I wish in a future chapter to show that this in fact is what we may hope to do, and that by following this line of development we may arrive at a more profitable method of studying English cadence than the sole study of metrical formulae.

The further stages of the argument must be put off, however, for the moment, while we take up certain questions concerning the occurrence of the cadences rather than their form.

✧ CHAPTER THREE ✧

WHERE DOES CADENCE OCCUR IN AN ENGLISH SENTENCE?

The question, *What are the usual and conventional places for the occurrence of cadence in English?*, has scarcely been considered at all, even by those who have treated the subject of the forms most fully. It has been assumed that the ear is a sufficient guide to the reader in determining his author's intention, and that the author himself is directed merely by his natural feeling for euphony and beauty. It may be, indeed, that we shall not succeed in avoiding a final appeal to tests as vague as these. But, on the other hand, it is clear that we should not neglect any opportunity to control them by facts or principles that are capable of definite formulation. For the chief danger that besets the student of cadence is the temptation to discover a proper place for cadence wherever he discovers the forms. He may too easily adjust his reading of his author's sentences to his preconceived ideas of cadence form. Indeed, we have already found, in our attempt to determine the principles acted on by Shelly in his search for cadence in the collects, a striking instance of the uncertainty of a merely subjective test.

I. The Final Positions

There is unanimous agreement on one point among all who have written on the subject, namely, that the places to look for cadence are at certain final positions, the *end* of the sentence, and the *ends* of certain parts of it. In the following section of this chapter I will hazard the suggestion that they may also be found, as part of the general rhythmic effect of a sentence, in certain other positions, not final in the sense in which the term is here used. But at least there is no doubt that they do occur in the final positions, and that these are much the most important places for them. Even though we had not the authority of the classical and medieval theorists to support us, we should expect to find cadence before pauses.

Where then do these pauses occur? What are the final positions in a sentence? This is evidently the all-important question. Until it has been answered as fully as the facts permit us to answer it, we have done almost nothing toward the establishment of a science of English cadence. Yet this question has not been even asked by those who have written on the subject, except by one American scholar who attempts an answer—professedly superficial—in a recent paper.[25]

The proper method of procedure is fortunately not far to seek. Cadence in classical and medieval Latin was a small and dependent part of oratorical style. It was a last touch of ornament which accented and completed a large design of "rhythm." The groundwork of this design was the rhetorical form of the "period." Periodicity and rhythm are often exactly identified in the ancient theory, or, when they are distinguished, they are related to each other as the means to the end. And this method of treatment is the only one that the student of modern cadence can profitably employ. We cannot hope to advance far in the study of the euphonious endings until we relate their occurrence, as far as the character of English prose permits, to the rhetorical design of the sentences in which they are used.

The theory of the period was a commonplace of rhetoric in the Renaissance, but hardly a vestige of it now remains in even the most formal of rhetorical treatises. It is partly for this reason that we are justified in reviving it here in connection with the subject of cadence, even though it is so familiar to historical students of rhetoric. But, besides this, Eugène Landry's careful studies in *La Théorie du Rhythme Français Déclamé* (Paris, 1911), would justify a new survey of the familiar field in view of the new precision which he has been able to arrive at in relating questions of rhythm and cadence to the doctrine of the period. The following summary will be found to owe a great deal to his treatment.

1. There is no better definition of the *period* than Hobbes' curt translation of Aristotle in his *Brief of the Art of Rhetoric* (1681):[26] "A period is such a part as is perfect in itself, and has such length as may easily be comprehended by the understanding." Aristotle's statement in full (*Rhetoric*, III, Ch. 9) is as follows: "I call a period a form of words which has independently in itself a beginning and ending, and a length easily taken in at a glance." Though the period ordinarily coincides with the sentence, theoretically it is not

25 F. M. K. Foster, "Cadence in English Prose," *JEGP*, XVI (July, 1917), 456-462. Professor Foster recognizes the important fact that the pauses are determined by breathing intervals necessary in oral delivery. He might, however, have stated the facts more simply, more accurately, and more completely if he had had recourse to the great tradition of rhetorical theory.

26 Published with Aristotle's *Rhetoric* in Bohn Classical Library (London, 1846). The passage quoted is from III, Ch. 8, p. 334.

the same, and in practice it may (in certain kinds of style)[27] consist of elements not syntactically connected. For it is not a syntactic or logical unit, but on the one hand a psychological, and on the other a rhythmical unit.[28] Here of course we are concerned with it as a unit of sound, a rhythmical unit. It may be simple, or undivided, as in "Socrates is mortal" (Landry's example, p. 235), or "I wonder you fear not their ends whose actions you imitate" (Hobbes' example, p. 334). But it may be divided and consist of parts.

2. The parts of a divided period are called *members* (*membra*) or *cola* (in medieval Latin also *distinctiones* or *versus*), and the number of these that may constitute a period is undefined, though Landry thinks that a larger number than eight is abnormal in the purely oratorical, or declamatory, style. The member rather than the period is treated by some writers as the true unit of oratorical style, since it is determined by the physiological laws of breathing, and hence has its length definitely limited. A member is followed by a rest, or pause, which is a breathing interval, and it very rarely exceeds twenty syllables in length, because the heightened energy of utterance required in public speaking cannot be maintained for a greater number of syllables than this without an opportunity fully to recover the breath. The number of emphatic accents varies from one to four.[29] It may be added, though the point is obvious, that a member is uttered during the *expiration* of breath, the pause being the period of inhalation.

The "harmony," "number," or "rhythm" of a period depends chiefly upon the relations between the members of which it consists: relations of length, form, and sound. In oratorical style there is always a tendency to arrange them in groups of two or more of approximately (but not exactly) the same length, and to point the effect of balance thus produced by similarity in the syntactic form of these members, by correspondences in sound between words in corresponding positions in them, and finally by parallel or related

[27] For instance, in the style of Seneca and in that of Montaigne, Bacon, Browne, and other "Anti-Ciceronians" and imitators of Seneca in the seventeenth century.
[28] Landry, p. 235.
[29] Landry (p. 216) finds that the average number of syllables is eleven and a half. It must be remembered, however, that in style not actually meant to be declaimed the member may be longer, both because the amount of energy expended in the utterance of a syllable is smaller and because speech is more rapid in such style. In Gibbon, whose style is not calculated for actual declamation, though it is made on the oratorical model, members of 23 or 24 syllables may be found.

rhythmic movements. Variations, however, from the regularity of a pattern thus suggested are, it must always be remembered, the chief resources of the orator in his quest of rhythmic and expressive beauty.

3. Some theorists give a place in the doctrine of the period to a phenomenon which is very frequent in every oratorical style in which there is a certain amplitude and dignity, namely, the combination of two members, related to each other syntactically in certain ways, to form a larger unit within the period. This double unit, consisting of two members, is called a *phrase*. It is not an essential part, however, of the theory of the period, since a single phrase cannot occur alone. Unless there are at least two phrases, balanced in form, we may describe the period as consisting merely of members. But in a style as copious and sonorous as, say, Isocrates' or Cicero's or Bossuet's or even Gibbon's, the phrase is very frequent; and though we shall not perhaps be called on to use it in the present discussion, it will often be of assistance in the study of the occurrences and forms of cadence.

4. A colon of a certain length may fall into two (sometimes even three) parts in utterance, the division between them being indicated by a pause shorter than that at the end of a colon. One of these parts, which, however, like the phrases, never occur singly, is called a *comma* (*caesum, incisum*, or sometimes in medieval Latin *subdistinctio*). The division of the *colon* into *commata* is not connected apparently with the physiological process of breathing, or at least is not primarily due to this, but is chiefly the effect of a law of beauty of sound which seems to demand such a break. Landry, therefore, and other theorists treat it as primarily a melodic phenomenon, rather than as a rhythmic one, though it serves also the purposes of rhythm. It corresponds, that is, to the division of the line made by the cesura in formal verse.[30]

Classical and medieval rhetoricians often define the *comma* in distinction from the *colon*, as "a part of discourse consisting of two or more words which taken separately from the context have no meaning."[31] This is too narrow a restriction,[32] but it serves to

[30] The part of a verse before or after the cesura is indeed sometimes called a *comma*; for instance, in the *Ars Rhetorica Clodiani* in Karl F. von Halm, ed., *Rhetores Latini Minores* [Leipzig, 1863], p. 590.

[31] So Martianus Capella, 39 (in Halm), and Aquila Romanus, 18 (*ibid.*).

[32] In some kinds of medieval style we often find successions of brief members, parallel in form and usually balanced in sound; they are characteristic, for instance, in the "rime-prose" of which so much has been written, and so little that is

indicate the fact that division into commas is not always marked by phrasal or syntactic form. Often of course it is: we can tell often where the pause comes by the sense. But sometimes it is *purely* a melodic and rhythmic phenomenon, and the orator makes his pause in contravention or disregard of meaning merely from his habit of rhythmic and melodic utterance.

This briefly is the doctrine of the period, as it was formulated by the Greek and Roman orators, and as it is sure to reappear whenever oratorical prose is studied with the purpose of describing its form. It began to be neglected in the theory of the eighteenth century—though not in its practice—and only a faint shadow of it now falls across the pages of our "College Rhetorics," where it is unintelligently assumed that there is but one kind of period, namely, that in which the sense is suspended until the end, and this is opposed to the so-called "loose sentence," which is called non-periodic. It would be interesting to trace the mistakes in theory and the evil results in practice that can be ascribed to this error, but this would lead us far away from our subject. We can only inquire here what the rhetoricians propose to do with the sentences of writers like Browne, South, Dryden, and Stevenson, which are characteristically "loose," yet are always periodic in the proper sense, and often of course very beautifully so.

The modern opinion is summed up, in short, by the clear and sensible Blair, who devotes a considerable passage in his Lecture XIII to demonstrating the fine sense of the music of speech among the ancients, and adds: "I am of opinion that it is in vain to think of bestowing the same attention upon the harmonious structure of our sentences that was bestowed by these ancient nations."[33] Of the exact truth of this statement there can be no question. But the conclusion that has been drawn from it by more recent rhetoricians, namely, that the form of the period cannot be usefully studied at all, is far from being Blair's, and equally far from being sound. The fact is that the neglect of this study has been due to the tendency to avoid the oratorical modes on which all the theory of rhetoric is formed, and to consider prose chiefly as it is addressed

---

enlightening. Whether these are to be considered *cola* proper, or (merely on account of their brevity) *commata*, is hard to say, and some medieval theorists were evidently thrown into utter confusion in their use of the terms by this phenomenon. See, for instance, Hugo of Bologna (Rockinger, p. 59).

[33] [Hugh Blair, *Lectures on Rhetoric and Belles Lettres* (Philadelphia, 1829), pp. 134-146.]

to the intellect, rather than as language spoken and heard. The characteristic prose of the nineteenth century has been the essay, rather than the address; and even in the eighteenth century, the great authority of the Addisonian model of style, especially as it was described in Blair's widely-used rhetoric, tended to outweigh the influence of Johnson, Gibbon, Burke, Robertson, and other writers of the latter part of the century, who wrote the more copious and sonorous language of oratory. It is natural that the exponents of such a style should lay more stress upon verbal propriety, grammatical precision, logical order, and the intellectual effects of prose than upon its rhythm and oral beauties.

This is not the place to discuss the merits of the modern tendency. We only need to observe that it is accompanied, as all similar tendencies in ancient and modern times have been, by a decline in the study of formal rhetoric, and that the student of prose cadence must therefore undo its effects upon his own mind in order to pursue his investigations with some hope of success. The prose that we should exclusively concern ourselves with in the present state of the subject of cadence is that which owes its form to the necessities and customs of public speech. For such prose is much more regular than essay prose in its periodicity, and can be more successfully analyzed according to the theory which has been outlined in the preceding pages.

Let us take some examples, then, of prose of this kind from various ages of English literature, and attempt to illustrate the application of the theory of the period, and its relations to the occurrence of the cadences.

The English collects themselves are the best possible *corpus* for such an experiment, first, because they fulfill ideally the conditions of an oral prose, and secondly, because they are made in close rhetorical imitation of Latin models in which the formal rules of the period were observed.

First, a very short and simply constructed prayer (2 Sun. after Ep.) which we may arrange in parallel columns in order to illustrate the close parallelism of form between the Latin and the English:

Omnipotens sempiterne Deus,	Almighty and everlasting God
qui coelestia simul et[34]	who dost govern all things in
terrena moderaris,	heaven and earth;

[34] [As printed in this article in 1919: *coelestia semper et.*]

supplicationes populi tui clementer exaudi,	Mercifully hear the supplications of thy people,
et pacem tuam nostris concede temporibus.	and grant us thy peace all the days of our life.

There are (after the address) three members, the middle one the longest, and in Latin (but not in English) subdivided into *commata*. There are therefore four opportunities for cadence in the Latin, three in the English. In Latin *cursus* forms occur at all the four places; in English there is but one *cursus* form, at the end of the second member (planus-2).

The Collect for the 4 Sun. after Ep. is more elaborate:

Deus qui nos in tantis periculis constitutos,
pro humana scis fragilitate   non posse subsistere:
da nobis salutem   mentis et corporis,
ut ea quae pro peccatis nostris patimur,
te adjuvante vincamus.

O God,
who knowest us to be set in the midst of so many and great dangers
that by reason of the frailty of our nature   we cannot stand
    upright;[35]
Grant to us such strength and protection
as may support us in all dangers,
and carry us through all temptations.

Here there are five members, two in the protasis, three in the apodosis, the apodosis however not being actually longer in syllables than the protasis, because it is made up of shorter members. In Latin the figures are: protasis, 15 + 17; apodosis, 12 + 13 + 8; total, 65: in English, 20 + 18; 9 + 9 + 9; total, 65. The members of the apodosis are too short and unified to permit of division into *commata*, except the first Latin member. In the protasis, a division of the second member is indicated, by phrasal form, after *fragilitate* and *nature*; whereas the continuous flow of sense through the first member seems to preclude division, though perhaps a reader would in fact make a melodic and rhythmic pause after *midst of* in

[35] [The word *always* ("we cannot always stand upright"), is included in recent American versions of the Prayer Book by revisors unaware of the strict attempt to secure though not imitate the Latin cadence observed by the translators of 1549; this inclusion would, of course, alter Croll's figures which follow. In them pl. refers to planus-1, and pl. 2 refers to planus-2.]

the English. Such arbitrary division will not, as we have already remarked, be found foreign to the custom of oral delivery. The cadences at the points thus indicated are: in Latin (1) *ve*; (2) ——, (3) *ta*; (4) pl., (5) *ta*; (6) ——, (7) pl.; in English, (1) pl. 2; (2) pl. 2; (3) pl.; (4) pl.; (5) pl.; (6) *ve*. (8-4-2).

We will take one more example from the collects (the Sun. next before Easter):

Omnipotens sempiterne Deus
qui humano genere   ad imitandum humilitatis exemplum,
Salvatorem nostrum carnem sumere   et crucem subire fecisti;
concede propitius,
ut et patientia ipsius   habere documenta,
et resurrectionis consortia mereamur.

Almighty and everlasting God,
who, of thy tender love towards mankind,
hast sent thy Son,   our Savior Jesus Christ,
to take upon him our flesh,   and to suffer death upon the cross,
that all mankind should follow the example of his great humility;
Mercifully grant
that we may both follow the example of his patience,
and also be made partakers of his resurrection.

Clearly there are disputable points here, and I have interpreted the relations of the members differently in English and Latin. Accepting the reading I have indicated, we have six members in Latin, eight in English. In English the protasis has been considerably lengthened, and its earlier members (as I think) made shorter in consequence, for the purpose, that is, of holding back the arrival of the rhythmical climax until the last long member of the protasis. In Latin, there are nine opportunities for cadence, six occurrences of the *cursus* forms, as follows:—(1) *trisp.*; (2) ——, (3) *pl.*; (4) ——, (5) *pl.*; (6) *ta.*; (7) *pl.* 2; (8) *pl.* 2; (9) *ve.* In English there are ten opportunities for cadence and three occurrences of the *cursus*-forms, as follows:—(7) *ve.* (9-5-3); (9) pl. 2; (10) *ve.* (8-4-2).[36]

When we turn from the collects to secular prose we lose the guidance of a tradition of oral delivery. But we must still choose

[36] The development of more regularity of rhythm towards the end both of protasis and apodosis, as here, seems to be a common feature of the collect usage.

our examples from forms of style controlled more or less directly by oratorical models. Gibbon's historical style is of this kind. The following passage from Chapter 49 illustrates the precision with which his periods are constructed. (A greater length of member is to be looked for in a style not actually meant for recitation.)

His treatment of the vanquished Saxons
was an abuse of the right of conquest;
his laws were not less sanguinary than his arms,
and in the discussion of his motives,
whatever is subtracted from bigotry,   must be imputed to
     temper.
The sedentary reader is amazed   by his incessant activity of
     mind and body.
and his subjects and enemies
were not less astonished at his sudden presence
at the moment when they believed him   at the most distant
     extremity of the empire;
neither peace nor war,
nor summer nor winter,
were a season of repose;
and our fancy cannot easily reconcile   the annals of his reign
with the geography of his expeditions.

The following list shows the form of cadence in each of the eighteen endings of this passage:—(1) 8-4-2, (2) 7-4-2, (3) 7-1, (4) 6-2, (5) 6-3, (6) 5-2, (7) 9-5-1, (8) 8-4-2, (9) 6-3, (10) 8-4-2, (11) 7-4-2, (12) 7-4?-2, (13) 3-1, (14) 5-2, (15) 5-1, (16) 6-3, (17) 5-1, (18) 9-6-4-2. It is surely significant that a passage, chosen only to illustrate typical periodic form, displays the *cursus* forms in thirteen out of the eighteen positions (i.e., in all but 3, 7, 13, 15, and 17). The fact tends to confirm the opinion that the study of period and the study of cadence are intimately connected.

For our last example we return to the period when English was often unconsciously translated Latin. It is the dedication of Robert Southwell's *A Foure-Fould Meditation*,[37] written by its publisher or editor, and has been chosen at random, rather than on the

---

[37] 1606, repub. 1695. [*A Foure-fold Meditation of the Foure Last Things. Composed in a Divine Poem. By R. S.*, ed. C. Edmonds. Isham Reprints, No. 4 (London, 1895) and attributed to Southwell by him, but it is assigned to Philip, Earl of Arundel. See C. S. Lewis, *Oxford History of English Literature*, III, 675.]

merits of its style, in order to illustrate the suitability of a ceremonious style for the study in which we are engaged.

Sir; as I with great desire   apprehended the least opportunity
    (6-3)
of manifesting toward your worthy self my sincere affection,
    (7-4-2),
so should I be very sory   to present anything unto you (7-4-3,
    or 7-4-2, if *unto* is accented on *to*),
wherein I should growe offensive, (7-4-2)
or willingly breed your least molestation: (5-2, or 7-4-2)
but these meditations, (5-2)   being Divine and Religious (5-2)
(and upon mine owne knowledge, (5?-2),   correspondent to
    your zealous inclinations) (6-2)
emboldened me to recommend them (8-4-2)   to your view and
    censure, (8-4-2)[38]
and therein to make knowne mine owne entire affection, (8-4-2?)
and serviceable love towards you. (8-4-2?)[39]

In this passage there is hardly room for a reasonable doubt as
to the occurrence of the pauses between the members; and in a
great deal of the formal prose of the fifteenth, sixteenth, and seventeenth centuries we should find the same controlled, regular, and
stately movement. The prose of this period of direct classical and
medieval influence is chiefly distinguished as displaying, along with
a comparative freedom from syntactic precision, a constant sense
of the weight and length of rhetorical members. It is rhetorically
construed, in short, rather than grammatically. Yet even in this
prose, it must frankly be admitted, there are no laws governing
the internal division of a period other than those of convenience
and beauty. We may be sure that a science of the rhythmic period
will never be discovered. And if it is true that even in our older
prose, composed in the regular manner of the rhetorical tradition,
we often find it necessary to defend by an appeal to personal preference our choice of this or that reading, it is certain that the
reader will find an ever-widening range for the exercise of his
artistic gifts of interpretation as he approaches the prose of our

[38] See below, the paragraphs in which footnotes 48 and 49 occur.
[39] The reader is requested to read the passage aloud in the manner appropriate
to it before passing judgment on the cadence of the last two members, remembering also that *towards* is probably two syllables.

own time. For the tendency of modern prose is to conceal rather than reveal rhetorical pattern—the more so of course as the custom of actual oral rendition grows more and more infrequent. The "phrasing" of many modern authors, therefore, is as difficult to interpret, compared with that of most authors of, say, the sixteenth century, as is that of a musician of a modern school when compared with that of the classicists who preceded Mozart and Haydn.

It is impossible, of course, to enter here into the details of this large subject. The passages analyzed above will serve to show in a general way the method by which we must proceed in studying the occurrence of cadence. There is nothing to add except an indication of the results of this method in the case of the collect cadences. For this purpose it will suffice to analyze the first twelve Sunday collects, beginning with the 1 Sun. in Adv. I find in these 65 opportunities for cadence; that is, ends of *cola* and *commata*—an average of almost 5.5 to a collect. But this average is higher than it would be if all the collects were counted, because the prayers in this part of the year are longer than in the Trinity season. The general average would probably be about 4.5, or a little less than that.

Of these 65 endings, 40, or 61½ per cent, prove to have *cursus* forms, as we have now interpreted the English usage with regard to these. In order to offer an opportunity to the reader to test my readings, I subjoin all of these 40 endings, marking one or two as doubtful:—

1 Sun. in Adv.:
    Cast away the works of darkness (8-4-2)[40]
    Visit us in great humility (9-5-3)
    Glorious Majesty (6-3)
    Rise to the life immortal (7-4-2)
2 Sun. in Adv.:
    Written for our learning (6-2)
    Grant that we may in such wise hear them (9-6-4-2)
    Inwardly digest them (6-2)
3 Sun. in Adv.:
    Who at thy first coming (6-2)
    Prepare thy way before thee (6-2)?

---

[40] That *away* does not have an accent is shown by the phrase *put upon us* in the parallel member that follows.

Stewards of thy mysteries (7-3)
Hearts of the disobedient (8-5-3)
4 Sun. in Adv.:
Raise up (we pray thee) thy power (5-2)[41]
Thy race that is set before us (7-4-2)
Thy bountiful grace and mercy (7-4-2)
Help and deliver us (6-2)
Sun. after Christmas Day:
Our nature upon him (5-2)
Born of a pure Virgin (6-2)
We being regenerate (7-3)
Renewed by thy Holy Spirit (7-4-2)
1 Sun. after Ep.:
Thy people which call upon thee (7-4-2)
2 Sun. after Ep.:
Supplications of thy people (6-2)
3 Sun. after Ep.:
Look upon our infirmities (8-5-3)
Dangers and necessities (7-3)
Help and defend us (5-2)
4 Sun. after Ep.:
So many and great dangers (6-2)[42]
The frailty of our nature (6-2)
Always stand upright (5-2)
Strength and protection (5-2)
Support us in all dangers (6-2)
Carry us through all temptations (8-4-2)
5 Sun. after Ep.:
Continually in thy true religion (10-6-4-2: trispondaic)
Defended by thy mighty power (8-4-2)
6 Sun. after Ep.:
The works of the devil (5-2)

[41] It may be thought that the member ends with *come among us (raise up (we pray thee) thy power, and come among us)*; in that case the cadence is *velox* (7-4-2). The proper explanation is probably that both cadences count in the rhythmic effect. See below, passages footnoted 48 and 49.

[42] The form of this ending is interesting because of the long syllable preceding the second accent. It produces an effect not unlike that of the classical Latin ending cretic-trochee (– ◡ – – ◡). See other examples in this prayer and that for the 6 Sun. after Ep. [But Croll has overlooked the possibility that a commonplace elision may enter into the *planus*; certainly *many and* constitutes an elidable situation in poetry, in which case the form, still highly interesting, might be 5-2.]

Grant us, we beseech thee (6-2)

Power and great glory (6-2)

Eternal and glorious kingdom (5-2: but see the first part of section II, below)

Sept. Sun.:

Lord, we beseech thee (5-2)

The prayers of thy people (6-2, or 5-2, according to the pronunciation of *prayers*)[43]

Punished for our offenses (7-4-2)

Delivered by thy goodness (6-2)

✧ II ✧

THE UNITARY PHRASE IN NON-FINAL POSITIONS

In all the discussions of cadence in either Latin or English it has been assumed that the only appropriate places for its occurrence are the final positions in the *cola* and *commata* of the period. I wish now to suggest, however, that it may also occur elsewhere, and that the euphony and flow that we hear in some kinds of prose is due to its occurrence in certain non-final positions as well as in the final ones. The positions meant are in a sense final, it is true, but they are not the ends of the parts of a period, as described above. They are independent of periodic structure. The principle may be stated as follows:—

The end of any phrase felt as having a unitary character may be cadenced, whether or not it coincides with the end of one of the divisions of a period.

Nearly all that needs to be said concerning this principle consists in explanation of the meaning of *unitary phrase*; and illustration will serve this purpose better than definition. Several types of the unitary phrase stand out as commoner than others.

1. A very simple type is that which consists of a noun preceded by its adjective. Examples:—

His glorious Majesty (1 Sun. in Adv.: ta.); an acceptable people (3 Sun. in Adv.: pl.); thy merciful guiding (5 Sun. after Easter: pl.); O Heavenly Father (4 Sun. after Tr.: pl.); (we) thine unworthy servants (A Gen. Thanksg.: ve.); thy bountiful goodness (24 Sun. after Tr.: pl.); thy manifold mercies ("A Prayer of Queen Elizabeth," Blunt, p. 66n.: pl.).

[43] [Certainly the likelihood is 5-2.]

335

2. More interesting is the phrase in which two words, often synonyms, are connected by *and*.[44] Examples:—

Sundry and manifold (4 Sun. after Easter: ta.); wills and affections (4 Sun. after Easter: pl.); almighty and everlasting (Tr. Sun., and passim: ve.);[45] defended and comforted (3 Sun. after Tr.: ta.); bountiful grace and mercy (4 Sun. in Adv.: ve.); honour and glory (Ibid. and passim: pl.); nature and property (*Deus cui proprium*, Blunt, p. 63: ta.); guided and governed (All Cond., Blunt, p. 65: pl.); sorts and conditions (Ibid.: pl.); merits and mediation (12 Sun. after Tr.: ve.); eternal and glorious (6 Sun. after Ep.: ta.); goodness and loving-kindness (A Gen. Th., Blunt, p. 65: ve.); holiness and righteousness (Ibid.: ta., 7-3); desires and petitions (St. Chrysostom: pl.).

3. The prepositional phrase; that is, a noun, adjective, or verb with a prepositional modifier following it, is an equally common form:—

Afflictions of thy people (Dearth and Famine: 6-2); prayers of thy people (Sept.: pl.); look upon thy people (5 Sun. in Lent: pl.); example of his patience (Sun. before Easter: pl. 2); the way of thy commandments (11 Sun. after Tr.: pl. 2); abundance of thy mercy (12 Sun. after Tr.: pl. 2); ordered by thy governance (5 Sun. after Tr.: 7-3); free from all adversities (22 Sun. after Tr.: 7-3).

A special case of type 3 is worthy of attention. In order to produce an equivalent of the amplitude of the Latin original the translators have frequently used phrases like the following: *the glory of the eternal Trinity* (10-5-3), *the fruition of thy glorious Godhead* (9-5-2), *the weakness of our mortal nature* (8-4-2), *protection of thy good Providence* (8-5-3), *serve thee in all godly quietness* (9-5-3), in all of which a prepositional phrase is expanded by giving an adjective to the noun which is the object of the preposition. The importance of such phrases in connection with the *velox* cadence has already been indicated in a former chapter. All of the passages just quoted do not, it is true, have the exact form of *velox*, even in the extended forms that we have agreed to recognize for that ca-

---

[44] [The reader may note that this type seems often to be connected with the rhetorical figures.]

[45] From an address frequently used: "Almighty and everlasting God," which translates *Omnipotens et sempiterne Deus*. After experiments by earlier translators, the authors of the 1549 Prayer Book have succeeded in securing exactly the syllabic and accentual form of the Latin except that the word *God* takes the place of the two syllable *Deus*.

dence. That they all produce the effect of *velox*, however, is a contention which cannot be justified here, but will be made clear in a succeeding chapter.

These three types of phrases have not been cited with the intention of making a complete list. They merely serve to show the character of the unitary phrase, and also perhaps that there is no difficulty in detecting the unitary character that distinguishes it. That it plays a *role* in connection with cadence can hardly be denied. In connection with the cadence of *final* positions, for instance, it has an importance that has not heretofore been explicitly recognized. Even in medieval Latin, where cadence is governed by prescriptive rules, the musical flow of the *cursus* ordinarily coincides with the syntactic flow of the phrase; but in English, which is without formal rules of cadence, it is obvious that the cadence form would not be heard unless it fell within a syntactic unit. It cannot, as Latin sometimes can, bridge a gap of any considerable breadth.

We are now concerned, however, chiefly with the *role* of the cadenced unitary phrase in non-final positions; that is, within the colon or comma of a period. Some difficulties arise in applying the principle in this case. For we shall often be in doubt whether the place where a unitary phrase ends is not also meant as the end of a comma, since the occurrence of such a phrase is in fact the commonest mark by which we detect the end of a cadenced division. But on the other hand there are many cases where there can be no doubt. For instance, in Class 2 among the forms of the unitary phrase specified above, are included a number of the phrases so familiar to students of sixteenth- and seventeenth-century prose, in which two words connected by *and* are used instead of a single word, for the sake of vocal amplitude and beauty. The typical case is when the two words are exact synonyms, but even when they are not quite synonymous the phrase is often evidently a mere melodic unit. Such phrases are not likely to end a member, especially if the two words are adjectives or verbs. But since their purpose is chiefly or solely euphonic, there is an evident probability that they will have a rhythmic character. And in fact it will be found that they fall with surprising frequency within the forms of cadence that we are here studying.

The examples cited above from the collects will serve to illustrate the point. But two illustrations from secular prose may be added to these. The first is from Raleigh's *History of the World,* and the whole sentence may be quoted because of its interesting rhythmic character. It is about the great conquerors of the world.

> They themselves would then rather have wished to have stolen out of the world without noise, than to be put in mind that they have purchased the report of their actions in the world, by rapine, oppression, and cruelty, by giving in spoil the *innocent and laboring* soul to the *idle and insolent,* and by having emptied the cities of the world of their ancient inhabitants, and filled them again with so many and so variable sorts of sorrows.

Here the adjective phrase "innocent and laboring" adds greatly to the rhythmic effect of the whole passage; and the special reason for citing it is that its cadenced character is expressly indicated by its parallelism with the phrase that ends the following comma: "the idle and insolent." Both are *tardus,* the first 7-3, the second 6-3, and the parallelism is further indicated by alliteration.

The other example is from President Wilson's Phi Beta Kappa address at Harvard in 1909. Of the college he says, in the midst of a long cadence period, that "its courses are only its formal side, its *contacts and contagions* its realities." It is evident that the underlined cadenced phrase is not meant to be final.

There is no authority, as I have already observed, among modern theorists for including the non-final unitary phrase among the cadenceable elements of a sentence. Nor is it mentioned by the medieval theorists of the *ars dictaminis.* But in medieval *practice* there seems to be the authority of analogy and precedent. For a careful examination of the Latin collects will show that the cadences are used in fact with much greater frequency than the rules require, and in the medial positions we are now considering as well as in the final ones. To prove this at length would take us outside of our proper field. But a single case will serve at least to show that the point is worthy the attention of medievalists who deal with our subject, a case that has special interest in the present discussion because it is paralleled, in part at least, as I will try to show, in English use.

In Latin there is often a slight pause before the verb in which a clause ends, due to the fact that in the suspended style which is characteristic of formal Latin discourse this verb has a closer connection with some earlier element in the clause (usually its object) than with the words that immediately precede it, these words often being phrases of a modifying character. Very often, it will be found, this pause before the final word of a colon is made the occasion of a *cursus* ending, though it usually occurs within another cadence, namely, the final cadence of the colon. An example will make this curious overlapping of cadences clear.

Familiam tuam (pl.),   quaesumus, Domine,
continua pietate (ve.)   custodi (pl.);
ut quae in sola spe gratiae coelistis innititur (ta.),
tua semper protectione (ve.) muniatur (trisp.: 11-8-6-4-2)

5 Sun. after Ep.

Here the second member ends in a *planus*; but the first accent of this *planus* also serves as the final accent of a *velox* which ends the phrase *continua pietate*. The last member ends in a trispondaic (four trochees preceded by a dactyl); but the phrase *tua semper protectione* ends in a *velox*, which falls within the bounds of the trispondaic.

Other examples are:—

Quos in soliditate (ve.) tuae dilectionis (ve.) instituis (ta.)
    2 Sun. after Tr.[46]
Promissiones tuas,
quae omne desiderium superant (ta.) consequamur (ve.)
    6 Sun. after Tr.
Quae pro nostra fragilitate (ve.) contraximus (ta.),
tua benignitate (ve.) liberemur (trisp.)
    24 Sun. after Tr.[47]

Many other cases of the cadenced non-final phrase besides the one that has been described could be cited, and it would be easy to show that the rhythmic effect of many passages in the Latin collects

[46] This example is interesting because it occurs at the end of a prayer. *Tardus* is a very rare ending for the final member; its occurrence here is probably due to the *velox* in the unitary phrase.

[47] Many examples will be found in the specimens of *proverbia* given by John Garland (d. ca. 1258) in *Poetria Magistri Johannis Anglici de Arte Prosayca Metrica et Rithmica* (ed. G. Mari, *Romanische Forschungen*, XIII, 1902, 883ff.); e.g., *a communione fidelium separari, veneno dulcedinis inquinatur*. This form, *tardus* plus *velox*, is the commonest form of the overlapping cadences. [See also Rockinger, I, 491-512.]

is chiefly due to it.[48] We need not, however, extend our inquiry further, since the case we have been considering will serve in English as well as in Latin to illustrate the importance of the non-final phrase. It is not to be expected that English would achieve the subtlety of interlaced cadence so often as Latin does. Yet even in this respect English usage will be found to offer interesting parallels to Latin, as in the following passages:—

That all things may be so ordered and settled (pl.) by their en-
    deavors (ve.). "Prayer for Parl.," Blunt, p. 64.
May evermore be defended (ve.) by thy mighty power (ve.: 8-4-2)
    5 Sun. after Ep.
Eternal and glorious (ta.) kingdom (pl.). 6 Sun. after Ep.
The successors of St. Peter and Constantine (ta.)
        were invested   with the purple and prerogatives (ta.:
    7-3) of the Caesars (ve.)   Gibbon, Chap. 49.
The object of her own amazement (ve.: 8-4-2) and terror (pl.).
    Ibid.
We have appealed to their native justice (ve.) and magnanimity
    (ve.: 8-5-3).   *Declar. of Indep. of the Am. Col.*
Deaf to the voice of justice (ve.) and of consanguinity (ve.: 9-5-3).
    Ibid.
The long-established practices   and long-cherished principles of
    international action (pl.) and honor (pl.).   Woodrow
    Wilson, "Letter to the Pope," Aug., 1917.
Its contacts and contagions (6-2) its realities (7-3).   Wood-
    row Wilson, *Phi Beta Kappa address at Harvard*, 1909.

But it is not necessary for our purposes to insist upon the frequent occurrence of the interlaced cadences in English. A simpler case arising from the tendency to cadence a non-final unitary phrase will prove, however, to be worthy of consideration. It is the case, apparently fairly common, of the cadencing of a unitary phrase immediately before the end of a member *instead* of the end of the member itself. The unitary phrase thus takes the place of preference

---

[48] In order to show how pervasive the endings of the *cursus* form may be I add an analysis of the commonest concluding formula of the collects: *Per Dominum nostrum* (pl.), *Jesum Christum* (trisp.), *qui tecum vivit et regnat* (pl.), *in unitate* (ve.), *Spiritus Sancti Deus* (ve.), *per omnia saecula* (ta.), *saeculorum* (ve.). In the body of a prayer such a minute subdivision would, of course, be impossible; but in a formula repeated often and with particular solemnity, all the rhythms would probably be heard, though in some repetitions some of them would be emphasized, in others, others.

in cadencing over the final syllables of the member, and the latter serve the purpose of breaking cadence and bringing back the tone of utterance to the common level of unrhythmic speech. A striking example from the Prayer Book will make clear what is meant.

The last clause of *Deus, cui proprium est* (Blunt, p. 63) has the interlocked cadence we have described:—*Miseratio tuae pietatis* (trisp.) *absolvat* (pl.). The English translation is: "Let the pitiful-ness of thy great mercy loose us." Here by great ingenuity the exact arrangement of accents and syllables in the original is preserved (not at all an uncommon achievement in the collects), as far as the ends of the words *pietatis* and "mercy"[49] (eleven syllables accented thus: / _ / _ _ / / / _, the strongest accent falling on the third syllable from the beginning). Thus the Latin trispondaic is preserved. But at the end the translators have departed from the form of the original, apparently with purpose. For they needed only to use the word of the old translations, *assoil*, which was still in use, or the newer *absolve*, which was well established, in order to con-tinue the Latin pattern. But the cadence of the phrase has been preserved, while that of the ending has not, and the effect produced is that the pause after "mercy" is lengthened, there is an abrupt break in rhythm, the words "loose us" are pronounced in a different tone, and the ear is brought back to the blunt style and the native words of plain prose.

A similar effect attained by the same means can be found very often in elevated English prose. In Gibbon, for example, it is so frequent as almost to constitute a mannerism, the peculiar fling of his irony being found in the words—added as if by an afterthought —that follow the cadenced phrase. For example, in Chapter 35 (the death of Jovian): "Dadastana was marked as the fatal term of his journey (pl.) and his life." Again, without the ironical tone: "The image of depopulation (ve.: 8-4-2) and decay." To these may be added an example from the American Declaration of Independence: "We have warned them from time to time of attempts by their legislature (ve.) to extend an unwarrantable jurisdiction (ve.: 8-4-2) over us"; and another from the Prayer Book: "In holiness

---

[49] To show the process by which this result has been attained, the earlier trans-lations may be quoted: "Late the merci of thi pitee assoile hem" (a 14th C. primer, repr. from a 15th C. MS [*The Prymer or Lay Folks Prayer Book*, ed. Henry Littlehales, MS Dd. 11, 82 ab. 1420-1430], *EETS* [1895-1897], p. 50); "The mercifulnesse of thi pitee asoile hem" (another 14th C. primer, ed. Maskell, quoted by Blunt, p. 64n.).

and righteousness (ta.) all our days" (General Thanksg., Blunt, p. 66).

Just how frequent this form may be there is no way of determining. The reader's ear must determine. At all events it is one illustration of the many ways in which the unitary phrase occurs, and it is in this alone that its value consists for the present purpose.

The point urged in this section of my paper certainly does not tend to simplify the subject of cadence. It tends rather to blur and disarrange some of the definite lines that have been drawn about it heretofore. The same remark may be made, indeed, about the preceding section; for the doctrine of the period, though it seems to be the only trustworthy guide through the uncertainties of cadence occurrence, is itself full of uncertainties, difficulties, and problems. But whatever complexities we have introduced into a theme that has been too simply handled arise from the effort to cope with the realities of the phenomena; and the errors that we are liable to when we do this are likely to be less serious than those that attend us when we trust too devotedly to trim arrangements and mechanical formulae.

Moreover, the principles we have discussed, in as far as they are sound, are evidently important. For they not only give us as much control through the study of the external phenomena of style as we seem likely to secure in the present stage of the development of the subject; they are also necessary to account for the rhythmic effects which our ears report. That is to say, the careful student of the prose which has a markedly cadenced sound should be aware that this sound cannot be explained as due to the widely separated endings studied, for instance, by Shelly in the collects. It must be due to cadences that occur with sufficient frequency to produce a pervasive and characteristic effect.

✧ CHAPTER FOUR ✧

THE RULES OF ENGLISH ORATORICAL CADENCE

We now return to the consideration of the *form* of the cadence.

In Chapter Two I tried to show that the differences between the metrical customs of Latin and English and the differences between their vocabularies would result in a relaxation of the exact syllabic requirements of the Latin forms when they were transferred to

English prose, and that the general tendency of these relaxations would be in the direction of a lengthening of the English cadences. Three examples of this were illustrated: First, the use of 7-3 as the equivalent of *tardus*; secondly, 8-4-2 as the equivalent of *velox*; thirdly, 8 (9)-5-3 as the equivalent of *velox*.

These three forms were specified as being nearer to the Latin forms than any other possible variations, and as being the most frequent in English use. It is evident, however, that they are not the only possible ones. *Tardus* and *planus*, it is true, cannot be extended further without losing their character. But within the larger limits of *velox* there is greater room for the kind of freedom we have described, and the time has come for the consideration of its full results in connection with this cadence.

An objection is sure to arise, however, at this point, perhaps has already risen during the previous discussion. If we are to vary so freely the form of the long cadence, we shall reduce the system of metrical scansion to an absurdity; at least the formula of medieval Latin, 7-4-2, will cease to be of any practical value for the study of English cadence. But this is an objection which we have foreseen and shall be glad to encounter. It is true that I do not think that the Latin formulae will cease to be of any value to us. But the object of the whole discussion of English freedom in a preceding chapter has been to show that the method of metrical scansion is unsatisfactory, when taken alone, in dealing with the English phenomena, and to prepare the way for the formulation of rules or principles of cadence which shall partly supplement and partly take the place of the formulae of scansion. The study of exact metrical forms which we have been pursuing, and shall have to continue to pursue a little further, is largely for the purpose of laying a firm foundation for such rules or principles.

In the present chapter, therefore, I will first consider, as briefly as possible, the further possible variations of the form of the long cadence which result from its adaptation to English custom and conditions, and will then attempt to draw up a set of rules, governing all the cadences, short and long alike, which will again, I hope, reduce the manifold facts to comparative simplicity.

I. Further Variations of the Long Cadence

The departures from the Latin form of *velox* which may appear in English without changing its essential character—in addition to those already treated—fall into two classes, in both of which the second half of the cadence (that is, the part corresponding to the last four syllables of Latin *velox*) is chiefly concerned.[50]

In the first class are forms in which the fall of accents in the second part is contrary to Latin rule. Two cases will include all the important forms.

(a) The first is that in which the two accents fall side by side, as in the forms 4-3-2-1, 4-3-2-1. Latin of course knows no such clashing of accents; but the forms are familiar to students of Anglo-Saxon verse as examples of the third type in Sievers' classification. Accustomed as English ears are to them, they would feel that no violence was done to the beauty of *velox* by introducing one of them within its general outline or framework. There is a striking example, or rather two examples, of the form 4-3-2-1 in a phrase of a Prayer of Queen Elizabeth:[51] "All other thy benefits and great mercies (7-3-2) exhibited in Jesus Christ (7-3-2)." The form 4-3 appears in: "Those things which we ask faithfully" (8-4-3) (23 Sun. after Tr.); "The power of the Divine Majesty" (8 or 9-4-3) (Tr. Sun.); "Almighty and most merciful (7-4-3) God" (20 Sun. after Tr.).

(b) The more important case in Class 1 is that in which the second part has an accent on the final syllable; that is, has one of the forms: 4-3-2-1, 4-3-2-1, 5-4-3-2-1, or even 6-5-4-3-2-1.[52] Some examples are: "Pureness of living and truth" (1 Sun. after Easter); "hope of thy heavenly grace" (5 Sun. after Ep.); "faithfully to fulfill the same" (1 Sun. after Ep.); "we may bring the same to good effect" (Easter); "thou dost put in our minds good desires" (Ibid.);[53] "serve thee with a quiet mind" (21 Sun. after Tr.); "always most thankfully receive" (2 Sun. after Easter).

This form could also be copiously illustrated from Gibbon, who displays a fondness for ending a rhetorical period in which the weak or trochaic endings have been prevailingly employed with this masculine iambic one, as in the following sentence from Chapter 49:

[50] *Velox* is properly a binary rhythm, with its accents on 7 and 2. The division here made use of is therefore justified only by its convenience for purposes of exposition.
[51] *Liturgies and Occasional Forms of Prayer put forth in the Reign of Queen Elizabeth*, Parker Soc., xxx (1847), 667; Blunt, p. 66n.
[52] Concerning the extension of *length* of the second part shown in these latter forms, see below, passages footnoted 56-57.
[53] As in other cases we have noted, so here the balance of members helps us to determine the cadence form intended.

His contemporaries of the fifteenth century (11-5-3)
were astonished at his sacrilegious boldness (10-4-2);
yet such is the silent and irresistible (8-5-3)   progress of
reason (pl.),
that before the end of the next age   the fable was rejected
(6-2)
by the contempt of historians and poets (6-2),
and the tacit or modest censure (ve.)   of the advocates of the
Roman church (8-3-1).

The ending 4-3-2-1 has often been noted as a favorite in English. Saintsbury finds it very common,[54] and Shelly has observed that it is more frequent in the Prayer Book than any other ending. Some critics therefore give it a place among conventional English endings, distinguishing it as a "native" ending in contrast with the Latin forms. It must in fact be recognized as having such a position in the theory of English cadence, but the point to be noted here is that it is often not to be treated as a complete ending in itself but as falling into place in the larger design of *velox*, the Latin ending, its first accent being lighter than the accent which precedes and thus marking itself as really the second and subordinate accent of a *velox*. Such cases have a peculiar interest as illustrating the process by which native customs reconcile and adapt themselves to a Latin tradition. There is a further interest also in the ending 7-4(3)-1 inasmuch as it brings an iambic movement into combination with the otherwise wholly trochaic inflections of the Latin cadences.

The second class of variations of the long cadence consists of those in which the latter part is *lengthened* by one or more unaccented syllables between its two accents, or after its second, or in both these places. We have already seen that an additional light syllable may follow the *final* accent without impairing the rhythmic effect (8 or 9-5-3). It is here asserted that one or even two such additional syllables may follow also the light secondary accent which precedes the final accent. Of course this cannot happen without destroying the balance of the cadence unless its first period is also correspondingly lengthened. The changes of form here considered therefore result in a considerable lengthening of the whole cadence, bringing it up sometimes to eleven syllables.

[54] [George Saintsbury, *A History of English Prose Rhythm* (London, 1912).]

345

Three cases will be illustrated:

(a) 5-2 Examples: The fruition of thy glorious Godhead (9-5-2: Ep. Sun.); eternal and glorious kingdom (8-5-2) (6 Sun. after Ep.); a happy issue out of all their afflictions (9-5-2) (All Cond. of men); partakers of thy heavenly treasure (9-5-2) (11 Sun. after Tr.); the meritorious race of the Carlovingian princes (10-5-2) (Gibbon, Chap. 49); the leaders of a powerful nation (9-5-2) (Ibid.); the pen of Laurentius Valla (Ibid.); left to our own proper resources (9-5-2) (Scott, *Rob Roy*, chap. 3); a late and ungracious compliance (8-5-2) (Ibid.); protection as well as amusement (8-5-2) (Ibid.).

(b) 6-2 Examples: By reason of the frailty of our nature (10-6-2) (4 Sun. after Ep.); mercifully to look upon thy people (11-6-2) (5 Sun. in Lent); those things which be profitable for us (10-6-2) (8 Sun. after Tr.); the contempt of historians and poets (9-6-2) (Gibbon, Chap. 49); the wealth of the palace of Ravenna (9-6-2) (Ibid.).[55]

(c) 6-3 Examples: Defended from the fear of our enemies (10-6-3) (2 Coll. for Peace, Evening Prayer);[56] the leaven of malice and wickedness (9-6-3) (1 Sun. after Easter); graciously to behold this thy family (11-6-3) (1 coll. for Good Friday); the revival of letters and liberty (10-6-3) (Gibbon, Chap. 49); the successors of St. Peter and Constantine (10-6-3) (Ibid.); without apprehending the future danger (velox) these princes gloried in their present security (10-6-3) (Ibid.).[57]

Still other examples of the expanded cadence could be illustrated. For example, I think that English often uses *three* light syllables after the last accent, even when the earlier periods of the cadence are not proportionately long. English, being fond of retrocessive accent, has many words such as *difficulty, hospitable, revocable*, which are foreign to the spirit of Latin pronunciation, but lend themselves in English to such forms as 9-6-4, which seem very far away from the Latin forms. But we will not go into details. The three forms

[55] This form is often hard to distinguish from the trispondaic, the only difference being that in the latter there is an accent on 4 which does not appear here.

[56] [In the most recent American version, simply "A Collect for Peace."]

[57] The balance of members in the last example serves to show the point at which cadence begins in the second member.

described are the most important illustrations of the kind of relaxation I have been discussing.

Before leaving them an objection which is certain to arise must be considered. Of the three forms described, the first, (a), apparently coincides in form with *planus*–1, the second with *planus*–2, the third with *tardus* in its Latin form 6-3. It may be said that in all the cases cited we have only examples of *planus* or *tardus* which happen to be preceded by a comparatively long period. But this is not the case, for the forms described seem to coincide with the forms of the short endings only because of the roughness of our method of notation. The difference is that when 5-2, for instance, is used to denote *planus*, there is a stronger accent on 5 than on 2, but when this formula is used to indicate, as in the above examples, the latter part of *velox*, this relation is reversed, and the accent on 5 is lighter than that on either 8 (9) or 2; for, as we have already said and as we shall have occasion to bring out more clearly a little further on, the second accent in *velox* is subordinate and even non-essential. The test then by which we may determine in a given case whether one of the forms described constitutes a complete cadence in itself or is part of a *velox* is to be found in the relation of its accents to each other.

II. The Rules of Cadence

But we have now reached the point, foreseen at the beginning of this section, where it is useless or confusing to continue the study of particular metrical forms. When *velox* may vary in length from seven to ten, or even more syllables, and its later accents move about as freely as we have been asserting they may, the method of scansion becomes absurd. It is true that a table might still be made of the forms that produce the required effect, and those that do not, but it is far simpler to state general rules which will allow for all the varieties of forms that we have discovered.

I have already said that the rules can be framed so as to include all of the forms of cadence, *planus* and *tardus* as well as *velox*. They are in fact meant (as will be seen) to reveal that these three are only varieties of a single rhythmic effect. However, I think that there is reason to observe a general distinction between the long cadence (related to *velox*) and the short cadence (related to *tardus*

347

and *planus*), because they are sometimes differentiated in English use. In certain kinds of style more copious and elaborate in form, the long cadence is characteristic; in others, in which shorter members and shorter phrasing prevail, the short cadence is very common, but the long one comparatively infrequent. Gibbon is a good example of the former, Macaulay of the latter. As regards their form, however, the long and short cadences are not essentially different except in the matter of length, as the rules will show.

The rules, then, are as follows:

1. The English cadence ordinarily begins on one of the syllables five to ten, counting from the end. It never begins later than the fifth, but sometimes the long cadence may begin as far back as the eleventh syllable, as in 11-7-3, or even on the twelfth, as in 12-8-4. These are, however, extreme cases.

2. The first accent is the strongest in the cadence, as marking its beginning. It is the climax as to height of pitch and strength of accent of the member in which the cadence occurs, and indicates the point at which the tendency to rhythmical form always observable in oratory, but restrained earlier in the phrase by the necessities of logical statement, is finally allowed to appear without check. It marks the moment of release of the rhythmic impulse which is half the secret of our delight in oratorical performance.

3. At this point a trochaic movement begins which carries through to the end of the phrase and cadence. The trochaic movement of the English cadence is alone enough to mark the influence of the classical cadences upon it, for it is not the nature of English prose, except under this influence, to keep to the same movement (rising or falling) throughout a phrase. It inclines to shift from one to the other, and perhaps prefers, on the whole, to end in a rising movement rather than a falling one.

Of course there is a striking exception to this rule in the case of the long cadence ending in 4-1 (or 3-1 or 5-1), which has been discussed above. But even in this case the first part of the cadence is enough to give it a general trochaic character, and a cesura can usually be detected at the point where the rising movement begins.

4. Each cadence has two accents, of which the first is stronger than the second, and is followed by a greater number of unaccented syllables, or by an equal number of syllables which makes the *effect* of being greater, than the second. Stated differently, this law is that there is an effect of decreasing length of period and strength of

accent from the beginning of a cadence to the end. This is the most important of the five rules and gives the clue to the character of all English prose cadence. The effect due to a three-, four- or five-syllable period followed by a two-syllable one, or of four syllables followed by three, seems to be constantly heard in all prose that is euphoniously and flowingly written.

The long cadence is covered by this law as well as the short ones, as will appear from the next rule, namely:

5. If the number of syllables following an accent exceeds three, a secondary subsidiary accent appears. This rule applies in practice only to the period of the first accent because if the second period contained more than four syllables it could not seem shorter than the first (see rule 4); that is, this rule explains the form of the long cadence. In the discussion of this cadence I have sometimes spoken as if it consisted of three parts, a longer and two approximately equal shorter parts. This has been done, however, only for convenience of description. Some writers seem, in fact, to think of it as having this character. But in this they are mistaken. *Velox* in Latin is a binary rhythm, the accent on 4 being only of importance as serving to prop up or carry on the long run of syllables between the accent on 7 and the accent on 2. The strength of the accent on it may vary from almost nothing to almost that of the final period. But it must never be actually as strong as this, because if it were so the effect of the undulating, long first period, which gives its character to *velox*, would be lost. Exactly the same principle applies to the long cadence in English. Like the short cadences it consists of two periods, a longer and a shorter.

It is in the placing of the subsidiary accent that the characteristic freedom of English usage comes into play. In Latin, of course, it always comes on the second syllable before the final accent; but in English its place depends upon the length of the first period, which may, with the help of this subsidiary accent, contain as many as eight syllables, and by considerations of euphony and convenience.

Heretofore I have assumed that the subsidiary accent must fall nearer to the second main accent than to the first; i.e., if the whole cadence has the form 8-2, the subsidiary accent must fall either on 4 or 5, if it has the form 7-2, or on 4 or 3; and this is the usual and regular case. However, I am not sure that English would always exact such fidelity to principle; 7-5-2 seems to occur occasionally with the effect of a long cadence; but, of course, the accent on 5 is very light.

III. The Theory of the Rules

Some concluding observations must be made about these laws, chiefly in order to show the effect of passing over from the method of scansion to the method of more general description. The phenomena described in the scansion method with which this paper began are not different from those covered by the laws. They are included in them. If the rules are observed with the utmost simplicity and brevity, the Latin forms necessarily result, the differences between the three being merely due to the differences in their length; that is, the difference between beginning to cadence on the fifth, sixth, or seventh syllable from the end. If they are observed with the utmost freedom allowable to English rhythmical custom, they still produce cadences which have the essential rhythmical (though not the exact metrical) character of these three Latin cadences.

There is, therefore, no opposition between the results obtained from the two methods of studying English cadence. As to the practical question, which of the two is to be preferred in the further study of the subject, no definite answer can be given, and none needs to be given at present. At the stage which the subject has now reached, it seems necessary to use both, to carry them along side by side. For in the various specimens of cadenced prose which properly come under our observation, and even in various passages within the same specimen, we shall find illustrations of an almost Latin regularity side by side with illustrations of the full play of the English freedom, and of almost every possible stage between these two extremes. If Gibbon, for instance, is nearly always precise in his cadencing, Newman, on the other hand, avoids pattern, and is now almost as regular as his medieval models, now as free as his sense for the form of English prose will allow him to be.

But the value of the rules does not lie wholly in the fact that they cover the English phenomena as the metrical formulae alone cannot do. They may prove also to open the way to a simplification of the problem of English cadence. I have already remarked, in stating the rules, that one of them, the fourth, has an importance altogether out of proportion with the others. This is the rule that a cadence consists of two accentual periods, of which the first is longer and carries a stronger accent than the second, or, stated more generally, that there is decreasing length of period and strength of accent from the beginning to the end of the cadence. Its importance consists in the fact that it states the general *character* of the English oratorical cadence—the nature of its movement in all the various forms of it that we have studied. The others chiefly state the limits of space within which this principle operates, or some necessary consequences of its application. But this principle taken alone, if it is a correct description of the facts, reduces all the varieties of cadence form to a single psychological, or, better, physiological, law of movement.

Zielinski has studied the "psychological bases" of the Ciceronian clausules. The most authoritative scholar in the field of prose rhythm, he has shown with practical conclusiveness—and with an even unnecessary elaboration of technical procedure—that there is in the Ciceronian clausule, whatever metrical forms it assumes, a single structural principle, "that it has no merely schematic significance, but an eminently psychological one; it was in fact—I repeat—a definite single thing in the consciousness of the orator, held together by understood principles of resolution" (*i.e.*, resolution of a long syllable into two short ones).[58] And on the basis of this conclusion Zielinski suggests that investigators may proceed in the discovery of the laws of rhythm in the various modern literatures. The conclusion which we have now reached in the present discussion has not been founded upon this hint from Zielinski.[59] It agrees, however, exactly with his conclusion concerning classical Latin cadence, and this fact may be accepted as evidence in favor of its soundness.

Zielinski has not attempted to describe "the psychological (or as I prefer to call it, physiological) significance" of the cadence at all

[58] Zielinski, "Der Rhythmus," p. 134. The same point is established in his well-known work, *Das Klauselgesetz in Cicero's Reden: Grundzüge einer Oratorischen Rhythmik* (Leipzig, 1904) [also in *Philologus*, suppl. vol. ix (1904). Croll makes no mention of Zielinski's complementary *Das Ausleben des Clauselgesetzes in der Römischen Kuntsprosa* (Leipzig, 1906) and "Der Constructive Rhythmus in Ciceros Reden," *Philologus*, suppl. vol. xiii (1914), or of A. C. Clark, "Zielinski's Clauselgesetz," *Classical Rev.*, xix (1905)].

[59] I regret that I had not read Zielinski's paper ["Der Rhythmus"] until I had already formulated my own practically as it stands. [Certainly the coincidence of conclusions on Latin cadence by Croll and Zielinski is remarkable, though there is no reason to believe that Croll made any major alterations in his work because of what he found in the latter's paper.]

fully. He draws up, however, a formula which he calls the "Integration-clausule," a single metrical formula which includes all the three types of Ciceronian cadence. It is this:

$$- \breve{\smile} - \mid - \smile, \; - , \; \smile, \; \cdots$$

Each comma in this formula indicates a point at which a cadence may end, the first the end of *planus*, the second of *tardus*, the third of *velox*.[60] In short, the meaning of this formula is that all the clausules consists of (1) a base, which is always a cretic (or molussus), and (2) a trochaic cadence.[61]

Base plus cadence: this formula has an evident kinship with the principle we have here arrived at, namely the principle of decreasing length of period and strength of accent from the beginning to the end of a cadence, the difference between the two being due to the fact that in a quantitative language the first period (cretic) has a somewhat different character from that which it has in a purely accentual system. It is, in fact, a level "base," after which cadence or fall begins. In English, on the other hand, it cannot be exactly that, and cadence or fall starts from the beginning of the movement—from the first (that is, the accented) syllable of the first period. But we need not go so far as English to find this departure from the classical Latin formula of Zielinski. Medieval Latin already shows exactly the English principle of decreasing length of period and strength of accents. That is, with no other change than from quantitative to accentual meter the difference between the Latin and the English principle is explained.

English, however, goes one step further than medieval Latin. It adopts the principle alone as the essential feature of its cadence. That is, it abandons all metrical prescription, and aims only at achieving the kind of *movement* characteristic of classical and medieval cadence. It has had the "integration-clausule" alone in its consciousness, but not the individual forms that it represents. It therefore reveals more clearly the character of the integration clausule than either classical or medieval Latin, and if our analysis of its phenomena has been correct we may hope to push further

[60] The reader must be referred to a careful study of Zielinski's paper for the explanation of the dots in this formula, and of certain other difficulties.

[61] Of course it is not apparent in the metrical scheme that the second part of *tardus* ($- \smile - / - \smile -$) is a *trochaic* cadence. But Zielinski considers this as having the effect of a trochee and a half. P. 129, q.v.

than Zielinski has done the explanation of the physiological law which underlies it. There is danger, it is true, in thrusting forward speculative theory at a time when the facts are still in need of verification. But at least the theory will have the merit of making clearer than it perhaps has been up to this point what is meant by the principle of decreasing length and strength.

The physiological explanation of verse is to be found in the dance in which it originated.[62] In the dance the regularity of the beats is the means by which energy is artificially maintained at a uniform level, higher than that of the ordinary human occupations and movements. In the same way in poetry the regularity of accent stimulates the energy of utterance, which always tends to flag and die away, and keeps it at an artificial height throughout a line or a stanza. And, of course, this energy of utterance accompanies, interprets, stimulates energy of emotion. Prose, on the other hand, even oratorical prose, cannot, does not aim to, move uniformly on this high level. Its foundation is laid on the basis of common and matter-of-fact speech: instead of forcing the physiological processes to adapt themselves to it, it yields and adapts itself to them. It rises constantly at certain points above the level of mere logical or matter-of-fact speech, heightening the intensity of its utterance to indicate the occurrence of these points, but it at once begins to fall away again toward it as the breath begins to fail, and the energy of utterance fails with it.

Cadence, then, is perhaps the euphonious way of accompanying in speech this natural fall of subsidence of energy. The particular forms of it that prevailed in Latin are the best and simplest ways of doing this; the principle we have been discussing describes collectively all the ways of doing it. Perhaps we may go further and find in the overlapping, or interlocking, of cadences of which we have spoken the impulse to protract this fall by partial successive renewals of the energy of utterance. Doubtless, indeed, an infinite variety of effect may be obtained by the ways in which this principle will interplay with the forms of words, the varieties of phrasal form, the varying demands of expression, the laws of balance and variation, and so on; and the varieties of style in different authors and different passages may be analyzed in terms of this interplay with useful results. But it is not our purpose here to touch these more difficult parts of the subject.

[62] [Croll explains his contention at greater length in his essay, *The Rhythm of English Verse*.]

A final point should be mentioned, though it cannot be discussed fully. We have been proceeding in this paper on the assumption that the laws of English cadence have been determined by imitation of Latin models. Is this a safe supposition? Is it true that the cadencing customs described in our five principles of cadence have been arrived at by a gradual relaxation, in accordance with the characteristic freedom of English use, of the metrical schemes handed down by medieval tradition from antiquity? Since we have drifted so far from these actual metrical schemes in following the facts of English practice, is it not safer to assume that the rules merely describe a necessary and universal tendency of oratorical style, and that the frequent occurrence in English of the exact metrical form of the Latin *cursus* is due, not to medieval tradition, but to the fact that these forms are the perfect and simplest manifestation of this tendency?

Several strong reasons could be urged in favor of the theory of direct Latin influence on which we have been working as a hypothesis. For instance, the mighty part played by the collects themselves, in which this influence can hardly be denied, in fixing the form of elevated prose at a time when it was still fluid and indeterminate, is in itself a consideration of great weight. But we need not now argue the point. For, even though the cadence of English were to be regarded as chiefly an independent development from the mere nature of oratory itself, yet the best approach to the knowledge of it would still be the theory and practice of the ancients, classical and medieval, because they regularized oratorical cadence in its most typical forms, and because they were exactly aware of their procedure, described it, and even to some extent, theorized it. In English, on the other hand, cadence has always, in the first place, been more irregular than in Latin, and subject to whimsical, individual preference, or even to the deliberate intention to break rhythm noticeable in many authors.[63] And, in the second place, it is not apparent that either the theory of cadence or its forms have been known to any English author; and those who have practiced it have either been controlled by an undefined feeling for the oral beauty of style, or else (as we have here assumed) by a tradition which was transmitted from Latin to English during the formative period of English prose style.

---

[63] With regard to this point, however, it should be observed that some Latin authors did the same thing; Tacitus, for instance.

Of course, there is also the possibility that we have misread the facts. We may have been deceived in our study of the English phenomena by a pre-determined belief in their similarity to those of medieval Latin. Even the unifying principle at which we have finally arrived may prove to be vitiated by the same error. This is a doubt which, of course, haunts all who study this subject with an open mind. But the question must now be left to the tests which future students of the subject may apply to our argument. It is to be hoped that they will be thorough enough to lead to some definite conclusions and place the subject of English cadences finally on a sound basis.

✦ CHAPTER FIVE ✦

IN WHAT KINDS OF PROSE MUST WE LOOK FOR CADENCE?

At best it must be recognized that we are still only in the fringes and outward edges of the subject of prose cadence, and even though the conclusions we have arrived at should prove to be generally sound there are many difficult questions which await solution. With regard to the form of the English cadence there is no doubt that investigations conducted by a different method from ours will cause some modifications in the principles we have stated. And with respect to its occurrences all that has hitherto been said must be regarded rather as indicating the method of study than as solving the problems. How do variations in the construction of a period affect its cadences? What effect do other rhetorical ornaments, such as balance, have upon the method of employing them? And what interactions can be discovered between them? Why do all authors cadence more regularly and euphoniously in some passages than in others? In some parts of a paragraph than others? And, to mention the largest question last, in what kinds of prose style are we justified in looking for the conventional kind of cadence; in what kinds are we not?

It is this last question alone that I will consider for a moment, and only in its most general aspect.

There has been a general tendency among students of prose rhythm in English to seek for some principle of universal applicability. It is assumed that a rhythmic law may be found which will explain all the prose which has literary character or beauty, that artistic prose as such has within it a principle of rhythm. The examples chosen for experiment are, therefore, representative of the most various kinds of prose-writing, from Gibbon's to Lamb's, from Gladstone's to Pater's, and there is even a marked disposition to choose them from writers of the most subtle or individual literary quality, such as De Quincey, Coleridge, Ruskin, Stevenson, and Pater, rather than from those who are most conventional and regular in their style. It would seem, indeed, that the farther prose has departed from its normal character, the more literary and non-oral it has become, the more attractive it has been to the investigators.

356

Judged by its results, however, this method must be declared to be at present in a state of bankruptcy. According to one student, the only law is the law of variability. According to another, prose rhythm is a subjective phenomenon, an effect unconsciously read into every passage of prose by the reader's natural love of rhythm, and otherwise not found there. Either of these results is equivalent to an acknowledgment that the principle sought for has not been found.

The method followed by those who begin from the study of Greek and Latin conventionalized cadence is wholly different from this. They do not postulate the existence of a natural and universal law of prose rhythm inherent in prose as such. They proceed, on the contrary, on the assumption that prose as such is without rhythmic law, and that it becomes rhythmic only as it is submitted to the control of some convention, a convention ultimately determined by particular customs of oral delivery. That is to say, all rhythm in prose is finally due, however subtle its variations may become, to certain regulated customs which have originated in the relations between a public speaker and his audience. The customs are undoubtedly rooted in universal facts concerning the powers of attention and the sensational susceptibilities of a crowd; and they may arise, therefore, independently in different times and places and languages. But when we consider how long a practice is necessary for their successful conventionalization into forms of art, when we remember further that they are inseparably bound up with a whole system of rhetoric, with the form of the rhetorical period, and the balances of parts within it, and with a certain kind of vocal delivery, we find ourselves less willing to reject the theory of the transmission of the laws of cadence by a steady current of tradition from the beginning of Greek oratory to the present day.

Now, it is evident that those who hold to this latter method of study will prefer, in the first place, to talk of the *cadence* of prose, rather than of its *rhythm*; for those who talk of *rhythm* are almost certain to think of regularities of recurrence, and of a movement running throughout the clauses and sentences of discourse; whereas Latin and English cadence is merely a euphonious fall and occurs only before certain pauses and at the ends of certain unitary parts of a sentence.

In the second place, they will narrowly limit their investigations to prose of an oratorical character. Of course they will not disregard the possibility—the probability, indeed, we may call it—that the form of every kind of normal artistic prose is ultimately oratorical. They hope, in fact, that by establishing the forms of oratorical euphony as definitely as possible they will be proceeding the directest way toward an explanation of the more subtle and literary forms of prose cadence. But they recognize also that the process is bound to be gradual and slow. For practical purposes there is a gulf fixed between the kind of prose in which the oratorical tone can be clearly heard and those various kinds which we may roughly describe as essay prose, and the latter should not be used at all in the effort to determine the elements of cadence.[64]

What is meant then by prose of an oratorical character? Of course, not only oratory in the limited sense; that is, prose meant to be spoken before a public audience. There is a great deal of good prose in English that falls under this caption. But there are also many kinds of writing not actually meant for public speaking in which the style is plainly formed in the mold of a conventional oratorical tradition. These kinds of writing are not peculiar to certain genres or types of prose; they may appear even in some works that are conventionally known as essays, just as some essays are actually entitled addresses or sermons. Unfortunately we are often compelled to decide by nothing but the form of the style itself. But this is a difficulty which cannot be avoided.

Yet the observation of genres is not altogether unprofitable. Works of certain literary types are on the whole more likely to display the oratorical manner than others. Oratory itself—sermons, addresses, political speeches, etc.—is evidently one of these. Most closely allied to it are various kinds of formal and ceremonious prose, such as dedications, "open letters," formal addresses to the readers of a book, proclamations, manifestoes, etc. The style of history as it was formerly written was often oratorical, as was Gibbon's, Robertson's, Macaulay's, for example; and, probably

[64] There are exceptions, however, Sir Thomas Browne, like his master Seneca, was fond of the cadences of oratory, and a profitable study of his form might be made by one who should be capable of interpreting the subtleties of a great master in variations. [See Norton Tempest, "Rhythm in the Prose of Sir Thomas Browne, *RES*, III (1927), 308-318, and E. L. Parker, "The Cursus in Sir Thomas Browne," *PMLA*, LIII (1938), 1037-1053.]

under the influence of historical writing, some novels and romances, among them Scott's, constantly betray the same stylistic character.[65]

[65] [Among the numerous other relevant works are Albert C. Clark, *Prose-Rhythm in English* (Oxford, 1913); W. M. Patterson, *The Rhythm of Prose* (New York, 1916); F. Novotný, *État Actuel des Études sur le Rhythme de la Prose Latine* (Lemberg, 1929); Norton R. Tempest, *The Rhythm of English Prose* (Cambridge, 1930); Sister Mary Rosenda Sullivan, *A Study of the Cursus in the Works of St. Thomas More* (Washington, 1943); P. F. Baum, *The Other Harmony of Prose* (Cambridge, Mass., 1952); M. Boulton, *The Anatomy of Prose* (London, 1954); G. C. Richards, "Coverdale and the Cursus," *Church Q.R.*, cx (1930); N. Denholm-Young, "The Cursus in England," pp. 68ff. in *Oxford Essays in Medieval History Presented to H. E. Salter* (Oxford, 1934).]

Foreword to Essays Eight and Nine

The two essays that follow represent Dr. Croll's contribution to what has become known as the theory of musical notation in prosody. Their chronological order has probably been reversed. The first, "The Rhythm of English Verse," Croll's major contribution to prosodical analysis, which has become a landmark in the study of that subject, was published in 1929, in mimeograph form, by the English Department at Princeton University. Presumably it was distributed primarily to the members of Croll's prosody seminar and perhaps to members of the Modern Language Association interested particularly in the subject. The only date for the essay is that in which the mimeograph appeared (1929), but it has been reported that a version of it existed at least as early as 1923, the date of the short, subsequent essay, and there are in fact certain indications in the latter that lead one to believe that much of the work of the greater essay had certainly already been accomplished. Croll's reference to double-time, for instance, is not especially meaningful without the explanation in the longer essay.

The importance of the date must be measured in reference to Croll's analysis of rhythm, in the longer essay, in relation to that of William Thomson in his book *The Rhythm of Speech*, the final version of which was printed at Glasgow also in 1923. Croll borrows fairly freely from Thomson in "The Rhythm of English Verse" at the same time claiming his own theory was well advanced before he became acquainted with Thomson's. In fact Thomson's theory was a decade in its generation and was certainly known in England. It is difficult to understand how Croll could have missed it until the publication of 1923, but the earlier essay credits only one prosodist of the school, Sidney Lanier, whose *Science of English Verse*—far less scientific than its title would indicate—was well known. One can only conclude that Croll was frank about his knowledge of Thomson in 1923 but that he employed his work rather freely in the six years that ensued between that date and the appearance of the mimeograph.

Thomson's is certainly the great name in the study of musical notation of verse, though Thomson himself disclaims that title. Like Croll in "Music and Metrics," he argues that the new system of notation is not really musical, though it has borrowed some time notation from that subject, but rather a rhythmical system of notation. He was unwilling to go so far as Croll and admit virtue to both systems of scansion, his own and the traditional syllable-counting method. Croll himself might have gone further and claimed that his system noted rhythm while the more traditional one was concerned with meter, but doubtless he was afraid of making such a hard and fast distinction. And surely he was right. He stopped short, then, claiming some merit for both systems, but arguing of course for the newer.

Neither Croll nor Thomson realized quite how old their method of scansion probably was; certainly both were preceded by Edwin Guest, *A History of English Rhythms*, 2 vols. (London, 1838), whose work was later re-edited by W. W. Skeat. And Guest was himself preceded by Joshua Steele's *Prosodia Rationalis*, the second and complete edition of which appeared in 1779. While there is no reason to believe that either might have known Steele, it seems unlikely that both Croll and Thomson would have missed Skeat's attention to the theory of Guest. But more recent prosodists often make the same sort of mistakes; J. C. Pope's *The Rhythm of Beowulf* (New Haven, 1942) pays tribute to Thomson without mention of Croll. Even *CBEL* does not mention the Croll mimeograph, which, while in many respects it reads like an abridgement and redaction of Thomson, often provides the clearest of insights.

Just how much credit the system of musical notation deserves it is hard to say. Certainly every such analysis provides grave difficulties, especially because no two readers pronounce syllables according them quite the same length. Put a poem on an oscillograph, or reproduce the sounds on smoked paper, and it is a hundred to one chance you will not reproduce anything closely resembling Croll's scansion, for in the final analysis syllabic length is a psychological rather than a physical matter. Greeks and Romans, for example, could distinguish between long and short syllables, apparently with great ease (a lost art), though in fact the syllables that they distinguished among, judging by their poetry, actually occupied a considerable gradation of times. There is no reason to assume, then, that the rhythmical system of scansion, though it breaks down in certain places, is not in fact psychologically as sound as we can expect. And certainly in some matters, especially the pointing up of rhythmical similarities, as between Virgil's *Aeneid*, "Arma virumque cano . . . ab oris" and Swinburne's "Out of the golden remote wild west, where the sea without shore is," the system is far more enlightening than that of conventional metrics. That is not the same as saying that many poets have written with rhythmical intentions, rather than the intention of filling a scheme of syllables and accents. In "Music and Metrics" Croll recognizes as much. Thomson, on the other hand, whose essay is more polemical, is not so willing to make admissions that might, conceivably, damage his system. That the system itself is useful can be seen from Pope's book, which is perhaps the only work on musical notation to have gained much academic credit.

Defects in scansion in which some measure of syllabic time is attempted are not of course confined to the Croll-Thomson system. English quantitativists of the sixteenth century had much the same trouble; while Spenser could produce an "Iambic Trimetrum" that is clearly recognizable for what it is, Gabriel Harvey complained it was not "altogether perfect for the feet," and Sidney's experiments in the *Arcadia* are almost impossible to follow even when he furnished diacritical marks with which to interpret. Even the Romans, for whom syllable length must have been a far easier psychological accomplishment, occasionally had troubles; otherwise why should they have invented the tricky concept of long by position?

As Croll most sincerely claims, however, in both essays, a definitive improvement in our methods of scansion awaits further study. Unfortunately the matter has been neglected since his day, notwithstanding some attention paid to principles in American periodicals. The reason for reprinting "The Rhythm of English Verse," however, is not its intrinsic merit as a method of analysis, nor even the insights Croll provides into certain verse forms, but rather the historical position occupied by the essay in the study of prosody. It has become an important document, and it is scarcely available. It is the editor's hope that this printing will fill a need long felt by students of the subject. And it is time such an important contributor received his due from bibliographers.

The ensuing version slightly alters Croll's wording from the mimeograph. Some abridgement has been made, usually for purposes of clarity, though some examples have been reduced to save space. The version included here is not, however, a redaction, despite the changes. On the whole, it faithfully represents Croll's intention, though in some places not his exact wording.* Justification for such a procedure must rest on two grounds: first, Croll was apparently not quite satisfied with the mimeograph, or he would, most likely, have seen it into print; and, second, the essay was more loosely written than Croll's other major works.†

The shorter essay, "Music and Metrics," is not of itself of sufficient interest to warrant reprinting, but as a companion piece to "The Rhythm of English Verse," and perhaps as an epilogue concerning the whole system, it provides an interesting note.

ROBERT O. EVANS
UNIVERSITY OF KENTUCKY

---

* All poems in the essay are given in Croll's version; minor variants from ordinary texts are his.
† I am indebted to Professor Ants Oras for his criticisms of Croll's theory and its psychological implications.

The Rhythm of English Verse

EDITED BY ROBERT O. EVANS

✧ AUTHOR'S PREFACE ✧

THE description of verse form in the following pages does not aim at completeness. It professes only to present the principles of *rhythm* in our verse, and for this reason it deals chiefly with lyric poetry. It is true that the elements of rhythm, described in Chapter I, are common to all kinds of English verse; but in "spoken" verse (blank verse, for instance) these are supplemented by certain conventions and usages which do not fall within the scope of the present study.

The principle that controls the discussion is the musical law of equality of time periods marked by beats. In several respects I have carried this principle and its implications further than any previous prosodist has done, and the second and third chapters must be regarded as largely a new extension of musical law in the field of verse. But of course all that I have done is based upon the studies of those who have preceded me during the last forty years, and it would not be just if I should not make an especial acknowledgment of my indebtedness to the great (if difficult) work by Dr. William Thomson, *The Rhythm of Speech* (Glasgow, 1923). My chapters were first written before this work appeared, but they have been several times rewritten since, and many of the changes they have undergone have been due to my study of it. *The Rhythm of Speech* is a new point of departure for students of English verse form.[1]

M.W.C.

[1] There follow acknowledgments to Dr. Croll's pupils at Princeton University, particularly Mr. Hamilton Cottier ('22) and Mr. Donald Goodchild ('18).

CHAPTER I

THE ELEMENTS OF THE RHYTHM OF VERSE

I. *Music as the Starting-Point*

The rhythmic form of verse is the same in its essential principles as that of the music of song, from which it is, in fact, derived in the first instance. In some kinds of verse, it is true, the form is much more remote from that of song than in others. For example, our English blank verse and the French Alexandrine line have been made, more or less deliberately, as unlike song as verse can ever be; and indeed all verse meant to be used in long poems or to be spoken in anything like the level of tone of prose discourse must have been treated in the same way. Still, the changes that have been introduced into our "spoken" verse, as we may call it, have not affected the fundamental principles of rhythm which it derives from song; they are merely additional procedures which restrict the operation of these principles within certain limits, without changing them in any way or adding new ones to them. Meanwhile a great deal of poetry continues and will always continue to be made as much like song as possible. Dancing and music are the arts of rhythm; they have nothing to learn about their own business from poetry; poetry, on the other hand, has derived all it knows about rhythm from them. The best way to approach the study of the rhythm of verse, therefore, is by way of the form of song.

The following lullaby first appeared in an Elizabethan play called *Patient Grissil*, sung to a tune, probably still older, called "Mayfair":

Larghetto

Golden   slumbers kiss your eyes

[There follow, beneath the musical staff, the additional lines: "Smiles a-wait you when you rise; Sleep, pretty wantons, do not cry, And I will sing a lul-la-by."]

There are a number of things in the music of this song that we are not concerned with. The symbols, for instance, that precede the time signature 3/8 [i.e., b-flat and e-flat] have to do with musical elements that do not appear in the poetry. We are not interested in the five parallel lines which make up the staff and are used to indicate the pitch of the various notes, for verse does not imitate the melody of music. Finally, even in indicating the *rhythm* of the words we cannot follow the notes exactly, because in singing words we can do things that cannot be done in saying them. For instance, the time occupied by the syllable—"gold"—in singing can be divided between two notes of different pitch; whereas in representing the form of the words as said it cannot be so divided. Taking account, however, of these differences, and using only as much of the musical notation as we need, we can represent the rhythmical form of the words as follows:

3/8   / Golden / slumbers / kiss your / eyes

or   / Sleep, pretty / wantons, / do not / cry /

In this case we have the music to guide us (or sometimes, to guard against). For the following lines from *Paradise Lost* there is of course no music, but the same method can well be used to indicate their rhythmic form:

3/8   / High on a / throne of / royal / state, which / far

Out / shone the / wealth of / Ormuz / and of / Ind /

II. Notation

The same symbols, then, can be employed in the notation of verse that are employed in music, and this is a method now employed by writers on prosody who hold views on the subject similar to those stated in the preceding paragraphs. No method, in fact, will represent the necessary facts about a great deal of our poetry that does not contain the essential elements of a musical notation. But there are certain serious practical difficulties in the printing and writing of the exact musical symbols for notes and rests in connection with verse; and there are, besides, some considerations of a theoretical kind which make it undesirable to do so. The following symbols, devised to meet these difficulties, will be employed throughout the present discussion, with one or two others which will be explained when the need for using them arises:

⌣ equals the half-note, ♩, of music.

— " " quarter-note, or crotchet, ♩.

⌐ " " eighth-note, or quaver, ♪.

⌐⌐ " " sixteenth-note, or semiquaver, ♪.

⌐⌐⌐ " " thirty-second note, or demisemiquaver, ♪.

A dot following any of these signs indicates that its time is increased by a half. Thus, — · indicates a quarter plus an eighth, or three eighths; ⌐· an eighth plus a sixteenth, or three sixteenths.

∧ equals a quarter rest, ✗ or <; that is, a rest equal in time to a quarter note.

∧ " an eighth rest, ⅞.

∧ " a sixteenth rest, ⅞.

∧∧ " a half rest; represented in music sometimes by two quarter rests, as here, sometimes by a special symbol.

A time signature at the beginning of a poem or passage, a fraction 3/8, 4/4, 6/8, etc., indicates the character of the rhythm; its meaning will be explained later. A time signature is not always necessary in verse, because 3/8 time is much the most frequent in our verse, and when no signature appears it may be assumed that the passage is in 3/8 time.

III. The Measure

Time. In the examples in I (above), each line is divided into parts by vertical bars. These mark divisions of time occupied in saying the line, and all the divisions of time so marked in a given line or passage are equal one to another or so nearly equal that the ear hears them as equal. The equality of time of these periods is the fundamental fact of rhythm; the rhythm of verse does not arise from equality or similarity in the number of syllables that occupy this time, for the number may vary greatly without disturbing the rhythm, and often silence (or rest) takes the place of one or more syllables. Indeed the interesting quality of the rhythm of English verse is largely due to the fact that equal times are occupied by syllables in different ways.

One of these periods is called a measure, because it is the number of times it is repeated that measures the form of a *line* of verse and gives it its name. Thus we call the line of the slumber song (section I) a four-measure line (or, if we prefer the Greek terms, a tetrameter line); the line of *Paradise Lost* is a five-measure (or pentameter) line, and so on. The English names require no further illustration. The Greek names are: dimeter, trimeter, tetrameter, pentameter, hexameter, heptameter, octameter.[2] It would be much better if we had worked out a consistent way of naming all the facts of verse in our own language, but many Greek terms have established themselves in our usage and sometimes prove convenient.

Stress or beat. There is another element in the form of a measure beside its time. For we could not hear the equality of time between successive measures, we could not be aware of the measures at all, unless there were something by which we could mark where one begins and another ends. We do this by uttering the first note or syllable of a measure with greater force than the others. There are several names for this greater force of utterance. *Accent* is the name usually given to it in grammar and phonetics. *Ictus* was the classical name, and it is sometimes employed by modern prosodists. We shall regularly call it *stress,* but no harm will be done if we often use also the word *beat*; for this is the word in everyday use, and it has the additional merit of calling attention to the close kinship of the rhythm of music and verse with other physical rhythms, the pulse of the heart, the beat of the feet of marching men, or of dancers, etc.[3]

The number of stresses, or beats, in a line may of course be just as conveniently used to describe the length of a line (four-beat lines, etc.) as the number of measures; and we shall often use this method, though the other is more strictly correct, since it is the measures and not the beats that constitute the line.

The wave-like movement of verse. It will be convenient to call attention to an error that causes a great deal of bad reading of

[2] [The Greek names, however, do not mean the same as the English. In the first place, Greek verse was constructed according to the principles of a quantitative meter (one in which the vital principle concerns the length of syllable, a long syllable being one with a long vowel or one in which a short vowel is followed by a consonant cluster); English verse, except for a few experiments, has traditionally concerned itself with the number of syllables and the position of accents; hence it is called syllabic (or more accurately syllabo-accentual) verse. Moreover, the Greek names adopted to describe English verse have undergone a change in meaning; for example, Greek iambic trimeter is quite different from English, the former being a meter which employs double feet. To this already complex situation, Professor Croll's willingness to adopt the traditional Greek names is likely to cause only added confusion.]

[3] [Prosodists do not always qualify their terminology with such scrupulous care; hence the use of the word *stress* may be objectionable because it implies loudness as well as force of utterance. But as whisper speech, in which loudness is not a factor, clearly contains accents, Prof. Croll is surely correct in his definition, though his decision to use the word *stress* may work against clarity.]

poetry. Any description of stress is likely to create the impression that there is a steady fall of force from the beginning of a measure to the end, a sudden rise at each new beat. This is not true. If it were, music and verse would consist of a succession of fresh starts, violent recoveries. Even a good machine does not work in so ugly a manner, much less music and verse, which have their origins in certain movements in the bodies and minds of men.[4] It is true that as soon as the stronger syllable is uttered a fall of energy follows; but during this fall new energy is being stored up in anticipation of the next stress, which we feel to be coming. That is, the gradual fall of stress is accompanied by a gradual rise toward the next stress. The movement of energy in verse is not: ⋀⋀⋀⋀⋀⋀ nor: ⋁⋁⋁⋁⋁⋁⋁; but rather ⌣⌣⌣⌣⌣⌣, though of course the swing of rhythm in music and verse is never so regular and uninteresting as this diagram would indicate.

In other words, the movement is neither a rise nor a fall, but an easy progress, a punctuated comfortable swing, in which there is a combination of both. The orchestra leader, who beats time exaggerating greatly the force of the stress, and the motion of the sea waves are in some ways a better parallel to musical rhythm than the thrusts of a piston rod. But of course a better parallel than either of these, because it is probably the source of musical and verse rhythm, is the motion of dancing. A dancer would certainly think it absurd to represent the rhythm of his performance by either of the first two diagrams above.[5]

Anacrusis, or catch-note. Closely connected with these facts is a phenomenon which may cause confusion in noting the form of verse unless it is properly understood. The stressed syllable or note stands at the beginning of a measure. But when a line or passage begins

---

[4] [While credible and often stated, Prof. Croll's theory that the origin of music and verse lies in dance is, of course, pure conjecture.]

[5] It is not desirable to enter into controversy, but the reader will observe that the statements made here imply that there is no difference between the kinds of verse traditionally called rising and falling (or iambic and trochaic). There is in fact no difference of rhythm between them, and the terms are useful only for the purpose of telling whether a line begins and ends with a stressed or an unstressed syllable. This is just as true of Greek and Latin verse as it is of English, and in the best recent discussions of it the line separating measures is always placed *before* the stressed syllable, just as it is in the best recent studies of English verse. See, for instance, C. F. Abdy Williams, *The Aristoxenian Theory of Musical Rhythm* (Cambridge, 1911). [It might be more accurate simply to say that fashions of marking measures, or feet, change; a system not unlike that employed by Prof. Croll was used by Edwin Guest in *A History of English Rhythms*, 2 vols. (London, 1838).]

exactly on the first note or syllable of a measure, it has an effect of abruptness or impetuousness; and in fact neither musician nor poet ever begins a composition or passage with the first note of a measure unless he wishes to express some particular character in the feeling of the piece by doing so. Generally he begins with one or more preliminary notes or syllables that are not parts of a complete measure (that is, are extra metrical) and are meant to prepare the ear for the first beat. Some long poems have been written, it is true, in which this practice has not been followed; in *Hiawatha*, for example, and a number of poems in imitation of the classical dactylic hexameter, each line begins on the stressed first syllable of a measure. But experience shows that this is usually an inappropriate method in English except in lyric, where, of course, a quick and impulsive effect is often desired.[6]

The preliminary syllable or syllables must be regarded, then, as a well established part of the form of English verse. The name for this is *anacrusis*, a Greek word meaning "upstroke" and originally applied to the first touching of the string of an instrument at the beginning of a piece.[7] In music it is sometimes called the catch-note.

Anacrusis has been spoken of above as extra-metrical, meaning that it does not form part of any measure. This is not a true description of it, however, except as applied to the first line of a poem or stanza, or when a single line is taken out of its context in a poem and considered alone. Otherwise it completes a measure left incomplete at the end of the preceding line. This can be most clearly shown by printing a passage of verse continuously, without regard to the division into lines:

/ Lo, the poor / Indian, // whose un / tutored / mind Sees / God in / clouds and / hears him // in the / wind

Pope, Essay on Man

If the reader of these lines allows more time for the measure / mind Sees / than for other measures, because "mind" ends a line, he must consider it as no more than the slight retard that often occurs at

---

[6] [Croll is speaking of what are known in usual metrical terminology as headless, or truncated, lines. For example, "Whan / that A/pril with / his shour/es soote"; this type of line is often taken for a distinguishing mark of Chaucerian prosody, though the matter is highly debatable. See Bernhard Ten Brink, *The Language and Meter of Chaucer* (London, 1901), or R. O. Evans, "Whan that Aprill(e)?," *N&Q*, N.S.IV:6 (June 1957), 234-237.]

[7] [From Gr. ἀνακρούω, meaning "strike the strings."]

a similar place in music; and in fact it will usually be found by careful time-beating that the slight delay on "mind" is almost made up for by an acceleration on "Sees," and that the beat of the following measure occurs but slightly after its proper time.

IV. Times and Stresses within the Measure

The measure is the unit ordinarily employed in describing the form of verse, and the smallest unit of time commonly taken account of in beating out its rhythm. It is, however, not the ultimate unit of time measurement; for it is itself—in verse, just as in music—composed of a number of equal time units, each of which has its own stress or beat; and there are different kinds of measures according to the number of measures. There is not, however, as great a range of difference, for all measures in English poetry are either two-time or three-time measures; that is, we count either twice or thrice while their time elapses.[8] But that is not all. The kind of measure will depend not only on the number of times or counts within it, but also on the length of time we must give to each count. A two-time measure may contain two eighths: ($\_\neg \_\neg$) or two quarters: (— —), and a three-time measure may contain three eighths, three quarters, or more rarely three halves.

The method to be employed here to show these facts is the same as that used in music, namely, a "time signature" placed at the beginning of a passage, describing the form of all the measures that follow. This is a number written in the form of a fraction, the denominator of which (always 2, 4, or 8) shows how many times this unit occurs in each measure. Thus 2/8 means that there are two eighths to a measure, etc.[9]

The reader of English verse is not conscious of the time division within the measure unless he has been specially trained to hear it. We do not ordinarily detect it when verse is read aloud to us. Nor does the poet in composing usually pay any deliberate attention to it. It might be supposed, then, that it is not a real part of the

[8] [In *The Rhythm of Speech* (Glasgow, 1923), William Thomson argues that only two-time and three-time measures are possible; e.g., a four-time measure would be philosophically only a double two-time measure, etc. It seems likely Croll is specially indebted at this point.]

[9] The five signatures (2/8, 2/4, 3/8, 3/4, 3/2) are the only ones that have to be employed in noting the form of simple measures in English verse. But in lyric poetry all of the measures so designated are frequently used in groups of two, constituting "double" or "compound" measures, and for such measures we shall employ signatures with numerators double those of the fractions given. [Note slightly revised; hereafter indicated by R in parentheses.]

373

rhythmic structure of the verse, as it is of Greek and Latin, that we are satisfied if the main beats of the various measures are always separated by equal periods of time, and we are not concerned with the way this time is partitioned within the measure. But this is not the case. Two-time (or its double, four-time) and three-time (or six-time) are different rhythms and produce different effects. Some poets are conscious of what causes the difference and take full advantage of the opportunities it offers them; others produce the difference, without being fully aware of the cause of it, by merely following traditional forms of song or verse; and if we are not able to determine in a given case whether to call a rhythm two-time or three-time, this is only because our powers of observation have not been sufficiently trained for the purpose.

If the syllables of a measure coincide exactly with its rhythmical times or beats, there would of course be no difficulty in this part of our subject; we should only have to count syllables. But they do not always, or even usually, do so. In a three-time measure there may be one syllable, two syllables (this is the case, for instance, in the usual iambic pentameter line), three, four, or even sometimes five; and rests may occupy the time of the whole or any part of the measure. In a two-time measure there is the same range of possibilities. There is no way to tell, then, except by beating or tapping the two or three times with unvarying regularity and listening for the way in which the syllables fall with reference to them. Since the speed with which a line must be said for this purpose must not be much less than that of a normal reading (else the time relations will be distorted), it will be seen that a fast tapping and very quick observation are necessary and that it requires a good deal of practice to learn to hear the times within a measure.

V. Three-Time Verse

In illustrating three-time verse we shall for the present disregard the distinction between 3/8, 3/4, and 3/2 time. Some of the following examples are in 3/8, some in 3/4, and time signatures will be employed to indicate the difference; but it is to be remembered that we are only concerned here with the general features of all three-time verse.

1. 3/8   I am / monarch of / all I sur / vey, ⌒/∧

My / right there is / none to dis / pute, ⌒/∧

From the / centre all / round to the / sea, ∧/∧

I am / lord of the / fowl and the / brute. ∧/∧∧/[10]

Cowper, *The Solitude of Alexander Selkirk*

2. 3/4   Flow / gently, sweet / Afton, a / mong thy green /

braes;

Flow / gently, I'll / sing thee a / song in thy / praise.

Burns, *Afton Water*

In these two examples is illustrated the fact that verse in three-time *may* be written in uniform three-syllable measures. The effect of this way of writing is of greater speed and smoothness, though the speed is actually the same when it is written with two syllables to the measure. In the eighteenth century a great deal of lyrical 3/8 verse was written with a uniform three-syllable arrangement of the time, even verse of a serious character; but it is now felt to be chiefly appropriate to sentimental, light, or humorous effects.

Until recently it was the universal custom of prosodists to speak of three-syllable measures of this kind as dactyls or anapests (dactyls if the lines begin without anacrusis, anapests if they begin with it). But this was a serious mistake which has done much to prevent readers from hearing the true rhythms of a great deal of verse. The dactyl and anapest are not three-time but two-time measures. The dactyl is: (2/4) /————/; the anapest is the reverse: (2/4) ——/—; there is plenty of English three-syllable verse in this kind of time, as we shall see; it will suffice for the moment to specify the verse of *Evangeline,* which, though many attempts have been made to read it in a rapid three-time movement, is actually written in genuine 2/4 dactylic measures. But verse like the lines of Cowper and Burns quoted above is of course not dactylic; on the contrary, it is three-time.

Though the three-syllable arrangement of three-time is possible, therefore, and common enough, it is not the most frequent or the standard English arrangement. Even in the most song-like lyric the two-syllable arrangement is, on the whole, more common; and in

---

[10] The rests that occur here, and elsewhere, will be explained in the chapter on double or compound measure. (R)

all our epic and dramatic verse it is the typical and normal form, the pentameter line which is the standard in such poetry being always, except for an occasional measure here and there, written in two-syllable measures.

3. 3/8   Night's / candles / are burnt / out, ⌃and / jocund / day

Stands / tiptoe /⌃on the / misty / mountain-/tops. ⌃/

Romeo and Juliet

This passage shows Shakespeare's blank verse in its more regular form; more regular, that is, in observance of the two-syllable rule. It offers a favorable opportunity, therefore, for the observation of the way in which three-time distributes itself in English between two syllables. This was a matter which was exactly controlled by rule in Greek and Latin verse; the trochee, for example, always had the form: /— ⌐/, the iamb ⌐/— ; English, on the contrary, has no rules for the distribution of the time between the syllables, and its freedom and variety in this respect are the most important differences between its verse form and that of the ancients. In the ten measures quoted above the time is distributed in six ways:

$$— \urcorner ; \; \urcorner — ; \; \urcorner \wedge \urcorner ; \; \urcorner \cdot \urcorner ; \; \wedge \urcorner \urcorner ; \; — \wedge :$$

it is evident that Shakespeare had no rule to guide him. Indeed he did not think about this subject at all; his practice was wholly uncontrolled by a theory of time distribution.

4.   That / father / lost, lost / his, ⌃and the sur/vivor / bound

    In filial obligation for some term

    To do obsequious sorrow: but to persever

    In obstinate condolement is a course

    Of / impious / stubborn/ness: ⌃'tis un/manly grief.

Hamlet

Here, in Shakespeare's later blank verse, we observe that the two-syllable rule, though not lost sight of, is much less strictly observed. In several measures there are three syllables, and in one four.[11]

[11] [However, the three-syllable measure indicated in the last line, / impious /, is probably a mistake; the practice of elision of contiguous vowels (*-ious*) permitted this sound combination to be considered as a single syllable. And probably such a pronunciation was common enough in Shakespeare's time.]

5. 3/4   By the / waters of / Babylon we sat / down and / wept
         Re/membering / thee,
         That for / ages of / agony hast en/dured and / slept
         and / wouldst not / see.∧/

Swinburne, Super Flumina Babylonis

6. 3/8   / Sweet for a / little ∧/ even to / fear, and / sweet,
         O / love, to / lay down / fear at / love's fair / feet. ∧/

Swinburne, Erotion

7. 3/8   Blown from / lips that / strow the / world-wide / seas
         with / death ∧/

Swinburne, Chorus in Erechtheus

These three passages are useful in illustrating the wide range of custom in the syllabification of English three-time verse. In the first there are numerous measures of one, two, and three syllables, and the second measure of each long line has invariably five syllables. On the other hand, in two passages that follow it, Swinburne has not only observed the two-syllable rule almost without variation; he has also written English three-time verse with as clear a consciousness of time division within the measure as if he were writing Greek or Latin poetry. It is probable, in fact, that he was deliberately attempting in both of these passages to reproduce in English some of the effects of the classical iambs.[12]

VI. 3/8 and 3/4 Measures

In the preceding section the general character of three-time has been considered without reference to the distinction between 3/8,

---

[12] The first measure in example 6 is apparently irregular because, according to common custom, the anacrusis has been absorbed into the measure; the third measure is perfectly regular if the word *even* is treated as a monosyllable; see Robert Bridges, *Milton's Prosody* (Oxford, 1921). (R) [The effect of classical iambs, however, was usually obtained, as in the meter of Greek tragic dialogue, by employing iambs in pairs, by dipody, in which the initial syllable of each pair might be either short or long.]

3/4, and 3/2 time. The length of the unit employed in the measure is as important, however, in determining the character of a verse rhythm as the number of times it occurs.

In beginning the study of this distinction, it will be well to observe two things concerning 3/8 time. *First*: It is a very fast time. Though the 3/8 measure occupies more time than the 2/8 measure, it is the fastest *three*-time measure that can be employed, because its unit (one eighth) is the shortest that our ears are easily capable of apprehending.[13] If we try to beat twice, instead of once, for this unit; that is, to beat six times in 3/8 measure, we find that it is practically impossible to do so; division of it is beyond the ordinary capacity. *Second*: The 3/8 measure is not only the fastest possible three-time measure: its length is a fairly stable quantity. That is, it is not long in one poem, short in another, but is of about the same length whatever kind of poem it is employed in. For instance, if we beat time in three different kinds of 3/8 time verse—first, a line of blank verse:

Things / unat/tempted / yet in / prose or / rhyme /
second, a line of folk song:
/ Oh / dear / what can the / matter be? /
third, a line of literary lyric:
/ Kentish Sir / Byng / stood for his / King /

giving to each passage the speed appropriate to it, we find that the measure does not appreciably change its time from one passage to another. The blank verse line may *seem* to be slower, partly because it is uttered in a speaking tone, whereas the others are appropriately said in something like the lyrical tone of song, and partly because the two-syllable arrangement of the measure in three-time always seems to make it slower. But the speed is actually not very different from that of the other passages and can only be made so by some deliberate effort of expression, which may temporarily impose an artificial *tempo*.

When we apply the same test to a number of passages in 3/4 time from different poems, we find the same result; namely, that the measure is of about the same length in all of them. It is much longer,

---

[13] It seems probable that this verse unit is determined by the length of the short syllables in our ordinary prose utterance; e.g., each of the short syllables except the last in the fast phrase "many men of many minds"; whereas the longer one-quarter unit of 3/4 and 2/4 time is similarly determined by the long syllables of speech, such as "minds" in the phrase just quoted. This is a subject, however, for theorists; our purpose is only observation of the facts.

however, than the 3/8 measure, and if not actually twice as long it at least approximates that length and perhaps would attain it in an ideal reading. A rough way of detecting the contrast between them is to observe that a three-syllable measure in 3/8 time has the effect of being a little faster than ordinary speech, because its unit is similar to that of the short syllables of speech; whereas the 3/4 measures seem to drag a little behind the speed of unpoetic speech, because their unit is the long syllable, or is at least like it. But the relation between them is more exact than this test indicates: it is ideally, if not actually, a two-to-one relation.[14]

In order to illustrate the difference properly, passages of considerable length would be necessary, because it is easy to force a line or two of a poem, read out of context, into an improper *tempo*. The hearer or reader must allow himself to be controlled by the movement of each poem as a whole and must usually be guided by the speed into which he has fallen at the end of a stanza or passage rather than by that with which he begins it. The following fragments of ¾-time verse must not be regarded, therefore, as adequate test passages when they are taken alone:

1.   For I / trust if the / Enemy's / fleet came / yonder / round
            by the / hill,

And the / rushing / battle-bolt / sang from the / three-
            decker / out of the / foam

That the / smooth-faced / snub-nosed / rogue would / leap
            from his / counter and / till,

And / strike, if he / could, were it / but with his / cheating /
            yard-wand, / home.[15]

Tennyson, Maud, I, 1

---

[14] Some rough experiments with a metronome seem to show that a 3/8 measure normally measures about 92, a 3/4 measure about 52. These facts justify us in assigning, for convenience in notation, a more or less fixed value for the eighth-note. In music, of course, the notes have no general absolute values.

[15] Regarding the measure / cheating /, observe that the verse beat always falls on the vowel of a syllable and therefore not always on the first letter or letters. Thus the measure is really / -eating y- /, and the time taken by "-ing y-" is fully the half-note shown in the notation. There are many interesting features of the time distribution in this passage. The frequent occurrence of measures with the form:

2.   / What's this dull / town to me? /

Robin's not / near.∧/

/ What was't I / wished to see, /

What wished to / hear?∧/

Robin Adair

3.   / March! / march! /₃ Ettrick and / Teviotdale! /

Why the deil / dinna ye march / forward in / order? ∧/¹⁶

Scott, *Blue Bonnets over the Border*

4.   By the / waters of / Babylon we sat / down and / wept

Re/membering / thee ∧/

Swinburne, *Super Flumina Babylonis*

5.   / You may es/teem him

A / child for his / might,

/ Or you may / deem him

A / coward from his / flight: ∧

But if / she whom Love doth / honour ∧

Be con/cealed from the / day, ∧

Set a / thousand guards up/on her, ∧

Love will / find out the / way. ∧

Song of the Early 17th Century

—·—· counteracts the smoothly fast effect of the ordinary three-syllable measure, but, indeed, Tennyson has prevented his verse from "cantering" by many
other kinds of variation from the typical measure of 3/4 time, which seldom
appears in his writing. (R)

¹⁶ The mark over the syllables "dinna ye" indicates that the three eighths are
said in the time of two eighths; such a run of three notes in the time of two is
called in music a "triplet." Another interesting example of it is in Kipling's *The
First Chantey*, where a triplet occurs at the same point in every line and is therefore to be regarded as a regular part of the rhythmic form of the poem: 2/4 /
Mine was the / woman to me, / darkling I / found her // Haling her / dumb from
the camp / held her and / bound her. /

6. He is gone on the mountain, // He is lost to the forest, // Like a summer-dried fountain // When our need was the sorest.

Scott, Coronach

7. The Assyrian came down like a wolf on the fold, // His cohorts all gleaming in purple and gold.

Byron, Sennacherib

The *tempo* of these poems is not always exactly the same. Some shading of the speed will doubtless occur for purposes of expression; some readers might try, for instance, to read Scott's *Coronach* slower than Byron's *Sennacherib* in order to emphasize a dirge-like quality in the rhythm, or the same reader might at different times vary his reading of either of them a little. And the same thing will happen in ⅜-time verse. But these expressive variations are very slight and will not conceal the fact that if the ¾-time verse is read properly its measure occupies normally nearly twice the time of that of the ⅜-time verse.

A useful way to test the truth of this statement is to read ⅜-time verse beating time for the alternate measures alone. For instance, if we read: "Of / man's first diso/bedience, and the / fruit" stressing only "man's," "-be," and "fruit," we shall find that the time intervals between these syllables are almost exactly the same as between those that have the stresses in: "That the / smooth-faced / snub-nosed / rogue would / leap from his / counter and / till."

This procedure is easier to follow in the comparison of poems more nearly the same character. Thus the beats in *Robin Adair*: "/ What's this / dull town to me? // Robin's not / near," coincide in time with the beats on "Byng," "King," etc. in Browning's: "Kentish Sir / Byng stood for his / King //[17] Bidding the / crop-headed Parliament / swing," and similarly the beats in Scott's: "/Why the deil / dinna ye march / forward in / order?" correspond with the alternate beats in Cowper's *Solitude of Alexander Selkirk*:

I am / monarch of ⸽ all I sur/vey ⌃⸽⋀/

My / right there is ⸽ none to dis/pute ⌃⸽⋀⌒.

In the 3/8 measure it is always extremely difficult to hear the three beats distinctly; the ordinary reader hears only the first beat of the measure and needs to hear only that in order to keep the right

[17] [In the case noted the double bar indicates the end of the line, as is usual, but not necessarily the end of a measure. Elsewhere the double bar indicates both the end of the line and the end of the measure. The complication is editorial, caused by setting the lines in paragraph form rather than separately; any apparent confusion can simply be resolved by counting the measures.]

rhythmic movement. But in 3/4 time the slower *tempo* permits and often compels one to hear the three beats distinctly, and it is often necessary to pay particular attention to the way they all fall upon syllables or pauses within the measure, because the character of the rhythm depends on this. For instance, in the last line of the stanza quoted above, "Love will find out the way," the syllable "Love" at the beginning has the third beat of a measure and is clearly heard as having it; and in the next to last line the three syllables, "Set," "thou," and "guards" have almost equal stresses, though "Set" takes a third beat, "thou" a first, and "guards" a second. Again, in Scott's *Coronach*, the last syllable of each of the four lines quoted has beat two in its measure, and the first syllable of the following line has beat three; the hearing of these inner beats of the measure with more or less clearness is essential to the steady movement of the rhythm. They have the effect of holding back the reader in his natural rush toward the next strong beat and so prevent the verse from falling into the inappropriate, fast 3/8 movement.

VII. The Charge of the Light Brigade

The marking of inner stresses in the 3/4 measure is interestingly illustrated in a lyric form which has had a remarkably long and glorious history in English poetry—the "tail rhyme" stanza employed by Tennyson in *The Charge of the Light Brigade*. The original form of the stanza is six lines rhyming *aabccb*, the *b* lines being the short tail-rhyme lines; and so it appears in a fourteenth-century song in praise of the Virgin Mary.[18] But in later song and in literary use the stanza is usually longer, and the tail-rhyme lines variously placed. Drayton's *Agincourt* has *aaabcccb*; this is a form often used by recent poets, as by Hodgson in his *Eve*. In *The Charge of the Light Brigade* Tennyson, with characteristic technical curiosity, varies the arrangement in different stanzas.

What may safely be called the characteristic distribution of stresses in this remarkable lyric form is illustrated in the first lines of the song *Robin Adair*:

/ What's this dull / town to me /

Robin's not / near.

[18] / Hail be thou / lady so bright // Gabriel that / said so right // "Christ is with / thee." Carleton Brown, *Religious Lyrics of the Fourteenth Century* (Oxford, 1924), No. 92.

In all the poems mentioned above the second measure of the line (except in the tail-rhyme lines) has usually the form shown here, a dotted quarter plus an eighth plus a quarter, and it is obvious that this gives the emphasis to the third beat of the measure which is demanded by the fact that it falls on a rhyming word. In the first measure of the line the arrangement shows a great deal of variation, and no general rule can be stated except that it is almost always so managed as to make a contrast with that of the second measure. Probably the form that is to be regarded as characteristic is that illustrated above: — — — ; but in *Agincourt* the movement is nearly always — — · —⌐ , the first two beats of the measure being distinctly heard, the third beat being syncopated and hence *not* distinctly heard.

/ Fair stood the / wind for France /

When we our / sails advance, /

Nor now to / prove our chance /

Longer will / tarry; ∧/

The same arrangement is very frequent in Hodgson's *Eve*, and prevalent in Calverly's *Ode to Tobacco*: "How those who use fuses // All grow by slow degrees // Brainless as chimpanzees // Meagre as lizards; // Go mad and beat their wives // Plunge, after shocking lives, // Razors and carving knives // Into their gizzards."

Much the most famous poem written in the kind of verse we are considering, since Drayton's wonderful epic lyric, is *The Charge of the Light Brigade*. Tennyson himself said that he had arrived at the rhythm of this poem by repeating to himself the phrase, "Someone had blundered," which he had read in a newspaper account of the battle of Balaclava.[19] The form of "Someone had blundered," which actually appears as a tail-rhyme line of the poem, is:

/— — — /— — ∧ /;

but Tennyson has not followed this even distribution very often in other lines. There is great variety:

/ Half a league, / half a league /

[19] Of course what he meant was that in saying over the phrase he discovered that it would go to the rhythm of a number of well-known songs and verses, such as *Agincourt* and *God Save the King*. See what is said below of the origin of Swinburne's *Super Flumina Babylonis*. (R)

Half a league / onward ∧/

/ Forward the / Light Brigade /

/ Theirs not to / make reply /

/ Into the / valley of Death /

Rode the six / hundred ∧/

VIII. 3/2 Measures

Finally, there is still a slower three-time, in which the unit is twice as long as in ¾-time, four times as long as in 3/8—to be noted as 3/2. This is a form which has not yet been studied by prosodists, and it is only very lately that its existence in English poetry has even been suspected. We can point to no more than four or five poems, therefore, in which we are able to assert positively that the measure is 3/2; but these are all so interesting in the way that time is distributed within the measure that they justify a careful observation. It is certain that many other poems of like character will be discovered by further study of the subject.

1. 3/2   With deep af/fection and recol/lection,

I often / think of those Shandon / bells, ∧

Whose sounds so / wild would

In the days of / childhood

Fling around my / cradle ∧ their magic / spells ∧∧∧∧

Mahoney, *The Bells of Shandon*

Two things are to be observed in this handling of 3/2 time. *First*: The time of the long unit (a half-note) is usually filled by two syllables instead of one: (— — or — · ⌐ being much more frequent than ⌐⌐); so that there are always five or six syllables in a measure. Of course this is an important element in the necessary slowing up of the measure. *Second*: The third beat of every measure is strongly marked to the ear, less strongly of course than the first, but more strongly than the second. The syllables "deep," "re-," "oft-," "Shan-," "sounds," etc. have an unavoidable stress. By these means a difficult form has been made easy for the ear to follow, and the observation of them will aid greatly in the comprehension of a much more difficult poem in the same time.

2. 3/2
As I / ride, ∧∧ as I / ride ∧∧
With a / full heart for my / guide ∧∧
So its / tide ∧∧ rocks my / side ∧∧
As I / ride, ∧∧ as I / ride ∧∧∧∧
That as / I ∧ were double-/eyed ∧∧
He in / whom our Tribes con/fide ∧∧
Is de/scried ∧∧ ways un/tried ∧∧
As I / ride, ∧∧ as I / ride. ∧∧∧∧

Browning, *Through the Hetidja to Abd-el-Kadr*

In another poem of Browning's 3/2 time is used with a markedly different effect. The reader familiar with classical verse will often recognize marked similarity to the Greek Ionic measure in its two forms: ⌐⌐⌐ — — and — —⌐⌐⌐.[20]

3.
That / fawn-skin dappled / hair of hers
And the / blue eye
Dear and / dewy, ∧
And that / infantine fresh / air of hers. ∧∧/
Why, with / beauty ∧∧ needs there / money be,
Love with / liking? ∧∧
Crush the / fly-king
In his / gauze, ∧ because no / honey-bee? ∧∧/

Browning, *A Pretty Woman*

[20] [Croll refers to the meter of Ionic Verse used by Sappho, Alaceus, sometimes

In the three examples cited the difficulty of keeping the long measure of 3/2 time at its proper slow speed has been met by a very frequent use of two syllables to each of the beats, the half-notes often being divided into quarters; and for this reason the verse does not sound very slow. But in the following the slow *tempo* is very distinctly heard, because there is ordinarily but a single syllable to the beat. It seems to be the unique example in English verse of 3/2 time written in this way, and it will be observed that in as many syllables as possible the author has taken advantage of both of the two elements that add length, namely, vowel length and accumulation of consonants.

4.　　/ Dawn talks to/day ∧∧

　　　　Over / dew-gleaming / flowers ∧∧∧∧

　　/ Night flies a/way ∧∧

　　　　Till the / resting of / hours ∧∧∧∧

　　/ Fresh are thy / feet ∧∧

　　　　And with / dreams thine eyes / glistening ∧

　　　Thy / still lips are / sweet ∧∧

　　　　Though the / world is a / listening. ∧[21]

O / Love ∧∧ set a / word in my / mouth for our / meeting

Cast thine / arms round a/bout me∧to / stay my heart's / beating∧

O / fresh day, O / fair day, O / long day made / ours. ∧∧∧/[22]

William Morris, Song in *Love is Enough*

IX. Two-time Verse

In two-time verse the faster form (2/8) and the form with the slower *tempo* (2/4), are about equally common.

Aeschylus (and in much modified form by Anacreon); the Greek meter, however, is double: either *falling* (— — ⌣⌣ — — ⌣⌣) or *rising* (⌣⌣ — — ⌣⌣ — —).]

[21] The symbol ⊏⊐ (rarely used) is equivalent to the whole note (○) in music.

[22] The reading of this and the two preceding examples is that of William Thomson who first pointed out the very slow three-movement in English verse.

1. 2/8   / All a/long the / valley / ⌃⌃ / stream that / flashest /

         white / ⌃⌃ /

       / Deepen/ing thy / voice / with the / deepen/ing of

         the / night / ⌃⌃ /

Tennyson, *In the Valley of the Cauteretz*

2. 2/4   / Out of the / golden re/mote wild / west, where

               the / sea without / shore is

   / Full of the / sunset, and / sad if at / all with the /

           fulness of / joy ∧

Swinburne, *Hesperia*

The relation between 2/8 measures and 2/4 measures is of course the same as between 3/8 and 3/4 in that the latter is double—or about double—the former; but in another respect, and an important one, it differs. For we cannot break up a 3/4 measure into two 3/8 measures, or at least not without difficulty and strain, because it has an odd number of units and the division would occur in the middle of one of them. On the other hand, an even or "square" time not only can easily be divided into two symmetrical parts with beats at the beginning and middle, but tends to divide itself thus, and to keep on subdividing itself in the same way until its lowest unit (the eighth note) is reached. We *want* to hear two-time; that is, in 2/8 measures, and a poet may of course permit and require us to do this by placing beats at all the possible division-points. On the other hand, if he wishes his measures to be in 2/4 time, he must prevent them from breaking up by writing them so that we cannot easily hear a strong secondary beat in the middle of the measure.

In the poems cited above, for instance, Tennyson has made the last subdivision of time and marked it clearly by stress. Swinburne, on the contrary, has so written his 2/4 time that many of the measures will not easily divide. In his method of doing this, both in *Hesperia* and in many other poems of similar form, there is no doubt that he has been influenced by the way in which 2/4 time is used in the Greek and Latin dactylic hexameter line, for he has mingled the two most important forms of the 2/4 measure: ‒ ⌐ ⌐ (dactyl), and ‒ ‒ (spondee), exactly as they mingle in a typical Greek or Latin line. If we compare the first line of the *Aeneid* with the first line of *Hesperia*, we can see how strong the resemblance is:

2/4 / Arma vi/rumque ca/no, Tro/jae qui /primus ab/oris

The only difference is that Vergil here has a spondee in the fourth measure, Swinburne a dactyl. The *Iliad* begins with a line of exactly the same form as the first line of *Hesperia*:

2/4   / μῆνιν ἄ/ειδε, θε/ά, Πη/ληια / δεω' Ἀχι/λῆος

And at the ends of the alternate lines Swinburne omits an unstressed syllable always, but for this there is also good classical precedent in the so-called elegiac verse.[23]

In the following example there has probably been no classical influence, and it shows how naturally "dactyls" and "spondees" may mingle in 2/4 verse controlled only by our native forms of song:

3.   To / whom used my / boy George / quaff else /∧

By the / old fool's / side that be/got him? /∧ ⌐

For / whom did he / cheer and / laugh else /∧

While / Noll's damned / troopers / shot him? /∧[24]

King / Charles, and / who'll do him / right now? /∧

King / Charles, and / who's ripe for / fight now? /∧

Give a / rouse: Here's, / in Hell's de/spite now, /∧

King / Charles! ∧/   Browning, *Cavalier Tunes*

[23] [The initial line of *Hesperia*, ending with the phrase "shore is," bears such close phonetic resemblance to the initial line of the *Aeneid*, ending "aboris," that one is inclined to jump to the assumption that Swinburne was imitating Vergil's rhythm; on the other hand, as Croll notes, Swinburne's form is really that of the Greek elegiac couplet in which the hexameter line was followed by a pentameter (or more exactly a hexameter in which the third and sixth feet were catalectic) (e.g., see Callimachus, Ennius, Tibullus, Propertius, Ovid—though there are certain refinements in the later Latin poets which Swinburne does not attempt to imitate, especially a restriction that the pentameter line must end with a disyllable or a word of five syllables).]

[24] There is probably meant to be a leveling-out of times here to express the bitterness of the speaker's utterance. Otherwise we should note the "troopers" as: ⌐ ‒ ·, "shot him" as ‒ ‒ ∧. The measure "in Hell's de-" (with its beat or

Another pair of examples will give further aid in distinguishing 2/8 and 2/4 time:

4. 2/8   / Loud / sang the / souls /⌒ of the / jolly / jolly /

    mari/ners ⌒

/ Plague up/on the / hurri/cane ⌒ that / made us /

    furl and / flee /

Kipling, The Last Chantey

5. 2/4   / Hail to the / Chief who in / triumph ad/vances

/ Honor'd and / blest be the / evergreen / Pine ⋀/

Scott, Boat Song (Lady of the Lake, ɪɪ)

A little beating of the time makes it clear that two measures of the Kipling poem are equal in time to one of Scott's. It is also clear that Scott means his unit to be 2/4, not 2/8, because he has written the measures so that the second minor beat in them can sometimes hardly be heard at all, while Kipling has constantly made us hear the stress that divides 2/4 into two 2/8 measures. It will be observed that Kipling's verse appears to move much faster than Scott's, though the actual time is really the same. (That is, one of Kipling's 8-beat lines occupies the same time as one of Scott's 4-beat lines.) 2/8 time always has this effect.

The verses so far quoted show clearly that syllable-counting is an unsafe guide to the detection of the times within a measure. In *Hesperia* there are many more three-syllable measures than two-syllable ones; in Scott's *Boat Song* all have three syllables except the last of each line, but to call these measures three-time would be the same mistake as to describe the Latin dactyl and spondee in the same way. The verses that follow show that syllable-counting is equally untrustworthy in the quick 2/8 times.

6. 2/8   / Early /⌒ one / morning /⌒ just / as the / sun was /

    rising /⌒

"in") will not trouble anyone accustomed to Browning's resolute way of handling word accents. William Thomson, however, reads the line: "Give a / rouse: here's, in / Hell's de/spite now."

389

I / heard a / maid / sing / in the / valley / ∧

be / low. / ∧ /

Folk Song

7. 2/8 / Come un/to these / yellow / sands

And / there / take / hands / ∧ /

Curtsied / when you / have and / kissed

The / wild / waves / whist / ∧ /

Ariel's song in *The Tempest*

8. 2/8   / I / had a / penny / ∧

A / bright / new / penny / ∧

I / took / my / penny / to the / Mar/ket- /

Square / ∧ /

A. A. M., in *Punch* (March 26, 1924)[25]

X. Thesis and Arsis

We have been considering what seems a small unit of time in
verse, the time from one beat to another within the measure. Even
this time, however, consists of two parts, a part in which a beat is
heard and then the release of the beat, just as in the ticking of a
clock we hear a sound plus a silence, constantly repeated; and it is
this alternation of beat and silence that makes rhythm. An illustration from dancing will make this clearer. On each of the two beats
of a measure of two-time, the dancer's foot falls; then it is raised,
in preparation for the next fall; and the rhythm of dancing consists
in this interchange. So, exactly, in verse. A two-time measure consists really of four parts, two of which are marked by the fall of
the beat, the other two, alternating with these, by the release
of the beat. For example, in Swinburne's line, "Out of the golden
remote wild west, where the sea without shore is," "golden re-"
consists of two parts, "gold-" and "-en re-," each of which occupies

25 For full notation, see Ch. III.

1/4 time; but each consists of two parts, a part in which the stress is laid on and a part in which it is released. The stress comes on the vowel in "gold-," and the rest of the syllable releases it; the stress falls on "-en," and "re-" releases it.

The Greeks named these parts of a rhythmic time *thesis* (meaning the fall of the foot in dancing) and *arsis* (the raising of the foot), and these terms will sometimes be convenient in discussing our verse. It is true that we do not often need to pay attention to the minute division of the times within the measure just described, but the measure itself is constituted in just the same way that each of the times within it is. It consists of a part in which a heavier beat (the measure beat) occurs and a part in which this heavier beat is released, and we hear only the fainter beats of the times within the measure. The former of these parts is the thesis of the measure, the latter the arsis. For example, in Swinburne's line the thesis of the second measure is "gold-," the arsis "-en re-"; the thesis of the third is "-mote," its arsis "wild," etc.[26]

These terms are chiefly useful in English in discussing two-time measures because in the unsymmetrical three-time measure we cannot tell where the thesis ends and the arsis begins. In any symmetrical unit, in fact, where half the time belongs to thesis, half to arsis, they are valuable terms, and we shall find it necessary to take them up again in treating double or compound measures, which are of course always symmetrical.

XI. Syncopation

The first line of *Paradise Lost* used to be scanned (though of course with a different notation from the one here used):

Of / man's first / diso/bedience / and the / fruit.

It is now recognized that this is a false representation of any possible reading of the line, and the first two measures, with which alone we are concerned for the time, are now usually shown thus:

/ man's / first diso-/

This is much nearer to the truth, but still a careful observation will show that it does not exactly correspond to the natural flow of rhythm. We do not hold the syllable "man's" quite so long; the

---

[26] [The reader should be cautioned that the terms *thesis* and *arsis* may exactly shift their meanings in the works of some modern prosodists. It would be desirable to restrict the terms to their Greek sense.]

word "first" has, it is true, the beat of the second measure, but we begin to say it before the time for this beat has actually come, and the time for the beat therefore occurs half-way through the syllable. We may note this phenomenon by a symbol which shows half the time of the syllable "first" in the first measure and half of it in the second, the vertical bar crossing it midway. Thus:

Of / man's fir/st / diso/bedience /‸and the / fruit.²⁷

Other examples are found in Browning's *Meeting at Night*:

The / grey se/a‸ and the / long bla/ck land /

And the / yellow ha/lf-moon / large and / low.‸

This phenomenon (the beginning of the syllable that has the beat before or after the time for the beat) we call *syncopation*. It occurs frequently in almost all English verse, and in some kinds of double-measure verse, as we shall see, at regular places in the line. In ordinary simple-time verse, as in blank verse, for instance, it comes without plan or prescribed arrangement. But in either case it is not to be regarded as an irregularity or as careless or unimportant. On the contrary, it is the cause of part of the pleasure we feel in good verse. It may be regarded as a momentary conflict between the rhythmic pattern and the actual run of words that fill it—a conflict that is resolved at a following (usually the next) beat, and meanwhile produces a pleasant sense of difference, of momentary freedom from law, of that "strangeness in the proportions" which has been said to be necessary to beauty.²⁸

In Milton's line the fourth measure:

/‸and the /

provides an illustration of a way of treating the measure, very com-

²⁷ [It should be noted that it is difficult to divide a monosyllable into parts, though the accent falls, it is true, on or near the vowel or diphthong and the rest may represent a falling away from the ictus. Croll's entire discussion of syncopation, it seems, is overly pedantic and moreover possibly caused by misreading, through modernization, of Milton's line; for example, the *-ience* in the word *disobedience* was certainly considered by Milton to represent no more than one syllable, according to the standard practices of elision of the period (in which contiguous vowels very frequently elide, or near enough to be considered metrically to have done so). And there is no reason to assume that Milton did not pronounce the word as having four syllables instead of five in his flow of speech; indeed English pronunciation often accords it four syllables to this day.]

²⁸ [The idea of "strangeness in the proportions" may arise from Aristotle's discussion of unity in variety, rudimentary as it is, in the *Poetics*, though it is more usually traced from Plotinus, from his denial that beauty can consist in mere symmetry: Bernard Bosanquet, *A History of Aesthetic* (London, 1892).]

mon in all kinds of verse, which may be regarded as a variety of syncopation. The place for the stress is here occupied by a rest. Stress, that is, for the moment drops out of the verse scheme. In the other examples it is merely weakened, or perhaps we should say diffused through two or more syllables, so that we cannot say exactly where it comes; but this is virtually equivalent to saying that stress has disappeared as an element of form. For instance, the three syllables "long black land," the three syllables "half moon large," in the Browning passage, are not only almost exactly equal to one another in time; the stress upon them is also so equalized that for the time we cannot tell thesis from arsis. In general, then, we note that the effect of syncopation in verse is to weaken or eliminate the beats affected by it. The time goes on regularly, but the time markers are not heard.[29]

Syncopation is of as frequent occurrence in music as in verse, and it is a more conspicuous thing when it occurs, because the pattern of beats which is being momentarily violated in one of the vocal or instrumental parts is kept steadily going by another or others, so that the contrast is very easily caught. Chopin, for instance, is said to have sometimes kept up a syncopation in playing the melody of a piece with his right hand while his left hand kept the regular time without variation. In verse, on the contrary, there is nothing to measure the departure by except as we are able to hear in our inward ears the regular beats going on.

Finally, it is to be observed that syncopation is a phenomenon that is not peculiar to the first beat of a measure but may, and constantly does, affect the beats within it. For instance, one of the measures of Scott's *Boat Song* is:

2/4   / triumph ad/vances

another:

/ Honor'd and /

In each case the second beat of the measure falls in the middle of the second syllable. This is a very common arrangement of the stresses in 2/4 time, but an excessive use of it produces an effect of monotony, as may be seen in certain passages of Longfellow's *Evangeline* (and other poems in similar verse):

---

[29] [The remarkable weaknesses of scansion in those parts of the essay dealing with syncopation seem to stem, at least partially, from Croll's eclectic (sometimes unscientific) interpretations of phonetic phenomena.]

/ So passed the / morning a/way. And / lo with a / summons

so/norous /

Sounded the / bell from its / tower, and / over the / meadows

a / drum beat. /

It is noticeable that Swinburne seldom syncopates the 2/4 time in this way, and it is a fact that more than anything else makes his verse so much more classical in effect than that of *Evangeline, Hermann und Dorothea,* etc. Of course there are several other ways of syncopating beats within the 2/4 measure, as, for instance, in the third measure of each of the lines from *Evangeline* just quoted.

In three-time measures also syncopation occurs in a variety of ways.[30] For instance, the measure of the form: — · ⌐— — , illustrated above in the discussion of *The Charge of the Light Brigade,* is very common, as is its equivalent in 3/8 time; ⌐· ⌐⌐ ⌐ ; and even more frequent is the form: — · — · or ⌐· ⌐· in which the time for both the second and third beats falls within syllables, as in the following:

/ candles /, / world-wide /.

A particular effect that may be won by the use of such measures at regular places in a line is shown by a line of Masefield's *Tewkesbury Road*:

3/8   Through the / grey light / drift of the / dust, /in the /

keen cool / rush of the / air. /

---

[30] There is another kind of syncopation in verse, though it would be confusing to discuss it at length. It is illustrated by the rag-time song:

2/4 There'll be a / hot time in the / old town to/night./

Here in the measures beginning "hot" and "old" the strong stress at the beginning of the measure is not disturbed; it occurs at the right place, but is immediately followed by another strong stress where there should be none (that is, in the arsis position). The effect is violent and exciting, quite different from that of the ordinary kind of syncopation. Additional examples from Browning, Kipling, etc. could be produced. (R)

✧ CHAPTER II ✧

THE DOUBLE OR COMPOUND MEASURE

I. Definitions

Double or compound measure in verse corresponds to music that is written in 4/4 or 6/8 time. In such music every measure consists of the sum of two simple measures equal in time: 2/4 plus 2/4, etc., of which each keeps its initial stress or beat. There are thus two beats in a double measure, but the first (called "primary stress") is stronger than the second (or "secondary"). For example, a line of Browning's *Love Among the Ruins*:

′ Where the / quiet-′colored / end of ′ evening / smiles

Each part enclosed between solid vertical lines constitutes a double measure, and the dotted vertical line indicates the division between its two constituent measures. In this case the line begins with the second half of a double measure; the first full double measure, therefore, is "quiet-colored."

The terms *thesis* and *arsis* may be used to describe the relation between the two parts of a double measure. As in a simple time measure the more stressed part is called the thesis, the less stressed the arsis; so we may call the first measure of a double measure, with its primary stress, the thesis, and the second measure, with its secondary stress, the arsis. Thus "quiet" is the thesis, "colored" the arsis.

It should be noted that the symbol employed to indicate the division between the parts of the double measure, the dotted bar, does not effect the application of the time signature. The time signature applies to a unit covering two measures and reaching from one solid bar to the next. In some respects, then, the form of the double measure might be better shown by omission of the dotted bar, and it may be omitted whenever it is desirable to do so.

Theoretically there are as many kinds of double measures as there are single measures: 2/8 measures compounded become 4/8; 2/4, 4/4; 3/8, 6/8, etc. And in fact all of the kinds of measures described in the preceding chapter occur frequently in their double or compound form except the extremely slow 3/2 measure.

II. Where to Look for Double Time

The presence of the double measure in some kinds of poetry

has been recognized (though it has been called by various names) in recent studies of English verse. But it is also treated as a late innovation. No earlier instance seems to have been cited than Campbell's *Battle of the Baltic*, and the conspicuous use of it in a large body of recent poetry, as in the ballads of Kipling, Masefield, and Noyes, has been regarded as probably a passing fashion, due largely to the imitation of Campbell's martial lyrics.

This is a wholly false account of the part played by double time (or compound time) in the history of our verse. It is not modern; on the contrary, it is a familiar phenomenon in the lyric verse of every period. It is not occasional and exceptional but it is so common that it is difficult to find a song-like lyric in English in which it does not appear. In short, it seems likely that when the subject has been adequately studied we shall have to conclude that compound time is the primary and fundamental form of the rhythm of the English lyric, to which it always goes naturally; that simple time, on the other hand, has to be learned by deliberate effort and practice and is always the sign of literary control and artistic sophistication.

These are far-reaching statements. Their validity must finally be tested, not by argument, but by the sensitive and trained hearing of many readers. Yet there are several arguments of an *a priori* nature which give them strong support.

1. The music of all the traditional forms of popular song, from which the form of the words is of course derived, is in double time; and the best illustration of this statement is the music of the ballad itself, which is apparently the fundamental form of our native lyric.[31]

2. Our involuntary rhythmizing of any uniform succession of sounds, such as the ticking of a clock, the throb of an engine, the click of car wheels, is always done in double time. We do not hear a clock's sound as "tick, tick, tick, tick, tick," but as "tick, tock, tick, tock." That is to say, the continuous repetition of the same kind of beat, with silence between, does not satisfy our natural desire of rhythm. The beats themselves must have the rhythm produced by alternations of stronger and weaker.[32]

[31] [Croll's contention depends somewhat on a naturalistic explanation of the origin of the ballad, upon which considerable doubt has been cast by Professor Arthur K. Moore, "The Literary Status of the English Popular Ballad," *Comparative Literature*, x, 1 (Winter 1958), 1-20. Moore's footnotes cite all of the pertinent bibliography.]

[32] [This subject receives much more extensive treatment in Thomson, *The Rhythm of Speech*.]

3. The analogy of Greek poetry is very important in the study of English verse because these are the two kinds of poetry in which the control of music is most strongly felt. It is now known that Greek iambic and trochaic verse was *always* written dipodically; that is, in double measures. Furthermore, the two other most important kinds of Greek measures, the dactyl and the anapest, are double time measures, whose time signature is 2/4.

The dactyl is $—\,{}_{-\!7}\,{}_{-\!7}$; the anapest ${}_{-\!7}\,{}_{-\!7}\,—$ ·

If the conclusion to which these arguments tend is sound, therefore, the logical method of treating our verse would be to begin with double time and then to show the development of single-time verse from it. But nothing so radical is attempted in the present discussion. The purpose of the following chapters is merely to illustrate the great prevalence of double time in English lyric, and especially to show how it is necessarily related to the simplest and fundamental line and stanza forms, which are in fact dependent upon it. In order to accomplish these purposes, we shall begin with the ballad form and gradually extend our view to the more literary kinds of stanza.

It is necessary to enter the *caveat* here that double time is not to be heard in "spoken" verse; that is, in the blank verse and rhymed pentameter couplet that are usually employed in our epic and dramatic poems or in the kinds of stanza that are used in long narrative, descriptive, and expository works. It is primarily a phenomenon of lyric verse and does not appear even in all lyrics, since a great deal of literary lyric follows the customs of "spoken" verse. In general it is not to be expected in verse written in iambic pentameter lines, though this is not an absolute rule because song-like lyrics are sometimes written in stanzas of such lines. It is possible indeed that, when we have fully grasped the nature of the double-time rhythm, we shall discover that its influence (though not its exact form) is constantly present in blank verse giving it the rhythmic variety and flexibility that we hear. But this possibility is at present merely a field for interesting speculation.

III. Ballad Stanza, or Common Meter: 4.3.4.3

The / sheriff ;′ dwelled in / Notting;′ham

He was / fain he ;′ was a-/gone ⌒;′⋀

And / Robin ;′ and his / merry ;′ men⌒

397

/ Went to ;' wood a-/non ⋀;'⋀⋀

A Gest of Robyn Hood

	Go we to	dinner said	Little-
For I	dread Our	Lady be	wroth with

John ⋀	Robin	Hood said	Nay ⋀ ⋀
me For she	sent me	not my	pay ⋀ ⋀⋀

Ibid.

6/8 For / Withering;'ton my / heart was ;' woe

That / ever he ;' slain should / be ⋀;'⋀

For when / both his ;' legges were / hewen in ;' two,

Yet he / kneeled and ;' fought on his / knee. ⋀;'⋀⋀/

Chevy Chase

These are three stanzas of well-known ballads, all alike in form, but printed in different ways to show different methods of notation. We have the melody (or *a* melody) to which each was sung, and the notations given above have been guided in part by the form of the music. When the ballad stanza is printed without music, it is now customary to consider it as four short lines, and for this arrangement there is good reason in the rhythmic structure. But it was originally, and is still sometimes,[33] treated as two long lines of seven stresses each. In discussing it, therefore, it is sometimes necessary to distinguish which arrangement is meant by the awkward terms "short-line" and "long-line."

Each long line has seven heard stresses, but as the notation shows, each of them has the time of eight measures. That is, there are four double measures in each long line, but a rest takes the place of syllables in the arsis of the last. This rest occupying the time of the arsis in a double measure is a very important element in the form-marking of the ballad stanza and its many derivative

[33] E.g., Kipling's *Rhyme of the Three Sealers* and *McAndrews' Hymn.*

forms. In the form illustrated above (known in hymnbooks as Common Meter, or c.m.) it occurs at the end of every long line. It may also occur at the end of each short line, taking the place of the arsis of the second double measure. That is, there are four places in the stanza where it may occur: in the arsis of the second, the fourth, the sixth, and the eighth double measure; and the chief variations of the ballad form arise from different placings of it. In a well-established form (which we shall call 6's) it occurs in all of the four possible places so that there are only three heard stresses in each short line, six in each long line; in another (the "Short Meter" of hymnbooks) at all of the four possible places except at the middle of the second long line, the first long line, therefore, having six heard stresses, the second seven; in another (the "Long Meter" of hymnbooks) there are no rests, and there are four heard stresses in each short line.

The rest, it is to be observed, takes the place of a secondary stress alone, not of a primary stress; or, to speak more exactly, of the arsis, not the thesis, of the double measure. For this there are two reasons. First, it is only the arsis, with its weaker stress, that *could* be omitted. The primary stresses are the main supports of the rhythmic structure. A pattern is usually clear even when they alone are heard; if only one of them is unheard it may become blurred or uncertain.[34] Second, when the secondary stress at the end of a line is unheard, the last heard stress is a primary, and the end of the line is strongly marked to the ear by its superior firmness and force. It will be seen, then, that double time, with its regular alternation of strong and weak stresses, plays an important part in the determination of line and stanza form.

The three variations of the ballad stanza described above are those which have firmly fixed themselves in our tradition. If there were no others, the problem of naming these three would be easy. But in fact there are a great many others, indeed almost an indefinite number, arrived at by combining the lines of the ballad stanza in different relations with one another and varying their number; and in order to describe these we must have some way of distinguishing all the possible forms of the short line and long line. The method cannot be that of syllable-counting employed in the hymnbooks (where 6's and 7's, for instance, means that some lines have

[34] What is said here applies only to popular or comparatively simple kinds of verse. In the works of subtle artists in rhythm a rest sometimes takes the place of a primary stress.

six syllables and others seven) because in most of the poems concerned the number of syllables to a measure varies freely. It must
be a method of beat-counting—or measure-counting, which is the
same thing. But here a difficulty arises: Should the number of beats
counted include that which falls in a silence or rest, or should it
not? In strict accuracy it should, for the silent measure is as much
a part of the line as any of the sounded ones. But the trouble is that
then every line would have to be called an 8-beat (or 4-beat) line,
and to distinguish one form from another, awkward and difficult
terms would be necessary. For this reason the method used here
will be to name the number of *heard* stresses. Short lines without
rest will be called 4's; with a rest at the end, 3's; 8's will mean
long lines without rest; 6's long lines with a rest at the middle and
one at the end.[35] These are not altogether satisfactory terms, it is
true; and in the future it will probably be necessary to devise a
system of naming based upon the double measure instead of the
simple measure.[36] Meanwhile the method of naming lines by the
number of their heard stresses will meet most practical needs. For
example, the stanza of Kipling's *The Last Chantey*:

4/8   / Thus ,' said the / Lord ,' in the / Vault a,'bove the /

Cheru,'bim ⌃

/ Calling ,' to the / Angels ,' and the / Souls in ,' their

de/gree ⌃,'⌃

'Lo! / Earth has ,' passed a/way ⌃,'⌃

In the / smoke of ,' Judgement / Day ⌃,'⌃

That Our / word may ,' be es/tablished ,' shall we /

gather ,' up the / sea? ⌃,'∧/

[35] The phenomenon of rest taking the place of stressed syllables was described
in Greek by the term *catalexis*, but in several ways the term is not adaptable to
English usage. [It is difficult to understand the reservation, for the term has
commonly been employed so in English; perhaps Croll means to object to the use
applied to rest in place of an *un*-stressed syllable.]

[36] The Greeks did this, their term *dimeter* meaning double measure; but it is
not desirable to domesticate this term in English. [In English *dimeter* usually refers
to a two-foot line.] The subject of the nomenclature of English verse should be
examined by some representative body of scholars and teachers, such as the
Modern Language Association of America or the National Education Association.
[The recommendation was written, of course, when MLA was smaller and a fairly
cohesive body; to expect such an association today to function as an academy
would, doubtless, be futile.]

consists of five lines of the form 8:7:3:3:7 respectively, or of four lines of 8:7:6:7, if the two short rhyming lines are considered one long line, as they well may be. It must be remembered, however, that the four long lines are in fact all of the same *length*, each consisting of four measures of double time, as the notation shows.

IV. Short Meter (3:3:4:3, or 6:7)

In this and the two following sections are considered the three variants of the ballad stanza that are most prevalent and may be regarded as independent fixed forms.

The first is the form known in the hymnbooks as Short Meter (s.m.), which is derived from the usual ballad form by introducing a rest in the place of syllables in the arsis of the second double measure; that is, at the end of the first short line. A stanza, therefore, has the form 3:3:4:3, or 6:7. In the sixteenth century, before the introduction of blank verse, this form was very popular in all kinds of poetry and was known, for a reason that is not clear, as Poulter's Measure (perhaps in allusion to the thirteen beats in each couplet of long lines, poulterers being supposed, like bakers, to be generous in counting their dozens).[37] For epic and dramatic purposes it was fortunately superseded at the end of that century by blank verse, for its strong musical beat is inappropriate for such uses. It is an excellent lyric form, however, as is shown by the variety of lyric uses to which it has been put by different poets. A stanza of a hymn will show one of its effects:

6/8   / Lord of the / harvest, / hear

Thy / needy / servants' / cry

/ Answer our / faith's ef/fectual / prayer,

And / all our / wants sup/ply /

Charles Wesley (1742)

This is three-time; Tennyson has used the same form (without stanzaic division, however) in two-time, with a variety in the syllable arrangement which would be inappropriate in a hymn:

4/8   / All a- / long the / valley / stream that / flashest /

white

37 [In the sixteenth century Gascoigne and W. Webbe advanced substantially the same reasons.]

/ Deepen- / ing thy / voice / with the / deepen- / ing of

the / night

/ All a- / long the / valley / / where the / waters /

flow

I / walked with / one I / loved / two and / thirty / years

a- / go /

. . . .

And / all a- / long the / valley / by / rock and / cave and /

tree /

The / voice / of the / dead / was a / living / voice to / me /

In the Valley of the Cauteretz

In Burns's *Bonnie Lesley* the short-meter stanza combines in a double stanza of 3's, the form being: 3:3:3:3:3:3:4:3. And a number of other combinations and variations could be mentioned. For example, the limerick form is really a stanza of S.M., but the third short line (of four beats) is broken into two 2-beat lines, which rhyme together, and hence, of course, the rhyme arrangement is different throughout.

V. 3's (6's)

3's. A longer discussion is called for of the stanza made up wholly of 3's, a rest taking the place of a measure at the end of every short line. A series of lines of three beats would have an unpleasant abruptness if they all ended on a stressed syllable, especially since the last syllable in this case would always have a primary stress; and for this reason the first and third short lines are usually written with a light syllable following the last stressed syllable (sometimes called "feminine ending") of the first and third lines of the stanza, as in the following:

> My soul, there is a country
> Far beyond the stars,
> Where stands a winged sentry,
> All skillful in the wars.
>
> Henry Vaughan, *Peace*

402

Good hap to the fresh fierce weather,
    The quiver and beat of the sea!
While three men hold together
    The kingdoms are less by three.

Swinburne, A Song in Time of Order

In the following the same arrangement will be noticed, and also the frequent syncopation of the secondary stress that is so characteristic of native English verse in many forms (often illustrated in the examples that follow):

4/8   He / came a,'l so / stille ;'/∧∧
        / To his ;' Mother's / bower ;'/∧
     As / dew ;' in A- / prille ;'/∧
     That / falleth ;' on the / flower ;'/∧∧

        / Mothe,'r and / maiden ;'/∧
     Was / never ;' none but / she ;'/∧∧
        / Well may ;' such a / Lady ;'/∧∧
        / God's ;' mother / be ;'/∧∧/

Carol (15th C.)

6's. The brevity of a stanza of four lines of 3's makes it difficult to handle and undesirable except in verses meant to be sung, or when a particular effect is sought; and for this reason 3's usually occur in stanzas of double the length of those just quoted. In hymns the doubling is usually effected in stanzas of eight short lines of 3's, but much the commoner arrangement in secular poetry is four long lines of 6's, each consisting of two 3's; and it is the remarkable increase in the number of poems so written during the last century that gives its present interest to the study of this form.

The following examples are all cited in illustration of 6's, but it will be seen that they are not all from poems written in stanzas of ballad length; that is, two long lines, or of double that length, four long lines. For 3's and 6's are not bound to stanza form so closely as the forms we have considered. We may have stanzas of

403

three lines of 6's, for instance, as in Lamb's *The Old Familiar Faces*, or short lines of 3's may mingle in some kind of pattern with long lines of 6's or 7's, as in Kipling's *The Last Chantey*, or we may have an indefinite number of lines, as in *The Revenge*, etc. It must be understood, then, that our subject is the line of six heard beats and not, as heretofore, a definite stanza form.

The following are two specimens of the form, both in 6/8 time; the second shows, like the fifteenth-century carol (above), syncopation of secondary stress at certain regularly recurring places in the stanza:

It is / good to be ,/ out on the / road /·/Λ and / going one ,/ knows
    not / where /·/Λ/

/ Going through ,/ meadow and / village, /·/Λ one / knows not ,/
    whither or / why /·/ /

Through the / grey light ,/ drift of the / dust /·/Λ in the / keen
    cool ,/ rush of the / air /·/Λ /

/ Under the ,/ flying white / clouds /·/ /and the / broad blue ,/
    lift of the / sky /·/Λ /   Masefield, *Tewkesbury Road*

/ I will ,/ make you / brooches ,/Λ and / toys for ,/ your
    de/light /·/Λ

Of / bird-so,/ng/ at / morning ,/Λ and / star-sh,/ine /at /
    night /·/Λ/

/ I will ,/ make a / palace ,/ΛΛ/ fit for ,/ you and / me /·/Λ

Of / green da,/ys/ in / forests ,/Λ and / blue da,/ys/ at /
    sea /·/Λ /   Stevenson, *Romance*

Syncopation in double-measure verse. Stevenson's poem offers a good opportunity to illustrate the peculiar role often played by syncopation in lyrics written in double measures. In single-measure verse it occurs irregularly; that is, at any place in a line and at different places in different lines. In double-measure verse, on the contrary, it is often used so regularly that it is necessary to regard it as part of the formal law or pattern of the verse. It occurs in the arsis of the first and third double measures of the second and fourth lines of each stanza. In the fifteenth-century carol (above) the regularity is not absolute, but a marked effect is produced by the prevalence of syncopation at the same place in the first line of the stanza. In the preceding chapter it has been shown that syncopation may affect not only the first beat of a measure, but also any of the beats within it, and in double-measure verse we may often observe the tendency to regularize and pattern its occurrence with reference to these inner beats. For example, it has already been pointed out that there is a regular contrast between the first and second measures of the line in Drayton's *Agincourt*.

6/4   ∕ Fair stood the / wind for France

∕ When we our / sails advance

∕ Nor now to / prove our chance

∕ Longer will / tarry ∧∧∕∧∧∧/

The contrast is, in fact, due to the different arrangement of the syncopation in the thesis and arsis of a double measure.[38]

Two poems by Yeats. A marked characteristic of 6's is the relatively large number of primary stresses that are heard in them— four in each long line; and when they are written, as they are in the above examples, in such a way as to bring into prominence the contrast between primary and secondary stresses, this effect is much heightened. It is a kind of rhythm, therefore, as obvious and emphatic as that of folksong and children's rhymes, and doubtless the popularity of many recent poems written in it is chiefly due to this fact. It may easily degenerate into doggerel. But on the other hand, like other kinds of double-measure rhythm, it is capable of the most varied and interesting effects when its opportunities are taken advantage of; as, for instance, when the contrast between its strong and weak beats is deliberately kept faint and elusive, when the regular 6's are mingled with other lines different from them but related to them in some proper numerical proportion, and, especially, when syllables and silences within the double meas-

[38] For a full discussion of this stanza see Ch. I.

ures are placed in some interesting and individual way in relation to the pattern of time beats. The following examples from well-known poems have been chosen in order to show some of its finer uses:

6/8

/ All things un/comely and / broken ;́, ∧⁄ / all things ;́ worn

out and / old,⁄;́∧

The / cry of a ;́ child by the / roadway, ;́∧ the / creak of a ;́

lumbering / cart,⁄;́

∧ The / heavy ;́ steps of a / ploughman, ;́∧⁄/ splashing the ;́

wintry / mould⁄;́∧∧

/∧ Are ;́ wronging your / image that ;́ blossoms a / rose in the ;́

deeps of my / heart.⁄;́∧⁄/

*The Lover Tells of the Rose in his Heart**

There may well be a difference of opinion as to the reading of the last line in this stanza, which is a refrain line. It is at least evident that the rest which regularly takes the place of syllables in the arsis of the second double measure in the other lines does not occur there in this line, and that the rhythm of the stanza owes its peculiar and beautiful quality largely to that fact.

6/8   / I will a/rise and / go no/w ∧ and / go to ;́ Innis / free⁄;́∧

And a / small ;́ cabin / build the/re, ∧ of / clay and ;́

wattles / made⁄;́∧

Nine / bean ro/ws will I / have the/re ∧ a / hive for the ;́

honey-b/ee ∧;́∧

And / live alo/ne in the / bee-loud ;́ glade.⁄/

*The Lake Isle of Innisfree**

Here again the fourth line is different from the others, but the relation is more apparent. The most interesting thing about the

* Reprinted with permission of The Macmillan Company, New York, Mr. William B. Yeats, and Macmillan & Co. Ltd., London, from *Poems* (copyright 1906 by The Macmillan Company; copyright renewed 1934 by William B. Yeats).

rhythm, however, is the frequent syncopation, which at one place seems to occur at a primary stress (end of the third line). It does not occur at regularly recurring places, as it often does in 6's, but at any place; and the effect it makes is of extreme informality and casualness, as if the verse were imitating familiar talk.

Morris's *The Wind*. There could be no better illustration of the varieties of music to which 3's lend themselves than the contrast between these poems of Yeats's and William Morris's *The Wind*, the musical pattern of which has been correctly displayed by William Thomson in *The Rhythm of Speech*:

6/8

Ah / no, no / it is / nothing /∧∧/ surely / nothing at / all ∧/

∧∧/Only the / wild-going / wind∧/∧∧/ round by the / garden /

wall∧/

∧ For the / dawn just / now is / breaking /∧ the / wind be-/

ginning to / fall∧/

∧∧/ Wind∧/∧∧/ wind∧/ thou art / sad∧/∧ art thou / kind∧/

∧∧/ Wind∧/∧∧/ wind∧/∧ un/happy∧/ ∧thou art / blind∧/

∧∧/ Yet∧/ still thou / wander/est the / lily / seed to / find ∧ /

Tennyson's *The Revenge*. The prevalent form of the line in Tennyson's poem is 6's, but this is constantly varied from, especially by lines which are without medial rests, and consist, therefore, of three, instead of four, measures of double time. Thus in the last section, the rising of the storm is portrayed in a succession of such lines (five heard beats plus one unheard at the end), but its climax and breaking is marked by the change, magnificently prepared for, to 6's, in the third line from the end.

6/8

And a / wave like the / wave that is / raised by an / earth-

quake / grew∧/∧

Till it / smote on their / hulls and their / sails and their / masts

and their / flags∧/∧

407

And the / whole sea / plunged and / fell on the / shot-shat-
tered navy of / Spain

And the / little Re/venge her/self went / down by the
island / crags

To be / lost ever/more in the / main.

Lamb's *The Old Familiar Faces*. Another poem, which has given great trouble to prosodists, seems to be in 6's, and William Thomson's reading of it confirms this impression, though the terms in which he describes and explains this and other poems are quite different from ours. The refrain line, in 4/4 time, is as follows:

/ All / all are / gone the / old fa/miliar / faces

But the poem seems to require the faster time of 4/8. There is an extraordinary variety in the way the syllables fall with reference to the time beats—what we may call the syllabic modulation of the rhythm—in this poem, and probably not all readers will agree with the following; the rhythmic form, however, seems to be clear.

4/8 / I have / had / play-ma/tes, / I have / had com/panio/ns

/ In my / days of / childho/od, / in my / joyful / schoolda/ys

/ All / all are / gone the / old fa/miliar / faces

/ Friend of my / bosom thou / more than a / brother

/ Why wert not thou / born in my / father's / dwelling

/ So mi/ght we / talk of the / old fa/miliar / faces

408

Meredith's *Love in the Valley*. In Lamb's poem and several others we have considered there are lines in which it is difficult to tell whether a secondary stress falls in the time of a rest or upon a syllable which by a slight protraction of its time might take it; for example, the second syllable of *playmates* and *childhood* above. Where we have music to which the verses have been written, it will indicate the proper reading; otherwise the choice depends upon the reader's taste, or upon the vigor with which he chooses to bring out the rhythmic pattern. Of course, if the syllable rather than the rest takes the stress in such cases, the line is not properly described as a 6-beat line, since seven or eight stresses are actually heard. And since this is a very frequent occurrence in what we call 6's, it is evident that the dividing line between this form and the other variants of the ballad form cannot always be drawn with certainty. In the poem from which the following passage is taken, for instance, it is impossible to say whether the typical line has six, seven, or eight beats.

4/8   / Shy / as the / squirrel / that / leaps among the /

pine- tops

/ Wayward / as the / swallow / over / head at / set

of / sun

/ She / whom I / love is / hard to / catch and /

conquer

/ Hard, but / O the / glory / of the / winning / were

she / won /   Meredith, *Love in the Valley*

Many of Kipling's ballads could be cited also to show how an artist may take advantage of the opportunities that this form allows him to mingle 6's, 7's, and 8's.

VI. 4's (Long Meter)

The third of the most important variations of the ballad stanza is that in which all of the four measures of each of the short lines are filled with syllables, and there are, therefore, no rests taking the place of beats. This is a commoner form in the hymnbooks (where it is known as Long Meter, or L.M.) than in secular song, because it is capable of a steadier and slower movement than 6's or 7's. But it appears nevertheless in many popular ballads, doubtless because of the form of the music to which they were sung; e.g.:

Had / Willie ,' had but / twenty ,' men

But / twenty ,' men as / stout as ,' he

Fause / Sakelde had ,' never the / Kinmont ,' taen

Wi' / eight score ,' in his / compa,'nie.

Kinmont Willie

In the following Elizabethan song, written certainly to a popular melody, the same form, except for a difference of rhyme, can be seen:

Come / live with ,' me and / be my ,' love,

And we will all the pleasures prove

That hills and valleys, dales and fields,

Or woods or steepy mountains yields.

Marlowe, *The Passionate
Shepherd to his Love*

In appearance the difference between this form and the common ballad form (7's) is very slight; it consists only in the fact that the rest at the end of each long line is filled with syllables. But this difference is really very important. For it is this rest which keeps the order of primary and secondary stresses: strong, weak, strong, weak, strong. Fill it with syllables and at once this arrangement begins to become weak or indeterminate; and presently a reverse arrangement: weak, strong, etc., may begin to declare itself. In popular song, and in all verse directly controlled by it, it is true, the strong beginning is prevalent, perhaps universal, in L.M., just as it is in C.M. and S.M.; but, on the other hand, there is a marked tendency in our literary lyric, and even in songs written under literary influence, to go over to the weak beginning. Two Elizabethan songs will illustrate this:

There ,' is a / lady ,' sweet and / kind,

Was never face so pleased my mind;

I did but see her passing by,

And yet I love her till I die.

> Ford, *Musick of Sundry*
> *Kinds* (1607)

Give me a / look, ,' give me a / face

That ,' makes sim/plici,'ty a / grace,

Robes loosely flowing, hair as free;

Such sweet neglect more taketh me

Than all the adulteries of art;

They strike my eyes, but not my heart.

> Jonson, *Simplex Munditiis*

It will be seen that the arrangement indicated in these passages is not always clear to the ear in all of the lines; there is a tendency to slip into the strong beginning of popular verse, even when the pattern is of the opposite sort. So marked, indeed, is this tendency that we feel the need of something in the sound of the verse to indicate the weak beginning when it occurs, and the method that is frequently employed for this purpose is the omission of anacrusis before the first stress; that is to say, a trochaic syllabification of the lines.

,' Shall a / smile or ,' guileful / glance

Or a sigh that is but feigned

Shall but tears that come by chance

Make me dote that was disdained?

No! I will no more be chained.

> Wm. Corkine's *Second*
> *Book of Airs* (1612)

Had we never loved so kindly,
Had we never loved so blindly,
Never met or never parted,
We had ne'er been broken-hearted.

Burns, *Ae Fond Kiss*

When the moon is on the wave,
    And the glow-worm in the grass,
And the meteor on the grave,
    And the wisp on the morass—

Byron, *Manfred*, Act I, Sc. 2

／ When we two / parted

    In ／ silence and / tears,

／ Half broken-/hearted

    To ／ sever for / years,

／ Pale grew thy / cheek and cold,

    ／ Colder thy / kiss;

／ Truly that / hour foretold

    ／ Sorrow to / this.

Byron, *When We Two
Parted*

Poems written like these, with regularly trochaic or dactylic syllabification, usually prove to have the weak beginning, but the rule is not universal. And there are other ways of indicating the place of the secondary stress. For example, in the following the secondary stresses in the refrain line are shown by the fact that there is but one syllable in the measure in which they occur:

The ／ tide / rises, the ／ tide / falls,

The twilight darkens, the curlew calls,

Along the sea-sands damp and brown

The traveler hastens toward the town

412

And the tide rises, the tide falls.

Longfellow, *The Tide Rises*

Other examples of weak beginning in four-beat lines (or two-beat lines that easily run together into four-beat lines) are Scott's *Coronach* ("He is gone on the mountain") and *Lochinvar*, Byron's *Sennacherib*, and Moore's *The Last Rose of Summer*.

VII. Illustrations of the Weak Beginning

So important is the phenomenon that we call weak beginning in the study of double-measure verse that it requires further comment and illustration. Usually of course it is found in forms in which there is an even number of beats in the line (2, 4, 6, or 8) because otherwise both the first and the last stress of every line is a secondary, and between the lines there must be a rest taking the place of a primary stress. Obviously such an arrangement would only be desired for some special purpose. Perhaps five-stress lines will be found to display it in a few poems, but at present no examples can be mentioned with confidence.

4's (or 8's). Browning uses the weak beginning in lines of four or eight beats with surprising frequency. *Home Thoughts from the Sea* is interesting because of a change of arrangement introduced into the second half of the last line:

4/4

/ Nobly, / nobly / Cape Saint / Vincent / ∧ to the / Northwest /

died a/way∧/∧∧/

/ Whoso / turns as / I, this / evening, / turn to / God to / praise

and / pray,∧

/ While Jove's / planet / rises / yonder, /∧∧/ silent /∧ over /

Afri/ca.∧/

A double purpose is served by the rest in the last half-line; it not only prepares the mind for the idea of the concluding words, it admirably breaks the uniformity of movement and leads to the dying cadence of the last double measure.

413

Love Among the Ruins is in 8-beat lines if the two lines of six and two beats respectively are taken as one:

6/8

;′ Where the / quiet-;′colored / end of ;′ evening / smiles ^;′ Miles

and / miles ^;′^

On the / soli;′tary / pastures ;′ where our / sheep ^;′ Half

a/sleep ^;′^ ^/

Here the omission of anacrusis helps to set the tune of the rhythm, and the exact syllabification (two syllables to a measure) keeps it steady; the same method is observed in *Cristina*:

4/8

;′ She should / never ;′ have looked / at me ;′ If she / meant I;′

should not / love her

;′ There are / plenty (etc.)

On the other hand, *The Laboratory* displays the freest variation both in the number of syllables and in the use or omission of anacrusis:

6/8

;′ Now that I, / tying thy ;′ glass mask / tightly,

May ;′ gaze through these / faint smokes ;′ curling / whitely

As thou ;′ pliest thy / trade in this ;′ devil's / smithy

;′ Which is the / poison to ;′ poison her, / prithee? ;′^ ^/

In Tennyson we may observe the same variety of practice, sometimes, as in *Locksley Hall*, an exact counting of syllables, sometimes, as in most of the sections of *Maud*, the utmost freedom in the syllabic modulation of the rhythmic pattern. A typical stanza of the former is:

;′ When I / dipt in;′to the / future ;′ far as / human ;′ eye could /

see

;′ Saw the / vision ;′ of the / world and ;′ all the / wonder ;′ that

would / be

414

The continuousness of the rhythmic impulse through the long 8-beat line, often noted as the peculiar technical excellence of this poem, is chiefly dependent upon the weak beginning and secondarily upon the regularity of syllabic number; both of these features of the form serving to distinguish the effect from that of the song-like ballad. Yet there are interesting variations of the pattern even here. For instance, in the second line of the first stanza we are perhaps meant to read in the same way as at the conclusion of Browning's *Home Thoughts from Abroad*:

/ Leave me / here and / when you / want me /∧∧/ sound up/on

    the / bugle-/horn /

And in the following an inversion of the regular order of the stresses is heard in the first and the third double measures:

/ Glitter / like a / swarm of / fire-flies / tangled / in a / silver /

    braid

In verse, as in music, such variations from pattern are not infrequent. They are the small swirls, eddies, or counter currents that enliven, without breaking, the forward movement of rhythm.

6's without rests. The form so described must be distinguished from that called sixes and discussed above as one of the forms of the ballad line. That has four double measures to the line; this has three, and it is a striking indication of the faultiness of our present nomenclature that we have no convenient way of naming this difference. Several illustrations of the form are to be found in Tennyson; e.g.:

Our / doctor had / called in an/other, I / never had / seen him

    be/fore

But he / sent a / chill to my / heart when I / saw him come / in

    at the / door;

Fresh from the / surgery / schools of / France and of / other /

    lands,

Harsh red / hair, big / voice, big / chest, big / merciless / hands.

                                           In the Children's Hospital

415

Wheer 'asta / bean saw long an' / mea liggin' 'ere a/loan?
Noorse? theert / howt o' a noorse: whey, / Doctor's a bean an'
a/goan.

Northern Farmer: Old Style

One of the most difficult poems in English, rhythmically considered, is Browning's *A Grammarian's Funeral*. Apparently there are six beats (three double measures of 4/4 time) in the long line plus the short line, which are evidently meant to form a single movement, or rhythmic phrase; and this movement unquestionably begins with a secondary stress. This is not an unusual form. But Browning has employed extraordinary variations in the way his syllables adapt themselves to this pattern, probably in order to suggest the labored climbing gait of the bearers of the body, first their effort for a firm foothold, then a pause as they gather their strength, then a rapid swing upward to the end of the movement. It will be observed that the syllable arrangement is the same in every line: ten syllables in each long line, five in each short one. But this arrangement is deceptive as regards the fall of the beats and the division of the time and is to be looked upon as a mechanical device of the author to aid him in a difficult rhythmical experiment rather than as a help to the reader in hearing the proper fall of the beats.[39] The following are two characteristic passages:

4/4

1. Let us be/gin and carry / up this corpse, Singing to/gether
   Leave we the / common crofts, the / vulgar thorpes, Each in its /
   tether

2. Sleep, crop and / herd! sleep, darkling / thorpe and croft, Safe
   from the / weather!
   He, whom we / convoy to his / grave aloft, Singing to/gether,
   He was a / man born with thy / face and throat, Lyric A/pollo!
   Long he lived / nameless: how should / Spring take note Winter
   would / follow?[40]

[39] [The paragraph on *A Grammarian's Funeral* illustrates Croll's system at its most perceptive point; while individual readers are bound to quarrel often with the scansions, the system, carefully applied, does allow for and even encourages psychological analysis of verse that is impossible with customary metrics.]

[40] The boldness of an attempt to explain a rhythm that has not been explained before justifies further comment. The singularity of Browning's use of 4/4 time here consists (if the explanation is correct) in the fact that not only the primary and secondary beats (the first and third in the measure) are heard distinctly, but also the off-beats (the second and fourth), and these are often equally important

It is, however, in Swinburne that 6's with the weak beginning can be studied to the best advantage. In both of the following the time is 4/4:

Out of the / golden remote wild / west, where the sea without /
shore is
Full of the / sunset, and sad, if at / all with the fulness of / joy,
Hesperia

And the / great King's high sad / heart, thy true last / lover,
Felt thine / answer pierce and / cleave it to the / core;
   And he / bowed down his hopeless / head
   In the / drift of the wide world's / tide
And dying, Thou hast / conquered, he said, Gali/lean; he said it,
and / died.
The Last Oracle

In another poem of Swinburne's, which has excited a great deal of interest, the time is 6/4. There can be no doubt that the poet arrived at the form of its line by repeating a well-known biblical passage until he had discovered the verse rhythm that came nearest to representing the actual prose movement of the words or that he wrote a poem in that rhythm in which each line preserved exactly the syllabic arrangement of the passage. Probably this is not an uncommon method of verse writers seeking for new rhythmical effects, and the interest in the present case is due to the fact that a certain measure in each line has five syllables. These five syllables do not come, however, in a formless rush; by beating out the time carefully it will be found that each of the three beats of the measure is heard.

---

with the others as determinants of the rhythm. This, the syllable that ends the longer of the two lines, has always an unmistakable beat, being indeed a rhyme word. But this beat is the second in its measure, not (as a false reading might make it) the third, for this third beat falls at the beginning of the short line that follows. Again in a large number of longer lines there is a long rest after the fourth and fifth syllable, and the important third beat of the measure falls in this rest; e.g.: " No! yonder / sparkle is the / citadel's Circling its / summit ." But there are astonishing varieties of syllabification in this part of the line, as in the following:

Grant I have / mastered learning's / crabbed test, Still there's the / comment
Let me know / all! Prate not of / most or least, Painful or / easy;
Even to the / crumbs I'd fain eat / up the feat, Aye, nor feel / queasy.

Whether Browning has asked too much of the reader's ingenuity is a question everyone must decide for himself. (R)

6/4

By the waters of / Babylon we sat down and / wept, remembering /
    thee

That for ages of / agony has endured and / slept And wouldst not /
    see.

By the waters of Babylon we stood up and sang, Considering thee,

That a blast of deliverance in the darkness rang, To set thee free.

Super Flumina Babylonis[41]

This is one of the poems cited by William Thomson in illustration of his theory that different measures in a line may occupy different times, provided these times are in a certain kind of ratio. He reads the five-syllable measure—"Babylon we sat"—and also a later measure in each line—"wept, Re-"—as having the time 4½ instead of the three-time of the other measures. This is a theory that not many of his readers are willing to accept, and in the present case, certainly, there is no need to evoke it. There is no more difficulty in saying these five syllables in the time of a three-fourths measure than there would be in singing five notes in the same kind of musical measure.

In many other poets besides those mentioned the weak beginning six (without rests) is a favorite form, and the explanation of its frequent use is not far to seek. The 6-stress line is apparently the longest that can be used without a breathing space in English verse, and even this needs to be made easy by the arsis beginning, which serves as an introduction or glide to the first primary stress.

[41] In some lines the opening two syllables might easily be considered only anacrusis, but there are enough lines (e.g., the last one quoted) to show that a secondary stress is meant to occur there. (R)

418

✧ CHAPTER III ✧

THE DOUBLY COMPOUNDED MEASURE

Among the examples used in the preceding chapter there are a number of which the rhythm is not fully, or indeed quite correctly, accounted for by the facts so far considered. For the relation of the beats within the double measures is more or less affected by, is partly dependent upon, a relation between the double measures themselves as members of a larger unit of which we have so far taken no account. This larger unit is the doubly compounded measure; that is, one which consists of two measures of double time. When this phenomenon occurs, its presence is detected by the greater strength of the primary stress in one of the double measures as compared with that in the other, and there are, therefore, four grades of stress in each doubly compounded measure: (1) the stress upon each of the two or three units of time of which every single measure is made up (for, though we do not usually pay any attention to this reading, it must always be remembered that it is the foundation upon which all musical and verse rhythm is built); (2) the stronger stress on the first of these two or three units, marking the beginning of a measure; (3) the still stronger stress marking the beginning of the thesis of the double measure, this being called the primary stress, as compared with the secondary which marks the beginning of the arsis; (4) a still stronger, marking the beginning of the doubly compounded measure and falling upon the primary stress of the first of the two double measures of which the doubly compounded measure is made up. Or—to state the same facts in different terms—one of the two double measures serves as thesis, the other as arsis, of the larger unit, just as one of the single measures serves as thesis, the other as arsis, of the double measure, and as the single measure itself also has its thesis and arsis.[42]

That the fourth grade of stress is in fact often heard, that a recognition of it is necessary to a true reading of many lyric poems, is quite certain; and nothing else is quite certain at present about this matter. It is a subject that has not been studied by prosodists, and the many questions it raises in the mind can at present be put

---

[42] These terms are very unsatisfactory. We call the highest stress in the double measure the primary stress; yet the still higher stress in the doubly compounded measure we have to call fourth grade of stress. This is confusing and is further evidence of the need of new terminology. (R)

only as questions. This is true of the most important question of all: How frequent an occurrence is the double compounding of measures? When are we to look for it? Is the fourth grade of stress an occasional phenomenon only, which may be used for particular effects, or, on the other hand, is it a fundamental fact of rhythm, always potentially present but usually allowed to remain latent—a fact, that is, whose omission, rather than its presence, should be noted? Music does not help us to an answer; for, though the thing is often heard, perhaps always heard, in popular song, there is no notation of it.[43] It does not enter into the formal scheme. It appears that ultimately we shall have to appeal to the theory of Greek verse for the aid we so much need in the study of double compounding, but this is still too little understood to be of much practical value.

There is, however, one guiding principle that we may safely appeal to: the length and form of the line in our verse is vitally connected with, and is apparently dependent upon, the double compounding of measures. The original and, as it were, the natural line of English verse, based upon the singing and dancing customs of the people, is the four-beat line; that is, the line of two double measures. And it is a common opinion that all other lines have been arrived at by some modification of this basic four-beat form. (The same thing is true of Greek verse, it seems, and probably of every kind of verse that has arisen from popular custom.)[44] That is, the length of a line is that of one doubly compounded measure; it is probable that its structure is also. A line cannot be a mere arbitrary numerical division of discourse; it must be a thing heard in some way as a rhythmic unit; and the fourth grade of stress, it seems, is what causes it to be heard; for it is this which elevates the two double measures (otherwise symmetrical) into members of a single rhythmic movement. The line, then, is produced by carrying further the same principle of doubling that appears in the double measure; the double line (as, for instance, the first and second, or third and fourth, short lines of the ballad, taken together as a unit) carries this compounding a step further, having eight measures (four

---

[43] That is, there is no notation of double compounding in popular music. But classical composers often indicate by their time signatures the double compounding of simple rhythms. 12/8 is a common signature (e.g., Beethoven's pianoforte sonata Op. 57); Bach in the *Well Tempered Clavichord*, Vol. 1, Prelude 15, uses the time signature 24/16, equivalent in this case to 8/8. (R)

[44] [Croll's idea of the origin of verse, English or Greek, seems today a little naïve, though there is no evidence to indicate it is wrong. We are no longer quite willing to accept his theory as the sole logical explanation.]

double measures, two doubly compounded measures); and the simplest form of the stanza, the ballad stanza of sixteen measures, is produced merely by continuing it to another stage. There is, however, no grade of stress to mark these further stages of reduplication. The fourth is the highest that can be obtained, and even this, as we have seen, is not always brought into play.

The usual position of the fourth grade of stress in a four-beat line is at the second primary stress; that is, in the thesis of the second double measure. It may also occur at the first primary stress, but there is no doubt of the prevalence of the other form, as in the following stanza, where the fourth grade of stress is marked by parallel vertical bars:

> / All day long and // every day
> From / Christmas Eve to // Whitsun- day
> With/in that chapel- // aisle I lay
> And / no man came a-// near.
>
> Morris, *The Chapel in Lyoness*

The reason our custom prefers this arrangement is evident. The fourth grade of stress is of the nature of a climax in the rhythmic movement of a line, and as a rule it will be gradually approached, instead of occurring early in the line, unless there is some special reason for proceeding differently.

In the stanza just quoted the fourth grade of stress is on the third heard stress of each line, because that is the primary stress of the second double measure. In the following the second primary is the fourth measure of each line, and this is also, therefore, the position of the fourth grade of stress:

> Had we / never loved sae // kindly,
> Had we / never loved sae // blindly,
> Never / met or never // parted,
> We had / ne'er been broken//hearted.
>
> Burns, *Ae Fond Kiss*

The difference is due to the fact that in these stanzas the lines begin with secondary stress; whereas in the preceding they begin with primary. It is due, that is, to the difference between strong and weak beginning; since this has already been treated under the subject of double measures, it need not occupy attention here. In the examples on the following pages the highest stress is usually in the third measure, but a few illustrations of its occurrence in the fourth measure will be given. The important point is that the last primary stress of a line is the customary position for the highest grade of stress, whether this occurs in the third or the fourth measure.

Medieval Latin verse. It will be well to begin the illustration of this fact by reference to medieval Latin church songs, since it is believed that not only the ballad form, but a number of other English forms in which the fourth grade of stress is most distinctly heard, originate in this kind of verse.[45] The first stanza of those quoted below has lines with strong beginning, and therefore with the fourth grade of stress in the third measure; the third has the weak beginning and the fourth grade of stress in the fourth measure, except in the refrain lines. In the second the two arrangements alternate (the two short lines being considered one long line of four beats) in a pattern:

1.   De/sidero to//millies;
                    Me, / Jesu, quando // venies?
                    Me / laetum quando // facies
                    Et / vultu tuo // saties?

2.   Que do/lore,
                     Que moe//rore
                     Deprimuntur // miseri   /
                     Qui a/byssis
                     Pro com//missis
                     Submergentur // inferi!   /

3.   Lachry/mosa dies // illa
                     Qua re/surget ex fa//villa
                     Judi candus homo // reus
                     Huic / erge parce // Deus
                     / Pie Jesu, // Domine,
                     / Dona eis // Requiem.   /[46]

The ballad form. The following lines of medieval verse have approximately the form of the English ballad stanza: two lines of eight beats each, the last beat falling in the time of a rest:

[45] [Not only English forms; e.g., see the chapter "La Dissolution de la Métrique Latine" in Georges Lote, *Histoire du Vers Français*, I (Paris, 1949).]

[46] Where there is a strong beginning, as in the first of these stanzas, anacrusis appears (except in refrain and tail-rhyme lines), but weak beginning passages, like the third stanza, have no anacrusis. A tendency toward the same principle in English verse has been mentioned. (R)

For/tunae rota // volvitur, de/scendo mino//ratus;
/ Alter in altum // tollitur, / minus exal//tatur.   /

According to one theory, medieval Latin verses of this form are not only like our ballad stanza but are actually the source of it. It is more probable, in fact, that both our ballad form and these Latin "septenaries" (or 7's) have their origin independently in the customs of popular singing and dancing, in which this form is natural and prevalent. Fortunately we are not concerned with questions of origin, and the purpose of quoting the above lines is only to show that one of the resemblances between the English and Latin forms is the fall of the fourth grade of stress.

1.   / "Go we to dinner," said // Little John
        / Robin Hood said   // "Nay;
    For I / dread our Lady be   // wroth with me,
    For she / sent me   not my   // pay."

                            A Gest of Robyn Hood

2.   O / little did my // mother think
        The / day she cradled // me
        What / lands I was to // travel through
        What / death I was to // dee

                            The Three Maries

3.   John / Gilpin   was a   // citi   zen
        Of / famous   London   // town
        A / train-band captain // eke was he
        Of / credit   and re- // nown   /

                        Cowper, *John Gilpin's Ride*

6's and 6's & 7's. That the fourth grade of stress is merely a typical or ideal feature of the ballad rhythm, often to be heard only with that inward ear which carries a pattern of rhythm through a run of words, could be shown by many examples. On the other hand, its reality is proved by countless poems in the forms of 6's and 6's & 7's, which, as we have seen, are varieties of the ballad form. In these forms the omission of so many secondary stresses has the effect of bringing the primary stresses into higher relief, and therefore of making the main outlines of the rhythmic pattern more apparent; and it is doubtless for this reason that the fourth grade of stress is likely to be more distinctly heard. In a section of the preceding chapter a number of examples of poems in these forms were scanned, but some lines of several of them may now be repeated with the addition of the fourth grade of stress in order to show how necessary to their proper rhythmic movement is the observance of this feature of their form:

1. / I will make you // brooches   and / toys for your de//light
Stevenson, Romance

2. / All a long the // valley   / stream that flashest // white
   / Deepening thy // voice with the / deepening of the // night
Tennyson, In the Valley of the Cauteretz

3. / Wind   // wind   unhappy thou art // blind   /
   / Yet stil thou // wanderest the / lily-seed to // find
Morris, The Wind

4. / I have had   // playmates   / I have had com//panions
   / In my days of // childhood   / in my joyful   // schooldays
   / All   all are // gone   the / old familiar   // faces   /
Lamb, The Old Familiar Faces

5. / Shy   as the // squirrel   that / leaps among the // pinetops
   / Wayward as the // swallow over/head at   set of   // sun   /
Meredith, Love in the Valley

Choral songs. Still more heavily struck is the fourth grade of stress in choral songs of all kinds, such as marching songs, glees, rowing songs, and chanteys, most of which are usually in 4/4 time.

4/4

        Hail to the   / Chief who in   triumph ad-   //vances
        Honor'd and   / bless'd be the evergreen   // Pine
        Long may the tree in his   banner that   glances
        Flourish, the shelter and   grace of our   line.
Scott, Boat Song (Lady of the Lake, II)

4/8

/ Loud   sang the // souls   of the / jolly   jolly   // mariners
/ Plague upon the   // hurricane that   / made us furl and // flee!
For the / war is   done be//tween us
In the / deep the Lord hath // seen us
    Our / bone we'll leave the // barracout and / God may sink
      the // sea
Kipling, The Last Chantey

Nursery rhymes and popular songs. In general, the more strongly marked the contrast between the primary and secondary stresses of the double measures, the more strongly marked also will be the fourth grade of stress. We are not surprised, therefore, to hear it clearly in children's rhymes and in popular song.

1. 6/8   / Baa, baa, // black sheep, / have you any // wool?
           / Aye, sir, // aye, sir, / Three bags // full.   /

2. 6/8   / Three blind // mice
           / See how they // run
           They / all ran after the // farmer's wife
           She / cut off their tails with a // butcher's knife
           Did you / ever see such a // sight in your life
           As / three blind // mice.   /

3. 4/8   / Early one // morning just / as the sun was // rising
           I / heard a maid // sing in the / valley be//low,
           / O don't de//ceive me   / O never // leave me
           / How could you // use a / poor maiden // so?   /

Fourth grade of stress in the fourth measure. In the poems cited thus far the fourth grade of stress has fallen uniformly in the third measure of the line, because this is where the last primary stress of the line occurs. But we have already observed that when a four-beat line has a weak beginning the place of the last primary stress is in the fourth measure, and this will, therefore, be the normal place for the highest grade of stress. The following examples illustrate this place of its occurrence, and it will be observed that in all of them there is trochaic syllabification, which has already been spoken of as a frequent sign of the weak beginning.

1.   Lamp of / Earth! where'er thou // movest
           Its dim shapes are clad with brightness,
           And the souls of whom thou lovest
           Walk upon the winds with lightness,
           Till they fail as I am failing,
           Dizzy, lost, yet unbewailing.
                Shelley, Song in *Prometheus Unbound*, II

2. Many a morning on the // moorland did we hear the copses //
      ring
   And her whisper throng'd my // pulses with the fulness of
      the // Spring.
                Tennyson, *Locksley Hall*

So also in the song in *Twelfth Night*:

> In delay there lies no plenty
> Then come kiss me, sweet and twenty,
>   Youth's a stuff will not endure

And in a song by Lorenzo di Medici (which Shakespeare may have been imitating):

> Quant e bella giovinezza
> Chi si fugge tuttavia
> Chi vuol esser lieta, sia,
> Di doman non o'e certezza.

The apparent and visible form of Browning's *Love Among the Ruins* is of a six-beat line followed by a two-beat line, but the actual heard rhythm is of an eight-beat line, or rather two four-beat lines of two double measures each, with weak beginning. What marks this form to the ear is the fourth grade of stress upon the fourth and eighth beats.

> Where the / quiet-colored // end of evening / smiles Miles and // miles
> On the solitary // pastures where our sheep Half a//sleep
> Tinkle homeward through the // twilight, stray and stop As they // crop
> Was the site once of a // city great and gay So they // say
> Our country's very // capital, its prince Ages // since
> Held his court in, gathered // councils wielding far Peace or // War.

Fourth grade of stress at the beginning of the line. Finally, there seems to be no theoretical reason why the highest grade of stress should not come in the first measure of the line, the first (instead of the second) double measure serving as the thesis of the doubly compounded measure. That the opposite arrangement is prevalent has been illustrated in many examples, and the practical reason for this custom is evident. But is it universal? Would not a desired effect of abruptness, or great vigor, or perhaps of naïveté sometimes be secured by beginning with the greatest force of utterance? For instance, is not the imitation of a child's speech successfully achieved in the following lines by just this method?

1. // I had a / penny
    A // bright new / penny
    I // took my / penny To the // Market square
    I // wanted a / rabbit
    A // little brown / rabbit
    And I // looked for a / rabbit Most // every/where

A. A. M. in Punch (March 26, 1924)

In very martial verse, again, the high stress seems to occur in the same position sometimes.

2. Of // Nelson and the / North
    Sing the // glorious day's re/nown
    When to // battle fierce went / forth
    All the // might of Denmark's crown
    And her // arms along the / deep proudly // shone;
    By each // gun the lighted / brand
    In a // bold determined / hand,
    And the // Prince of all the / land
    Led them // on.

Campbell, The Battle of the Baltic

3. And they // praised him to his / face with their // courtly
      foreign / grace;
    But he // rose upon their / decks and he // cried:
    'I have // fought for Queen and / Faith like a // valiant man
      and / true,
    With a // joyful spirit / I Sir   // Richard Grenville / die.'
    And he // fell upon their / decks and he   // died /   //

Tennyson, The Revenge, XIII

In both these poems the way that lines of various length work into the stanza movement seems to depend upon the regular recurrence of the fourth grade of stress in the first and fifth measures, as here marked.

Similarly, in lines with five heard stresses in lyric verse the highest stress, if heard at all, will regularly occur in the first and fifth measures of the line, as in the last strophe of *The Revenge*:

When a // wind from the land they had / ruined awoke from
// sleep,
And the // water began to / heave and the weather to // moan

427

And or // ever that evening / ended a great gale   // blew
And a // wave like that wave that is / raised by an earthquake
           // grew

So also in the alternate lines (the second and fourth) of a stanza-like movement that occurs several times in the famous chorus in Swinburne's *Erechtheus*:

4/4

But she / knew not his coming for // terror   she / felt not her
    wrong that he // wrought her

6/8

When her // locks as leaves were / shed before his // breath

4/4

And she / heard not for terror his // prayer   though the / cry
    was a God's that be//sought her

6/8

Blown from // lips that strew the / world-wide seas with //
    death   /[47]

Conclusion. In the preceding pages we have studied the rhythmic form of our lyric verse, beginning with the first and simplest unit of time, within the measure, proceeding thence to the form of the measure itself, thence again to the larger unit, the double or compound measure, and finally to the doubly compounded measure which includes the smaller units in one large and complex movement. To complete the pattern of the rhythmic form of our verse it would be necessary to show how the process of doubling units produces stanzas. But that part of the subject lies beyond our present purpose. We have seen enough, at least, to realize that one rhythmic impulse controls even the smallest units of a line and holds them all together in a single rhythmic relation with one another. At every stage we have had to admit our ignorance and incapacity concerning some of the most vital features of the rhythm

[47] This poem has engaged the attention of prosodists by the remarkable changes of rhythm that occur in it, and the most extraordinary skill with which they are effected. The first and third lines of the passage are 6's with rests at the middle and end (that is, four double measures, with six heard stresses); whereas the second and fourth lines are 6's without rests (that is, three double measures). Lines 1 and 3 are in 4/4 time; lines 2 and 4 are in 6/8 time. We have to shift, that is, from two-time to three-time in passing to the second and fourth lines. Probably we are intended to make a very long rest at the ends of lines 1 and 3, no less in fact than the length of a whole double measure.

of our verse, for we have all been so long under the domination of a mechanical and inadequate prosody that we are only beginning to learn the real truth concerning the time relations of even our simpler lyric forms. As we become more skillful in interpreting what we hear, many of the problems that now baffle us will solve themselves.[48]

[48] [In all fairness it might be noted that Dr. Croll's hope for our future understanding of lyric verse has not, since 1929, resulted in any major revision of the ordinary, or mechanical, method of scansion. The more complex time theories remain about where he and Thomson left them, and with the exception of J. C. Pope's book, *The Rhythm of Beowulf* (New Haven, 1942), scarcely a single piece of literary criticism has shown dependence on these methods of interpretation. Their value as historical curiosity in the still little understood subject of prosody remains unquestioned; whether their usefulness as a means of analysis can further be justified remains for future scholars to show.]

Music and Metrics: a Reconsideration*

EDITED BY ROBERT O. EVANS

❖ I ❖

IN 1880 Sidney Lanier published the *Science of English Verse*, in which he tried to show—we may now certainly say *showed*—that the rhythmic principle for verse is the same as that of song, and of music in general; or in other words that its rhythm is due to the quality or *time* occupied in the utterance of the measures. The full applications of this idea were not seen by Lanier himself; they are frequently disregarded by more recent metrists who acknowledge the general ability of the principle; but it was in fact revolutionary in two particulars. First, it implies that rhythm is not dependent upon the number of syllables, which may vary greatly in different measures of the same line. Secondly, it implies that the old distinction between iambic and trochaic (rising and falling) rhythm was unreal. In music, there is no such distinction; there it is understood and has always been recognized that rhythm merely moves from one stressed point to another, in waves, not in a series of sudden falls or rises, abruptly begun or abruptly ended. The musical theory of verse requires us to recognize in verse the same indifference to the old distinction between rising and falling movements.

This second point of difference was not understood by Lanier, and is still less clearly recognized than the first; but it has gradually worked itself to the foreground of controversy, and is now probably the chief difficulty that stands in the way of a reconciliation of the old and the new scansion. In fact there is no difference in the importance of the one and the other; they are inseparable, and must equally be taken into account in any attempt to show how the time principle of music is related to the rules concerning number and arrangement of syllables that were accepted, until forty or fifty years ago, as an adequate description of our verse.

It is extremely discreditable to our scholarship that almost no attempt of this kind has yet been made. I shall hardly need to call

---

* First published in *Studies in Philology*, xx (1923), 388-394.

attention to the situation at which we have arrived after all the controversy aroused by Lanier and his successors: it is apparent in nearly all the prosodic treatises issued for general and popular use, during the last fifteen years, and in many addressed to the more critical attention of scholars. These manuals, almost uniformly, begin with a statement of the time principle of the new scansion which they accept as sound and of universal application. Some of them proceed to show that this principle destroys the old rules of syllable-counting and the old distinction of rising and falling rhythm. Yet in later pages, or wherever description takes the place of theory, the old terms and the old ideas reappear, without apology made or reason given, and all that has formerly been said is disregarded and implicitly denied. I will not characterize this method of procedure except by saying that it is exactly characteristic of the undetermined state of mind in which most of us have been content to linger. Without being quite aware of it, we seem to be holding two contradictory opinions at once concerning the same set of facts. There is something in the new scansion, of course; there is something, however, in the old also. But what it is that is in either of them, and what the relation between them may be, we cannot particularly say, and apparently we do not particularly care.

This confusion of ideas is the cause, I am convinced, of the suspension of progress which has been so noticeable in metrical study of late years, after the vigorous forward impulse which it received from the first clear statements of the time principle; and the purpose of my paper is to state, in terms of the barest simplicity, what I think the relation between the old and the new scansion is.

✧ II ✧

It frequently happens in controversy that two statements are set against each other in an artificial opposition which conceals their true relations. Both are true; there is no real conflict between them because they apply to different kinds of facts or apply in a different way. But in the midst of a quarrel such adjustments and discriminations are not likely to be made. Two sets of phenomena come to be regarded as mutually exclusive though they are not really so, and whatever credit is given to one is written in as a debit against the other. Many useless controversies have arisen, in short, from an unwillingness to acknowledge that in any important subject of discussion the facts arrange themselves in different planes of truth.

The controversy which is now delaying the progress of metrical inquiry is of this kind. The new, or musical, interpretation of our verse form is the correct statement of its rhythmical law. Moreover, it is a complete statement and needs no supplementation by any statements drawn from the old syllabic system. Syllable-counting is *not* a rhythmic phenomenon; the difference described by the terms iambic and trochaic, and dactylic and anapestic (in short, by the terms *rising* and *falling*) is not a *rhythmic* difference. The facts described by these terms and by all the others of the old scansion are real facts of course; but they are not facts of rhythm. They may and frequently do occur without causing rhythm, as, for example, in passages of verse written by beginners or by writers lacking a musical ear. On the other hand, they may and do fail to occur in the verse which is still correctly, regularly, and beautifully rhythmical,[1] as for example, in *Christabel*, the later blank verse of Shakespeare, and passages of *Samson Agonistes*, none of which can be correctly described either by the number or the arrangement of the syllables.

If these are not facts of rhythm, then what kind of facts are they? In brief they belong to a certain system of verse rhetoric which has been found wholesome and useful in the writing of some poetry. They should not be stated as parts of the fundamental law of verse form; strictly speaking, they cannot be stated as laws of any kind; for they are merely optional modes of procedure, customs that may be observed or not at pleasure. This does not mean of course that they are less important in certain kinds of poetry and as means to a desired effect than the laws of rhythm themselves; but they operate in a different way and on a different plane from these laws; and the error of the older prosodists—in as far as they were in error— consisted in assuming, if they ever did really assume this, that they cause the rhythm of verse or involve a rhythmical principle.

✧ III ✧

I do not offer this distinction as if it were a discovery. It is un- avoidable, I think; and the reason that it has not been mentioned by

---

[1] The reference here is not to sung verse and lyric, in which of course the rules of the old scansion have always been freely disregarded, but to "spoken verse" (epic, dramatic, philosophical, etc.) alone. The distinction between these two kinds is extremely important in the study of verse form. The limits of this paper do not permit the discussion of it; but it may be taken for granted that whatever is said here of spoken verse is still more plainly true of lyric.

the metrists of the last forty years, beginning with Lanier, must be that they have taken it for granted. Yet I cannot but think that this avoidance has been the cause of our present confusions and controversies, and is now the chief hindrance to the progress of inquiry; and at all events it must be my excuse for entering into a little further explanation of the relations between the old and the new scansion.

The desire of rhythm within us is very strong, because it is primary, instinctive, physical. It is the way in which our hampered and fretted energies seek release in free and ideal activity. And for this reason, when it has found some pattern to set it free, it is likely to expand and exhaust itself quickly in excessive exercise, just as a spirited horse will run itself out when it is turned loose in a field. The tendency of rhythm, in short, is to rush to the height of energy and speed. Now in a song or a song-like lyric there is no reason why it should not be allowed to waste itself in this way, because the purpose of such a poem is to express an emotion as fully as it can in a short time and be done with it. But, on the contrary, the writer of a long poem must always conserve the energy of his reader, as the rider of a spirited horse must restrain his paces if he is to bring him in unwearied after a day's travel. He must be sure that the desire for rhythm is never allowed its full freedom, because a height of energy must be followed by a corresponding fall to lassitude and dullness. He secures continuity of power only by a constant moderation of it; and the chief purpose of his versifying must be, not to heighten the rhythmic impulses of his verse, but always to curb and check them.

It is in the principle of *resistance* to rhythm, then, that I think the regular rhetoric described in the old prosody has its explanation and justification. Let us consider the rule of syllable regularity first. It is evident that the occurrence of stressed and unstressed syllables in mathematical alternation is not a procedure that derives its validity from the nature of the rhythmic impulse. The analogy of music tends to show rather that the rhythmic instinct is best satisfied by a variation in the number of notes that fill the prescribed measure of time; and, in fact, the history of our verse itself shows that it tends to syllabic freedom whenever the curb of artificial restrictions is taken off. To control this tendency by conventional limits conventionally imposed has been one of the first considerations in all those periods in which the need of a level and continuous rhetoric for long poetic discourse has been most strongly felt, as, for example, in the time of Chaucer, again in the third quarter of the sixteenth century (when Gascoigne first stated the rules of the syllabic scansion[2]), and once more in the second half of the seventeenth century, when the licenses of Shakespeare's successors had dissolved these rules in the drama, and they were beginning to dissolve in other genres. At all of these points in our literary history the natural tendency of our verse toward syllabic freedom had destroyed the rhetorical firmness which is appropriate to spoken verse; and in each case a two-syllable convention imposed itself upon verse of this kind as a means to its recovery. In the latter part of the seventeenth century a three-syllable convention, complementary to this, first established itself; but in practice this confined itself almost solely to lyrical verse, and seems to have been gradually disappearing since the end of the eighteenth century. Nothing more need be said of it here.

The other feature of the old scansion, the distinction between so-called rising and falling movements, presents a more interesting subject of discussion. If it is true, and most prosodists, I believe, now admit the fact, that there is no difference of rhythm between the two kinds, what actuality of verse composition is represented by the traditional terms iambic and anapestic, on the one hand, and trochaic and dactylic, on the other? The answer is again made clear by comparison with music. The rhythm of a line of music, like that of a strain of music, does not begin until the first stressed note, or syllable is heard. How could it? But in verse, as in music, it is generally not desirable to begin abruptly on the stress, unless for some particular expressive reason. Such a beginning produces an effect of uncontrolled, or at least unmoderated energy, and sometimes of breathless speed, which cannot be corrected in the following measures without a particular effort. In this fact is to be found the explanation of the prevalent "iambic" line of English spoken verse. In this line there is no more a rising movement than there is a falling one in the "trochaic" line. It is like the trochaic line except that it begins with an extra-metrical syllable, which may be called "anacrusis" in Greek, or "catch-note" in the terms of music; and when the use of such a syllable is prescriptive, as it is in ninety-

[2] [George Gascoigne, *Certayne Notes of Instruction Concerning the Making of Verse or Rhyme in English, Written at the Request of Master 'Edouardo Donati'* (London, 1575). Rptd. G. Gregory Smith, *Elizabethan Critical Essays*, i (London, 1904).]

nine out of a hundred long English poems, the impulsive and rebellious spirit of rhythm is even more effectively curbed than by the syllable-counting rule.[3]

These two are not, of course, the only devices that our spoken verse employs to resist and control the freedom of rhythm. The handling of pauses at the ends of lines and within them, conflicts between the pattern of the verse stresses and the fall of the natural, or prose, emphases, difficult or slow combinations of consonants and vowels, are other means to the same end. But it is unnecessary to discuss any of them. Enough has been said perhaps to illustrate the difference between the laws of rhythm and the conventions of style that have been and are so prevalent in a great part of our poetry.

✧ IV ✧

The distinction is perhaps too obvious to justify so deliberate a statement. But the results that would follow from a careful observation of it are, as it seems to me, of the utmost importance; and in conclusion I will state two or three of them.

In the first place, it would make possible a revision of the nomenclature of our prosody and the settlement of the confused condition of metrical notation that now prevails. The conflict between the musical and the syllabic theories has resulted in a half-hearted and apologetic use of the older terms in various ways that are admitted to be either inadequate or inexact; it has almost banished notation from schoolroom and treatise. The former of these subjects is too large and too puzzling to be touched on here; there is great need of a serious and long-continued examination of it by a number of literary students working in co-operation and chosen by various representative bodies of English and American scholars. The subject of notation is not so difficult and should perhaps be considered first. The Modern Language Association of America has indeed already begun a study of it through a committee of five. What success will attend their efforts does not yet appear; but either through their agency or some other, adequate methods of portraying the rhythm of our verse must soon be agreed upon, or the teaching of the oral beauties of poetry will still further diminish in our schools and colleges.

---

[3] In so brief a statement I have omitted the discussion of the "trochaic" convention because, in spite of some famous attempts, it has not shown itself a good one for spoken English verse.

Secondly, a clear recognition of the fact that the old scansion states the terms of a rhetoric rather than the laws of rhythm would lead to the abandonment of many impractical attempts to reduce its operations to an exact and scientific statement. The laws of rhythm are simple, and music provides us with the means of stating them and discussing them intelligibly; but the ways in which these laws mingle with a rhetoric of expression and yield a variety of effects are beyond all formulation; for these are not subject to law; they are the part of poetry that escapes the thumb and finger of science. For instance, the grouping of syllables in speech units about the stresses, the conflict of sense emphases with verse stresses, the relations of sense divisions and verse patterns, are examples of such phenomena.

Finally—and this is the most important result—the disappearance from our minds of the fictitious opposition of the old scansion and the new may lead to a further extension of the study of the relations of verse form and music. We have but tangled our fingers in the fringes of this great subject. How inadequate, for instance, is our knowledge of what we should call "double-time" verse—though the prevalent term is still, I believe, "dipodic" verse; are we not on the verge of discovering that double time is the standard and prevalent form in our lyric poetry, as it was in the Greek and Latin, and as it always has been in the music of our song, instead of an occasional diversion of Browning, Swinburne, Kipling, and some other recent poets? And this is but one part of a vast field of inquiry in which prosodic study may not only be of great service to the readers of poetry, but may even hope to assist the poets themselves toward the discovery of new modes of formal beauty.

Index

The Index lists names of persons and a selection of leading ideas, technical terms, and the like. An italicized page number indicates that on that page, either in the main text or in the notes or both, either once, twice, or more times, there is bibliographical material relevant to that entry. In other words, the common practice of giving separate references to footnote material has not been followed. Since such information involves the use of italicized titles, the reader will have no trouble in finding it by glancing over the main text and footnotes on that page. The listings under subject-headings such as *brevity* and *courts* could have been multiplied but are intended only to serve as an *entrée* into what Croll has stated concerning them. The task of indexing his works is an exceptionally difficult one, not only because of his wide-ranging erudition and his changing terminology but especially because of his frequent brief but usually significant allusions to authors and ideas; for example, he names Montaigne on at least a hundred pages of the present volume; and on page 98 there are 31 references which had to be recorded in the Index, despite its selectivity.

No attempt has been made to enter subjects such as *rhetoric* which are so continuously treated throughout the volume that almost every page in it would have to be listed.

It is hoped, however, that the Index will provide a key to Croll's most important insights and to the development of his thought and reading. For example, it reveals that although scholars have remarked on his use of *baroque*, they have overlooked his perhaps equally significant use of the terms *positive* and *positivist*.

INDEX

444

77
147,150

h 175

184 process of thought +, 206-210, 220-222, 229-230, 232
y. 215, 190